||||| |||| || ||||||| ||||||||| ||||| |||

☑ **S0-BIQ-858**

Punc	error in punctuation	*Shift*	shift (inconsistency) in pronoun form 7.6 in verb tense 8.1
No Punc	punctuation should be omitted		

Punctuation Symbols

⊙	period 10.1	*SL*	sentence length ineffective 24.2
!	exclamation mark 10.3	*Sp*	spelling error 17
?	question mark 10.2	*Sub*	faulty subordination 3, 25.2
⌃	comma 11 with co-ordinate clauses 11.1 after introductory element 11.2 with non-restrictive modifiers 11.3 with interrupting elements 11.3 in a list or series 11.4 for clarity 11.5 conventional uses 11.6	*T*	error in use of tense 8.1
		Trans	needs better transition 21.3
		Trite	trite expression 28.3
		Var	ineffective or insufficient sentence variety 25.1
		Vb	error in verb form 8
		Wdy	wordy 24.3
No ⌃	omit comma 11.7	*WW*	wrong word 17.2, 27.3
⌃;	semicolon 12.1	//	elements should be parallel in form
⌃:	colon 12.2	⌒	close up space
/--/	dash 13.1	#	separate with a space
(/)	parentheses 13.2	∧	omission
⌄⌄	quotation marks 14.1	X	careless error
⌐/⌐	brackets 13.3	✓	good
/.../	ellipses 14.2		
/=/	hyphen 15.2		
⌄	apostrophe 6.2, 15.3		
Ref	reference of pronoun unclear 7.1		
Rep	careless repetition 24.5		
Rest	error in punctuation of restrictive or non-restrictive modifier 11.3		

Canadian Cataloguing in Publication Data

    Corder, Jim W., 1929-
      Handbook of current English

    Includes index.

    ISBN 0-7715-5697-7

    1. English language—Rhetoric.   2. English
language—Grammar—1950-   I. Moore, Michael
David, 1947-   II. Avis, Walter S., 1919-1979.
III. Title.

PE1408.C67 1983   808′.042   C82-094803-9

Co-ordinating Editor: Joan Kerr
Editors: Alicia Meyers, Geraldine Kikuta
Assembly: Susan Weiss, Keith Murray, Jean Galt
Cover Design: Brant Cowie/Artplus

ISBN: 0-7715-**5697-7**
1 2 3 4 5 WC 87 86 85 84 83
Printed and bound in Canada

More Gage Books in English

HANDBOOK OF CURRENT ENGLISH

SECOND CANADIAN EDITION

MICHAEL D. MOORE
Wilfrid Laurier University

The late WALTER S. AVIS
Royal Military College of Canada

JIM W. CORDER
Texas Christian University

gage PUBLISHING LIMITED
TORONTO ONTARIO CANADA

Contents

Paragraph and Sentence Writing

Preface

The second Canadian edition of the *Handbook of Current English* sustains certain convictions that have marked the book from its beginning: that selective and thoughtful use of language is important in every part of everyone's life; that some forms of expression are more effective and more appropriate in given situations than others; that a "good" language is a language suited to its speaker or writer, to the subject at hand, to the readers of the language, and to the context in which all come together. This edition has been revised to retain nearly all the coverage of the former edition, to expand some portions, and to add some new material. Most of the changes respond to suggestions made by many users of the popular first Canadian edition and to recent developments in our theories of language and of writing instruction. All changes, I hope, are in aid of clear, straightforward, and sufficient advice to Canadian students.

New material appears in various ways. Some chapters of the first edition, especially in Part One, needed only slight clarifications or updating. These relatively minor revisions make meaning fuller and plainer without noticeably altering arrangement or emphasis. In Part Two, the sections on outlining, on preparing a first draft, on using a dictionary, on the meaning of words, and on research essays are also basically unchanged.

Other chapters, however, have been extensively rewritten. For example, in chapter 19 the discussion of the relationship among writer, subject, and audience, and of the different types of writing is expanded and altered for more natural use. The chapter on revising has also changed. In former editions, that section focussed too narrowly on correcting a paper after it has been returned. The new first part of the section concentrates on the need for revising while the writing is still in progress. The chapter on practical writing tasks now includes fuller coverage of business correspondence and a new part on reports. A similar scale of revision is to be found in the chapters on sentence length and on the effect of words. The order (and hence the numbering) of the chapters in Part Two has also been modified to reflect better this book's assumption that, in rhetorical matters, purpose precedes and governs form. The sequence does not, however, preclude starting with words (26, 27, and 28) and working up to sentences (24 and 25) and paragraphs (22 and 23).

In a few important places, almost wholly new discussions or emphases are provided to replace or develop parts of the first edition. In chapter 18 (Discovering What You Have to Say) the treatment of "prewriting" techniques is, I think, appreciably strengthened. The new edition's advice on paragraphing is also improved by being divided into two fully explained and illustrated chapters. Likewise, the approach to sentence styling in the second edition is more systematic.

A different sort of change is the increase in examples and exercises. One significant alteration in this respect is the general substitution of Canadian (and some broadly international) references and sample passages for American material. The examples also range more widely in subject matter and complexity, and there is a higher proportion of excerpts by women writers.

Of special significance in the Canadian edition is the shift to the metric system in conformity with the Canadian adoption of Le Systeme International d'Unités (SI); moreover, the Celsius scale replaces the Fahrenheit. Again, where instructions are offered for addresses relating to correspondence, the designations established by Canada Post for abbreviating the names of provinces and territories are used—as is the proper form and position of the Canadian Postal Code. Finally, in the treatment of figures and dates, the designated metric formula is also followed—as is the 24-hour system for specifying the time of day.

Throughout the revision, my purpose has been to make material accessible. I believe the present sequence is good and usable; at the same time, I believe that the sections can be rearranged according to the needs of particular teachers and particular classes, and that they can stand alone as reference sources. The organization and features of the *Handbook of Current English* are designed to make the text easy and effective to use, as the following discussion explains.

THE DESIGN OF THE BOOK AND ITS FOCUS ON WRITING

The first seventeen chapters of this book are about particular features of the English language—grammar, usage, punctuation, and other conventions. These sections describe the way edited English typically behaves as a system of language. The remaining chapters are chiefly about the written uses of language. The first seventeen chapters are a kind of *reference* or guide to language; the rest are about the *process* of writing.

No perfect order exists for talking about language and writing. It is possible to start almost anywhere and find a useful way of exploring the subject. As the book is arranged, the first seventeen chapters may be used for study in their own right or as continuous reference for writing assignments. The remaining chapters reflect, to some extent at least, a sequence of events that many of us go through as we write, from discovering what is to be said, through the first efforts at planning and drafting, to concern about particular features of the writing, and on to completed works.

Much that is said throughout the book applies to both speaking and writing, but the focus here is upon writing. Most of us will go on talking, but there are fewer reasons to write. Telephones, computer-assisted communication, and increasingly sophisticated multiple-use television suggest that we will have many ways to communicate without writing.

Still, we need to write, for a variety of reasons. Some school and job assignments, of course, require it, but there are more compelling reasons for writing. Writing is almost inevitably a more conscious and deliberate act than speaking. Accordingly, writing gives us a chance to be more precise and more thorough than we are in speaking; we have in writing an opportunity to organize our thoughts and experiences deliberately, to establish connections carefully, to speculate and draw conclusions thoughtfully. Furthermore, writing is both portable and permanent; it can be taken easily to other times and other places. Through it we can remember what we have been and imagine what we will be. By its nature writing is an effort to go beyond the written structures that others have created, to seek what is still possible to say, to say what hasn't yet been said.

Introduction: The Languages We Use.   The introduction is a discussion of the English language; it includes an account of distinctions between speaking and writing and of some varieties of English and the ways they can be used. The introduction suggests some ways of moving among varieties of English according to the principle of appropriateness. Some recommendations made throughout the text may be clearer if students read this material at the start of the course.

Part One: Conventions of the Language.   Chapters 1 through 9 (Grammar and Usage) review the grammar of English sentences and the functions of various kinds of words and word groups. Chapters 10 through 16 (Punctuation and Other Conventions) discuss and illustrate the principles governing the use of punctuation, mechanics, and other conventions, as well as various customs for using capital letters, apostrophes, abbreviations, and numbers. The final section (Spelling) suggests ways to overcome various spelling problems.

The sections in this first half of the *Handbook* treat single, definite topics. Grammatical definitions are included where they are relevant and necessary to the discussion. Many particular matters of usage are discussed at the point where they relate to general principles, but many more are included in the Glossary of Usage.

Part Two: The Writing Process. The second half of the *Handbook* serves as a brief rhetoric and as a practical guide to college and university writing. Chapters 18 through 21 (Prewriting) focus on the processes of discovering what can or should be written and on the first steps in giving shape and character to the writing. Chapters 22 through 25 (Paragraphs and Sentences) discuss means by which sentences and paragraphs can be managed and controlled to shape meaning; they show ways of using various sentence patterns and various patterns of paragraph construction to develop ideas. Chapters 26 through 28 (Diction) discuss the dictionary and deal with appropriate and effective uses of words. Chapter 29 (Revising and Submitting the Project) suggests ways of altering emphasis, mood, tone, and direction to suit the needs of the writing at hand. It also describes some conventional practices in preparing a manuscript for submission.

Part Three: Practical Writing Situations. The two chapters of this section consider a few specific writing tasks that arise frequently in school or on the job. Chapter 30 is devoted to the problems and techniques of research writing, and contains a sample research paper written by a student. Chapter 31 discusses and illustrates other writing situations such as examinations, correspondence, and reports; a sample report, prepared by a student, is included.

Glossary of Usage. The Glossary gives succinct advice about the words and constructions that most often cause confusion in college and university writing.

Exercises. Where possible, the exercises call for students to do some writing themselves, rather than to respond to another person's writing or to underline or to fill in blanks. The exercises characteristically appear, not bunched at the ends of sections, but within the sections, immediately following the pertinent material. Colored triangles mark exercises wherever they occur within the section.

Marginal Tabs and Correction Charts. The colored marginal thumb tabs correspond to each of the six main divisions discussed above. In the margin of each right-hand page is also the pertinent correction symbol or abbreviation to indicate the material on those pages.

Papers can be marked by using either the correction symbols or the section numbers; the two are co-ordinated in the correction chart on the inside front cover as well as on the marginal tabs. In the text itself, the handwritten correction symbols appear with specific suggests for revision, printed in color. Students should study the text that follows each suggestion whenever they are not sure why revision is necessary.

Appearing on the inside back cover of the book is a checklist for revision; it should be helpful for students to go over their papers with these questions in mind before they hand in their work.

Acknowledgments

I have sometimes used plural pronouns in the text, not because I think of myself as an editorial "we," but because I'm glad to remember the contributions of my co-authors, Walter S. Avis and Jim W. Corder. The first Canadian edition of the book was prepared by Walter Avis, the eminent linguist at Royal Military College who died in December 1979. This second edition extends and broadens that work, and is dedicated to his memory. Jim Corder is the author of the American text (now in its sixth edition) upon which this book was originally based. Although the two versions of *Handbook of Current English* are now independent and increasingly dissimilar, they share much of Jim Corder's spirit and style.

I cannot list all the teachers, scholars, and friends to whom I am indebted, but I want to mention some. Users of the *Handbook* whose valuable suggestions deserve acknowledgment include Stephen Adams (University of Western Ontario), Lilian Falk (St. Mary's University), and Jack Lewis, D.H. Parker, and D. Wallace (Laurentian University). Equally important was the help and encouragement extended by colleagues at Wilfrid Laurier University, especially John Chamberlin, Meg Hancock, Ed Jewinski, and Charlotte Cox. I also thank editors Joan Kerr, Alicia Myers, and Geraldine Kikuta at Gage Publishing for their kindness and patience.

Most of all, I'm grateful to my family—Patty, Jennifer, Julie, and Emily—for managing to put up with me while I completed this project in hours, days, and weeks that should have been theirs.

Michael D. Moore
Wilfrid Laurier University

Canadian English

Walter S. Avis

Language in Canada, as in most countries, is taken for granted. Some people, however, especially recent arrivals from the United Kingdom, refuse to accept the fact that the English spoken in Canada has any claim to recognition. Others, who themselves speak Canadian English, are satisfied with the view that British English is the only acceptable standard. To these people, the argument that educated Canadians set their own standard of speech is either treasonable or ridiculous.

One Canadian I know had his eyes opened in a rather curious way. While shopping in a large Chicago department store, he asked where he might find chesterfields. Following directions to the letter, he was somewhat dismayed when he ended up at the tobacco counter. He soon made other discoveries as well. Blinds were "shades" to his American neighbors, taps were "faucets," braces "suspenders," and serviettes "napkins."

Before long his American friends were pointing out differences between his speech and theirs. He said *been* to rhyme with "bean," whereas for them it rhymed with "bin"; and he said *shone* to rhyme with "gone," whereas for them it rhymed with "bone." In fact, their Canadian friend had quite a few curious ways of saying things: *ration* rhymed with "fashion" rather than with "nation"; *lever* with "beaver" rather than "sever"; *z* with "bed" rather than "bee." Moreover, he said certain vowels in a peculiar way, for *lout* seemed to have a different vowel sound from *loud*, and *rice* a different vowel from *rise*.

The English are also quick to observe that Canadians talk differently from themselves. For example, the English don't pronounce *dance*, *half*, *clerk*, *tomato*, *garage*, or *war* as Canadians do; and they always distinguish *cot* from *caught*, a distinction that few Canadians make. They also find that many of the words they use in England are not understood by people in Canada. Suppose an Englishman gets into a conversation about cars. Says he, "I think a car should have a roomy boot." No headway will be made till somebody rescues him by explaining that in Canada the boot is called a "trunk." Before the session is finished, he will probably learn that a bonnet is called a "hood' and the hood of a coupé is "the top of a convertible." Similarly, he must substitute *muffler* for *silencer*, *windshield* for *windscreen*, *truck* for *lorry*, and *gas* for *petrol*.

The examples I have mentioned suggest, quite correctly, that Canadian English, while different from both British and American

English, is in large measure a blend of both varieties; and to this blend must be added many features which are typically Canadian. The explanation for this mixed character lies primarily in the settlement history of the country, for both Britain and the United States have exerted continuous influence on Canada during the past two hundred years.

As the several areas of Canada were opened to settlement, before, during, and after the Revolutionary War in the 1770s, Americans were prominent among the settlers in many, if not in most, communities. American influence has been great ever since: Canadians often learn from American textbooks, read American novels and periodicals, listen to American radio programs, and watch American television and movies. Moreover, Canadians in large numbers are constantly moving back and forth across the border, as emigrants, as tourists, as students, and as bargain hunters. Finally, Canada shares with the United States a large vocabulary denoting all manner of things indigenous to North America. One need only leaf through the unabridged (or the concise) *Dictionary of Canadianisms* or the *Dictionary of Americanisms* to appreciate this fact.

On the other hand, Britain has also made an enormous contribution to the settlement of English-speaking Canada. For more than a century and a half, Britishers in an almost continuous stream and speaking various dialects have immigrated to Canada. In most communities, especially those along the Canadian-American border (where most of Canada's population is still concentrated), these newcomers came into contact with already established Canadians; and, as might be expected, their children adopted the speech habits of the communities they moved into. Only in certain settlement areas where relatively homogeneous Old Country groups established themselves did markedly British dialectal features survive through several generations. Such communities may be found in Newfoundland, the Ottawa Valley, the Red River Settlement in Manitoba, and on Vancouver Island. For the most part, however, the children of British immigrants, like those whose parents come from other European countries, adopt the kind of English spoken in Canada. Yet in the very process of being absorbed, linguistically speaking, they have made contributions to every department of the language.

That part of Canadian English which is neither British nor American is best illustrated by the vocabulary, for there are hundreds of words which are native to Canada or which have meanings peculiar to Canada. As might be expected, many of these words refer to topographical features, plants, trees, fish, animals, and birds; and many others to social, economic, and political institutions and activities. Few of these words, which may be called Canadianisms, find their way into British or American dictionaries, a fact which should occasion no surprise. British and American dictionaries are based on British and American usage, being primarily intended for Britons and Americans, not for Canadians.

Prominent among Canadianisms are proper nouns, including names of regions: *Barren Grounds*, *French Shore*, *Lakehead*; names given to the natives of certain regions: *Bluenoses*, *Newfies*, *Herringchokers*; names associated with political parties: *New Democratic Party*, *Parti Québécois*, *Union Nationale*. In addition, there are a host of terms identified with places or persons: *Digby chicken*, *McIntosh apple*, *Quebec heater*, *Winnipeg couch*.

Languages other than English have contributed many Canadianisms to the lexicon: (from Canadian French) *brulé*, *caribou* (a drink), *joual*, *lacrosse*, *Métis*, *portage*; (from Amerindian) *babiche*, *Dene*, *kokanee*, *pemmican*, *shaganappi*; (from Eskimo) *atigi*, *Inuit*, *komatik*, *kuletuk*, *ulu*, *oomiak*. Sometimes the origin of such loan-words is obscured in the process of adoption; thus *carry-all*, *mush*, *siwash*, *snye*, and *shanty* derive from Canadian French *cariole*, *marche*, *sauvage*, *chenail*, and *chantier*.

Other Canadianisms are more or less limited to certain regions —to Newfoundland: *jinker*, *nunny bag*, *screech*, *tickle*, *tilt*; to the Maritimes: *aboideau*, *gaspereau*, *longliner*, *sloven*; to Ontario: *concession road*, *decker*, *dew-worm*, *fire-reels*; to the Prairie Provinces: *bluff* (clump of trees), *grid road*, *local improvement district*; to British Columbia: *rancherie*, *saltchuck*, *skookum*, *steelhead*; to the Northland: *bush pilot*, *cat-swing*, *cheechako*, *utilidor*.

Hundreds of Canadian words fall into the category of animal and plant names: *caribou*, *fool hen*, *inconnu*, *kinnikinnick*, *malemute*, *oolichan*, *saskatoon*, *sockeye*, *whisky-jack* or *Canada jay*. Many more fall into the class of topographical terms: *butte*, *coulee*, *dalles*, *sault*. Yet another extensive class includes hundreds of terms of historical significance: *Family Compact*, *Klondiker*, *North canoe*, *Red River cart*, *wintering partner*, *York boat*.

For many terms there are special Canadian significations: *Confederation*, *francization*, *Grit*, *height of land*, *reeve*, *riding*, *warden*. From the sports field come a number of contributions, especially from hockey and a game we used to call *rugby*, a term now almost displaced by the American term *football: boarding*, *blueline*, *convert*, *cushion*, *dasher*, *puck*, *rouge*, *snap*. And in the same area there are a number of slang terms that merit mention: *chippy*, *homebrew*, *import*, *rink rat*. Other slang or informal terms include: *fuddle-duddle*, *horseman* (mountie), *moose pasture*, *peasouper*, *redeye*.

In pronunciation, as in vocabulary, Canadians are neither American nor British, though they have much in common with both. Although most Canadians pronounce *docile* and *textile* to rhyme with *mile*, as the British do, it is probable that most pronounce *fertile* and *missile* to rhyme with *hurtle* and *missal*, as the Americans do. And no doubt Canadians pronounce some words in a way that is typically Canadian. Most of us, for example, would describe the color of a soldier's uniform as *khaki*, pronounced (kär′kē). Yet no non-Canadian dictionary recognizes this Canadianism. Americans say (kak′ē), while the British say (kä′kē). In Canada, many people put flowers in a vase, pronounced (vāz); Americans use a (vās) and the British a (väz). To be sure, a number of Canadians say something like (väz), especially if the vase is Ming.

If we take imported dictionaries as our authority, such pronunciations as (kär′kē) and (vāz) are unacceptable. But surely the proper test of correctness for Canadians should be the usage of educated natives of Canada. Here are some other examples of pronunciations widely heard among educated Canadians; many of them are not recorded in imported dictionaries: *absolve* (ab zolv′), *arctic* (är′tik), *armada* (är mad′∂), *chassis* (chas′ē), *culinary* (kul′∂ ner′ē), *evil* (ē′v ∂l), *finale* (f∂ nal′ē), *fungi* (fung′gi), *jackal* (jak′∂ l), *longitude* (long′g∂ tūd), *official* (ō fish′∂l), *opinion* (ō pin′y∂n), *placate* (plak′āt), *plenary* (plen′∂ rē), *prestige* (pres tēj′), *resources* (rizôr′s∂z), *senile* (sen′īl), *species* (spē′sēz), *Trafalgar* (tr∂fol′g∂r).

Of course, not everyone uses all of these forms; yet all are used regularly by educated Canadians in large numbers. Who can deny that (ri zôr′s∂z) and (spē′sēz) are more often heard at all levels of Canadian society than (ri sôrs′∂ z) and (spē′shēz), the pronunciations recommended in nearly all available dictionaries? Surely, when the evidence of usage justifies it, forms such as these should be entered as variants in any dictionary intended to reflect Canadian speech.

Another of the functions of a dictionary is to record the spellings used by the educated people of the community. In spelling, as in vocabulary and pronunciation, Canadian usage is influenced by the practice of both the Americans and the British. In areas where American and British practices differ, Canadian usage is far from uniform. Until recent years, British forms have predominated in most instances, for example, in *axe*, *catalogue*, *centre*, *colour*, *cheque*, *mediaeval*, *plough*, *skilful*, and *woollen* (and words of similar pattern), in spite of the obvious practical advantages of the

American forms: *ax*, *catalog*, *center*, *check*, *color*, *medieval*, *plow*, *skillful*, and *woolen*. In some cases, however, American spellings have asserted themselves to the virtual exclusion of the corresponding British forms, as in *connection*, *curb*, *jail*, *net*, *recognize*, *tire*, and *wagon* for *connexion*, *kerb*, *gaol*, *nett*, *recognise*, *tyre*, and *waggon*.

American spellings are becoming more commonly used in Canada. Many have, for example, been long ago adopted by Canadian newspapers, especially those in the larger centres, and by magazine and book publishers. Young people seem to use such spellings as *color*, *center*, *defense*, *medieval*, *program*, *skillful*, and *traveler* much more frequently than was formerly the case, the implication being that some American forms are accepted as proper in many Canadian schools. The fact is that educated usage is very much divided, varying from province to province and often from person to person. For the most part, however, Canadians respond to these variants with equal ease. Under such circumstances, a Canadian dictionary should include both forms, for here, as elsewhere, the lexicographer's obligation is to record usage, not legislate it.

It has been argued in these pages that there is such a thing as a distinctive variety of English that is Canadian; yet it should be observed that this distinctive variety is referred to as "Canadian English" and not as "the Canadian language." The fact is that Canadians share one language with Britons, Americans, Australians, and a host of other people, both inside the Commonwealth and beyond it. To claim that there is a Canadian language, or, as many Americans do, an American language, is to distort the meaning of the word *language* for nationalistic purposes. On the other hand, it is bullheaded to insist, as many do, that "English is English" and that only fools "dignify the slang and dialect" of Canada by giving it serious attention.

Introduction

The Languages We Use

There is no substitute for learning to write. Speech will not do as a substitute because it lets us off the hook too easily—both speaker and listener—through the persuasive shorthand of gesture, facial expression, and intonation. . . . Hence the great importance traditionally (and correctly) placed in humane education upon writing. There is really no other way of coming to terms seriously with language than by trying to write it well. To accept the proposition that writing is outmoded, that society is no longer "verbal" enough for skilful conduct of writing to be "relevant," is to arrest the development of those who . . . are unaware how easily— by "reading badly"—they can be made mute victims of cynical manipulation (social, commercial, and political) and could become emotional cripples and intellectual dwarfs. — George Whalley, "Picking up the Thread"

Everyone who will use this textbook speaks English. Those who are native speakers of English know the language long before it is studied in school. We can usually understand sentences that other people utter, even though we may have never heard words in precisely those combinations before. By the time older people will admit that we have learned to talk, we can say sentences that we have never heard or said before. In fact, we can say sentences long before we know that there are such things as sentences. But even if we know English before we study it, there is ample reason to study it in school and throughout our lives. It is a medium through which we can conduct our affairs, whether trivial or important. We need to know what we can about the language and work toward using it wisely and well.

Paradoxically, English is both easy and difficult to study: easy, because we already do know the language; difficult, because English isn't one thing, but many things. It is varied; it changes. When we speak, we don't all sound alike, and when we write, we don't all write in the same way. Each of us knows English in various versions, and each of us uses one version when talking to a close friend, say, and another when speaking to a forty-year-old English teacher. In the talk that we hear every day, we understand many different ways of speaking; and we can read and understand still other ways of speaking in print.

Yet using a language well depends on more than an awareness of our abilities to speak and understand different varieties. It is also more than writing "complete" sentences, using correct verb forms, making verbs agree with their subjects and pronouns with their antecedents. Beyond these forms and conventions, using a language well is a matter of choosing from the broad range of that language the words and constructions that will best convey our ideas to a particular audience in a particular situation, that will best enable us to present ourselves fully and honestly to another. But no one can make choices unless choices are available; no one can choose among beans, corn, and broccoli unless beans, corn, and broccoli are on the table for the choosing. To make good choices in language, we must recognize the different versions of English and know the various ways English is used in contemporary writing and speaking.

THE ELEMENTS OF LANGUAGE

Basically a language consists of a system of sounds, a collection of words, some changes in word forms, and some patterns into which the words fit to convey meaning. It may or may not have a system of writing and printing.

Sounds

English has between thirty and thirty-five distinctive speech-sounds (about eighteen vowels, the rest consonants) and variations in pause, pitch, and stress. Each sound is used with slight modifications in actual speech; for example, some people have a full *r* and others a very slight indication of the sound. The pronunciation of words varies considerably among the different regions in which English is used, so that we can easily identify some people as being from Newfoundland, say, or Cape Breton, or the Ottawa Valley.

Words

Counting everything from slang and local words to rarely used words and limited scientific terms, English has a vocabulary of well over two million words. Many of these are used in several different senses—one dictionary giving forty different meanings for the word *check*. An unabridged dictionary has about 500 000 entries; a college dictionary has about 150 000 entries; a university student probably uses or recognizes over 50 000 basic words, not including derivatives made by adding syllables like *-ed* and *-ly*. English forms many new words by adding prefixes (*in-*, *anti-*, *re-*, *super-*) and suffixes (*-er*, *-ish*, *-ship*, *-teria*), and it makes compounds freely by putting two or more words together (*bookcase*, *streamlined*).

Word Forms

Some languages are *inflected:* that is, their words change form to express grammatical relations in case, number, gender, person, tense, and the like. Latin and German, for example, are highly inflected. English uses very few changes in word forms: only a few endings, like the *-s* or *-es* of nouns (*boys, churches*), the *-s, -ed, -ing* of verbs (*asks, asked, asking*), *-er* and *-est* for comparing adverbs and adjectives (*hotter, hottest; nearer, nearest*), and a few internal changes, like the changes in vowels in *man-men, sing-sang*. These changes in form are one basis for grouping words into parts of speech.

Constructions

English has two basic ways of combining words into groups; by phrases centred on nouns or their equivalents (*in the morning; crossing the street*) and by clauses centred on verbs (*he runs the forty-yard dash; when she saw the results*). We interpret the meaning of these familiar patterns very largely from the order in which the words stand, an order that we pick up naturally as children and follow almost instinctively. Out of these simple word groups, we build sentences of varying length and complexity. The study of the relationships between words and word groups in sentences is *syntax*, the principal division of *grammar*.

Conventions

English, which, like other languages, first existed as speech, is represented in writing and printing by the twenty-six letters of the alphabet, a dozen or so punctuation marks, and such devices as capitals and italics. Our accepted practices of spelling, punctuation, capitalization, and so on were developed mostly by printers and serve chiefly to represent the spoken language in a conventional form.

These are the *materials* of language. What we do with them is another matter. This book is about *current* English, which appears in many forms. The book by and large uses — and usually recommends — *standard English*. This is the kind of English expected from an educated person who has spoken, heard, written, read, and examined English enough to know its traditional characteristics and the ways it is habitually used in books, magazines, classrooms, and public meetings. Another way to describe standard English is to say that those who use it will generally have accepted the judgments on usage made by many people in many places over a long period of time.

There is good reason to use standard English when writing. When you talk to other people, you are with them; they can watch your face and your hands; they see whether you lean toward them or turn coolly away; and they know instantly whether you are speaking uncertainly or boldly. But when someone else reads what you have written, you can't count on being there. More often than not, you are *not* there. That may mean that you will want or need to address your readers in a language whose characteristics you can confidently expect them to understand. You and your readers may not ever be together unless you hold a language in community property. Qualities that a language has accumulated in many places over a period of some time are likely to be clearer to readers, more accessible to them, than forms and usages that belong only to you or to you and a close circle of friends.

VARIETIES OF ENGLISH USAGE

Living languages undergo continual growth and change. Ordinarily the changes are slow and barely noticeable—slightly different pronunciations, new shadings in the meaning of words, and gradual shifts in grammatical constructions—but their cumulative effect can be dramatic. The works of Shakespeare, written four centuries ago, present difficulties to the modern reader: many of the words are unfamiliar and the grammar occasionally seems strange. The writings of Chaucer, who lived two centuries earlier, are hard to read without a large glossary and a grammar guide. Still earlier works, like *Beowulf*, can be understood only by specialists who have studied Old English much as they would study a foreign language. Yet all these works are written in a language that can claim to be called English and have been admired by many generations of readers of English.

Obviously our language has passed through many changes in the course of its history, and it will go on changing from generation to generation. But the language doesn't just change as time passes; at any given moment in its history, it also shows many internal variations. The work and worry and play of everyday life include all kinds of activities and situations, and English, both spoken and written, must serve them all. There are differences in the words and constructions typically used in various kinds of publications, even within a range no wider than that from newspapers to textbooks, and we use different language in writing or speaking to different people and for different purposes.

For instance, if in your writing you needed to say something about an object presented as something that it is not, you might use any one of the following words: *simulated*, *spurious*, *fraudulent*, *counterfeit*, *imitation*, *false*, *sham*, *pseudo*, *phony*, *bogus*, perhaps *put-on*. When you use one of the words, you may not think of it as an act of choice, and it may not be. You may simply use the word that you are most accustomed to using, or to hearing. If you do make a deliberate choice, however, the choice depends on many things — who you are, where you live, the people you spend most time with, the audience that will receive what you say or write, how much of your own personal language you are willing to use, and other factors. But you do have some choice among the words in this series, and in most other instances, especially when you write.

Since choices in vocabulary and construction are often available, it seems foolish to rely only on what we already know about language and to take for granted that the way we use words is going to be sufficient. Yet there is not always one "right" choice to make; no language should be forced into or kept in a neat mold. Until fairly recently, it was common for students and teachers of language to assume that "good" English was fixed, that departure from an inflexible set of rules governing its use was automatically "bad" English. This highly *prescriptive* approach to language study reflected the belief that there was some ideal form of English, orderly and uniform. Students had merely to learn the laws and apply them, just as they would in studying physics or chemistry. Although the prescriptive approach often produced good results, both practical experience and modern linguistic scholarship — called *descriptive* because it studies and describes the language as it *is* — have shown it to be less than satisfactory. No single system of conventions and rules can accurately describe a complex, changing language. Whether we like it or not, our language is changing and varied, and because it is, it offers choices.

But choices are not choices unless we know what they are. There is no perfect way of describing or listing all the possible forms of spoken English. *One* way to catch the variety of spoken English is to start with highly personal language, and then see what happens to personal language in groups, in special times, in special places.

Idiolects

Everyone has a personal language. It may be remarkably different from the language of someone who lives two hundred miles away, or even next door; it may be scarcely distinguishable from another person's language. This personal language is called an *idiolect*, a modern word formed by the blending of two Greek forms *idio-* (originally meaning "personal" or "one's own") and *-lect*, taken from *dialect*, which originally meant "talk" or "speech" although today it refers to one of the several varieties of a language. An idiolect, then, is the total language stock — words, grammar, pronunciations, and so on — of one speaker or writer at a given point in his or her life. In fact, no idiolect is identical with any other, for each grows in the context of an individual's life and as the circumstances of that life change, so the idiolect changes. Each of the speakers in the passage that follows begins to be recognizable, even in a few lines. The first speaker's language, in particular, tells something about his age, his location, and the manner of life he has led.

> "Ain't no whoopin' cranes nowadays," the old man said disconsolately.
>
> Lee spoke very slowly now, trying hard to be patient. "At Becker's slough. Honest. I saw the black tips of his wings just as clear!"
>
> "And you feel like you want to go, too," Grandpa said. "Breaks your heart almost, you want to go that bad, when you hear the thunder right over your head — like a big, long freight train passin' in the nighttime."
>
> His voice rose in an unexpected harsh croak. "At Becker's slough, you say? A whoopin' crane — a real, honest-to-gosh whooper? Boy, I ain't seen a whooper for forty years!" — Edward McCourt, "Cranes Fly South"

The writer in the passage below, however, owns and uses a different language. It is a language that is both active (some fifteen verbs and a number of nouns or modifiers made from verbs — *spincasting*, *calling*, *shielded*) and easy, with familiar pronoun references and pleasantly varied sentences that range from six to fifty-seven words.

> Trotlines from shore to shore get you more fish and bigger ones, but they're also more labor. After I'd finished with the line I worked along the beach, spincasting bootlessly for bass. Four Canada geese came diagonally over the river, low, calling, and in a moment I heard a clamor at the head of the island, shielded from me by the island's duned fringe and by willows. I climbed up through them to look. At least 200 more honkers took off screaming from the sand bar at the upper end of the bare plain. The passenger ran barking after them. Calling him back, I squatted beside a drift pile, and in the rose half-light of dusk watched through the field glass as they came wheeling in again, timid but liking the place as I liked it, and settled by tens and twenties at the bar and in the shallows above it where the two channels split. — John Graves, *Goodbye to a River*

One's idiolect is not necessarily restrictive. For although each of us speaks an idiolect—our own personal language—we can easily understand other idiolects we hear and read, and almost everyone at times shifts from one way of speaking to another. Nevertheless, it is possible for a personal language to be so uniquely personal as to be incomprehensible to a hearer or reader—as in forms of baby talk, or in some kinds of family lingo.

Intro

Dialects

When a community of speakers and writers uses idiolects that have much in common in pronunciation, grammar, and vocabulary, the combined idiolects are often referred to as a *dialect*. Usually we think of a dialect only as the language of a particular geographical region, but we can use the word to name any gathering of idiolects that share essential characteristics. A dialect is almost like a code: speakers and writers of a dialect can usually converse with and write to speakers of the general language, but they also know the special language of some group or region. For example, when a speaker says, "He jumped aboard of that dory some quick, eh?" he or she is using a dialect common in the Maritimes. But dialects occur everywhere; people who live and work on farms sometimes use distinguishable dialects, to be sure, and so do people who teach the third grade, and so do people whose language is often supposed to be remarkably proper.

Regional dialects.   There are, of course, many *regional dialects;* some of them are readily recognizable. Migration habits, work habits, geographical features, plant and animal life, and other characteristics of a particular region sometimes help to create a language for the region that is easily distinguishable from other dialects. A regional dialect may be marked by special words; people in the Prairies, for example, have more occasion to talk about *sloughs* and *coulees* than people in Ontario do, because of western topography.

A regional dialect may be identified at times by special pronunciations of ordinary words. After the election of Georgian Jimmy Carter as President of the United States in 1976, American newspapers often printed pieces on "how to speak Southern," with definitions—"bard" means *borrowed*, "gull" means *girl*, "stow" means *store*, "ahmoan" means *I am going to*, as in "Ahmoan go eat dinner."

A regional dialect may be marked, too, as in the following passage, by characteristic constructions (*folks begin to git their eyes open*), by pronunciations (*infarnal, leetle*), and by words not commonly used elsewhere (*consate*):

> Then mimicking his voice and manner, he repeated Allen's words with a strong nasal twang. " 'A' most time for you to give over the clock trade, I guess, for by all accounts they ain't worth havin', and most infarnal dear, too; folks begin to git their eyes open.' Better for you, if you'd 'a had your'n open I reckon; a joke is a joke, but I consate you'll find that no joke. The next time you tell stories about Yankee pedlars, put the wooden clock in with the wooden punk-inseeds, and hickory hams, will you? The Bluenoses, Squire, are all like Zeb Allen: they think they know everythin', but they get gulled from year's eend to year's eend. They expect too much from others, and do too leetle for themselves. . . . " — T.C. Haliburton, "Gulling a Bluenose"

Occupational dialects.   There are professional languages, craft languages, and shoptalk, all of which might be called *occupational dialects*. A wide range of such dialects is before us a good part of the time. We frequently borrow words from occupations for use in conversation, less frequently for use in writing — for example, *feedback*, *input*, *bug*, *huddle*, *fade-in*, *fade-out*, *close-up*, or *program* (as used with computers). Occupational dialects, of course, would occur most frequently in speech or writing in the discussion of particular occupations and their work, but as the words listed above may suggest, parts of some occupational dialects have come into common use and no longer call attention to themselves as forms of dialects. But occupational dialects occur in many ways. In professional journals and specialized books, for example, we may expect to find languages that are common to people within given occupations. The passage below, though it appeared in a fairly popular publication, depends heavily on language taken from studies in education and psychology:

> The child-centred syndrome sounded humane and friendly enough and took its force from a swing of opinion among educators against rigid curricula, bad instruction, and inflexible methodology. The new fashion was intended to contrast with, rather than rejuvenate, subject-centred and teacher-centred instruction. This new panacea was given added urgency by the cry for greater student freedom and the desire for increased course choices. Students knowing nothing of the ingredients were to write their own recipes. Government alarm at rapidly escalating classroom costs, inevitable if instructional excellence was to be maintained in small classes and in traditional curricula, further augmented these changes. A highly educated and literate population can be achieved only at enormous cost. — Joseph Gold, *In the Name of Language*

General English

Most of the language you hear or read, however, probably doesn't belong to any one of these dialects. If we take into account all of the language you hear or read in a week, from television, classrooms, friends, overheard conversations, radio disc-jockeys, books, newspapers, magazines, and elsewhere, a good part of it doesn't have the distinctive character of personal idiolect, regional dialect, or occupational dialect. Much of it is in that broad range of language so commonly used that it attracts no attention to itself, and of course there are varieties of language within that range. These varieties we might call *general dialects*. In writing, the vocabulary and sentence structure of the general dialects seem natural — and close to those of speech. Punctuation is usually relatively light, and sentences are likely to vary widely in length and complexity.

In the following passage, the author talks about our capital, Ottawa, but the language he uses is the community property of English-speaking people everywhere:

> Early September in Ottawa makes the residents forgive and forget too easily the brain-numbing harshness of the winter months. September evenings are long and somnolent. The air moves softly, caresses the bared skin. For those who live downtown, the Rideau canal is the focal point of these evenings. The paths and parkland that stretch beside the canal become crowded with strollers taking the evening air. Families crowd the park benches until long after their children's bedtimes, finally surrendering the benches to couples who will linger until the early morning hours. Here and there, runners, dressed in flimsy shorts and undershirts, lope silently through the knots and clusters of people. — Ian Adams, *S, Portrait of a Spy*

General dialects are not limited to transmitting matters of general interest; they will also carry specialized information in a way that can readily be understood by any educated speaker of English:

> Boat size is a critical factor in analysing the development of the inshore fishery. Almost all the boats between 31 and 65 feet in length are 'Cape Island' boats — a locally designed and built vessel ideally suited to carrying heavy loads in open seas. The boats are made of wood, although fibreglass construction at significantly higher cost is a growing trend. The wooden boats can cost up to $100,000, depending upon size and equipment. (The most frequently built boat is a 39 footer which, with Loran navigational equipment, ship-to-shore radio, radar, sonar, and auto-pilot, will range in cost between $50,000 and $75,000.) Because of heavy use of the boats in all weather conditions, the most productive fishermen usually sell them after three or four years, either to new fishermen locally or to fishermen from outside the southwest area. To give a sense of the

scale of capital investment involved and of the backward linkages to the local economy, a conservative estimate would have some ten million dollars of boat construction in the county annually. —Rick Williams, "Inshore Fishermen and Unionisation"

While general English may sometimes seem flat or uninteresting, it may also be interesting and precise. In the following passage, the language is a compressed form of what any of us might say (except perhaps the words *fraught*, *bilious*, and *turgid*). It is non-fiction, yet it does evoke the quality of vivid feeling that we associate with literature:

The next day the snails came out of their shells. We had spent the night in Sparta and returned to Mystras early in the morning. The rain had stopped, but the ground was still chill and damp; the sky was fraught with windblown clouds and patches of a frightening kind of blue. The first snail I saw was in the doorway of the mansion of Lascaris; the thing was sitting there, protruding more than halfway out of its shell, green and bilious, possibly the most hideous thing I'd ever seen. The same green as the ghastly jungle plant with its tendrils clinging to the slope, the turgid green of too much rain and history. — Gwendolyn MacEwen, *Mermaids and Ikons: A Greek Summer*

Dialect Modifications

Most of the English that we hear, read, speak, and write falls within what we have called the *general dialects*. Some versions of language within this range are far more casual and informal than others. Many of us, even if our speech or writing shows no other distinguishing marks (such as the work we do, or the place we live), use language that is breezy and often uncomplicated. Sentences are often short, and words and phrases may be more characteristic of speaking than of writing: *cop*, *deadpan*, *biffy*, *chancy*, *phony*, *peeve*, *whodunit*. Such words as these and others we use may be labelled *informal* (or colloquial) in dictionaries, which means that they occur more often in casual speech than in writing.

When writing or speaking informally, we are likely to make some use of *slang:* newly made words (*stagflation*, *shortfall*, *groupie*), or old words with new meanings (*cool*, *straight*, *trip*), or phrases conspicuously overused (*good deal*, *bottom line*). For many reasons, a continuing flow of such words and phrases enters the language. Sometimes we adopt one or another of them because we want to be different or because we feel that new experiences need new names; sometimes we want to set ourselves apart from some other group (parents, say) by adopting expressions they don't use. Most slang is short-lived, but some proves useful enough to be absorbed into the general vocabulary.

If being informal, we are apt to use quite a few *localisms*, words or phrases characteristic of a certain region and often associated with a *regional dialect*. People often use regional names for common things (*coal oil* or *kerosene; gaspereau* or *alewife; shadberry, saskatoon berry*, or *juneberry*), special names for certain occupations (*longlinerman, draegerman, boom man*), or special names for features of the landscape peculiar to a region (*tickle, bogan, thrum-cap, butte, bench, muskeg, bluff* "clump of trees"). Some of these words are old forms put to new uses; others are borrowings from Canadian French or from Amerindian languages.

Intro

Non-standard English

Some of the varieties of language mentioned above are *non-standard* forms of English. A *standard* may be defined as an accepted measure of quality. If a measure of quality is accepted, that means it has wide use. Idiolects, dialects, and the various dialect modifications are associated with particular people, particular groups, particular places, particular times. In this special sense then, they are *non-standard*, not languages for wide use.

Any language may appear in non-standard form. If grammatical errors occur, if spelling is inconsistent, if punctuation is inadequate, if usage is that not widely accepted, such language may be called *non-standard*. Errors in form mean that the language is not meeting an accepted measure of quality. Indeed, you should already know that the most common way of judging a person's language is by its propriety and consistency in grammar, spelling, punctuation, pronunciation, and usage. Moreover, each of the varieties of language — those primarily spoken forms already mentioned and the primarily written forms discussed in the following sections — can become unacceptable and therefore non-standard because it contains contradictions, ambiguities, and other violations of clear thinking. In short, we can consider as non-standard any language that is inconsistent within itself and fails to communicate as effectively as possible.

You should also remember that language can be misused to deceive, to betray, to oppress. Some styles of language are *non-human* and thus unacceptable. If a speaker says "From the beginning of our contact session, I want to get you programmed to give me instant feedback," then no matter what his or her intention is, the speaker is thinking of us as objects, electronic machines. An educator who says "We must get the new students conditioned to the self-paced learning programs" is, whether he or she intends to or not, visualizing students as Pavlovian dogs. Some such styles may also be *mean-spirited*. They focus on the speaker and his own interests and associates, excluding all others from the circle of communication. Some styles are simply agencies for falsehood or intimidation; the growing prevalence of ambiguous "big words" and misleading jargon in public expression is dangerous because such language deliberately evades clear meaning. (See also 28.1, Formal Words.)

EDITED ENGLISH

No perfect system exists for classifying and naming all versions of the English language. The idiolects, dialects, and versions of language mentioned above are examples only. All of them are forms of spoken English. Some of them can also be written effectively.

But for use in writing, almost any language has to be edited because it is ordinarily being presented publicly. Such public presentation—as opposed to private conversation or personal note-making—requires careful preparation and revision; in short, it needs editing. *Edited English* is a version of the language that you may associate with schools, good newspapers, good books, or good public speakers. It is an idiolect or dialect that has been modified to produce a measure of uniformity consistent with the grammatical standards traditionally taught in Canadian, British, and American schools, using a vocabulary shared by people in different places and different times. Edited English has been produced by a kind of filtering process. In this process, what separates people from each other linguistically is supposed to be trapped and discarded, while what binds people together linguistically is left free for use. Few people consistently *speak* edited English, but many *write* it most of the time. What we should keep in mind is that though edited English is just another available variety of language, it is one of the most important for effective communication.

We do not, of course, mean that all forms of edited English are alike. The forms of spoken English mentioned above, when edited for public presentation, can become appropriate edited English. The casual language of our private conversations, of our idiolects and dialects, can be written as a kind of *informal* edited English. The general spoken English that was described earlier is the foundation for *general* edited English. The *formal variety* of usage, found chiefly in writing, is principally a development from general spoken English but still more fully edited and more complex than general edited English. It is more influenced by reading and follows more closely the conventions built up by writers and editors in the past. It usually occurs in discussions of specialized topics and in writing addressed to somewhat limited audiences.

The vocabulary of formal English includes most of the general words but very few from regional dialects. Necessarily, formal English uses the specialized vocabulary of the subject matter being discussed; it also may use a good many abstract words. The grammatical constructions tend to be fuller than in general English, and very often the sentences are somewhat longer and more complex. Formal writing tends to follow older practices in punctuation and to use *close* punctuation—more frequent marks than are typical in general English, and *heavier* ones, such as a semicolon where a comma might serve.

Intro

The formal English used in academic, scientific, technical, and scholarly writing is usually impersonal. Good formal writing, however, is not stilted or dull. This account of the mapping of Switzerland shows the single-minded attention to the subject, the compact and orderly statement of ideas, and the moderate use of technical terms that characterize impersonal formal English:

> The heroic task of making a topographic survey and map of Switzerland fell to the lot of General Guillaume Henri Dufour (1787-1875). Under his personal supervision the work was begun in 1830 and the first sheet was published in 1842. Thirty-four years later the entire survey, on a scale of 1 : 100,000, was finished and the last of the 25 sheets came from the press. Soon after, the map appeared in atlas form, published at Berne. Far from being a pioneering effort that would require immediate revision, the Dufour atlas proved to be a model of accuracy and artistic delineation, not only for future map makers of Switzerland, but for cartographers at large. The sheets of the atlas were used as a basis for later surveys on different scales, and on the sheets of Switzerland's new survey references were made to the corresponding sections and subsections of the original Dufour map. The art work and conventional signs on the new map were almost identical with those on the Dufour originals. The lettering and bench marks (figures denoting heights), prominent buildings, roads, boundaries and forests were printed in black. Small slopes and passes, ravines and narrow defiles that could not be shown by equally spaced contour lines were printed in brown hachures. Black hachures were used to indicate rocky prominences and precipices, the general effect being a pictorial representation by oblique lighting. Horizontal surveys were shown in bronze and water was indicated by shades of blue. — Lloyd A. Brown, *The Story of Maps*

A more personal type of formal English is shown in the following passage. Some of the words and phrases are formal—*inert knowledge*, *radical error*, and *delicate*, *receptive*, *responsive to stimulus*. The constructions are full: note the sentence beginning *Who-*

ever was the originator and the following sentence, beginning *But whatever its weight of authority*. But some constructions (*I appeal to you*, *as practical teachers. So far, so good*.) carry an unmistakable personal emphasis and keep us aware that the writer is expressing himself as an individual:

> I appeal to you, as practical teachers. With good discipline, it is always possible to pump into the minds of a class a certain quantity of inert knowledge. You take a text-book and make them learn it. So far, so good. The child then knows how to solve a quadratic equation. But what is the point of teaching a child to solve a quadratic equation? There is a traditional answer to this question. It runs thus: The mind is an instrument, you first sharpen it, and then use it; the acquisition of the power of solving a quadratic equation is part of the process of sharpening the mind. Now there is just enough truth in this answer to have made it live through the ages. But for all its half-truth, it embodies a radical error which bids fair to stifle the genius of the modern world. I do not know who was first responsible for this analogy of the mind to a dead instrument. For aught I know, it may have been one of the seven wise men of Greece, or a committee of the whole lot of them. Whoever was the originator, there can be no doubt of the authority which it has acquired by the continuous approval bestowed upon it by eminent persons. But whatever its weight of authority, whatever the high approval it can quote, I have no hesitation in denouncing it as one of the most fatal, erroneous, and dangerous concepts ever introduced into the theory of education. The mind is never passive; it is a perpetual activity, delicate, receptive, responsive to stimulus. You cannot postpone its life until you have sharpened it. Whatever interest attaches to your subject-matter must be evoked here and now; whatever powers you are strengthening in the pupil, must be exercised here and now; whatever possibilities of mental life your teaching should impart, must be exhibited here and now. That is the golden rule of education, and a very difficult rule to follow. — Alfred North Whitehead, *The Aims of Education*

Altogether, then, there are many versions of our language — countless idiolects, many dialects, general, public, edited English, and formal language. Each version can be used to move or to inform; each can be warm, generous, and powerful; each can be used with point and precision; and each must be used with due regard for meaning since effective communication cannot be achieved without a firm grasp of this important aspect of language.

To ignore this principle of *effectiveness* is to be indifferent to the dangers of misunderstanding that lie in the abuse and misuse of language and to forego the deep satisfaction that comes from using good language in a clear, concise, and pleasing way. In what follows, we will examine the question "What is 'good' language — especially with reference to written English?"

THE SEARCH FOR "GOOD" LANGUAGE

A "good" language is not just a gathering of specific practices in vocabulary, grammar, and usage that you must invariably follow. Many varieties of English are available to you, all equally reputable and, in certain circumstances, all equally "good." The objective in writing is not first to conform to some previously established system of usages, but to use the resources of the language to communicate fully, precisely, and honestly. Good writing is not born of a system of rules and usages; systems of rules and usages are born of good writing.

Intro

SOME VERSIONS OF ENGLISH — A SUMMARY

Spoken language

IDIOLECT: an individual's personal language, influenced by environmental factors (geographical area, occupation) and internal factors (age, sex, personality).

DIALECT: the combined idiolects of a *community of speakers*. Dialects can overlap, but can be classified by such terms as regional and occupational.

DIALECT MODIFICATIONS: slang, localisms, fad words.

GENERAL ENGLISH includes the languages above and might be called the dialect of the great majority of speakers of Canadian English without the strong modifications of other dialectal factors.

NON-STANDARD ENGLISH does not meet the accepted measure of quality in usage, grammar, pronunciation, meaning, and so on.

Written language: Edited English

INFORMAL ENGLISH is characterized by short sentences and "breezy" style; it includes personal correspondence and journal-keeping.

GENERAL ENGLISH is characterized by the constructions and vocabulary of general English, more attention being paid to grammatical form; it is found in most books, newspapers, and magazines.

FORMAL ENGLISH is characterized by full constructions and specialized vocabulary; it is generally impersonal, found mostly in academic, scientific, technical, and other scholarly writing.

NON-STANDARD ENGLISH: see above.

A language can enable us to remember our experiences and get them straight in our minds. A language can enable us to put our experiences in order and establish connections between them. A language can enable us to speculate on our experiences and draw conclusions from them. A language can enable us to praise or to blame. As the previous section suggests, many varieties of language are available to serve these purposes, each suitable in particular circumstances. Each of these varieties may have its own distinct structure, and each can be written.

It is here that writers meet a special problem, already noted. When we speak to someone, we are there. We can "finish out" our words by gestures and sounds. The tone of voice, a shift of shoulders, a gesture with the hands, a movement of the eyes—all these complement the words. And when we speak to people, often we can tell if they are comprehending or accepting what we say by their expressions; if we sense that they are not fully understanding us, then we have the immediate opportunity to start over, speaking in a different way and using different words to get over the difficulty.

But when it comes to writing, we are rarely present when someone reads what we have written. Our meaning and intention rest entirely in the words on the page, and these are sometimes inadequate. No language we use permits us to communicate two things at once under normal circumstances; when we say one thing, we're *not* saying another; if we acquire the capacity to use a formal language, we often risk losing the rich words that name particular local features in a regional dialect. When we write, there is a further problem, for written words have to stand on their own. We are not there to explain, to modify, to fill in, to shift emphasis. We should, then, give our greatest care to writing, to insure the precision and the fullness of our meaning. Readers are likely to be people much like ourselves who have their own varied interests and preoccupations. They think their own thoughts. They can't be expected to fill in gaps we leave out. They can't be expected to attend closely just because we've written something.

Writing is a kind of *contract* between writer and reader. The writer asks the reader to spend time in reading; in return the writer is obliged to give care to the writing. The reader requires of the writer some worth in what is written and owes the writer at least a little curiosity, a little patience, a little willingness to listen. Any language that clearly demonstrates precision and fullness of meaning and also promotes rapport between reader and writer is likely to be "good" language.

APPROPRIATE LANGUAGE

This *Handbook* customarily recommends what we earlier called *Intro*
edited English, for several sound reasons. In the first place, as
already mentioned, no single handbook can fully describe all the
versions of English; it is doubtful that a single handbook could
describe *two* versions or even a *single* version of the language fully.
Since this book can't describe all, or even some, versions of the
language fully, it sets out to describe and recommend the kind of
language that appears most commonly in print, that is, the primary
medium of communication in most books, newspapers, and magazines in Canada. Edited English is valuable because it is widely
used, and it is widely used because it is flexible and will serve many
purposes. It is a language suitable to sociological research and to
cookbooks, to personal letters and to political commentary. We
recommend it, finally, because it is a language we can speak, hear,
and read in common. Its widespread use in publications and in
schools makes it accessible to most people. The language does not
belong to any single person, or to any single group or region.
Widely used and commonly accessible, edited English is a shared
language which most readily facilitates mutual understanding. We
have not tried to list here all the characteristics of edited English:
the rest of this *Handbook* tries to show what edited usage is like.
When we say, "Many writers prefer to..." or "It's usually best to
say..." or "Try to avoid...," we are recommending general
Canadian English edited for written use.

Any language, in principle, can be a "good" language if used
appropriately. Consequently, edited English can be governed by a
standard of appropriateness. When you write a language, the
choice of vocabulary, usage, and construction is, in a way, not
yours alone. The subject you are talking about makes certain
demands. The audience you reach may have certain expectations
and these merit your respect. When we make our choices from the
range language offers, we must use words in trust and place
ourselves in community with others. We cannot use language solely
as if it were our private toy. Not can we use language solely to
please others. If we are to use a language well, we must use it so
that it is appropriate to us as speakers or writers, appropriate to its
audience, and appropriate to the particular situation we find ourselves in.

Appropriateness to Speaker or Writer

As a writer, you dominate the writer-reader relationship; your judgment and sense of fitness control the language you use. Whatever your purpose in writing, express your ideas in language that seems natural. Your writing, in fact, should be an honest expression of your own character. Your language alone is what presents you to a reader; you cannot be everywhere your writing is, and only your language can bring a distant reader and you into any accord. The most fitting language for you, then, is that which gives you and your ideas fullest and most effective expression.

This does not mean that the idiolect or dialect that you already speak is a language you can rest content with. Nor does it mean that your idiolect is necessarily "bad" language. It does mean that you should strive to master other versions of general English because they are appropriate in situations you may expect to face in future. One place to start the process of choosing an appropriate language is in your own present language. How well do you understand the way you already speak and write? What is your present language like? Does it have special traits that you can't reasonably expect other people to understand? Are you sure of yourself in spelling, punctuation, sentence structure? When you write a paper for a course, do you choose the best part of your natural language, or do you try to imitate some entirely different variety of English? If you return to a paper that you wrote some time ago and read it aloud, does it sound at all like something you would or could say? If it doesn't, can you tell what happened to your language in the paper? Or what has happened to it since?

The suggestions and the pressures of teachers or critics may have some brief effect on the way you use language, but in the long run you set your own standard. The language you use is your responsibility. Good English is not primarily a matter of rules, but of judgment. You are not struggling under a series of *don'ts* but trying to discover among the wide resources of modern English the language that best suits your purpose, your audience, and yourself.

Appropriateness to Reader or Listener

If you are trying to reach particular types of readers, you may have to adjust your subject matter and your manner of expression more or less to their expectations. You have to be more than merely understandable; you may have to meet your readers, who are real people, largely on their own ground. If your language—though right for you—is not language your readers can use and respond to, then they will not get your meaning. You can enjoy in cold comfort the knowledge that you are right in what you say, but you can hardly expect applause from those who are unable to understand much of what you say (or *intended* to say). Meeting readers on common ground, or even on their ground, is not as hard as it may appear at first. After all, some adjustments in language are made *Intro* almost automatically in letters, for one naturally writes in different ways to different people. The big problem lies in having to write without knowing who will be reading the words. Yet you must learn to overcome such difficulties through practice under critical direction. In writing a class paper, try to direct it to some particular audience—your classmates, for example, or people who disagree with you, or your best friend. Avoid writing vaguely "to whom it may concern." Imagining a specific audience will help you judge what words and what kinds of sentences are appropriate. In this way, you will learn to choose language that is clear, interesting, and most suitable for the occasion.

Clarity. Since the aim in writing is to communicate, you must select clear and exact words that your readers will understand. If the subject demands unfamiliar words, try to use them so that the meaning is clear; if necessary, include a concise explanation. Occasionally, you may have to provide a formal definition. Clarity also calls for sentences that are not excessively long and that have a natural, direct movement—though you also must remember the demands of the subject and situation. Experienced readers can grasp more elaborate sentences than those who read little or read hurriedly. Nevertheless, everyone finds pleasure in reading direct, straightforward sentences.

Careful attention to punctuation is also necessary if you are to make your statements clear to your readers. The various marks—commas, dashes, semicolons, periods and so on—indicate the groups of words that are to be understood as units and often show the relationship between these units. Omitted or misused marks may force readers to go over a passage two or three times to get its intended meaning; superfluous marks may prevent them from recognizing words belonging together or may slow their reading-speed to the point of exasperation.

Correctness. Part of a writer's duty to his or her readers is to meet their expectations in language by taking care to avoid thoughtless, elementary errors. Such blunders will certainly convince some readers that you are not giving them the consideration they deserve; they may very well refuse to take you seriously. When you finish writing a paper, take time to check it carefully for errors in grammar, spelling, punctuation, and other matters of usage.

Interest. All readers appreciate some liveliness in what they read, both in the writer's expression and in the choice of material. Too many students seem to feel that serious writing requires flat, pompous language. On the contrary, in striving for liveliness, there is no need to seek novelty through words that are out of the ordinary. Instead, use just those words you might use in an intelligent, reasonably animated conversation. Avoid monotonous sentences that drag; vary their length and pattern so as to please active, alert minds. Attract your readers' interest by making reference, when appropriate, to things people have actually said and done, and use details to illustrate your ideas.

One warning is needed: in gearing your writing to your readers' background and expectations, don't underestimate their intelligence, thus compromising yourself and insulting them. Visualize them at their best and write for them at that level.

Appropriateness to Purpose and Situation

The teacher in your writing class may be interested in seeing essays and other forms of writing in which you use a wide variety of language types and styles, exercises in your own idiolect that use dialect forms, and so on. But most of your other teachers will not be so receptive to such experiment in the papers they assign. In all probability, they will expect — and appreciate — well-written edited English, as described earlier. Here again you must accept responsibility for choosing appropriate language. Good judgment is essential to good writing.

The standards of written usage in a composition course are about the same as what would be expected in published material of similar nature. This means that papers about personal experiences, school activities, or your own private reflections might be suitably set forth in general English. It also means that papers required in other courses will usually be formal, revealing less of your own personality and attitudes; such papers focus with greater concentration on an impersonal subject and require the writer to meet other expectations and objectives.

This standard for college and university writing is not the result of an arbitrary decision that a given variety of language is nicer or more correct than others. When you are able to use a more formal variety of language, you have, by acquiring that ability, mastered a larger vocabulary, a wider variety of sentence structures, and a greater degree of control. Such mastery of mature language is necessary if you wish to say anything of merit about academic subjects. Consider this single instance. Suppose you are in a philosophy course where one of your assignments is to write a critique of a book on philosophy, including an examination of the author's premises, the mode of his argument, and the style of his presentation. To complete the assignment requires, among other things, that you know what a *critique* is, and also that you must command a language that will let you talk accurately about *premises*, *modes of argument*, and *styles of presentation*.

Intro

The rather technical language that will enable you to discuss these things may not, however, be useful in a meditative essay about sitting on the prairie at midnight under hosts of twinkling stars. If you pay attention to purpose and situation, you should be able to treat most subjects in appropriate language. Inexperienced writers frequently use language that is too heavy to be appropriate to them or to their subjects. For example, a student who wanted to say that he had rebelled against his parents despite having come from a happy home wrote:

> Although my juvenile domestic environment was permissive and munificent and my sibling relationships were auspicious, I found it incumbent upon me to express my generation's mores in reaction to paternal supervision.

The student may seriously have believed that this inflated kind of writing was better than a simple statement. He would almost certainly object to being told that his sentence was *bad English*, worse perhaps than if it contained some inaccurate or illogical expressions. Inaccuracies can be quite easily corrected, whereas inflated and inappropriate language must be completely replaced if the paper is to be effective. The artificial "formality" of such language is not found in good formal writing, and it should be avoided in student papers.

Once you find the tone that is right for your situation, you should stay with it unless there is some special reason for changing. Although the lines between the varieties of usage cannot be drawn precisely, conspicuous shifts from one to another should ordinarily be avoided, as in the second of these two sentences:

> In the distant pines the rising wind whined as it played among the needles. And when the storm broke, the rain came down in buckets.

Superficial consistency is not so important as fundamental appropriateness, but ordinarily one variety of English should be used throughout a piece of writing.

Reading the work of practised writers is one good way to increase your sensitivity to language and its various uses. Before attempting to write for an unfamiliar situation, read and study some good examples of writing done for a similar purpose. After all, it makes little sense to try to write an article for a magazine you have never read or to try to write a technical report or reference paper without ever having seen one. First you must learn what is typically done in a given situation. When you have learned, follow the accepted practices unless there is good reason to do otherwise.

▶ EXERCISE

A good part of the time most of us take for granted the language we use and hear regularly. We may not pay much attention to language differences unless we hear words or phrases that are new to us or startling in their context. One way to work toward using your language thoughtfully and well is to pay close attention to what you say and hear, thus becoming more conscious of the many ways language is used in the world around you.

1. What are the identifying marks of the variety of language used by those people you were closest to in your early years? List words, expressions, special ways of saying things that you have heard from family and friends, but do not commonly hear elsewhere.

2. If you are in school, list new expressions and ways of saying things that you have heard since starting school. Which of them have you started using yourself?

3. Which words and expressions that you use or hear appear to have been popularized by their use on some television program?

4. Which words and expressions are used to express approval by your family? Your friends and associates now? Which words and expressions are used to express disapproval by your family? By your current friends and associates?

5. Which words and expressions seem to recur most frequently around you?

6. Which words and expressions that you use or hear seem to be associated with some particular region in Canada?

PART ONE

Conventions of the Language

1

Grammar of Sentences

*. . . the right to utter a sentence is one of the very greatest liberties; and we are
entitled to little wonder that freedom of utterance should be, in every society, one
of the most contentious and ill-defined rights. The liberty to impose this formal
unity is a liberty to handle the world, to remake it, if only a little, and to hand it to
others in a shape which may influence their actions.* — Richard Weaver, *The Ethics
of Rhetoric*

The *sentence* is the primary constructed unit in edited English as it
is in all other varieties of English. Indeed, a sentence form of some
kind exists in most, if not all, languages.

What appears to happen in the English sentence form is that two
or more kinds of experience are combined to make a new and more
complete statement of experience. You may know what *pants* are
and what *tearing* is, but when you read the sentence "My pants are
torn," you can understand it without stopping to think about the
separate things, *pants* and *tearing*. The sentence is something new
and different from the kinds of experience that it includes. In the
common sentence form the two (sometimes more) kinds of experience are stated, usually one as a subject, the other as a verb.
Sometimes, however, one or the other or both of the experiences
are not stated, but supplied by the context:

> He went to town yesterday. [In this sentence, the different kinds of
> experience or reality included are the person referred to as *He* and the
> act of *going*.]

> Why weren't you there? [In this sentence the two are the person
> referred to as *you* and the idea of *being in some place*.]

> Please try to be on time. [In this sentence, one is omitted, but since we
> can understand that the speaker is talking directly to someone, we
> know that what is left out is *you*.]

> Why not? [Here all of the experiences are omitted from the sentence,
> and we would have to depend on the circumstances in which the
> words appear to know what the experiences are. They might, for
> example, be a shortened form of "Why can't I go to town?"]

> Good! [Here again we would have to depend on the circumstances in
> which the word appears to know what the statement is.]

All these constructions are sentences, though they look very
different from each other. A written sentence is a message of one or
more words punctuated as an independent unit. A sentence, then, is
made complete by its grammatical form and meaning or, in special
circumstances, by the context in which it appears.

A writer has to twist and turn sentences this way and that so as to get the message across most effectively. In order to take full advantage of what sentences can do, however, you must understand how different kinds of sentences are made. If you know the inner structure of sentences and the way the parts fit together, your control of the several kinds of sentence will improve and so will the quality of your writing. This section reviews the basic grammatical terms needed in analysing and describing sentences and in discussing the relations between the several parts.

Further explanation of the effective use of sentence types—how you can give your style emphasis, control, and variety—is provided in chapter 25. That advice depends, however, on your having a basic knowledge of common sentence elements and constructions.

1.1 ◀

1.1 MAIN SENTENCE ELEMENTS

Most English sentences are made with a subject and a verb. You may see this pattern referred to as the "major" or "favorite" sentence type in English.

The Subject

The subject (s) of a sentence is a noun or noun equivalent (pronoun, noun clause, gerund, infinitive) that is the starting point of the sentence. The *simple subject* is a single word, like *students* in the first sentence below. The *complete subject* consists of the simple subject together with its modifiers—*Hurried students:*

       s
Hurried **students** often make careless mistakes. [noun]

 s
She runs faster than her brother does. [pronoun]

      s
What he doesn't know is that he talks too much. [noun clause]

 s
Talking is his only exercise. [gerund]

 s
To listen is to suffer. [infinitive]

The Verb

A verb (v) is a word which has forms like *ask*, *asks*, *asked* or *sing*, *sang*, *sung*, *singing* and which in a sentence agrees with the subject. In the typical sentence, the verb follows the subject and, like the subject, is often a nucleus for modifying words. The verb may consist of one or more words:

S   V
Hurried students often **make** careless mistakes.

V   S   V
Does he **listen** to what she says?

S   V
Leslie Jones **has driven** for twenty years without getting a ticket.

S   V
Perhaps the defendant **should be given** the benefit of the doubt.

The *predicate* is the verb and whatever words are related to it, such as objects, complements, and modifiers. In the following sentences, the complete predicate is in boldface type, the verb itself being marked with a v:

S   V
Hurried students **often make careless mistakes.**

S   V
The doorbell **rang.** [The verb is the complete predicate.]

S   V
After finishing his second year, George **spent two long sessions talking with his advisor about his major.**

The Object

The *direct object* (O) of a verb is a noun or noun equivalent that completes the statement. It answers the question asked by adding "what" or "whom" after the verb. (Hurried students often make what? Careless mistakes.):

S   V   O
Hurried students often make careless **mistakes.** [noun]

S   V   O
The Sherwoods have decided **to buy a home.** [infinitive phrase]

S   V   O
He wondered **what he should do.** [noun clause]

The *indirect object* (IO) is used with verbs of telling, asking, giving, receiving, and so on. It names the receiver of the message, gift, or whatever, answering the question "to whom or what" or "for whom or what." It comes *before* the direct object:

S   V   IO   O
He gave the **church** a memorial window.

The same meaning can usually be expressed in a prepositional phrase placed *after* the direct object:

   S   V   O
He gave a memorial window **to the church.**

1.1 ◀

The Complement

A complement (C) is a noun or an adjective in the predicate which follows a linking verb (LV). In contrast to an object, a complement is related to the subject rather than to the verb, because a linking verb (sometimes called a *copula*) expresses a condition rather than direct action. A noun used as a complement is called a *predicate noun*; an adjective used as a complement is called a *predicate adjective:*

      S   LV   C
Mary Enderby is a skilled **architect.** [predicate noun]

      S   LV   C
The tenor sounded a little **flat.** [predicate adjective]

The most common linking verb is *be* in its various forms: *is, are, was, were, has been, might be.* Other linking verbs include *seem* and *appear* and, in some contexts, *feel, grow, act, look, smell, taste,* and *sound.*

See also 9.2, Predicate Adjectives.

▶ **EXERCISE**

List both the main sentence elements (subject, verb, direct object, indirect object, complement) and the complete predicate of each sentence in the paragraphs below.

At Flowerlea the channel is so narrow the summer cottagers can lean over and assess the deckhands' breakfast bacon. In the fall the last of the cottagers sit around their barbecue pits with a liner in the front yard, the shipmaster pacing about above them, cursing them and their hot dogs, the handiest things to curse. He is afraid of the Flowerlea channel, so narrow, and of the weight of waters astern hurrying him along, the navigation season waning and his insurance rate about to jump sky-high if he doesn't clear the locks by the appointed day. — Hugh Hood, "Three Halves of a House"

The land still draws me more than other lands. I have lived in Africa and in England, but splendid as both can be, they do not have the power to move me in the same way as, for example, that part of southern Ontario where I spent four months last summer in a cedar cabin beside a river. "Scratch a Canadian, and you find a phony pioneer," I used to say to myself in warning. But all the same it is true, I think, that we are not yet totally alienated from physical earth, and let us only pray we do not become so. I once thought that my lifelong fear and mistrust of cities made me a kind of old-fashioned freak; now I see it differently. — Margaret Laurence, "Where the World Began"

Word Order

In English, we identify the main sentence elements chiefly by their position in the sentence — that is, by word order. Although the form of the words is the same, it makes a lot of difference whether their order is "the ball hit the boy" or "the boy hit the ball."

Typical word order.   The typical order of the main elements is subject-verb-object (or subject-linking verb-complement). This is the order in which we make most statements and the means by which we understand them.

In "The class congratulated Rachel," we know through experience that *class* is the subject of *congratulated* because it comes before the verb, and that *Rachel* is the object because it follows the verb. When the verb is in the *passive voice* (a past participle following some form of the verb *be*), the order of sentence elements remains subject — verb: "Rachel was congratulated by the class."

So familiar is this order that we recognize it even though the statement itself may be gibberish, or "jabberwocky," as in these lines by Lewis Carroll:

> . . . the slithy toves
> Did gyre and gimble in the wabe. . . .

Whatever the meaning, most people would agree that because of the order of the words, the subject is *toves* and the verbs are *did gyre* and *gimble*.

Inverted order.   The typical order of sentence elements is reversed in questions, exclamations, and emphatic statements:

           V   S   O
QUESTION: Have you a minute to spare?

                    C   S LV
EXCLAMATION: How wasteful these meetings are!

                      O   S   V
EMPHATIC OBJECT: A better job I never had.

In sentences with *there* or *it* as an *anticipating subject* (AS), or *expletive*, the real subject comes after the verb:

AS LV C S
It is a difficult choice.

  AS LV C   S
There are several reasons for the difficulty.

1.1

Gr s

When the usual order of elements is reversed, the subject of the sentence can be found by locating the verb and identifying what word answers the question formed by putting "who" or "what" before it. Thus in the expression "A lot he knows about it," *knows* is the verb, and since the answer to "*Who* knows?" is obviously *he*, *he* (rather than *lot*) is the subject.

Main Sentence Elements

SUBJECT: A noun or noun equivalent that performs an action or is in a particular state of being; it usually appears before the verb and determines the number (singular or plural) of the verb.

VERB: A word that is inflected to show tense, person, and number. It signifies the action or state of being of the subject.

PREDICATE: The verb and all words related to it.

DIRECT OBJECT: A noun or noun equivalent that answers the question asked by adding *what?* or *whom?* to the verb.

INDIRECT OBJECT: A noun that names the receiver of some action, answering the question *to whom or what?* or *for whom or what?* added to the verb. It comes before the direct object.

COMPLEMENT: A noun or adjective in the predicate, following a *linking verb*; it refers to the subject rather than the verb, because a linking verb expresses a condition rather than direct action.

Examples:

    S   V   DO
Careless drivers may injure pedestrians.

   S   V   IO   DO
Charity may give the needy financial aid.

     S LV   C
Some drivers are often careless.

   S LV   C
Charity is often the last resort of the needy.

   AS LV C   S
There are many hotels in Vancouver.

1.2 SECONDARY SENTENCE ELEMENTS

In addition to the main sentence elements (subject-verb-object or subject-linking verb-complement), most sentences also contain secondary elements. Secondary elements are typically used as modifiers (M)—they describe, limit, or make more exact the meaning of main elements. The table on page 32 shows the various ways in which modifiers—single words, phrases, and clauses—might be used to qualify or expand a simple statement.

Adjectives and Adverbs as Modifiers

Single words used as modifiers are ordinarily related to the element they modify by means of word order. *Adjectives* relate to nouns and usually stand before the words they modify, but sometimes they come immediately after; in both examples, *climb* is the word modified:

>   M   M
> It was a **slow, dangerous** climb.

>   M   M
> The steepness of the slope made the climb **slow** and **dangerous.**

Adverbs are more varied in position because often they relate to the sentence as a whole. However, when they modify a particular word (verb, adjective, or adverb) they usually stand close to it:

>   M
> They **particularly** wanted to go. [modifies *wanted*]

>   M
> He came home from the movies **quite** late. [modifies *late*]

See 9, Adjectives and Adverbs.

Other Words and Word Groups as Modifiers

In English a noun often modifies another noun: *glass* jar, *ski* pants, *dance* hall. Nouns used in this way are usually called *modifiers* (not adjectives) or, more exactly, *nouns used attributively.* (See 6.4, Nouns as Modifiers.)

Prepositional phrases function as modifiers in the majority of English sentences:

>   M
> An apartment dweller **in a large city** [modifies *apartment dweller*]

>   M   M
> can live **in the same place** [modifies *can live*] **for a year** [modifies *in*

M
the same place] and never speak **to his next-door neighbor.** [modifies *speak*]

Verbal phrases and subordinate clauses also can function as modifiers:

M
Finding no one at home, he scribbled a note and left it under the front door. [participle phrase modifying *he*]

M
He needed a way **to make money.** [infinitive phrase modifying *way*]

M
People **who live in glass houses** shouldn't throw stones. [subordinate clause modifying *People*]

(See 3, Subordinate Clauses and Connectives, and 4, Verbals and Verbal Phrases.)

Appositives

An appositive (A) is a noun or noun equivalent placed beside another noun to supplement or complement its meaning. It has the same grammatical function as the noun to which it relates. In speech, it is marked by a pause and a change in pitch:

A
Your lawyer, **Mr. Jenkins,** is on the telephone.

A
The story takes place in Thebes, **a city in ancient Greece.**

(See 11.3, page 150, Appositives.)

Modifiers of Modifiers

Words, phrases, and clauses that modify the main sentence elements may themselves be modified. These expressions are called *modifiers of modifiers:*

MM   M   S   V   M   M   O
The **local** high-school orchestra played several difficult selections

MM M
very well.

▶ EXERCISE

Notice how the sentence *The girl sang* can be expanded to make this sentence: *The delicately beautiful girl, made even more attractive by her nervousness, sang so sweetly that every person in the audience hoped she would win the contest.*

Modifiers

Modifiers of the subject:

M   S

A WORD: The **local** orchestra played a selection.

S   M

A PHRASE: The orchestra, **consisting largely of amateurs,** played a selection.

S   M

A CLAUSE: The orchestra, **which had practised hard for several weeks,** played a selection.

Modifiers of the verb:

V   M

A WORD: The orchestra played the selection **badly.**

V   M

A PHRASE: The orchestra played the selection **with more enthu-siasm than technique.**

V   M

A CLAUSE: The orchestra played the selection **as if they had never rehearsed together before.**

Modifiers of the object:

M   O

A WORD: The orchestra played a **difficult** selection.

O   M

A PHRASE: The orchestra played a selection **of old folk-tunes.**

O   M

A CLAUSE: The orchestra played a selection **which no one in the audience had ever heard before.**

Modifiers of the main clause:

M

A WORD: **Nevertheless,** the orchestra played the selection.

M

A PHRASE: **Considering their lack of experience,** the orchestra played the selection fairly well.

M

A CLAUSE: **Since there were no other requests,** the orchestra played the selection.

Expand the following sentences in a similar way, using modifiers, to at least twelve words each:
1. Dogs bark.
2. This typewriter works well.
3. The car runs.

1.3 ◀

Gr s

1.3 PHRASES AND CLAUSES

English sentences are constructed of single words, phrases, and clauses. Main (or independent) clauses form the principal grammatical units of sentences; they express completed statements and can stand alone. Phrases and subordinate clauses, on the other hand, are dependent on other sentence elements and are used very much like single words.

Phrases

Phrases are groups of related words connected to a sentence or to one of the elements in it by means of a preposition or a verbal. A phrase has no subject or predicate and cannot stand alone.

Prepositional phrases.   A prepositional phrase consists of a preposition (*at, from, by, in, of, under,* etc.) followed by a noun or noun equivalent and whatever modifiers that it may have. It functions like an adjective or adverb, depending on what element it modifies:

> He came **from a small town** [modifies the verb *came*] **in northeastern New Brunswick** [modifies the noun *town*].

Verbal phrases.   A verbal phrase consists of a participle, gerund, or infinitive (none of which has full verb function) plus its object or complement and modifiers. A participle phrase functions as an adjective; a gerund phrase as a noun; and an infinitive phrase as either a noun, an adjective, or an adverb. (See 4, Verbals and Verbal Phrases.)

> Sentences **containing several unrelated ideas** [participle phrase modifying *Sentences*] are seldom effective.

> **Containing the enemy** [gerund phrase used as subject] was their first objective.

> The easiest way **to understand grammatical construction** [infinitive phrase modifying *way*] is **to analyse your own sentences** [infinitive phrase used as complement].

Clauses

A *main* (or independent) clause contains a subject and predicate and is the grammatical core of a sentence. In the three sentences below, the main clauses are in boldface. Each is a complete expression and could stand alone as a sentence:

>   S   V
>   **I laughed** because I couldn't help myself.

>   S   V   O   S   V   O
>   **She hated English,** but **she needed one more course to graduate.**

>   S   V   O
>   If I were you, **I would find a new job.**

A *subordinate* (or dependent) clause also has a subject and a predicate, but it functions as *part* of a sentence. It is related to the main clause by a connecting word that shows its subordinate relationship, either a relative pronoun (*who, which, that*) or a subordinating conjunction (*because, although, since, after, if, when*, etc.):

> I laughed **because I couldn't help myself.**

Subordinate clauses are used like nouns (as subjects, objects, or complements), like adjectives (modifying nouns or pronouns), or like adverbs (expressing relationships of time, cause, result, degree, contrast, and so forth). The subordinate clauses are emphasized in the following examples:

> He confessed **that he loved me.** [noun clause, object of *confessed*]

> Many of the criminals **whose cases crowded the docket each year** were third- or fourth-time offenders. [adjective clause modifying *criminals*]

> **After you plant the seeds,** you should water the garden right away. [adverb clause of time]

> The peas in his garden were stunted **because he did not water them soon enough.** [adverb clause of cause]

See 3, Subordinate Clauses and Connectives.

▶ **EXERCISE**

Start with this sentence: *She walked*.

1. Add a *phrase* that tells where she walked.
2. Add a *phrase* that tells how she walked.
3. Add a *phrase* that tells when she walked.

4. Add a *phrase* that tells where she walked and a *clause* that tells why she walked there.

5. Add a *clause* that tells when she walked, a *phrase* that tells where she walked, and a *clause* that tells to what place she walked.

1.4

Gr s

1.4 SENTENCES CLASSIFIED BY CLAUSE STRUCTURE

An understanding of grammatical elements enables us to give convenient *names* to the different kinds of sentences we have at our disposal. In chapter 25 of this book, for example, where effective choices in sentence style and variety are discussed, sentences are referred to mainly in terms of their *form* (arrangement) and *structure* (the kind and number of clauses). The four main structures are the following:

Simple Sentences

Compound Sentences

Complex Sentences

Compound-Complex Sentences

Simple Sentences

A simple sentence contains one independent clause and no subordinate (dependent) clauses:

The man went across the street.

Although simple sentences contain only one clause, they need not be limited to a minor idea. They may, moreover, contain a number of modifiers, and either the subject or the predicate (or both) may be compound:

Colleges and universities do not exist to impose duties but to reveal choices. [compound subject, compound object] — Archibald MacLeish, "Why Do We Teach Poetry," *The Atlantic Monthly*

He got off the northbound train at the first stop after Manawaka, cashed in his ticket, and thumbed a lift with a truck to Winnipeg. [compound predicate] — Margaret Laurence, "Horses of the Night"

Adam and Padre Doorn climbed out of their jeep and went inside. [compound subject and compound predicate] — Colin McDougall, *Execution*

Compound Sentences

Compound sentences contain two or more main clauses and no subordinate clauses:

> We of the steerage were careless in our dress [first main clause], but he was always clad in immaculate white linen, with pointed, yellow shoes to match his complexion. — John Buchan, *Prester John*

Each clause in a compound sentence is independent and is *co-ordinate* (of equal rank) with the other clauses. The clauses may be joined (or separated) in one of three ways:

With co-ordinating conjunctions. Independent clauses are most frequently linked by the co-ordinating *and, but, or, nor, for, yet* or the correlatives *either . . . or, neither . . . nor, both . . . and, not only . . . but (also):*

> It rained all morning, **but** it cleared up for the picnic.
> **Either** you play to win **or** you don't play at all.

Without connectives. Independent clauses not joined by co-ordinating conjunctions are conventionally separated by semicolons:

> They are generous-minded; they hate shams and enjoy being indignant about them; they are valuable social reformers; they have no notion of confining books to a library shelf. — E. M. Forster, *Aspects of the Novel*

With conjunctive adverbs. The clauses in a compound sentence are sometimes linked by a conjunctive adverb such as *accordingly, also, consequently, however, nevertheless, therefore, then.* However, the function of these connectives is one of modification. When they come between one clause and another, they are preceded by a semicolon:

> The urban renewal program has many outspoken opponents; **nevertheless,** some land has already been cleared.

See 12.1, Semicolons.

Complex Sentences

A complex sentence consists of one main clause and one or more subordinate clauses:

> As far as I could determine [subordinate clause], Paris hadn't changed at all [main clause] since I last visited it ten years before [second subordinate clause].

In published writing today, complex sentences are used far more frequently than the other three types are. Often, as many as half of the sentences in a particular piece of writing are complex. Complex sentences offer more variety than simple sentences do; it is often possible, for example, to shift subordinate clauses around in the sentence in order to get different emphases or different rhythms. Look at the example above again. It could be changed in various ways by keeping essentially the same words but changing the emphasis:

1.4 ◀

Gr s

> Since I last visited Paris ten years ago [subordinate clause], it hadn't changed at all [main clause], as far as I could determine [subordinate clause].
>
> Or,
>
> Paris hadn't changed at all [main clause], as far as I could determine [subordinate clause], since I last visited it ten years ago [second subordinate clause].

The tone changes slightly in these examples: in the first example the idea emphasized is that Paris hadn't changed at all; the second sentence emphasizes the visit ten years before; and the third places more doubt on the idea of Paris not changing because *as far as I could determine* gets heavier emphasis. And complex sentences are often more precise than compound sentences are: a compound sentence gives two ideas equal weight; a complex sentence establishes a more exact relationship.

Compound-Complex Sentences

A compound-complex sentence contains two or more main clauses and one or more subordinate clauses:

> When two men fight a duel [first subordinate clause], the matter is trivial [first main clause], but when 200 million people fight 200 million people [second subordinate clause], the matter is serious [second main clause]. — Bertrand Russell, *The Impact of Science on Society*
>
> Because they can sometimes become unwieldy [first subordinate clause], compound-complex sentences occur less frequently than other types [first main clause], but they can be very useful [second main clause] when you want to unite several related ideas [second subordinate clause] as Russell does in the example above [third subordinate clause].

As explained in chapter 25, there will be times when you want to "complicate" the form of a statement—for emphasis, subtlety, or variety. On such occasions a compound-complex sentence may be especially suitable.

▶ **EXERCISES**

1. Combine the short sentences in each group below into a single sentence by reducing some to phrases or subordinate clauses. Arrange the parts in any way necessary to create sentences:
   a. He left before sunrise. He reached his old country-home by noon. He had time to look around a while. He went on to his aunt's house.
   b. The ball took a bad bounce. It hit the second-base player in the eye. She picked it up anyway. She threw it to first base. The runner was out. The second-base player fell to her knees.
   c. The wind died. It was sunset. The night was clear. The wisp of moon was not out yet. There were stars. It was still. The crackling of the fire was the only sound.
2. Write one sentence on each model shown below. An example of each is given:
   a. compound: main clause + conjunction + main clause
      He ate the squash, but he didn't like it.
   b. complex: subordinate clause + main clause
      When he had planted the beans, he marked the row with two stakes.
   c. compound-complex: subordinate clause + main clause + conjunction + main clause
      After he bought the car, he regretted his haste, but then it was too late.
   d. complex: main clause + subordinate clause
      He disliked the car because it used too much gas.
   e. compound-complex: main clause + subordinate clause + conjunction + main clause + subordinate clause
      He went to the country whenever he could, and he visited as many of his old friends as possible.
3. Compare any twenty successive sentences from *your* last essay with any twenty successive sentences from this book's introduction, "The Languages We Use." First, calculate the average number of words per sentence in each sample. Then count the number of Simple, Compound, Complex, and Compound-Complex sentences in each sample. What does this tell you about your own writing?

1.5 SENTENCES CLASSIFIED BY PURPOSE

All sentences are also conventionally classified by meaning or purpose as follows:

Statements   (often called *declarative sentences*):

> Jim laughed.
> Most of the sentences we speak and write are declarative.

1.6

Gr s

Questions:

> At what temperature does water boil?
> Why do you ask?

Commands   (including requests and instructions):

> Write soon.
> When the water boils, turn off the burner.

Exclamations   (feelings, facts, or opinions expressed in an emphatic way):

> How lucky you are!
> He should be thrown out!

1.6 UNORTHODOX FORMS

While the great majority of independent forms are complete sentences, some are not. In speech, for example, we often express ourselves by a single word ("Yes." "Oh?") or phrase ("In a minute.") or clause ("If you say so."). Exclamations like "Ouch!" and "How terrible!" or short answers ("Yes." "Not if I can help it.") are likewise complete thoughts but really aren't sentences. All such expressions are punctuated as if they were sentences; the first letter of the first word is capitalized, and the end punctuation is a period, question mark, or exclamation point.

By convention, commands and direct requests generally do no have subjects ("Don't let me hear you say that again." "Please try."). The implicit subject, *You*, is obvious.

These unorthodox forms are somewhat informal and, except in dialogue, rarely appear in written English. Nevertheless, unlike sentence fragments (2.1), they are regarded as *complete* constructions.

Intentional Sentence Fragments

Strictly speaking, all *incomplete* constructions (known as sentence fragments) may be considered grammatical errors. See 2.1, Fragmentary Sentences. But under certain circumstances they can be used deliberately to create special impressions. Consider the following statements:

> **And so on to Bangkok. Spit and hiss of water, the gramophone quiet. The lights out along the deck, nobody about.** — Graham Greene, *The Shipwrecked*

> They took no interest in civilized ways. **Hadn't heard of them, probably.** — Clarence Day, *Life with Father*

> What is a hero? **The exceptional individual.** How is he recognized whether in life or in books? **By the degree of interest he arouses in the spectator or the reader.** — W. H. Auden, *The Enchaféd Flood*

> To understand what a fine place Montreal is when spring is coming you must know the winters that come first. **Chill grey mornings; sun bright in the cold noon sky but giving off no heat to speak of; skies darkening again early in the afternoon; long frosty nights with that window-banging wind whipping in burning hard from the north, pushing people before it like paper, making dunes and ridges that hurt the eye to look at on the mountain snows, burning children's cheeks red and cutting like a knife across flat frozen ponds. Old men blowing on their wrinkled hands, boys with blue lips and women with running noses all huddled up and knocking their feet together in the bitter cold waiting for liquor commissions to open and banks to shut, late dates, street cars....** — Mordecai Richler, *Son of a Smaller Hero*

None of the expressions printed above in boldface type is a complete sentence. Still, each is meaningful and stylistically effective. Those "unorthodox" forms are being used consciously by skilled writers to achieve emphasis or informality, to imitate dialogue, to avoid colorless, repetitious verbs, or to make descriptive details more vigorous as impressionistic images. They are justified by their context.

You must remember, however, that this kind of construction is a minor type in English, an *exception* to the typical pattern of subject and predicate. In most of the writing you are likely to do, then, fragmentary sentences should be employed rarely if at all.

2

Common Sentence Errors

Probably the three most conspicuous errors in sentence construction are fragmentary sentences, comma faults, and fused sentences. These three faults are very common. Should they occur in your writing, they will be critized because they suggest either that you are unable to recognize and distinguish independent grammatical constructions, or that you have not checked your writing carefully.

2.1 FRAGMENTARY SENTENCES

Frag Revise the fragment marked by joining it to another sentence, by making it into a complete sentence, or by rewriting the passage.

A *fragmentary sentence* is a grammatically incomplete statement —a phrase or clause—punctuated as if it were a sentence. A complete sentence must have, as a minimum, a main subject and a main predicate. When one of these requirements is missing, we have a partial sentence only—a fragment.

Fragmentary sentences occur frequently in our speech, and they often make good enough sense there, as responses to what someone else has said, for example, or as additions to what we have already said. Indeed, even in writing the incomplete form tends to be some sort of afterthought or stray idea—something added clumsily to qualify the previous statement:

> Here is an example that illustrates, firstly, a complete sentence. And, secondly, a fragment.

Notice that the second construction above lacks *both* a main subject and a main verb. It should probably have been combined with the first statement.

The idea expressed in a fragmentary sentence needs to be completed or joined with another idea in a grammatically sound sentence. The various ways of making this correction are outlined below. (See 1.6, Unorthodox Forms, for a discussion of the occasional effective use of fragments.)

Joining a Fragment to Another Sentence

A fragmentary construction usually belongs to the preceding sentence. If you read the passage aloud, you will probably notice that you pause only slightly before the sentence fragment and do not drop your voice as noticeably as you do at the end of complete sentences. This confirms that the fragment should be joined to the preceding sentence, usually with a comma. Sometimes it should also be rephrased.

> SENTENCE FRAGMENT: The next afternoon we made our way through Caen. **That town in Normandy which became famous during World War II.**

> REVISED: The next afternoon we made our way through Caen, a town in Normandy which became famous during World War II.

Phrases as fragments.   Phrases are partial and subordinate sentence elements and should not be presented as if they were complete sentences:

> FRAGMENT: I cite these examples to show you how interesting accounting can be. **And to give you an idea of the kind of problems an accountant has to solve.** [The fragment has no main subject and verb. It is an infinitive phrase — *to give* belongs in the first sentence parallel with *to show*.]

> REVISED: I cite these examples to show you how interesting accounting can be and to give you an idea of the kind of problems an accountant has to solve.

> FRAGMENT: For the past five years I have been contributing annually to the Heart Foundation. **Without ever suspecting that one day a member of my own family might benefit from my contributions.** [prepositional phrase]

> REVISED: For the past five years I have been contributing a small amount annually to the Heart Foundation, without ever suspecting that one day a member of my own family might benefit from my contributions.

> FRAGMENT: Professor Brown suddenly glanced up from his notes. **His eyes twinkling with suppressed laughter.** [Twinkling is a participle, not a full verb.]

> REVISED: Professor Brown suddenly glanced up from his notes, his eyes twinkling with suppressed laughter.

Explanatory phrases beginning with *such as, for example, that is, namely,* and similar expressions belong in the same sentence as the statement they explain:

FRAGMENT: Their mother had a hard time cooking for them because they disliked so many things. **For example, squash, sweet potatoes, beets, okra, cabbage, apricots, and peaches.**

REVISED: Their mother had a hard time cooking for them because they disliked so many things, for example, squash, sweet potatoes, beets, okra, cabbage, apricots, and peaches.

2.1

Frag

Subordinate clauses as fragments. *Subordinate clauses* are only parts of sentences and should not stand alone. A relative pronoun (*who, which, that*) or a subordinating conjunction (such as *although, because, if, when, while*) indicates that what follows is a subordinate clause and that it should be combined with a main clause:

FRAGMENT: At the time, my old rowboat with its three-horsepower motor seemed a high-speed job to me. **Although it only attained a speed of about twelve miles an hour.** [adverb clause, beginning with *Although*]

REVISED: At the time, my old rowboat with its three-horsepower motor seemed a high-speed job to me, although it only attained a speed of about twelve miles an hour.

FRAGMENT: The whole area is honeycombed by caves. **Many of which are still unexplored.** [adjective clause, introduced by *which*]

REVISED: The whole area is honeycombed by caves, many of which are still unexplored.

Making a Fragment into a Sentence

If the idea expressed in the fragment deserves special emphasis, it can be made into a complete sentence by inserting a subject and a predicate:

FRAGMENT: He talked for fifty minutes without taking his eyes off his notes. **Apparently not noticing that half the class was asleep.** [*Noticing* is a participle, not a verb.]

REVISED: He talked for fifty minutes without taking his eyes off his notes. Apparently he did not notice that half the class was asleep. [The subject is *he*; the predicate is the verb *did notice* plus the words related to it.]

FRAGMENT: National elections and student elections may be compared as closely as an object and its photograph. **The only difference being in size.** [*Being* is a participle, not a verb.]

REVISED: National elections and student elections may be compared as closely as an object and its photograph. The only difference is in size. [*Is* is the verb, and *difference* is the subject.]

Rewriting a Fragment

Sometimes involved or hopelessly snarled sentence fragments have to be completely revised. The following attempt at a long "sentence" has three phrases that seem to be subjects, but there is no *main* verb. A number of verbs appear, but each one is in a subordinate construction:

> FRAGMENT: **The people** who only said, "Oh, too bad," on seeing the lifeless puppy, **the small boy** who removed the dead puppy from the gutter, and the **middle-aged man** who kept saying that people were making a greater fuss about this incident than had been made over his own accident at this same corner a year ago, when he was almost run over by a taxi.

> REVISED: When the small boy removed the dead puppy from the gutter, some people only said, "Oh, too bad." But the middle-aged man kept saying that people were making a greater fuss about this incident than they had made over his own accident at this same corner a year ago, when he was almost run over by a taxi.

► EXERCISES

1. Sentence fragments often appear in advertisements. The name of a product by itself is sometimes followed by a period to create emphasis. Short phrases punctuated as if they were sentences may seem more direct and to the point. When words and phrases are punctuated as sentences, they can be more readily moved around for purposes of design and visual effect. Find three advertisements that depend on fragments (advertisements by automakers are good places to look) and rewrite the text with complete sentences. Be prepared to discuss which you think is more effective.

2. Rewrite the following sentences so that they contain no fragments:
   a. Statistics are not yet available to show the actual decrease in accidents. Since this program is still in the process of being completed and traffic has doubled in the past few months.
   b. The area thrives on competition since the same kind of shops are all grouped together. An example of this being the three supermarkets, which are within a mile of each other.
   c. Public transportation will have to be subsidized by the government. Because it will be too expensive for people to ride otherwise.
   d. A popular person usually has three good personality traits. A good sense of humor, considerateness of others, and good grooming.
   e. The professor was obviously displeased with the performance of the class. His eyes looking as angry as lightning bolts.

2.2 COMMA FAULTS

C F   Change the marked comma to a period or semicolon or revise the passage to make an acceptable sentence or sentences.

A *comma fault* (or a *comma splice*) occurs whenever two independent statements are written with only a comma between them. There are several good ways of linking two related statements, but a comma by itself (as in the following example) is not sufficient:

> The card catalogue is the key to the books in the library, many large libraries have separate catalogues for certain collections of books.

Each of the two clauses joined here is a main clause that could stand alone as a simple sentence. The clauses should either be separated by a period or joined into a compound sentence by a semicolon or an appropriate connective:

> The card catalogue is the key to the books in the library. Many large libraries have separate catalogues for certain collections of books.

> The card catalogue is the key to the books in the library; many large libraries have separate catalogues for certain collections of books.

> The card catalogue is the key to the books in the library, and many large libraries have separate catalogues for certain collections of books.

Those who understand clause structure and know how and when to use clauses will not have much trouble with comma faults. If you make this error often, review 1.4, Sentences Classified by Clause Structure. You may also find it helpful to read your papers aloud. If your voice drops or if you pause noticeably at a comma, check the sentence to see if it is actually two independent statements. For example, read this sentence aloud to see how much more marked the pause is at the comma following *past* (a comma fault) than at the comma following *17:30*:

> The long shopping days along downtown streets are a thing of the past, the stores now open for business at 10:00 and close at 17:30, including Saturdays.

The marked pause indicates that there are two separate statements here; a new sentence should begin after *past*.

Making Two Sentences

A comma fault may be removed by using a period instead of the comma, making two full sentences:

COMMA FAULT: He took a couple of steps, stopped, reached out, and turned a valve, as he did so he told us the valves had to be checked daily.

REPUNCTUATED: He took a couple of steps, stopped, reached out, and turned a valve. As he did so, he told us the valves had to be checked daily.

This is usually the best solution when the ideas are clearly distinct or when there are many commas in either or both statements. However, correcting a comma fault by putting a period between two very short, closely connected statements may result only in two weak sentences:

I opened the door noisily, he didn't move. [Here joining the clauses by **but** is preferable to making each a separate sentence.]

Using a Semicolon

Comma faults may sometimes be corrected by substituting a semicolon for the comma. This is appropriate when the ideas expressed in the two clauses are closely related:

COMMA FAULT: Charley then crossed the room and threw a switch which started the motor, returning, he wiped the sweat from his forehead with the back of his hand.

REPUNCTUATED: Charley then crossed the room and threw a switch which started the motor; returning, he wiped the sweat from his forehead with the back of his hand.

A great many comma faults in student papers occur with "conjunctive" adverbs such as *however, accordingly, consequently, therefore*. When such adverbs appear at the junction of two independent clauses, the conventional punctuation is a semicolon. Although such words show the connection between ideas in the clauses, their connective function is weak.

COMMA FAULT: The person with a university degree has an education far beyond that to be obtained solely from books, **therefore** his or her chances for success may be greater than are those of a person without this education.

REPUNCTUATED: The person with a university degree has an education far beyond that to be obtained solely from books; therefore, his or her chances for success may be greater than are those of a person without this education.

Other uses of adverbs like *however* and *therefore* are discussed on page 162.

2.2

CF

Revising the Passage

Often the best way to remove a comma fault is to revise the sentence, using a connective that will show the relation between the statements. The connective may be a co-ordinating conjunction (such as *and* or *but*), a subordinating conjunction (*although, because, if, since, when*), or a relative pronoun (*who, which, that*) referring to a noun in the first statement. Sometimes one statement can be revised as a phrase, as in the third example:

> COMMA FAULT: It is a personal matter, everyone has to cope with it sooner or later.
>
> REVISED: It is a personal matter **that** everyone has to cope with sooner or later.
>
> COMMA FAULT: I enjoy being in the midst of a party, particularly if I feel some responsibility for its success, conversation is a stimulant more powerful than drugs.
>
> REVISED: I enjoy being in the midst of a party, particularly if I feel some responsibility for its success, **because** conversation is a stimulant more powerful than drugs.
>
> COMMA FAULT: Many companies are looking for experts in pollution control, this is a rapidly expanding field.
>
> REVISED: Many companies are looking for experts in pollution control, a rapidly expanding field.

There are many ways of correcting comma faults. The revision chosen in most situations will depend on the writer's intention and understanding of the passage where the fault occurs. Consider this comma fault:

> The war provided the setting for many novels, three of them were especially outstanding.

Suppose this occurs in the opening paragraph of a paper in which you intend to review a number of war novels very briefly and then focus at some length on three that you think are outstanding. You might revise the sentence as shown below, subordinating the first statement to show that the review of several novels is less significant in the paper than the close study of three (see 3 and 25.2):

> While the war provided the setting for many novels, three of them were especially outstanding.

If you intend in your paper to give equal time and attention to the review of several novels and to the close study of three, you might revise the fault in this way:

> The war provided the setting for many novels. Three of them were especially outstanding.

If the review of a number of novels is what is most important in your paper, and the three novels are simply being used as examples, then you might revise in this way:

> The war provided the setting for many novels, including three that were especially outstanding.

▶ **EXERCISE**

Comma faults can often be corrected in several different ways, as the example below suggests. Study the example, and then correct the following sentences in the way that you feel is most effective. Be prepared to discuss your revisions.

Comma fault: The Oilers voluntarily raised Wayne Gretzky's salary, it was a wise move.
Revised as a compound sentence: The Oilers voluntarily raised Wayne Gretzky's salary; it was a wise move.
Revised as two sentences: The Oilers voluntarily raised Wayne Gretzky's salary. It was a wise move.
Revised by rewriting: It was a wise move for the Oilers to raise Wayne Gretzky's salary voluntarily.
When the Oilers voluntarily raised Wayne Gretzky's salary, they made a wise move.
Raising Wayne Gretzky's salary voluntarily was a wise move by the Oilers.

1. I'd like to own a bigger car, I don't think I could afford the gas.
2. Bricklayers were hired on a contingency basis, that is, they weren't paid until the building was finished.
3. Jim hit a single down the right-field line, David scored from second base.
4. Julie is an excellent guitarist, she taught herself.
5. The electricity went off during the storm, we could not read or watch television.

2.3 FUSED SENTENCES

 Use a period or semicolon between the two statements, or revise the passage to make an acceptable sentence or sentences.

A *fused sentence* is the same kind of error as a comma fault, except that no punctuation at all appears between the main clauses. It should be corrected in the same way as a comma fault:

1. make two sentences of the fused sentence;
2. use a semicolon to separate the two main clauses;
3. rewrite the passage.

> FUSED SENTENCE: Two volumes of this work are now completed the first will be published next year.

2.4

Mix

> POSSIBLE REVISIONS: Two volumes of this work are now completed. The first will be published next year.
>
> Two volumes of this work are now completed, the first **of which** will be published next year.

▶ **EXERCISE**

1. The birds began to sing it was late in the afternoon.
2. The steak was very expensive prices have been going up lately.
3. "What is the purpose in this?" he asked he did not believe in fraternity initiations.

2.4 MIXED CONSTRUCTIONS

Mix   **Revise the mixed construction to make an acceptable sentence or sentences.**

When several sentence faults are combined or when a construction is not one of the standard sentence types, the result is sometimes called a *mixed construction*. Repunctuating cannot correct errors of this kind; the whole passage must be rewritten into acceptable sentence units:

> MIXED CONSTRUCTION: I had always admired his novels, and when I had a chance to meet him, a real delight. [independent and subordinate clauses improperly joined by *and*]

> POSSIBLE REVISION: I had always admired his novels and was delighted when I had a chance to meet him.

> MIXED CONSTRUCTION: Charles was a hard worker, but I wondered how was he going to get everything finished on time? [shift from statement to question]

> POSSIBLE REVISION: Although Charles was a hard worker, I wondered how he was going to finish everything on time.

> MIXED CONSTRUCTION: Of course, the Haitian diet is quite different from ours, this is obvious consisting largely of beans and rice. [a comma fault and a misplaced modifying phrase]

POSSIBLE REVISION: Of course, the Haitian diet, consisting largely of beans and rice, is quite different from ours.

Since mixed constructions usually involve a combination of errors, their variety is almost infinite. The only sure way to avoid them is to learn the principles of sentence construction thoroughly and to check with a critical eye the form and meaning of every sentence you write.

3

Subordinate Clauses and
Connectives

A *subordinate clause* is a secondary sentence element expressing an idea that modifies the statement made in the main clause. A subordinate clause must have its own subject and predicate, but it is shown to be a dependent or incomplete statement (a subordinate part of the whole sentence) by the special kind of *connective* word that relates it to the main clause. In the following sentence, the main clause is *few people outside Manitoba thought*; the connectives, each introducing a subordinate clause, are *when* and *that*:

> **When Sterling Lyon ran for re-election in 1981,** few people outside Manitoba thought **that he could lose to the NDP.**

Subordinate (dependent) clauses are used in sentences as modifiers, subjects, objects, or complements. Depending on the grammatical function they serve, they are classified as adjective clauses (3.1), adverb clauses (3.2), or noun clauses (3.3).

About half the sentences in most kinds of writing contain one or more subordinate clauses, for subordination shows the relationship between ideas much more exactly than a series of simple or compound sentences. Effective use of subordinate clauses is discussed at the end of this section. For a further discussion of subordination and style, see 25, Sentence Variety, Control, and Emphasis.

3.1 ADJECTIVE CLAUSES

A clause that modifies a noun or pronoun is an adjective clause. The relative pronouns *who, which,* and *that* (p. 91) are the words most frequently used to introduce adjective clauses; these pronouns also serve as subjects or objects within the clause:

> Some people **who buy modern paintings** are interested in them more as investments than as art. [*Who* is the subject of the clause, which modifies *people*.]

> The goals **for which he had fought all his life** no longer seemed important to him. [*Which* is the object of the preposition *for*; the clause modifies *goals*.]

> Many books **that are commercially successful** do not qualify as serious literature. [*That* is the subject of the clause, which modifies books.]

He received a letter from an uncle **whom he had not seen for twenty years.** [*Whom* is the object of the verb *had seen*; the clause modifies *uncle*.]

Adjective clauses may also be introduced by the relative adverbs *when, where,* and *why:*

It was a day **when everything went wrong.** [The clause modifies *day*.]

She returned to the town **where she had lived as a girl.** [The clause modifies *town*.]

The reason **why these early settlements disappeared** has never been explained satisfactorily. [The clause modifies *reason*.]

Clauses Without Relative Words

Sometimes an adjective clause is a restrictive modifier, a modifier that is essential to the sentence because it limits the meaning (see 11.3). In this case, the connective or relative word is often omitted, especially when the following word is a pronoun or proper name:

The only books [that] Alice read in high school were those [that] her teacher assigned.

He is a person [whom] everyone admires.

These subordinate clauses with *implied* connectives have long been used in English and are acceptable in all varieties of writing.

And Which

And is sometimes needlessly used between an adjective clause and the rest of a sentence. The relative pronoun *who, which,* or *that* is the only connective needed; the use of *and* or *but* is superfluous and obscures the subordination:

CARELESS: The sea anemone is a fascinating creature **and which** looks more like a plant than an animal.

REVISED: The sea anemone is a fascinating creature which looks more like a plant than an animal.

The appropriate use of *and which* and *but which* is illustrated in the following examples:

The expedition finally reached the famous Great Slave Lake, which lay on the main fur-trading route **but which** no white man had previously seen.

Multiple-choice examinations, which are easy to score by machine **and which** most students find easy to answer, may not be the best way to measure learning.

3.2 ADVERB CLAUSES

A subordinate clause that modifies a verb, adjective, adverb, or main clause is an adverb clause. It usually expresses a relationship of time, place, direction, cause, effect, condition, manner, or concession:

> He lived abroad for seventeen years but returned to Canada **when war broke out.** [The clause modifies the verb *returned*.]

> During her husband's absence she managed the business better **than he had.** [The clause modifies the adverb *better*.]

> He becomes very stubborn **when he meets opposition.** [The clause modifies the predicate adjective *stubborn*.]

> **Because she was a woman of principle,** even her opponents respected her. [The clause modifies the main statement, *even her opponents respected her*.]

English has many connectives for expressing these adverb relationships. The following are among the most common:

after	because	since	unless
although	before	so	until
as	if	so that	when
as if	in order that	though	where
as long as	provided that	till	while

Frequent use of sentences including these words usually indicates a logically effective style. (See also 3.4, Using Exact Connectives, and 25, Sentence Variety, Control, and Emphasis.)

3.3 NOUN CLAUSES

Because they function as nouns, subordinate clauses used as subjects, objects, complements, and appositives are called noun clauses. Most noun clauses are introduced by *that*, but *whatever*, *whoever, who, what, why, when, where,* and *whether* are also used.

As Objects

Noun clauses are most frequently used as direct objects:

> The Prime Minister said **that his meeting with the Inuit representatives had been fruitful.**

> No one knows **why these early settlements disappeared.**

> They wondered **what would happen next.**

Noun clauses also serve as objects of prepositions:

> From **what you have told me,** I think he is making more money than he deserves.
>
> There is a prize for **whoever gets there first.**

In the last sentence, *whoever* is the correct form rather than *whomever* because the pronoun is the subject of the clause.

As Appositives

Noun clauses are quite often used as appositives:

> Most people still accept the myth **that progress is inevitable.**
> The fact **that he might lose** never occurred to him.

As Subjects

Sentences beginning with a subject clause introduced by *that* or *whether* sometimes seem rather stilted, especially if the clause is relatively long. In most kinds of writing, constructions of this kind can more easily appear *after* the verb:

> STILTED: **That he could raise his grade by studying harder** had never occurred to him.
>
> REVISED: It had never occurred to him **that he could raise his grade by studying harder.**
>
> STILTED: **Whether or not we should revise our foreign policy** was the principal topic of discussion.
>
> REVISED: The principal topic of discussion was **whether or not we should revise our foreign policy.**

Subject clauses introduced by other words are common in all levels of writing:

> **Whatever is worth doing at all** is worth doing well.
> **Where he disappeared** is a matter of conjecture.

As Complements

Noun clauses sometimes occur as complements, particularly in definitions and explanation. Such constructions are often awkward, however, and it is often better to substitute a different wording:

AWKWARD: Usually the winner is **whoever has the most endurance.**

BETTER: The person with the most endurance usually wins.

OR: Whoever has the most endurance usually wins.

AWKWARD: Our materialism is **why some Europeans criticize us.**

BETTER: Some Europeans criticize us for our materialism.

OR: Our materialism is criticized by some Europeans.

3.4 ◀

Sub

After "The reason *is* (or *was*)..." the preferred connective in formal and general writing is *that* rather than *because* (*because* means "the reason that"):

> The reason he lost the election was **that** [preferable to **because**] he lacked organized support.

▶ EXERCISE

Combine the following pairs of sentences by making one of the sentences into a subordinate clause:

1. The hamster is a handsome animal. It looks like a bundle of fur.
2. He was a strong man. He was feared and admired.
3. The rain has fallen for two days. It has washed the bridge way.
4. Those delegates are not here yet. They attended a big party last night.
5. He was fourteen years old. He began to shave.

3.4 SUBORDINATION FOR EXACT STATEMENT

Sub **Show the intended relationship between ideas by using appropriate subordination, or correct the faulty subordination.**

Ideas that deserve equal emphasis should be expressed in grammatically co-ordinate forms (as in *My son is in high school and my daughter is in university*). But an important part of writing is discriminating among ideas that do *not* deserve equal emphasis. Statements that describe or explain another statement or tell how, when, where, or why something happened should be expressed in subordinate constructions whenever the relationship is not immediately clear from context. For example, there is no reason why three separate sentences should be made of these obviously related ideas:

> Mozart made his first trip to Italy in 1769. He was thirteen years old. His father went with him.

If the first statement is the one the writer wants to emphasize, it can stand as a main clause while the other two are reduced to a secondary level:

1. In 1769 Mozart made his first trip to Italy
2. when he was thirteen years old
2. accompanied by his father

Then the sentence would look like this:

In 1769, **when he was thirteen years old** [subordinate clause], Mozart made his first trip to Italy [main clause], **accompanied by his father** [verbal phrase].

Showing the Relative Importance of Ideas

A subordinate clause usually indicates that the matter subordinated is less important to the subject being discussed than the main statement. To judge the rightness of subordination, then, it is necessary to know what the intended emphasis of the passage is. For instance, in joining the two statements "The lightning struck the barn" and "Mother was setting the table for supper" the first would be the main statement if your purpose was a general account of the event:

The lightning struck the barn [main clause] just as Mother was setting the table for supper [subordinate clause].

But if the point to be emphasized is what Mother was doing when the lightning struck, the sentence would probably be written like this:

When the lightning struck the barn [subordinate clause], Mother was setting the table for supper [main clause].

In this case the paragraph would probably go on to tell what Mother did in the crisis.

In revising sentences, then, it is important to see that the parts are related according to their relative importance.

Using Exact Connectives

Subordinate clauses are exact because their connectives show a precise and specific relationship to the main clause. Co-ordinating conjunctions, especially *and*, are much less definite in meaning than adverb connectives like *because, since, when, while* or the adjective connectives *who, which, that*:

CO-ORDINATE STATEMENT: Sandra was waiting for the bus and she saw a purse on the sidewalk.

ONE STATEMENT SUBORDINATED: **While she was waiting for the bus,** Sandra saw a purse on the sidewalk.

CO-ORDINATE STATEMENT: "Anglosaxon Street" is one of Earle Birney's best-known poems, and it has been reprinted in many anthologies.

ONE STATEMENT SUBORDINATED: "Anglosaxon Street" **which is one of Earle Birney's best-known poems,** has been reprinted in many anthologies.

3.4 ◀

Sub

In speaking we tend to rely on only a few of the conjunctions available for expressing adverb relationships (see 3.2), but in writing greater exactness is expected. Notice in the following sentences the difference that is made whenever one word—the connective—is changed:

Ralph sat gloomily in the corner *because* Lynn began to flirt with all the men at the party.

Ralph sat gloomily in the corner *while* Lynn began to flirt with all the men at the party.

Ralph sat gloomily in the corner *until* Lynn began to flirt with all the men at the party.

Ralph sat gloomily in the corner *although* Lynn began to flirt with all the men at the party.

Always choose the connective word that exactly expresses the relation you see between the subordinate clause and the main clause. Weak connectives like *and* or *as* or *for* usually don't convey such meanings fully or clearly.

Using *as* and *so*. Particular care should be taken to avoid overusing the common conjunctions *as* and *so*. For instance, *as* may introduce various kinds of adverb clauses and mean something different in each case:

DEGREE OR MANNER: I went **as fast as I could go.**

TIME: Our guests arrived **as the sun was setting.**

CAUSE: **As it was getting dark,** we turned on some lights.

COMPARISON: Lettuce is not **as** fattening **as spaghetti is.**

ATTENDANT CIRCUMSTANCE: **As the fire spread,** the sky grew darker.

The variety of its meanings makes *as* a word to be watched in writing. In some instances it is the proper and only connective to use—to express comparisons, for example (We went as far *as the others did*), or in clauses of manner (*As the twig is bent*, so grows the tree). But in many other constructions, *while, when, since,* or *because* would be more exact and emphatic:

While [not *as*] we were walking, he told us stories.

The war was almost over **when** [not *as*] he was captured.

As is especially weak when used in the sense of *because*. To introduce clauses of reason, purpose, or result, *since* or *because* is clearer and more decisive in most writing:

He refused to join in the square-dancing **because** [not *as*] he was afraid of making a fool of himself.

Like *as*, the connective *so* (or *and so*) is overworked and often inexact. In most writing it should be replaced by a more definite word:

INEXACT: She couldn't find a job, **so** she decided to go to summer school.

REVISED: **Since** she couldn't find a job, she decided to go to summer school.

INEXACT: He was new to the district, **so** he had few friends.

REVISED: **Because** he was new to the district, he had few friends.

The inexact sentences are not wrong; in both, *so* means *therefore* or *consequently*. But the revised sentences are better; *since* and *because* are signals alerting the reader at the outset that cause-effect relationships occur in the sentences.

In clauses of purpose, *so that* is preferable to *so*:

He went to Toronto **so that** [not *so*] he could find a job in publishing.

▶ EXERCISE

Combine the following pairs of sentences, choosing one of the statements to be the subordinate idea. Use a connective that accurately shows the relationship.

1. They pawned his big pocket watch. They needed money for groceries at the end of the month.

2. They knew what to expect of the weather. They had lived on the prairies for forty years.

3. The angry farmers had assembled and now stood shouting in front of the Peace Tower. The Prime Minister came out to address them.

4. He got the garden planted by April 15. It cost him forty dollars for fertilizer, a new hoe, and a sore back.

3.5 FAULTY SUBORDINATION

Faulty subordination usually results from a careless stringing together of ideas as they happen to come into the writer's mind.

Consider, for example, the haphazard use of dependent constructions in the following sentence:

> Because her mother died when Barbara was five years old, and since her father lived a solitary life, Barbara had a very unhappy childhood, having no family to confide in.

3.5

Sub

The elements in this cluttered statement might be rearranged to establish a better sense of order and proportion:

> Barbara had a very unhappy childhood. She was five years old when her mother died, and since her father led a solitary life, she had no family to confide in.

When you go over the first draft of your papers, revise any loose subordinate elements that weaken your sentences or obscure their meaning.

Tandem Subordination

It is usually best to avoid statements in which a series of dependent clauses are strung together, one after another. Too many clauses beginning with similar connectives (*who, which, that; when, since, because*), each built upon the preceding one, are called tandem subordination, or "house-that-Jack-built" constructions:

> TANDEM SUBORDINATION: He had carefully selected teachers **who** taught classes **that** had a slant **that** was specifically directed toward students **who** intended to go into business.

> REVISED: He had carefully selected teachers who specifically slanted their courses toward students intending to go into business.

> TANDEM SUBORDINATION: The recordings **which I** bought last week were scarce items **that** are essential to people **who** are making collections of folk music **which** comes from Spain.

> REVISED: Last week I bought some scarce recordings that are essential to collectors of Spanish folk music.

Sentences that begin and end with the same kind of subordinate clauses are awkward because of their seesaw effect:

> **When** he came home from work, Dad would always complain **when** the children weren't there to meet him.

Such constructions can be improved by changing one of the connectives. Usually it is possible to choose a connective that is more exact:

> When he came home from work, Dad would always complain **if** the children weren't there to meet him.

Inverted Subordination

Putting the main idea of a sentence in a subordinate clause or phrase ("inverting" the proper relationship between statements) may result in an awkward or incongruous statement:

> INVERTED: She was eighteen when her hands were severely burned, which meant that she had to give up her goal of becoming a concert pianist.

> MORE ACCURATE: When she was eighteen, [main clause:] **her hands were severely burned.** As a result, [main clause:] **she had to give up her goal of becoming a concert pianist.**

Inverted or "upside-down" subordination frequently occurs in sentences that trail off into weak participle phrases:

> The road was blocked, **causing us to make a twenty-mile detour.**

Such sentences can be improved by putting the less important statement in an adverb clause:

> We had to make a twenty-mile detour **because the road was blocked.**

▶ EXERCISE

Practise further with subordination by rewriting the first three to five paragraphs of several newspaper articles. You should be able to combine some sentences by turning short ones into subordinate clauses.

4

Verbals and Verbal Phrases

The three kinds of *verbals* (participles, gerunds, and infinitives) are special forms derived from verbs to perform the grammatical functions of nouns or modifiers. As its name suggests, a verbal is "verb-like" in certain respects; it typically expresses action or some state of being, and it can greatly resemble the verb from which it originated. But its grammatical purpose or status in a clause corresponds in fact to that of a noun or adjective or phrase, never to that of an actual verb (see 8, Verbs). For example, the *verb* in the following sentence (*is eating*) establishes the tense (the time of the action, in this case the present) and governs the predicate:

> Patty is eating peanuts.

However, *eating* is not a verb in any of the following examples. In every case it is a *verbal* because it functions as a noun or modifier, never determining the main tense or governing the predicate:

> Patty likes **eating** peanuts. [verbal as object]
>
> **Eating** peanuts is one of life's pleasures. [verbal as subject]
>
> Slowly **eating** peanuts, Patty eyed us curiously. [verbal in phrase]
>
> The **eating** area of the kitchen was strewn with peanut shells. [verbal as adjective]
>
> She longed to be **eating** peanuts. [verbal as adverbial modifier]
>
> She has only one hobby, **eating** peanuts. [verbal as appositive]
>
> The woman **eating** the most peanuts will receive a prize. [verbal in phrase]

Verbals, then, are used in sentences as nouns (subjects, objects, complements) or modifiers. They have many qualities of verbs, but they cannot serve as full, finite verbs to make sentences or clauses. In many sentences, however, verbal phrases function very much like subordinate clauses in showing the relationship between main and subordinate ideas:

> **When she graduated from Acadia,** she went to Halifax in search of a job. [subordinate clause]
>
> **Having graduated from Acadia,** she went to Halifax in search of a job. [verbal phrase, modifying *she*]

Verbals are classified by form and function as

1. **infinitives** (*to ask, to buy, to be eating*), which can serve either as nouns or as modifiers;

2.   **participles** (*asking, asked, buying, bought, eating, eaten*), which modify nouns and pronouns;

3.   **gerunds** (*asking, buying, eating*), which are verbal nouns.

Although the present participle and the gerund are identical in form, they can be distinguished by the way they are used in sentences:

PARTICIPLE: a **dancing** figure [modifier]

GERUND: **dancing** takes skill [noun]

The forms and principal uses of verbals are illustrated in the table on page 63. (See also 8, Verbs.)

4.1 USING VERBAL PHRASES

Verbal constructions are considered *phrases* because, unlike clauses, they don't express full verb functions. Verbals can, however, take objects, complements, and adverbial modifiers. In some constructions they also take a subject, if the meaning of that term is stretched a little:

Slowly weaving its way from twig to twig, the spider built its nest. [*way* is the direct object of the participle *weaving*, which is modified by the adverb *slowly; way* is modified by the prepositional phrase *from twig to twig*; the entire participle phrase modifies *spider*, the subject of the sentence]

He avoided the accident by **running his car onto the shoulder of the road.** [*car* is the direct object of the gerund *running*, which is modified by the phrase *onto the shoulder of the road;* the verbal phrase is the object of the preposition *by*]

She wanted **to be an architect or industrial designer.** [*architect* and *designer* are complements of the infinitive *to be;* the verbal phrase serves as object of the verb *wanted*]

Subjects with Infinitives

An infinitive phrase often has an expressed subject:

He wanted **the whole department** [subject of the infinitive] **to be reorganized.**

If the subject of an infinitive is a pronoun, it is in the object form:

They asked **him** [subject of the infinitive] **to be secretary.**

Their mother told **them** [subject of the infinitive] **to behave.**

Subjects with Gerunds

When a noun or pronoun precedes a gerund, serving as its "subject," some questions of usage arise: sometimes the possessive form is used, sometimes the common form. The writer must depend partly on the sound in choosing the form that seems more natural, but the following principles should serve as guides:

4.1

Vbl

Forms and Uses of Verbals

Infinitives

An infinitive is (1) the base form of a verb (with or without *to*) or (2) any verb phrase that can be used with *to* to function in a sentence as a noun, an adjective, or an adverb.

Forms:	Active	Passive
PRESENT	(to) ask, (to) be asking	(to) be asked
PAST	(to) have asked, (to) have been asking	(to) have been asked

Principal uses:

SUBJECT: *To be called* to the principal's office makes little boys nervous.

OBJECT: He does not like *to express his opinion*.

MODIFIER **(adjective):** I have plenty of work *to do*. (Modifies *work*)

MODIFIER **(adverbial):** The students came *to learn French*. (Modifies *came*)

ABSOLUTE PHRASE MODIFYING THE MAIN CLAUSE: *To tell the truth*, he is a bore.

Participles

A participle is a verb form, typically ending in *-ing* or *-ed*, used as a modifier.

Forms:	Active	Passive
PRESENT	asking	being asked
PAST	having asked	asked, having been asked

Principal uses:

MODIFIER OF A NOUN: a *smiling* candidate; a *clogged* drain

PARTICIPIAL PHRASE MODIFYING A NOUN: The Candidate *getting a majority of the votes* will be nominated.

ABSOLUTE PHRASE MODIFYING THE MAIN CLAUSE: *Everything considered*, a portable typewriter seems the most practical gift.

Gerunds

A gerund is a verb form, typically ending in *-ing* or *-ed*, used as a noun.

Forms:	**Active**	**Passive**
PRESENT	asking	being asked
PAST	having asked	having been asked

Principal uses:

GERUND AS SUBJECT: *Having been asked* made him happy.

GERUND PHRASE AS SUBJECT: *Taking anthropology* opened a whole new field.

GERUND AS OBJECT: She taught *dancing*.

GERUND AS COMPLEMENT: Seeing is *believing*. (*Seeing* is also a gerund.)

GERUND AS A MODIFIER OF A NOUN: the *dining* room, a *fishing* boat

GERUND AS APPOSITIVE: He had only one hobby, *collecting stamps*.

1. When the subject of a gerund is a personal pronoun or a proper noun, the possessive form is generally used:

   The less said about **his** singing, the better.

   They insisted on **Bob's** playing the piano.

2. When the subject is stressed, the common form is usually preferred with nouns and the object form with pronouns:

   Did you hear about the **mayor** being arrested for speeding?

   I can't imagine **him** winning an award.

3. When the subject is a plural noun, the common form is usually preferred:

   The manager disapproves of **people** smoking in meetings.

   The staff will not tolerate **visitors** coming and going at will.

4. If the subject is abstract, the common form is used:

   It was a case of **panic** getting the upper hand.

   There is a danger of the **temperature** dropping suddenly.

5. When the subject is modified by other words, the common form is used:

   There was something suspicious about the **daughter** of the sponsor winning the $10 000 prize.

   At the beginning of the election, no one in Ottawa foresaw the possibility of the **Finance Minister,** who had angered so many people with his tax bill, retaining his seat in the Commons.

6. With other noun forms, usage is divided. If you are writing a formal paper, it is usually best to use the possessive form, but the common form of the noun is widely used in general English:

> FORMAL: The neighbors complained about the **dog's** barking at night.
>
> GENERAL: The neighbors complained about the **dog** barking at night.
>
> FORMAL: Jones worried about his **secretary's** taking another job.
>
> GENERAL: Jones worried about his **secretary** taking another job.

4.1

Vol

▶ **EXERCISE**

Write sentences that include the terms shown below. Let the noun or pronoun be the subject of the gerund.

Example: Richard/strumming on his old guitar
Sentence: The dog howled at the sound of Richard's strumming on his old guitar.

1. the cousin of the senator/getting the contract for the highway
2. orchestra/talking during rehearsal
3. pronoun referring to Richard/giving up
4. my mother/saying such things
5. fear/overcoming his sense of responsibility

4.2 IDIOMATIC USE OF INFINITIVES AND GERUNDS

Sometimes we say things in a particular way, not because it is grammatically proper, but simply because it is a way of speaking or writing that has been customary for a long time. When we say that we *put up with* something, the expression doesn't make much sense logically, but we know that it means *tolerate* because it is an *idiom* that we are familiar with. Although systematic rules cannot be given to explain these traditional habits of the language, maintaining idiomatic usage is just as important as following any of the more obviously "logical" grammatical procedures of English. See also *Idioms* in the index. Expressions involving verbals tend especially to be governed by idiomatic custom.

Some of these expressions are regularly completed by infinitives ("privileged *to attend*"), others by gerunds ("the privilege *of attending*"). When one form is substituted for the other, the result is an unidiomatic construction: for example, "eager *to join*" is a standard idiom, but "eager *of joining*" is not. Here are typical expressions, some that call for a gerund, others for an infinitive.

(You will find others in your dictionary under the main word of the construction):

Gerund	Infinitive
cannot help going	compelled to do
capable of working	able to work
skilled in writing	the desire to write
the habit of giving	the tendency to give
successful in getting	manage to get
ignore saying	neglect to say
my object in paying	my obligation to pay
satisfaction of doing	satisfying to do

With many words, especially common ones, either a gerund or an infinitive is idiomatic: "a way *of doing* it" or "a way *to do* it."

Avoiding *the* and *of* in Gerund Phrases

Gerunds are more direct when they are not preceded by *the* and when they are completed by a direct object rather than an *of* phrase:

AWKWARD: In **the** revising **of** the first draft, writers should check their spelling.

DIRECT: In revising the first draft, writers should check their spelling.

To with Infinitives

Most infinitive constructions are introduced by *to*, "the sign of the infinitive":

She needed time **to think.** They hoped **to get** home before dark. His efforts **to be promoted** failed.

To is not used, however, after auxiliary verbs (*can, may, must, shall, will*):

I can **see.** You must **try** it. We may **go** to Europe next fall.

With a few verbs (*do, dare, help, need,* etc.) usage varies:

I did see him. It did me good **to see** him.

I helped him [**to**] **learn** to drive.

Split Infinitives

If an adverb comes between *to* and an infinitive (I don't want *to ever see* him again) the phrase is called a *split infinitive*. A writer should avoid split infinitives that are obviously awkward or that call undue attention to themselves:

AWKWARD: I will not describe the circumstances of our meeting, or even attempt **to** physically **describe her.**

BETTER: I will not describe the circumstances of our meeting, or even attempt **to describe** her physically.

But split infinitives are not always awkward. When the normal position of the adverb is after the word *to*, a split infinitive is standard usage (The receptionist asked them *to please sit* down). Putting the adverb modifier immediately before or after the infinitive would be clumsy or misleading in some statements:

CLUMSY: Autumn is the time **really to see** Europe.

BETTER: Autumn is the time **to really see** Europe.

4.3

m m

4.3 MISRELATED MODIFIERS

m m Revise the sentence so that the expression marked is clearly related to the word or statement that it modifies.

When verbals, either as single words or in phrases, are used as modifiers, they usually refer to individual words:

I first noticed him **sitting alone in a corner.** [present participle, modifying *him*]

The city hall, **completely renovated four years ago,** always impresses visitors. [past participle, modifying *city hall*]

He still had three years **to serve in prison** before he would be eligible for parole. [infinitive, modifying *years*]

Like other modifiers, verbal modifiers must be clearly related to the words that they modify. When a verbal construction seems from its position to refer to a word that it cannot sensibly modify, it is said to be *misrelated*, or *misplaced*. Participle phrases usually give writers the most trouble:

MISRELATED: On the other side of the valley, **grazing peacefully like cattle,** we saw a herd of buffalo. [the participle phrase seems to refer to *we*]

REVISED: On the other side of the valley **we** saw a herd of buffalo, **grazing peacefully like cattle.** [the phrase clearly refers to *buffalo*]

Misrelated modifiers may be momentarily confusing to the reader (or unintentionally humorous) and should therefore be avoided.

Sometimes the correction can be made by putting the modifier immediately before or after the word it is meant to modify, as in the example above, but often it is better to rewrite the sentence completely:

> MISRELATED: One early-day western politician is said to have passed out campaign cards to the voters **pinned together with five-dollar bills.** [the participle phrase seems to refer to *voters*]

> REVISED: One early-day western politician is said to have pinned five-dollar bills to the campaign cards he passed out to voters.

Occasionally modifiers are placed so that they seem to refer to either of two elements in the sentence. These constructions (sometimes called *squinting modifiers*) can be avoided by changing the position of the modifier or by otherwise revising the sentence:

> SQUINTING: The woman who was standing in the doorway **to attract attention** dropped her purse.

> REVISED: The woman who was standing in the doorway dropped her purse **to attract attention.**

> OR: The woman, standing in the doorway **to attract attention,** dropped her purse.

Other types of misrelated modifiers are discussed in 9.5, Position of Adverbs.

4.4 DANGLING MODIFIERS

Dm   Revise the sentence to include the word to which the dangling modifier refers.

A modifier must always refer directly to some particular thing in the sentence, either a word or (as explained in 4.5, Absolute Modifiers) a distinct idea. When we cannot identify a specific word or idea that it could sensibly refer to, the modifier is said to be *dangling*. Like misrelated modifiers (4.3), dangling modifiers make a sentence confusing and often laughable:

> **Having moved at fifteen,** his hometown no longer seemed familiar.

The above sentence declares that the hometown moved; no other literal meaning is possible. Obviously that meaning was not intended, but it is a writer's obligation to be alert, during revision, for such slips. This kind of error often occurs when passive rather than active verbs are used:

DANGLING: **In painting four of these pictures,** his wife was used as his model.

REVISED: **In painting four of these pictures, he** used his wife as his model.

DANGLING: **To find the needed information,** the whole book had to be read.

REVISED: **To find the needed information, I** had to read the whole book.

4.5 ◄

abs m

Usually the easiest way to correct a dangling modifier is to name the agent or "doer" of the action immediately after the phrase, as in the revisions shown above. It is often better, however, to revise the sentence entirely, making the relationships more accurate by using other constructions. Changing the verbal phrase to a subordinate clause often improves the sentence:

DANGLING: **Having been delayed by a train accident,** the leading role was played by a local actress.

REVISED: **Because the leading lady was delayed by a train accident,** her role was played by a local actress.

4.5 ABSOLUTE MODIFIERS

A writer should distinguish clearly between verbal modifiers that obviously dangle, such as those cited above, and *absolute modifiers* —participle or infinitive phrases that modify the statement as a whole and thus do not need a specific reference word in the main clause. As the word *absolute* suggests, these modifiers are complete and independent; their form does not depend on anything else in the sentence.

A number of absolute constructions are commonly used expressions:

Everything considered, this plan seems best.

To make a long story short, we bought the house.

Considering the cost of lumber, the price is reasonable.

Absolute modifiers can usually be converted easily into subordinate clauses: *When everything is considered*, this plan seems best.

An absolute phrase with a subject is sometimes called a *nominative absolute*. This construction is often used effectively in descriptive and narrative prose for adding details or parenthetical material:

The class roared and several children started a violent handslapping on their desks. Mr. Edwards, **a green look** [subject] **returning** [participle] to his face, bent his shoulders helplessly and waited. . . . Ava looked wretched. I now saw something which a few hours ago I would have declared to be impossible. The girl's lips were trembling and her black eyes, **their mocking beleaguered look** [subject] **gone** [participle], were slowly filling with tears. Her famous composure was beginning to crumble. Yet her voice was steady. —Irving Layton, "A Plausible Story"

Everyone was preparing to go home, **mothers** [subject] **buttoning** [participle] their children's coats, **children** [subject] **clutching** [participle] . . . their balloons and whistles and paper baskets full of jelly beans. —Alice Munro, "The Shining Houses"

▶ **EXERCISE**

Some of the sentences below contain misrelated or dangling modifiers. Rewrite the sentences to make the relationships clear. The sentences with absolute modifiers need no revision. Notice that the sentences needing correction can be revised in more than one way. In the first revision below, the subject *their actions* is dominant; in the second revision, using *I* as the subject makes it dominant.

Example: Having grown tired of them, their actions no longer concerned me.

Revision: Because I had grown tired of them, their actions no longer concerned me.

Revision: Having grown tired of them, I felt that their actions no longer concerned me.

1. Being thoroughly persuaded of them myself, the beliefs I hold seem to me to be obviously true.
2. My spirits often sink in despair, however, trying to find ways to convince others of these truths.
3. After having convinced a friend against his will, both he and I find that our friendship is in doubt.
4. It does not really persuade anyone to accept my beliefs by citing authorities to prove my point.
5. To be honest about it, my friends have grown weary of my arguments and often try to avoid me.
6. After having satisfied my own mind in every detail of an argument, the decision I reach seems incontrovertible.
7. My position tends to harden very rapidly, my decision having been reached, and I am not likely to change my mind.
8. To be perfectly frank, it is unwise for you to pretend that you are convinced by what I say to be polite.
9. Above and beyond the call of mere friendship, being more important, truth is what matters.
10. To do justice to any friendship based on truth, it takes absolute candor on both sides.

5

Agreement of Subject and Verb

Agr Make the marked verb agree grammatically with its
subject.

In English, parts of speech that change form to show number,
gender, or person should *agree*, or correspond, when they are
related to each other. Pronouns agree with their antecedents (see
7.2) and verbs with their subjects. Agreement, or correspondence,
means, in this case, that if a subject is plural, then its verb ought to
be plural as well.

Agreement between subject and verb is not always a problem in
general English because most verbs seldom change form. The verb
be is an exception, for it has several forms; but other verbs have
only two forms in the present tense and only one form in the past
tense. Although we say *I swim* and *you swim*, we change the form
for the third person singular to *he swims, she swims*, or *it swims*. In
the past tense, we use *swam* for all situations. See 8, Verbs, for a
discussion of English verb forms.

Questions about agreement of subject and verb are most likely to
arise when verbs have compound subjects or collective nouns as
subjects, or when the number of the subject (singular or plural) is
obscured by other words occurring between the subject and verb.
These problems are discussed in the following sections.

5.1 VERBS WITH COMPOUND SUBJECTS

A compound subject is made up of two or more words, phrases, or
clauses joined by *and, or, nor*. The number of the verb depends on
which conjunction is used and on the meaning of the subject.

Subjects Joined by *and*

The conjunction *and* is used to join co-ordinate items, to link them.
Accordingly, subjects joined by *and* usually take a plural verb:

> **Bob, Ted,** and **Sandra swim** with the national team.

> The first **draft** of your paper and the **version** finally turned in might
> **differ** in several ways.

Exception: When the words of a compound subject refer to the same person or are considered together as a unit, the verb is usually singular:

> His warmest **admirer** and severest **critic was** his wife.
>
> **Law and order means** different things to people with different political opinions.

Subjects Joined by *or, nor*

Compound subjects joined by *or, nor, either . . . or, neither . . . nor* sometimes take singular verbs and sometimes plural. Here are some ways to tell the difference:

1.   When both subjects are singular, the verb ordinarily is singular:

> **One** or the **other is** certainly to blame.
>
> Neither **Premier Davis** nor **Premier Blakeney was able** to attend the federal-provincial conference.

In general usage, exceptions to this rule are sometimes made. In questions, where the verb precedes the subject, general usage tends to use a plural verb:

> **Are** [formal: *Is*] either **Clark** or **Broadbent** supporting the bill?

A plural verb may also follow two singular subjects if they are not considered as separate:

> Neither **radio** nor **television provide** [formal: **provides**] adequate news coverage.

Bear in mind that the *formal* usage in these cases is always appropriate; choose it whenever you are in doubt.

2.   When both subjects are plural, the verb is plural:

> No artificial **colorings** or **preservatives are used.**

3.   When one subject is singular and the other plural, usage varies. In formal writing, the verb usually agrees with the nearer subject:

> One major **accident** or several minor **ones seem** to occur at this corner every weekend.
>
> Neither the **revolutionists** nor their **leader was** to blame.

In general usage, a plural verb is often used even if the nearer subject is singular:

> Neither the **revolutionists** nor their **leader were** to blame.

4. When the subjects are pronouns in different persons, formal usage requires that the verb agree in person and number with the nearest subject. In general usage (and even in formal usage if the alternative is awkward), the verb is usually plural:

> FORMAL: Either **you** or **she is** likely to be elected.

> GENERAL: Either **you** or **she are** likely to be elected.

> FORMAL AND GENERAL: Neither **you** nor **I are** trained for that job. [*Am* would sound unnatural.]

5.1

agr

Such problems of agreement can usually be avoided by substituting a different, more natural construction:

> **One** of you **is** likely to be elected.

> **Neither** of us **is** trained for that job.

Subjects Followed by *as well as*

In formal usage, a singular subject followed by a phrase introduced by *as well as, together with, along with, in addition to* ordinarily takes a singular verb:

> The **treasurer as well as the president was held** responsible for the mismanagement of the company.

But a plural verb is often used in these situations when the added phrase is clearly intended as a compound subject:

> Both the **production** of small cars, **together with the supply** in the dealers' showrooms, **have been outstripped** by the demand.

A simple solution—and one that may make the statement more direct—is to use *and* wherever appropriate:

> Both the **production** of small cars and the **supply** in the dealers' showrooms **have been outstripped** by the demand.

▶ **EXERCISE**

Write sentences using the subjects given below, making sure that the verb agrees with the subject.

Example: backaches, dizzy spells, and blinding headaches
Sentence: Backaches, dizzy spells, and blinding headaches *are* signals that you should see a doctor.

1. beer, wine, and champagne
2. neither codeine nor magnesia tablets
3. both alligators and crocodiles

4. neither drugs nor tobacco
5. the teacher together with the class

5.2 VERBS WITH COLLECTIVE NOUNS AS SUBJECTS

Words that refer to a group of people or objects but are singular in form are called collective nouns or group nouns: *army, audience, choir, committee, crowd, faculty, gang, group, government, jury, mob, orchestra, public, team.* Verbs and pronouns used with collective nouns are either singular or plural, depending upon the meaning of the group word.

Nouns Referring to the Group as a Unit

Singular verbs and singular pronouns are used with collective nouns that refer to the group as a unit:

> **Class is** dismissed.
>
> The **committee has** already held **its** first meeting of the year.
>
> The **audience is** requested to remain seated during intermission.

Nouns Referring to Individuals in a Group

When a collective noun refers to the members of the group, especially if it represents them as acting individually, a plural verb and plural reference words are used:

> The graduating **class have** all agreed to have **their** pictures taken.
>
> The **committee are** arguing among **themselves.**
>
> The **audience have** taken **their** seats.

Sentences like these often sound rather unnatural, and in most cases it is better to substitute a clearly plural subject (the committee *members*, the *members* of the audience).

Verbs with Measurements and Figures

Expressions signifying quantity or extent (*kilometres, litres, years, grams*) take singular verbs when the amount is considered as a unit:

> **Five dollars is** too much to pay for a book in that condition.
>
> **Four litres** of oil **is** all the crankcase holds.
>
> **Three months passes** in no time at all at the coast.

When the amount is considered as a number of individual units, a plural verb is used:

> **Two more dollars are** missing from the till this morning.
>
> There are **two litres** of milk in the refrigerator.
>
> The last **three months have been** the driest in Saskatchewan's history.

5.2

Agr

In expressions of addition and multiplication, usage is evenly divided:

> Five and seven **is** [or **are**] twelve.
>
> Five times seven **is** [or **are**] thirty-five.

A singular verb is used in expressions of subtraction and division:

> Twenty-five from thirty-one **leaves six.**

Verbs with *data, number, public*

Data is a plural form and is generally so considered in formal, particularly scientific, writing; but since the singular *datum* is rarely used, *data* is often used for both singular and plural in general writing; agreement often depends on context:

> SINGULAR IDEA: The **data** the president needs **has been analysed** by his assistant. [*data* refers to a body of facts]
>
> PLURAL IDEA: After the **data** [individual facts] **have been gathered** and **analysed,** you can decide which elements are most essential to your study.

Number as a collective noun may be either singular or plural: preceded by *the*, it refers to the total sum and takes a singular verb; preceded by *a*, it refers to the individual units and takes a plural verb:

> **A number** of pages **are** badly torn.
>
> **The number** of pages assigned for daily reading **was** gradually increased to twelve.
>
> Physicians were disturbed to find that **an** alarming **number** of bacteria **were** developing a tolerance to penicillin.

Public takes a singular verb if the writer wishes to signify the whole group (The *public is* invited to attend); it takes a plural verb if the writer is considering the individual members (The *public are* invited to express their opinions).

Words Ending in -ics

Physics, mathematics, economics, civics, linguistics, and similar *-ics* words that refer to a science, art, or a body of knowledge are usually considered singular; other words ending in *-ics* that refer to physical activities (*athletics, acrobatics*) are generally treated as plurals.

SINGULAR FORMS: **Physics was** my most difficult subject in high school.
Ballistics is the study of the motion of projectiles.

PLURAL FORMS: **Athletics have** been virtually abolished from some smaller schools.
New **calisthenics are** designed for older people.

Some words ending in *-ics* (*ethics, politics, acoustics*) may be used in either a singular or plural sense, according to the context:

SINGULAR IDEA: In almost every group, **politics is** a controversial subject.

PLURAL IDEA: Radical **politics were** offensive to the Family Compact.

SINGULAR IDEA: **Acoustics is** a branch of science that is growing fast.

PLURAL IDEA: The **acoustics** in this room **are** not all they might be.

When you are in doubt about the number of a word ending in *-ics*, consult a dictionary.

5.3 BLIND AGREEMENT

Sometimes writers make a verb agree with a nearby expression rather than with its actual subject. Since this often occurs when a writer accepts the nearest convenient word or phrase that looks like a subject, it is frequently referred to as "blind agreement." The error usually occurs in the following situations:

Plural Nouns Between Subject and Verb

A singular subject followed by a phrase or clause containing plural nouns is still singular:

Here and there a **man** [subject] such as Columbus, Galileo, and others **has** [not *have*] ventured into the unknown physical and intellectual worlds.

The **lumberman** [subject] who previously sold only to carpenters and builders now **finds** [not *find*] hundreds of amateurs eager to build their own homes.

I decided to see exactly how **one** of those new cars **is** [not *are*] put together.

5.3

Agr

one of those who

In formal English, the verb in clauses that begin *one of those who* (or *that*) is plural:

He is one of those men who never **care** how they look. [The verb is plural because its subject *who* refers to *men*, not to *one*.]

Godfrey's "The Hard-Headed Collector" is one of those stories that **leave** you more puzzled when you finish than when you began. [*Stories* is the antecedent of *that*.]

Although a singular verb is common in spoken English ("one of those girls who *plays* in the band") and in a good deal of published material, the plural verb is customarily used in formal English.

Exception: When *the only* precedes *one of those who* the verb is singular, since the pronoun *who* then refers to one person or thing only:

She is the only one of those women who **plays** bridge well.

there is, there are

When a sentence begins with the introductory (or "dummy") word *there* (sometimes referred to as an "anticipating subject"), the number of the verb is determined by the subject which follows:

There **are** conflicting **opinions** [subject] about smoking in the classrooms.

There **is** great narrative and dramatic **power** [subject] in most of the novel.

At our camp there **were** at least a dozen **men** [subject] who were familiar with the mountain trail.

In this construction a singular verb is frequently used before a compound subject, especially if a plural verb would be unidiomatic, as in the second example below:

There **is food** and **drink** enough for everyone.

There **was nothing** he could do and **little** he could say.

Verb and Complement

A verb agrees with its subject and not with its complement or its object:

> Our chief **trouble** [subject] **was** [not *were*] the black flies that swarmed about us on the trip.
>
> The **black flies** [subject] that swarmed about us on our trip **were** [not *was*] our chief trouble.
>
> The **material** [subject] that was most interesting to me when I worked on my reference paper **was** [not *were*] the books that stated the facts forcefully.

When subject and complement differ in number, the sentence usually sounds less awkward if the subject and verb are plural, as in the second example above.

Inverted Word Order

When the word order is inverted, care must be taken to make the verb agree with its subject and not with some other word:

> Throughout the story **appear** thinly disguised **references** [subject] to the author's own boyhood.
>
> **Is** any **one** [subject] of these pictures for sale?
>
> Accompanying the actress **were** her **secretary** and two **members** of her legal staff. [The verb has a compound subject.]

Subjects like *series, portion, part, type* take singular verbs even when modified by a phrase with a plural noun:

> A **series** of panel discussions **is** scheduled for the convention.
>
> A substantial **portion** of the reports **is** missing.
>
> The most interesting **part** of the investigations **was** the discovery and identification of the forged letters.

▶ EXERCISES

1. Find the subject of the italicized verbs in the following paragraph. If the subject is a pronoun, indicate what word or idea it refers to.

    Epidemics *have taken* a great toll of lives in past generations. Death in infancy and early childhood *was* frequent and there *were* few families who didn't lose a member of the family at an early age. Medicine has changed

greatly in the last decades. . . . The use of chemotherapy, especially the antibiotics, *has contributed* to an ever decreasing number of fatalities in infectious diseases. Better child care and education *has effected* a low morbidity and mortality among children. The many diseases that have taken an impressive toll among the young and middle-aged *have been conquered*. The number of old people *is* on the rise, and with this fact come the number of people with malignancies and chronic diseases associated more with old age.
— Elisabeth Kubler-Ross, from *On Death and Dying*

5.3

agr

2. Determine the subject of each of the following sentences and select the verb form that agrees with it. If there is any problem of agreement, explain your choice of verb in terms of the points made in this section.

a. The wages of sin (is, are) death.
b. All (is, are) well.
c. Comparison of things that are unlike and that, by their uniqueness (produces, produce) a sense of wonder in us, (show, shows) that the writer is just displaying his or her own cleverness.
d. Too many metaphors (is, are) a sign of a young writer.
e. "Patience and fortitude," though describing virtues, (is, are) a motto often used to counsel sloth.
f. The United States (enjoys, enjoy) good relations with Canada.
g. He is one of those people who (is, are) always making trouble.
h. To have loved and lost (is, are) an experience most of humanity (has, have) suffered.
i. Many of our tax dollars (go, goes) to defence commitments.
j. Neither metaphor nor simile (is, are) useful if the image is confused.

3. Write sentences that include the following items:

a. *Three semesters*, meant as a single unit, used as the subject
b. The word *ethics* used as the subject in a plural sense
c. A singular subject followed by a phrase that includes a plural noun
d. *There are* at the beginning of the sentence
e. The expression *one of those who*
f. *A part of the audience* used as the subject

6

Nouns

Nouns are naming words used in sentences chiefly as subjects of verbs, objects of verbs or prepositions, as complements following a linking verb, as appositives, or as modifiers of other words. They change their form to show number (by adding *-s, -es,* etc.) and possession (by adding *'s, s'*). A noun may designate a person (*Henry Cartwright, child*), a place (*Spain, home*), a thing (*pencil, steak*), a quality (*beauty, rage*), an action (*hunting, logrolling*), or an idea (*justice, reality*).

The table on the next page shows the forms, functions, and customary ways of classifying nouns. The following sections focus on the common problems that writers may have with nouns: how to use plural and possessive forms conventionally, when to use *a* or *an* before nouns, and how to spot unidiomatic or clumsy noun modifiers.

6.1 PLURALS OF NOUNS

 Change the marked noun to a standard plural form.

Most English nouns form the plural simply by adding *-s* to the singular form (*cats, girls, books, things*). If the plural makes an extra syllable, *-es* is added to the singular form (*bushes, churches, kisses, Joneses*).

A few nouns preserve older methods of forming the plural adding *-en* (*children, oxen*) or changing the vowel (*feet, teeth, geese, mice*). Some nouns, such as the following, have the same form of both singular and plural:

1. the names of some animals, such as *deer, fish, mink, sheep*;
2. all words ending in *-ics,* such as *athletics, civics, mathematics*;
3. a number of words rarely or never used in the singular, such as *barracks, headquarters, measles, trousers, scissors.*

There are few hard-and-fast rules for troublesome plurals, however, and writers should learn to consult the dictionary whenever they are unsure of a plural form. If the plural of a noun is irregular, it will be shown under the entry for the singular form; if no plural is given, the plural is formed in the usual way, by adding *-s* or *-es.*

Nouns: Forms, Functions, and Classes

Forms

6.1

Noun

SINGULAR AND PLURAL FORMS
Singular: boy, mother, box, child, goose, hero, baby, phenomenon
Plural: boys, mothers, boxes, children, geese, heroes, babies, phenomena

COMPOUND NOUNS OR GROUP WORDS, two or more nouns (written as one word, as two words, or hyphenated) functioning as a single unit: bookcase, football; pine tree, high school; father-in-law, hangers-on

POSSESSIVE FORM: boy's, Harriet's, girls', cats'

GENDER. A few nouns in English have one form for the masculine, one for the feminine: actor, actress

Functions

SUBJECT OF A VERB: The *tires* squealed as the *car* skidded around the corner.

OBJECT OF A VERB: The new company manufactured *toys*.

COMPLEMENT: A whale is a *mammal*. He became *president*.

OBJECT OF A PREPOSITION: The acrobats were performing inside the *tent*.

INDIRECT OBJECT: He gave the *church* a memorial window.

APPOSITIVE: Mr. McDermott, the insurance *agent*, is here.

MODIFIER OF A NOUN: He thought *cigarette* holders looked silly. *Mr. Tyler's* car was stolen.

MODIFIER OF A STATEMENT: *Each year* we make new resolutions.

Classes

PROPER NOUNS, names of particular people, places, and things, written with an initial capital, or upper-case letter: Anne, George W. Loomis, Halifax, Monday

COMMON NOUNS. In contrast with these proper nouns, all the other groups are common nouns and are written entirely in lower-case letters

CONCRETE NOUNS, names of objects that can be seen and touched: leaf, leaves, road, panda, manufacturer

ABSTRACT NOUNS, names of qualities, actions, ideas that are perceived mentally: kindness, hate, idealism, fantasy, concept

COLLECTIVE NOUNS, names of groupings of individuals: fleet, army, company, committee, bevy

MASS NOUNS, names of material aggregates or masses not defined as individual units: food, money, intelligence, justice

COUNT NOUNS, names of things perceived as individual units: car, shelf, pencil, cow, vase

Since writers ordinarily know when a plural form is needed, the chief problems with noun plurals are related to spelling. Section 17.3, Spelling Troublesome Plurals, shows some groups of nouns whose plurals may cause such problems.

▶ **EXERCISE**

Write a sentence using the plural form of the following words. If you can use more than one of them in a single sentence, do so: *father-in-law, apparatus, commander-in-chief, sheaf, medium, phenomenon, berry, handful, thesis, tomato, auto, governor-general*.

6.2 POSSESSIVE (GENITIVE) CASE

Case refers to the form a noun or pronoun takes that shows its relationship to other words in the sentence. In English, nouns have only two case-forms, the common form (*dog, book, Ross*) with its plural (*dogs, books, Rosses*) and the possessive (*dog's, book's, Ross's*) with its plural (*dogs', books', Rosses'*). These forms are all pertinent to the written or printed language.

The "possessive" relationship may also be conveyed by using a prepositional phrase governed by *of* (*of the dog, of the book, of Ross*), although one is not always interchangeable with the other in idiomatic usage.

Uses of the Possessive

The possessive case is typically used to indicate ownership (the *student's* book) or close association or identification with (the actor's mannerisms). But it also shows other relationships:
1. **Description**: a *day's* work, a *suit's* style, *yesterday's* paper.
2. **Doer of an act**: the *wind's* force, the *dean's* permission.
3. **Recipient of an act**: the *bill's* defeat, the execution *of a spy*.
4. **Subject of a gerund**: (see page 63): the *doctor's* warning.

Forms of the Possessive

The possessive and plural forms of common nouns are identical in sound so that in speech they can be distinguished only by the way they are used: the possessive is followed by another noun (The *boy's work* was finished), whereas the plural is not (The *boys worked* hard). It is impossible for the ear to distinguish between the singular and plural possessive except in the large context of what is being said.

6.2

Noun

In writing, the apostrophe signals the possessive case, and the position of the apostrophe (*boy's, boys'*) ordinarily tells us whether a possessive is singular or plural.

Insert an apostrophe where it belongs in the marked word or take out the unnecessary apostrophe.

Position of the Apostrophe

Most singular nouns form the possessive by adding *'s*, as do the few plural nouns that do not end in *-s* (such as *men, women, children*):

> the **teacher's** remarks (the remarks of the *teacher*)
>
> a **day's** work (the work *of a day*)
>
> the **children's** playground (the playground *of the children*)

Plural nouns ending in *-s* form the possessive by adding an apostrophe alone:

> the **teachers'** meeting (the meeting *of teachers*)
>
> the **musicians'** union (the union *of musicians*)
>
> the **Joneses'** relatives (the relatives *of the Joneses*)

Singular nouns ending in *-s* either form the possessive by adding an apostrophe alone, just as plural nouns do, or by adding *'s* if an extra syllable occurs in the pronunciation. Either way is acceptable; consistency is, however, desirable.

Mr. **Jones'** [or **Jones's**] business	the **hostess'** [or **hostess's**] gown
Delores' [or **Delores's**] father	the **actress'** [or **actress's**] role

Group words.   With group words or compound nouns the *'s* is added to the last term:

> the **Queen of England's** duties   the **attorney general's** job
> her **mother-in-law's** address   **someone else's**
> responsibility

Nouns in series.   When two co-ordinate nouns (joined by *and, but,* or *nor*) are in the possessive, the apostrophe usually is added only to the last one if there is a joint relationship: *Ann and Tom's* mother. But if there is an individual relationship, the apostrophe is used with both nouns: *Ann's and Tom's* bicycles, *neither Ann's nor Tom's* teacher.

Plural nouns as modifiers.   The apostrophe is not used in some expressions in which the plural noun is considered a modifier (*savings* plan, *Parks* Department, *sales* manager, capital *gains* tax, *serials* index). Since plural noun-modifiers are being increasingly used, careful attention should be paid to letterheads, signs, official publications, and the like to determine the proper form in specific cases.

Using *of* Phrases and *'s* Forms

The *'s* form of the possessive is customarily used with reference to living things (my *uncle's* house, a *cat's* paw) and an *of* phrase with reference to non-living things (The door *of the room*, an angle *of inclination*, the beginning *of the end*). But in many instances, either form may be used, the choice depending largely upon the sound and intended emphasis of the expression (the *book's* cover, the cover *of the book*). Some idiomatic expressions are usually stated in one form only (a *week's* wages, a *moment's* hesitation, an embarrassment *of riches*, the wages *of sin*).

Awkward use of *'s* forms.   An *of* phrase is sometimes preferable to an *'s* form to avoid a clumsy or unidiomatic expression or a statement that may be ambiguous. When the modifying noun is separated from the word it refers to by a phrase or a clause, an *of* phrase should be used:

> The apartment **of the woman** who won the contest was ransacked last night. [not *The woman who won the contest's apartment* nor *The woman's apartment who won the contest*]

The *of* phrase is useful in distinguishing between the recipient and doer of an act, particularly if the meaning is unclear in context. *John's photographs* might mean either photographs *of* him or photographs taken *by* him; but *the photographs of John* would ordinarily mean that John was the subject of the pictures.

The double possessive.   In a few statements both the *of* and *'s* forms of the possessive are used, an idiom of long standing in English: that boy *of Henry's* , some friends *of my father's* , a remark *of the author's* .

▶ EXERCISE

Indicate which of the italicized nouns in these sentences are correctly written with *-s* endings and which should have *-'s* or *-s'*.

1.   The *energies* of our system will decay, the *suns* glory will dim, and the earth will not tolerate the race that has disturbed *its* peace.
2.   A wit of *Barries* said, "Facts were never pleasing. . . . He was never on *terms* with them until he stood them on their *heads*."
3.   The din from the *childrens* playground tried the *Joneses* patience.
4.   The king was "the *peoples* prayer . . . and the old *mens* dream."

6.3 USE OF *a* AND *an* WITH NOUNS

Whether *a* or *an* is used before nouns and noun phrases depends on the following *speech sound* . Use *a* before a consonant *sound*: *a* car, *a* yard, *a* Union, *a* European nation, *a* history book (also *a* historical novel, where *h* may be unpronounced). Use *an* before a vowel *sound*: *an* ape, *an* oar, *an* hour, *an* honest woman.

6.4 NOUNS AS MODIFIERS

Nouns are freely used in English to modify other nouns. Since they thus assume some of the functions of adjectives, such modifiers may be called *adjectivals* (or attributive nouns). In fact, many compound nouns are made up of just such sequences: *textbook, dog-train, maple sugar*. (See the table on p. 81.) Most compound nouns are today written in block, that is, as one word, though practice varies according to whether the block form is awkward in appearance, open to misreading, and so on: *book agent, motor inn, language laboratory, grab bag* .

   In speech, such established compounds are tied together by a special pitch-stress pattern, the first noun bearing louder stress than the second, as *flypaper, fly swatter*. (See 15.2 for details about hyphenating compounds). Once such sequences are commonly written as one word or with a hyphen, the adjectival loses its identity, having been absorbed into the compound-noun category.

Nevertheless, the free use of adjectivals remains typical of English syntax: *murder mystery, kitchen utensils, student council*, where the usual meaning is "of, related to, or having to do with." On occasion, however, adjectivals take on specialized meanings, as illustrated by *toy poodle*, the modifier *toy* designating a miniature type of the breed. Such specialized meanings are entered in dictionaries, as are many adjectival + noun sequences with special meanings, for example, *snow fence* and *water cooler*.

Most adjectivals are singular in form, just as adjectives always are: one *maple* leaf, two *maple* leaves; one *balloon tire, two balloon* tires. Note also that singular forms are used for compound (and therefore hyphenated) adjectivals expressing measurement: a *two-litre* jug, a *three-metre* jump, a *thirty-degree* temperature.

In certain situations, a writer may choose either an adjective or an adjectival: an *atomic* bomb or an *atom* bomb; but such freedom of choice is not always available or appropriate. In many situations, the adjective is preferable to a clumsy, imprecise, or unidiomatic adjectival: use *medical* (not *doctor*) school; *Canadian* (not *Canada*) money.

In proper names, as of government agencies, business firms, and so on, the adjectival *Canada* has long been in use alongside the adjective *Canadian*: *Canada* Council, *Canada* Cycle and Motor Co., Ltd. (CCM), *Canadian* Broadcasting Corporation, *Canadian* Tire Corporation Ltd.

Moreover, Canadians should be aware of a peculiarly native innovation wherein the adjectival *Canada* occurs after the noun it modifies in such names. This development in Canadian English reflects French syntax and owes its origin to the federal government's policy of promoting bilingualism nationally: Air *Canada*, Parks *Canada*, Statistics *Canada*, and so on. Indeed, the practice has spread to other institutions of various kinds where national scope is implied: Loto *Canada*, Unity *Canada*. It has recently become fashionable even among business firms, domestic and multinationals: Career *Canada* Ltd., Bell *Canada*. Even magazines follow the vogue: *Nature Canada*, *Ski Canada*. Rapid growth of this syntactical Canadianism make such a sentence as the following quite idiomatic: "Canadian hockey players got support from Hockey Canada when playing for Team Canada in the Canada Cup series."

Just as nouns function as adjectives in some respects (adjectivals), so nouns function as adverbs, though much less often. A noun as adverb, called an *adverbial*, occurs in this sentence: *He walked home*, where the noun could be replaced by *there, quickly*, or some other adverb.

► **EXERCISES**

1. Ability to discriminate between one style and another in the use of nouns improves with experience in reading and exercise in writing. Count and classify the nouns occurring in any three paragraphs in each of the following sources according to these categories: plural, possessive, concrete, abstract, compound, adjectival.

   a. An article in a news magazine such as *Maclean's*
   b. An article in an opinion magazine such as *Canadian Forum*
   c. An article in a newspaper
   d. An editorial in a newspaper

2. Select the noun form you consider appropriate in each of the following sentences. Where the choice is not optional, create a sentence in which the inappropriate form would be appropriate. If need be, consult your dictionary.

   a. The (major-generals, majors-general) agreed on two possible (hypothesis, hypotheses).
   b. Their (enemies, enemys) stormed into the (valleys, vallies).
   c. All the (data, datum) were sent to the managers of the (auditoria, auditoriums).
   d. "Television," she said, "is one of the (media, mediums) that contribute to a permissive attitude toward violence."

3. Proofread the following sentences carefully, correcting all errors in the use of noun forms:

   a. The father-in-laws temper was aroused when wine was spilled on a bride's-maid dress.
   b. Muskoxes are native to the Arctic's tundra.
   c. The governor general of Canadas office is held by a Canada-born person of recognized merit.
   d. He used a two-horses wagon to carry his potatos to market.

6.4

Noun

7

Pronouns

The word *pronoun* means *for a noun* or *instead of a noun*. A pronoun is a word similar to a noun in function, but it does not directly name a person, place, thing, or idea. Usually it is used as a substitute for a previously stated noun, called its *antecedent*. A pronoun refers to its antecedent for its specific meaning, which is generally evident from the context:

> My uncle phoned last night. **He** is coming by plane.
>
> Men over forty are invited to join. **They** may apply by mail.
>
> Joe heard that credit cards cause many financial problems. **This** interested **him**.
>
> My friend and I are invited to a party with her cousins. **We** are going to **it** with **them**.
>
> I am using your pen because I lost **mine**.

Pronouns eliminate the need to repeat nouns every time a person, place, thing, or idea already designated is referred to. They also, help bind statements together, for when a pronoun in a sentence refers to a noun in the preceding sentence, there is a natural connection between the two sentences. Notice how the pronouns in the following passage help give it continuity:

> The young man has formed an ideal of saving **his** money and **he** considers the bank the best place to accomplish **his** purpose. **He** understands the essentials of banking, if not the details; **he** understands how **he** appears to others (confused, incompetent, helpless, etc.) and also *why* **he** appears so; **he** understands what **he** does wrong while **he** does it; and above all **he** understands **himself** thoroughly, past and present, both **his** inner self and **his** outer appearance. —R.E. Watters, "Stephen Leacock's Canadian Humor"

Pronouns should be used more carefully in writing than they sometimes are in speaking. Remember that a reader cannot see the writer or hear his change in tone. Readers need to see pronouns in the form that indicates their function so that they will be able to follow a pronoun's reference to its antecedent without confusion. The following sections discuss the most common problems in using pronouns. The table on page 91 lists the various kinds of pronouns and their forms.

7.1 REFERENCE OF PRONOUNS

Ref   **Change the marked pronoun so that its reference will be exact and obvious; if necessary, substitute a noun for the pronoun or revise the sentence.**

7.1

Ref

Pronouns Referring to a Definite Antecedent

The antecedent of a pronoun should be clearly stated, not merely implied, and the pronoun should refer specifically to this antecedent:

> INACCURATE: He had been vaccinated against typhoid, but **it** did not protect him. [No antecedent for *it*]
>
> ACCURATE: He had a typhoid **vaccination**, but **it** did not protect him. [*Vaccination* is the antecedent of *it*]

Instead of changing the antecedent, it is often better to substitute a noun for the inexact pronoun:

> INACCURATE: She couldn't understand how to make the cake until I wrote **it** out.
>
> ACCURATE: She couldn't understand how to make the cake until I wrote out **the recipe**.

A simple test for accurate reference is to see whether the antecedent could be substituted for the pronoun. If not, the sentence needs revision.

> INACCURATE: She talked a lot about the technique of horsemanship although, as a matter of fact, she had never ridden **one** [horsemanship?] in her life.
>
> ACCURATE: She talked a lot about the technique of horsemanship although, as a matter of fact, she had never ridden **a horse** in her life.

The antecedent of a pronoun should not be a noun used as a modifier or a noun in the possessive form:

> INACCURATE: To make an attractive tulip border, plant **them** close together. [*Tulip* is used as a modifier.]
>
> ACCURATE: To make an attractive border of **tulips**, plant **them** close together.
>
> INACCURATE: Bill provided a lot of excitement one afternoon when he was skipping rocks across the pond and cut open a young **girl's** head **who** was swimming under water. [A noun in the possessive functions as a modifier.]

ACCURATE: Bill provided a lot of excitement one afternoon when he was skipping rocks across the pond and cut open the head of a young **girl who** was swimming under water.

Ambiguous Reference

Sometimes the meaning of a pronoun is unclear because the pronoun could refer to two different antecedents. To eliminate such ambiguity, either substitute a noun for the pronoun or clarify the antecedent:

CONFUSING: When Stanton visited his father in February, **he** did not know that **he** would be dead within two months.

CLEAR: When Stanton visited his father in February, **he** did not know that **the old man** would be dead within two months.

Sometimes ambiguous reference may be avoided by making one of the antecedents singular and the other plural:

AMBIGUOUS: In the nineteenth century, many businessmen [plural] exploited the workers [plural] at every opportunity, not caring whether **they** were making a living wage, but only whether **they** were making a lot of profit.

CLEAR: In the nineteenth century many businessmen [plural] exploited the worker [singular] at every point, not caring whether **he or she** was making a living wage, but only whether **they** were making a lot of profit.

Using the same pronoun for different implied antecedents is particularly annoying to a reader and should be avoided:

CONFUSING: We pulled out our spare, which was in the trunk, and put **it** on. **It** dampened our spirits for a while, but we decided to go on with **it**. [The first *it* refers to the tire, the second to the mishap, the third to the trip.]

REVISED: We pulled out our spare, which was in the trunk, and put the tire on. Having to change a flat dampened our spirits for a while, but we decided to go on with the trip.

Identifying the antecedent by repeating it in parentheses after the pronouns is a wordy and makeshift practice that should be avoided:

CLUMSY: Boswell first met Johnson when **he** (Johnson) was fifty-four.

REVISED: Johnson was fifty-four when Boswell first met **him**.

Ambiguity sometimes results from a careless use of possessive pronouns:

AMBIGUOUS: Mrs. Hurst was a very popular woman and **her accusa-**

tion scandalized everyone in town. [Was Mrs. Hurst the accuser or the accused?]

REVISED: Mrs. Hurst was a very popular woman and **the accusation she made** [or **the accusation made about her**] scandalized everyone in town.

7.1

Ref

Pronouns Referring to Ideas and Statements

This, that, which, and *it* are often used to refer to ideas or situations expressed in preceding statements:

Always do right. **This** will gratify some people and astonish the rest.
— Mark Twain

Kinds of Pronouns

Personal pronouns

	Subject	Object	Possessive
First person			
Singular	I	me	my, mine
Plural	we	us	our, ours
Second person			
Singular and plural	you	you	your, yours
Third person			
Singular			
masculine	he	him	his
feminine	she	her	her, hers
neuter	it	it	its (of it)
Plural	they	them	their, theirs

Relative pronouns

who	whom	whose
that	that	
which	which	whose, of which

Interrogative pronouns

who	whom	whose
which	which	whose, of which
what	what	

Reflexive and intensive pronouns: myself, yourself, himself, herself, itself, oneself, ourselves, yourselves, themselves

Demonstrative pronouns: this, these, that, those

Indefinite pronouns

all	both	everything	nobody	several
another	each	few	none	some
any	each one	many	no one	somebody
anybody	either	most	nothing	someone
anyone	everybody	much	one	something
anything	everyone	neither	other	such

Reciprocal pronouns: each other, one another

Numeral pronouns: one, two, three...first, second, third...

I just am a Canadian. **It** is not a thing which you can escape from. **It** is like having blue eyes. —Robertson Davies

They criticized me sometimes for being too much concerned with the average Canadian. I can't help **that**. I'm just one of them. —John Diefenbaker

In such constructions, the idea to which the pronoun refers must be obvious.

Use of *who, which, that*
The relative pronoun *who* refers to persons, *which* generally refers to things, and *that* refers to either persons or things.

Students **who** [or *that*] plan to enter the university in the fall should forward transcripts of their records to the registrar.

In five minutes he solved a problem **that** [or *which*] I had struggled with for nearly five hours.

This is a matter about **which** more information is needed.

That always introduces restrictive clauses. *Who* and *which* are used both restrictively and non-restrictively. See 11.3, Commas to Set Off Interrupting Elements.

The use of *which* to refer to persons is not idiomatic English. *Which* is often used, however, to refer to impersonal organizations of people like groups, clubs, companies, and so on:

The provincial legislature, **which** [not *who*] passed the act despite the lieutenant-governor's protest, had its eye on getting more votes.

The Plowrite Company, **which** manufactured farm implements, has gone into bankruptcy.

Use of *he* or *she*

It can be a problem to decide which *gender* of pronoun (*he*, *she*, *him*, *her*, *his*, *hers*) to use when the antecedent is a singular noun or pronoun that includes persons of both sexes (*student*, *teacher*, *clerk*, *supervisor*, *everyone*, *anyone*, *somebody*). Clarity, accuracy, and fairness demand, for example, that a woman never be implicitly referred to as *he*, or a man as *she*. Consider the following examples:

7.1

Ref

> Each entering first-year **student** must write the mathematics aptitude test before choosing **his** science courses.
>
> Every **employee** of Nadir Pharmaceuticals should ensure that **she** has filled out a pension plan form.

If we can assume that the requirement announced in each of the above statements applies to both men and women, the use of gender-specific pronouns (*his* and *she*) is inexact and needlessly confusing. The practice of always using masculine forms (*he*, *him*, *his*), when referring to "people in general" used to be widely regarded as preferable to the wordy *his or her* and *he or she*, but it has become increasingly rare.

The best solution in all such cases is to rewrite the sentence using plural nouns and pronouns that don't take masculine or feminine forms:

> All entering first-year **students** must write the mathematics aptitude test before choosing **their** science courses.
>
> All **employees** of Nadir Pharmaceuticals should ensure that **they** have filled out a pension plan form.

If for some reason you cannot change the sentence to substitute plural forms you should either use *his or her* or *he or she* to agree with the singular antecedent:

> Each entering first-year **student** must write the mathematics aptitude test before choosing **his or her** science courses.
>
> Every **employee** of Nadir Pharmaceuticals should ensure that **he or she** has filled out a pension plan form.

The "slash" forms *his/her* and *he/she*, a kind of bureaucratic shorthand, are generally considered non-standard. Don't use them unless you're sure they will be acceptable to your audience. There is a third possibility, for *they* (*their, them*) as a common-gender singular is already widespread in spoken English, and may in time occur more frequently in writing, especially when the antecedent is an indefinite pronoun like *everyone* that includes both sexes: "Everyone who wishes to can get *their* textbooks at the university bookstore."

▶ **EXERCISES**

1. Use pronouns to replace the repetitious nouns and make a single, smoother sentence.

   Example: John saw the sports car. John knew at once that he must own the
   sports car.

   Revision: John saw the sports car, and he knew at once that he must own it.

   a. Christopher lit George's cigar. The cigar glowed brightly.
   b. "My goodness, yes." Susan's husband said. "Susan's husband will tell you about Susan. Susan has left town."
   c. The second baseman told the first baseman that the second baseman wanted to take the first baseman to dinner after the game. The first baseman said no.
   d. When the teacher gave the students the students' assignment, the students groaned. Then the students did the work.

2. Revise each of the following sentences in which the reference of pronouns is inexact, misleading, or otherwise faulty.

   Example: A general-interest bookstore would probably do better in this town
   than an obscure one.

   Revised: A general-interest bookstore would probably do better in this town
   than a bookstore that specialized in obscure books.

   a. After he had studied *kung fu* for three months, he began to boast that he was an expert one.
   b. An exercise room is available in the basement of the new physical-education building which can be used by both students and faculty.
   c. Tolliver's wild-flower text is useful, but its description of the high-plains crocus is vague.
   d. Football is a more complex game now than in the past, with its play books and game movies, but many are still brutally rough.
   e. When the women were about to leave the exhibit of quarter horses, they ran into their husbands.

7.2 AGREEMENT OF PRONOUN AND ANTECEDENT

agr   Make the marked pronoun agree in form with the word to which it is related.

To be clear in meaning, a pronoun must agree in number with its antecedent—the particular noun to which it refers. When a pronoun serves as subject, the number of the verb is determined by the pronoun's antecedent. (See also 5, Agreement of Subject and Verb.)

7.2

agr

Personal Pronouns

Personal pronouns, like nouns, have both singular and plural forms, as listed in the table on page 91. A personal pronoun referring to a singular antecedent should be singular; one referring to a plural antecedent should be plural. Errors in agreement are most likely to occur when a pronoun is separated from its antecedent by some intervening element:

> INACCURATE: Although the average **Canadian** believes theoretically in justice for all, **they** sometimes fail to practise it. [*Canadian* is singular; *they* is plural.]

> ACCURATE: Although the average **Canadian** believes theoretically in justice for all, **he or she** sometimes fails to practise it. [*Canadian* and *he or she* are both singular, as are their verbs.]

> INACCURATE: After reading his **arguments** in support of abolishing property, I found that I was not convinced by **it**. [*Arguments* is plural; *it* is singular.]

> ACCURATE: After reading his **arguments** in support of abolishing property, I found that I was not convinced by **them**. [Both *arguments* and *them* are plural.]

When a pronoun's antecedent is a collective noun, the pronoun may be either singular or plural, depending on the meaning of the noun (see 5.2):

> The **class** planned **its** next field trip.

> The **class** had **their** pictures taken.

A pronoun referring to co-ordinate nouns joined by *and* is ordinarily plural:

> When **Linda and Gail** returned, **they** found the house empty.

Usually a singular pronoun is used to refer to nouns joined by *or* or *nor*:

> **Dick or Stan** will lend you **his** car.

In general, the principles governing agreement between a pronoun and co-ordinate nouns are the same as those governing agreement between a compound subject and verb; see 5.1, Verbs with Compound Subjects.

Relative Pronouns

When a relative pronoun is used as the subject of a dependent clause, an antecedent of the pronoun determines the number of the verb and of all reference words:

> George is one of those people who **have** trouble making up **their** minds. [The antecedent of *who* is the plural *people*, which requires the plural verb, *have*; *who* also requires the plural reference *their* for the same reason.]

> George is a person who **has** trouble making up **his mind**. [The antecedent of *who* is *person*.]

Indefinite Pronouns

A number of words of greater or less indefiniteness often function as pronouns: *some, all, none, everybody, somebody, anybody, anyone*. Some of these words are considered singular; others may be singular or plural, depending on the meaning of the statement. In revising your papers, be sure that verbs and reference words agree in number with indefinite pronouns.

Everyone, anybody, somebody.   *Everyone, everybody, anyone, anybody, someone, somebody, no one, nobody* are singular forms and are used with singular verbs (Everyone *has* left; Somebody *was* here; Nobody ever *calls*).

Spoken usage and written usage, however, often differ in the form of the pronouns used with these words. In writing, a singular reference word is standard (Everyone brought *his* book); in speaking, a plural reference word is often used.

> WRITTEN: Not **everyone** is as prompt in paying **his** bills as you are.

> SPOKEN: Not **everyone** is as prompt in paying **their** bills as you are.

But more writers are using either *his or her* or accepting the plural reference that occurs often in speech. And in some statements a singular reference word would be puzzling or nonsensical with the indefinite pronoun:

> When I finally managed to get to my feet, everybody was laughing at me, and I couldn't blame **them** [*him* would be impossible] because I was a funny sight.

All, some, none.   *All, any, some, most, more* are either singular or plural, depending upon the meaning of the statement:

All of the turkey **has** been eaten.

All of these questions **were** answered.

Some of the dialogue **is** witty.

Some of the farmers **have** opposed marketing boards.

7.2

agr

The word *none* may be either singular or plural, depending upon the context. In current usage, it is commonly used with a plural verb, but formal usage still prefers a singular verb unless the meaning is clearly plural.

None of our national parks **is** more scenic than Banff.

None of the changes **has** been proved.

None of the new homes **are** as well constructed as the homes built twenty-five years ago. [The sentence clearly refers to all new homes.]

The emphatic *no one* is always singular:

I looked at a dozen books on the subject, but no one **was** of any use to me.

Each.   *Each* is a singular pronoun and usually takes a singular verb and singular reference words:

Each of the players on the football team **has his** own idea about physical training.

Although the use of the plural form to refer to *each* is considered informal (*Each* of the children ran as fast as *their* legs could carry *them*), this construction is sometimes found in writing when the plural idea is uppermost:

Each of these people undoubtedly modified Latin in accordance with **their** own speech habits. — Albert C. Baugh, *History of the English Language*

However, unless you are prepared to justify your use of plural forms with *each*, you should use singular verbs and pronouns. See also 9.3, Demonstrative Adjectives, for agreement of *this* and *that* (*this kind, that sort*).

▶ EXERCISE

Rewrite the following sentences, changing the words indicated. Make all other changes that would naturally occur, including those in pronoun, noun, and verb forms.

Example: Change *an athlete* to *athletes*. When an athlete gets out of shape, he is probably insuring the end of his career and the end of his team's winning record.

Rewritten: When *athletes* get out of shape, *they* are probably insuring the end of *their* careers and the end of *their* team's (or *teams'*) winning record (or *records*, if *teams'*).

1. Change *a person* to *people*. When a person weaves in and out of traffic lanes, he is endangering the lives of other motorists as well as his own.

2. Change *Another* to *Other*. Another grocery store also reports that its meat sales have fallen off.

3. Change *anyone* to *everyone*. My sister wanted to be able to help anyone who looked insecure or troubled, and to make him feel at ease, no matter who it happened to be.

4. Change *one* to *some*. One actor may interpret the role of Hamlet one way, another another way: if one decides that the role is pathetic, another may decide that his view — the tragic one — is correct.

5. Change *each* to *all*. Until the law determining the age of legal majority was changed, each student was expected to provide her home address so that her grades could be sent to her parents.

7.3 CASE OF PRONOUNS

Case   Change the form of the marked pronoun to show how it functions in the sentence.

Subject and Object Pronouns

Most personal pronouns and the relative or interrogative pronoun *who* have one form when they are used as subjects (*I, she, he, we, they, who*) and another when they are used as objects (*me, her, him, us, them, whom*). A simple test may help you know which pronoun form to use. In a sentence like this, "He left the books for Sarah and (I, me)," omit *Sarah and*. Then it becomes clear that *me* is the form to use. Subject and object forms are listed in the table of pronoun forms on page 91.

After prepositions.   The object form of a personal pronoun is used after a preposition (a letter for *him*; among *us* three). When a pronoun immediately follows a preposition, there is seldom any question about the proper form, but when there are two pronouns, or when a noun is used with the pronoun, writers are sometimes tempted to use a subject form:

INCORRECT: The work was divided between **she** and **I**.

REVISED: The work was divided between **her** and me.

INCORRECT: The same is no doubt true of what European and Asiatic nations have heard about **we** Canadians.

REVISED: The same is no doubt true of what European and Asiatic nations have heard about **us** Canadians.

After *than* in comparisons.   In written English, *than* is considered a conjunction, not a preposition, and is followed by the form of the pronoun that would be used in a complete clause, whether or not the verb appears in the construction:

I am older than **she** [is].

John dances better than **I** [do].

I like him better than **she** [does].

I like him better than [I like] **her**.

In speech, the object form is common with *than* when the pronoun stands alone (I am older than *her*; My room-mate was taking more courses than *me*). It is occasionally found in general writing, especially fiction, but in most college and university writing the subject form is preferable in these constructions.

***It is I* and *it's me*.**   Formal English prefers the subject form after the linking verb *be*:

It is **I**.

That is **he**.

But educated as well as uneducated people frequently say "*It's me*" or "*That's him*." *Me* is more natural in this expression because the pronoun stands in the normal position of the object, right after a verb. All authoritative grammars and dictionaries now consider "it's *me*" acceptable general usage. However, this construction seldom occurs in writing, except in dialogue, where "It is *I*" would sound stilted.

The notion that *I* is somehow more "correct" or polite than *me* sometimes leads people to use the subject form even when the pronoun is the object of a verb: "Father took Jerry and *I* to the game." The object form should always be used in such constructions: "Father took Jerry and *me* to the game."

Who, whom.   The distinction between *who* and *whom* is rarely made in informal speech (the *Oxford English Dictionary* says *whom* is "no longer current in natural colloquial speech") and it may eventually disappear in writing. For example, in the construction *Who* are you taking to the concert?, most would agree that *who* seems natural, since it is in the subject position, even though formal usage would require *whom*, as the direct object (You are taking *whom* to the concert?).

In most writing, it is probably best to make the distinction between *who* and *whom*: *whom* is the standard form when it is the object of a preposition and comes immediately after the preposition (To *whom* were you speaking? He was a man in *whom* we placed great trust). In other objective constructions *whom* is also used; use *who* when it is the subject of a verb, even in subordinate clauses which may themselves be in the objective case:

> Taxes will go up no matter **whom** we elect [*whom* is the direct object of the verb *elect*].

> Taxes will go up no matter **who** is elected [*who* is the subject of the verb *is elected*].

The easiest way to check your usage is to arrange the elements in the clause in a subject—verb—object order (we elect *whom*; *who* is elected): *whom* serves as object, *who* as subject. Sometimes intervening words cause problems, but the principle still holds:

> He made a list of all the writers **who** [subject of *were*] he thought were important in that century.

Possessive Pronouns

In writing, the chief problem in the use of possessive forms of pronouns is the apostrophe. Remember that an apostrophe is not used with the possessives of personal pronouns (a relative of *ours*; the tree and *its* leaves), nor with the possessive of the relative pronoun *who* (a boy *whose* name was Tom).

Possessive of personal pronouns.   Personal pronouns have two forms for the possessive (see p. 91): one is used as a modifier before a noun (*my* roommate, *her* favorite hat); the other is used (by itself or in a phrase) after a noun (That pencil is *mine*; a friend of *hers*). While either form may be used in many statements (*our* government, this government of *ours*), there are some constructions in which one form is obviously better than the other:

> CLUMSY: We decided to pool **their** and **our** resources.

> REVISED: We decided to pool their resources with **ours**.

Its and it's.   *Its*, without the apostrophe, is the possessive form of *it*; *it's*, with the apostrophe, is the contraction for *it is* or *it has*:

> Everything should be in **its** proper place.

> **It's** [it is] an ill wind that blows no good.

> **It's** [it has] been a long time.

One of the mistakes most frequently marked in student papers is the use of *it's* for *its*. If you tend to confuse these two forms you should check each instance of *its* (*it's*) when revising your papers: for example, if you've used *it's*, read the word as *it is* or *it has*; your meaning will reveal any errors.

7.3

Case

Possessive of indefinite pronouns.   Several of the indefinite pronouns (*all, any, each, few, most, none, some*) are used only in *of* phrases for the possessive:

> They were both happy when things were going well, but adversity brought out the best side **of each**.

The apostrophe and *s* are used with the possessive forms of other indefinite pronouns, just as they are with nouns:

> **Anyone's** guess is as good as mine.
>
> One man's meat is **another's** poison.
>
> **Somebody's** books were left in the classroom.

When indefinite pronouns are used with *else*, the apostrophe and *s* are added to *else* and not to the preceding word:

> These notes are somebody **else's**.
>
> Anyone **else's** offer would have been accepted.

Possessive of *who* and *which*.   *Whose* is the possessive form of the relative pronoun *who*. *Who's*, the informal contraction for *who is* or *who has*, is not used in most writing.

> A well-known Canadian painter is A. Y. Jackson, **whose** paintings are familiar to thousands.
>
> It is the white-collar worker **who is** [informal: *who's*] least likely to be affected by seasonal unemployment.

Although *whose* usually refers to persons and *of which* to things, *whose* is regularly used to refer to inanimate things when *of which* would be awkward:

> . . . we would cross a room in which no one ever sat, **whose** fire was never lighted, **whose** walls were picked out with gilded mouldings. — Marcel Proust, *Remembrance of Things Past*

▶ **EXERCISE**

Read the following sentences and correct any pronouns used incorrectly.
Example: She answered the phone, trying to sound very dignified, and said,
      "Would you like to leave a message with I?"
Revised: *I* should be *me*.

1. She divided what was left of the cake equally between Margaret and I.
2. A book in which a man and a woman collaborate should deal accurately with human nature, for between him and her they represent the two sexes.
3. Most of the other actors have had more experience than me and make fun of my stage fright.
4. Whom do you think is going to be chosen as editor?
5. A letter came for Paul and I inviting us to a committee meeting.

7.4 REFLEXIVE AND INTENSIVE PRONOUNS

The reflexive form of a personal pronoun is used to refer back to the subject in an expression where the doer and recipient of an act are the same:

> I had only **myself** to blame.
>
> He hurt **himself** skiing.

The same pronoun form is sometimes used as an intensive to make another word more emphatic:

> The award was presented by the Governor General **himself**.
>
> Life **itself** is at stake.

In certain constructions, *myself* is mistakenly considered by some people as more polite than *I* or *me* (My wife and *myself* accept with pleasure), but in standard English the reflexive form is not used as the subject or as a substitute for *me*:

> Another fellow and **I** [not *myself*] saw the whole thing.
>
> Sam invited John and **me** [not *myself*] to dinner.

Hisself and *theirselves* are not standard English forms.

7.5 CHOICE OF PERSONAL PRONOUN FORM

Personal pronouns indicate the person or persons speaking (first person: *I, we*), the person spoken to (second person: *you*), or the person or thing spoken of (third person: *he, she, it one, they*). In writing, the choice of form may be a problem since the writer can refer to himself or herself as *I, one,* or *we*. Some questions that frequently arise in using these pronouns are considered here.

I and we.   When writing as an individual, the usual way to refer to yourself is to use the first-person singular pronouns *I*, *me*, *my*, *myself*, and *mine*. If you happen to be writing as a member of a group, employ the first-person plural pronouns *we*, *our*, *ourselves*, and *ours*.

> **I** often treat **myself** to **my** favorite appetizer: smoked oysters.
>
> After writing **our** last exam, **we** went to the pub.

7.5

Pron

There is no reason to avoid using these first-person pronouns, even in formal writing. If used frequently, however, they do draw more attention to the *writer* than to the subject — an emphasis that is not always desirable (or intended). For this reason, many authorities suggest that such forms be avoided whenever a relatively impersonal or "objective" approach is appropriate, as in scientific reports. In such situations you will usually want to concentrate on the generalized needs of your subject and your reader, not on your incidental impressions. The fewer times you refer to yourself, the less subjective or self-centred your style will seem.

But remember that all writing is done by a person, that is, by an "I" with particular experiences and a particular voice. Eliminating personal pronouns does not, in itself, make statements objective or conclusive, and the roundabout wording of supposedly "impersonal" assertions can be extremely clumsy. It is often better to present the fact plainly and honestly, rather than to try to get around the natural use of "I" by awkward passive constructions:

> AWKWARD: After exploring the subject **it is concluded that** that mass hysteria is a rather common occurrence.
>
> REVISED: After exploring the subject **I find** that mass hysteria is a rather common occurrence.

Of course, if a teacher or supervisor specifically insists that you avoid first-person pronouns in formal writing (or if you have been warned that your style tends to be too personal and arbitrary), try hard during revision to reduce the number of self-referential expressions you use.

We is useful for general reference (*We* are living in an atomic age), but as a substitute for *I*, the "royal" or "editorial *we*" is out of place in most writing:

> AWKWARD: The conclusions in **our** essay are based upon information **we** obtained from the local police.
>
> REVISED: The conclusions in **my** essay are based upon information **I** obtained from the police.

You.   Overuse of the generalizing *you* (meaning people in general) should be avoided. Don't write *you* unless you really want the pronoun to refer specifically to your reader. Otherwise, the unintentionally implied reference to the reader may be irritating, misleading, or both:

> AWKWARD: When **you** begin reading *The Waste Land*, **you** are totally confused.

> REVISED: When **I** began reading *The Waste Land*, **I** was totally confused.

> AWKWARD: In my business **you** have to work evenings.

> REVISED: In my business **I** have [or **one** has] to work evenings.

In the awkward versions above, the writers obviously did not mean *you* (their readers) at all. Use of the informal generalized *you* should be confined instead to situations which genuinely apply to everyone:

> When **you** suddenly enter a dark room, it takes a while for **your** eyes to adjust.

You can be used successfully, as in a familiar essay, when the writer seeks to establish a close relationship with the reader. Similarly, a reader can be addressed personally as *you* throughout publications (such as this *Handbook*) in which the author is employing a social and fairly informal voice.

One. The pronoun *one*, meaning "a person" or "anyone," is used when you want to refer to people in general (or at least to all people who are assumed to share your attitudes):

> Watching the scene on television, **one** senses the drama of the situation.

> **One** can never forget the intense blue of the Aegean Sea.

But this use of *one* is impersonal, rather stiff, and often ungainly, especially when *one* is repeated several times. General English characteristically uses personal pronouns in such expressions:

> Watching the scene on television, **I** [or *you*] can sense the drama of the situation.

> **I** can never forget the intense blue of the Aegean Sea.

In current Canadian usage, it is standard practice to refer to *one* (meaning the writer or anyone) by the third-person *he* and *his* or *she* and *her*:

> **One** should be cautious if **he** wants to avoid offending his friends.

> **One** never knows when **her** purse may suddenly be snatched.

7.6 AVOIDING SHIFTS IN PRONOUN FORM

Shift   **Make the marked words or constructions consistent in form. Pronouns should be consistent in person and number; verbs should be consistent in tense.**

7.6

Shift

In using pronouns for general reference, be consistent and do not make unnecessary shifts from singular to plural forms or from *we* to *you* or *one*:

> INCONSISTENT: After **one** has selected the boat **he** is going to learn in, it would be a good idea if **you** first learned the theory of sailing. Most of **us** have at least seen a sailing boat, but seeing one and sailing one are two different things. **One** might think that a boat can sail only with the breeze and not against it. Or **they** might think that a stiff breeze is necessary to sail a boat.

> CONSISTENT: After **you** have selected the boat **you** are going to learn in, it would be a good idea if **you** first learned the theory of sailing. **You** have probably seen a sailing boat, but seeing one and sailing one are two different things. **You** may think that a boat can sail only with the breeze and not against it. Or **you** may think that a stiff breeze is necessary to sail a boat.

The pronoun *one* is more likely to lead to a shift in construction than are the other forms. Unless you intend to be impersonal and feel confident in your use of *one*, use *you, we, he, she*, or a noun substitute in these situations.

▶ **EXERCISE**

Revise the following sentences to correct the needless shifts in person or number.

Example: The modern car is very complex, and they are always breaking down.
Revised: The modern car is very complex, and *it is* always breaking down.

Or: Modern cars *are* very complex, and they are always breaking down.

1. Some writers think teachers use grammar as a means to block your creative abilities.
2. When a person has enjoyed a year of travelling, one is reluctant to return home to an ordinary job.
3. When a student has spent a lot of time on his compositions, they are apt to be disgruntled if all they get is grammatical criticisms.
4. Anybody would feel the same way if you had a teacher like mine.
5. Although a pocket dictionary can give some help, they cannot replace a standard desk dictionary.
6. Nobody in the class seemed very sure of their ability to analyse style.

8

Verbs

 Change the marked verb form so that it conforms to standard usage.

In meaning, verbs indicate action (*run, manufacture, write*), condition (*am, feel, sleep*), or process (*become, grow*). In form, they may be one word (*do*) or a phrase (*should have done*), and may add letters (prove*s*, prove*d*) or change internally (s*i*ng, s*a*ng, s*u*ng) to indicate person, number, tense, and voice. Except in questions, verbs usually follow the subject.

This chapter discusses some of the most common problems in the use of verb forms. Charts and lists are also provided to illustrate the principal characteristics and uses of verbs and verb phrases. (See also 4, Verbals and Verbal Phrases, and 5, Agreement of Subject and Verb.)

8.1 TENSE

Make the tense of the marked verb conventional in form or consistent with others in the passage.

By means of the different tenses, writers set the *time* of the situation they are describing (as happening in the past, going on at present, or occurring in the future) and also show the continuity of the action or explanation. Consistent and conventional use of tense keeps the sequence of your writing in order and enables a reader to follow the time relationships.

Tense Forms

The appropriate form of a verb should be used to indicate each of its tenses. Problems seldom arise with regular verbs, because the past tense and past participle are the same (*walked, imagined, meant*) and derive consistently from the base form (*walk, imagine, mean*) by the endings *-ed, -d,* or *-t.*

In irregular verbs, however, the base form changes in the past tense or past participle, or both (*draw, drew, drawn; drink, drank, drunk*). (See 8.2, Irregular Verbs, and 8.3, Auxiliary Verbs.)

Besides the simple present tense (*walk*) and simple past tense (*walked*), there are various distinctions of time that can be indicated by adding auxiliary verbs. (See 8.3.) In the future tense, for example, the base form is preceded by the auxiliary verb *will* (*will walk, will draw, will grow*). Other variations of tense are formed by combining auxiliary verbs with present or past participles (*am walking, have drawn, will be boiling*) or by using adverbial expressions (for example, *about to go* as a future). Consult the charts and lists in this chapter for illustrations of the tenses and auxiliary forms used most frequently in time distinctions.

8.1

Time and Tenses

The various tenses in English serve to indicate particular moments or periods in past, present, or future time:

PAST TIME:
Past tense — **I cooked** meat pies yesterday. [indicates something that happened at a particular time in the past]

Past progressive tense — **I was cooking** meat pies when they came in. [indicates something going on during a period of time in the past]

Perfect tense — **I have cooked** meat pies many times. [indicates something that has happened at various times in the past]

Past perfect tense — **I had cooked** meat pies long before I found the recipe I use now. [indicates something that happened before some time in the past]

PRESENT TIME:
Present tense — **I cook** meat pies. [indicates something that happens, as customary practice, or that can happen in the immediate present]

Present progressive — **I am cooking** meat pies. [indicates something that is going on at the present time]

FUTURE TIME:
Future tense — **I will cook** meat pies for dinner tomorrow. [indicates something that can happen at some time in the future]

Future perfect tense — **I will have cooked** the meat pies before she gets home with the wine. [indicates something that will take place before some particular time in the future]

Notice how the tenses are used to indicate differences in time in these sentences:

He **has finished** supper [perfect] and **is looking** [present progressive] at television.

He **had finished** supper [past perfect] and **was looking** [past progressive] at television.

Most Frequently Used Active Verb Tenses

	I	he, she, it	we, you, they
Present tenses			
PRESENT (immediate present)	ask	asks	ask
PRESENT PROGRESSIVE: (continuing present)	**am** asking	**is** asking	**are** asking
Past tenses			
PAST	asked	asked	asked
PAST PROGRESSIVE (continuing period in past)	**was** asking	**was** asking	**were** asking
PERFECT (past time extending to the present; past participle with *have* or *has*)	**have** asked	**has** asked	**have** asked
PAST PERFECT (a time in the past before another past time; past participle with *had*)	had asked	had asked	had asked
Future tenses			
FUTURE (future time extending from the present)	will ask **am** going to ask	will ask **is** going to ask	will ask **are** going to ask
FUTURE PERFECT (past time in some future time; future tense of *have* with past participle)	will have asked	will have asked	will have asked

He **had finished** supper [past perfect] when **I arrived** [past].

He **finished** supper [past] when **I arrived** [past].

When the verb of a main clause is in the past or past perfect tense, the verb in a subordinate clause is also past or past perfect:

They slowly **began** to appreciate what their teacher **had** [not *has*] **done for them.**

Up to that time I had never **seen** Slim when he **hadn't** [or *didn't have;* not *hasn't*] a wad of tobacco in his mouth.

Exception: A present infinitive is usual after a past verb:

I would have liked very much **to attend** [not *to have attended*] her wedding, but I was out of town.

8.1

Consistent Use of Tenses

Shift

Make the marked words or constructions consistent in form. Verbs should be consistent in tense; pronouns should be consistent in person and number.

Careless shifts in tense (as from the present to the past, or the past to the future) confuse the sequence of your writing:

UNNECESSARY SHIFTS: **I sit** down at my desk early with intentions of spending the next four hours studying. Before many minutes **passed**, **I heard** a great deal of noise down on the floor below me; a water-fight **is** in progress. **I forgot** about studying for half an hour, for it **is** quite impossible to concentrate on French in the midst of all this commotion. After things **quieted** down **I begin** studying again, but **had** hardly **started** when a magazine salesman **comes** into my room. [mixture of present and past]

CONSISTENT: **I sat** down at my desk early with intentions of spending the next four hours studying. Before many minutes **had passed**, **I heard** a great deal of noise down on the floor below me; a water-fight **was** in progress. **I forgot** about studying for half an hour, for it **was** quite impossible to concentrate on French in the midst of all that commotion. After things had **quieted** down **I began** studying again, but **had** hardly **started** when a magazine salesman **came** into my room. [past tense throughout]

In single sentences inconsistencies in verb tenses often occur when a writer shifts the form of two or more verbs that should be parallel:

SHIFTED: For years **I have been attending** summer camp and **enjoyed** every minute of it.

CONSISTENT: For years **I have been attending** summer camp and **enjoying** every minute of it.

8.2 IRREGULAR VERBS

Some of the most commonly used verbs in English create problems in writing because of their irregular forms or optional uses. A writer sometimes departs from the standards of edited English when he forms certain tenses of the irregular verbs. Such deviations are most likely to happen when he uses some dialect form or other non-standard form (He *seen* the show last week), or when he confuses forms with similar spellings (*choose, chose*).

Irregular Verb Forms

The following list shows the principal parts of irregular verbs that sometimes cause problems. The *past tense*, second column, is used in the simple past (She *wrote* a letter). The *past participle*, third column, is used with the auxiliaries to form verb phrases (The bird *had flown* away; Soon this *will be forgotten*; The chimes *are being rung*). (See 8.3, Auxiliary Verbs.) The past participle cannot be used alone as a full verb in the past tense.

When two forms are given, both are acceptable (He *lighted* a cigarette; He *lit* a cigarette). Verbs marked with an asterisk (*) are discussed in the sections following. For verbs not given here, consult a recent dictionary. Caution: If your dictionary labels the form in question *non-standard, obsolete, archaic, dialect,* or *rare,* that form is not suitable for most general writing.

Infinitive	Past tense	Past participle
arise	arose	arisen
bear (carry)*	bore	borne
bear (give birth to)*	bore	borne, born
begin	began	begun
bite	bit	bitten, bit
blow	blew	blown
break	broke	broken
bring	brought	brought
burst	burst	burst
catch	caught	caught
choose	chose	chosen
come	came	come
dig	dug	dug
dive	dived, dove	dived
do*	did	done
drag	dragged	dragged
draw	drew	drawn
dream	dreamed, dreamt	dreamed, dreamt
drink	drank	drunk
drive	drove	driven
eat	ate	eaten
fall	fell	fallen
fly	flew	flown

Infinitive	Past tense	Past participle
forget	forgot	forgotten
freeze	froze	frozen
get*	got	got, gotten
give	gave	given
go	went	gone
grow	grew	grown
hang (a person)	hanged, hung	hanged, hung
hang (an object)	hung	hung
know	knew	known
lay (place)*	laid	laid
lead	led	led
lend	lent	lent
lie (recline)*	lay	lain
light	lighted, lit	lighted, lit
lose	lost	lost
pay	paid	paid
prove	proved	proved, proven
ride	rode	ridden
ring	rang, rung	rung
rise	rose	risen
run	ran	run
see	saw	seen
set*	set	set
shake	shook	shaken
shine	shone, shined	shone, shined
show	showed	showed, shown
shrink	shrank, shrunk	shrunk
sing	sang, sung	sung
sink	sank, sunk	sunk, sunken
sit*	sat	sat
slide	slid	slid, slidden
slink	slunk	slunk
speak	spoke	spoken
spring	sprang, sprung	sprung
steal	stole	stolen
swim	swam, swum	swum
take	took	taken
tear	tore	torn
throw	threw	thrown
wake	woke, waked	woke, waked
wear	wore	worn
wring	wrung	wrung
write	wrote	written

8.2

Vb

born — borne

The past participle of *bear* in the sense of "carry" is spelled *borne*: a leaf *borne* by the wind, he had *borne* many hardships. In the sense of "give birth to," the spelling is *born* in the passive voice, *borne* in the active: *born* in Truro, a *born* loser, a child *born* to her (but, she had *borne* a child).

do — did — done

Speakers of some dialects use *done* as a past-tense form (He *done* his best) where edited English requires *did*, the standard form. Particular care should be taken with the past tense and the past participle:

PRESENT TENSE: I, we, you, they **do**; he, she, it **does**

PAST TENSE: I, you, he, she, it, we, they **did**

PAST PARTICIPLE: I, you, we, they have (had) **done**; he, she, it has (had) **done**

The verb *do* can also have auxiliary functions (see 8.3) in negative and emphatic phrases ("I *do not* believe Harriet, but I *do* believe you.").

don't — doesn't.   *Don't* is the contraction for *do not* (I *do not*, I *don't*), *doesn't* is the contraction for *does not* (he *does not*, he *doesn't*). The substitution of one form for the other (*Don't* she look pretty?) is not consistent with edited forms of the language.

Idioms with *do*.   *Do* is used in many standard idioms (set expressions): *do* without, *do* away with, make *do*. In college and university writing, it is best to avoid informal expressions with *do*, like these:

When the Dean of Women arrived, she seemed **done in** [better: *exhausted*].

They **did** [better: *cheated*] the government out of $50,000.

Consult a dictionary whenever you are unsure about the appropriateness of a particular expression with *do* or *done*.

get — got — gotten

The principal parts of the verb *get* are *get, got,* and *gotten* or *got*. Both forms of the past participle are used in Canada:

He could have **gotten** [or *got*] more for his money.

Her efforts had **gotten** [or *got*] no results.

Used with *have* to show possession (see below), the form is always *got*. In other constructions, *gotten* is quite common.

8.2

Vb

have got, have got to.   *Have got* in the sense of possession (I *haven't got* a black tie) or obligation (We *have got to* finish this experiment today) is widely used in speech and is acceptable in most kinds of writing. Some writers of formal English avoid the expression, regarding *got* as redundant and preferring *have* alone (I *haven't* a black tie; We *have to* finish this experiment today). Although *have* alone carries the meaning, it is so frequently used as a mere auxiliary of tense that it is not often considered as a verb of full meaning; in such cases either *have* or *have got* is considered acceptable.

Idioms with get.   In many common idioms *get* is standard usage for all levels of speaking and writing:

STANDARD:	get up	get along with (someone)
	get away from	get over (an illness)
	get ahead	get tired

Other expressions with *get* are considered informal and would best be avoided in college or university writing:

INFORMAL: Long-winded discussions **get** on my nerves.

This modern music **gets** me.

Some people seem to **get** away with murder.

A stray bullet **got** him in the shoulder.

When you are in doubt about the standing of an idiom with *get*, consult a recent dictionary.

lie — lay

The verbs *lie* and *lie down* (meaning *recline*) do not take an object. The principal parts are *lie, lay, lain*: You *lie* on the bed, or *lie down* on the job; Yesterday he *lay* in bed all morning; The log had *lain* across the road for a week. The present participle of *lie* is *lying*: The log was *lying* in the road; I found him *lying* in bed.

    Lay and *lay down* (to put or place) take an object. The principal parts are *lay, laid, laid*: She *laid* her purse on the table; He should *lay down* his cards; The cornerstone was *laid*: The robin *laid* an egg. The present participle of *lay* is *laying*: He was *laying* the foundation.

sit — set

The verb *sit* (as in a chair) does not take an object. Its principal parts are *sit, sat, sat*: I like to *sit* in a hotel lobby; He *sat* there an hour; I have *sat* in the same chair for three semesters.

The verb *set* (meaning to put something down) takes an object. Its principal parts are *set, set, set*: *Set* the soup on this pad; They *set* the trunk in the hall yesterday; She has *set* candles in the windows.

8.3 AUXILIARY VERBS

There are two kinds of *auxiliary verbs*, irregular verbs that can (or must) combine with other verbs in various ways to change or add meanings. One kind of auxiliary verb works with one or more participles to indicate additional distinctions of tense (*am* drinking, *had* touched, *will* arrive, *was* being told, *will have* been spanked). The other kind of auxiliary can join with the base form of a different verb to establish special meanings (*can* fight, *would* like, *should* apologize, *did* succeed). The two kinds of auxiliaries sometimes appear in the same phrase (*should have been* apologizing).

Remember that some auxiliary verbs such as *be, have,* and *do* can be used either as auxiliaries or as distinct forms ("I *have* forgotten my pencil, but I *have* my ruler."). Certain other words (*will, would*) are rarely used except as auxiliaries, however, and others (*shall, should*) are used only as auxiliaries.

Forms of the Verb *be*

Forms of *be* and *have* are the most frequently used auxiliary verbs in English. The verb *be* has eight forms, three more than any other verb in English. In addition to the infinitive, there are three forms in the present tense, two in the past tense, the present participle, and the past participle:

	I	he, she, it	we, you, they
PRESENT TENSE:	am	is	are
PAST TENSE:	was	was	were
PRESENT PARTICIPLE:	being		
PAST PARTICIPLE:	been		

The forms of *be* are not troublesome in ordinary situations, at least not for those reasonably well acquainted with edited English. Some speakers of dialect (in Newfoundland, for instance) do use the auxiliary *be* in a different way, as in *she be singing*. These forms are usually not found in general written English, however.

Ain't.   *Ain't* is a dialectal and, in Canada, a non-standard negative contraction of the various forms of *be; aren't* and *isn't* are the standard forms. In questions with *I, am I not*? is formal; *aren't I*? is the form most often used. Since the forms are rarely needed in writing except in dialogue, the form most natural to the speaker would be used.

Choice of *can* or *may*

In all levels of usage *can* is used for ability (This car *can* do better than 150 kilometres an hour; He *can* walk with crutches), and *may* is used to indicate possibility (That *may* be true; We *may* get there before dark).

To express permission, formal English and edited general English use *may* (*May* I go now? You *may* have any one you like.). Although general spoken English increasingly uses *can* in such expressions (*Can* I go now? You *can* have any one you like.), in writing it is best to use *may*.

shall — will

In current Canadian usage, *will* is generally used with all persons of the verb for the future tense (I *will* leave tomorrow. He *will* arrive at six. We *will* return later.). To express determination or for emphasis, usage is divided about *will* and *shall* (I *will* not permit it. They *shall* pass.). Some writers make the following formal distinctions between *shall* and *will*:

Simple future

FIRST PERSON:	I shall ask	we shall ask
SECOND PERSON:	you will ask	you will ask
THIRD PERSON:	he, she, it will ask	they will ask

Emphatic future

FIRST PERSON:	I will ask	we will ask
SECOND PERSON:	you shall ask	you shall ask
THIRD PERSON:	he, she, it shall ask	they shall ask

Such distinctions are seldom heard in conversation nowadays and rarely met at all except in very conservative formal writing. Observe that the distinctions are eliminated in conversation where the contractions are used: *I'll* ask; *we'll* ask; and so on.

shall and ***will*** **in questions.**   In questions, *will* is used in all persons, but *shall* is often used, especially in formal English, if there is a notion of propriety or obligation:

> **Will** I go? Where **will** we go next? What **will** you do now?
>
> OBLIGATION: **Shall** I go? What **shall** she wear?

Some writers use *should* and avoid both *shall* and *will*:

> Where **should** we go next? **Should** I go?

In the negative, *won't* is the regular form:

> What **won't** they think of next?
>
> Why **won't** you go?

Overuse of *shall*.   *Shall* should not be used in statements where *will* is the standard form:

> Whether or not Parliament **will** [not *shall*] pass the bill is not for me to guess.

Some people apparently think that *shall* is a more correct (or elegant) form than *will*. It is not.

should — would

Should and *would* are used in statements that carry a sense of doubt or uncertainty:

> It **should** be cooler by evening. [Contrast with the meaning of: It *will* be cooler by evening.]
>
> I wasn't ready as soon as I thought I **would** be.

Should, like *shall*, is often used to express the idea of propriety or obligation:

> You **should** wash your hands before meals.
>
> I **should** answer her letter this week.

In polite or unemphatic requests, both *would* and *should* are used for the first person and *would* for the second person:

> I **would** be much obliged if you could help me.
>
> I **should** be much obliged if you could help me.
>
> **Would** you please give this your earliest attention?
>
> I wish you **would** write more often.

In indirect discourse, *would* and *should* serve as the past tenses of *will* and *shall*:

> DIRECT DISCOURSE: Mary said, "I will go."
>
> INDIRECT DISCOURSE: Mary said that she would go.
>
> DIRECT DISCOURSE: "Shall we adjourn?" the president asked.
>
> INDIRECT DISCOURSE: The president asked if they should adjourn.

8.3

Vb

Terms Used in Describing Verbs

VERB FORMS (8.1) English verbs have three principal parts:

INFINITIVE (the base form)   PAST TENSE   PAST PARTICIPLE

ask (to ask), go (to go)   asked, went   asked, gone

REGULAR AND IRREGULAR VERBS (8.1 and 8.2). Regular verbs add -*ed* to form the past tense and past participle (ask, asked, asked). Irregular verbs change form in other ways (sing, sang, sung; go, went, gone).

TENSE (8.1). The "time" of a verb's action as expressed in the form of the verb:

PAST: I went   PRESENT: I go   FUTURE: I will go

For other tenses, see the table on p. 108.

TRANSITIVE AND INTRANSITIVE.

A verb is **transitive** when it has an object: The teacher *demanded*(v) *order*(o).

A verb is **intransitive** when it does not have an object: He *slept*(v) well.

ACTIVE AND PASSIVE VOICE (8.4). A **passive** verb is a form of *be* and a past participle: *is believed, was believed, had been believed, will be believed*. All other verbs are **active**.

MODE (8.5). The manner in which a statement is expressed (an almost obsolete distinction now):

The **indicative mood** expresses a fact or a statement: I *am* thrifty.

The **subjunctive mood** is used in some conditions (as those contrary to fact: If I *were* king.) and in such constructions as: It is necessary that he *be* twenty-one.

AUXILIARY VERB (8.3). A verb used in a verb phrase to show tense, voice, etc.: *am* going; *had* gone; *will* go; *should have been* done.

LINKING VERB OR COPULA (1.1). A verb that "links" its subject to a predicate noun or an adjective: She *is* a teacher. the days *became* warmer.

FINITE AND NON-FINITE VERBS. A **finite verb** (from the Latin *finis*, meaning "end" or "limit") can be limited (5 and 8):

In **person** by a pronoun or subject (I *sing*, she *sings*)

In **time** by a tense form (she *sings*, she *sang*)

In **number**, by a singular or plural form (he *sings*, they *sing*)

Finite verbs are full verbs in sentences and clauses: I *had gone* before he *came*.

THE NON-FINITE VERB FORMS (participles, infinitives, gerunds) are not limited in person or number and are ordinarily used in phrases (4): Before *leaving* I thanked our host. She needed a hat *to wear* to the party.

Writers sometimes use *would* with another verb to suggest continuous or habitual action: The man *would* always be waiting at the corner. He *would* give me a quarter for candy. I *would* refuse it. It's generally better to depend on the accurate verb tense of the primary verb: The man *was* always *waiting* at the corner. Every time he saw me he *offered* me a quarter for candy. I always *refused* it.

▶ **EXERCISES**

1. Rewrite this paragraph, filling in the proper forms of the verbs indicated in parentheses, including any necessary auxiliary verbs.

   As the action begins, it is clear that the old man (perfect of *rise*) and (perfect of *bid*) the young soldier enter. The audience is aware that the young soldier (perfect of *know*) for a long time that it was the old man who (past perfect of *slay*) his father. When the soldier (past perfect of *return*) from the war, his mother (past prefect of *forsake*) her deathbed to tell him how the old man (past perfect of *steal*) into the house, (past perfect of *find*) the loaded gun on the night table, and, even as the mother (past of *shrink*) into the corner of the room, (past perfect of *shoot*) her husband. Laden with this heavy sorrow, her heart (past perfect of *burst*). Within the next few moments of action, the young soldier (future perfect of *bind*) the arms of the old man and (future perfect of *begin*) to lead him from the room.

2. Supply the proper form of the verbs in parentheses in each of these sentences. Some of the constructions may call for an infinitive, participle, or gerund (see 4, Verbals).

   Example: Last night the wind (whip) the leaves so that they (spin) like the arms on a windmill.

   Answer: whipped, spun

   a. Once she had (do) the exercises, she (do) her reading with much greater pleasure.
   b. In the saloon, the dark-bearded cowboy pushed aside his beer and slowly (draw) his gun.
   c. He could have (get) a higher grade if he had worked a little longer on the project.
   d. Within minutes the police officer (ride) up to investigate.

   e. Before he called, she had (lie) down to rest a few minutes.
   f. A low moan was (wring) from his lips.
   g. He had (rid) the town of many criminals before.
   h. At the hitching post the horse (shake) his mane and nervously (paw) the ground.
3. Write sentences following the instructions below.
   a. a single sentence that uses both *can* and *may*
   b. a sentence that uses the past tense of *sit*
   c. a sentence that uses the past tense of *set*
   d. a sentence that uses *should* to express an obligation
   e. a sentence that uses *would* as the past tense of *will*
   f. a sentence that uses *should* as the past tense of *shall*

8.4

V.b

8.4 ACTIVE AND PASSIVE VOICE

When writers use the *active* rather than the *passive voice*, they do so because they wish the doer of the action denoted by the verb to be the subject of the sentence:

ACTIVE VERB: Jim's father **gave** him a car.

PASSIVE VERB: Jim **was given** a car by his father.

The passive consists of a form of *be* plus the past participle (*is given, are chosen, was taken, have been corrected*).

Appropriate Passives

The great majority of English sentences use active verbs, but sometimes the passive is appropriate. Passive constructions are apt if the actor is unknown or unimportant to the statement:

The game **was postponed** because of rain.

The expressway **will be completed** by spring.

One of the advantages of the new tank is that the engine **can be removed** and **replaced** in far less time than the same operation took for the old one.

A passive verb may also be appropriate if the writer especially wants to emphasize the object or the act rather than the doer:

The fire **was discovered** by the watchman.

The bill **is supported** by members of all parties.

But passives should not otherwise be used without a good reason (such as variety in sentence patterning). Active constructions are normally much more economical and decisive.

Inappropriate Passives

Pass   Change the passive verb or verbs to active.

Passive constructions are often weak or awkward and should usually be changed in revision to the more direct active voice:

> WEAK PASSIVE: A distinction **is made** by sociologists between achieved and ascribed status.
>
> ACTIVE: Sociologists **make** a distinction between achieved and ascribed status.
>
> PASSIVE: All of the major Russian novelists **were studied** in my comparative literature course.
>
> ACTIVE: I **studied** all of the major Russian novelists in my comparative literature course.

It is sometimes awkward or ambiguous to combine an active and a passive verb in the same sentence:

> AWKWARD: The city **needs** more money to build new schools, and it **will** probably **be raised** through a bond issue.
>
> REVISED: The city **needs** more money to build new schools and **will** probably **raise** it through a bond issue.

Some writers habitually employ the passive voice in order to avoid having to identify the person responsible for an action:

> Your scholarship application **has been rejected**.
>
> I'm afraid my drink **has just been spilled** on your carpet.
>
> He **is considered** an unreliable witness.
>
> **It has been concluded** that the pub **should be closed**.

Unless you have a good reason for resorting to one of these supposedly "tactful" evasions (see, for example, 7.5 regarding personal pronouns in scientific reports), use forthright *active* constructions whenever possible.

► EXERCISE

Revise the sentences below so that they will still mean the same thing, but are in the active voice.
Example: It has always been felt by me that the study of biology is boring.
Revised: I have always felt that studying biology is boring.
1. Biology is thought by students to be very time-consuming.
2. It is also felt that cutting up dead frogs is disgusting to some students.
3. Sometimes tests are given by biology professors which are thought to require too much memorizing.

4. Also, it is costly to some to pay the lab fees.
5. For these reasons, it is an opinion of mine that the abolishment of required biology should be considered by school authorities.

8.5 USE OF THE SUBJUNCTIVE MOOD

The word *mood* is a variant of the word *mode* and indicates manner. A verb in the subjunctive mood, then, is a verb used in a particular manner, to express a future contingency or a condition contrary to fact. Certain instances of atypical verb forms are known as the subjunctive mood: he *ask* instead of *asks*; I, he, or she *were* instead of *was*; I, he, she *be asked* instead of *is* or *was asked*.

Use of the subjunctive forms in current English is quite limited and inconsistent, even in formal English. There is almost always an alternative construction, often with auxiliary verbs; therefore, writers seldom need to use the subjunctive.

In Hypothetical and Conditional Statements

The subjunctive is sometimes used, especially in formal English, to express contrary-to-fact, impossible, or improbable conditions:

> If I **were** in your position [I'm not], I wouldn't accept his offer.
>
> He said that if he **were** in power [he isn't], he would remove them.

The subjunctive may also be found occasionally in conditional statements:

> If the subject of a verb **be** impersonal, the verb itself may be called impersonal.

This use does not contribute to meaning and seems unnecessary; the verb *is* would be preferable.

In *that* Clauses

The subjunctive is used in many set expressions (usually in a formal, often legal, context) for recommendations, demands, and so on:

> FORMAL: It is required that the applicant be over twenty-one.
>
> STANDARD: The applicant must be over twenty-one.
>
> FORMAL: I ask that interested citizens watch closely the movements of these suspicious persons.

STANDARD: I ask interested citizens to watch closely the movements of these suspicious persons.

In Formulas

The subjunctive is found in numerous formulas and set phrases, locutions surviving from a time when the subjunctive was used freely:

If I were you	If only she were here	As it were
God be with you	Be that as it may	Come what may

▶ **EXERCISE**

Complete the following sentences using subjunctive verb forms.
1. If I. . . .
2. She said if she. . . .
3. Were he to. . . .
4. It is necessary that each student. . . .
5. What would you do if she. . . .

8.6 IDIOMS WITH VERBS

 Change the marked word or expression so that it will be idiomatic.

An idiom is a usage that has become established through custom rather than rule. Verbs and verb phrases should be both idiomatically correct and appropriate to the general level of a writer's style. The chart that follows lists some verb forms that should be avoided because they are clumsy or not in good edited form. Others are acceptable in informal or general usage but inappropriate in formal edited written English.

Troublesome Idioms

ABLE TO: A clumsy and unidiomatic expression when used with a passive infinitive: "This shirt **can be** [not *is able to be*] washed without shrinkage."

AGGRAVATE, IRRITATE: In formal usage **aggravate** means to intensify or make worse; **irritate** means to vex or annoy: "The seriousness of his crime was **aggravated** by the prisoner's implication of innocent people." "Stop **irritating** me with those silly questions." Informally **aggravate** is used in the same sense as **irritate**: "I was never so **aggravated** in my life." The distinction between the two words should be observed in college writing.

BEING THAT: To introduce a dependent clause of reason or cause, **being that** is an unacceptable substitute for **because, since,** or **for**: "Randy decided to major in pharmacy **because** [not *being that*] his uncle was a successful pharmacist."

8.6

CONTACT: Many people dislike this verb as a substitute for "get in touch with someone," although it is widely used in business: "Will you **contact** our Mr. Hubble?" In general and formal writing "call" or "see" is ordinarily used.

ENTHUSE: Most dictionaries label **enthuse** informal, preferring **be enthusiastic about** or **show enthusiasm**. While **enthuse** is in fairly common use, it is generally better to use another form.

FIX: In general usage, **fix** commonly means repair or prepare (**fix** a broken clock, **fix** lunch for three). It also means to make fast or establish (**fix** the tent to its pegs, **fix** tariff prices). **Fix** is informal in the sense of to **get even with** (I'll **fix** you for that).

LEAVE, LET: **Leave** means to depart or to abandon; **let** means to permit: "They won't *let* us *leave*." Using **leave** for **let** is inappropriate edited English.

PREDOMINATE, PREDOMINANT: **Predominate** is a verb: "The captain's will **predominated** throughout the voyage." **Predominant** is an adjective: "His **predominant** characteristic is laziness."

SUSPECT, SUSPICION: **Suspect** is the verb meaning to distrust or imagine: "The police **suspected** foul play." **Suspicion** is a noun, and when used for **suspect** is a localism, inappropriate in edited English except in dialogue.

TRY AND, TRY TO: Both are accepted idioms: **Try and** is the more common in general English, especially in informal speech (**Try and** get in on time); **try to** is the preferred form otherwise (**Try to** get in on time).

WANT, WANT TO, WANT THAT: In the sense of **ought** or **should, want** is informal: "You **should** [rather than *want to*] review your notes before the test." In statement of desire or intention, **want to** is the standard idiom: "**I want you to get** [not *for you to get* or *that you get*] all you can from this year's work." In such constructions, **want that** and **want for** are not standard.

▶ EXERCISE

Correct any faulty verb forms that you find in the following sentences. Some of the constructions call for verbals (see 4).

Example: He often had came to the same bar.
Revised: He often *had come* to the same bar.

1. The students were not use to seeing the Chancellor in Duffy's Tavern, ordinarily a student hangout.
2. It was raining hard, and he had almost drowned before he come upon a place to find shelter.
3. He was wet through and through, and he said that his feet were nearly froze.
4. Having rode across the prairie all day, Lonesome Jim was thoroughly wore out and could not get his legs unbended.
5. It is regretted that you be informed that your work has been considered unsatisfactory.
6. Having born a pack, a shovel, a canteen, a map case, and a notebook for thirty miles, Jim laid down and went to sleep immediately.
7. There don't seem to be any way to keep him from sleeping when he is tired.
8. His grandfather believed that the family had originally came from northern Alberta.
9. He sat the overdue books on the counter and waited to pay the fine.
10. They got up before dawn, drunk coffee and ate rolls, checked the map, and taken side roads west for the next stage of their journey.

9

Adjectives and Adverbs

Use the appropriate form of the marked adjective or adverb.

The basic parts of a sentence—the simple subject, the verb, the object—do not always convey the full sense of what is intended. Adjectives and adverbs are supplementary words that function as qualifiers, calling attention to a more specific quality of the thing or action referred to by the word they modify. Note the difference in meaning signalled by the adjectives in the following sentence:

> The can on the shelf contains gas.

> The **red** can on the **lowest** shelf contains a **poisonous** gas.

By *expanding* the sentence, the adjectives *restrict* its meaning: the sentence is a statement about a particular can on a particular shelf containing a particular substance.

Adjectives and adverbs enable a writer to specify, to distinguish more exactly (not *shelf*, but *lowest shelf*). These modifiers may add descriptive details (a scene of *pleasant* memories; he laughed *loudly*), limit or make more specific the meaning of a key word (the *first* book; he left *immediately*), or qualify statements (*Perhaps* you've had enough).

In sentences an adjective or an adverb is identified by finding the word or word group to which it is related: remember that an adjective normally modifies a noun, while an adverb modifies a noun, an adjective, or another adverb.

> ADJECTIVE: the **lucky** dog [modifies the noun *dog*]

> ADVERB: He **luckily** won the third round. [modifies the verb *won*]

> ADJECTIVE: The car is **fast**. [modifies the noun *car*]

> ADVERB: She drove **fast**. [modifies the verb *drove*]

Other forms and uses are discussed in the sections that follow.

9.1 POSITION OF ADJECTIVES

Most writers have few problems with adjectives. The forms of adjectives are relatively simple, and they are usually easy to place in a sentence. The typical position of adjectives (and of participles and nouns used as adjectives) is immediately before the words they modify, though other positions are sometimes possible:

> An **unoccupied** farmhouse had been put at the bishop's disposal by a member of the congregation, on account of the **great** scandal the church was suffering. It was provided with . . . **simple** furnishings, and the owner wanted no remuneration for it. Nearby, there lived an **old** woman who had agreed to look after the bishop. . . . — Wilfred Watson, "The Lice"

> So on **Saturday** afternoons the **well-to-do** Jews walked up and down Decarie Boulevard which was their street. A street of **sumptuous** supermarkets and banks **built** of granite . . . , and delicatessens **rich** in **chromium** plating. — Mordecai Richler, *Son of a Smaller Hero*

Two or more adjectives are often placed after the word they modify to gain emphasis or to avoid a clumsy expression:

> He was hesitating awkwardly there at the door, **tall** and **dark**, in his fine expensive city clothes. . . . — Morley Callaghan, "Father and Son"

> . . . the sailors thronged the streets in flapping blues and spotless whites — **brown, tough,** and **clean.** — Thomas Wolfe, *Look Homeward, Angel*

If an adjective is in a phrase, it often follows the noun:

> The old man, exceedingly **weary** from his trip, lay down to rest.

9.2 PREDICATE ADJECTIVES

Predicate adjectives (adjectives that follow linking verbs) refer back to the subject (see 1.1). The common linking verbs are the forms of *be* (*am, is, are, was, were, has been*), *seem, appear, become, grow, prove,* and verbs describing sensations like *taste, feel, smell, look, sound*.

> The children looked **unhappy.** [predicate adjective, describing *children*]

> Overnight the weather turned **cold**. [predicate adjective, modifying *weather*]

Sometimes these linking verbs are followed and modified by adverbs (The weeds grew *rapidly*). To determine whether a predicate adjective or an adverb should be used, see whether the word modifies the subject or the verb. When it modifies or refers to the subject, use an adjective (as above); when it modifies the verb, use an adverb:

> As the rain continued to fall, the children looked **unhappily** out the window. [adverb, modifying *looked*]

> He turned **abruptly** when he heard his name called. [adverb describing the way in which he *turned*]

9.2 ◀

Adj

good — well

Good is an adjective (a *good* time; This cake tastes *good*). *Well* is either an adjective (He was a *well* boy; Are you feeling *well*? All is *well*), or an adverb (He writes *well*). Either *good* or *well* may be used as a predicate adjective with the verb *feel*, but with different connotations:

> Don't you feel **well**? [referring to a state of health, meaning *not ill*]

> It made him feel **good** to pack his own bag and get into the front seat and drive his own car. [referring to a general attitude of satisfaction — comfort, happiness, well-being]

Do not use the adjective *good* in place of the adverb *well*:

> The team played **well** [not *good*] for five innings.

bad — badly

As an adjective, *bad* is the usual form after linking verbs:

> She feels **bad**. The milk tastes **bad**. The situation looks **bad** to me.

But the adverb *badly* is also used when the emphasis is on the verb: I feel *badly* [or *bad*] about your troubles. Remember, however, that *I feel badly*, when used by itself, also means *My sense of touch is poor*. Beware also of laughable ambiguities such as *I want to play the violin badly*.

▶ **EXERCISES**

1. Write sentences following the directions given below.
   a. Write a sentence in which *good* is used as a predicate adjective.
   b. Write a sentence in which *bad* is used as a predicate adjective.
   c. Write a sentence in which *glad* is used as a predicate adjective.
   d. Write a sentence in which *good* is used as a predicate adjective and *well* is used as an adverb.
2. List five magazine advertisements or television commercials that use sentences with predicate adjectives, such as *Boffo is best*.

9.3 DEMONSTRATIVE ADJECTIVES

This and *that* (called *demonstrative* adjectives) are the only adjectives with plural forms: *this* idea, *these* ideas; *that* project, *those* projects. *This* and *these* usually refer to something nearby, or something the writer is more closely associated with or more interested in. *That* and *those* usually refer to something farther away, or something the writer is less immediately interested in:

This car is easy on gas.

That car is a lemon.

These books are required for this course.

Those books are recommended for further reading.

This and *that* are often used with *kind* and *sort*, (see *kind*, p. 553), which are singular nouns and should be preceded by singular modifiers:

I like **this kind** of cake best.

Jokes of **that sort** annoy me.

9.4 FORMS OF ADVERBS

Although a number of common adverbs have unique forms (*now, quite, there, too*), most adverbs are made by adding the suffix *-ly* to an adjective: accidenta*lly*, rea*lly*, apt*ly*, mere*ly*. In some cases it is necessary to alter slightly the ending of the base form before adding the suffix; for example, an adjective ending with *-y* or *-ble* or *-ple* is usually changed (see 17.4, Some Principles of Spelling):

easy – easily	sensible – sensibly
happy – happily	noticeable – noticeably
sleepy – sleepily	horrible – horribly

A few other adverbs have exactly the same form as the adjective, either ending in *-ly* (*early, likely*) or without any characteristic ending (*fast, hard, late, better*). Notice that *hardly* (meaning *not quite*) has developed a sense different from *hard* (meaning *strenuously*). The adverb *late* (meaning *tardily*) also has a different sense from the adverb *lately* (meaning *recently*).

Some standard adverbs have been formed by adding *wise* to another word, as *likewise, otherwise, clockwise*. However, the practice of adding this suffix to a noun to mean "with regard to" — as in *budget-wise* or *recreation-wise* — is considered jargon and should be avoided.

Long and Short Forms of Adverbs

Some adverbs have two forms: one with the *-ly* ending (long form), the other without (short form): *slow — slowly, loud — loudly, tight — tightly*. Adverbs used with or without the *-ly* ending include:

9.4
adv

bright	deep	fair	quick	sharp	straight
cheap	direct	loose	rough	slow	tight
close	even	loud	second	smooth	wrong

The long and short forms are often interchangeable:

> Go **slow**. Go **slowly**.
>
> Don't talk so **loud**. Don't talk so **loudly**.
>
> The rope was drawn **tight**. The rope was drawn **tightly**.

But such is not always the case. For example, the *-ly* form is expected between a subject and its verb (He *slowly* walked up the stairs.).

Formal writers tend to use the long forms more often; other writers the short forms. Since a comprehensive rule cannot be given, the choice between a long form and a short form is usually a matter of personal judgment, depending on the rhythm of the sentence and the tone of the writing.

Bobtailed Adverbs

The various forms and choices involved in using adverbs occasionally cause confusion and error. A "bobtailed" adverb, for example, is actually an *adjective* that has been mistakenly used instead of the expected adverb form. When an adverb properly has only the *-ly* form, take care not to drop the ending from such adverbs as *seriously* and *differently*:

> Twenty-five dollars is **considerably** more than I want to pay. [not *considerable*]
>
> People often told him that he should take things more **seriously**. [not *serious*]
>
> She worked **differently** from the others. [not *different*]

Dropping the *-ly* in such words is a dialectal characteristic and is a non-standard practice. If there is doubt, use a dictionary. The bobtailed adverbs most often encountered are terms of emphasis (*real, sure, awful*) or of quality (*bad* and many others). In general or edited English, these forms are adjectives only; the adverbs have *-ly* endings:

It was a really [not *real*] exciting performance.

They were surely [not *sure*] enjoying themselves.

She was awfully [not *awful*] sore after the trail ride.

He danced so badly [not *bad*] that his partner was embarrassed.

The team played superbly [not *superb*] in the first period.

almost — most

Almost is an adverb meaning "very nearly":

I **almost** lost my mind. [adverb, modifying the verb *lost*]

The train was **almost** always on time. [adverb, modifying the adverb *always*]

Most is an adjective meaning "the greatest number":

Most fishermen are optimists. [adjective, modifying *fishermen*.]

You'll sometimes hear *most* used as an adverb in casual speech: "This train is *most* always on time." In writing, however, use *almost*.

9.5 POSITION OF ADVERBS

Adverbs Modifying a Single Word

When an adverb modifies a single word, its typical position is immediately before that word:

The party ended **quite** late. [modifies *late*]

They **never** finished the job. [modifies *finished*]

Unlike adjectives, adverbs can have various positions in the sentence. Try to place them in a position that clearly indicates your intended meaning and desired emphasis.

They **hastily** finished the math assignment.

They finished the math assignment **hastily**.

Hastily they finished the math assignment.

They finished **hastily** the math assignment. [awkward]

Sentence Adverbs

Many adverbial modifiers — single-word adverbs, phrases, or clauses — cannot sensibly be related to another single word in a sentence. It is conventional to say that these adverbs "modify the

9.5

m m

whole sentence" and to call them *sentence adverbs*. Their position is variable:

> **Unfortunately**, they had already left.
>
> They had already left, **unfortunately**.
>
> They had **unfortunately** already left.

This flexibility makes it possible to shift the position of many sentence adverbs for variety as well as for emphasis.

Misplaced Adverbial Modifiers

m m   Revise the sentence so that the marked expression is clearly related to the word or statement it modifies

Be careful not to misplace a modifier so that the meaning of a statement becomes ambiguous or even ludicrous:

> AMBIGUOUS: Archibald has almost insulted every woman he knows. [*almost* seems to modify *insulted*]
>
> CLEAR: Archibald has insulted almost every woman he knows.

> AMBIGUOUS: She tried to understand Archibald unsuccessfully [*unsuccessfully* seems to modify *understand*]
>
> CLEAR: She tried unsuccessfully to understand Archibald.

Adverbs are sometimes confusingly placed so that they could modify either an element that precedes or one that follows; these are sometimes called "squinting modifiers":

> The workers decided to strike at twelve o'clock.
>
> [*At twelve o'clock* could refer to either *decided* or *strike*]

In some constructions, misplacing a modifier may alter the intended meaning:

> My habit of overeating even embarrasses me. [intended meaning: *embarrasses even me*]

See also 4.3, Misrelated Modifiers, and 4.4, Dangling Modifiers, for a discussion of the placement of verbal modifiers.

Position of *only* and Similar Adverbs

In formal usage, limiting adverbs like *only, merely, hardly, just* are placed immediately before the element they modify:

> I need **only** six more pledges to make a full hundred.

The audience seemed **hardly** to breathe when the girl began speaking.

In informal spoken usage such adverbs usually stand immediately before the verb:

I **only** need six more pledges to make a full hundred.

The audience **hardly** seemed to breathe when the girl began speaking.

This latter pattern, typical of speech, is also acceptable in general writing as long as no misunderstanding of the author's meaning could occur:

When the brilliant lightweight boxer, Kid Lewis, stood for Parliament in his native borough, he **only** scored a hundred and twenty-five votes. — George Orwell, *The English People*

He **only** remembers one verse of the song and he has been repeating it. — Eugene O'Neill, *A Moon for the Misbegotten*

▶ **EXERCISE**

Examine the following sentences and decide where you would place the indicated modifier within each sentence. If more than one position is possible, explain what change of meaning or emphasis would result from shifting the modifier.
Example: Add *almost*: The fire had burned down to nothing.
With modifier: The fire had *almost* burned down to nothing.
Alternative: The fire had burned down to *almost* nothing.

1. Add *certainly*: The fields were carpeted with snow that had fallen in the night, for there had been none yesterday.
2. Add *scarcely*: Some had landed, oddly enough, on the back patio, where the wind was now blowing.
3. Add *almost*: Farther out in the yard, the doghouse was covered to the roof so that it looked like a small mound of cotton.
4. Add *even*: The garden walks were so obliterated by drifts that my father, who had laid out the garden, did not know where they were.
5. Add *more or less*: You could tell where the path went by following the clothesline, which had a ridge of snow that made it visible from the house.
6. Add *only*: Yesterday I had seen the yard with a few flowers growing.
7. Add *definitely*: "It's beautiful to look at," my father said, "but you'll have to shovel the walks because your mother will want to hang out the wash she did last night."
8. Add *better*: Picking up the battered shovel, I went out into the bitter wind, knowing I would be able to get the job done before the snow hardened.
9. Add *hardly*: Although I walked on the white snow-blanket softly, I had taken a few steps when I fell in a position from which I could extricate myself.
10. Add *merely*: Because it was a moderate snowfall, I laughed and went on with my work.

9.6 DOUBLE NEGATIVES

A statement in which a second negative needlessly and confusingly repeats the meaning of the first negative is called a *double negative*: "The trip will *not* cost you *nothing*." In this example the apparently intended meaning ("nothing") has actually been reversed ("not nothing"). Two-part negative constructions do appear in other languages. In French, for example, two words (*ne* and *pas*) are usually needed to make a negative. In edited English, however, one negative is quite adequate: "The trip will cost you *nothing*" or "The trip will *not* cost you anything."

Obvious double negatives like *not* with *nothing* seldom cause problems. Watch out for concealed double negatives, when *not* is part of a contraction (*won't, can't*) or when it is used with *but* or with adverbs of negative meaning such as *hardly, barely, scarcely.*

Can't hardly, couldn't scarcely.   Such common non-standard expressions as "I can't hardly hear you" and "There wasn't scarcely enough money left to pay the taxes" are confusing double negatives because *hardly* and *scarcely* in this sense mean *almost not*. The standard idioms that should be used in writing are, "I *can* hardly hear you" and "There *was* scarcely enough money left to pay the taxes."

Can't help but.   The construction *can't help but* (or *cannot help but*) has become an established idiom. Many writers, however, consider it illogical and prefer to use instead one of the following expressions:

I **cannot but** feel sorry for him.

I **can't help feeling** sorry for him.

Irregardless.   *Regardless* is the standard usage. The suffix *-less* is a negative ending; the addition of the negative prefix *ir-* in *irregardless* creates a double negative, a confusing non-standard usage.

Not...nor.   This common double negative ("Fido is *not* a dog *nor* a cat; he is an iguana.") probably results from confusion with the construction *neither...nor*. Any of the following standard usages would be preferable:

Fido is *not* a dog *or* a cat; he is an iguana.

Fido is *neither* a dog *nor* a cat; he is an iguana.

Fido is *not* a dog, *nor* is he a cat; he is an iguana.

9.7 COMPARISON OF ADJECTIVES AND ADVERBS

 Make the comparison of adjectives or adverbs more accurate or more appropriate.

Most adjectives and adverbs have three different forms to indicate degrees of the characteristic they name. These degrees are called the positive (*happy; boring*), the comparative (*happier; more boring*) and the superlative (*happiest; most boring*).

Forms of Comparison

Most adjectives and adverbs are compared in one of two ways: by adding *-er, -est* to the positive form, or by prefixing *more, most* (or *less, least*).

	Positive	**Comparative**	**Superlative**
ADJECTIVES:	hot	hotter	hottest
	brilliant	more brilliant	most brilliant
	expensive	less expensive	least expensive
ADVERBS:	near	nearer	nearest
	sincerely	more sincerely	most sincerely
	often	oftener, more often, less often	oftenest, most often, least often

In general, *-er, -est* forms are used with words of one syllable (*long, longer; dry, driest*), and *more, most* with words of more than two syllables (*more interesting, most rapidly*). With two-syllable words, a writer often has a choice of either form (*abler, more able; easiest, most easy*). In some cases, the desired rhythm of the sentence may determine which form is chosen:

> After a night's sleep, his eyes were **steadier** and less **bloodshot**; his bearded face seemed **handsomer** and his voice **more resonant**.

A few common modifiers form the comparative and superlative degrees irregularly:

Positive	**Comparative**	**Superlative**
bad	worse	worst
good, well	better	best
far	farther, further	farthest, furthest
little	less, lesser, littler	least, littlest
many, some, much	more	most

See the Glossary of Usage for distinctions in meaning between modifiers such as *farther* and *further*.

Use of the Comparative Form

The comparative form of an adjective or adverb is ordinarily used when just two things are compared:

> You're a **better** man than I am, Gunga Din!
>
> Blood is **thicker** than water.
>
> She works **more diligently** than her sister.

In certain familiar expressions the comparative form is used although no actual comparison is mentioned (higher education, the lower depths, Better Business Bureau). Usually, however, an incomplete comparison is unfair to the reader ("Look *younger*, live *longer*" . . . than what?). Writers of advertising copy are particularly fond of this use of the comparative because of the favorable inferences a hasty reader may draw: "Smoke a *milder* cigarette"; "More protection for *fewer* dollars"; "Sudso gets clothes *cleaner*." Such constructions are evasive or meaningless and should be avoided in edited English.

Use of the Superlative Form

The superlative form ordinarily indicates the greatest degree among three or more persons or things:

> He was voted the member of his class **most likely** to succeed.

> Many critics consider *King Lear* the **greatest** of Shakespeare's tragedies.

In spoken English, the superlative is occasionally used for comparing two things (Put your *best* foot forward). But in writing it is usually better to keep the superlative for comparisons among three or more things.

Superlative forms also occur in expressions in which no direct comparison is implied (*best* wishes, *deepest* sympathy, *highest* praise, *most* sincerely yours). The form with *most* is frequently used as an intensive to signify a high degree:

> For example, Herbert Spencer (1820-1903), a **most** influential English philosopher. . . . —Melvin Rader, *Ethics and Society*

The informal use of a heavily stressed superlative to indicate nothing more than general approval is an affectation that should be avoided in serious writing:

> Hasn't she the **sweetest** voice? (Better: Hasn't she a **sweet** voice?)

Comparison of *unique* and Other Absolutes

Some people regard words such as *unique, perfect, dead, empty* as logically incapable of comparison or qualification because those words express absolute states. Ordinarily, we wouldn't expect that something could be *more unique, more perfect, deader,* or *emptier,* but in actual usage these terms are often qualified or modified by comparative forms, as in the following examples:

> . . . The **more unique** his nature, the more peculiarly his own will be the coloring of his language. — Otto Jespersen, *Mankind, Nation, and Individual from a Linguistic Point of View*

Whether words like *unique* should or should not be qualified is a matter that can be determined only by appropriateness. In college and university writing, such words probably should not be qualified because, used with their full meaning, they are valuable words that say something precisely.

More exact comparisons are acceptable in these instances. If you say that A is *more nearly unique* or *more nearly perfect* than B, you are not talking about absolute states that should not be qualified; you are saying that A is closer to being unique or perfect than B is.

9.8 MAKING COMPARISONS IDIOMATIC

 Change the marked expression so that it will be idiomatic.

In writing, expressions of comparison should be more carefully and more fully stated than they often are in speaking. Non-standard expressions that might pass unnoticed in conversation (such as *the slowest of any runner on the team*) are too slipshod to be used in careful writing (where the same idea would be expressed: *the slowest runner on the team*).

Comparing Comparable Things

When using comparisons in your writing, make certain that the things compared are logically comparable:

> TERMS NOT COMPARABLE: The rhinoceros has a hide almost as tough as an alligator. [*hide* and *alligator* are not comparable]
>
> COMPARABLE TERMS: The rhinoceros has a hide almost as tough as that of an alligator [*or* **as an alligator's**].
>
> TERMS NOT COMPARABLE: One reviewer compared these short stories

to Stephen Leacock. [*stories* and *Stephen Leacock* are not comparable]

COMPARABLE TERMS: One reviewer compared these short stories to those written by Stephen Leacock [*or* **to Stephen Leacock's**].

9.8

Completing Comparisons

Statements involving comparisons should be written out in full, particularly if any misunderstanding might arise if any part is left out:

AMBIGUOUS: I owe him less than you.

CLEARER: I owe him less than I owe you. *Or*: I owe him less than you do.

AMBIGUOUS: He admires Eliot less than other modern poets.

CLEARER: He admires Eliot less than other modern poets do. *Or*: He admires Eliot less than he does other modern poets.

Double comparisons with *as . . . as, if . . . than* should always be filled out in writing:

He is **as** tall **as**, **if** not taller **than**, his brother. [*not*: He is as tall if not taller than his brother.]

The styles vary **as** much **as**, **if** not more **than**, the materials.

Since the *if not . . . than* construction ends to interrupt sentence movement, it is usually preferable to complete the first comparison and then add the second, dropping *than*:

He is as tall as his brother, if not taller.

The styles vary as much as the materials, if not more.

Use of *other* in Comparisons

Other is used when the comparison involves things of the same class, but not when the things being compared belong to two different classes:

She is a better dancer than any other girl in school.

She is a better dancer than any [not *any other*] boy in school.

The Ecstasy of Rita Joe was more successful than the **other** plays we produced.

I think movies are more entertaining than any [not *any other*] book.

Other is not used with superlative comparisons:

Pavlova was the best of all the [not *all the other*] Russian ballerinas.

The Egyptians had attained the highest skill in medicine that had up to that time been achieved by any [not *any other*] nation.

Use of *like* or *as* in Comparisons

To introduce a prepositional phrase of comparison expressing similarity, *like* is standard usage:

They are **like** two peas in a pod.

He looks **like** his father.

Bicycle riding, **like** golf, can be enjoyed at almost any age.

But notice the ambiguity of a statement such as "She wanted to be a doctor *like her father*." A reader will not know whether the phrase is intended to mean "as her father was" or "of the same kind [e.g. surgeon, or wealthy] as her father."

To introduce a clause of comparison with a definite subject and verb, it is best to use *as, as if, as though* instead of *like*:

She wanted to be a doctor **as** her father had been.

He acted **as if** he didn't feel well.

She took to skiing **as** a duck takes to water.

Avoid the mistake of substituting *as* for *like* or *such as* in prepositional phrases like the following:

Some Canadian authors **like** [or *such as*, but not *as*] Buckler and Garner take their material from a particular region.

Like [not *As*] Hamlet, you are indecisive. [*As Hamlet* would mean *playing the role of Hamlet on stage*]

The expression *to feel like* is very commonly used in speech, but it can be unclear when the conventional meaning of *like* (in this context, *similar to*) is not really intended by the speaker. While we can say "I feel like a fool" without much chance of being misunderstood, the statement "I feel like a cold drink" is potentially laughable. "I feel like a blindfolded person" is ambiguous because different meanings of *feel* are possible. A casual and non-standard usage sometimes heard is "I feel like these new fashions were designed for grandmothers" or "We feel like we are the better team"; this habit should be avoided when writing.

Other colloquial uses of *like* as a conjunction have increased in recent years, but standard constructions (*as, as if, as though*) are probably preferable:

He fights well, **as** [not *like*] a champion should.

Sue talks **as though** [not *like*] she knows everything.

I'm going to tell it **as** [not *like*] it is.

In general, you can avoid the possible difficulties of *like* if you simply form the habit of using the word only as a preposition and only when you mean *similar to* or *such as*.

9.8

fd

▶ **EXERCISES**

1. Some of the adjective and adverb forms and expressions of comparisons in these sentences would be inappropriate in most college and university writing. Revise each sentence to improve it.

    a. The ship lay in the cove like it was a natural fixture.
    b. It had been there so long that the weather had turned it more grey.
    c. Many things would be needed to refurbish it, as caulking, paint, new masts, and glass for portholes.
    d. We couldn't scarcely imagine how differently it must have looked in its prime.
    e. The ship looked as much if not more pathetic than an old hound lying forgottenlike nearby a deserted farmhouse.
    f. Still, the scene was real fine artwise, and camera enthusiasts were taking pictures most every clear day of the year.
    g. Picturesque as the sight was, everyone agreed it was the saddest.
    h. I thought wistfully of how trim and noble the ship must have been in her heyday, what with her tall masts and most every sail stretching out to catch the wind.
    i. The reason for its being there was most unique; the owner had died before he could convert it into a museum.
    j. A sailing ship is the most romantic, because it pits man against the elements more than any other motorized boat does.
    k. To sit on the wharf and watch the old ship rot, that's what made me feel badly.
    l. The most dreariest of sights is watching anything lose its former beauty.
    m. I only wished I could have seen her in her prime, when she was shipshape.
    n. Her prow was cut sharp back, so that she could cleave the waves like a knife through hot butter.
    o. She was clearly the best designed of all the other ships I have ever seen, bar none.

2. Fill in the modifiers called for in the paragraph below, choosing modifiers that will help create a consistent tone for the paragraph.

    Sometimes, late in the evening, when I have worked (adverb) and (adverb) at my desk, I stop and lean back in my (adjective) chair and hear night sounds (adjective) and (adjective) in the distance. Sometimes I hear a (adjective) car passing, or someone calling far away, or (adjective) music from some car radio, or a bird song, (adjective) and (adjective). Then I remember that there is a world outside my window (adjective) (adverb), and I go to the door and stand a moment, looking out (adverb).

End Punctuation

Every complete sentence requires a mark of punctuation at the end, either a period (.), a question mark (?), or an exclamation mark (!). The great majority of sentences are statements, requiring a period (also known as a full stop) at the end. All direct questions are followed by a question mark, while expressions conveying excitement or especially emphatic statements are ended with an exclamation point (or mark).

Periods and question marks also have several conventional uses in addition to their function as end signals.

10.1 PERIODS

 Insert a period at the place marked.

Periods are the most common end stops; they mark the end of all sentences that are not direct questions or exclamations.

Periods After Statements

> Madagascar is an island off southeast Africa.
> "Where is he now?" she asked. "Tell me."
> "Oh." [Where no question or exclamatory force is intended.]

Periods After Indirect Questions and Courtesy Questions

An indirect question is really a statement *about* a question, and thus is followed by a period, never by a question mark:

> He asked us where we got the money. (A direct question would be *Where did you get the money?*)
>
> They wanted to know what I had been doing since I graduated.

An exception is often made in the case of *courtesy questions* (polite requests phrased conventionally as direct questions) in letters. Either a question mark or a period may be used:

> Will you please return this copy as soon as possible.
>
> May we hear from you at your earliest convenience?

Periods After Abbreviations

A period is conventionally used after most abbreviations:

Mr. H.L. Matthews	Oct.	Ph.D.	i.e.
Ms. K.A. Austin	D.D.S.	etc.	Ave.

An abbreviation within a sentence may be followed by additional punctuation (*After she gets her M.A., she might go on to get her Ph.D.*), but at the end of a sentence, no additional mark is needed unless the sentence is a question or exclamation (*Does he have a Ph.D.?*)

Periods are sometimes omitted from abbreviations, especially if they are made from initial letters: UNESCO, NDP. Consult an up-to-date dictionary for the preferred form of particular abbreviations. If usage is divided (R.M.C. or RMC), follow a consistent style throughout any one piece of writing. (See 16.1, Abbreviations).

Periods with Figures

A period (decimal point) is used before fractions expressed as decimals and between whole numbers and decimals, and to separate dollars and cents:

.05	4.6	3.141 59	95.6%
$4.98	$.98	*but* 98 cents	*or* 98¢

(See 14.2 for periods used as ellipses to mark interruptions or the omission of words.)

10.2 QUESTION MARKS

? Punctuate this sentence or sentence element with a question mark.

After Direct Questions

A question mark is used after a sentence expressing a direct question:

How much can your platypus eat in two minutes?

What should we do?

Did Napoleon dislike Elba?

Really?

When a sentence begins with a statement but ends with a question, the ending determines the punctuation:

> Perhaps this explanation is poor, but is there a better one?

After Questions Within a Sentence

A question mark stands immediately after a question that is included within a sentence:

> "Are you engaged?" he blurted.

> Someone once remarked (wasn't it Mark Twain?) that old second-hand diamonds are better than no diamonds at all.

When a question mark and quotation marks occur together, the question mark goes *inside* the quotation marks if the quotation is a question. The question mark goes *outside* the quotation marks if the whole sentence is a question:

> He asked himself, "Is this the best of all possible worlds?"
> Do you agree that this is "the best of all possible worlds"?

To Indicate a Doubtful Statement

A question mark is used, with or without parentheses, to show that a statement is approximate or questionable:

> Geoffrey Chaucer, 1340? — 1400
> Geoffrey Chaucer, 1340(?) — 1400

Sometimes writers place a question mark in parentheses to indicate humor or mild sarcasm:

> She gave him an innocent (?) wink over her menu.

But this use of the question mark should probably be avoided. If humor or sarcasm requires so obvious a signal for the reader to recognize it, it would be best to revise the entire passage.

10.3 EXCLAMATION MARKS

> **/** Insert or remove exclamation mark at the place
> **¡** indicated.

An exclamation mark is used after an emphatic interjection (Oh!

Ouch! Fire! Help! No, no, no!) and after statements that are genuinely exclamatory:

> The building had disappeared overnight!
>
> What torments they have endured!

There is seldom need for exclamation marks unless you are writing dialogue. Don't use an exclamation mark unless the statement is genuinely emphatic; it will not lend weight to a simple statement of fact, nor will the use of double and triple exclamation marks add anything.

10.3

▶ **EXERCISE**

Rewrite the following items, changing any inappropriate end punctuation. Make any other changes you need in order to use different end signals.

1. My first job, as an elevator operator, was the most thrilling I've ever had! To me it was almost as if I were an actor, waiting my cue to speak and move!! My audience responded! How could they help it. They had to get off!!
2. What fear he must have felt while he swayed there?
3. "Aren't you ready to leave yet," he asked?
4. Will the government have the nerve to call an election this year.
5. How I hope we will win!
6. Could you please get off my foot.
7. Win one of sixteen luxurious all-expense paid vacations in Quebec!
8. He asked us where we got the money?
9. Didn't the customs officer say, "Have you anything to declare"?
10. Our immediate problem is how do we get the cork out of the wine bottle.

11

Commas

 Insert a comma at the place indicated.

Commas mark a slight separation between grammatical units, similar to brief pauses in speech. They are highly important to the *meaning* of all kinds of sentences, and they are also valuable in determining the pace and tempo of reading. About two-thirds of all punctuation marks used are commas.

To use commas well, you must know not only when to use them but also when to omit them. The principal uses of the comma are the following:

1. to separate clauses linked by **co-ordinating** conjunctions (*but*, *and*, *yet*, *so*, *for*, *or*, and *nor*);
2. to separate **introductory** elements from the rest of the sentence;
3. to separate **interrupting** elements from the rest of the sentence;
4. to separate different items or elements in a **series**;
5. to **clarify** a sentence by separating elements that could, if not kept apart, confuse the writer's meaning or emphasis.

This chapter describes each of these functions more fully. Attention is also given to optional or special uses and to some of the more frequent comma errors.

11.1 COMMAS BETWEEN CO-ORDINATE CLAUSES

A comma is customarily used before the conjunction linking the co-ordinate clauses in a compound sentence. Notice that the comma always comes *before* the co-ordinating conjunction, not after it:

> This down does not actually exist, **but** it might easily have a thousand counterparts in America or elsewhere in the world. —Rachel Carson, *Silent Spring*

> They were lost as to what to do at first, **so** I provided a kind of verbal running commentary to accompany them. —Joseph Gold, "A Word to the Wise"

The origin of things is the mystery of mysteries, **and** every civilization that has risen above brute nature has tried to explain it. — S.K. Heninger, Jr., *The Cosmographical Glass*

No naked boys swam or dived here, **nor** had they since 1947 when the Rotary Club swimming pool had been built in town. — W.O. Mitchell, *How I Spent My Summer Holidays*

Bear in mind that commas are used in this way only when the linking words (*but*, *and*, *yet*, *nor*, and so forth) function as co-ordinating conjunctions. Those words can have other kinds of connective uses in which the comma is not required. In the following sentences, for example, commas would *not* be used unless the writer happened to want a dramatic pause between the paired elements (see 11.5, page 156, dramatic pauses):

After the accident she was sadder **but** wiser.

Safe climbing requires proper planning **and** proper equipment.

She wants to be an accountant **or** a missionary.

Short Clauses Joined by *and, or, nor*

The comma may be omitted before the conjunctions *and*, *or*, *nor* in compound sentences if the co-ordinate clauses are short and closely related in thought:

Life is short [　] and time is fleeting.

He had to get home [　] or his father would be furious.

Nancy didn't like her [　] nor did I.

General writing often omits the comma where formal writing would use one, as between the two independent clauses in this example:

From time to time the room swayed around him and he was glad he wasn't the one who would have to drive home. — Mordecai Richler, *The Apprenticeship of Duddy Kravitz*

Clauses Joined by *for*

A comma is necessary between clauses joined by *for* used as a conjunction, so that it won't be confused with the preposition *for*:

He was an easy target, for anyone could pull the wool over his eyes. [*for* as a conjunction]

He was an easy target for anyone who wanted to take advantage of him. [*for* as a preposition]

11.2 COMMAS AFTER LONG INTRODUCTORY ELEMENTS

Adverb clauses and long modifying phrases are usually set off by a comma when they precede the main clause. When these elements come at the end of a sentence, a comma may or may not be necessary.

Commas After Introductory Adverb Clauses

Adverb clauses (see 3.2) are often placed at the beginning of a sentence for variety or emphasis. In this position they are usually separated from the main clause by a comma:

> **When he said that we would be expected to write an essay every week,** I nearly collapsed.

> **Before penicillin and other antibiotics were developed,** pneumonia was often fatal.

The comma is often omitted after a short introductory clause closely related to the main clause, especially if both clauses have the same subject and provided no ambiguity or confusion results:

> **When I lived in Toronto** [ ] I went to the theatre every month.
> **After he seized control** [ ] the situation changed drastically.

When an adverb clause *follows* the main clause, no comma is used (as a general rule):

> I nearly collapsed [ ] **when he said that we would be expected to write an essay every week.**
> Pneumonia was often fatal [ ] **before penicillin and other antibiotics were developed.**

If, however, such an adverb clause is only loosely related to the main clause and would be preceded by a distinct pause in speech, it is separated from the main clause by a comma:

> The new gym will be finished by spring, **unless, of course, unexpected delays occur.**
> The college and the cadets were undoubtedly popular, **though it was a popularity not unmixed with envy.** —R.A. Preston, *Canada's R.M.C.*

Commas After Introductory Modifying Phrases

Long modifying phrases are generally punctuated in the same way as adverb clauses. When they come before the main clause, they are followed by a comma:

> **To fully understand the impact of Einstein's ideas,** one must be familiar with those of Newton. [infinitive phrase]
>
> **Leaning far out over the balcony,** he stared at the waves below. [participle phrase]
>
> **In such a situation,** the wisest thing to do is run. [prepositional phrase]

When the phrases are relatively short and create no ambiguity or confusion, the comma is often omitted:

11.2

> **In this context** [ ] the meaning is entirely different.
>
> **To evade the draft** [ ] he moved to Canada.

Commas

Commas are used:

1. Between co-ordinate clauses (11.1)
   a. When they are joined by *but*, *yet*, *so*, *for*
   b. When they are joined by *and*, *or*, *nor* if the clauses are long or not closely related
2. After long introductory elements (11.2)
   a. When an adverb clause precedes the main clause (usually optional if the introductory clause is short and closely related)
   b. When a modifying phrase precedes the main clause (usually optional if the phrase is short and closely related)
3. To set off interrupting elements (11.3)
   a. To set off *non-restrictive* clauses and phrases (these do not limit, define, or restrict the meaning of the term they modify)
   b. To set off appositives
   c. To set off conjunctive adverbs such as *however*
   d. To set off inserted expressions and names in direct address
4. To separate co-ordinate items in a series (11.4)
   a. In a series of words, phrases, or clauses not joined by conjunctions (optional before *and* joining the last item in a series)
   b. In a series of co-ordinate adjectives, all modifying the same noun
5. To separate constructions for clarity or emphasis (11.5)

6. In certain conventional places (11.6)
    a. In numbers
    b. In dates
    c. In addresses
    d. With titles and degrees
    e. In correspondence
    f. With phrases identifying direct quotations

Commas should *not* be used (11.7):

1. Between main sentence elements
2. Between two words or phrases joined by *and*
3. Between main clauses without a connective
4. With restrictive modifiers
5. After the last item in a series

When the modifying phrase *follows* the clause, commas are unnecessary if the thought seems to flow smoothly from one to the other:

> One must be familiar with Newton's ideas [ ] **to fully understand the impact of Einstein's.**

> Special treatment may be necessary [ ] **in case of severe malnutrition.**

> The local residents often saw Elgin [ ] **wandering among the ruins.**

But if the phrase is only loosely related to the clause or if it modifies some distant expression, a comma should be used to prevent confusion:

> Wilson nervously watched the man, **alarmed by his silence.** [The phrase modifies *Wilson*, not *man*.]

▶ **EXERCISES**

1. Complete the sentences started below, punctuating wherever necessary.
    a. When she hit. . . .
    b. If I can. . . .
    c. Although he. . . .
    d. At this particular time and place. . . .

2. Read the following sentences carefully. In which of the places marked with brackets would you insert a comma? In which do you consider a comma optional? Not appropriate? Give specific reasons for your choice of punctuation.
    a. When a man has done me an evil turn once [1] I don't like to give him the opportunity to do so twice. — Sir John A. Macdonald

   b. Let us all be happy and live within our means [1] even if we have to
       borrow money to do it. — Artemus Ward
   c. Whenever punctuation problems arise [1] it is a good idea to consult the
       text [2] and determine the proper usage.
   d. Walk right in [1] and sit right down.

11.3 COMMAS TO SET OFF INTERRUPTING ELEMENTS

11.3

A word, phrase, or clause that interrupts the movement of a
sentence is usually set off by commas or other appropriate marks.

Non-Restrictive Clauses and Phrases

A *non-restrictive* modifier is a phrase or clause that *does not limit
the meaning* of the term it refers to. It interrupts a clause, expressing some extra idea that could be omitted without affecting the
sentence's basic meaning. Non-restrictive modifiers are always set
off by commas to indicate their interjected (or incidental) relationship to the sentence's main idea:

Last night's audience, **which contained a large number of college
students,** applauded each number enthusiastically.

The people of India, **who have lived in poverty for centuries,**
desperately need financial and technical assistance.

Vasari's history, **hovering between fact and fiction,** is not a reliable
source.

Notice that the modifiers in the three preceding sentences are not
essential to the terms they modify. Although some information
would be lost if they were removed, the central meaning of each
sentence would not change.

A *restrictive* modifier, on the other hand, provides information
that *does* limit or define the meaning of the term it refers to. It is not
merely interjected; it is essential to the basic idea the sentence is
expressing. Without it, the sentence would take on a different
meaning or become difficult to understand. Since this kind of
modifier is *not* extra to the sentence's meaning, it is *not* set off by
commas:

He is a man **who thinks for himself.**

Corte's discovered many temples **which were pre-Toltec in origin.**

The questions **that he did not answer** were the most interesting ones.

Almost all clauses beginning with *that* are restrictive. All clauses in which the relative pronoun may be omitted are restrictive (the questions *he failed to answer*, the book *I read*).

Distinguishing between restrictive and non-restrictive elements can be extremely important for clarity of meaning. You must carefully consider the nature of the term modified and the context in which it occurs. If the term is fully defined in itself and cannot be confused with another, the modifier that follows is non-restrictive. But if the term is vague or ambiguous without the modifier, the modifier is restrictive. Compare the function of the modifier in each of these passages:

> Children **who can't swim very well** should stay off the diving board.
>
> Children, **who can't swim very well,** should stay off the diving board.
>
> Last month I read a novel and a biography. The novel, **which especially appealed to me,** was written by Hugh Hood.
>
> Last month I read several novels and a biography. The novel **which especially appealed to me** was written by Hugh Hood.
>
> While in Rome, I took photographs in the vicinity of St. Peter's. The square, **designed by Michelangelo,** is perfectly symmetrical.
>
> While in Rome, I took photographs of squares designed by Michelangelo, Bernini, and Borromini. The square **designed by Michelangelo** is perfectly symmetrical.

Whenever you are in doubt about such elements, the "logical" test is to consider whether the modifier is *extra* or *supplementary* to the clause's clarity or meaning. If it is, set it off with commas. See also 11.7, Misused Commas.

Another test that some writers find helpful is to read the passage aloud. If your voice drops slightly in pitch and you hesitate briefly before and after the modifier, the modifier is probably non-restrictive and requires commas. If you read the passage smoothly without a pause, the modifier is probably restrictive and needs no commas.

Appositives

Appositives — nouns or noun equivalents that extend the meaning of a preceding expression — are usually non-restrictive modifiers and are set off by commas:

> Thomas Malthus, **author of the first serious study of population growth,** foresaw one of our greatest modern problems.

> We visited Queenston Heights, **the site of a crucial battle in the War of 1812.**

Notice that such appositives, like other non-restrictive modifiers, must be set off by *two* commas when they occur in the middle of the sentence.

Restrictive appositives and those used as part of a person's name require no commas (close apposition):

> I thought the question referred to Lewis **the novelist** rather than to Lewis **the politician.**
>
> William **the Conqueror** invaded England from Normandy.

11.3

Adverbs that Compare or Contrast

Conjunctive adverbs that relate what is being said to some preceding idea (*however*, *therefore*, *consequently*, *too*, *also*) are generally set off by commas when they occur within a sentence:

> When in good shape, **moreover,** Paul has been known time and again to jump up in the air, kick both caulked feet against the ceiling, and come down again on a chalked mark. —J.D. Robins, "Paul Bunyan"
>
> How, **then,** may the pronunciation of Canadian English be characterized?—Mark M. Orkin, *Speaking Canadian English*

When such words appear at the beginning of a sentence, they may or may not be followed by a comma, depending on the emphasis desired and the rhythm of the sentence:

> **Thus** the way was cleared for further explorations.
>
> **Nevertheless,** work did not always proceed according to plan.

When a clause beginning with such an adverb is joined by a preceding clause, the *semicolon* must be used, since these words are not conjunctions. They are sequence signals, which relate ideas in various ways but do not join them grammatically (see 12.1, page 162, Semicolons Between Clauses Linked with a Conjunctive Adverb):

> Business recessions take place periodically; **however,** they are generally short-lived.
>
> The natives are incredibly poor; **moreover,** they have little hope of bettering their lot.

When adverbs that closely modify the verb or the entire sentence (*perhaps*, *so*) begin the sentence, they should not be followed by a comma. Similarly, conjunctions are part of the clauses they introduce and should not be set off from them:

Perhaps a solution can still be found.
But the average Canadian cannot afford such luxuries.

Inserted Expressions

When a sentence is interrupted by an incidental or loosely related
expression (*of course*, *at any rate*, *after all*, *if you ask me*, and so
forth), the inserted element is usually set off by commas:

> In part, **no doubt,** such demands reflect the hardening of opinion
> against Soviet policy in Europe. — J.A. Corry, "Free Trade in Ideas"

> I spoke, **I remember,** on *The Value of Imbecility in Education*. It was
> more or less the same kind of talk that I had given at Port Arthur under
> the title *Our National Heritage*. — Stephen Leacock, "No Vote of
> Thanks"

> Failure, **after all,** is the sugar of life: the more lumps you take, the
> sweeter you are. — Eric Nichol, *A Scar is Born*

To decide whether or not to set off these *disjunctive phrases* with
commas, read the passage aloud with the kind of emphasis you
want to give it. If your voice drops and you pause slightly before
and after the phrase, commas should be used. But if the phrase
seems to run naturally into the rest of the sentence, probably no
commas are necessary:

> Machines are useful, **of course,** in doing complex calculations.

> Machines are **of course** incapable of what we call creative thought.

Weak exclamations (*well*, *oh*, *say*) and *yes* and *no* sometimes
occur as modifiers, particularly at the beginning of a sentence.
They are conventionally separated from the sentence they modify
by commas:

> **Well,** not much can be done about it now.

> **Yes,** times have changed.

> That was a difficult climb, **eh**?

> I'd much rather eat cauliflower than, **say,** beets or carrots.

Names in Direct Address

Names which occur as interrupters in direct address are also set off
by commas:

> I firmly believe, **fellow citizens,** that justice will prevail.

> I seems to me, **George,** that your attitude is poor.

> **Workers of the world,** unite!

▶ **EXERCISES**

1. The following sentences contain both restrictive and non-restrictive modifiers. Punctuate each sentence appropriately. If the sentence makes sense either way, explain the difference in meaning between the restrictive and the non-restrictive modifier.

    Example: The alligator which was often hunted for its hide is in danger of becoming extinct.
    Correction: insert commas after *alligator* and *hide*

    a. The wall which was built by Hadrian served its purpose for many years.
    b. Diamonds which are synthetically produced are more perfectly formed than natural diamonds which have serious flaws.
    c. American movies that are exported abroad are popular in countries that have no movie industry of their own.
    d. The French chef whose accomplishments are well known is eagerly sought by expensive restaurants and hotels.
    e. The oboe which is a woodwind instrument is played by means of a reed inserted in the mouthpiece.
    f. The early settlers who were exposed to severe winters and who expected Indian attacks usually constructed forts many of which can still be found.
    g. Drunk drivers who are responsible for many traffic fatalities obviously do not consider the value of human life.
    h. The common belief that science can solve everything is another example of the naive optimism that most people are prey to.

2. Provide any necessary punctuation in the following sentences to set off interrupting elements or clarify meaning:
    a. The steep Kicking Horse Pass named for an accident involving a surveyor's animal was a continuing problem for the railway builders.
    b. The change in government policy will not however close all unfair tax loopholes.
    c. Her attorney was clever and eloquent nevertheless the evidence presented by the Crown was overwhelming.
    d. Cockfighting outlawed by the authorities still takes place in areas where the police seldom turn up.
    e. There is no doubt a logical explanation for these strange occurrences.
    f. No dogs cannot climb trees children.

11.4 COMMAS TO SEPARATE ITEMS IN A SERIES

Words, Phrases, or Clauses in a Series

A comma is the mark ordinarily used to separate co-ordinate words, phrases, or clauses in a list or series:

He affected a nicely greying mustache and goatee, leather patches on the elbows of his houndstooth jacket, an ascot around his neck, a battered old pipe in his hand. — *Maclean's*

We were taught how to sit gracefully, how to walk, how to converse politely.

Although usage is divided, most writers prefer to use a comma before a connective joining the last item in a series:

The twisted features, the soft coloring, and the design of the whole mask were so blended as to produce an effect between terror and comedy. — Douglas Leechman, *Native Tribes of Canada*

He couldn't decide whether to visit London, Paris, or Rome.

In some informal writing, especially in newspapers, this final comma is omitted if no misinterpretation is possible. However, because there is quite often the possibility of misreading, it's generally better to use a final comma:

At the rock concert we heard Blackberry Wine, Golden Gate Bridge, Red Eye and the Bull Dogs. [Is Red Eye and the Bull Dogs one group or two?]

If each of the items in a series is joined by a conjunction, commas are ordinarily omitted. The following sentence illustrates two series without connectives:

It doesn't mean that our great corporations or cartels or combines are necessarily sinister and morally debauched and without any social responsibility. — Arthur L. Phelps, "Christmas This Year (1949)"

(See also 12.1, page 163, Semicolons to Separate Elements Containing Other Marks.)

Co-ordinate Adjectives

Commas are used to separate adjectives in a series when they modify the same noun. Since each performs the same function, such adjectives are called *co-ordinate*. In a co-ordinate series each member could sensibly be joined by *and* instead of a comma, or the order of modifiers could be reversed:

Never did man talk as **dark, robust, dynamic, bespectacled** Robert Charbonneau talks. — W.E. Collin, "On Writing in French Canada"

Commas are not used when the adjectives are arranged so that each one modifies the entire following expression. Such items cannot be joined by *and* or reversed in order:

She made a **tasty** [   ] **Hungarian** goulash.

He spoke longingly of the **good** [ ] **old** [ ] **prewar** days.

Notice that a comma is never used between the last adjective in a series and the noun it modifies.

▶ **EXERCISE**

In which of the places marked with brackets would you insert a comma? In which do you consider a comma optional? Not appropriate?

a. If a man can write a better book [1] preach a better sermon [2] or make a better mousetrap [3] than his neighbors [4] though he builds his house in the woods [5] the world will make a beaten path to his door. — Ralph Waldo Emerson

b. Put your trust in God [1] my boys [2] and keep your powder dry. — attributed to Oliver Cromwell

c. When I was a child [1] I spake as a child [2] I understood as a child [3] I thought as a child: but when I became a man [4] I put away childish things. — 1 Corinthians

d. Professor Tillman [1] author of several books [2] gave a series of lectures on the depression.

11.4

11.5 COMMAS TO SEPARATE FOR CLARITY OR EMPHASIS

Commas tend to keep distinct the constructions they separate and should be used wherever necessary to prevent misreading or to indicate meaningful pauses. They are useful in the following situations:

1. When the subject of a clause may be mistaken for the object of a verb or preposition that precedes it:

    As far as I can **see, the results** have not been promising.

    When the rains are **over, the fields** are ploughed in preparation for planting.

2. When a word has two possible functions, a comma can guide the reader in interpreting it properly. Words like *for, but,* and *however,* for example, may be used in several ways:

    The surgeon's face showed no emotion, **but** anxiety and a little nervousness must have been hiding behind that impassive mask. [. . . showed no emotion but anxiety . . .]

    Sharon was thoroughly embarrassed, **for** her parents treated her like a child. [. . . was thoroughly embarrassed for her parents . . .]

    However, I interpreted his remarks liberally and continued my work.

    However [ ] I interpreted his remarks, they made no sense.

3. A comma is sometimes necessary for clarity when one expression might be mistaken for another:

   After he broke his **hand, writing** was very difficult for him.

4. When the same word occurs consecutively, a comma may be used, although usage is divided on this:

   Whatever **is, is** right.

5. A comma can indicate a dramatic pause, as before an afterthought, even though no punctuation is grammatically needed. Depending on the emphasis you want to signal, sentences like the following could be written with or without commas:

   The meal was expensive [ ] but delicious.

   She entered the room [ ] and suddenly collapsed.

   This new Canadian wine is robust [ ] yet mellow.

6. Certain constructions, notably ones expressing emphatic contrast, need to be separated by commas from the rest of the clause: *I want the car keys, not a lecture on safe driving.*

11.6 COMMAS IN CONVENTIONAL PLACES

Current practices should be followed in the use of commas in conventional places. Such commas help the reader quickly recognize distinct units of information.

Numbers.   Commas have been conventionally used to group numbers into units of threes in separating thousands or millions (2,853 84,962   3,542,869).

In the *metric system,* however, it is conventional to use **spaces,** not commas, between groups of three digits to the left and right of the decimal point. The space is unnecessary if there are only four digits to the left or right of the decimal, unless such numerals are listed in a *column* with other numerals of five digits or more:

	Column of numerals:
Canada's area is 9 976 139km^2	
1 mile = 1.609 344km	56 113.74
This is the year 1978.	9 825.36
1 cal = 4.1868J	12 377.40

Spaces do not appear in such numbers as serial numbers (My car's serial number is 982101776.) or addresses (I live at 11850 Oak St.).

For any such numbers follow the style of the original source.

Dates.   Commas separate the day of the month and the year:

> February 8, 1928   November 21, 1975

When only the month and year are given, a comma is not necessary, although it is frequently used:

> October 1929 *or* October, 1929

In the all-numeric form, however, commas have been replaced by hyphens or by spaces and the order of year, month, and day is always maintained.

11.6

> 1982-08-26 *or* 1982 08 26

Addresses.   Commas in addresses separate cities or towns from provinces or territories and/or countries. No comma precedes the Canadian postal code (or the codes of other countries). Notice the following examples of customary format:

Canada:	Edmonton, Alberta
	T6G 2E5
United States:	Toledo, Ohio 43601
Britain:	Bromsgrove, Worcestershire B60 1BS

Titles.   Commas separate proper names from titles and degrees:

> S.R. Bonnycastle, B.A., Ph.D.
> Colonel (Retired) J.M. Smithers, D.S.O., C.D.
> Raven I. McDavid, Jr.

Notice that the final element in dates, addresses, and titles is followed by a comma if it falls within a sentence:

> He was born on September 10, 1929, ten years before Canada entered World War II.
>
> She was born in Paris, Ontario, and lived there ten years.
>
> Syl Apps, Jr., followed his father into professional hockey.

Letters.   Commas are conventional after the salutation (greeting) in informal letters (Dear Shirley, Dear Uncle Joe,) and after the complimentary close of most letters (Yours truly, Sincerely yours,). A *colon* is used after the salutation of a formal or business letter (Dear Mr. Miller:).

Quotations.   A comma is customarily used after expressions that introduce direct quotations:

Guy Lombardo said, "Corn is always green—like money."

If the phrase interrupts a sentence in the quotation, it is set off by two commas:

"Corn," Guy Lombardo said, "is always green—like money."

No comma is needed with very short quotations, exclamations, or phrases closely built into the structure of the sentence:

Father always said "Time is money."

She began to scream "Fire!" as soon as she saw the smoke.

One famous novelist likened Canada to "two solitudes."

11.7 MISUSED COMMAS

No Remove the superfluous comma at the placed marked.

Students frequently use too many commas because of a mistaken notion that the more punctuation, the better. Remember that too many commas are as bad as too few, and be prepared to justify every comma you use. The most common misuses of commas are described below.

Misused Comma Between Main Sentence Elements

Since a comma is a mark of separation, it should not ordinarily be used between those elements of a sentence that naturally go together: subject and verb, verb and object (or complement), preposition and object. There should be no marks where the brackets stand in the following sentences:

SUBJECT AND VERB: Sometimes students who have attended expensive preparatory schools [ ] have trouble adjusting to large public universities.

VERB AND OBJECT: I have often noticed [ ] that a person's physical characteristics may influence his personality.

VERB AND COMPLEMENT: Whenever the dogs in the kennel appeared [ ] restless or hostile, the trainer took steps to pacify them.

PREPOSITION AND OBJECT: Nothing troubled her except [ ] that her friendship with Swift was causing gossip.

Misused Comma Between Two Words or Phrases Joined by *and*

Except for co-ordinate clauses (11.1), two items joined by *and* or by one of the other co-ordinating conjunctions are not ordinarily separated by a comma. Commas would be out of place in the following compound constructions:

> Primitive agricultural tools [ ] and bits of clay pottery were found. [compound subject]
>
> He either talked too much [ ] or else said nothing at all. [compound predicate]
>
> In his senior year he was captain of the football team [ ] and secretary of his class. [compound complement]
>
> She wanted more time for study [ ] and contemplation. [compound object of preposition]

11.7

Misused Comma Between Main Clauses Without a Connective

A comma alone is an inadequate mark of separation between two main clauses. If the clauses are not joined by a co-ordinating conjunction, they *must* be either separated by a semicolon or punctuated as individual sentences. See 2.2, Comma Faults.

Misused Comma with Restrictive Modifiers

A restrictive modifier is one that is essential to the meaning of the sentence (see 11.3); it should not be separated from the element it modifies by a comma. The boldface elements in the following example are restrictive and should stand as they are here, without commas.

> The conenose, or kissing bug, is an insect **whose painful bite can draw blood.**
>
> The book **that I left at home** is the one I really need for class.

Misused Comma After the Last Item in a Series

A comma is never used between the last adjective in a series and the noun it modifies:

> He imagined himself as a **rich, handsome, successful**[ ] man of the world.

A comma is also not used after the last item in other kinds of lists or series:

> The acting ability of such stars as Olivier, Guinness, Plummer, and Fonda [   ] is generally acknowledged.

▶ **EXERCISE**

Commas have been omitted from the following passages. Copy the paragraphs, punctuating with commas wherever you think appropriate; be prepared to account for the commas you insert.

1. There was once a man and his wife who had long wished in vain for a child and at last they had reason to hope that heaven would grant their wish. There was a little window at the back of their house which overlooked a beautiful garden full of lovely flowers and shrubs. It was however surrounded by a wall and nobody dared to enter because it belonged to a witch who was feared by everybody.

2. From that point day after day up the steep slopes some thirty men toiled under burdens of tools forges ironware cables ropes rolls of sail canvas fittings and rigging and anchors saws axes sledges caulking merchandise such as bolts of cloth beads hatchets knives guns ammunition seven cannon tin plates cooking pots and kettles beads bright braids and buckles and supplies of flour corn beans molasses tea and kegs of brandy and other spirits. It was back-breaking exhausting work a carry of more than ten miles. After the ridges came thick forests deep in snow. At all times the temperature was near zero and frequently biting winds swept in from Lake Erie. — Adapted from John Upton Terrell, *Lasalle: The Life and Times of an Explorer*

12

Semicolons and Colons

Both semicolons (;) and colons (:) are strong marks of punctuation, but their functions are completely different and should never be confused. They cannot be used interchangeably. The semicolon is a mark of *separation*. The colon is a mark of *anticipation* directing the reader's attention to something that follows.

12.1 SEMICOLONS

 Use a semicolon at the place marked to separate co-ordinate sentence elements.

As a mark of separation, the semicolon is much stronger than a comma and almost as definite as a period. If the following passage is read aloud at normal speed, the voice should fall in pitch, pausing almost as for a period, after *crossroad* and after *tumble-down*:

> Our haunted house was not strictly in the best haunted-house tradition. It was not a ramshackle pile standing at a lonely crossroad; it was on a street inside the town and was surrounded by houses that were cheerfully inhabited. It was not tumble-down; it was a large, well-built mansion of brick, and it still stands, good as new. — Frank Sullivan, *The Night the Old Nostalgia Burned Down*

Like a period, a semicolon separates two independent statements, but it enables a writer to imply a much stronger *relation* between them than making them into two distinct sentences would indicate. The kinds of constructions in which the semicolon is appropriate are described below. Notice that in all its uses the semicolon marks a separation between *co-ordinate* elements (elements of equal rank).

Semicolons Between Main Clauses Without an Expressed Connective

A semicolon must be used to separate main clauses that are not joined by one of the co-ordinating conjunctions (*and*, *but*, *for*, *or*, *nor*, *so*, *yet*):

> The penalty for not turning work in on time is a lowered grade; the penalty for not turning it in at all is failure.

These clauses are clearly separate in thought and structure and *could* be punctuated as separate sentences. A semicolon is used to combine such clauses when the writer considers them parts of one idea. Sometimes the second clause continues the thought of the first:

> Toward the end of the French régime, one had only to take a canoe trip along the St. Lawrence and the Richelieu rivers for an almost complete enumeration of Canadian homes; the waterfront or shore-line was synonymous with settled country. — Marcel Rioux and Yves Martin, *French-Canadian Society*

Sometimes the second clause presents a contrasting idea:

> But however immature they are, these lovers are not dull characters; on the contrary, they are hauntingly and embarrassingly real. — Arthur Mizener, *The Far Side of Paradise*

The use of a comma rather than a semicolon or period between main clauses without an expressed connective is considered a serious error in writing. (See 2.2, Comma Faults.)

Semicolons Between Main Clauses Linked with a Conjunctive Adverb

A semicolon is used before conjunctive adverbs like *however*, *therefore*, *consequently*, and *nevertheless* when they occur between clauses:

> On your income-tax return you can deduct the cost of meals and lodging for business trips; **however,** you cannot deduct the cost of meals if you were not away overnight.

> And, in fact, absence of intellectual content is the mark of the sentimental genre; **conversely,** it is because of her intellect that Jane Austen is never sentimental. — Brigid Brophy, "A Masterpiece, and Dreadful"

The use of heavy conjunctive adverbs between long clauses is probably more characteristic of a formal style, as the second example above may indicate. Many writers prefer to make such clauses into separate sentences as in the following example:

> Logic is often powerless against emotion. Nevertheless, we should try to base important decisions on facts and careful reflection.

Semicolons with Co-ordinating Conjunctions

A semicolon is sometimes used (instead of a comma) between main clauses connected by co-ordinating conjunctions under one or more of the following circumstances:

1. the clauses are unusually long,
2. the clauses are not closely related,
3. one or more of the clauses contain commas, or
4. the writer wishes to show an emphatic contrast between statements:

> This new variety was related, of course, to the mother dialects of the British Isles, and preserved many of the features of its forbears; but it exhibited also an increasing identity of its own during the course of several centuries. — G.M. Story, "Newfoundland Dialect: An Historical View"

> Only in a modern university, for example, could large sums be spent on television equipment to make a lecture course available in many rooms; and only a modern academic would be surprised to find the television sets performing to empty seats. — Geoffrey Durrant, "The New Barbarians"

Semicolons to Separate Elements Containing Other Marks

In addition to separating co-ordinate sentence elements, semicolons are often used in lists and series to separate elements that contain commas or other marks. In the following sentence, for example, the semicolons are necessary for clarity:

> Words of unknown or uncertain origin [include] *bangbelly*, a type of pudding; *callivances*, a species of white bean; *chronic*, an old stump; *cracky*, a little dog; the *diddies*, a nightmare; *dido*, a bitch; *gandy*, a pancake; *pelm*, light ashes; *shimmick*, a term of contempt for one who attempts to deny his Newfoundland origin.... — Mark M. Orkin, *Speaking Canadian English*

Notice that here, just as with main clauses, the semicolon separates *co-ordinate* elements. It is never used between elements of unequal rank, such as phrases and clauses or main and subordinate clauses.

▶ **EXERCISE**

Commas and semicolons have been omitted from the sentences below. Insert the appropriate punctuation.

1. In the summer she visited Munich Heidelberg Frankfurt and Slazburg and in early fall she went on to Albania Greece and Egypt.
2. The weather was hot humid and miserable all day however a west wind cooled the air after dark.

3. Orchestra rehearsal begins at seven she will be there even though she needs to study.

4. The storm knocked out the electricity consequently we could not read or watch television.

5. She knew her parents were worried about her accordingly she called in to let them know she was all right.

12.2 COLONS

 Insert a colon at the place marked, or change the misused colon.

A colon is a strong mark of anticipation, directing attention to what follows:

> Sciences normally begin in a state of naïve induction: they come immediately in contact with phenomena and take the things to be explained as their immediate data. — Northrop Frye, "The Function of Criticism at the Present Time"

Although inexperienced writers sometimes confuse them, the functions of colons and semicolons are entirely different. The distinction is simple: a colon *introduces* what is to follow; a semicolon *separates* co-ordinate elements. The following passage illustrates the correct use of both marks:

> The community that gathered round each country church soon came to have an organic unity about it: the parish became the natural subdivision of the countryside, comprehending most of the life of its people; their social occasions, their religious occasions, their marryings, their buryings and their business went on within its bounds, and often within earshot of the church bell. — A.R.M. Lower, *Colony to Nation*

Anticipatory Use of Colons

A colon may be used after a main clause to indicate that a list, an illustration, or a summation is to follow immediately:

> Needless to say, there are many slang terms native to Canada, quite a number of them relating to the sports arena: *deke*, *chippy*, *homebrew*, *import*, *rink rat*. — W.S. Avis, "The English Language in Canada"

> The characteristic problem of the first missionaries had been to win the acceptance of pagan tribes: to acquire the skills of the woodsman; to learn new languages; to endure squalor, privation, fatigue and

loneliness; to win a hearing in the face of hostility or ridicule; perhaps to face death. — S.R. Mealing, *The Jesuit Relations and Allied Documents*

The colon is used as an anticipatory mark only after grammatically complete expressions. Do not use a colon between verbs and their objects or complements, or between prepositions and their objects:

> COLON: He visited the following cities: Moncton, Quebec, and Sarnia.
> NO COLON: He visited Moncton, Quebec, and Sarnia. [objects of verb]
> COLON: The string section consists of four instruments: violin, viola, cello, and bass.
> NO COLON: The four instruments in the string section are violin, viola, cello, and bass. [complements of verb]

Colons Between Main Clauses

A colon may be used between two main clauses when the second clause is an illustration, a restatement, or an amplification of the first:

> His opposition was never a match for him: neither in men nor in organization did the Liberals approach him. — A.R.M. Lower, *Colony to Nation*
>
> I was impractical: I wanted to marry a poet. — Lillian Hellman, *Pentimento*

In such a case the first clause *directly introduces* the second, and would seem incomplete without it. The colon between them is a mark of connecting and completing, not of separation. When two clauses do not rely on each other in this way, however, a semicolon should be used instead. (See 12.1, Semicolons.)

Colons Before Quotations

A colon is generally used between an introductory statement and a grammatically complete quotation, especially if the quotation is more than one sentence:

> Here is a well-known verse from *Ecclesiastes*: "I returned and saw under the sun, that the race is not to the swift, nor the battle to the strong, neither yet bread to the wise, nor yet riches to men of understanding, nor yet favour to men of skill; but time and chance happeneth to them all." — George Orwell, "Politics and the English Language"

The saying of a cynical friend flashed suddenly across my mind: "A saint may be nothing but a whitewashed sepulchre and the charity of the philanthropist a mere cloak for the pride of humility." — James A. Roy, "Brother Andre"

When a short quotation is built closely into a sentence, it may be preceded either by a comma (as in dialogue) or by a colon, depending on how it is introduced:

As Alexander Pope said, "A little learning is a dangerous thing."

She reminded him of the words of Pope: "A little learning is a dangerous thing."

Colons in Conventional Places

A colon is also customary in the following places:

1. After an expression directly introducing examples or a large body of material (as after *places* in the preceding sentence).
2. Between hours and minutes expressed in figures: 11:30
3. In formal footnotes and bibliographies:

    Between volume and issue: *Sidney Newsletter* 2:1
    Between chapter and verse of the Bible: Matthew 4:6
    Between the title and subtitle of a book: *China: A Modern Enigma*

4. After the salutation in a formal letter:

    Dear Sir: Dear Professor Jones:

See page 186 for use of capital letter after colons.

▶ **EXERCISE**

Either find and copy from your reading or write sentences according to the directions below:
1. a sentence with a colon preceding a list of information or examples
2. a sentence with a colon between two main clauses
3. a sentence with a colon before a quotation

13

Dashes, Parentheses, and Brackets

Dashes, parentheses, and brackets are all special marks used to separate interrupting elements from the main thought of the sentence. Dashes are ordinarily used when the interruption is abrupt or emphatic. Parentheses are used when the interruption is an aside or explanatory remark. Brackets are conventionally used when an editorial comment interrupts quoted material.

13.1

/ – – /

13.1 DASHES

/ – – /   Use a dash or dashes to set off the expression marked.

On the typewriter a dash is made with two unspaced hyphens; there should likewise be no space on either side of the dash, between it and the words it separates.

Dashes are used to set off parenthetical expressions and abrupt interruptions in thought. The dash is a useful mark of separation, but since it is a more emphatic way of setting off elements than either commas or parentheses, it should not be used to excess or in places where another mark (or none) would be more appropriate. Dashes are customarily used in the situations shown below.

1.   To set off parenthetical expressions and abrupt interruptions:

In reality, the whole idea of a specifically feminine—**or, for the matter of that, masculine**—contribution to culture is a contradiction of culture.—Brigid Brophy, "Women Are Prisoners of Their Sex"

2.   To mark sharp turns in thought:

He praised Ann's intelligence, her efficiency, her good taste—**and then proposed to her sister.**

He is a humble man—**with a lot to be humble about.**

3.   To enclose parenthetical elements (usually to give greater emphasis to elements that could also be set off with commas):

Still we do condemn—**we must condemn**—the cruelties of slavery, fanaticism, and witch-burning.—Herbert Muller, *The Uses of the Past*

> With our love of record keeping — **doubtless a mark of our business society** — the origin of almost everything is known or easily discoverable. — Jacques Barzun and Henry Graff, *The Modern Researcher*

For clarity, dashes are sometimes used instead of commas to set off parenthetical elements that have internal punctuation. Note that *two* dashes are necessary to enclose a parenthetical element that falls in the middle of a sentence.

4.   To set off an expression that summarizes or illustrates the preceding statement:

> He founded a university, and devoted one side of his complex genius to placing that university amid every circumstance which could stimulate the imagination — **beauty of buildings, of situation, and every other stimulation of equipment and organisation.** — Alfred North Whitehead, "The Idea of a University"

5.   To serve some special uses:
   a.   To precede a credit line, as at the end of the quoted passages in this *Handbook*.
   b.   After introductory words that are to be repeated before each of the lines following:

> We pledge —
> To uphold the Monarchy.
> To obey the laws of Canada.

   c.   To separate questions and answers in testimony:

> Q. — Did you see him?
> A. — No.

   d.   To indicate interrupted dialogue (usually *two* dashes separated by a space are used):

> "Well, I had always assumed that — — "
> "I don't care what you assumed," John snapped.

13.2 PARENTHESES

   Use parentheses to enclose the expression marked.

Parentheses are curved marks used chiefly to enclose incidental or explanatory remarks as shown below.

1.   To enclose incidental remarks:

> Her young man was a gifted carver, who had been sent out into the

desert by the cruel pharoah **(pharoahs were always cruel — of this I was positive)** in order to carve a giant sphinx for the royal tomb. — Margaret Laurence, "The Mask of the Bear"

2. To enclose details, brief definitions, and examples:

For seven long years **(1945-1952)** austerity was the key word in British economic life.

Inside the walls was a three-storey redoubt **(a strongpoint armed with three two-pounder cannon and one eight-pounder)** towering above the walls of the fort so that its cannon could fire into the country beyond from all sides. — Pierre Berton, "The First Commando Raid"

13.2

(/)

3. To enclose figures or letters used to enumerate points:

The main questions asked about our way of life concern **(1)** the strength of our democracy, **(2)** our radical practices, **(3)** our concept of modern economy, and **(4)** the degree of materialism in our culture.

No punctuation marks are used before a parenthetical *statement* that occurs within a sentence. If a comma or period is needed after the parenthetical material, it is placed *outside* of the *closing* marks:

There is talk with music (tapes and records), talk with film and tape (movies and television), talk with live public performance (demonstrations and "confrontation"). — William Jovanovich, "A Tumult of Talk"

When the parenthetical statement comes between sentences, the appropriate end punctuation is placed *inside* the closing mark:

If we could get off by ourselves on a continental island, far away from the wicked Americans, all we should achieve would be to become a people like the Australians. (And even then the American goblin would get us in the end, as he is getting the Australians.) — Frank H. Underhill, "Notes on the Massey Report"

13.3 BRACKETS

[/]   Use brackets to set off any insertion in quoted material.

Brackets are square marks used to insert brief editorial comments and explanations in material quoted from other writers:

Lest it be thought that I am exaggerating, listen to Mencken: "The impact of this flood **[of common-speech, non-fashionable Americanisms]** is naturally most apparent in Canada, whose geographical

> proximity and common interests completely obliterate the effects of English political and social dominance."—Eric Partridge, *Slang Today and Yesterday with a Short Historical Sketch and Vocabularies of English, American and Australian Slang*

Comments or directions may be bracketed in conversation or in other quoted material to show that the speaker didn't actually say the enclosed words:

> Although very formal speeches usually begin with a ceremonial greeting like "Madam [or Mister] Chairperson, distinguished guests [if there are any], ladies and gentlemen...," such remarks are unnecessary in more casual situations.

The Latin word *sic* (meaning *thus* or *so*) is sometimes inserted in brackets within quoted material to mark an error in spelling, usage, or fact that appeared in the original:

> The author's next letter was headed "St. John [sic], Newfoundland, Oct. 6, 1854."

Since many writers feel that the insertion of *sic* to mark the errors of others is more snobbish than scholarly, the practice has declined in recent years.

In this book, brackets are used with examples of writing to enclose words that might better be left out of a sentence, to suggest an improved expression, and to comment on a construction. These special uses are illustrated below:

> At the end of an hour and a half we arrived at [the spot where] the red flag [was situated].
>
> He looks **similar to [like]** his father.
>
> **Most** fishermen are optimists. [adjective, modifying *fishermen*]

Occasionally, brackets are used for parenthetical material that falls within parentheses—thus ([ ])—but such constructions are awkward and can usually be avoided. Consult the preceding section to be sure that you don't confuse the normal uses of parentheses and brackets (see 13.2, Parentheses).

▶ EXERCISE

In each numbered space in the following sentences, which mark of punctuation (if any) would you consider most appropriate: a comma, a semicolon, a colon, a dash, or a parenthesis? Is punctuation necessary in all cases? If more than one choice is possible, list the marks in order of your preference.

a. Let us begin by looking [1] at the two countries where population pressures are most severe [2] India and Pakistan.

b. The finalists in diving were [1] Wilkins [2] U.S.A. [3] and Boyes [4] Canada [5] no one else had qualified.

c. To Ahab the white whale became an obsession [1] even Starbuck [2] the first mate [3] could do nothing to shake him out of it.

d. Reisman divides behavior into two major classes [1] inner-directed [2] directed toward pleasing the self [3] and other-directed [4] concerned with pleasing others [5].

e. The Edsel was [1] the most carefully planned and lavishly promoted new car in automobile history [2] but it was a total failure.

f. Someone [1] was it Carlyle [2] ironically used a truss factory [3] as a symbol [4] of modern [5] industrial progress.

g. Some industries have established good relations with their unions by increasing benefits [1] vacations, insurance, pension plans [2] but many manufacturers feel that there is only one permanent solution to their chronic labor problems [3] increased automation.

h. The key word in the essay [1] *faction* [2] is carefully defined by the author at the beginning [3] then he goes on to explain [4] what forms it may take.

i. An audience is basically one of three things [1] although various mixtures are also possible [2] friendly, hostile, or indifferent.

j. When Cadwallader quit talking [1] the chairman snorted [2] tugged at his ear [3] and spoke [4] "If you ladies and gentlemen [5] there were no ladies present [6] believe that I will support this recommendation [7] then you have lost your minds."

13.3

[/]

14

Quotation Marks, Ellipses, and Italics

In general the more common punctuation marks—periods, question marks, commas, semicolons, and so on—indicate intonation and degrees of interruption that would occur if the material was read aloud. They show how the writer wants the words grouped together for meaning and emphasis.

The three marks discussed in this chapter—quotation marks, ellipses, and italics—are somewhat different in purpose. They are visual guides that tell the reader at a glance such things as whether the words are a writer's own and whether they are being used in a special way. Compare the following pairs of sentences:

> He said I was a fool. [He accused the *writer* of being a fool.]
> He said, "I was a fool." [He called *himself* a fool.]
>
> He spoke of Watson's moral decline. [the moral decline of Watson]
> He spoke of Watson's *Moral Decline*. [a book by Watson]

Although quotation marks, ellipses, and italics are used less often than other punctuation, it is important to know how to use them correctly. They are often necessary in writing that is likely to contain references to the writing of others.

14.1 QUOTATION MARKS

 Make the quotation marks and accompanying punctuation conform to conventional usage.

Quotation marks are necessary to set off direct speech and material quoted from other sources. They are also used around some titles and around words used in special ways.

Usage varies, but double quotations (" ") are the usual marks in Canadian publications. Students should follow this convention. Use single marks (' ')—made on the typewriter with apostrophes—only for a quotation within a quotation (see p. 174). Whether double or single, quotation marks are always used in *pairs*, before and after the quoted material.

Quotation Marks to Enclose Direct Discourse

Statements representing actual speech or conversation are enclosed by quotation marks. The following passage illustrates typical punctuation for direct discourse. Notice not only the quotation marks but the positioning of the punctuation used with them:

> My father came back in from shovelling snow, his face red from exertion and annoyance.
>
> "Blasted snow gets heavier every year," he growled. "Why does any sensible person stay in this country?"
>
> Mother said, "You shouldn't be shovelling at all. The doctor told you to let the boys do it."
>
> "Well, there's plenty out there now for them to shovel. The snowplow just came by and filled in the driveway again."

In dialogue the words of each speaker are normally indented like paragraphs, as in the example above. But when short speeches or statements are quoted to illustrate a point in exposition, they are usually included in the relevant paragraph:

> Some of the constructions were typically Cree or Ojibwa. I have heard, "Bye me I *kaykatch* [nearly] killed it two ducks with wan sot." That would be pretty good Cree translated literally into that language. Again, "John James Corrigal and Willie George Linklater were sooting in the marse. The canoe went *apeechequanee*. The watter was sallow whatefer but Willie George kept bobbin up and down callin, 'O Lard save me.' John James was on topside the canoe souted to Willie and sayed, 'Never mind the Lard just now Willie, grab for the willows.'" —S.O. Scott, "Red River Dialect"

Only *direct discourse*, which represents the actual words of the speaker, is enclosed by quotation marks. *Indirect discourse*, which gives the substance of what the speaker said but not his exact words, is *not* enclosed in quotation marks:

> DIRECT DISCOURSE: The coach said, "Get in there and fight."
>
> INDIRECT DISCOURSE: The coach told us to get in there and fight.
>
> DIRECT DISCOURSE: "At the present time," the minister replied, "I haven't made up my mind about the bill."
>
> INDIRECT DISCOURSE: The minister replied that he had not yet made up his mind about the bill.

Quotation Marks Around Quoted Material

Words taken directly from another writer or speaker must be clearly set apart, either by enclosing them within quotation marks or by using some other conventional typographic device such as printing them in reduced type. Whether a writer is quoting a phrase or several paragraphs, he should make certain that he follows the exact wording and punctuation of his source.

Short quotations.   Quotation marks are used around quoted phrases and statements that are included within the body of a paragraph. The quoted material may be worked into the structure of a sentence or may stand by itself:

> Creighton has written of his arch-foes, the proponents of the "liberal" or continentalist interpretation of Canadian history, that they "will tell our children how Edward Blake exposed the serpentine machinations of Sir John Macdonald and how Mackenzie King finally slew the hideous dragon of British imperialism with the glittering lance of national autonomy." — T.D. MacLulich, "Creighton's *John A. Macdonald*: History as Heroic Romance"

> While Iago, for example, is gulling Roderigo, he scoffs at him with superb disdain: "I have rubb'd this young quat almost to the sense / And he grows angry." (*Othello*, 5.1.11 – 12). — Maurice Charney, *How to Read Shakespeare*

> New begins by confessing that the last line of the novel "haunts" him. "The ambivalence of it puzzles, irritates, confuses." — Morton L. Ross, "The Canonization of *As for Me and My House*: A case study"

Long quotations.   When quoted material is relatively long — more than one full sentence from the original source or more than four lines in your paper — the passage is usually indented and single-spaced but *not* enclosed in quotation marks:

> A British member of Parliament, A.P. Herbert, also exasperated with bureaucratic jargon, translated Nelson's immortal phrase, "England expects every man to do his duty":
>
>> England anticipates that, as regards the current emergency, personnel will face up to the issues, and exercise appropriately the functions allocated to their respective occupational groups.
>
> — Stuart Chase, *The Power of Words*

A quotation within a quotation.   Use single quotation marks around quoted material that appears within a quotation which is itself enclosed in double marks:

> If they depended solely on economic theory to guide them, they would be in the position of the man John Williams mentions: "About the practical usefulness of the theory, I have often felt like the man who stammered and finally learned to say, 'Peter Piper picked a peck of pickled peppers,' but found it hard to work into conversation." — C. Hartley Grattan, "New Books"

In the rare instances when a third quotation occurs within a second, double and single marks are alternated, like this:

> In the next passage he gives an example of Mill's uncontrolled temper: "Mill attached Beaton with a poker after reading his comment that 'A work of genius is not, as Mr. Mill says, "a spontaneous outflowing of the soul"; it is the product of intellectual discipline, a quality Mr. Mill notably lacks.' "

Such a proliferation of quotation marks is confusing and can usually be avoided, either by indenting and single-spacing the main quotation or by paraphrasing some of the material:

14.1

> In the next passage he gives an example of Mill's uncontrolled temper, telling how Mill attacked Beaton with a poker after reading his comment that "A work of genius is not, as Mr. Mill says, 'a spontaneous overflowing of the soul'; it is the product of intellectual discipline, a quality Mr. Mill notably lacks."

Quoted verse.   A short quotation of verse (a phrase or portion of a line) may be built directly into a sentence and enclosed by quotation marks, as is this phrase from *Romeo and Juliet:*

> "A plague on both your houses" was the general attitude toward the parties in any conflict, no matter what the outcome. — Percy Finch, *Shanghai and Beyond*

If the quoted passage extends over several lines of the poem, it is best to line it off exactly as it appears in the original, single-spaced and indented. Quotation marks are unnecessary:

> Milton opens *Paradise Lost* by announcing that he will write
>
> > Of Man's first disobedience, and the fruit
> > Of that forbidden tree whose mortal taste
> > Brought death into the World. . . .

If two or three lines of verse are being incorporated into the body of your paragraph, the passage is enclosed in quotation marks and the line breaks are indicated by diagonal lines (/):

> Milton opens *Paradise Lost* by announcing that he will write "Of Man's first disobedience, and the fruit / Of that forbidden tree whose mortal taste / Brought death into the World."

Quotation Marks with Other Punctuation

The following conventions govern the use of other punctuation with quotation marks:

1. Commas and periods are always placed *inside* the closing quotation mark:

   "Yes," Roger agreed, "It's too late to worry about that now."

   Her watch case was described as "waterproof," but "moisture-resistant" would have been more accurate.

2. Semicolons and colons are placed *outside* the closing quotation mark:

   This critic's attitude seems to be "I don't like any movie"; on a few occasions, though, he has said kind words for a travelogue or a documentary film.

   Fully a third of the railway passengers were what trainmen call "deadheads": people who ride on passes and never tip.

3. Question marks, exclamation points, and dashes are placed inside *or* outside the closing quotation mark, depending upon the situation. They come *inside* when they apply to the quotation only:

   Mother looked at me and asked, "Why do you say that?"

   He gave me a skeptical look which seemed to mean "Look who's talking!"

   Terrence interrupted, "No, listen to this — " and proceeded to recite a poem none of us had ever heard before.

They are placed *outside* the closing quotation mark when they apply to the entire statement:

   Who was it who said that "good guys finish last"? [The whole sentence is a question.]

   And to top it all off, she refers to her automatic dishwasher as "essential equipment for gracious living"!

End punctuation is never doubled. If a quotation ends your sentence, the end punctuation within quotation marks also indicates the end of the sentence:

   This lack of response is, of course, an action from Laura, which forces him to a further question, "You got any objections?" — Brian Meeson, "The Language of Public Performance"

Notice that no period is added after the final quotation mark, even though the sentence is a statement, not a question. Occasionally it is necessary to use double marks *within* a sentence to avoid a possible misreading, as in the following sentence:

   At singles bars, uninspired opening lines like "Do you come here often?", "What's your sign?", and "Is anyone sitting here?" are heard hundreds of times each evening.

Quotation Marks Around Titles

Quotation marks are used to set off the titles of single poems, essays, short stories, articles, and brief compositions published as part of larger works. The titles of books and the names of newspapers and magazines, however, are printed in *italics* (or, in the case of typed and handwritten work, underlined):

> Two of the poems by Bliss Carman that appear in *Literature in Canada Volume 1* are **"A Windflower"** and **"Easter Eve."**

> Judith Blake and Kingsley Davis have contributed an article titled **"Norms, Values, and Sanctions"** to *The Handbook of Modern Sociology,* edited by Robert E.L. Faris.

> Roch Carrier's *The Hockey Sweater and Other Stories* (originally published in French as *Les Enfants du bonhomme dans la lune*) includes his most famous tale — "The Hockey Sweater."

(See 14.3, Italics, and 30, The Research Paper.)

A few titles are neither set off by quotation marks nor underlined for italics: the Bible, the Old Testament, the British North America Act, the Canadian Tire Catalogue, the Regina Telephone Directory (or any other catalogue or directory).

Quotation Marks to Set Off Expressions

Words and phrases used in a special way as popular or unusual *expressions* are often set apart by quotation marks. This form (sometimes known as an *apologetic* quotation) shows your reader that you know there is something unconventional or even questionable about that usage. Depending on context, the quotation marks signify roughly the same thing as a phrase like *in a manner of speaking* or *so-called* or *in a special sense* or *popularly known as*. A few of these occasions are described below.

Popular and slang expressions. In serious situations, good writers avoid overfamiliar popular terms (*lifestyle, bottom line, game plan, modern rat race*) and slang phrases (*get it together, busted by the narcs, blow your mind*), mainly because these expressions are so worn out and unoriginal. But if you do occasionally want to employ the popular associations of a vogue word or non-standard usage, put it in apologetic quotation marks as in the following examples:

> The disheartening outcome of recent international conferences has convinced some of our politicians that certain nations consider us as little more than "fall guys."

Woodhouse tried in his fashion to build a bridge between the wholly "ivory tower" life which could have been his and the busy complex society which poured past the university gates. — John A.B. McLeish, *A Canadian for All Seasons*

The quotation marks in these illustrations indicate to the reader that the writer is, in effect, "quoting" currently or formerly fashionable expressions from popular culture. You shouldn't, however, use trite or colloquial phrases without a specific reason; apologetic quotation marks will not restore their freshness or precision or transform slang into standard English.

Unusual usages.   Notice that the second-last sentence in the above paragraph has the word *quoting* in quotation marks. This is an apologetic form acknowledging that the word's ordinary or literal meaning is being extended or twisted for a special purpose. The same method of emphasis can also signal or clarify various other kinds of unusual effects:

Sir John A. Macdonald was famous for "tomorrowing" his way through hostile Parliamentary question periods. [adaptation of an existing word]

Larocque's most "inflammatory" speech actually induced his hearers to set fire to the computer building. [verbal pun]

Some professors may have to be "re-tooled" to teach new subjects. [analogy]

To *revise* an essay is to "see again" what you have written. [etymological emphasis]

Naturally you should keep special or unusual usages to a minimum, especially in formal writing. Such effects are most successful when used infrequently.

Nicknames.   When a real or imaginary person is commonly referred to by a famous nickname, it is not set off by quotation marks. Less familiar nicknames should, however, be in quotation marks, as should *all* nicknames that are included (within parentheses) as part of a full reference to the person.

Rocket Richard	Maurice ("Rocket") Richard
Babe Ruth	George Herman ("Babe") Ruth
Joey Smallwood	Joseph ("Joey") Smallwood
"Old Tomorrow"	Sir John A Macdonald ("Old Tomorrow")
"Slag" Smith	Alphonse ("Slag") Smith

Words used derisively.   Sometimes a writer may use quotation marks around a term to show that it is being used derisively or sarcastically:

> This remarkable piece of "art" consists of a large canvas covered with mud and old bus transfers.
>
> She was so "genteel" that she avoided any reference to the human body.

It's generally better, however, to try to make the tone of the whole passage derisive rather than to rely too much on quotation marks.

A word used as a word.   Some people put quotation marks around a word that is being used as a word or as an example rather than for its meaning (that is, as a *citation form*):

14.1

> People often confuse the meanings of **"allusion"** and **"illusion."**

But *italics* are preferable to quotation marks for this purpose (see 14.3). As the following passage illustrates, different kinds of word emphasis in a single sentence can require the carefully distinct use of both italics and quotation marks:

> In that same generation *nationality* became a key-word in politics. If Germany or Italy hitherto were only a political idea, and were now becoming "nations", everyone wanted to know the meaning of *nation*, and this was best observed by students of language and of history. Every civilized country was suddenly more interested in its "national origins". — Owen Chadwick, *Catholicism and History*

The italicized words above (*nationality* and *nation*) are simply formal citations. They are presented as words only. On the other hand, the terms within quotation marks ("nations" and "national origins") are to be understood as popular expressions of the day — names embodying the broad ideas that people were talking about.

▶ **EXERCISE**

Write sentences according to the directions below.
1. a sentence naming any published poem, essay, or story *and* the title of the book in which it appears.
2. a sentence that includes a short quotation from something you have read.
3. a sentence in which you identify a speaker and the speaker says something as direct discourse.
4. the sentence above converted to indirect discourse.
5. three sentences giving dialogue between two speakers as direct discourse.
6. the three sentences above converted into indirect discourse.
7. a sentence including either a colloquial (slang) expression or a word used sarcastically.
8. a sentence using a word in citation form — a definition, perhaps.

14.2 ELLIPSES

/.../   Use an ellipsis to indicate any omission in quoted material.

A punctuation mark of three spaced periods, called an ellipsis (plural: *ellipses*), indicates that one or more words have been omitted from quoted material. If an ellipsis comes at the end of a sentence, the sentence period (or other end punctuation) is retained, and the three periods of the ellipsis follow it. There is no space between the last word and the end punctuation:

> There are those...who fear the ignorance of the people of Upper Canada; I...stand more in dread of rulers who are virtually independent of them.... — William Lyon Mackenzie (1826)
>
> ...my roots are entirely Canadian. I'm as Canadian as you'll ever find. Whatever that means. — Donald Sutherland

To indicate that an entire paragraph or more or an entire line or more of poetry has been omitted, a full line of ellipses is used:

> That's my last Duchess painted on the wall,
> Looking as if she were alive....[two words are omitted here]
> ....[two lines omitted]
> Will 't please you sit and look at her?
> — Robert Browning, "My Last Duchess"

Ellipses are sometimes used, especially in dialogue, to indicate interruptions in thought, incompleted statements, or hesitation in speech, as in the doomed heroine's unsteady utterances near the end of George Ryga's *The Ecstasy of Rita Joe*:

> It was different where the women were...It's different to be a woman...Some women was wild...and they shouted they were riding black horses into a fire I couldn't see...There was no fire there, Jaimie!...One time I couldn't find the street where I had a room to sleep in...Forgot my handbag...had no money...An old man with a dog said hello, but I couldn't say hello back because I was worried an' my mouth was so sticky I couldn't speak to him....

14.3 ITALICS

Ital   Underline the word or expressions marked to correspond to the conventions for using italic type.

Words that have special status or that require emphasis are set off in most published works by printing them in slanting type called *italics*. In handwritten or typed papers, such words are underlined:

The article first appeared in <u>Saturday Night</u> and was

reprinted in <u>The Fredericton Gleaner</u>.

Italics for Titles

The names of newspapers and magazines and the titles of books, plays, films, long poems, and other complete works published separately are conventionally italicized (or underlined):

Maclean's	*The Toronto Star*
The Diviners	*Accounting Principles*
the novel *Execution*	*Hamlet,* Act III
The Senior Dictionary	the movie *Ben Hur*
	Dante's *Divine Comedy*

14.3

Ital

Titles of articles, short stories, poems, and other short pieces of writing that are part of a larger work are usually enclosed in quotation marks:

Atwood's "Further Arrivals" is a poem in *Literature in Canada.*

(See 14.1, page 177, Quotation Marks Around Titles, and 30, The Research Paper.)

The names of specific ships, trains, aircraft, and so on are always put in italics:

She took a cruise on the *Princess Patricia.*

The *Royal Scotsman* was a famous locomotive.

Such names are usually preceded by the unitalicized definite article *the*, as above, but this word is not formally part of the name and is sometimes omitted:

He was an officer on [*or* in] HMCS *Athabasca.*

In 1875 the German immigrant ship *Deutschland,* bound for Canada, ran aground in the mouth of the Thames.

Canadian scientists and technicians developed the communications satellite *Anik.*

Italics for Words and Phrases Used as Examples

Words used as words or as examples rather than as parts of a sentence should be italicized.

A few slang terms move into the general language: *crestfallen* and *mob* are examples; some live a long life as slang, never becoming quite respectable; *dough* for "money" is over a hundred years old, and *boozing* goes back to the 1500's. — P.G. Penner and Ruth E. McConnell, "What's the Usage?"

Quotation marks are occasionally used for this purpose, but italics are preferable. (See 14.1, page 179, A word used as a word.)

Italics for Foreign Words

Words from foreign languages that have not been absorbed into English should be italicized (or underlined), not set off by quotation marks:

> In Antiquity every tree, every spring, every stream, every hill had its own *genius loci,* its guardian spirit. —Lynn White, Jr., "The Historical Roots of Our Ecological Crisis"

> Its own natural bird, too, it had, *die goldene pawe,* the gold parrot, winging its way to the ghetto from lands remote. . . . —A.M. Klein, "The Yiddish Proverb"

Foreign expressions that would ordinarily be underlined for italics include terms like *coup d'état, Weltschmerz, deus ex machina, carissime, mañana.* In most books and formal writing, the accents and other customary marks must be reproduced: *français, bête, élève, leños, espléndido, römisch, così.*

The following passage illustrates two different usages of words taken from a foreign language (in this case, from French):

> There used to be a schoolroom exercise called "writing the précis." I gather from contact with many students that such old-fashioned discipline is no longer inflicted on them. This is to be regretted, for working at a précis is as valuable to a writer as *barre* exercises are to a dancer. —Olive Holmes, *Thesis to Book: What to Get Rid Of*

The first French derivation above, "précis," is anglicized (has become widely accepted as part of the English language) and thus need not be italicized. The second French word in the passage, *barre*, is italicized, however, because it is not at present absorbed into general English. Common anglicized terms include the following:

bourgeois	debut	laissez-faire	sputnik
chalet	debutante	prima donna	status quo
chic	fiancée	slalom	vice versa

Although dictionaries usually designate words that are now anglicized (have become part of the English language) and those that are not, their usage tends to be conservative. If you are certain that an expression marked "foreign" is familiar to your readers, you need not underline it. See 17.5, Variant Spellings, regarding *accents* in anglicized words, and 28.2, Technical and Foreign Terms, regarding overuse of foreign words.

The scientific names of plants, insects, and so on are Latin words and are always italicized:

> The highbush cranberry (***Viburnum opulus***) is also called the moose-berry.

Abbreviations of the less common Latin words and phrases used mainly in reference works are sometimes italicized, but Latin abbreviations in general use are not:

> e.g. et al. etc. ca. i.e. vs. viz.

Italics for Emphasis

14.3

Ital

Italics (or underlining) can be used to indicate a word or phrase (or even a sound) the writer particularly wishes to stress. If the sentence were read aloud, the italicized words would be heightened by the voice for emphasis:

> Since we cannot have our fill of existence by going on and on, we want to have ***as much life as possible*** in our short span. — Susanne K. Langer, "Man and Animal: The City and the Hive"

> There is not, however, the slightest doubt that the primary struggle in the novel is to decide which ***white man's*** concept of human society is to prevail. — Robin D. Mathews, "The Wacousta Factor"

> De-clock de-***clack*** de-clock de-***clack*** de-clonk de-clonk de-clonkety ***clack!*** [sound of a freight train's wheels] — Malcolm Lowry, *October Ferry to Gabriola*

In most writing, however, italics for emphasis should be used sparingly. When used excessively or with words that do not deserve special stress, this device may strike a reader as affected. There are also better ways of making key words or ideas prominent in a sentence; see, for example, 25, Sentence Variety, Control, and Emphasis.

In certain kinds of explanatory publications (such as this *Handbook*), italics are used for emphasis especially often. Important terms and distinctions are highlighted in this way to correspond to the stress that a speaking voice would naturally employ when presenting complicated ideas:

> At its best science is statistical. This means that "scientific laws" do not express ***with certainty*** how nature behaves: scientific laws merely describe how nature ***has*** behaved ***within limits*** and how it is ***likely*** to behave within limits again, under similar conditions. — G. Milton Smith, *A Simplified Guide to Statistics*

This "exaggerated" stress would probably be unnecessary and

inappropriate in ordinary writing situations. Unless you are writing a textbook or making very subtle distinctions, it is best to achieve emphasis in more natural ways.

▶ **EXERCISES**

1. Write sentences following the directions below:
   a. a sentence in which you quote two lines of a poem.
   b. a sentence in which you use quotation marks to set off a single word.
   c. a sentence in which you quote something you have read with ellipses to indicate that you have omitted something.
   d. a sentence that includes a word or phrase italicized for emphasis.

2. All the quotation marks and indentations have been removed from the following passage from a short story. Rewrite the passage, using quotation marks and indentations to show dialogue and changes in speaker.

This is Adelaide, George said. Adelaide, Adeline — Sweet Adeline. I'm going to call her Sweet A, Sweet A. Adelaide sucked at her straw, paying not much attention. She hasn't got a date, George said. You haven't got a date have you, honey. Adelaide shook her head very slightly. Doesn't hear half what you say to her, George said. Adelaide, Sweet A, have you got any friends? Have you got any nice, young little girl friend to go out with Dickie? You and me and her and Dickie? Depends, said Adelaide. Where do you want to go? Anywhere you say. Go for a drive. Drive up to Owen Sound, maybe. You got a car? Yeah, yeah we got a car. C'mon, you must have some nice little friend for Dickie. He put his arm around this girl, spreading his fingers over her blouse. C'mon out and I'll show you the car. — Adapted from Alice Munro, "Thanks for the Ride"

15

Capital Letters, Hyphens, and Apostrophes

Capital letters, hyphens, and apostrophes are convenient signals that adapt words to special uses. These signals are not, however, just habits: writing in which capitals are improperly used may seem sloppy or affected to readers; words incorrectly hyphenated may be difficult to read, and can cause faulty modification; misuse of apostrophes often makes the writer seem careless.

15.1 ◀

Cap

15.1 CAPITAL LETTERS

Cap   **Capitalize the marked word; be consistent in the use of capital letters.**
lc   **Write the marked word with a lower-case (small) letter.**

Most uses of capital letters are standard conventions; writing in which capitals are used inconsistently or unconventionally may focus attention on the wrong words and interrupt the natural flow of thought.

The following sections describe the most frequent uses of capital letters. A complete listing of all forms is obviously impossible. Consult a recent dictionary or style manual if you are in doubt as to whether a particular word requires a capital.

Capitals to Mark Units of Expression

Capital letters are used to draw the reader's attention to the beginning of a statement or to individual words in titles.

First word of a sentence. Capitalize the first word of every sentence or expression punctuated with an end stop (period, question mark, or exclamation mark):

> Has the change helped? Not much. The reason is obvious.

First word of a line of poetry. In traditional verse style, the first word of each line is capitalized:

> Mrs. McGonigle's boys enjoy the sun
> By gogglesful, and stare along the beach
> Whose innocence is almost all Elaine,
>   Almost, but not quite, all.
>   — George Johnston, "Elaine in a Bikini"

Bear in mind that many modern poems do not follow this convention. Always transcribe poetry exactly as it appears in the published version.

First word of a quotation.   The first word of a direct quotation that is in itself a complete sentence is capitalized:

> He said, "The future of humanity cannot be left to chance."
> "The crisis is here," she said. "We must act now."

But no capital is used when the quotation is fragmentary or built into the structure of the sentence, or when the second part of a quoted sentence is interrupted by an expression such as *he said:*

> According to the advertisement, it was the "most spectacular picture of the year."
> "The argument is based," he said, "upon a false premise."

In parentheses.   A complete sentence enclosed in parentheses is always capitalized when it stands alone, but when enclosed *within* another sentence, it usually is not:

> The broadcast, sponsored by a local store, was frequently interrupted by lengthy commercials. (Apparently the sponsor doesn't believe that silence is golden.)
> Fitzhugh was the member of a prominent family (his mother was the granddaughter of Sir Thomas Wyatt) and was received in the highest circles.

Sometimes after a colon.   A complete sentence standing after a colon is not usually capitalized when the connection with the preceding clause is close:

> Indeed, if Galileo had not been so expert an amateur theologian he would have got into far less trouble: the professionals resented his intrusion. — Lynn White, Jr., "The Historical Roots of Our Ecological Crisis."

The sentence after the colon is sometimes capitalized if it is distinctly separate or if the writer wants to give it emphasis:

> Quite a few teachers in the departments of science would tell the

student: **We** scientists deliver the laws of nature to the philosopher, who has to interpret them. — Philipp Frank, *Relativity: A Richer Truth*

In titles of written material.   The first word, the last word, the principal parts of speech (nouns, pronouns, verbs, adjectives, and adverbs), and prepositions of more than five letters are capitalized in the titles of books, magazine articles, themes, and so on:

> *Land of the Silver Birch*   *The Loved and the Lost*
>
> *Canadian Business: Its Nature and Environment*
>
> *Flames Across the Border*

15.1

Cap

I **and** *O.*   The pronoun *I* and the exclamation *O* are always capitalized to prevent their being read as parts of other words:

> Give a man a girl he can love,
>
>   As **I, O** my love, love thee. . . . — James Thomson, "Gifts"

The exclamation *oh* is not capitalized unless it stands first in a sentence.

Capitals for Proper Nouns and Their Derivatives

The names of specific people, places, and things, and the words derived from them are conventionally capitalized (Karl Marx — Marxism; Africa — African sculpture; Lent — Lenten menu). Examples of the most frequent types of proper nouns are given in the following sections.

In a few cases, words originally derived from proper nouns have dropped the capital in the course of frequent use (*pasteurized milk, jersey cloth, french fries*). Usage differs about the capitalization of others (*diesel, levis*). Up-to-date dictionaries provide a guide in such matters, as do the practices of current publications.

Names and titles of people.   A person's name or nickname is capitalized:

William Lyon Mackenzie	Nellie McClung	Wayne Gretzky
Laura Secord	Mindy	Mike Pearson

A title should be capitalized when it is used as part of a person's name, but not when it is used as a descriptive term. A few titles of high rank are usually capitalized whether or not the officeholder is named: the Prime Minister, the Pope, the Queen of England, the Chief Justice of the Supreme Court. Titles referring to a position or an office rather than to the specific person holding it are not capitalized:

Capitals	No capitals
Professor Townsend	Francis Townsend is a professor.
Sergeant David Moore	A sergeant maintains discipline.
Judge **R.A.** Snow	She was appointed judge.
The Captain of the *Skeena* assembled the crew.	The captain of a ship is in full command.
The Queen addressed the opening session of Parliament.	England has had several queens.

Names of family relationships are usually capitalized when used with a person's name or when used as proper nouns standing for the name. They are not capitalized when used as common nouns or when preceded by a possessive:

Capitals	No capitals
Grandma Seton	She is a grandmother.
Aunt Sarah	My aunt's name is Sarah.
I showed Mother the card.	I showed my mother the card.
Whatever **F**ather said, we did.	His father was demanding.

Names of groups.   Names referring to racial, national, linguistic, political, or religious groups are capitalized:

Negro	German	Liberal	Catholic
English	Italian	Conservative	Jew
French	Pole	New Democrat	Moslem
Israeli	Indian	Creditiste	Baptist

Names of social and economic groups are not capitalized (except occasionally for stylistic emphasis):

the middle class   the intelligentsia   the bourgeoisie

Names of organizations.   Names and abbreviations of business associations, clubs, political parties, and other organizations are capitalized:

Canadian Manufacturers Association (**CMA**)
Independent Order of Foresters (**IOOF**)
New Democratic Party (**NDP**)
Canadian National Institute for the Blind (**CNIB**)

Names of places. Words that designate specific geographical divisions or particular places and areas are capitalized:

Asia	Ghana	Hyde Park
European	Albertan	Cabbagetown
Latin America	Victoria	Third Avenue

When the names of directions are used to identify geographic areas, they are generally capitalized. When they merely indicate direction, they are not:

Capitals	No capitals
the old West	west of Suez
a Southerner	a southern exposure
the Far East	eastern Manitoba

15.1

Cap

Names of institutions. The names of specific public and private institutions and their divisions and departments are capitalized. Names that apply to a whole class of institutions are not:

Capitals	No capitals
Fredericton Public Library	a public library
Ontario Health Ministry	public health problems
Smith Falls High School	our high school

Names of government departments are generally capitalized although some newspapers have discontinued the practice:

Department of Recreation   Treasury Ministry

Specific high-school, college, or university courses are capitalized; general subjects are not, except for language courses:

Capitals	No capitals
Modern French Literature	literature
Advanced Narrative Writing	composition
Chemistry 101	chemistry

Names of specific objects. Names of specific objects, such as ships, planes, structures, famous documents and artifacts, and brand-name products are capitalized.

HMCS Nipigon	the Ambassador Bridge
the *Ocean Limited*	Brock's Monument
Chevrolet	Magna Charta

Names of units in time. Capitalize words designating specific periods, events, months, days, and holidays:

the Stone Age	the Norman Conquest	Thursday
the Renaissance	the Battle of Waterloo	Labor Day
the June Ball	January	

Names of seasons are not generally capitalized:

winter   summer   spring   fall   autumn

Sacred names.   References to deities and to sacred texts are capitalized. Pronouns referring to the Christian Trinity are also usually capitalized:

God	Holy Ghost	Talmud
Genesis	Bible	Koran
Virgin Mary	New Testament	Buddha

Abstractions.   Such abstractions as ideas, qualities, or conditions may be capitalized to show that they are being discussed in some ideal or absolute state. Sometimes abstractions are personified, particularly in poetry:

Throughout recorded history, Man has responded to the challenge of Nature.

The pursuit of the Good Life is a persistent human preoccupation.

In general writing, capitalized abstractions are seldom appropriate. Students should confine their use to formal papers of critical analysis or philosophical theory and follow the practices found in readings assigned in the course for which the papers are written.

Distinguishing proper and common forms.   Some words can be spelled either with or without capitals. It is important to distinguish between these forms because they often have different meanings:

Capitals	No capitals
a Conservative (a member of the Conservative Party)	a conservative (one who believes in tradition
a Liberal view (of the Liberal Party)	a liberal view (of a moral issue)
Orthodox beliefs (of the Greek Orthodox Church)	orthodox beliefs (conventional)
Catholic sympathies (of or with the Catholic Church	catholic sympathies (broad; universal)
Romantic poetry (of the Romantic Period)	romantic poetry (concerning romance or love)

▶ **EXERCISE**

In the sentences below, all capital letters have been replaced by lower-case letters. Supply capitals and any other necessary marks wherever you think they are appropriate.

1. added opposition leader joe clark: "this is no time to show weakness."
2. the town of belmonte, perched atop a rocky hilltop in northern portugal, is dominated by a giant stone cross, a ruined castle and the roman catholic church of the holy family.
3. french choreographer maurice bejart had a difficult time casting his ballet rendition of goethe's faust.
4. life's little dilemmas department: the videotaped house of commons question period is being rerun tonight on channel 11 at precisely the same time that channel 5 is broadcasting the stanley cup playoff game.

15.1

Cap

15.2 HYPHENS

Hyph **Insert or remove the hyphen between the marked words to conform to current usage.**

Hyphens are used to connect two or more words used as a single expression (*heavy-hearted, will-o'-the-wisp*) and to keep parts of other words distinct (*anti-inflation*).

Hyphens are needed in some instances to prevent misreading (*un-ionized*) or to differentiate between the same words used in different ways (a *drive in* the evening, a *drive-in* theatre). But generally they are used as a matter of convention (*brother-in-law, hocus-pocus*).

In printed matter the use of hyphens varies considerably: relatively few hyphens are found in newspapers and magazines; more are found in formal writing. The important thing to look for in proofreading is consistency. If an expression is hyphenated the first time it occurs, it should be hyphenated throughout.

This section lists the most common uses of hyphens. (See also 26.2, page 409, Spelling and Word Division.)

Hyphens in Compound Words

A hyphen is used between two or more words considered as a single unit in certain expressions, as discussed below.

Names for family relationships.   Some compound names for family relationships are hyphenated; others are not:

HYPHENATED: father-in-law, great-grandfather, sister-in-law

ONE WORD: stepson, stepmother, grandfather

TWO WORDS: half brother, second cousin

Compound numbers. A hyphen is used in numbers from twenty-one to ninety-nine. Fractions are hyphenated except when the fraction already contains a hyphenated number:

thirty-three

one hundred twenty-eight

twenty-first birthday

four-fifths of a box

one-half inch

one thirty-second of an inch

Compounds with *self*. Most group words beginning with *self* are written with hyphens (*self-contained, self-pity, self-support, self-government*); some words beginning with *self* are written as one word: *selfsame, selfless, selfhood*. Consult an up-to-date dictionary to find out which form is preferred.

Standard compound nouns. A number of compound nouns are regularly written with a hyphen: *bull's-eye, city-state, jack-o'-lantern, secretary-general*. Other similar compounds are written as one word, that is, in block (*beeswax, newsprint, policyholder*) or as two words (*intelligence test, labor union, shipping point, water cooler*).

Since practice is likely to vary with many such compounds, the hyphen is often optional. Where no misreading is apt to arise, some writers would omit the hyphen. Nevertheless, block forms are increasingly common, especially where the first element of the compound carries a heavier stress than the second. When in doubt, consult an up-to-date dictionary.

Hyphens in Group Modifiers

When two or more words act as a closely linked modifier immediately before another word, they are often hyphenated to suggest the close relationship:

gray-green eyes

a **well-kept** lawn

a **nineteenth-century** poet

an **all-out** effort

A hyphen should always be used to prevent a possible misreading:

a **slow-motion** picture

a **navy-blue** uniform

a **pitch-dark** room

some **reclaimed-rubber** plants

When the first word of a group modifier is an adverb ending in -*ly*, no hyphen is used after it:

richly deserved praise   openly antagonistic attitude

Compound modifiers formed with present or past participles are usually hyphenated when they precede a noun:

a **good-looking** man   a **well-planned** attack

Such phrases are not usually hyphenated in other positions:

Her father was good looking.   The attack was well planned.

15.2

Hyph

Long phrases or clauses used as modifiers are hyphenated:

. . . and he offers dramatic recitals about guerrillas (whom he didn't meet) and possible ambushes (which he didn't find), all of it pretty much in the **gosh-we-could-even-hear-the-guns-in-the-distance** school of war reporting. — G. Barrett, "Korean Scenario"

This practice is commonest in informal writing.

Hyphens with Prefixes

Hyphens are used after certain prefixes to follow convention or to prevent ambiguity. Consult an up-to-date dictionary.

1. Between a prefix and a proper name:

    pre-Renaissance   post-Confederation
    anti-Communist   un-Canadian
    ex-Premier Bourassa   pro-German

2. Between some prefixes that end with a vowel and a root word beginning with a vowel, especially if the root word begins with the same vowel:

    re-elected   semi-independent   re-ink   pre-exist

Practice varies at present with respect to certain words beginning with a prefix that is followed by a similar vowel:

co-operation   cooperation   coöperation
re-establish   reestablish   reëstablish

For such words, the best policy is to be consistent in any given piece of writing.

3. To avoid confusing words of similar shape but different meaning; in speech, the prefix of such words is stressed by separating it from the root word with a hyphen:

to **re-cover** a sofa (to *recover* from an illness)
to **re-sort** buttons (a seaside *resort*)

Stressed prefixes also occur in terms like *ex-wife*, *all-Canadian*, *do-gooder*, *Pan-African*.

Suspension Hyphens

The suspension hyphen is often used to carry the modifying expression from one word over to the next:

Two-word forms first acquire the hyphen and later are printed as one word. Quite frequently the transition is from the **two-** to the **one-word** form, bypassing the hyphen stage.

Unnecessary Hyphens

Don't hyphenate a term that is currently written as a single word or as two words. Even if your dictionary lists as alternatives such old-fashioned forms as *to-night* and *post-man*, use the first or preferred form. Here is a brief list of words that you might be tempted to hyphenate:

One word	Separate words
anybody (pronoun)	all right
basketball, baseball, football	class president
bookkeeping	grade curve
footnotes	high school
himself, myself, ourselves	"How do you do?"
nevertheless	motion picture
outdoor	no one
outwit	press agent
overlooked	report card
roundabout	school days
semicolon	single file
taxpayer	six o'clock
timetable	tax rate
today, tomorrow	water pressure
throughout	weather office
weatherman	

▶ **EXERCISE**

Indicate which of the following expressions should be written as separate words, which should be one word, and which should be hyphenated. The words in parentheses indicate the sense in which the expression is intended.

a lot (of work to do)   non communist
base ball   not with standing (a conjunction)

dark horse	over look (to slight or neglect)
every one (is present)	out and out (outright)
flame thrower	pipe wrench
gilt edged	re written
give and take	school board
hydro therapy	self satisfied
in so far as	semi colon
jet black	some body (is missing)
left overs (food)	space craft
man hunt	ten word (telegram)
man of war (a ship)	three quarters (of an inch)
may be (perhaps)	un Canadian
never the less	where abouts (at what place)

15.2

Hyph

15.3 APOSTROPHES

 Insert an apostrophe where it belongs in the marked word, or take out the unnecessary apostrophe.

An apostrophe (') is used in contractions, to mark the plural form of some expressions, and to indicate the possessive case of nouns. Although it is a minor mark that seldom affects the reader's interpretation of a statement, its omission or misuse is noticeable.

Apostrophes in Contractions

Contractions are an attempt to represent the rhythms of speech in written discourse. They are appropriate in dialogue, informal writing, and nowadays in much general writing. Although they are used from time to time in this *Handbook*, remember that many teachers, editors, and readers think that contractions are out of place in formal writing and academic papers.

When a contraction is appropriate in writing, an apostrophe is used to indicate the omission of one or more letters:

can't	I'll	it's (it is)	wasn't
don't	I'm	o'clock	we're
haven't	isn't	shouldn't	won't

Notice that *till* (as in "from morning till midnight") is *not* a shortened form of *until* and no apostrophe is used with it.

An apostrophe is used with dates from which the first figures are omitted (the class of '59, the gold rush of '98). Normally, in formal writing, dates are written in full.

Apostrophes with Possessive Case Forms

An apostrophe is used with the singular and plural forms of nouns and indefinite pronouns to mark the genitive case:

John's car   children's games
Victoria's parks   your parents' permission
a stone's throw   anybody's guess

An apostrophe is *not* used with the possessive forms of the personal pronouns *his, hers, its, ours, yours, theirs:*

the city and **its** suburbs   these seats are **ours**

(See 6.2, page 83, Forms of the Possessive, and 7.3, page 100 Possessive Pronouns.)

Apostrophes for Plurals of Letters and Figures

An apostrophe may be used before an *s* to indicate the plurals of figures, of citation forms, and of letters of the alphabet:

the early 1900's [*or* 1900s]
several size 16's [*or* 16s]

There were three *and*'**s** and two *but*'**s** in that sentence.
There are two *s*'**s** and three *a*'**s** in Saskatchewan.

Apostrophes for Letters Dropped in Representing Speech

An apostrophe is commonly used to indicate the omission of sounds in representing speech:

"Then comes harvest, and that is proper hard work—mowin' and pitchin' hay, and reapin' and bindin' grain, and potato-diggin'. . . ."
—T.C. Haliburton, "The Blowin' Time"

It is unnecessary in representing speech to indicate all such omissions; too many apostrophes make for difficult reading.

▶ **EXERCISE**

In the two paragraphs below, capital letters, apostrophes, and hyphens have been omitted. Insert them where you think they are appropriate.

1. it had been established that the girl had been strangled at about three oclock in the morning. mrs. agnew had declared that she had heard some one moving around the girls apartment shortly before that time, and later had heard

someone with a slow heavy step going along the hall. she had looked out the window; a heavy set man had gone down the street, he didnt walk like a negro, he didnt look like a negro. as far as she was concerned he certainly wasnt a negro. — Morley Callaghan, *The Loved and the Lost* (Macmillan, Laurentian 9, p. 213)

2. armstrongs solution is surely the correct one: if a new model car shows a high incidence of brake failure, we do not conclude that the manufacturer should stop putting brakes into his automobiles, but that he should put in better working ones. armstrong is implicitly arguing, it seems to me, for a wide ranging reform of graduate education, one which would reinstate the ph.d. as a symbol of scholarly and intellectual competence. . . . This is the only answer: the much discussed unease professor peyre describes is real, but it is mostly the dissatisfaction of people who dont know why theyre doing what theyre doing, and who are unhappily convinced that its too late to change. — Adapted from William C. Dowling, "Avoiding the Warmed-Over Dissertation"

15.3

16

Abbreviations and Numbers

Abbreviations and numbers are useful and appropriate in technical, business, and legal documents, as well as in some specialized instances, such as reference works and scholarly footnotes. In a general writing, however, words and figures are usually written out. This chapter discusses the conventions followed in using abbreviations and numbers in most writing.

16.1 ABBREVIATIONS

Ab **Write in full the abbreviation marked or, if an abbreviation is appropriate, change it to the correct form.**

Dictionaries list most current abbreviations, either as regular entries or in a separate section, but they don't indicate when these forms should be used. The following sections discuss the kinds of abbreviations that are appropriate in formal and general writing as well as some forms that should not be used. If you are in doubt whether a particular abbreviation is appropriate, you will usually do better to avoid it.

Abbreviations for Titles, Degrees, and Given Names

The courtesy titles *Dr., Mr., Ms., Mrs.,* and *Messrs.* are always abbreviated when used with proper names, as are *Jr.* and *Sr.: Mrs.* Jean C. Holt, *Mr.* Claude C. Sampson, *Jr.* The convenient *Ms.,* used as a courtesy title equivalent to *Mr.* in addressing a woman without regard for her marital status, must remain an abbreviation, since it was devised as an abbreviation and does not stand for any word. Academic degrees are also generally abbreviated: *M.A., Ph.D., LL.D., M.D., D.D.S.*

Abbreviations of degrees or honorary titles are often placed after a name in formal writing situations. But this is not appropriate if the information added after the name merely duplicates the meaning of the courtesy title used before the name:

William Carey, **M.D.** *or* **Dr.** William Carey [not *Dr.* William Carey, *M.D.*]

James T. Holloway, **Esq.** *or* **Mr.** James T. Holloway [not *Mr.* James T. Holloway, *Esq.*]

If there are different (or variable) kinds of status or qualifications involved, however, it is appropriate to include both references when you want to be very formal:

Professor Jane Campbell, Ph.D.

Professor Michael Purves-Smith, M.Mus.

Reverend Hans Kouwenberg, M.A., B.D.

16.1

ab

In formal writing, titles like *Reverend, Professor, General, Senator, Admiral* are usually written out in full. In most other styles, they may be abbreviated *if* the first name or initials of the person are used:

Standard forms	Forms to avoid
The Reverend James T. Shaw	The Rev. Shaw
The Reverend Mr. Shaw	Rev. Shaw
Rev. J.T. Shaw	The Reverend delivered a sermon.
Professor Jane Campbell	Prof. Campbell
Professor Campbell	Jane Campbell is an English Prof.
Prof. Jane L. Campbell	
General Williams	Gen. Williams
Gen. John Williams	The Gen. was given a new command.

Spell out given names (also known as first names or Christian names) in full, or use initials. Avoid such abbreviations as *Geo., Thos., Chas., Wm.:*

George Thompson *or* G.F. Thompson [not *Geo.* F. Thompson]

Forms of *Saint* are almost always abbreviated when used with a name:

St. Francis, **Ste.** Catherine, **SS.** Peter and Paul, Sault **Ste.** Marie

(Note: **St.** John's, NF, but Saint John, N B)

Abbreviations for Agencies and Organizations

If a government agency or other organization is known primarily by its initials (or by some other shortened name), the writer should generally use the familiar abbreviation rather than the full name:

CBC	CHR	CNIB	CTV Network
NRC	NDP	OHIP	RCMP
UIC	CMHC	IODE	*GPO Style Manual*

Abbreviations that are pronounced as words (called *acronyms*) have become very common: UNESCO, CUPE, CUSO, NATO, DREE, NORAD.

See pages 202 and 203 for discussions of the use of capitals and periods in abbreviations.

Abbreviations for Place Names and Dates

The names of countries, provinces, months, and days are usually written out except in reference works:

Canada	Ghent, Belgium	Wednesday, November 3
United States	Brandon, Manitoba	Christmas [not *Xmas*]

Words like *Street, Avenue,* and *Boulevard* should be written out in general writing, not abbreviated as they might be in addressing a letter.

A few unusually long place names are customarily abbreviated even in rather formal writing: the *USSR;* Barbados, *B.W.I.* (British West Indies); *NT* (Northwest Territories).

Metric abbreviations for the names of the provinces and territories of Canada are as follows:

AB	Alberta		NS	Nova Scotia
BC	British Columbia		ON	Ontario
MB	Manitoba		PE	Prince Edward Island
NB	New Brunswick		PQ	Quebec
NF	Newfoundland		SK	Saskatchewan
NT	Northwest Territories		YT	Yukon Territory

Abbreviations for Units of Measurement

In consecutive writing, most expressions for time, mass, volume, and length are customarily written out in full:

in a second	**rather than**	in a s
in a minute		in a min
hour		h
year		a
four grams		4 g
ten litres		10 L
twenty hectares		20 ha
sixty centimetres		60 cm

The metric units are used in directions, recipes, references, and technical writing: 1 kg butter, 60 cm ribbon, 1 L milk, and so on. No period is used with these metric units.

Abbreviations for Scientific and Technical Terms

Some scientific words, trade names, and other expressions are referred to by their abbreviations when they are familiar to readers and would be needlessly long if written out:

> DDT (in place of **d**ichloro-**d**iphenyl-**t**richloro-ethane)
> ACTH (in place of **a**drenocortico**t**ropic **h**ormone)
> Rh factor (**Rh**esus factor)
> DNA (**d**eoxyribo**n**ucleic **a**cid)
> FM radio (**f**requency **m**odulation radio)

16.1

Ab

If an abbreviation is to be used repeatedly and may not be familiar to every reader, explain it the first time it is introduced:

> The International Phonetic Alphabet, known as the IPA,. . . .
>
> *A Dictionary of Canadianisms on Historical Principles (DCHP).* . . .

Measurements expressed in technical terms are abbreviated when they are used with figures:

> Tests show the car's highest speeds to be 50 km/h [kilometres per hour] in low gear, 70 km/h in second, and 150 km/h in third.
>
> The turntable can be adjusted to play records at either 78, 45, or 33⅓ **rpm** [revolutions per minute].

Expressions of this kind are written without periods. (Note the oblique stroke in km/h.) They are not abbreviated when used without figures:

> The speed of a ship is usually given in knots rather than in **kilometres per hour**.

Other Standard Abbreviations

There are a few standard abbreviations that are used in all levels of writing:

a.m.* and *p.m.   The expressions a.m. (*ante meridiem*, "before noon") and p.m. (*post meridiem*, "after noon") are always abbreviated: 6:00 a.m., 12:24 p.m. Current usage prefers small letters for these abbreviations, but they may be capitalized. Periods are required.

The abbreviations a.m. and p.m. are used only in referring to a specific time:

STANDARD: He had an appointment at 3:00 p.m.

NOT: He had an appointment in the p.m.

The 24-hour clock is coming into general use. The approved form for noon is 12:00 in this system and midnight is 24:00 (or 00:00 the next day): *The sun will set today at 19:27*.

B.C. and A.D.   These expressions are used to distinguish dates in history in reference to the birth of Christ; they are always abbreviated, and periods are required. B.C. means "before Christ," and follows the date; A.D. stands for *anno Domini*, "in the year of our Lord," and *precedes* the date when it is necessary to use it at all.

836 B.C.   A.D. 76   A.D. 1984 (usually 1984 only)

Commonly used Latin expressions.   English has absorbed a number of Latin expressions that are conventionally abbreviated. The following are in common use and should not be italicized:

cf.   *confer* — compare (with another source)
e.g.   *exempli gratia* — for example
etc.   *et cetera* — and so forth (never *and etc.*)
i.e.   *id est* — that is

Many writers prefer the English equivalents for these and similar expressions. In student writing, the overworked catchall *etc.* should be avoided. It is best to use *and so forth* (*and so on, and the like*) or rephrase the list, introducing it with *such as* or a similar qualifier. See also 30.8, page 487, Other abbreviations in footnotes.

The ampersand.   In student writing the ampersand (&) should not be used as a substitute for *and* unless it appears in an official printed expression or title that you are copying: *Quill & Quire, Clarke Irwin & Company, Limited*.

Capitals with Abbreviations

Abbreviations are capitalized when the words they stand for are capitalized or when the abbreviation represents a title:

IODE (Imperial Order Daughters of the Empire)
CAHA (Canadian Amateur Hockey Association)
RCR (Royal Canadian Regiment)
St. Matthew, St. Thomas Aquinas
32 degrees C (Celsius)

When an abbreviation stands for words that would not be capitalized if they were written out, no capitals are needed unless the
abbreviation begins a sentence.

Periods with Abbreviations

A period should be put after the abbreviation of a single word and
usually between the letters of abbreviations for longer terms:

16.1

p.	doz.	M.A.	c.o.d.	Nov.	e.g.
ch.	Lt.	B.A.	Ph.D.	hp.	O.E.D.

Ab

Usage is divided about the punctuation of abbreviated names made
of two or more letters written as a unit. Some publications prefer
periods (*R.M.C., C.B.C.*), but a growing number are using the
solid form (*RMC, CBC*), especially when the abbreviation is
generally used instead of the full name. Some dictionaries list
optional forms. It doesn't make much difference which form you
use as long as you are consistent throughout your paper.

When an abbreviation falls at the end of a sentence, only one
period is used: *He owned a hundred shares of C.G.E.*

16.2 NUMBERS

Num   **Follow conventional usage for words or figures for
numbers; be consistent in the treatment of numbers.**

There are few rules about using figures or words for numbers
occurring in most writing. In general, books and magazines write
out all numbers of one or two digits and also larger numbers that
can be written in two words (*one hundred, six thousand, three
million*). This style is usually appropriate for college papers and for
most other kinds of general and formal writing. Newspapers and
magazines generally use figures for all numbers over ten, and some
scientific and technical publications use figures exclusively.

GENERAL AND FORMAL: four, ten, fifteen, ninety-four, 114, 2000,
22 500, thirty thousand, five million [but usage varies]

INFORMAL: four, ten, 15, 94, 114, 2000, 22 500, 30 000, 5 000 000
(or 5 million)

There are a few special situations (described below) in which figures are always customary. In other cases, use the form that is appropriate not only for your readers but also for your material. In general, write out all simple one-digit and two-digit numbers and round numbers that can be easily read; use figures for numbers that cannot be written in two words and for series of numbers that are to be compared:

WORDS APPROPRIATE: He shot three quail and one rabbit.

FIGURES APPROPRIATE: The next ship unloaded 1500 kilograms of king salmon, 460 kilograms of chinook salmon, and 100 kilograms of crab.

WORDS APPROPRIATE: Five votes were cast for the class president's proposal, twenty-one against it.

FIGURES APPROPRIATE: In Alberta we sold 17 003 units; in Quebec, 10 750; in Ontario, 10 547. Our share of the national market was 87.2 percent.

WORDS APPROPRIATE: If I had ten dollars for every time I've broken one of my resolutions. I would have at least a thousand dollars by now.

FIGURES APPROPRIATE: Dresses in the $25-$35 range were selling well, those from $36-$50 fairly well, and those over $50 hardly at all.

Whichever form you use, be consistent. Don't change needlessly from words to figures or from figures to words in the same piece of writing:

INCONSISTENT: When I was 15, I thought anyone over thirty-five was old.

CONSISTENT: When I was fifteen, I thought anyone over thirty-five was old.

Conventional Uses of Figures

Figures are customarily used in all the following situations:

1. Dates are always written in figures except in formal social correspondence, such as wedding invitations. The forms *1st, 2nd, 3rd*, and so on are sometimes used in dates, but only when the year is omitted:

    October 10, 1976   Oct. 10, 1976   October 10   October 10th

2. Hours are written in figures before a.m. or p.m., but they are spelled out before *o'clock:*

7 a.m.	18:00 hours (24-hour system)	twelve noon
11:35 p.m.	one o'clock	twelve midnight

3. Mathematical and technical numbers, including percentages:

3.141 59	longitude 74°02′E.
99.8 percent, 99.8%	.410 gauge shotgun

Except in dates and street numbers, a space is used to separate thousands, millions, and so on, although it may be omitted in four-digit figures: **16.2**

Num

    1365 (or 1 365) years   8 393 624   17 016

Many people still use commas (instead of spaces) for this purpose. (See 11.6, Commas in Conventional Places.)

4. Page numbers and similar references:

pp. 183-86	page 12
chapter iv	Genesis 39:12
Ch. 19	Act III, scene iv, line 28 (III, iv. 28)

5. Sums of money, except sums in round numbers or, in formal style, sums that can be written in two or three words:

Figures	**Words**
a bargain at $4.98	two thousand a year
The British pound was once worth $4.85.	a dollar a litre

6. Street numbers (with no spaces between thousands):

2027 Fairview North   Apartment 3C, 1788 Grand North

7. Statistics and series of more than two numbers, especially when the numbers are to be compared:

The survey showed that the class contained 24 Liberals, 18 Conservatives, and 12 New Democrats.

Numbers at the beginning of sentences.   These numbers are written out unless they are dates:

Two to 3% of loading and up to 10% is common and 20 to 30% in specially surfaced papers. . . . — "Paper Manufacture," *Encyclopaedia Britannica*

1960 was a year of devastating drought in China.

Arabic and Roman Numerals

Arabic numerals (1, 2, 17, 96) are used in almost all cases where numbers are expressed in figures. Roman numerals, either lower case or capitals (i, ii, cxlvi; I, II, CXLVI), are occasionally used to number outlines, chapters, acts of a play, or formal inscriptions. Lower-case roman numerals are used to number the front matter of a book, pagination in Arabic numerals beginning with the body of the book.

In Roman numerals a small number preceding a larger is to be subtracted from the larger (ix = 9, xc = 90). The following table shows the common Roman numerals (lower-case):

1	i	10	x	50	l	200	cc
2	ii	11	xi	60	lx	400	cd
3	iii	15	xv	70	lxx	500	d
4	iv	19	xix	80	lxxx	600	dc
5	v	20	xx	90	xc	900	cm
6	vi	21	xxi	99	xcix	1000	m
7	vii	30	xxx	100	c	1500	md
8	viii	40	xl	110	cx	1900	mcm
9	ix	49	xlix	199	cxcix	1983	mcmlxxxiii

Cardinal and Ordinal Numbers

Figures indicating number only are *cardinal numbers: 1, 2, 3, 72, 135*. The numbers indicating order (*first, second, seventeenth*) are *ordinal numbers*. Except in routine enumeration, ordinals should be spelled out rather than abbreviated to *1st, 2nd, 17th*.

Since the ordinals can be either adjectives or adverbs, the forms ending in *-ly (firstly)* are unnecessary and are now rarely used.

▶ **EXERCISE**

Read the following sentences carefully, keeping in mind the principles stated in the preceding section. Rewrite faulty forms making whatever changes are necessary. Since there is sometimes a choice in usage, remember that one of the principles of using numbers and abbreviations is to be consistent:

1. When we arrived at the theatre on Yonge St., we found that the evening's performance would start an hr. late.
2. The University recently added 2 new members to its faculty — Jos. Blumenthal, MA, and Mary Persons, Doctor of Philosophy.
3. Six members of the RCMP conferred recently with Canada's U.N. Representative at his office in N.Y.

4. Fifty-five to 60% of U. of M. students approved the 02:00 curfew; about 30% were violently opposed.

5. His monument to St. Francis, a remarkable piece of sculpture, weighed over 2500 lbs. and rivalled his monument to Saint Peter.

6. P. 237 of the manual lists the home addresses of Members of Parliament & p. 298 lists their Ottawa addresses.

7. On Dec. 23 CBC will dramatize the most celebrated Xmas story of recent times — "The Christmas Carol" by Chas. Dickens.

8. Dr. Roscoe Caries, D.D.S., reported that in an experiment involving two thousand and forty-two children, tooth decay was not significantly reduced.

9. Lee had 4 sisters (ranging in age from sixteen to 31 yrs.) and a widowed mother.

10. After 10 months the RCMP finally tracked Groark to Springwater, SK where they found him suffering from d.t.'s in the barn of the Rev. John Gantry.

16.2

Num

17

Spelling

This recommendation of steadiness and uniformity [in spelling] *does not proceed from an opinion that particular combinations of letters have much influence on human happiness; or that truth may not be successfully taught by modes of spelling fanciful and erroneous. . . . Language is only the instrument of science, and words are but the signs of ideas; I wish, however, that the instrument might be less apt to decay, and that signs might be permanent. — Samuel Johnson*

Sp   **Correct the spelling of the marked word.**

For college and university writing, and for much other writing, this text recommends edited English, as typical in Canada. One purpose of editing is to make the use of language consistent, so that, for example, if a writer uses the word *co-exist* seven times in an essay, it will always be spelled in the same way. Another purpose of editing is, if it does not interfere with some purpose of the writer, to eliminate errors and unconventional usages.

One feature of language that often requires careful editing is spelling. Sometimes people talk about spelling as if it were some monstrous and unnatural act. It isn't that, but it isn't always easy. Some people spell well; others do not. Accurate spelling doesn't appear to have any direct connection with good writing. But good *edited* writing is characterized by accurate spelling. Out of regard for yourself and for your reader, you should make certain that whatever you write is as free from error as possible. You want your reader to see the same word that you intended to write, and your reader is entitled to expect that you will follow the conventions of spelling. Misspelled words seldom interfere with meaning, but they may distract the reader from what you are trying to say, or, worse, lead him or her to assume that if you don't care about your spelling, you don't care about what you are saying.

17.1 OVERCOMING SPELLING PROBLEMS

English spelling would be easier if each sound used in speaking were represented by a single letter or even by a combination of letters. But the way a word is pronounced and the way it is spelled do not always match. The same letter or combination of letters may represent a variety of sounds, as does the *a* in *fare, hat, many, lay, far, war, human*, or the *ou* in *though, bough, enough, through*. And one sound may be represented in a variety of ways: b*ee*, beli*e*ve, prec*e*de, s*ea*, mach*i*ne. As a further complication, a number of English words are written with silent letters: lam*b*, *p*sychology, *k*nife, r*h*ythm, *w*rote. Others, called *homonyms*, sound alike but are spelled differently: *meat, meet, mete; sight, site, cite; write, right, rite; peace, piece*.

Obviously, absolute correctness in spelling is not easy to achieve in English. Most mistakes can be avoided, however, if you are willing to take the time and effort necessary

1. to learn the spelling of difficult words,
2. to use the dictionary when you are in doubt, and
3. to proofread what you have written.

Eliminating Careless Mistakes

17.1

Carelessness undoubtedly accounts for the majority of misspelled words in student papers. It may result from too rapid writing (as in papers written in class) or from failure to proofread the finished copy carefully. Typical examples of careless misspelling are *their* for *there, to* for *too, who's* for *whose, it's* for *its, fourty* for *forty*— basic words that you learned before entering high school. Most people make careless mistakes when writing rapidly, but conscientious writers eliminate them by proofreading.

Accurate proofreading requires careful word-by-word reading. If you have difficulty checking your own writing, try following each line with a pencil point, so that you have to look at every word separately. Some people find it helpful to read their papers aloud, pronouncing each word distinctly. Any method is useful if it makes easier the obligation to be accurate as to what has actually been put down on paper.

Using a Dictionary

If you are uncertain about the spelling of a word, consult your dictionary. The trial-and-error method of writing a word several ways until it "looks right" (*curiousity? couriousity? curosity?*) is unreliable.

For papers written outside class, it is probably best to check spelling in *revision*. If you stop to look up the spelling of every doubtful word while you are writing a first draft, you may lose the flow of thought or interrupt the sentence movement. Put a check in the margin or over the word as you are writing; then when you are ready to revise, look up each word you have marked.

Learning to Visualize Words

People who do a good deal of reading tend to be better spellers than those who read little, for seeing a word on the printed page tends to fix it in the mind. Sometimes, however, we learn to recognize a word in reading without noticing how it is spelled. Very few Canadians, for example, ever learned to spell the last name of Nikita Khrushchev, the former Soviet premier, though they saw it in their newspapers every day for years. Many people have a similar problem with such common English words as *occasion*, *occurrence*, and *precede*. When you meet a new word—or when you have to look up a familiar word—look at it carefully, noticing each syllable, and try to fix it in your mind for future use.

Writing Practice

If you are willing to take the time, you can often get the spelling of troublesome words straight in your mind by writing them until you spell them right without hesitation. It sounds like a tedious process, but probably worth the time if it enables you to become comfortable with words so that you can use them. If you are uncertain about the spelling of *embarrass*, for example, write or type the word ten, twenty, or more times, in its various forms, until the spelling becomes automatic: *embarrass, embarrassed, embarrassment, embarrassing.*

Separate into syllables words that you find difficult to spell (consult your dictionary for the proper divisions). Stress those letters or combinations of letters that trouble you:

em baR Rass	par aL Lel
oC Ca sion al ly	preJ U dice
o MiT Ted	rep E ti tion
op tI mist	sep A rate

It helps to say the word as you write it, either aloud or to yourself. The combination of (1) seeing a word letter by letter, (2) writing it carefully, and (3) pronouncing it will overcome most spelling problems.

Learning New Words

Learn to spell new words as you meet them, especially in your courses. A new or unfamiliar expression is of little use in writing until you can spell it with confidence. Make a note of the words you may have to use in essays, reports, or examinations. Underline key words in textbooks and observe their spelling on the blackboard. Then write them out in syllables, pronouncing them as you do so:

ba cil lus	de men tia prae cox	pro pri e tar y
bi par tite	Gen ghis Khan	u ni cel lu lar
car bon if er ous	me tath e sis	

When instructors in various courses complain that their students can't spell, they are usually referring either to very common words or to words that make up the essential vocabulary of their subject.

Keeping a Spelling List

You can help yourself in proofreading if you will keep a list of words you have misspelled or that you have trouble spelling. The words should be spelled correctly and should be easy to find so that you can refer to them when proofreading your papers. The purpose of such a list is to prevent the same mistakes from occurring in one paper after another. When the same word occurs more than once in your list, mark it in some way that will call it to your attention.

17.2 ◀

Sp

17.2 COMMON SPELLING ERRORS

The following list contains one hundred words frequently misspelled in student papers. Each word is divided into syllables so that you can see more clearly how it is put together.

ac com mo date	din ing room	lei sure
ac quaint ed	dis ap pear ance	li brar y
a cross	dis ap point	lik a ble
a gree ment	dor mi to ry	main te nance
all right (two words)	em bar rass	man u fac tur er
al read y	en vi ron ment	mis spelled
a nal y sis	e quip ment	mo not o nous
ap pear ance	ex ag ger ate	mys te ri ous
ar ti cle	ex ist ence	nec es sary
ath let ics	ex treme ly	no tice a ble
at tend ance	fa mil iar	oc ca sion al ly
be lieve	fas ci nate	oc cur rence
ben e fit ed	for eign	o mit ted
Brit ain	for mer ly	op por tu ni ty
bus i ness	for ty	par tic u lar ly
change a ble	gram mar	pas time
choose	height	per form
com par a tive	hin drance	pre ced ing
con ceive	im ag i nar y	prej u dice
con science	im me di ate ly	priv i lege
con tin u ous	in ci den tal ly	prob a bly
de ci sion	in de pend ent	pro ce dure
def i nite	in tel li gent	pro nun ci a tion
de gen er ate	ir re sist i ble	pro por tion
de scrip tion	judg ment [*or* judge ment]	psy chol o gy
de vel op	knowl edge	quan ti ty

re ceive	sim i lar	trag e dy
re fer ring	soph o more	tru ly
rep e ti tion	suc ceed	un doubt ed ly
re sem blance	sym pa thize	un til
sched ule	tem per a ment	u su al ly
sec re tar y	tend en cy	val u able
seize	there fore	writ ing
sep a rate		

You may find this list useful in testing your spelling ability and in checking and correcting errors in your papers. A spelling list of your own, however, will be more profitable to study than lists made by others, because it will help you to concentrate on your individual problems.

Errors Caused by Faulty Pronunciation

Although faulty pronunciation is not a major cause of misspelling, it is responsible for some very common mistakes:

Correct spelling	Misspelling
ath let ics	athaletics
priv i lege	privlege
en vi ron ment	enviroment
mis chie vous	mischievious
pre scribe	perscribe
dis gust	discust
re mu ner a tion	renumeration

Pronounce each syllable to yourself when writing longer words (*ac-com-pa-ny-ing, par-tic-u-lar-ly, stud-y-ing*). Also notice that many longer words contain letters that are neutralized or lost in speech: tem-per-*a*-men-tal, ac-ci-den-*tal*-ly, lab-*o*-ra-to-ry.

Omission of Final -ed

One of the most common spelling errors is the omission of *-ed* at the ends of words. This sometimes occurs because of analogy to speech, where the *-ed* sound often is lost in rapid conversation by assimilation to the following sound. To catch such errors in writing, you will have to rely on your eye rather than your ear. There are three principal trouble areas:

In verb forms.   Regular verbs form their past tenses and past participles by adding *-ed*. Be careful not to drop these letters, especially before words beginning with *t*, like *to*. *Used to* and *supposed to* are commonly misspelled.

I **used to** [not *use to*] misspell words.

He is **supposed to** be [not *suppose to* be] an authority.

In verbal modifiers. The past participle is often used as a modifier (*stewed prunes, raised platform*). Here too the tendency in pronunciation is to drop the *-ed*, and many such shortened forms have become established: *grade school, oilcloth, cream cheese, roast chicken*. Others are sometimes found in print but are debatable: *bottle beer, whip cream, advance headquarters*. In college and university papers, use only shortened forms that are generally accepted. In less formal writing, more latitude is allowed, but dictionaries, current written practice, and appropriateness to the paper should serve as guides.

17.2

In modifiers from nouns. Adjectives are often formed by adding *-ed* to nouns: *long-haired, heart-shaped, two-faced*. When the *-ed* is dropped in such forms—a growing tendency in current English—the result is a noun modifier (see 6.4): *king-size bed, hard-surface road, high-heel shoes*. Established forms like these are appropriate in all writing. It's usually better, however, to keep the *-ed* (as in *advanced courses, middle-aged, old-fashioned*) unless you have seen the form without the *-ed* in edited English.

Confusion of Words That Sound Alike

Be careful not to confuse words of identical or similar sound. It is easy when writing rapidly to put down *their* for *there*, *its* for *it's*, *maybe* for *may be*, but conscientious writers will check their finished work closely for errors of this sort. Substituting one form for another may suggest an idea that the writer did not intend:

> Psychiatric treatment changed Bobby from a withdrawn, unhappy child to a normal, happy boy **excepted** by his group.

The following pairs of words are often confused in writing. See if you can distinguish between them.

accept-except	coarse-course	principal-principle
advice-advise	credible-creditable	quiet-quite
affect-effect	desert-dessert	stationary-stationery
aisle-isle	its-it's	than-then
allusion-illusion	lead-led	their-there
birth-berth	loose-lose	to-too
capital-capitol	passed-past	their-there
choose-chose	peace-piece	weather-whether
cite-site	personal-personnel	who's-whose
conscience-conscious		

▶ **EXERCISE**

Make up sentences that will illustrate clearly the differences in meaning in the paired words above.

Examples: Everyone *except* Sam *accepted* the invitation.
It's difficult for the leopard to change *its* spots.
The ceremonies will be held *whether* or not the *weather* is fair.

Separate Words and Combined Forms

Observe the distinctions between expressions that are written as
one word and those written as two. These forms frequently need to
be checked in revision:

all ready [adjective phrase]: The girls were at last **all ready** to leave.

already [adverb of time]: It was **already** dark when they arrived.

all right [adjective phrase, conventionally written as two words]: The
seats seemed **all right** to me. (The forms *alright* and *alrite* are not
accepted in edited usage.)

all together [adjective phrase]: We were **all together** at the depot.

altogether [adverb, meaning wholly]: That's **altogether** another
matter.

a while [noun]: They talked for **a while.**

awhile [adverb]: Can't you stay **awhile** longer?

may be [verb phrase]: He **may be** the next mayor.

maybe [adverb, short for *it may be*]: **Maybe** you'll have better luck
next time.

Certain phrases may be mistakenly written as one word through
analogy with other forms or because they are often run together in
speech:

The assignment was **a lot** more difficult than I expected. [not *alot*,
which is a non-standard form]

The judge **threw out** his testimony. [not *throughout*]

The puppy was always there at his owner's **beck and call**. [not
beckon call]

17.3 SPELLING TROUBLESOME PLURALS

Nouns Ending in -y, -o, or -f

Nouns ending in -y following a vowel form the plural regularly by
adding -s (*toys, bays, joys, monkeys*). But nouns ending in -y
preceded by a consonant change y to i and add -es to form the
plural:

apology, apolog**ies**	curiosity, curiosit**ies**	library, librar**ies**
company, compan**ies**	ferry, ferr**ies**	study, stud**ies**

Exception: In forming the plural of proper names, the -y is retained
and -s added: all the *Kellys*, both *Marys*.

Nouns ending in *-o* preceded by a vowel form the plural by adding *-s (folios, studios, tattoos)*. If the final *-o* is preceded by a consonant, the plural is usually formed by adding *-es*, but a few nouns add *-s* only:

echoes	potatoes		pianos	sopranos
heroes	tomatoes	But:	solos	tobaccos
cohoes	vetoes		banjos	Eskimos

A few nouns ending in *-o* add either *-s* or *-es* to form the plural: *cargos, cargoes; hobos, hoboes; zeros, zeroes*. Because no rule can be given for adding *-s* or *-es*, a writer must either memorize the plurals or consult a dictionary.   **17.3**

Nouns ending in *-f* or *-fe* often form the plural regularly (*beliefs, chiefs, fifes, roofs*). But some common words ending in *-f* form their plurals by changing *-f* to *-ves:*

calf, calves	knife, knives	self, selves
half, halves	leaf, leaves	thief, thieves

The plural of a few nouns ending in *-f* may be either *-s* or *-ves: elfs, elves; hoofs, hooves; scarfs, scarves; wharfs, wharves*.

Group Words and Compound Nouns

Most compound words and group words form their plurals by adding *-s* to the last word of the group, whether the expression is written as one word or two:

Singular	Plural
baby-sitter	baby-sitters
cross-examination	cross-examinations
major-general	major-generals

But when the significant word is the first term (as it often is in hyphened compounds), that word is the one made plural:

daughters-in-law	passers-by
men-of-war	courts-martial

The plural of nouns ending in *-ful* is made by adding *-s* to the last part of the word: ten *handfuls* of rose petals; several *shovelfuls* of topsoil; three *teaspoonfuls* of paprika; two *pocketfuls* of marbles.

17.4 SOME PRINCIPLES OF SPELLING

Chaotic as spelling is in English, some principles are helpful for spelling common words. Listed below are guides to spelling that you have probably heard before. If you *know* that you know them, you might better spend your time on some other aspect of writing. But if you aren't quite certain about these general principles, review them and perhaps consult the spelling section in the front pages of a dictionary for detailed information.

Final -e

Words ending in silent -e generally retain the -e before additions (called *suffixes*) beginning with a consonant (-*ment, -ly, -some, -ness*), but drop the -e before additions beginning with a vowel (-*ing, -able, -ous, -ary*).

-e retained before the consonant:

arrange-arrangement	nine-ninety
awe-awesome	require-requirement
definite-definitely	shape-shapeless
hope-hopeless	spite-spiteful

Exceptions:
argument   awful   duly   ninth   truly

-e dropped before another vowel:

argue-arguing	imagine-imaginary
arrive-arrival	shape-shaping
conceive-conceivable	value-valuable
grieve-grievous	write-writing

Exceptions: In a few words, -e is kept before a vowel to avoid confusion with other forms or to indicate pronunciation:

dye	dyeing	(compare *dying*)
singe	singeing	(compare *singing*)

Words ending in -ce or -ge retain the final -e before additions beginning with *a, o,* or *ou* (so that the final -c or -g will not suggest the "hard" sound):

changeable	noticeable	unmanageable
courageous	outrageous	vengeance

-ie- and -ei-

The familiar jingle learned by most schoolchildren is helpful in spelling -*ie*- and -*ei*- words: "Write *i* before *e* except after *c*, or when sounded as *ā* as in *neighbor* and *weigh*."

Words with -ie-.   Words with -*ie*- are more common than words with -*ei*-. The typical sound of -*ie*- is *ē*:

achieve	chief	grievous	niece
believe	field	hygiene	siege

Other -*ie*- words are *mischief, sieve,* and *view.*

Words with -*ei*-.   After *c,* and also to spell the sound *ā,* -*ei*- is generally used:

ceiling	perceive	eight	reign
conceive	receipt	freight	vein
deceive	receive	neighbor	weigh

The long *ē* sound is spelled -*ei*- (rather than -*ie*-) in a few words: *either, leisure, neither, seize, weird.* Other sounds spelled -*ei*-: *counterfeit, foreign, height, heir.*

17.4

Sp

Doubling the Final Consonant

Double the final consonant before a suffix beginning with a vowel (-*able,* -*ed,* -*er,* -*ing*) with (1) words of one syllable ending in a single consonant after a single vowel (*brag, hit, sit*) and (2) with words of more than one syllable, ending the same way and accented on the last syllable (*commit, forget, prefer, occur*).

One-syllable words			Words of more than one syllable		
bat	batter	batting	commit	committed	committing
grip	gripping	gripped	control	controllable	controlled
pin	pinned	pinning	occur	occurrence	occurred
spot	spotty	spotted	omit	omitted	omitting
wet	wetter	wettest	prefer	preferred	preferring

The consonant is *not* doubled (1) in words with two vowels before the final consonant (*daub, daubing; keep, keeper; spoil, spoiled*), or (2) in words ending with two consonants (*help, helped; peck, pecking; lurk, lurked*), or (3) when the accent of the lengthened word shifts to an earlier syllable (*infer', in'ference; prefer', pref'erable; refer', ref'erence*).

Usage is divided about doubling the final consonant of some words not accented on the last syllable, but Canadians generally prefer the forms having doubled consonants:

bias-biassed	quarrel-quarrelling
counsel-counselled, counsellor	travel-traveller, travelled
diagram-diagrammed	worship-worshipped, worshipping
kidnap-kidnapping, kidnapper	

Final -*y*

A final -*y* preceded by a consonant regularly changes to *i* before all suffixes except those beginning with *i:*

body-bodies	happy-happiness
busy-business	lonely-loneliness
carry-carried, carrying	marry-marriage, marrying
duty-dutiful	mercy-merciful
easy-easily	study-studious, studying
envy-envious	Tory-Tories

Final -y preceded by a vowel remains unchanged when a suffix is added:

boy-boys, boyish	enjoy-enjoyable, enjoyment, enjoying
delay-delayed, delayer	play-playful, playing, played

See also 17.3, Spelling Troublesome Plurals.

-cede, -ceed, -sede

Only one word ends in -sede: supersede. Only three end in -ceed: exceed, proceed, succeed. All other words of this sort end in -cede: precede, recede, intercede, secede, and so on.

-able, -ible, -ance, -ence

Words with these endings should be carefully checked for correct spelling. Those ending in -able (such as advisable, desirable, improbable, suitable) are much more common than those ending in -ible (such as audible, divisible, horrible, visible). But since no English rules govern the spelling of these endings, and each has a similar neutral vowel in pronunciation, the individual words should be looked up in a dictionary whenever there is doubt. The same is true for words ending in -ance, -ant, -ence, and -ent (such as attendance, confidence; defendant, existent).

17.5 VARIANT SPELLINGS

For a number of historical reasons, many English words have two spellings in current use, for instance, whisky, whiskey; storey, story (of a building); extol, extoll; skilful, skillful. A good dictionary indicates which is the more usual by placing that form first (as expellant or expellent). Secondary spellings that are archaic or rare will be given at the end of the entry, as will variants having much less currency than the form or forms given as entry words.

Students should make a habit of using the word given first (such as *judgment* rather than *judgement*), but they must remember that the editors are presenting as preferable the form used most commonly in the speech community the dictionary is intended for, as the United Kingdom (British usage), the United States (American usage), or Canada (Canadian usage).

As explained in this *Handbook*'s prefatory article entitled "Canadian English" (page xvi), Canadians have special spelling dilemmas as a result of being exposed to those strongly influential patterns of spelling, British and American. As a result, Canadian usage in spelling certain words and classes of words is divided. In some words, we use spellings similar to the British pattern, in others to the American pattern.

17.5

This Canadian way of spelling, largely followed in printed matter, slavishly follows neither the British nor the American way. This being the case, Canadian dictionaries are much more reliable than any others for Canadian writers of English. Unfortunately, there are very few such dictionaries so that Canadians often buy dictionaries not specifically intended to reflect usage in Canada. If you must use a non-Canadian dictionary, then be aware of what you are using and make allowances for the intent of those who compiled the dictionary.

In most situations, either of two possible current spellings may be used; the important point is to remain consistent in using the chosen form throughout any one piece of writing. Thus one may choose *honor* or *honour, centre* or *center, plough* or *plow* as long as one spells those words (and any others in the same class) in a consistent way; thus if you choose to spell *honor* with *-or*, you should also spell *labor, color*, and so on in the same way.

Certain forms are not at all commonly used in Canadian writing; these should be avoided, as *ax, adz, sox* (for *socks*), *check* (for *cheque*), *connexion, gaol*, and many more. On the other hand, *draft* or *draught, mold* or *mould, medieval* or *mediaeval, program* or *programme, plow* or *plough*, and so on are widely met with in Canada, where certain spellings are preferred because of their associations; *defence* (not *defense*) is the traditional spelling in government circles, as in the *Department of National Defence*. And *Inuit* (not *Innuit*) is gradually displacing *Eskimo* in official circles. Many French words having accents in the spelled form (*Québec, Montréal, parti Québécois*) are nowadays accepted with or without accents when used in English contexts. Accents should be retained in some anglicized words; for example, the noun *résumé* (an outline of personal data) might otherwise be confused with the verb *resume* (to begin again).

Simplified spellings such as *thru* for *through, enuf* for *enough*, *thoro* for *thorough, nite* for *night*, and so on are not acceptable in edited English anywhere.

For the spelling of proper names (the British *Labour* Party; the *Center* for Applied Linguistics) and for direct quotation (Prime Minister Winston Churchill described it as "a *humourless* situation"; President Carter said he would "give the bill the *ax*"), the spelling of the original should be used; but in normal circumstances, Canadian forms should be used.

▶ EXERCISES

1. This exercise should help to fix some of the general principles of spelling in your mind. Copy the words in each of the following groups, making the additions or changes indicated:

    a. Supply *-ei-* or *-ie-* as required for correct spelling:

    all— —d   counterf— —t   fr— —ght   n— —ther   th— —r
    bel— —ve   for— —gn   l— —sure   s— —ze   w— —rd

    b. Add *-ed* to the following verbs to show whether the final consonant is doubled or not. If there is a choice of forms, indicate both of them:

    bargain   clot   drop   quarrel   travel
    bias   ship   differ   refer   occur

    c. Adding *-ing* to each of these words, making any necessary changes in the root form of the word:

    become   control   endure   hurry   use
    centre   dine   hope   prove   write

    d. Change each of these words to an adjective ending *-ous:*

    continue   courtesy   glory   mischief   sanctimony
    courage   dispute   grieve   outrage

    e. Add *-able* or *-ible* to the following words, changing letters wherever necessary to conform with accepted spellings:

    accept   contempt   enforce   repair   train
    advise   digest   justify   sense

    f. Add *-ance, -ant* or *-ence, -ent* to these words, making any other necessary changes:

    ascend   confide   depend   maintain   vigil
    compete   defend   exist   resist

2. Copy the following paragraph, correcting the misspelled words. Feel free to consult a dictionary. You may first wish to see how many mistakes you can find and correct without a dictionary.

    The principal that every great man is a national tradgedy is easily defensable. It is difficult to conceive that strong, independant men will not irresistably impose upon their countrymen their own exagerated eccentricities and prejadices. Napoleon, for example, beleived that he had a definate destiny to succede, a "star" guiding him personaly and France to great heighths. He did not dream of hinderance from the other nations of Europe. His plans were to seperate them one by one and to seize all power and priveledge. Only Britian refused to acommodate itself to his grandoise schemes.

PART TWO

The Writing Process

18

Discovering What
You Have to Say

The rule is, first think, and then write; don't write when you have nothing to say or, if you do, you will make a mess of it. — John Henry Newman, "The Idea of a University"

All of us have things to say, although often we don't know it. What we have to say on any particular subject is rarely at the front of our minds, fresh, fully realized, compelling, ready to be expressed. This unprimed condition is perfectly natural, not something that anyone should find embarrassing or discouraging. In fact, even the frustrations of "writer's block," when properly understood, are more likely to yield a useful or satisfying analysis of any complex matter than instant opinions are. Most easy answers have little substance, sincerity, or value, and lucky inspirations strike few of us when we need them. Although general impressions and familiar facts can usually be produced at a moment's notice, a worth-while *idea* is generated only through thoughtful questioning of what we know.

Even on matters of special interest to us (a personal experience, a hobby, a career objective, an anxiety), our thoughts are surprisingly vague and chaotic until something prompts us to begin sorting them out more exactly in words. The nature of that "something" inducing us to start calling up and clarifying our undeveloped ideas can vary greatly, but normally it is in the pressure of some specific need or occasion (a course project, a problem assigned at work, a public issue, or perhaps even a personal whim). Whatever the situation is, and no matter how long or short the paper is expected to be, we nearly always have to work at *discovering* in advance what to say. We can't interest a reader until we have interested ourselves, and this means exploring our place in the world, testing our personal resources, weighing our judgments and hunches, and evaluating our information. By such a wide-ranging process, made efficient through experiment and practice, we learn how to coax something worth saying out of a profusion of indistinct thoughts and feelings.

It should be kept in mind that this part of the book will be concerned with a somewhat different conception of "good writing" than was covered in Part I. The various chapters of Part I described the basic forms and conventions of the English language itself, and a sound grasp of those matters is certainly essential for successful writing. But in Part II we will see how even the most conventional or "correct" English can be considered "poor writing" if it isn't doing its job; that is, if it expresses little or nothing that is worth reading. A truly effective treatment of any subject begins long before you need to worry about editing, and no amount of "proper" usage will make up for the slightness of a paper thrown together without energetic forethought. Good writing begins when you start looking hard at your experiences and knowledge to determine what they add up to, when you gradually realize what parts of your subject matter to you, and when those emerging insights take some distinctive shape in your own words. Only after this *prewriting* process of discovery and sifting, of sorting and selecting is it sensible to turn to the planning, composing, and, finally, the editing of the product itself.

18.1

18.1 FINDING SOMETHING YOU WANT TO SAY

Plan

From the start, whether you are in a university course or doing some other work that requires writing, you can expect to spend more time in preliminary thinking and hunting than you do in drafting the paper. Of course, your exploratory work will almost certainly involve writing things down—miscellaneous rough notes, scribbled ideas, tentative lists, even half-controlled free writing or doodles. But all this precedes your first continuous draft. Hence, this chapter describes what is often called *prewriting*, the stage of inquiry and struggle that most experienced writers go through in one way or another even before attempting a rough draft.

Forming a habit of more or less systematic prewriting activities can make all the difference between successful and unsuccessful projects. Ancient rhetoricians called this deliberate searching process *invention*, and it's a good word to use. It comes from a Latin verb, *invenire*, which has several shades of meaning:

1. to discover or find;
2. to come upon or meet with, to encounter;
3. to fabricate mentally, to create or devise in the mind.

Hence, *invention* is the name for the mental actions by which you come upon, or meet, your own experiences and thoughts, the things you know, and the things other people know. You *make* something out of them in your mind by examining what they mean to you and how they fit together. In short, you learn what your attitude towards and knowledge of the assigned subject really is; this is the first step in deciding what you want to say.

The commonest habit of ineffective writers is working aimlessly, or beginning a draft too soon. They simply accept and express whatever facts, impressions, and opinions first come to mind, and they seem to have nothing in particular to say *about* those things. The problem is that having a topic doesn't always make it possible for you to write, or give you a reason for writing. If you are assigned a vague topic like "My Last Summer Job" or "The Energy Crisis," you must somehow decide in advance what you have to say and why it is worth while to say it. Writing without a reason is a waste of your time (and your reader's). Consider the following brief essay, composed in a first-year university writing course:

My Theatre Experience

I worked at a theatre before coming to university. When my parents started managing the drive-in, they drafted me to do the odd jobs there.

While working in the cafeteria, box office, and the projection booth, I met many new people. One man said that he came to get away from his wife and kids. Many boys and girls came to have dates. A few people, however, actually came to watch the movie.

At the drive-in, I felt different emotions because of the actions of my customers. One lady claimed that her son, who was six feet in height, was under twelve years of age. A boy eleven years old does not have to pay admission; therefore her son was admitted free. One boy tried to hide in the back floor of a car, under a quilt, while the driver drove into the theatre. I am aware of such tricks, and the boy was caught. One girl caught her slacks on the barbed wire while climbing over the fence at the back of the theatre. She never came over the fence again.

I experienced entertaining and enlightening experiences at the drive-in theatre.

The author of this piece knows roughly where his subject is, and he has put some promising things on paper in "correct" English. But he doesn't appear to have looked at his experiences very closely, and we're left wondering what the *purpose* of the paper might be. Generalities like "enlightening" or "entertaining" or "I met many new people" don't tell us much. What is really unique about working at a drive-in theatre? Exactly what "different emotions" did the writer feel? What is the relevance of that girl who caught her slacks on the fence? What is the writer's attitude towards all these things? How has his drive-in experience entered his life or "enlightened" him about human nature? And what is a reader supposed to conclude from so offhand an account? Has either the writer or the reader gained anything from the paper? Altogether, it would seem that more time should have been spent before writing in remembering episodes and behavior patterns and in reflecting on what they might mean.

But how should prewriting be done? How do you get invention started? And when is it time to actually begin writing? This chapter makes some suggestions, but there is no way to tell which of these (or other) approaches will work best for you. Every person probably has a different style of exploration, and much also depends on the nature of the subject concerned. Some techniques are quite formulaic, while others that may seem haphazard can turn out to be equally fruitful. Be prepared to experiment with (and adapt or combine) the methods explained in the following pages, remembering that you will eventually establish your own strategies of invention by seeing what succeeds for you.

18.1

Collecting Your Impressions

Plan

The two different stages of prewriting are *finding* and *exploring*. It is obviously impossible to explore something before you have found it, yet to find is not the same thing as to explore (as the drive-in essay shows). The rest of this section is about ways of *finding* something worth exploring—generating and collecting enough details (facts, impressions, experiences, opinions) to stimulate and support the more thorough examination of your subject that will come later. (See 18.2, Some Ways of Thinking About Your Subject.)

Keeping a journal.   This activity which may help you with your writing requires daily attention over a long period of time. Some composition teachers may require that you *keep a daily journal*; if your teacher does not, you might try on your own. What we're suggesting is that you commit yourself to making daily entries in some kind of notebook. The entries may be words, phrases, sentences, paragraphs, essays, poems, bits and pieces. The point is to record in some way things that matter to you or puzzle you or cause you to wonder. Put down what you see and learn and feel and know. A journal can get you in the habit of expressing yourself comfortably and honestly on paper.

To make a journal work as it should, you need to make daily entries: saving up for a week and writing a group of entries won't give you an account of what you were conscious of on *different* days. Don't be hesitant in making journal entries, and don't imagine that every entry should be something important. If a song you hear on the radio moves you, write about the song and try to say why and how it moved you. If something goes sour in one of your classes, try to figure out what it is by recalling what different people said and did.

Making abstractions concrete.   A second thing you can do requires some practice, and could be a part of your journal. Try writing concrete phrases and sentences that locate and *embody* the abstract ideas and impressions that come to you. The purpose in doing this is for you to get in the habit of putting your ideas and impressions into quite specific settings for quite specific terms, as in the following examples:

>   EASE AND RELAXATION: an unhurried visit to the National Art Gallery in Ottawa.

>   FEAR: the whirring of a bat when you can't see it; the taste of brass in your mouth after an out-of-control car just misses you.

>   COMFORT: some good, fresh pipe-tobacco and some exciting books on a Friday evening with the weekend still ahead.

>   ANXIETY: a message to call home without any indication of what it's all about.

Practice in creating particular scenes and terms to accompany ideas and impressions may help you avoid falling back on standard phrasings and clichés when you are trying to express yourself on paper. (See also 27.4, Concrete and Abstract Words.)

   Neither the journal nor this practice in making ideas and feelings concrete guarantee that you will always find good subjects to write about. Both may help by letting you see which way your thoughts and impressions are likely to run, which topics are likely to appear and reappear in journal notes, and which kinds of topics seem to matter to you most.

Free writing.   Another method of generating specific information to work with—and of getting in touch with what you know and feel—is simply to write *randomly* about your subject for a few minutes. Never mind "good English," and don't stop to ponder the significance or triviality of what pours out of you. Reject nothing. Just keep the flow of free association going. The jumble of disconnected impulses, vaguely remembered facts, names, places, opinions, events, questions, and so forth will grow into a page or more of *data*—raw materials that you can then examine for possible ideas. Much of it will be useless, of course, especially when you first try the technique. But this more or less uncontrolled process of free writing can often uncover things that you would not otherwise notice or remember. Printed below is a good example of worthwhile free writing, excerpted from a first-year student's preparatory work for a Research Ethics assignment:

> . . . torture and death of lab animals—medical research, test drugs, cosmetics, other products—not just vivisection—electric shock (psych), cancer transplant, blinding—mutilation—all in the name of progress, big business, glamor (–but this angle bores me)—is morality and pain irrelevant?—animals suffer (plants too?)—but this isn't just sentimental or religious or squeamish—cute bunnies blinded by cosmetic tests or cuddly puppies—is there no right and wrong in science and business (end justifies means—strong cruel to weak)—definition of "progress" as technology and profit—but be fair: scientists need to learn about safety, doctors practice surgery—Ruth Casey told me about open-heart surgery dogs, cancer cures—also remember Thalidomide disaster; drugs must be tested. But why animals rather than people? Same arg for retarded persons. Or remember Jews in concentrn camps. Maybe psych worse—monkeys, pigeons, rats screwed up—arrogance of humans—can I prove all this (ask Doug's father? Humane Society?)—Science Today article on genetic DNA tampering—get view of other side—periodicals in Library? alternatives? can't stop progress? who decides? compare Pollution debate for ideas . . .

18.1

Plan

That muddle is typical of three pages of scribbling that only the writer herself could decipher or fully understand. But in fact those sheets of chaotic and uncertain jottings, written in a single sustained burst, did enable the student to realize which aspect of the assigned topic interested her. She also gradually recognized that she opposed indiscriminate research on animals, and that the issue could be examined on logical rather than emotional grounds. At the same time, of course, she had generated many more examples (or potential examples) *on both sides of the argument* than her essay itself would probably require. She was ready to proceed.

Free writing is just one of several types of swift, unrestrained prewriting that are known as "brainstorming." A related method, for example, is to let your pen freely produce lists of *words* in the same energetic, almost random manner. The trick is to avoid interrupting or challenging the process of spontaneous suggestion. All such techniques assume that a few minutes of rapid, uninhibited association of ideas can often provide a rich abundance of details and possibilities much faster than other approaches can. Some kinds of brainstorming are used regularly by *groups* of people, especially to resolve academic or business problems that require a wide choice of fresh insights or answers in a hurry.

The free-writing approach doesn't always work, but it is worth trying if you are the sort of person who tends to have trouble getting started or thinking of details and implications. Remember, however, that the hodgepodge produced by free writing is *not* a rough draft; it is just a mass of material from which you can start *finding* possible ideas for further development.

Seeing patterns and connections.   There are some other things you can do to help discover what you're going to write about and to help in thinking about assigned subjects. The questions and observations that follow may help you see patterns and connections in your own ideas and impressions, and to relate these patterns to things around you.

1. Do you notice which things seem to *recur* in your experience? Actions, attitudes, emotional reactions, and other experiences may never be exactly repeated, but there are likely to be recognizable likenesses and patterns among your experiences. If there are, they may help you to find a subject, or to see an assigned subject in a new way.

2. How do you look at your experiences? What do you *focus* on? How and when does your focus change? When you first entered your writing class, did you see and hear individuals, or did you respond to the class as a whole? How do you look at it now? Shifting your focus from long range to close range, looking at one part, then at another, than at both in relation to each other enables you to see and know what's around you, and what happens when your focus shifts.

3. How do your experiences *differ* from others? How varied is your experience? How do the things you are familiar with appear to other people? Answering questions like these may also help you understand your own ideas and impressions and learn what there is in them that has significance for you.

4. What can you learn about an idea, an event, or an experience by looking at it in three different ways? If you regard a subject as something *fixed*, you can examine its parts. If you regard your subject as *changing and dynamic*, you may see the relationships among the parts. Or, your subject may be *part of a larger context*, and you may want to see how it fits into this larger scene. Any (or all) of these different perspectives can make a general topic yield up something worth pursuing.

5. What is there in your experience that can be *shared* with another? Can you find a way of presenting your experience that will make it possible for another to share? How can you use the knowledge and values that others have so as to connect them with you and your subject?

Once again, you should note that asking and answering these questions does not guarantee that you will always find good subjects. Like other varieties of prewriting, however, they may remind you to look for something specific and worth while. It is possible to write *competently* without much forethought, but *good* writing won't occur until something matters enough that the writer feels the need to speak out.

Private resources. For some papers that you will write you already know enough to treat the subject well. Your own experience will provide subjects and material for many of your essays: what you have done in school and out, the jobs you have held, your hobbies, the people you know, the places you have visited, and the courses you are taking. Consider this brief list of topics and see how many you could write on from your own experience:

Overcoming Self-Consciousness	Living Within a Budget
A Job I Disliked	Considerations in Buying a Car
Advice to a High-School Student About to Enter the University	A Successful Amateur Play
	Building a Record Collection
	How to Run a Meeting

18.1

Plan

You need not feel that a paper based upon your personal experiences will be boring to others. Some beginning writers are afraid that their own experiences have been too limited, or that their opinions and attitudes are too commonplace to be of interest to anyone but themselves. But much published material is based upon incidents and attitudes that are in no way unique or sensational ("Making Your Hobby Pay," "The Most Unforgettable Character I Have Met," "Diary of a City-Bred Farmer"). If you are *interested* in what you have to say, your readers probably will be too. A fresh and lively account of the experiences of a baby-sitter is more readable than a dull description of a journey up the Amazon.

In most situations, you will be able to tell whether or not your present knowledge, opinions, and attitudes are sufficient material. For papers based on personal experience, ask yourself as many questions as you can think of about the subject. If, for example, you are going to explain how a person should apply for a job, recall and analyse your own experiences in looking for work. How did you find out what jobs were available? How did you decide which jobs to apply for? Did you apply in person or by letter? If you were not hired, what were the probable reasons? What mistakes, if any, did you make either during an interview or in your letter of application? If you were going to apply for another job, would you go about it in the same way?

A similar analysis will help you gather material for papers presenting personal opinions or attitudes. If you decide to enumerate the qualities of a good teacher, think of two or three of your teachers who were outstanding and try to discover what qualities they had in common: a sound knowledge of their subject? a genuine interest in students? a willingness to help the slower students? fairness in grading? a sense of humour? You could extend your analysis by considering also one or two teachers who were definitely unsatisfactory, to see what qualities they lacked.

Public resources.   Not all papers can be written entirely from personal opinion or experience. Many subjects call for information that must be gathered by reading, by observation, or through personal interviews. Some subjects will demand thorough research and formal presentation. Others may require only the addition of your casual reading (newspapers and magazines) as support. It is quite permissible to use factual knowledge from casual reading for any occasion that requires it—not as in a formal report with documentation, but as the natural supplement to what you wish to say.

In using outside resources to develop material for a paper, read critically, and think about what you read. Be careful to distinguish between verifiable *facts* (the cost of living index in Saskatoon and in Halifax) and *opinions* (the reasons for the rise of separatism in Quebec). On controversial subjects, read and weigh the opinions on all sides of the question before arriving at a firm opinion of your own.

Make the effort to understand and assimilate material from published sources before using it in a paper. Instead of merely copying an author's words, think about the ideas he is expressing. Do you agree or disagree with them? Why? (See 30.4, Evaluating your Material.) Moreover, proper acknowledgment should always be made for borrowed material—in a footnote if the paper requires formal documentation, or informally if the situation warrants it—as for the quotations opening the sections of this *Handbook*. (See 30.8, Documenting the Paper, for details on using materials from printed sources.)

Limiting Your Subject

The main aim of collecting lots of impressions and information—more material than your essay itself will require—is to give yourself a wide choice of possible approaches. Sooner or later, however, you must decide which aspect of the general subject strikes you as especially interesting or important. Remember that most assigned topics are deliberately vague. The writer is expected to narrow the topic into a more specific, manageable form by selecting from some worth-while *focus* or *point of view*. This decision is the final step in finding something definite to work on, and it conveniently limits the amount of exploring that remains to be done.

There is seldom any danger that the focus you select will be too narrow. It is large subjects, such as "Canadian Foreign Policy," "The Aims of Higher Education," and "The Role of Women in Contemporary Society" that lead to difficulty. On such ambitious subjects, most writers can only repeat commonplace judgments and empty generalities, and after writing a paragraph or two, they find that they have nothing more to say.

18.1

Plan

Limit the subject you select so that you can develop it fully in the required number of words. Most college and university essays are short—a thousand-word essay that would fill only one newspaper column. Because even ten thousand words would not be enough to cover most large subjects ("Justice," "Crime Prevention," "Forestry"), break down such subjects into topics you can handle. "TV Police Stories," for example, might be limited to "The Effect of TV Police Stories on Children." But since there are many children and several programs about police, you might write a more interesting paper and offer more interesting judgments by focussing specifically on your little brother and TV police stories.

The suggestions made above about ways of looking for subjects are also ways of limiting your subject—the more specific you are in asking about a subject, the narrower your final topic is likely to be. It is best to concentrate on a single, well-defined aspect of the subject rather than on the subject as a whole:

General subject	More specific topic
Voting as an obligation of citizenship	Arousing student interest in voting
Sportsmanship	How sportsmanship differs in tennis and baseball
Pollution control	The efficiency of pollution control devices on cars

As you gather information, your topic may change slightly—and it may continue to change through all the preliminary stages of your thinking. The important thing to remember at first is to make the topic specific and to *avoid lapsing into a general approach*.

► **EXERCISE**

Using (or adapting) one or more of the *finding* techniques discussed in 18.1, generate a page or so of specific ideas and information about one of the following very general subjects. The purpose of the experiment is to see if you can efficiently discover a particular aspect that *you* wouldn't mind writing about.

1. Airports
2. City Traffic
3. Labor Unions
4. Snow
5. Education

18.2 SOME WAYS OF THINKING ABOUT YOUR SUBJECT

Once you have determined what your own focus is going to be, it is time to *explore* more thoroughly the nature and possibilities of that approach. The information and ideas you have already gathered are a good start, but the real significance of that material still needs to be investigated. Having a good subject does not in itself give you a reason for writing; you don't yet know what you want to say about it. In other words, it is time to discover and clarify your *purpose*.

There are various ways of analysing what you have found that may help you to see what is most interesting or useful or valuable in it. The methods summarized in this section can be effective as you first begin probing the topic and also after you have developed a specific proposition, or thesis, and are seeking a way to support or explain it. These (and other) strategies can also assist you to recall knowledge that you already have about the subject, or draw your attention to information you still need to find. Some may help you to understand principles or implications or relationships inherent in the subject. All aim at encouraging the conscious and subconscious processes by which we notice connections, pursue insights, and make judgments.

Asking Questions

Posing a systematic series of questions about the topic is one good way of probing its significance. The clue to what you really want to say may suddenly (or gradually) emerge if you make yourself *write* answers to questions like those suggested below. A suitable method of organization (comparison, for example), may also suggest itself during the inquiry.

1. What can you learn by *definition*? To what class does your subject belong? How does it differ from other members of the same class? Can definition help you determine just what your main point is? If you have determined what your main point is, does definition give you a way of organizing your discussion?

2. Will *comparison* with something you know well help you understand your subject? Can you detect similarities in your subject and one or more other things? Does detecting differences between your subject and a similar thing help you understand your subject? Does your subject differ in degree from similar things?

3. Studying *relationships* may tell you something about your subject and show you a way to organize your discussion. How is your subject connected with a cause? How and why did your subject come to be? Is your subject to be studied as an effect of some causes, or as a cause of later effects? What are the antecedents of your subject? What consequences are likely to follow from your subject? With what ideas or things is your subject incompatible? Are there ideas that are contradicted by your subject?

4. Is there expert *testimony* about your subject that you can call on? Are there laws, principles, precedents, or other kinds of testimony that will help you understand your subject and validate it to others?

18.2

Plan

Suppose, for example, that the general subject of *sportsmanship* interests you. Perhaps you're interested in athletics, or perhaps you've just seen an episode of bad sportsmanship, or perhaps you've simply wondered why people behave differently in games. The questions mentioned above may help you discover how to discuss sportsmanship, a first step is to determine what class of things it belongs to. Is sportsmanship a *virtue*, a *mark of civility*, a *quality*, a *social disguise for aggression*? The problem of defining sportsmanship, in other words, may get to be so important that you decide that this is your subject and you don't have to look further. Each of the sets of questions above may lead to a specific way of writing about sportsmanship.

Tracing Relationships

Another set of suggestions for exploring your subject lies in seven relationships that give coherence to discussions. These relationships put in the form of questions may be as follows:

1. With what does your subject *co-ordinate*? What can be linked to your subject by *and*?

2. From what is your subject *observably different*? What can be linked to your subject by *but*?
3. What can be cited as a *cause* for your subject? What can be linked to your subject by *because* or *for*?
4. What can be cited as a *result* of your subject? To what conclusions does your subject lead? What can be linked to your subject by *therefore* or *so*?
5. What are the *alternatives* to your subject? What can be linked to your subject by *or*?
6. What does your subject *include*? What examples, narratives, or episodes can be linked to your subject? What can be linked to your subject by *also*, *for example*, or *furthermore*?
7. What *sequences* exist within your subject? Is your subject part of a larger sequence? What can be connected to your subject by *then*, *next*, or *in future*?

It is quite important that you *write* a few lines in each case. Start with one or another of those transitional words and trace out the different or additional possibilities that are brought to mind. The very process of writing things down may give you the idea or logical direction you want for your paper.

To see how these questions might work, go back to the sample subject that started off as "TV Police Stories," then became "The Effect of TV Police Stories on Children," and finally became "TV Police Stories and My Little Brother." If you say "My little brother watches all of the TV police stories *and* . . . ," when you finish the sentence in your own way you'll probably have to name some other things he does that are like watching the police stories. If you say "My little brother watches all of the TV police stories *but* . . . ," when you finish the sentence you'll probably find yourself talking about ways your little brother is different from other children who watch these programs. If you ask what sequences there are in your little brother's actions, that may lead you to discuss how he behaves after watching the programs, or the ritual he goes through to get ready to watch the programs.

Structuring the Analysis

Another methodical way of getting your subject to reveal its potential is to organize and examine the information according to some formal structure. Such approaches are commonly used in report-writing or problem-solving situations in which orderly inquiry and practical conclusions are the writers' main objectives.

You may even have a standard format or checklist of categories that must be followed, as in the typical laboratory experiment report (Purpose, Hypothesis, Apparatus, Method, Observations, Conclusions). If no conventional structure exists in your subject area, use your own judgment in predicting which aspects of the topic an impartial reader would reasonably expect to see explored or explained.

The journalist's pentad.   A method of probing used routinely by reporters to help themselves collect and assimilate information is known as the journalist's pentad or the "W5" structure. It consists of seriously applying the questions *what*, *who*, *when*, *where*, and *why* to any assigned topic.

Answering these apparently simple questions shrewdly and concisely can be a lot more challenging (and therefore more profitable) than you might expect. It is valuable to make yourself define exactly *what* your focus is, identify *who* is directly or indirectly involved in or affected by it, limit it accurately as to time and duration (*when*) and place (*where*), and explain convincingly *why* it is happening or is important. Until you have tried jotting down responses to such questions, don't assume that you "know" your subject. Avoid superficial impressions and hasty opinions; attempt to imagine how another intelligent writer might answer those same questions differently than you do.

If your topic were Newsprint Recycling, for example, the question *what* would require you to decide which particular aspect of recycling you are going to discuss: its advantages? its costs? its problems? the mechanical processes? the uses of recycled paper? The question *what* can, of course, be asked in many different ways:

What happened?	What is it an example of?
What is happening?	What is its background?
What will happen?	What is interesting about it?
What could happen?	What is indirectly related to it?

Obviously, this method can be used both to generate and to analyse information. The questions *who*, *when*, *where*, and *why* would similarly expand your awareness of the topic's implications and of the many possible approaches a paper or report might adopt. Additional queries, such as *how*, *what next*, or *who cares*, are also productive ways of entering more fully into the details or wider significance of any subject. As long as you remember that you must eventually choose a single unified purpose for your essay, there is no harm in seeing how many extra ideas a structured exploration can provide.

18.2

Plan

The case method.   The outline below illustrates another way of structuring an analysis. Known as the "case method," it is commonly used in various forms as a problem-solving technique in fields such as town planning and business administration. It can readily be adapted, however, to almost any writing situation that requires the logical sorting out and evaluation of unfamiliar or complicated information. If you have trouble seeing the relationship of ideas or weighing opinions, this sort of approach may help you organize your thinking:

1. Background information [*brief summary of situation*]
2. Statement of the Problem [*what essential question needs to be answered?*]
    (a) Primary Problem [*the main question*]
    (b) Secondary Problems [*related questions*]
3. Implications of the Problem [*why it matters*]
    (a) Primary Implications [*most important effect*]
    (b) Secondary Implications [*other effects*]
4. Possible Solutions [*all reasonable answers to the question(s)*]
    (a) Possibility A — advantages
                    — disadvantages
    (b) Possibility B — advantages
                    — disadvantages
    (c) Possibility C — advantages
                    — disadvantages
5. Decision [*the best solution or answer*]
    (a) Full Statement of Decision [*your thesis*]
    (b) Summary [*why your solution best answers the questions and their implications*]
6. Implementation [*what should happen next, and how?*]

The advantage of structured analysis *as an exploratory technique* is that it assists you to clarify the issues and to impose some form onto all your different ideas and impressions. It may also remind you that certain essential information still needs to be obtained. Of course, the method will not miraculously *give* you the issues or answers, and it can lead other writers to quite different conclusions about the same topic.

Suppose, for example, that you have gathered information for a medium-length essay on landlord-tenant conflict. Because this controversial subject has so many apparently contradictory aspects, it would not be surprising if you were unable to see clearly your own position or to choose some particular approach for your paper. A structured analysis might be a good way to figure out the significance of your ideas. You must somehow assemble and arrange a wide variety of facts and viewpoints in order to decide what you think the main issue is and to develop a thesis that can be explained adequately in an essay of that length. While you could not realistically attempt to cover every aspect of the tenancy problem, and while another writer may not agree with your breakdown of its key features, you will be able to offer one coherent way of looking at it.

Bear in mind that this technique is being recommended here as a potentially helpful *prewriting* method, not as an appropriate format for the draft of your paper. Always transform the results of a structured analysis into a more fully developed and original presentation of the topic. Remember too that a structured approach won't be ideally suited to every kind of assignment; many subjects cannot (or should not) be reduced to the status of a practical problem or experiment. A hard-nosed, strictly mechanical examination of the landlord-tenant question, for example, would probably strike most readers as oversimplified. It is usually best to combine a structured analaysis with other exploratory techniques to ensure that you are not limiting your choice of criteria or possible directions.

18.2
Plan

A Checklist of Suggested Methods
for Finding a Subject
and Locating Material

For Help in Finding a Subject

1. Keep a journal and record ideas and information.
2. Practise making abstractions concrete.
3. Generate ideas with spontaneous free writing or free association.
4. Look for patterns and connections:
    a. What things recur in your experience?
    b. How do you look at things? When and why does your focus change?
    c. How does your experience differ from that of others?
    d. What do you learn when you look at an experience or possible subject as fixed? as changing and dynamic? and as part of a larger context?
    e. What can you share with someone else?

5. Draw on private resources: your own knowledge, experience, and feelings.
6. Refer to outside or public resources such as newspapers, periodicals, and so on.

For Help in Thinking About a Subject

1. Ask questions:
   a. What can you learn by definition?
   b. Will comparison reveal something about the subject?
   c. What kind of relationships does your subject have with other things?
   d. Is there testimony available about your subject?
2. Trace relationships by asking:
   a. What can be linked to your subject by *and*?
   b. What can be linked to your subject by *but*?
   c. What can be linked to your subject by *because* or *for*?
   d. What can be linked to your subject by *therefore* or *so*?
   e. What can be linked to your subject by *or*?
   f. What does your subject include?
   g. What sequences occur in your subject?
3. Use some kind of structural organization to order the information to be examined:
   a. Ask the five questions: *what*, *who*, *when*, *where*, and *why*.
   b. Organize ideas via the case method.

▶ **EXERCISE**

Using (or adapting) one or more of the *exploring* techniques discussed in 18.2, prepare an outline (at least four main points) for an essay you wouldn't mind writing about one of the following topics. Be sure to indicate the overall purpose of the proposed paper, and list a couple of specific examples for each of the main points.

1. Amusing Characters in Airports
2. Bicycling in City Traffic
3. Strikes in Essential Public Services
4. Snowmobiles
5. Campus Architecture

18.3 LOCATING A THESIS

When you have gone far enough in your thinking and planning to select a specific topic and you know pretty well what you want to say about it, it is necessary to compose a *thesis statement*. This is a sentence that defines exactly what you think your paper can demonstrate. It puts precisely into words the result of your prewriting—the conclusion you have finally reached about the subject. Hence, the thesis statement is the most important sentence you will write during the whole project; it will govern both the writing and the reading of your paper.

Phrasing the thesis statement can be considered the final step in prewriting. It confirms that you have developed a clear focus and that you can firmly declare your *main point* itself. Construct this sentence carefully, perhaps trying out several variations until you're satisfied that your central or controlling idea is accurately and decisively expressed. Don't be vague or timid. Much of your prewriting efforts will have been wasted if you let yourself slip back into weak generalities at this point:

18.3

Plan

WEAK: Some movies made for theatres are censored before being shown on television. [*merely a fact, not a point of view*]

WEAK: This essay will examine the arguments for and against censoring movies on television. [*merely a restatement of the subject*]

WEAK: The censoring of movies shown on television is a controversial topic. [*slightly better, but still too indecisive and self-evident*]

WEAK: I am opposed to the censoring of movies shown on television. [*merely a personal opinion, emphasizing the writer instead of the subject*]

BETTER: Movies made for theatres should not be censored before being shown on television. [*a definite viewpoint, but no reason is implied*]

BEST: The censoring of movies shown on television violates the producer's right to freedom of artistic expression and the viewer's right to freedom of choice. [*a distinct position, with reasoning implied*]

Notice how specific that final thesis statement is. Whether or not you agree with the idea it expresses, you can certainly see exactly what the paper will attempt to prove and, to some extent, the kind of arguments that will be advanced. Vagueness and half-heartedness are the enemies of good thesis construction. Before you can prepare an outline and rough draft, you must be able to write a sentence that answers the question "What, exactly, is the main idea that I want to communicate to my reader?"

Writing a thesis statement requires you to stop and really think about your subject and to decide what is important or interesting. The personal essay "My Theatre Experience" (see page 224) might have been given direction and focus by a good thesis statement.

The author, with more thought and digging in his memory, could have written several different essays about what he observed at the drive-in. To name just one possibility, he might have decided finally that the assignment was a chance to write about the way people behave in the dark when they think no one is watching, at least no one they know. Such a focus would have taken the writer beyond the mere facts, providing instead an interesting interpretation or analysis of the incidents. With this clearer aim in mind, he could more easily have asked himself what his *point* was — what he wanted to say about people's behavior in the dark. Writing a thesis statement makes a writer decide exactly what the paper's central thought is to be, and demands that it be said in a single sentence. Here are some thesis statements that could have been developed out of that one approach to "My Theatre Experience":

> My experience working in a drive-in theatre taught me that people behave differently in the dark, resorting to trickery, deceit, and foolishness.

> I learned from my work in a drive-in theatre that public manners and private manners are not the same.

> Darkness seems to make people do things they would not do in the broad light of day.

Any of these (or other) possibilities would certainly have helped the author produce a paper worth writing and worth reading. Even a personal essay needs a thesis statement to define the *idea* that gives meaning or importance to an otherwise pointless profusion of facts.

Testing the Thesis

It is important to be critical of your own thesis statement — to "test" its clarity and accuracy — before proceeding to base an outline and rough draft upon it. Does it declare completely and unambiguously your real point of view? Does it cover all the particular points you expect to present in the paper? Is it specific enough to be explained and illustrated within the limits of your assignment's prescribed length? Are you sure it isn't just a statement of self-evident fact or merely a rewording of the assigned subject? Is the idea your own, or are you simply repeating what you have often heard or what you hope is a safe answer?

One good way of checking the strength of a thesis statement is to review briefly the points that can be given in its support. A thesis about television censorship, for example, could perhaps be assessed by briefly jotting down in a series of "*because* clauses" the writer's reasons:

Movies should not be censored before being shown on television

because a movie's producer has the right to artistic freedom and the right to retain control over how his or her work is used

because television viewers have the choice of watching another channel, and hence are able to do their own censoring

because nobody should have the authority to force their definition of "unacceptable" material onto other people

because...

Unless you can foresee some such basis of support for your thesis, you shouldn't begin writing the essay. More exploratory prewriting would be necessary to give you a firmer grasp of your subject, your position, and the kinds of illustrative material you need.

On the other hand, if you are satisfied with the wording of the thesis and feel confident that it can be effectively explained and developed, there is a further "test" you can perform. Try to anticipate the possible objections of readers who might not share your point of view. This should be fairly easy to do if your prewriting has led you to consider all sides of the question, not just your own opinions or preferences. The rough "*because* clauses" of an imagined counter-argument favoring television censorship could look something like this:

18.3

Plan

Some movies should be censored before being shown on television

because certain excellent movies could not otherwise be televised at all

because many viewers lack maturity and cannot censor for themselves or for their families

because "unacceptability" can be adequately defined for the vast majority of people, and public media should serve that general audience

because...

Re-examine your own thesis and main points in the light of such counter-arguments, rephrasing your ideas if necessary. Occasionally you may even change your mind, a development that would confirm the value of systematic prewriting as a way to discover what you really believe. (See also 20.2, page 272, Thesis-Sentence Outlines, for illustrations of how preliminary work can lead to additional discoveries and to a more worth-while thesis.)

At this point any thesis statement is still in its draft form. No matter how carefully you have composed it, further thinking and planning may suggest changes. But at least you now have a thesis statement that will enable you to make a definite start on developing the paper itself. (See also 21.2, page 286, Using Sentences to Control Direction, and 21.4, page 291, Effective Openings.)

► **EXERCISES**

1. Which of the following sentences are too vague, obvious, or confused to be effective *thesis statements*? Suggest ways of improving the ones you consider inadequate.
   a. The qualities of a good administrator are many.
   b. I intend to examine the idea that private schools may not be altogether superior to public schools.
   c. Objective examinations are limited because they give undue weight to memory and not enough to the ability to relate facts to one another.
   d. These two poems are about beauty.
   e. Subjects like philosophy are irrelevant in today's society.
   f. Sex education should be compulsory for everyone.
   g. The purpose of this essay is to discuss nuclear power.
   h. Pierre Berton's books about the building of the railway are good because he shows the dangers of nitroglycerine.
   i. I strongly believe that the showing of gory films on news broadcasts is disgusting and that I have a right to be protected from offensive subjects.
   j. *Start With a $1000* contains financial information on how to invest one thousand dollars.

2. Compose two substantially *different* thesis statements for possible essays on *each* of the topics in the Exercise on page 238.

3. Each of the two following topics has a thesis statement that can lead to an interesting paper, but some of the points listed do not have any bearing on the controlling idea and should be changed or eliminated. Arrange the ideas in groups that belong together, eliminating or changing them as necessary.
   a. *Salmon Fishing*: Salmon fishing is a thrilling and inexpensive sport.
      Requires skill
      Prizes offered for biggest fish
      Equipment need not be expensive
      Boats can be rented cheaply
      Salmon fight to the last breath
      Fraser and Restigouche Rivers two of the best locations
      Conservation efforts have paid off
      Baked salmon is a delectable dish
      How the Indians prepare salmon
      No thrill equals that first strike.
   b. *Regulating Children's TV Habits*: Although some TV programs are undesirable, parents should not regulate what children watch.
      There are some excellent educational programs
      Developing good judgment depends on practice in choosing
      TV often takes place of baby-sitter
      Children want to watch what playmates watch
      Some TV programs bad for immature minds
      Children resent too much discipline
      Outdoor exercise also important
      Free play of curiosity develops intellect
      Violence fascinates children
      Overprotection in youth produces distorted ideas of reality

19

What Writing Will
Let You Do

What is written without effort is in general read without pleasure. — Samuel
Johnson

Chapter 18 suggested some ways of discovering and exploring a
subject's potential. The result of such efforts is the thesis statement
—a clear expression of your main point. At this stage you may also
have a few strong impressions about how that idea could be
developed in an essay, and you may feel ready to start a rough draft.
First, however, you should decide on the *relationship* you want the
paper to establish between yourself, the subject, and the reader. It is
also important now to consider which of various possible *methods*
of writing would be best suited to what you want to accomplish.

19.1

Writ

This chapter will examine different ways of choosing an
approach and method for your paper. Such decisions should be
made (at least tentatively) before you try a serious draft, so that you
will waste less time writing disorganized false starts. Some experimental or trial-and-error work can be helpful, of course, but a full-
length draft produced haphazardly is a very inefficient technique
for finding a coherent "voice" and strategy. As a minimum, you
ought to think over the options and opportunities that your particular subject affords. A *controlled* draft, composed with a consistent
point of view and type of presentation, will assist you to see pretty
well the form in which your ideas could appear in the final version.

19.1 THE MEETING PLACE OF AUTHOR,
SUBJECT, AND AUDIENCE

Some kinds of writing you may do for your own sake—diaries,
notes, and the like. Some kinds of writing you may do for the sake
of the subject—laboratory reports, case histories, meditative
explorations. Usually, however, an audience of some kind is
waiting, and you must find a just and happy balance among the
material and arguments available on a subject, the interests, needs,
and peculiarities of an audience, and your own character. You must
be honest to yourself, do justice to a subject, and earn an audience.

The Writer's Position

Before you begin writing the first draft of a paper, you must discover where *you* stand with regard to your subject and to your audience. Have you engaged yourself in the subject enough to make it interesting to others? Have you weighed it to give it worth? What position will you take toward your subject in presenting it to your audience? Must you address the audience in strictly logical and impersonal fashion? Or does the subject justify a more emotional presentation? Or should you concentrate rather on the impression of yourself that will emerge through your writing? Can you combine these tactics in such a way that you and your audience will come together and share an idea?

If you imagine yourself, a subject, and an audience at the three points of a triangle, you'll be able to visualize some of the problems in determining where to stand. If you stand too close to your subject, you may forget the need of sharing it with an audience. If you stand too far from your subject, you may not see it clearly. If you stand too close to your audience, you may start sounding too chummy. If you stand too far from the audience, you may seem remote and aloof.

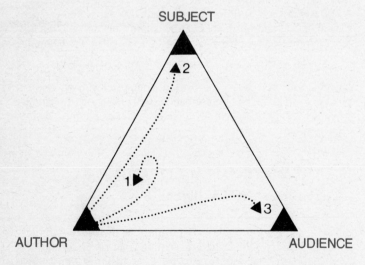

The numbered lines in the diagram indicate the three basic things that writing will let you do. You can write for your own sake (line 1), for the sake of the subject itself (line 2), or for your reader's sake (line 3). But it is almost impossible for any unified piece of writing to emphasize more than one of these. Depending on your purpose (and on the nature of the assignment), you will want to stick quite consistently to just one type of approach. Mixing them together, or shifting back and forth between them, is likely to result in a confusing paper that doesn't satisfy the needs of *any* element in the triangular relationship.

This differentiation of three basic kinds of writing, explained more fully below, is indebted to James Kinneavy's work in *A Theory of Discourse*.

Expressive writing.   In many kinds of writing the author is dominant; the writing is by the author and, in many ways, for the author. As line 1 in the diagram shows, this kind of writing leaves the author and returns to the author. It may be called *expressive writing*, for the author's need to express appears to be the primary motive in such writing.

You should note two things about *expressive writing*. First, there are many different kinds. Personal letters, diaries, and journals often seem intended chiefly as personal expression; some descriptive writing is the author's account of learning to see. Some expository and argumentative writing turns out to be *expressive writing* when the author, instead of seeking to explain or to persuade, uses the occasion for meditative purposes to work out personal thoughts about a subject. Second, expressive writing offers some opportunities and sets some limits that other kinds of writing don't. You are probably free, for example, to write more informally than you might otherwise and to use looser forms of organization. On the other hand, you may not be free to enter into a technical discussion of something that has taken your interest. You are your own prime object of attention in this kind of writing; you must first of all be honest with yourself.

But in other kinds of writing, the subject deserves primary attention, and you must get out of the way. Because expressive writing doesn't involve *communicating* facts and information, it is usually unsuitable for the sorts of projects ordinarily assigned at college, university, or your place of employment.

Referential writing.   As line 2 indicates, some writing is focussed on the subject, with the author and any possible audience fading into the background. Kinneavy calls this kind of writing *referential writing*; it refers to something outside and independent of both the author and the reader. It aims at the orderly presentation of facts, not opinions or feelings, and is most commonly used in report-writing of various kinds. Newspaper stories are referential,

19.1

Writ

though editorials and opinion columns are not. Most business letters and memos are referential; their purpose is to exchange specific information about a subject as efficiently as possible. Laboratory reports, factual book reports, and other research projects are referential writing, as are most examination answers. Essay assignments may call for referential writing, but in many subjects an argumentative (or even a personal) approach may be required instead.

You have less freedom in this kind of writing than you might with *expressive writing*; the subject must be dealt with, and that may require tighter organization, more technical use of language, and closer control of your own opinions. But you need not think of *referential writing* as only limiting; sometimes it is a great advantage to get outside yourself and plunge into the exploration of a subject. (See also 19.2, Exposition.)

Persuasive writing.   In other kinds of writing, which Kinneavy classifies as *persuasive writing*, the audience is the proper target of attention. Rather than explain a subject, such writing aims to move or to persuade an audience. In addition to presenting facts clearly, the author must constantly consider how best to convince the reader that those facts *prove* or *mean* something beyond themselves. In other words, persuasive writing is used in situations in which there is some disagreement about how the subject should be interpreted.

Argumentative essays belong to this group. So do newspaper and magazine editorials, columns of commentary, film reviews, and so forth. Persuasive writing also includes letters of recommendation, critiques, sermons, suggestions, and some kinds of public letters (for example, letters of protest). On such occasions the writer is urging the reader to believe something or to take some sort of action. Projects of this type make particular demands on you; they require clear, careful reasoning that an audience can easily follow, and sure, specific evidence that will support your assertions. (See also 19.3, Argumentation.)

Adjusting to the Audience

Kinneavy's general scheme of organization, including *expressive writing, referential writing,* and *persuasive writing*, is a reminder that the language you use, the style you use in sentences and paragraphs, the forms of organization you depend on, the relationship you establish among yourself, your subject, and your audience, may vary according to what the writing you are doing is intended to do. It makes a difference in the way we talk and write whether we are talking about ourselves, some subject outside ourselves, or to an audience. Speakers and writers sometimes go astray when they forget what they are supposed to be doing. We've all been in classrooms where teachers have become so involved in their subject (referential discourse) that they have forgotten their audience of students (requiring persuasive discourse). We've all heard salespeople and politicians so intent on selling themselves to us (persuasive discourse) that they have forgotten to learn very much about their subject (requiring referential discourse).

As you are planning a piece of writing, you may need to keep in mind the interests and needs of a particular audience. It is easy, of course, to forget your readers and to think only about your subject in some of the writing you will do as a student. The announcement of an assigned subject does not necessarily give you a purpose for writing; and unless you *discover* a purpose and relate it to your audience, even a dutiful fulfilment of the assignment will amount to little. If there is an audience for your work and you ignore it, your work is in vain, no matter how correct.

19.1

Writ

It is difficult, when you are writing alone at night, for example, even to think of an audience. The easiest thing to do is to get the paper written without bothering about an audience; but usually when you write something, somebody else reads it. When you are writing for a class, it's easy to assume that your teacher is your only audience. Often it is better to write instead for your class, or for people who read habitually, or for people like yourself, or for an ideal audience of readers who are willing to set aside their own views and heed what you have to say.

One way to get in the habit of thinking about your audience, if your assignment permits it, is to specify a particular audience for what you are writing and indicate at the first of the paper who the audience is: "Those of you who are partial to TV police stories may never have thought about their effect on a twelve-year-old boy." There is little point, however, in imagining so vague a readership as "people in general" or "all TV viewers." The trouble with always writing "to whom it may concern" is that you usually end up with something so general that nobody (including yourself) will really care about it.

If the subject you are dealing with is controversial, and if both you and your audience are likely to have intense feelings about the matter, you may have particular problems in finding the right approach to an audience. On matters we care deeply about, where feelings and emotions are taut—politics, ethical practices, religion, conservation and ecology, personal relationships, social, professional, or sexual, for example—we have difficulty hearing each other, and we're not always likely to listen to logic. How can we meet an audience in such a situation? There is no easy way.

One thing you can do, if you encounter this situation, is to move over into the shoes of your audience. You can begin by looking at the issue at hand from your audience's view. You can, for example, try to describe something as another person might see it—some scene or object, say, that is displeasing to you but pleasing to another. Or you can try to impersonate another and write an explanation or argument as the other person would.

You can still be authentically yourself and yet open to others. You can acknowledge opposing views and work to understand them. If people disagree with us, it's usually because they see things in a different way, and we can try to see it as they do, without sacrificing our own views. It takes time and patience to search for the space where you and an audience can be together, but that is a courtesy we owe each other.

The terms we've been using—*expressive writing, referential writing,* and *persuasive writing*—are useful because they are a reminder of these relationships in writing among an author, a subject, and an audience. They are not, however, the only terms that can be used to discriminate among different kinds of writing. In the following sections we'll use another set of terms to discuss some of the special problems and opportunities of different kinds of writing: *exposition, argumentation, description,* and *narration.* The two sets of terms are related, although the latter set is more traditional and less concerned with relationships. Argumentation is persuasive writing. Exposition is usually referential writing, although a writer might explain (write exposition) in order to express himself or herself. Description and narration are often referential, but they may also be expressive. But in any case, knowing what others have done in these modes of writing— knowing what is possible—is a way of learning what you can do when you set out to write.

19.2 EXPOSITION

The purpose of exposition is to *inform* your readers, to carry their knowledge of something beyond its present point, to help them understand a situation or a process, to give them factual information about an idea or belief. It ranges from the explanation of small personal matters ("How to Select a Summer Wardrobe") to complex scientific treatises ("The Effect of Ultraviolet Light on

Steroids") and to factual summaries of theories ("The Bank of Canada's Anti-inflation Policy") or of controversies ("The Battle over Pesticide Spraying in New Brunswick"). Here, for example, is a well-developed expository paragraph of historical analysis:

> With the Métis along the Saskatchewan, who had drifted west from the settlements of the Red River, all the mistakes of government had been repeated. There had been no provision for the effects of the railway's coming, nor for other and deeper change. The nomad hunters no longer followed the buffalo, for the buffalo had disappeared. The Indians said the earth had swallowed them up. Yet the half-breed squatter, forced to become a farmer, had no security for his land; civilization and the survey chain were steadily closing in. His narrow strips of river frontage were being carved into square blocks; he no longer owned what he thought he owned and there were strange men in his fields. They were denying him the use of other lands that had long been held in common, and they were appropriating some of the best. He could not understand the process, had no means of preventing it, and for years his complaints and petitions had been almost totally ignored. He lived, a French Indian in the view of a remote government, an obstacle in the course of settlement to be absorbed or brushed aside. — Joseph Schull, *Edward Blake: Leader and Exile (1881–1912)*

19.2 ◀

Exp

Skill in exposition is essential in all school work. You will probably do more expository writing, where you inform your reader, than any other kind of writing. Most of the texts read in college and university, except in literature courses, are also expository. Increasing skill in expository writing, then, is a major aim of composition courses. (See also 23.2, Expository Development.)

Gathering Information

Whatever your subject and whatever the length of your paper, you will have to exercise judgment in deciding what resources to use and in gearing your information to your particular audience and situation. (See 30, The Research Paper.) Some of the short expository papers you will be assigned as a student can be based entirely on your own knowledge and experience. (See 18.1, page 229, Private Resources.) Other papers will require that you gather and evaluate information from various sources in order to develop your subject adequately. (See 18.1, page 230, Public Resources.)

Even when you base your paper on a personal experience, such as building a boat or working in a drive-in theatre, you may find it useful to add to your information by reading in the library or by talking to people who have had similar experiences. It is a good idea in planning such a paper to make a list of points about which your memory is hazy or about which you lack adequate information. Then, to fill in the gaps, you can extend your observations or read what others have reported about the subject.

For typical information papers on subjects such as "The Canadian Senate" or "Devices for Controlling Air Pollution," you will usually need to consult a variety of printed sources—books, magazines, newspapers—to find information you cannot gather first-hand.

Relating Specialized Information to Your Reader

In gathering and selecting additional facts to use in an expository paper, be particularly careful to consider your audience. If you are writing a paper for experienced bridge players, you probably need not define terms like *point count* and *slam* or explain how a *finesse* is made, since your readers would be familiar with such fundamentals. But if you are writing on bridge for an English class, you cannot expect the typical student to have this knowledge; to make sure that your audience understands, you must take the time to insert brief definitions or explanations. If you do not, the whole paper may be puzzling or even incomprehensible to general readers. Remember that you are writing the paper in hopes of telling them something new, of adding to their knowledge in an area where they do not have your background. Put yourself in their place: what words or ideas might be unfamiliar to them? How can you explain these things so that they will understand them?

The following passages show effective and ineffective ways of relating specialized information to general readers:

> INEFFECTIVE: If the bleeding becomes severe or there is a chance of infection, you may have to cauterize the wound.

> EFFECTIVE: If the bleeding becomes severe or there is a chance of infection, you may have to cauterize the wound by searing it with a piece of metal that has been held over a flame until it is red hot.

> INEFFECTIVE: There are various ways to bridge the gap from one solo to the next. The trumpeter may play a series of riffs accompanied only by the rhythm section. This is probably the most common method.

> EFFECTIVE: There are various ways to bridge the gap from one solo to the next. Probably the most common method is for the trumpeter to play a series of short, conventional jazz phrases, called "riffs," accompanied only by the rhythm section—piano, bass, and drums.

Documenting Your Information

When your own observations form the basis of the paper, be sure to tell the readers why you consider your statements to be fairly authoritative. Otherwise they may not be sure how much value to attach to them. Somewhere near the beginning of the paper, state the circumstances under which you gathered your facts:

> Since I was sixteen, I have spent my summer vacations working in a local department store, first as a stock clerk and later as an assistant display manager. During that time, I have become familiar with the typical organization of a large retail store. . . .

> My home is only nine miles away from the Blackfoot Indian reserve, and I have had many opportunities to meet and talk to members of the Blackfoot people. . . .

> In gathering examples for this paper, I spent ten hours listening to radio programs featuring rock-and-roll records and copied down the lyrics of a dozen of the current favorites. . . .

19.2

Exp

When you incorporate published material into your paper, you must reproduce it accurately and credit the sources, whether you quote them directly or not. It is not honest to offer someone else's experiences or observations as if they were your own. In a research paper, credit is given formally by means of footnotes (30.8, Documenting the Paper), but in a general paper mention may be made informally. The following are some typical examples of how such acknowledgments can be handled:

> Franklin Soames, the author of *Zapotec Culture*, found that. . . .

> At a recent medical convention, H. L. Matthews, the noted urologist, was quoted as saying. . . .

> But according to Morris Wolfe, in a recent article in *Saturday Night*, ...

Sources which have been used extensively (and summarized in your own words) may be cited in a note at the beginning or end of the paper:

> Much of the material for this paper was taken from Donald Creighton, *Dominion of the North* (Toronto: Macmillan, 1957).

This convenient practice is unacceptable, of course, if you have used material word-for-word from your source. In such cases you must specifically acknowledge all borrowed phrases or passages. When in doubt whether documentation is necessary, it is safest to take the time to give credit. Don't ever give a reader any reason to suspect the originality or honesty of your work.

▶ **EXERCISES**

1. Look for several pieces of expository writing and bring them to class for discussion. Notice in particular how much detail different writers use, how writers convey specialized information, how much time they spend on different parts of their subject. Try to find selections that illustrate different relationships between the writer and the subject (involved? dispassionate? aloof? distant? close?). Explanations are likely to occur in many interesting places; look at the labels of jars and cans, the owner's manual that comes with some appliances or a car, a popular magazine for crafts and mechanics, textbooks, a book on how our language developed, the jacket commentary for a record album.

2. Notice the difference between the kind of writing employed on any fairly large newspaper's front page and the kind of writing used on inside pages in the editorial section, in letters to the editor, and in columns of expert opinion. See if you can find two different treatments of the same subject (for example, political or economic matters often appear in both *expository* reports and *argumentative* editorials).

19.3 ARGUMENTATION

Whereas the purpose of exposition is to *inform* your readers, the purpose of argumentation is to *convince* them. The two kinds of writing have much in common, and both are based on facts or impressions gathered from various sources. But expository writing simply *presents* information, while argumentative writing *uses* it to support or test a belief.

Remember that a statement of fact is not in itself an occasion for argument, since presumably facts can be checked. An argument is similar to a statement of opinion, in that it represents a judgment the writer has made; but an opinion is not an occasion for argument unless it is based on *facts* instead of mere preference, for only then can its validity be proved. A paper describing current fashions in clothing, the social habits of bees, or the history of the fur trade will be *expository* in method because these are factual matters and the reader is being invited to share the writer's knowledge. On the other hand, a paper attacking film censorship or urging a change in landlord-tenant laws will be *argumentative* because, although it is based on facts and reasons, it expresses a debatable opinion and tries to convince the reader to agree with it.

Like exposition, argumentative writing can range widely, from matters close at hand ("Down with Large Classes") to major public concerns ("Let's Get Rid of the CBC") or to matters of historical interpretation ("The Fairness of Louis Riel's Trial"). The following passage, from a student paper, offers a thoughtful (though not indisputable) argument against restricting the right of government employees to strike:

> Workers in essential public services ought to have the same protection and opportunities as workers in other fields. This security should, if necessary, include the right to strike. In a just society there can be no excuse for putting any group at a legal disadvantage simply because it is highly convenient to "the public" to do so. This does not mean, however, that service cannot be maintained; equal protection may be provided by different means. If we forbid public employees the right to strike, we must in fairness compensate them for this loss by guaranteeing some other effective bargaining position such as salaries automatically "pegged" to private-sector settlements. The issue is, however, not merely a moral, legal, or economic one. Repressive legislation would make public service careers very unattractive to the capable, self-respecting people we want to have in government work.

In the above passage the student has defined the problem, taken a definite position, and presented philosophical and practical reasons in support of that point of view. We may not share the writer's opinion (that is, we may weigh these or other factors differently), but the paragraph does present its case well. Of course, argumentation can also be more complicated, or based on conclusions reached only after doing some research. The following example is an economist's attack on the assumptions underlying Canada's production of military goods:

19.3
Arg

> The promotion of defence production in order to improve the balance of payments is also open to criticism. It is true that the stationing of troops abroad under the NATO agreement and the purchases of major weapons systems abroad are a significant drain on foreign exchange reserves, and thus constitute grounds for the active promotion of exports. They do not, however, provide a special reason for promoting the export of defence goods. Exports of any kind are sources of foreign exchange, and thus are equally useful for offsetting the drains arising from the defence program. Government policy-makers often appear to be preoccupied with the balance of foreign payments in particular economic sectors, such as defence, or the tourist trade, or automobiles, but there is no economic justification for this preoccupation. A sensible policy of export promotion would concern itself with those lines in which the prospects for stable growth are most promising. Most defence exports are probably not in this category. Their market is highly volatile since it is affected by rapid technological obsolescence, sudden shifts in military strategy, and political considerations — Gideon Rosenbluth, *The Canadian Economy and Disarmament.*

Specific discussion of patterns in argumentative paragraphing can be found in 23.3, Argumentative Development.

Locating the Argument

An argumentative paper *proposes* something. Whether it calls for action or simply asks for the recognition of a point of view, it centres on a proposition that the writer must be prepared to prove. This assertion (which will be your thesis statement) should express clearly and emphatically the idea you want the reader to accept. Compose it carefully, making sure that it is worded in an argumentative form and that it describes your position accurately. Ordinarily it needs to be simple—composed ideally of a single subject and a single predicate. If you argue, for example, that "The municipal government must be put into new hands on election day and reformed to keep provincial and federal agencies from encroaching on local authority," you have, by using a double predicate, introduced two arguments, both of which must then be proved.

You should find the suggestions in 18.3, Locating a Thesis, helpful in formulating an arguable proposition.

Using Resources and Evidence

When we state our opinions in informal situations, we often give little or no evidence to support them: "John is a reckless driver"; "The cost of living is going up every day"; "Divorce is the main cause of juvenile delinquency." This vagueness does not mean that we have no good reasons for so believing, but simply that our reasons are usually known and accepted by our listeners. On occasions when our opinions are questioned, we may attempt to support them with facts drawn from our experience and reading: "John had two accidents last month, and he always drives too fast." "Steak is up sixty cents a pound, and a refrigerator costs almost twice as much today as it did six years ago," "Psychologists say that emotional stability depends on a secure family life." Such evidence is considered acceptable or even convincing in informal situations, usually because the listener's personal regard for the speaker lends some weight to the evidence.

In writing, however, the relationship with your audience is far more impersonal; authority must rest much more on the facts themselves. Readers who know neither John nor you will want to know what kind of accidents John had and who was at fault; they will wonder whether "too fast" means in excess of speed limits; they may suspect that "always" is an exaggeration. Before accepting your opinion in regard to the relation between divorce and delinquency, they may want to hear what psychologists say in their own words, to be sure you are not misinterpreting their remarks or ignoring opposed opinions.

The more facts supporting your opinion that you can gather from experience or from the written statement of others, the more reason you can give your readers to accept that opinion. You will probably not be able to present absolute *proof*, but the greater the weight of your evidence, the more probable it will seem to them that your belief is the best one.

Types of Arguments

Some traditional kinds of argument may suggest certain ways of thinking about your material that will lead you to the evidence you need. One is the *argument from nature*. A young man who wished to call attention to inadequacies in the campus guidebook petitioned to have his name placed on the ballot in an election for winter carnival queen. He maintained that he was eligible on the grounds that the guidebook stipulated only that candidates should be students under twenty-one; sex was not mentioned in the body of the rules. The young man's petition was denied through an argument from nature. Pointing out that the rules came under the heading "Eligibility requirements for winter carnival queen," his opposition seized on the meaning of the word *queen* —by nature a female—to deny his eligibility. An argument from nature may be developed by a number of techniques: by defining the nature of a thing; by studying the meanings attached to the key words in a proposition; by classifying the subject in order to establish a frame of reference in terms of which it can be discussed.

19.3

Arg

People cannot always agree on the nature of things, of course, and for that reason they have often turned to other kinds of argument. The *argument from analogy* brings a subject and argument into a reader's knowledge by suggesting its similarity to something better known, as in the fairly common—but usually ineffective—analogy of government and business. The evidence you bring to this kind of argument must show that the comparison is both significant and accurate.

The *argument from consequence* enforces a proposition by examining cause and effect, antecedent and consequence. This is a useful kind of argument, but it is limited by the fact that human affairs are not ordered by certain laws of causality. Poverty *sometimes* breeds crime; prolonged tyranny *frequently* leads to revolution; honesty is *occasionally* rewarded. Before expressing an opinion about the outcome of some course of action, or about the cause of some event, make sure that the weight of evidence lends probability to your statement.

The *argument from authority* depends upon the testimony of respected persons, the authority of institutions, the weight of important documents. This is probably the least popular of the traditional kinds of argument, for most audiences prefer to feel that the truth is *discovered* in the course of an argument, rather than that it has been *pronounced* by authority.

Taking the Argument to Your Audience

Whatever kind of argument you use, and those above are only samples, remember that your readers have some confidence in their own intelligence and judgment and are likely to resent a writer who attempts to make up their minds for them. (See the discussion of author-audience relationships in 19.1) State your facts as specifically as possible—so that your readers can check them for themselves if they want to—and give your reasons for whatever conclusions you draw. Compare the following statements for effectiveness:

VAGUE: A few years ago, the president of a large company said that taxes were too high.

SPECIFIC: In a speech to the Kingston Chamber of Commerce on April 14, 1981, Oscar Winslow, president of the Winslow Paint Company, said, "Corporation taxes today are so high that they are destroying business incentive.

VAGUE: In many of his newspaper articles, H. L. Mencken made slighting references to democracy. Anyone can see that he despised it.

SPECIFIC: In his articles for the Baltimore *Sun*, H. L. Mencken frequently referred to democracy in terms such as these: "the domination of unreflective and timorous men, moved in vast herds by mob emotions" (July 26, 1920); "it may be clumsy, it may be swinish, it may be unutterably incompetent and dishonest, but it is never dismal" (July 14, 1924).

In trying to persuade readers to accept your opinion, you will naturally want to gather facts that will support your position. It is not fair to your readers, however, to suggest that *all* evidence reinforces your belief. They may be familiar with contrary evidence; even if they are not, its absence may make them suspect that you are stacking the deck in your favor. In a court of law, an attorney who deliberately suppresses evidence damaging to his or her case may be disbarred from future practice. The consequences to writers are usually not so serious, but they may also lose the case.

When you come across facts that do *not* support your opinion, give them as careful consideration as you do those that do. Is their source authoritative and relatively free of bias? Do they offer serious and relevant reasons to question your present opinion? Do they outnumber the facts you can find to support it? It may be that you will want to alter or modify your proposition after taking opposing facts into account. You may decide that your original opinion was wrong; many writers are unaware of the flimsy basis of their beliefs until they begin trying to substantiate them.

Even if the facts you gather do not change your opinion, it is unfair to simply discard those that fail to support it. In fact, it will strengthen your position in the readers' eyes if you frankly admit unfavorable evidence along with your reasons for being unpersuaded by it. Remember that the readers are your jury. If you have arrived at an opinion by weighing opposing evidence sensibly, they should be able to do the same.

19.3

Arg

Testing the Argument

One way to test your argument, or to examine the argument of another writer or speaker, is to scrutinize it for flaws in reasoning and in the use of evidence. The most common flaws in logic are known as *fallacies*. These typical blunders are mistakes of carelessness or of prejudice or (sometimes) of dishonesty. It is important to realize that incorrect reasoning can occur, accidentally or otherwise, and that its presence will seriously weaken your credibility in the reader's mind. The general label *non sequitur* ("it does not follow") applies to such errors of reasoning in which the conclusion does not follow from the evidence presented. Sometimes a step in reasoning has been omitted, and the fallacy can be corrected by supplying the missing link. But sometimes the conclusion is drawn from evidence that has no bearing on the issue: that actress Mary Starr uses a particular toothpaste has nothing to do with its quality; that a man does not beat his wife has nothing to do with whether he is a good husband; that the army teaches useful skills has nothing to do with the wisdom of sending troops to other countries.

A few of the most common fallacies are outlined below. Use this summary to check your own arguments as well as those you read in published writing. The technical names of the errors are not important, but you should notice that several different kinds of faulty thinking can undermine a paper's persuasiveness.

Hasty generalization.   In informal situations, we often overgeneralize from the facts: "She's *never* on time"; "Advertising is *only* a pack of lies." A little consideration shows us that in reality absolute situations are rare; reality is more accurately described in terms of finer shadings and degrees. Most readers are aware of this, and although they will accept and make statements like the above uncritically enough in conversations, they are suspicious of them in writing.

Be especially cautious in using terms like *all, always, everybody, nobody, never, none, only,* and *most*. Before making such all-inclusive statements, make sure that they are justified. If there are any exceptions to some assertion you make, modify your language to make it more accurate. Don't say that *all* young people want a home and family: *some* or *many* might be more accurate. Before you say that *most* early marriages end in divorce, ascertain from some reliable source whether more than 50 percent actually do; otherwise you are not justified in using *most*. Keep in mind that the English vocabulary provides you with a wealth of qualifying terms (*some, few, often,* to name only a few) and choose those that most accurately describe the number, extent, and frequency of the facts you are asserting.

Compare the following two statements for precision of expression. Both are based on the same facts (of the delinquents in the Provincial Training School, 75 percent come from low-income families, 45 percent have used narcotics at some time, and 20 percent have IQ scores over 100):

> OVERGENERALIZATION: **Almost all** delinquents in the Provincial Training School come from homes **on the verge of starvation. Most** of them are **dope addicts**, and **very few** are **brilliant.**
>
> ACCURATE STATEMENT: **Three out of four** delinquents in the Provincial Training School come from **low-income homes. Almost half** of them have **at least experimented** with narcotics. **A significant minority** are **above average mentally.**

False analogy.   Comparison and analogy are effective means of arguing, but only if there is really a basic similarity between the compared terms. If, for example, a university administrator sets out to argue for new rules and economies in his or her school on the basis that it should be run like a business, we should probably reject that argument on the grounds that the analogy is not valid, for similarities between a business and a university seem only incidental, not essential.

Post hoc, ergo propter hoc. This fallacy (literally, "after this, therefore because of this") is the fairly common one of assuming that two events or things are causally related simply because they are related in time. The young man who gets a raise a week after using a new deodorant probably owes his success to something else.

False extremes. This fallacy oversimplifies an issue by reducing it to just two possible answers: "The Department must either raise its grading standards or bury forever the ideal of academic excellence." Choices are almost never so clear-cut, though bullies and enthusiasts often express themselves in such terms. Also known as the "either-or" fallacy, the "black-or-white" fallacy, or the "false dichotomy," this kind of argument misleads by ignoring the existence of other, less extreme, possibilities. For instance, to say "Canadians should either actively support the monarchy or go and live in the United States" illogically excludes the obvious possibility that patriotic Canadians may nevertheless be anti-monarchists (or neutral). Like most false dichotomies, that statement also implies a threat in the extravagant alternative to the writer's position.

19.3
Arg

Begging the question. This term applies to an argument that assumes the truth of what needs to be proved. A politician who claims "Our feeble municipal government, greatly in need of reform, must be placed in new hands on election day" is begging the question unless he goes on to *prove* that the present government is feeble and in need of reform.

Ignoring the question. This is a broad term that applies to all arguments that are irrelevant, as when a premier argues that his government is not corrupt because the provincial budget is balanced. Another way he might ignore the issue would be to resort to an *argumentum ad hominem* ("argument against the man"), attacking the integrity of his opponents rather than the charge of corruption. Or he might use *glittering generalities* such as "my devotion and dedication to the fine people of our beloved province" to draw his audience into acquiescence by the emotional appeal of glowing sentiments and flattery. Another kind of evasion is *big words* —the use of jargon or pretentious language to confuse or intimidate the audience (see 28.1, Formal Words). All strategies that employ emotional means to persuade an audience to arrive at a judgment without examining the evidence are ways of ignoring the question.

When you have finished the first draft of an argumentative paper, examine it carefully for flaws. Have you weighed the available evidence? Are your generalizations supported by fact? Are your inferences valid? Make sure that your argument is both honest and sound.

▶ **EXERCISES**

1. Look for several pieces of argumentative writing and bring them to class for discussion. In each, try to determine just what the central topic of debate is and what kind of evidence the writer uses. Notice what kind of relationship the writer works to establish with the audience. Test the argument against your own judgment and common sense and against the fallacies listed above. You may find it helpful to look at newspaper editorials, letters to editors, advertisements, television commercials (if you can get the words down on paper), graffiti, bumper stickers, government announcements, political and social commentary in magazines.

2. Explain why each of the following statements is illogical. Try to distinguish between the different *kinds* of fallacies you notice:

    a. He behaves arrogantly because, like all rich people, he had an unhappy childhood.
    b. This article about the proposed irrigation dam is convincing because it's easy to understand.
    c. A woman who cannot keep her own household in order is obviously unfit to govern this country.
    d. No thinking person can be opposed to the time-honored free enterprise system which has brought greatness to our homeland.
    e. All red-haired women are hot-tempered.
    f. The seal hunt is not cruel, because it provides badly needed jobs in an economically troubled region.
    g. Since everyone else does it, there is nothing wrong with my making private calls on the company's long-distance telephone line.
    h. The denial of funding for our neighborhood swimming pool proves that the petty bureaucrats controlling the provincial government are incompetent.
    i. I'm sure Gary is an efficient administrator, because I've never heard otherwise.
    j. Being overweight obviously has a detrimental effect on academic work; twenty percent of the students who failed last spring were at least ten pounds overweight.
    k. The compulsory use of seat belts is a bad law because my best friend was seriously injured in an accident when her seat belt kept her from being thrown to safety.

19.4 NARRATION

Narration is the kind of writing that relates *action* or tells some kind of story. While exposition aims to inform, and argument to persuade, the purpose of *narrative* is to recreate a past experience or series of events. It moves through time, giving a sequence of happenings. The time covered by the narrative may be very long, as in summaries of historical processes such as the settlement of North America or the debates over the new Canadian Constitution. But you are likelier to find yourself writing about particular experiences that occur over a much shorter period. In the following vivid recollection of the Halifax Explosion of 1917, the time that elapses is just a few moments:

> The effects in the classroom were swift and destructive. The windows vanished. The thick opaque glass in the upper half of each door, with wire netting embedded to prevent ordinary breakage, flew out whole. Behind my row of desks a door-glass tipped forward, shot horizontally over our heads, and sliced deeply into the wall in front of us. Fortunately we were sitting by that time. Had it been twelve inches lower it would have decapitated most if not all of us in that row. The big clock on the wall just missed the headmaster and shattered on his desk. All the plaster sprang off the walls in large and small chunks, and filled the room with a fog of white dust. We jumped to our feet, staring at each other. One girl screamed (her cheek was cut from mouth to ear), but I don't recall much crying out. For a few seconds we stood like a lot of powdered clowns with badly applied daubs of red paint here and there; then with the instinct born of routine fire-practice the boys and girls dived through their separate cloakrooms, snatching coats and headgear off the hooks or off the floor and clattering away downstairs to run home. —Thomas H. Raddall, *In My Time*

19.4

Narr

Notice that effective narration is characterized by vigorous active verbs (*vanished, flew out, tipped, sliced, shattered, clattering,* and so forth). Once you have decided to treat your subject as a story (a series of events that illustrates or embodies an idea), be sure to emphasize action and specific details. Keep factual generalizations to a minimum so that your narrative won't lapse into exposition. (See also 23.4, page 350, Narrative Development.)

Point of View

The particulars of narrative writing are reported to an audience selectively through a given point of view. Ordinarily it is neither possible nor desirable to present every action in a sequence of events. Rather, you should focus on those aspects of an experience that, from your point of view, make it worth preserving.

Most of the narrative writing you do will be presented as the narrative of either a first-person observer or participant or of a third-person observer. Personal narratives and autobiographical sketches are ordinarily told in the first person, but it will depend on the story you tell whether you present yourself as participating or observing. In historical writing, reports, and case histories, you will ordinarily present the action in the third person, letting the events speak for themselves.

Whether you report an action as a participant or as an observer, try to focus attention directly on what went on. In the following passage the narrator unwisely draws attention to *himself* rather than to the event he is narrating:

> I was riding with a friend late one night, returning from a long weekend trip. I was extremely tired, and I am sure he was too, and as a result we weren't very observant about traffic lights. I did notice in the distance one very red blinker-light, though. I also saw a car directly in front of ours, like a slow-moving ship in a submarine's sights. I knew immediately that we were going too fast to stop, so my natural reaction was to brace myself for a crash. It seemed to me that I could hear the tires squealing for minutes before anything happened. I was surprised to find during those actually few short seconds that I was seeing a variety of vivid colors that I hadn't even noticed before. I was aware of the yellow dividing strip of the highway, and still off in the distance, the brilliant red flashes of the traffic signal. There were also the browns and greys and whites of the surrounding buildings, that I hadn't seen a few moments before, but now were things of sharp beauty.

This narrative should be tightened up, and the *I*'s made less conspicuous, by revising some of the sentences:

> Late one night I was riding with a friend. We were both extremely tired after a long weekend trip and not very watchful of the traffic lights. But I was dimly aware of one very red blinker-light in the distance. Suddenly a car loomed up in front of us, like a slow-moving ship seen through a submarine's sights. We were going too fast to stop, and instinctively I braced myself for the crash. Our tires squealed for what seemed minutes. Actually, only a second or two passed, but in that brief instant, all the color of the scene jumped into view—the bright yellow dividing strip of the highway, the brilliant red flashes of the traffic light, the browns, greys, and whites of the nearby buildings. For one sharp moment everything took on a strange an.l fearful beauty.

A reader will understand your experience more clearly if you concentrate on the events as they happened instead of on your feelings about them.

Use of Tenses

In narrative writing events are typically written down in chronological order, with verbs and adverbs controlling the movement:

> . . . **After a long half hour,** the rain **eased** a bit and the clouds **rose. I relaxed** a little. **I was showing** them that a rookie **could get through.**
> **Just then,** the engine **stopped** cold. As a rule, **when** an engine **fails,** it **will give** some warning. The water temperature **will rise,** or the oil pressure **will drop,** or there **is a knocking or clanking.** Even if it **is only for a minute or two,** it **gives** the pilot a chance **to look around** and **head for** a field or open place. However, **when** the timing gear in a Liberty engine **failed, one second** it **was roaring along** even and strong, and **the next** there **was** a tremendous silence. **I quickly twisted** all the knobs and gadgets in the cockpit, but there **was** no response, and the engine **stayed** dead. **While** my hands **were trying to restart** the engine, my neck **was stretching** and my eyes **searching** for some sort of field to **land in. I was surrounded** by heavily forested, sharply rolling hills. To my left **was** a cuplike basin with a small clearing. It **was** downwind, but my gliding radius **didn't allow** much choice. **I went** for it. — Dean C. Smith, "Flying by Guess and by God"

Most narrative writing uses the past tense, but the present (or "historical present") can occasionally be used instead to give a lively sense of events actually happening, as in this paragraph:

> The meeting dissolves in charges and counter-charges, loud arguments erupting in every corner of the room. "Order, now, order!" shouts the chairman. Things subside. It goes to a vote. The meeting votes that all outside work be stopped so that the full energies of the strikers can be brought to bear on the struggle. — Silver Donald Cameron, *The Education of Everett Richardson*

The most familiar use of the historical present is in writing about things that occur in literature and other works of art. It is standard practice to assume that the action of a novel, play, or film is always happening. For instance, in discussing Margaret Laurence's *The Diviners*, it would be appropriate to write "Morag suddenly *feels* [not *felt*] torn between the two loyalties that *have* [not *had*] governed her life until *now* [not *then*]." The following passage of literary history properly employs both the past tense and the historical present:

19.4

Narr

The writers of the early twentieth century **were** prolific, by Canadian standards, and the nature of their fictional garden **varied**, but some of its consistent features **can** be isolated. One quality it **shared** with the frontier of American fiction **is** a moral simplicity—an innocence which **is** not necessarily purity but an absence of civilized sophistication. As the wise old doctor in Nellie McClung's *Purple Springs* **says**, "this big west is new and crude and distinct—only the primary colors are used in the picture, there are no half tones, no shadows, and above all—or perhaps I should say behind all—no background. A thing is good or bad—black or white—blue or red." This **is** essentially the moral perspective which **underlies** the fiction of Stead and Stringer too, and in the work of Connor and McClung particularly it **is** accompanied by the sort of naive social conscience which **provides** the complex human problems of the West with superficially logical solutions like prohibition, industry, thrift, and simple piety. It **is** also the moral perspective of most sentimental romance, which **was** quite predictably the genre in which these writers **worked**.—Dick Harrison, "Cultural Insanity and Prairie Fiction"

Because the author of the above passage is primarily writing history, the main or controlling tense is the *past*. That is, actual past events are presented as *completed* action ("were...varied... shared...worked"). However, because the fictional action and typical features of the literature itself are considered timeless or enduring, these matters are discussed in the *present* tense ("says...underlies...provides"). The changes in focus are so clear that the shifts from past to present tense are not confusing. The paragraph below, however, illustrates the confusion that may result when a writer jumps from one tense to another:

The characters in *The Double Hook* **are** [present] all afraid of Old Lady Potter. Even after she **died** [past] they **are** [present] obsessed by her memory and imagine that they **could** [past] still see her fishing up and down the creek. But her death **seems** [present] to liberate the community from its catatonic passivity; the people **began** [past] to communicate with each other for the first time in many years. The narrator's words, "They'd turned their living flesh from her as she'd turned hers from others," **reinforce** [present] this impression that no good **will** [future] come to the town as long as Mrs. Potter's domination **persisted** [past].

Including Adequate Details

If your narrative is to come alive for your reader, you must include enough details to make it interesting and understandable. Avoid any statement that might leave the reader wondering "What?" or "Why?" or "When?" or "Who?" In the following paragraph, for example, the narrator fails to tell *what* his teacher said or *why* "the results of the contest were disappointing":

> On the night of the final judging, I was so nervous I could hardly move my fingers. As I waited backstage for my turn to appear, I was sure I had forgotten the opening notes of my number completely. I began thinking of ways to escape; maybe I could faint or pretend to be violently ill. But then at the last minute my piano teacher came by to wish me luck and **said something that suddenly changed everything.** When my turn came, I played with ease and confidence. **Although the results of the contest were disappointing, I** was pleased that I had conquered one of my major enemies — stage fright.

In selecting details, choose those that illuminate or enliven significant actions. A narrative should not be loaded down with minute and unimportant details. You can usually make your point and still keep the action moving by selecting two or three lively incidents, as in this example:

> The big fisherman started pounding his fists up and down in the air. "He just doesn't mean anything to me at all," Michael said quickly. The fisherman, bending down, kicked a small rock loose from the road bed and heaved it at the hangman. Then he said, "What are you holding there, Michael, what's under your arm? Fish. Pitch them at him. Here, give them to me." Still in a fury, he snatched the fish, and threw them one at a time at the little man just as he was getting up from the road. The fish fell in the thick dust in front of him, sending up a little cloud. Smitty seemed to stare at the fish with his mouth hanging open, then he didn't even look at the crowd. That expression on Smitty's face as he saw the fish on the road made Michael hot with shame and he tried to get out of the crowd. Smitty had his hands over his head, to shield his face as the crowd pelted him, yelling "Sock the little rat. Throw the runt in the lake." The sheriff pulled him into the automobile. The car shot forward in a cloud of dust. — Morley Callaghan, "Two Fishermen"

19.4

Narr

The effectiveness of specific detail in non-fictional narrative is well illustrated in Thomas Raddall's paragraph about the Halifax Explosion (see page 261). (See also 22.2, page 319, Continuity in Narrative Paragraphs.)

▶ EXERCISE

Look for several pieces of narrative writing and bring them to class for discussion. Who is doing this narration? Where is he or she in relation to the action? How do you know you can trust the writer to give you an accurate account of the action? When is the pace fast? When is it slow? Look at a variety of different kinds of narration: check the sports pages in your newspaper for accounts of different hockey games and notice how the narrative of a headlined game differs from that of a game assumed to be less interesting or important. Look at a history text or at some good books on an area of history that interests you. Notice how a movie critic summarizes the action of a movie, or how *TV Guide* summarizes the action of a variety show.

19.5 DESCRIPTION

The purpose of descriptive writing is to enable a reader to see an object, person, or scene as you have seen or imagined it. This requires specific *visual details* that will create a mental picture for your reader. Effective description demands an eye for significant details as well as a knack for putting sense impressions into words. Description is often written for its own sake, as a form of artistic expression, but it may also be an important part of other kinds of writing, from long research papers to technical reports and case histories. (See also 23.4, page 350, Descriptive Development.)

Seeing Your Subject Clearly

To make a description vivid to a reader, you must first of all know where you stand, physically and mentally, in relation to the thing you are writing about. How did you see your subject? From what angle? Under the weight of what mood? How can you define your subject, distinguishing it from similar things in the same class? What makes this particular sunset, for example, different from all others?

Descriptive writing succeeds only when you show your audience the specific, identifying details of object or scene. This requires that you see it clearly yourself, that you understand what you see, and that you say *precisely* what you see, as the writer has done in this passage:

> More than in people, India lay about us in things: in a string bed or two, tattered, no longer serving any function, never repaired because there was no one with the caste skill in Trinidad, yet still permitted to take up room; in plaited straw mats; in innumerable brass vessels; in wooden printing blocks, never used because printed cotton was abundant and cheap and because the secret of the dyes had been forgotten, no dyer being at hand; in books, the sheets large coarse and brittle, the ink thick and oily; in drums and one ruined harmonium; in brightly coloured pictures of deities on pink lotus or radiant against Himalayan snow; and in all the paraphernalia of the prayer-room: the brass bells and gongs and camphor-burners like Roman lamps, the

slender-handled spoon for the doling out of the consecrated 'nectar' (peasant's nectar: on ordinary days brown sugar and water, with some shreds of tulsi leaf, sweetened milk on high days), the images, the smooth pebbles, the stick of sandalwood. — V.S. Naipaul, *An Area of Darkess*.

No two persons look at a scene in exactly the same way. What makes one writer's description more vivid than another's is the kind of details selected and the way they are arranged.

Selecting and Arranging Details

Good descriptive writing is precise. If in describing a person you write "I first noticed this lady because she was wearing a funny hat," your description won't mean much to the reader because there are many kinds of funny hats. State in specific terms what the hat looked like: perhaps it was a black velvet beret covered with sea shells or perhaps it was a miniature merry-go-round.

19.5

Desc

Notice how lifeless the description is in this paraphrase, from which the specific expressions have been removed:

> Gabriel watched as she ran her hand over her blonde hair, as girls do in some parts of France. Her mother's hair had been black, and Chantal was not nearly as pretty as her mother had been, for she had a snub nose and a rather big mouth. Yet she was as graceful as her mother in her movements.

By way of contrast, compare the description as it was written:

> Gabriel . . . watched her pass a slender hand over hair which most people called blonde but which he thought of as French-blonde because its basic chestnut was highlighted with pale-silver in a way he associated with girls of northern France. Her mother's hair had been ebony against a very white, soft skin. Chantal was not as handsome as her mother had been; her mouth was wide and her nose was somewhat snubbed, but she moved with her mother's grace and was so supple she seemed double-jointed. — Hugh MacLennan, *Return of the Sphynx*

Being specific in descriptive writing doesn't mean that you should overload your sentences with adjectives and adverbs. While such words are used to "describe" or qualify other words, too many of them can be disastrous to any piece of descriptive writing. To refer to Lake Louise as "*absolutely* the *most marvellous* sight I have *ever* seen in my *entire* life" may give your readers some hint about your emotions, but it won't tell them much about Lake Louise or help them re-create your impression of it. Such language isn't descriptive because it isn't *visual*; neither are vague words like *beautiful*, *fantastic*, *impressive*, *amazing*, *ugly*, and *boring*.

A descriptive passage should contribute something to your project. Even in literary writing, its purpose is not merely ornamental. The details you select must work together to create a central impression that will clarify or illustrate a key idea in your paper. For example, well-chosen visual images will give a much sharper and more convincing picture than abstract generalities, as in the following sketch of a person:

> One photograph of John Hornby preserves for anybody who has ever heard anything about the man an indelible and tantalising image... The date must be the late spring or early summer of 1919. And there sits John Hornby on a log in a rare instant of repose: shock-headed, bearded, hawk-nosed, moccasined, the strong lean hands holding a thick illustrated catalogue. He is reading, it seems, with almost insolently withdrawn concentration. What the photograph does not show clearly — though it implies this in the way that some pen drawings can imply colour — is that John Hornby is a short wiry man, little more than five feet tall; that his eyes are an intense and memorable blue, and disconcerting because often vague in intention and always apparently looking at something a long way away. — George Whalley, *The Legend of John Hornby*

To give focus to a description, you may find it useful to adopt one of the methods for developing material discussed in 21.2. For example, a spatial arrangement that takes you from left to right in picturing your subject, or from high to low, or from near to far, may help you create order in your description.

Often objects attract attention to themselves and deserve to become subjects for description because of some special impression they make. Thus, an interesting way to organize description is to focus attention on the dominant impression, subordinating all else. In the following passage the impression of quiet laziness, idleness, dominates the scene:

> The Mausoleum Club stands on the quietest corner of the best residential street in the City. It is a Grecian building of white stone. About it are great elm trees with birds — the most expensive kind of birds — singing in the branches. The street in the softer hours of the morning has an almost reverential quiet. Great motors move drowsily along it, with solitary chauffeurs returning at 10:30 after conveying the earlier of the millionaires to their downtown offices. The sunlight flickers through the elm trees, illuminating expensive nursemaids wheeling valuable children in little perambulators.... And through it all the sunlight falls through the elm trees, and the birds sing and the motors hum, so that the whole word as seen from the boulevard of Plutoria Avenue is the very pleasantest place imaginable. — Stephen Leacock, "A Little Dinner with Mr. Lucullus Fyshe"

Good descriptive writing demands restraint and discrimination. It also takes practice to get the exact effect that you want. One way to get additional practice is to study published examples of descriptive writing that appeal to you, observing what kinds of details the writers use and how they present them.

▶ **EXERCISE**

Look for several pieces of descriptive writing and bring them to class for discussion. Spend some time taking note of how many of the sentences contain specific sensory details and impressions. Notice the arrangement in each selection, and see if you can determine what the description is for. Where is the writer in relation to the subject? Check advertisements, stage directions in printed plays, passages in novels, fashion magazines, craft magazines, textbooks, merchandise catalogues.

19.5 ◀

Desc

20

Organizing Your Material

Once the plan is made and the material parcelled out, then the dry skeleton of this structure should be hidden beneath a surface which is all variety and interest. — Herbert Read, *English Prose Style*

Before you begin to write your draft, spend some time thinking through the *order* in which you intend to present your material. With some subjects the material itself will determine organization. For example, narratives and papers that describe personal experiences usually follow the order of events, and an explanation of a process follows a step-by-step pattern of presentation. In descriptive writing ("A Trip Through the Agawa Canyon") the normal order may be from one point to another (leaving Sault Ste. Marie, entering the canyon, arriving at Bridal Veil Falls) or from a general impression to the specific details that give rise to it, arranged more or less in the order of prominence.

The order of presentation may require more thought with other topics, such as "A Criticism of Olivier's *Hamlet*" or "Repression and Rationalization as Defence Mechanisms." Whether you select the subject or your instructor assigns one, in most instances you will have to examine the material carefully to find the best order for your special purpose. (See 21.2, Developing Your Material, for suggestions about choosing a pattern of development.) *Outlining* your material is one good way to determine its best organization.

20.1 THE OUTLINE IN RELATION TO THE PAPER

The usefulness of an outline depends on the material in it. No matter how elaborate the form—in numbering, punctuation, and structure—if the outline doesn't help in writing your paper, it serves no purpose. You can make a pretty outline *after* you've written the paper if you just want to have an outline to turn in. Of course, that's a waste of your time. Outlines are useless unless you take them seriously. Outlines in themselves are no great matter. No one reads outlines for entertainment and education. There is no gold medal for the best outline of the year. What matters about outlines is that they represent a writer's care about the subject and possible readers. Taken seriously, they represent a writer's effort to think a subject through and get information and ideas together in the best relationship.

You can learn a number of things from a good outline. From the main divisions in a good outline you can estimate the number and relative length of the paragraphs in your paper, although usually the paragraphs will not correspond exactly to the headings. You can frequently construct topic sentences for these paragraphs by rephrasing or expanding the outline headings. The divisions will show where transitions are needed and suggest the kind of development that will be possible: contrast, comparison, illustration, or others. (See 23, Patterns of Paragraph Development, and 21.2, Developing Your Material.)

An outline should be long enough to suit your purpose, and no longer. It should be no more complex than the material demands. The number of main headings for most papers ranges from three to five. A larger number of main headings for a thousand-word paper, for example, suggests that the division is haphazard or that the organization is faulty. The same principle applies to subheadings. Outlines that contain numerous levels of subheads need revision, for no single topic ordinarily needs such minute subdivision. And except for very complex material, there is seldom any need to go beyond the third-level subheading.

20.1

Org

When you are asked to submit an outline with your paper, it should represent the plan that you actually followed. Your outline serves then as the table of contents. You may find it necessary in writing the paper to depart occasionally from your original plan; if so, make the corresponding changes in the final outline before handing it in.

20.2 TYPES OF OUTLINES

Four kinds of outlines are widely used: the scratch outline, the thesis-sentence outline, the topic outline, and the sentence outline. Sometimes your instructor will tell you which form to use. When you have no specific instructions, select the form that best suits your method of working and the kind of paper you are writing. In planning a long paper, especially one involving research, you will probably want to make a topic or sentence outline. For short papers and extemporaneous writing, informal notes or a scratch outline will generally serve the purpose. Even for long papers, you may find it useful to work informally for some time before committing yourself to a final, detailed plan. It is not uncommon, for example, for writers at work on long projects to draft key passages—an opening paragraph, a closing paragraph, a passage developing the central idea—and then to fit these bits of writing into a more formal plan, along with jotted notes, sentences, and other scraps of ideas. Whatever techniques you use, the important thing is to develop a plan that will guide you in writing your paper.

Scratch Outlines

A scratch outline is a series of notes—single words or phrases— jotted down to refresh your memory as you write. An outline of this sort is useful when time is limited, as when you are writing examinations or brief papers in class. The following is a sample scratch outline for a theme on the subject "The Value of Summer Jobs":

> Earning money for clothes and school
>
> Sense of responsibility
>
> Learning to budget own time and money
>
> Opportunity to learn about different kinds of jobs
>
> Develop good work habits and maybe learn practical skills

The exact form of a scratch outline is not particularly important, since ordinarily you will be the only one who sees it. If the list is longer than five or six items, you may need to arrange the entries in some logical order (or number them) before beginning to write.

Thesis-Sentence Outlines

If you have developed a thesis statement (page 238), you may be able to use its parts as the terms of your outline. This can be especially helpful for short papers and essay examinations. Suppose, for example, that upon arriving in class you are given an assignment to write a short theme during the class period, and that one of the possible topics is "Campus Fashions." Suppose further that your experience and observation enable you within a few moments to jot down the following ideas on this general subject:

> Most people dress pretty much alike. Conformity.
>
> Nearly everyone is in jeans or cords most of the time.
>
> There are some variations, like camp style, athletic wear, wild new fashions, the "slob" look.
>
> Something like "hippie" dress is still occasionally seen.
>
> "Conservative" casual dress is getting more common these days— the "straight" look.
>
> Women do tend to "dress up" more often than men do—the "classy" look is returning—style-conscious, feminine.

Actually, a lot of men (especially in faculties like Law and Business) are starting to cultivate the "professional" look—suit and tie—costume of the successful?

I guess on any given day there's a lot of variety, with a general trend towards increasingly conservative dress.

It is possible to arrange these notes as a scratch outline, as suggested above. Another moment's reflection, however, might enable you to exercise tighter control over your theme by formulating a thesis statement such as this:

While campus dress still has a generally homogeneous look (mostly jeans and cords, plus a few interesting fads), fashions are gradually becoming more varied and more formal or conservative.

If you can get this far quickly, you can use the thesis statement as your outline. The sentence above, for example, could forecast a fairly brief, six-paragraph theme, each paragraph developing in sequence the structural units of the thesis statement:

20.2

Org

PARAGRAPH 1: a brief introduction (mainly about the popularity of jeans and cords) that ends with the thesis statement (new trend)

PARAGRAPH 2: the interesting fads and eccentric looks (this, judging from the form of the thesis, is an interesting but minor part of the theme)

PARAGRAPH 3: the increasingly "straight" look, even in casual wear

PARAGRAPH 4: "classier" women's styles—traditional femininity

PARAGRAPH 5: "professional" costume of ambitious males

PARAGRAPH 6: a conclusion on the increasingly conservative and formal tendency in campus dress

One particular advantage of this method of organizing is that you can plan the shape and emphasis of your theme by planning the shape and emphasis of your thesis statement. Your observation might lead you to revise the thesis statement above in this way:

The gradual trend among students towards more traditional and conservative habits of dress probably reflects a decline in casual, anti-establishment attitudes about education and careers.

A short essay developed from this sentence would have a totally different emphasis from the one suggested above.

Topic Outlines

The topic outline, the most frequently used kind of formal outline, is helpful in organizing papers of more than five hundred words. It consists of brief phrases or single words (not sentences) that are numbered or lettered to show the order and relative importance of the ideas.

The first thing to do is to get all your ideas down on paper. On the subject "The Forces as a Career for Young Men and Women," your preliminary thinking might produce this rough, unsorted list of ideas:

Security

Promotion slow but steady

Many different branches appeal to different interests

Low pay

Commissioned ranks open to men and women graduates

Can't be fired

Cost of uniforms

Discipline often annoying

Frequent moves hard to adjust to

See interesting places and people

Social life restricted to small circle

Good retirement benefits

Annual vacation with pay

Military job training useful in civilian careers

Determining the central idea.   A quick glance at the list above reveals that some points stress the advantages of a service career; others, the disadvantages. The next step then is to divide the notes into two columns:

Advantages	**Disadvantages**
Security	Low pay
Promotion slow but steady	Cost of uniforms
Many different branches appeal to different interests	Discipline often annoying
Can't be fired	Frequent moves hard to adjust to
See interesting places and people	Social life restricted to small circle
Good retirement benefits	
Annual vacation with pay	
Commissioned ranks open to men and women graduates	
Military job training useful in civilian careers	

In this form the relationship between the various ideas is not shown (What is the relationship between "Promotion slow but steady"

and "Many different branches appeal to different interests"?) and
there is no clear balance between the two columns (Is "Security"
supposed to balance "Low pay"?). In analysing the columns,
however, you can see that there are two main ideas in each—the
financial aspect of a service career and the living conditions that go
with service life. You might then balance the notes in this way:

I. Financial aspect
   A. Disadvantages
      1. Low pay
      2. Cost of uniforms

   B. Advantages
      1. Security
      2. Promotion slow but steady
      3. Commissioned ranks open to men and women graduates
      4. Can't be fired
      5. Good retirement benefits
      6. Annual vacation with pay
      7. Military job training useful in civilian careers

II. Social aspect
   A. Disadvantages
      1. Discipline often annoying
      2. Frequent moves hard to adjust to
      3. Social life restricted to small circle

   B. Advantages
      1. Many different branches appeal to different interests
      2. See interesting places and people

20.2

Org

When the notes are arranged in some system, decide on a main
point you want to make in your paper. "The Forces as a Career for
Young Men and Women" doesn't tell what you are going to say
about the subject; it is a title, not a central idea.

   At this stage you can see that there is more and stronger material
on the financial advantages of a military career than on its disadvantages. On the other hand, the disadvantages of living conditions
seem to outweigh the advantages. But assuming that you want to
treat the subject fully and in a favorable light, you could frame a
tentative statement of purpose: "Although there are definite disadvantages to a career in the forces, the advantages outweigh them."
This statement now governs the reworking of the outline. At this
stage it is still tentative and can be changed as the purpose becomes
clearer in your mind.

Revising the outline.   With the central idea as your guide,
arrange the outline so that every part of it contributes directly to the
purpose of the paper. Examine each heading to see if it needs to be

strengthened or elaborated upon, if it repeats or overlaps another heading, or if it is unrelated to the central idea.

In the first part of the outline "Cost of uniforms" seems to be a weak point. Aren't officers given allowances for their uniforms? Possibly "Expense of frequent entertaining" is a stronger point; if so, substitute it for "Cost of uniforms."

The financial advantages of a career in the forces seem to stand out, but looking at these entries closely, you will see that some overlap or are actually minor parts of other points. the heading "Security" obviously covers "Slow but steady promotion," "Commissioned ranks open to men and women graduates," and "Can't be fired." Closer examination reveals that "Annual vacation with pay" is an aspect of living conditions rather than of finances; it should therefore be shifted to the second main heading.

Under "Advantages" in the second main heading, the first entry, "Many different branches appeal to different interests," seems out of place or badly phrased. Perhaps the point is that service people may be able to find jobs they like or are best fitted for.

As the plan now stands, the first part seems stronger. To make the argument more convincing, it would be a good idea to reverse the present order: begin with "Living conditions," and then end on an emphatic note—the training that the armed forces provide for other fields. After these changes have been made, and after some headings have been reworded to make them parallel in form, the final outline might be:

Thesis sentence: Although from the standpoint of finances and living conditions there are some disadvantages to a service career for men and women, the advantages outweigh them.

I. Living conditions
    A. Disadvantages
        1. Discipline often annoying
        2. Frequent moves hard to adjust to
        3. Social life restricted to a small circle
    B. Advantages
        1. Opportunity to find the job one is suited for
        2. Annual leaves with pay
        3. Chance to travel, to see new places, and to meet new people
II. Financial considerations
    A. Disadvantages
        1. Relatively low pay
        2. Frequent entertaining expensive
    B. Advantages
        1. Security
            a. Slow but steady promotion, including commissions for men and women graduates

      b. Permanent employment
      c. Good retirement benefits
   2. Preparation for civilian careers on retirement

The outline now can be the basis for an orderly paper that makes a definite point.

Sentence Outlines

A sentence outline is developed in the same way as a topic outline, but the ideas are more fully expressed. Each heading is expressed as a complete sentence, usually consisting of just one main clause:

> Thesis sentence: Although from the standpoint of finances and living conditions there are some disadvantages to a service career for young men and women, the advantages outweigh them.
>
> I. Living conditions are a major consideration in choosing a career.
>   A. Service life has several shortcomings in this respect.
>   1. The strict discipline imposed is often annoying.
>   2. Frequent moves are hard on an officer's family.
>   3. Social life is usually restricted to a small circle of service families.
>   B. On the other hand, there are certain advantages to service life.
>   1. The armed forces, with its wide range of occupations, give one an opportunity to find the job he or she is best suited for.
>   2. There are generous annual leaves with pay.
>   3. Wide travel opportunities can introduce one to new places and people.
>
> II. Financial considerations are also of major importance.
>   A. Two disadvantages are apparent.
>   1. The pay is low compared with that in many civilian jobs.
>   2. Officers are burdened with the cost of frequent entertaining.
>   B. The advantages, however, are more striking.
>   1. The armed forces offer a high degree of job security.
>   a. Promotions are slow but steady, with commissions open to men and women graduates.
>   b. There is almost no danger of dismissal.
>   c. Retirement benefits are good.
>   2. A career in the armed forces provides excellent preparation for civilian careers on retirement.

20.2

Org

Each heading is a complete sentence, and only one sentence—not two or three. All sentences are in the form of statements. All are in the same tense and reasonably parallel in structure.

    The chief advantage of a sentence outline is that the ideas will have to be clear and fully thought out before they can be stated in complete sentences. For that reason, it is sometimes assigned for training in writing long formal reports such as reference (or library) papers.

► **EXERCISES**

1. Choose three of the following general subjects, narrow them to a topic specific enough for a 500-word theme, and write a scratch outline for each: *population growth, separatism, summer activities, effects of television, automobile safety standards, automation, popular myths.*
2. Write a scratch outline on any one of the following topics that appeals to you, or choose your own. When you have jotted down all your notes, frame a thesis sentence and put the notes in the form of a topic outline:

Should Physical Education Be a Required Program?	Speaking in Public
Income Is Not the Primary Goal of Education	Unusual Place Names
Our Local Parking Problem	Forecasting Election Results
	I Prefer Bach

20.3 STANDARD OUTLINE FORM

Numbering, indentation, punctuation, and other physical aspects of outlines follow certain conventions, particularly when the outlines are to be read by someone other than the writer. When you are required to turn in an outline with your paper, use the type of outline your instructor specifies and put it in standard form.

Numbering and Indentation

Make the numbering of your headings consistent throughout. This is the typical method for numbering and indenting a topic or sentence outline:

```
Thesis sentence:_____
        _____   (Sentence statement)
    I. _____   (Roman numeral for main head)
        A. _____   (Capital letter for subhead)
            1. _____   (Arabic numeral for second
            2. _____    subhead)
                a. _____   (Lower-case letter for third
                b. _____    subhead)
        B. _____
    II. _____
```

The main heads (I, II, III...) are set flush with the left-hand margin. The subheads are indented four or five spaces in typed copy and about three-quarters of an inch in longhand, or they may be indented so that they are directly under the first word of the preceding heading, as shown in this book.

When a heading runs over one line, the second line is indented as far as the first word of the preceding line:

    I. The photo-electric cell, known as the "electric eye," has been put to a variety of practical uses.
        A. It is used in elevator doors to enable the elevator to stop at exactly the right level.

When you make an outline, avoid overelaborate and confusing systems. There is rarely any need to go farther than the third subhead (a, b, c...). Two levels of headings are often enough for a short paper.

20.3

Org

Punctuation and Capitalization

In a topic outline, capitalize only the first letter of the word beginning the heading (and all proper nouns), and do not put any punctuation at the end of the entry because these headings are not complete sentences:

    I. Present need for physicists
        A. In private industry
        B. In government projects
        C. In colleges and universities

Punctuate every heading in a sentence outline just as you would punctuate the sentences in your paper: begin with a capital letter and end with a period. Except for proper nouns, other words in the heading are not capitalized (a heading is not a title):

    I. The advantages of specialization are numerous.
        A. Students can set goals for themselves.
        B. They can obtain more knowledge about their subjects.

Content of Headings

Each heading in an outline should be specific and meaningful:

Vague and useless	**Specific**
The Profession I Want to Follow	The Profession I Want to Follow
I. Introduction	I. Lifelong interest in veterinarian's work
	A. Grew up with animals on a farm
II. Why I prefer this work	B. Saw importance of veterinarian's work
III. What the opportunities would be	C. Worked with a veterinarian last two summers
IV. The chances for success	II. Many opportunities in veterinary work today
	A. In rural areas
	B. In cities
V. Conclusion	III. Worthwhile and well-paying profession

Headings like "Introduction," "Body," and "Conclusion" aren't useful unless you indicate what material belongs in these sections. Instead of using general labels such as "Causes" and "Results," indicate what the causes or results are; it will save time later.

Putting headings in the form of questions or in statements that will have to be filled in later is not efficient practice. The necessary information will have to be supplied when you write, so you might as well supply it in the planning stage:

Indefinite	**Definite**
I. The Wars of the Roses	I. The Wars of the Roses
A. When they began	A. Started 1455
B. Why?	B. Caused by rivalry between Houses of Lancaster and York

Dividing the Material

Generally, if a heading is to be divided at all, it should be divided into more than one part. When there is only one heading under a topic, it usually repeats what is in the topic and should therefore be included with it:

Unnecessary division	**Accurate division**
The Hudson's Bay Company	The Hudson's Bay Company
I. Chartered by English king	I. Chartered by Charles II King of England, in 1670
A. Charles II	
1. In 1670	

The heads of an outline should represent equally important divisions of the subject as a whole, and should be parallel in grammatical form and tense. In a topic outline, if *I* is a noun, *II* and *III* are also nouns; if *I* is a prepositional phrase, so are *II* and *III*. The same principle applies to subdivisions. A sentence outline should use complete sentences throughout and not lapse into topic headings:

Unequal headings	**Equal headings**
Growing Roses	Growing Roses
I. Preparing the soil	I. Preparing the soil
II. Planting	II. Planting
III. Growing the plant	III. Watering
IV. Mildew	IV. Fertilizing
V. Insect pests	V. Spraying
VI. Using a spray gun	

The subdivisions should also designate equally important and parallel divisions of one phase of the main divisions:

20.3

Org

Unequal subheads	**Equal subheads**
I. Job opportunities in Alberta	I. Job opportunities in Alberta
A. Raising crops	A. Agriculture
B. White-collar work	B. Business
C. Dairy farms	C. Industry
D. Factory jobs	
E. Breweries	

Headings of equal rank should not overlap: what is in *II* should exclude what is covered in *I; B* should be clearly distinct from *A*.

Overlapping	**Accurate**
Ways of transporting freight	Ways of transporting freight
I. Water	I. Ship
A. Ships	A. Passenger ships
B. Freighters	B. Freighters
II. On the ground	II. Truck
A. Trucks	III. Railroad
B. "Piggyback" in trucks	A. Loaded into cars
III. Railroads	B. "Piggyback" in trucks
IV. In the air	IV. Airplane

Whatever form of planning you do for your paper, take it seriously. Use your plan as an opportunity to see your subject and its parts, and as an opportunity to try different arrangements. Remember that any outline is tentative; you may learn a better way of planning as you proceed.

▶ **EXERCISE**

Check the following outlines from the standpoint of effective and useful planning. Then state specifically what you consider to be the unsatisfactory aspects of each one, in form and content. Revise the outlines accordingly:

1. Types of Canadian schools
    I. Schools open to everyone
        A. Elementary schools
        B. There are many colleges and universities
        C. Secondary or high
        D. Providing technical instruction
        E. Private schools

2. Why everyone should be able to swim.
    I. Everyone should learn to swim.
        A. As early as possible.
            1. Children have been taught as young as three years
    II. The ability to swim may save your life.
        1. never swim alone
        2. don't show off in the water
        3. Many schools require students to pass swimming tests.
            a. my experiences
            b. Red Cross lifesaving test

3. Increasing automation in industry presents many problems.
    I. Unemployment
        A. Permanent layoffs
        B. Shorter working hours
        C. Decreases job opportunities
    II. What is automation?
        A. Definition
        B. Uses
            1. Where it cannot be used
        C. There are many advantages to automation
    III. Increased leisure time
        A. Recreation
            1. Hobbies
            2. Travelling
            3. Adult education classes
    IV. New skills are required.
        A. Trained technicians
        B. The unskilled workers are laid off.
            1. Providing government benefits
            2. Providing added training
    V. Is automation here to stay?

21

Writing the First Draft

. . . The great thing is to last and get your work done and see and hear and learn and understand; and write when there is something that you know; and not before; and not too damned much after. — Ernest Hemingway, *Death in the Afternoon*

No matter how certain you are about the material and the order of presentation, a complete first draft is important if the final paper is to represent your best work. You probably shouldn't expect to be completely satisfied with your preparation and planning. Even with long and careful preliminary work, you won't always have a good sense of everything that you are going to say until you do the writing itself.

Sometimes, of course, when you have studied a subject and thought it out, you will be able to lay out a plan for a piece of writing that has in it everything you wish to say in the order you wish to say it, and your own attitude toward your subject matter will already be clear. If that happens, the actual writing may be easier than usual: you may have little to do but complete your outline or plan by adding illustrations and transitions.

Often, however, even when you have thought your subject through and have a good, thorough, workable plan, you still won't have a good sense of all that's to be said: you still won't know exactly which illustrative material you may need to use to fill out parts of your plan, and your own attitudes toward the material may not be clear until you have found the words for them. It has often been remarked that we do not always know what we think until we hear what we say.

For this reason, when you are composing papers outside the classroom, it is usually best to write them out in rough draft first.

Up to this point, you have been dealing with ideas in abbreviated forms as rough notes or outline headings, even though you may have written bits and pieces in complete form. Now you are ready to put it all down in full sentences and paragraphs, to see the whole paper as your reader will, and to make whatever changes may be necessary for continuity and effective expression.

21.1

Draft

21.1 GETTING STARTED

Begin writing the first draft as soon as you have decided on the content and organization of the paper. Don't wait for "inspiration" or the proper mood: write while the ideas and information are still in your mind; an outline that you put away for three hours or three days can look cold and unfamiliar if your mind isn't still turning in the same way. For almost everyone, writing is work, and you must often begin writing when you would much prefer to do something else. If you wait until the last minute, your first draft may have to serve as your final paper, and the cracks and loose screws in it will show.

The beginning of a paper is often the most difficult part to word effectively. If you can't think of a good opening sentence, begin with some other part; if the wording of a good first paragraph doesn't come to you at once, turn instead to a part that comes more easily. You shouldn't waste time trying to get an ideal opening; as you work, a good start will often occur to you.

Once you have broken the ice by writing two or three sentences, you'll often find it easier to go on, even without that elusive "inspiration." Writing, like many other activities, calls for a warm-up, and you may have to do a few laps and some wind sprints before you are ready to go.

As a rule, write the first draft as rapidly as you can. Your paper will have more life if you put your ideas down one after the other without pausing to worry about correctness. At this stage, you should concentrate on getting down the gist of what you have in mind. You are the only one who will see your first draft, and matters of spelling, punctuation, and wording can be taken care of in revision. (See 29.2, page 452, Revising a draft.)

Plan to spend at least some time at uninterrupted writing. When you are working on a paper that is too long to be written in one sitting, it sometimes helps to stop in the middle of a paragraph or a passage that is going easily and well, perhaps even in the middle of a sentence. This practice will make it easier to get started again when you come back to your work. Take time to read over what you have already written before you begin writing again.

Leave plenty of space in the first draft for making corrections and changes. There should be ample margins on both sides of the page and space between lines for insertions and corrections.

21.2 DEVELOPING YOUR MATERIAL

Make the first draft as complete as possible. Write down *more* than you will probably use in your final paper; be generous with explanations and illustrative examples. It is much easier to cut out material later, during revision, than it is to look for more to satisfy the requirements of length or completeness of presentation. Papers that are heavy with material added at the last moment always seem disjointed. Those that have been pruned down from, say, fourteen hundred to a thousand words are likely to be more compact and to the point.

Put in any good ideas that occur to you when you are writing the first draft, even though they may not have come up in prewriting or in the original plan. In this stage, an outline does not need to be followed down to the last minor subdivision. Frequently a sentence written on paper will bring to mind an aspect of the topic that you overlooked when your material was in the form of notes. If the new idea turns out to be irrelevant, it can be omitted in revision; but if it is important, you can alter your outline to include it.

Kinds of Development

As the full paper grows from the organization plan you have decided on, it should follow the form of development that best suits the topic and that will be clearest to the reader. If you have made an unusually complete plan for your paper, the plan itself may tell you how to develop and amplify each part. Often, however, an outline or some other kind of plan will tell you only what is to be in each part of your paper, not what to *do* with it, or *how* to write it out.

21.2

Draft

The patterns of development discussed in chapter 23 on paragraph types may be useful to you in developing whole papers, though adequate development of a whole paper may require a combination of different kinds of paragraphs. Which kind predominates is determined by the needs of the paper. These are some of the most commonly used types of order:

1. **Time and sequence:** describing events in the order of their occurrence. This approach is apt in narrative writing (a report of an athletic contest, an account of an incident in history) or in describing a process (the construction of a log cabin, stages in the development of a frog).
2. **Space:** describing objects as they exist within a certain area, often used in descriptive expository writing (a description of a city from outskirts to centre, of a mural from left to right).
3. **Increasing complexity:** beginning with the simple or familiar and proceeding to the more complex or unfamiliar (discussing wind instruments beginning with the toy whistle, continuing to simple recorders, and ending with orchestral instruments like the flute and oboe).

4. **Comparison and contrast:** discussing all the features of one idea or situation, then all the features of another, and ending by drawing a conclusion about the two ("Television and Newspapers As Sources of News," "Public Schools and Private Schools"). If such a plan seems to make the paper break in the middle, present a sequence of comparisons and contrasts on each major point—not all the features of public schools and then of private schools, but in some such order as this: 1. Cost of attendance, 2. Curriculum, 3. Facilities.

5. **Support:** beginning with a general statement or impression and then supporting it with specific examples, details, reasons. This method is often useful in argumentation and for such topics as "The Value of Studying Foreign Languages," "The Problems of Increasing Automation," "First-year Composition Courses Should Be Required."

6. **Climax:** beginning with a specific fact or situation and unfolding the subject until it stands completed at the end. A paper about the development of the polio vaccine might begin with the need for the vaccine, then take up the problems facing researchers, go on to explain how solutions were found, and end with the production of an effective vaccine.

7. **Cause to effect or effect to cause:** beginning with an analysis of causes, culminating in a statement of effect, or stating the effect first, then moving to the analysis of cause. The subject should determine which pattern is better: if you are writing about your city's traffic mess, for example, you might want to describe that problem briefly at the beginning as an effect already known, then proceed to an analysis of the causes, which are probably less well known.

The working draft should employ the kind of development most appropriate to your subject. Often two kinds of development are used in combination: a narrative could follow both the order of time and that of climax; the method of support might be used effectively with comparison or climax. the essential thing, however, is that you do present your material in some sensible order.

Controlling Direction

One way to get into your draft and develop your meaning— especially if you are having trouble starting your paper or a particular section of it—is to use a sentence to direct the development. In your opening, for example, you can use your thesis sentence to indicate the development of your theme as a whole.

(See 20.2.) And in the body of your paper, you can similarly work with sentences to direct the development of each section.

Suppose that you have developed this topic outline as the basis for a paper:

The Profession I Want to Follow

Thesis sentence: I want to become a veterinarian because of my life-long interest in veterinary work, because of the many opportunities it offers, and because it is a worth-while and well-paying profession.

I. Lifelong interest in veterinarian's work
   A. Grew up with animals on a farm
   B. Saw importance of veterinarian's work
   C. Worked with a veterinarian last two summers

II. Many opportunities in veterinary work today
   A. In rural areas
   B. In urban areas

III. Worth-while and well-paying profession

The thesis sentence is a guide, directing the development of the outline and the theme. It could be used, for example, to introduce a climactic development that places increasing stress on the series of three factors.

21.2

Draft

The separate sections of the theme could also be directed by opening sentences. For example, we can assume that Section I will require at least three paragraphs. To control the relationships among them, the writer could introduce the section like this:

> Although I grew up with animals on a farm and saw the importance of the veterinarian's work. I didn't really understand all that a veterinarian does until I worked with one the last two summers.

This sentence, which might be used to open the first paragraph of the first section or might be used alone as an introduction, shows how the ideas in Section I are related and gives the writer a direction: there is a time sequence which suggests that the three paragraphs might be narrative; the last paragraph should probably get the dominant stress.

The first section closes with the idea that the writer is aware of the value of the veterinary profession. Section II, then, might open with a sentence like this:

> The needs for veterinary work are great in the country and surprisingly varied in the city.

This sentence, which makes the rural and urban needs co-ordinate, could forecast a balanced treatment by the method of comparison. The section would probably be developed in two paragraphs. Section III might then be directed in this way:

> Because the needs for veterinary medicine are great, the work is worth while; because the work is needed, the pay is good.

This balanced introductory sentence could lead the writer into a balanced, judicious paragraph stating an effect—the causes having been analysed in Sections I and II. (See also 22.1, Paragraph Unity.)

Sometimes a writer can also use particular patterns of paragraph development (see 23) to determine a means of expanding the material; this approach can be helpful in writing short themes. Suppose you arrive in your writing class some Monday morning to find an assignment on the blackboard for an in-class essay. One of the suggested subjects invites your response to the idea of an honor system. If you are familiar with the patterns of paragraph development, you might be able very quickly to settle on a design, a means of developing your paper. Not everyone has participated in an honor system; not everyone knows what it is. You might therefore decide that the purpose of your paper would be to explain what an honor system is. Knowing the pattern of definition, you could develop your explanation in this way:

PARAGRAPH 1: entirely **illustration**, describing an honor system in action

PARAGRAPH 2: **comparison** of honor system with similar things, such as codes of behavior in clubs

PARAGRAPH 3: **contrast**, an account of how honor system is unlike other codes

The sequence of three paragraphs forms a definition: the first by illustration identifies the *term*; the second by comparison puts the term in a *class*; the third by contrast shows how it *differs* from other members of the same class. With this three-paragraph definition, you might then be able to write a fourth, concluding paragraph of evaluation.

▶ **EXERCISE**

For each of the three topics listed below, write out five sentences to show how you would develop the topic according to the suggested pattern of development, as shown in the example.

Example: *Topic*: Origins of Contemporary Pop Music. *Pattern*: Time.
   a. In the 1950's Elvis Presley changed the direction of pop music by combining traditional blues with the noisy new energy of rock and roll.
   b. The 1960's made rock an electrical sound-and-light show, and gave folk music its greatest commercial success.

c. Developments in the early 1970's featured fuller orchestration, a newly polished country sound, and the insistent dance beat of disco.

d. The late 1970's saw the more aggressive and discordant tones of "heavy metal" and "punk" music.

e. Popular music in the 1980's is blending and reconciling many of the qualities that have emerged during the past thirty years.

1. *Topic:* Building a new shopping centre downtown. *Pattern:* space
2. *Topic:* Opinion is divided on the harmfulness of marijuana. *Pattern:* comparison and contrast
3. *Topic:* The discovery that the world is round changed both science and everyday life. *Pattern:* cause to effect

21.3 RELATING PARAGRAPHS IN SEQUENCE

As your write your first draft, remember that you are going to have to take a reader with you. Your individual paragraphs should represent a progressive development of the subject. If there is too wide a gap in ideas between the end of one paragraph and the beginning of the next, the reader may not be able to follow your line of thought. You must provide clear transitions.

21.3

Draft

Showing the Connection Between Paragraphs

Connect paragraphs by linking the topic of each new paragraph with the topic of the preceding one. This is not as hard as it may sound; usually it's easy — and natural — to phrase the opening statement of a paragraph so that it grows out of what you have just said. In the paragraphs below, linking words are in boldface type:

For most individuals, the **study** of **theology** — in particular, the **study** of the differences between Christian denominations, present and past — is undertaken in the manner of a **science** . . . For our forefathers, **theology** was queen of the **sciences** but science (*scientia*) for them still had its Latin meaning: an area of **knowledge**. It was the noblest of all the disciplines.

A careful **scientific** approach to **theology** is, of course, necessary: but it is equally necessary, perhaps more so, to insist that **theology** is an **art**. No **student** of literature, one hopes, would dare claim **knowledge** of Milton after reading a plot outline of *Paradise Lost*. He might well know of the broad parallels made between heaven and hell, and he might note how certain characterizations developed through the epic, but he would not have come to grips with the distinctive Miltonic **tone**. He would not realize the significant difference between the **poem** he was to **study** and its source in Genesis. He would then know the **structure**, but not **understand** the life of the piece.

> **Theological structures** are much like **poems** or paintings. Themes run through them which stand in varying perspectives and recur with varying frequencies. They have color and rhythm; they must be grouped as wholes and experienced as such, or they cannot be **understood**. It is as impossible to read a dogmatic outline of a specific denomination and experience its spiritual **tone** as it is to read a book on symphonies and experience Beethoven. In both cases careful **study**, open ears, and, above all, a willingness to experience a work of **art** as a whole are of first importance. — Adapted from Peter C. Erb, *Schwenckfeld in His Reformation Setting*

Definite links between paragraphs are made here by directly repeating key words and ideas (*study, theology, science, art, tone, structure,* and so forth). As a result, the development of the subject goes smoothly and logically from paragraph to paragraph.

Showing the Relation to the Topic of the Paper

It is also essential to show the relation between each paragraph and the thesis of the paper. This keeps all your paragraphs going in the same direction. For example, the following discussion of stylistic problems in journalism achieves unity by clearly identifying the contribution of each new paragraph to the main topic:

PARAGRAPH 1: As a result of twentieth-century developments Canadian newspapers have arrived at a writing style appropriate to the news presented. [four sentences follow]

PARAGRAPH 2: Haste causes most of the flaws of style to be found in the newspapers. [four sentences follow]

PARAGRAPH 3: Some of the style weaknesses of Canadian newspaper writing grow out of the special conditions under which newspapers are written. One such press-originated convention is the inverted pyramid construction of the news story. [six sentences follow]

PARAGRAPH 4: The inverted pyramid construction begins with an opening paragraph or "lead" which contains the most important details of the news event. [three sentences follow]

PARAGRAPH 5: There are three main reasons why, under modern production conditions, factual news stories should be constructed in this way. For one thing, . . . [five sentences follow]

PARAGRAPH 6: The inverted pyramid convention is particularly useful to the headline writer. [nine sentences follow]

PARAGRAPH 7: A third justification for the inverted pyramid style of news story relates to the common North American practice of holding the front page open to receive important up-to-the-minute news as late as possible. [twelve sentences follow]

PARAGRAPH 8: Whatever the justification of the inverted pyramid, it is susceptible to the criticism connoted by the word "journalese." [thirteen sentences follow]
— Adapted from W.H. Kesterton, *A History of Journalism in Canada*

In the above example, each new paragraph opens with a specific reference to the main topic, *style*. And in every case a further step in the logical arrangement of the ideas is clearly signalled. Although the fourth, fifth, sixth, and seventh paragraphs actually interrupt the main argument in order to explain the "inverted pyramid" structure in detail, specific links enable a reader to keep track of each idea's relation to the overall thesis. The more complicated your subject is, the more important it is to make distinct connections.

21.4 OPENING PARAGRAPHS

The first paragraph of a paper usually has three functions: to introduce the *subject*, to state (or strongly imply) the *thesis*, and to catch the reader's *interest*. It tells the reader exactly what you are writing about, what you have to say, and why it matters.

A good opening is important, even at the draft stage. Don't regard the introduction as a merely ornamental or formulaic flourish that makes no real difference to your paper. A good start, with a clear sense of direction, is essential if your paper is to develop coherently and efficiently. It will give you something specific to which all other paragraphs can be related. Writing it also forces you to think yet again about the wording and significance of your thesis.

If, after finishing your first draft, you find that you have written an obviously weak beginning, see if the second or third sentence, or even the second paragraph, may not provide a better starting point. Often the first few lines of writing are simply a warm-up, and the paper actually begins a few sentences later.

Effective Openings

No matter what you are writing about, the beginning of your paper should catch the readers' interest and get them into the subject. What this really means is that you must be able to show right away that you have a worth-while topic and an original idea about it. Some of the ways to accomplish this are discussed below.

A statement of purpose or point of view. This should not be a mechanical statement ("In this paper I am going to give you my reasons for majoring in political science.") or a flat rewording of the assignment, but a natural lead into the topic:

> When I decided to enter the university, like most undergrads I had only the vaguest notion of what subject I intended to major in. But now after two terms of haphazardly chosen course work, and after a good deal of self-analysis, I have decided that **there are at least four good reasons why I should major in political science**.

If your purpose is to discuss one aspect of some general subject, the first paragraph can make the limits of your paper clear:

> The Great Lakes are among the major lake systems of the world. Through the centuries many large cities have grown up along their perimeter as people recognized their value for inland navigation, water supply, and recreation. Pollution of their waters by industrial wastes has also inevitably increased through the years, until now it presents a serious threat. **The pollution problems in Lake Erie are typical of those of the Great Lakes area as a whole**.

A definition.   If your paper deals with some subject which has a variety of meanings for different readers, it is good to make your definition clear at the outset. There is no need to start with such a trite statement as "According to the *Gage Canadian Dictionary*, a hobby is 'something a person especially likes to work at or study apart from his main business.' " Try a definition that fits your own approach to the subject:

> A hobby, as I see it, is an activity that takes up most of your spare time and all of your spare money. At least that has been my experience since I became interested in photography. . . .

An important fact.   One of the quickest and clearest ways to open a paper is with the statement of an important fact that will lead to the general topic. This is a natural opening for a discussion of ideas:

> Throughout North America, 10.5 million people are out of work, factories are closing their doors, and "backbone" industries such as automobiles, housing, steel, and rubber are throwing themselves on the mercy of anyone who will float them a loan. Meanwhile, a new financial elite is taking shape: the expanding core of entrepreneurs who are turning a $5-billion-a-year profit peddling pornography to the millions of North Americans seeking cheap thrills in an increasingly unaffordable society. —Olivia Ward, in the *Toronto Star*

> My cultural loyalities, like just about everyone else's in this schizoid country we call home, are confusing. I was born in the province of Quebec, a Jew, my nationality Canadian, and the demands on my heart being made by each group seem to me increasingly contrary. — Mordecai Richler, in *Maclean's*.

A reference to personal experience.   If your subject is one with which you have had some personal experience, a reference to your connection with it provides an appropriate beginning. In an essay on the complex problems of the decline in literacy, for example, a university professor begins in this way:

> When I let it slip among ordinary company that I'm a professor of English, you can guess what the reaction is: "Oh-oh," they say with nervous smiles, "I'd better watch my language." . . . And the truth is, of course, that we are — we must be — concerned with language. It is the medium both of the works we study, and of our attempts to teach it. If language should decay far enough, the study of literature becomes difficult or impossible. . . . So I worry a good deal about language myself. And I think the most useful way to put my worries before you is to pursue that automatic reaction: "Oh-oh, I'd better watch my language." — Michael Hornyansky, "Is English Destroying Your Image?"

21.4

Draft

A lively detail or illustration.   A good way to arouse the reader's interest and curiosity is to begin with a lively detail — perhaps with an anecdote, an apt quotation, or an allusion to some current topic. Such material should of course be related to the subject of the paper, as is this beginning of an article on conservation:

> Millions of years ago, a volcano built a mountain on the floor of the Atlantic. In eruption after eruption, it pushed up a great pile of volcanic rock, until it had accumulated a mass a hundred miles across at its base, reaching upward toward the surface of the sea. Finally its cone emerged as an island with an area of about 200 square miles. Thousands of years passed, and thousands of thousands. Eventually the waves of the Atlantic cut down the cone and reduced it to a shoal — all of it, that is, but a small fragment which remained above water. This fragment we know as Bermuda. — Rachel Carson, *The Sea Around Us*.

Openings to Avoid

The opening paragraph should mark the actual beginning of the paper and be clearly related to the subject. If it does not create interest in the subject or get it under way, it probably does not belong in the paper. These common mistakes make poor beginnings:

A naked statement of purpose.   One of the weakest openings commonly found in student writing is the bald announcement of intention: "In this essay I intend to compare and contrast the advantages and disadvantages of. . . . " Your purpose must be made clear, of course, but it should *not* be expressed in the form of a promise or prediction or hope. Don't write "The purpose of this paper is to analyze. . . " or "I shall provide arguments in favor of. . . " or "I hope to be able to prove that. . . . " Such statements are unnecessary. Moreover, they are usually vague, tiresome, and inefficient—especially when given *instead of a clear thesis or idea*.

> POOR: This essay will present evidence supporting the argument that political factors are involved in the acid rain problem.

> BETTER: Political tensions between Canada and the United States are complicating the resolution of the acid rain problem.

As a rule, general statements of purpose are appropriate only in very long and complex essays, or in certain kinds of formal reports. In all other writing, a well-constructed thesis statement will more than adequately convey the writer's intentions. Even an *inductively* organized paper (thesis not fully revealed until the end) needs to have some distinct idea or issue presented at the beginning:

> POOR: I intend to provide arguments regarding the relative importance of various factors in the acid rain controversy.

> BETTER: The important issue in the acid rain controversy may not be economic or environmental after all.

Remember, then, to start by presenting a point of view, not a promise. A decisive beginning will help you write, and it will spare your reader a lot of frustration.

Beginning too far back.   If you are discussing the organization of the United Nations, there is no need to begin with the reasons for the failure of the League of Nations, nor is there any reason to begin a paper on Trudeau as Prime Minister with an account of his world travels. The shorter your paper, the more direct should be the beginning. A statement of the thesis or a rewording of the central idea is the simplest way to begin a paper written in class.

Too broad a generalization.   "Science in the last fifty years has made more progress than any other branch of knowledge" is a generalization far too sweeping to explain or prove in a five-hundred-word or even a five-thousand-word paper. Statements such as this are likely to be more impressive to the writer than they are to the reader. Wherever possible, begin with a specific statement: "Though smaller than your thumb, an electronic device called the transistor has had a tremendous effect on radio and television sets."

A self-evident statement. Avoid starting a paper with a remark so obvious that it need not be made at all: "Canada has many resorts and parks." And resist the temptation to open your paper with some commonplace observation that gives no hint of your own subject: "It has been said that the only thing constant in life is change." If you do decide to start with a very familiar or general remark, be sure that the sentence immediately following is a strong introduction to your particular topic and approach:

> POOR: Beauty is in the eye of the beholder. Different things are considered beautiful by different people. It is a matter of opinion...

21.4

Draft

> BETTER: Beauty is in the eye of the beholder. And when I behold my shiny bald head in the mirror, my eye sees beauty. Hair is...

Of course, broad generalizations and familiar sayings should be used only occasionally as openers. A more direct lead into your subject is usually preferable.

An unnecessary definition. Although a definition can occasionally be an effective opener (see page 292), it is ordinarily a rather tedious and uninformative way of introducing your idea. Use it only if your thesis directly involves the meaning or interpretation of words. Pointless definitions at the start of an essay are misleading and may even seem childish. It would not be necessary or appropriate, for example, to begin an essay on Shakespeare's *Macbeth* with a dictionary definition of *tragedy* or *drama* or *murder* or *king* unless the argument is going to focus exactly on the technical implications of such terms. Similarly, a paper on training skunks should not open with a definition of *skunk* unless, for instance, the writer is concerned with correcting the dictionary's description of skunk behavior.

The purpose of an introduction is to present your main idea and to engage the reader's interest. It is not the proper place for incidental definitions or for formal explanations of specialized terminology. If you must define or clarify unusual language, do so in a subsequent paragraph.

An apology or a complaint.   A statement such as this is discouraging to most readers: "Being a mere undergraduate, I'm afraid that what I have to say on this topic won't be of much value...." Complaints are also better left unwritten: "Before I started to write this theme, I thought I could find some interesting material on it in the library, but there wasn't any...." Remember that readers are interested only in the ideas that you present, not in the difficulties or disappointments you may have had while writing the paper.

▶ **EXERCISE**

Revise the following opening statements so that they at least tell readers what the paper is about. Try also to correct errors of wording and logic, and to make the statement lively enough to catch the readers' interest:

Example: In your modern world of today, personal hygiene has become very important for success in the modern complex world of business.
Better opening: These days, if you want to get ahead, it probably helps to look good and smell good.
Even better: Each year, Canadians spend millions on creams, deodorants, aftershaves, soaps, and other products designed to make them look and smell good. It is a sad reality that one's success in the world is probably determined as much by grooming as it is by talent.

1.   There are many topics of importance in the news these days. One of the many important topics is how we are going to control inflation.
2.   I have always liked certain kinds of hobbies. One of the most interesting hobbies I enjoy writing about is training horses, which is a very interesting hobby.
3.   The abolishment of seat-belt legislation and some of the reasons why I support it is the subject of this paper.
4.   The morning was dark and grey. A fog enshrouded the campus and reflected my mood as I sat at my desk, grimly clutching a pen, and approached the delicate topic of required physical education.
5.   "There are two sides to every question," says the proverb. This is not so in the case of the controversy over whether or not to register handguns. Only one opinion can be substantiated with facts. According to one dictionary, a handgun is a "gun which can be held in one hand easily, usually a pistol."

21.5 CLOSING PARAGRAPHS

The ending of your paper—the place at which you leave your readers—should be among the most interesting and forceful parts of the essay. Plan your paper so that it won't trail off or leave your reader up in the air. The final paragraph should round out your discussion in such a way that the reader will know you have said all you intended to say and that you have not stopped because you were tired of writing or because time ran out. Remember that the total effect of your paper may depend largely upon the way you end it.

Conclusions have three functions: to tie together the ideas you have been developing, to emphasize the paper's thesis, and to leave a strong final impression of your main point's importance or interest. Don't forget this third requirement; if the essay has been worth writing, you should be able to say why. If you can't, a reader may feel entitled to respond to your work by asking "So what?" or "Who cares?" There is no need to offer extravagant claims in this regard, but make some effort to indicate thoughtfully the significance of your topic or approach.

Effective Conclusions

Look at the closing paragraphs (and last sentences) of good books, chapters, magazine articles, or speeches to see the range of possibilities you might imitate or adapt. The important thing is to bring your paper to a definite, interesting resolution. Some suggestions for effective conclusions follow:

21.5

Draft

A climax. Make your final paragraph the culmination of the ideas you have been developing, or save the most important idea for the last. The concluding paragraph thus becomes the climax of the paper. A student paper of about a thousand words, which has described in detail the operation of a large used-car lot, brings all the details to a focus in this conclusion:

> This used-car lot was sponsored by an organization which sells thousands of cars a year, so it was by no means a fly-by-night affair. Although no sloppy repairs were done, and no highly crooked deals were tolerated, there was just a slight suspicion that the company was getting the best of every customer on every deal. Such mistrust typifies the bad public image from which Canadian used-car dealers seem unable to free themselves.

A prediction or suggestion. In certain situations it can be very effective to end your paper by looking to the future. You could offer a prediction, a warning, or a positive suggestion for action, as in this paragraph:

> The fact that this preliminary study has turned up even a few differences between Montreal and Ontario English suggests that further, more exhaustive surveys in these areas would be fruitful. Since differences in the speech of other areas of Canada may be just as

> great, the indications are that a linguistic atlas of Canada would be a worthwhile and almost necessary complement to a dictionary of Canadian English. — Donald E. Hamilton, "Notes on Montreal English"

A prediction or proposal of some sort is especially appropriate if your paper has raised a controversial issue or described a problem. A criticism of campus parking regulations, for example, might close by suggesting a specific alternative or by urging the victims of the present system to organize a protest. However, avoid calling blandly for "further study of the problem" — unless, like Hamilton in the above example, you can recommend particular approaches.

A summary statement.   Longer and more formal papers are sometimes concluded by restating the main points of the discussion. In the following conclusion to a lengthy book review, for instance, a brisk recapitulation of the reviewer's ideas and opinions leads naturally to the final comment:

> O'Hagan's distinction in these tales and the novel is that he shows us not only what it's like to live in the wilderness, but how we ought to behave in its presence. Where his style is firm he gives us observations of nature that are more accurate than those of any other Canadian writer I know of. Where his dramatization is successful he offers useful guides to manners and morals of life in the wilderness. We should have been attending to him for many years. — John Thompson, "Manners and Morals in the Wilderness"

But for most papers written in composition courses, it is seldom necessary or advisable to summarize what has already been said. The result is often a weak and mechanical ending.

Tying the ending to the beginning.   The final paragraph may repeat, in different wording, the opening idea. This method is useful in longer papers, both to remind the reader what the main outlook has been and to give it final emphasis. It is also helpful, if not overdone, in shorter papers, where the repetition of key ideas, key words, or key images may give the reader a sense of a circle neatly closing. The two paragraphs below are the opening and closing of an essay in which the author reminisces about his instructor in writing:

> When I was a freshman, *Gulliver's Travels* taught me more about writing than any other book. Other freshmen might find little to learn from it, but that is because they do not have Craig LaDriere for a teacher. . . .
>
>   Freshman English is not supposed to be a source of innocent

merriment. Its object all sublime is to make thought yield to words. Nobody quite learns how, but I went farther with Jonathan Swift and Craig LaDriere than ever before or since. — Francis G. Townsend, "A Freshman in Lilliput," *College Composition and Communication*

Endings to Avoid

Avoid unemphatic, inconclusive, or contradictory endings. Here are some typical pitfalls to avoid in your closing paragraphs:

A blunt summary.   The weak ending most frequently used by inexperienced writers is the direct restatement of the paper's argument or intention: "In conclusion, I have attempted to show that..." Like the naked opening (see page 294), a mechanical summary at the end is unnecessary and unsatisfying. There is rarely any good reason, in a short or medium-length project, to conclude with a mere repetition of what your reader has already been told. Instead, say something *about* your thesis to indicate why it is important or interesting.

21.5

Draft

An apology.   Ending a paper with an apology for its shortcomings serves only to emphasize them:

> I am sorry this paper is so short, but I always have a difficult time putting my ideas on paper.

If you carefully work out your ideas before writing and then present them as effectively as you can, you will not need to apologize for your efforts.

A qualifying remark.   If the last sentence of a paper is an exception or a qualifying remark, it weakens everything that has been said before:

> Although I haven't answered why some people refuse to face facts, I have come to the conclusion that not facing facts may be a natural part of human nature. Of course, this can be carried to extremes.

There may be two sides to every subject, but when the purpose or scope of your paper is limited to the arguments for one side only, don't suddenly shift to the other side in your conclusion. If, for example, you have been presenting every argument you can think of in support of price controls or strict ecological legislation, don't end like this: "Of course, there is much to be said for the other side also." If you feel such a qualifying statement is necessary, make it earlier in the paper.

Minor details or afterthoughts.   A paper describing the role of the pitcher in baseball shouldn't end with a remark about other aspects of the game:

> Baseball is one of our favorite sports, and to spend an afternoon at Olympic Stadium watching two great pitchers battling for a victory is an exciting experience. What I have said about pitching gives you an idea what a pitcher must keep in his mind while out there on the mound, or as a substitute on the bench. **There are eight other players on the team besides the pitcher and the same can be written about each individual player and his position.**

Some concluding statements make a reader wonder whether the writer actually finished his paper or abandoned it in the middle of an idea:

> I could go on for pages describing the other interesting people I met on the ship, but the length of this paper doesn't permit it.

Instead of putting a sentence such as this at the end of your paper, round out the description fully, or if the topic is already developed sufficiently, see if the next to the last sentence wouldn't make a respectable conclusion.

21.6 WRITING A TITLE

Word the title of your paper so that it gives a definite and accurate idea of the subject matter in as few words as possible. A title need not mystify or startle the readers, although it may perhaps arouse their curiosity or appeal to their sense of humor. Interesting titles are always appreciated, but one that is brief, simple, and exact will serve the purpose; it is, after all, the label on the product.

A title should not suggest more than the paper actually covers. If you are discussing your tastes in music, avoid such sweeping titles as "Modern Jazz" or "Music of Today"; use instead "Music I Like" or "I Prefer Bruce Cockburn." A report on the experiences of a baby-sitter scarcely deserves the title "Child Psychology" or "The Care of Infants"; "Experiences of a Baby-Sitter" will be good enough if you cannot think of a better title.

Unnecessarily long titles are not satisfactory, especially those that merely repeat the assignment: "An Experience in Childhood That Left a Lasting Impression on Me." Moreover, the thesis statement of your paper is not intended to serve as a title. Instead of writing a sentence (Reading Taught by Sound Should Replace Sight Reading), name the subject (Reading by Sound).

The title is not part of the paper, and it should not be referred to by a pronoun in the first sentence. If you want to mention the title in your opening, rephrase it slightly.

Unsatisfactory	**Satisfactory**
Becoming a Citizen	Becoming a Citizen
This is not a difficult process in Canada. . . .	It is not difficult for an immigrant to become a citizen of Canada. . . .

▶ **EXERCISE**

Below are four sample beginnings and endings from student papers. For each one, write two or three sentences criticizing the writing, including the title, if necessary. (Point out effective writing, too.) Then, pick two and rewrite them yourself.

Example: Beginning paragraph from a paper entitled "Good Policy or Bad"

21.6 ◀

Draft

Since I myself have never been outside of Canada, it would be foolish of me to think I can make any useful suggestions about Canada's Latin American policy. However, I have read about recent events in the Caribbean and South America with great interest, and, if you will bear with me, I would like to comment at some length on our present policy.

Critique: (1) The writer doesn't complete his thesis statement (2) The writer needlessly emphasizes his own weaknesses, which turns off the reader. (3) The title might be too general.

Rewrite: Recent events in the Caribbean and South America have stirred up a great deal of interest in the press about Latin America. It seems to me that we should take this opportunity to re-examine Canada's role in these events, and perhaps our entire Latin American policy.

1. *Beginning paragraph from a paper entitled "Modern Chicken Farming"*

    The world today is not what it was fifty years ago. Just think of all the amazing technological changes that have taken place. The automobile has replaced the horse and buggy; radio and television have revolutionized communications; modern medicine has conquered disease. And in 1945 the atomic age was born. Chicken farming, too, has changed drastically from what it was in 1920. I would like to describe some of those changes in the pages that follow.

2. *Closing paragraph from a paper entitled "What a Liberal Education Means to Me"*

    But the greatest value of a liberal education is a personal one; it goes beyond politics and economics. Besides helping the individual to live in his world, it helps him to live with himself. Liberal studies stimulate a love of reason and a flexible, inquiring attitude toward the great questions of mankind. They keep the mind strong and alert and stimulate a well-rounded intellectual development which is as essential to a full life as physical development. A liberal education, in the deepest sense, is an education for life.

3. *Closing paragraph from a paper entitled "The Population Explosion"*

All the statistics indicate that the future is bleak for the human race if the population explosion is not checked. Food, water, and other essential resources are even now inadequate. Living space is dwindling fast. Of course the picture may not be as dark as it looks. Maybe science will find a solution before long, or maybe the explosion will just taper off.

4. *Closing paragraph from a paper entitled "Population Pressures"*

An architect recently suggested that cities could be built in the sea to house the extra millions. They would consist of concrete buildings like silos attached to pontoon islands, and could extend as far below the water as they do above. People who lived on the lower levels could then watch the fascinating underwater world through their living room windows! People have never even begun to exploit the sea and know very little of its hidden wonders.

22

Basic Paragraphing

If a paragraph is to make its proper contribution to the whole paper, it must do something. . . . [It] must first of all make a point — convey an idea or impression. — Porter G. Perrin, "Writer's Guide and Index to English"

Good paragraphing helps writers write and helps readers read. The more fully you realize what an effective paragraph is and does, the easier you will find it to write one. At the same time, a grasp of the basic principles of paragraphing will make you a more perceptive and efficient reader. The important thing to understand is that a paragraph is not just a "lump" of loosely related statements.

A paragraph can be taken as a form of punctuation — a signal. The indentation of the first line of a paragraph tells your reader that you're taking a new step, shifting attitude, turning to a new feature of your subject, looking at some part of your subject in a different way. If a piece of writing shows a mind at work, then paragraph indentations are the major signs that let a reader follow the mind's methodical movement from point to point.

But good paragraphs do more than help you separate and arrange different facts, ideas, intentions, or steps. After all, the sorting of your various points should have occurred at the outlining stage (see 20, Organizing Your Material). Only the most careless writers are likely to let everything become mixed together again. But a plan is just a skeleton, or scaffolding. The real effectiveness of any piece of writing depends ultimately on what you put *into* its individual paragraphs and on *how* these sections of the paper actually cover the different points made in your thesis and outline. In other words, each paragraph can be regarded as an almost self-sufficient "mini-essay" that identifies, develops, and illustrates one specific aspect of the main thesis.

The three ingredients of any good paragraph, then, are the same qualities we expect in all extended writing. The first and most important of these is *unity* — singleness of effect. A paragraph should present and stick to just one idea, identifying it distinctly and showing its relation to the main thesis. Aimlessness or inconsistency, the worst faults a paragraph can have, may be signs of inadequate prewriting or outlining, but often the real problem is vague expression. The second internal requirement is *continuity* — connectedness of thought. Each step in the explanation or argument should be linked clearly to the preceding step so that the reader can easily follow your thinking. Inexperienced writers tend to overlook the disruptive effect of gaps in logic or unexpected shifts of focus, yet even a unified paragraph needs to have its sentences specifically related to each other to maintain coherence. Thirdly, a paragraph must treat its subject with *thoroughness*. In particular, you should provide plenty of details to clarify and illustrate general statements; a paragraph without concrete examples, elaborating remarks, and complete reasoning will invariably seem superficial and unconvincing.

This chapter gives further consideration to these three basic characteristics of all good paragraphing—unity, continuity, and thoroughness. The following chapter (Patterns of Paragraph Development) suggests ways to build and relate various *kinds* of paragraphs.

22.1 PARAGRAPH UNITY

An effective paragraph concentrates entirely on *one* specific topic, is composed with *one* purpose in mind, and employs a definite method or approach. This essential "oneness" of subject, aim, and method is called *unity*. A unified paragraph contributes one distinct point or perspective to the overall development of a paper's main idea. Whenever the writer decides to introduce a new topic or purpose, it is time to end that paragraph and begin another.

One paragraph in a report on "Noise Pollution in Cities," for example, might focus on traffic noise (*topic*), presenting medical evidence about its harmful effects (*method*) in order to convince the reader that traffic noise should be legally regulated (*purpose*). Unrelated matters (such as airplane noise, non-medical effects, or explanation of how noise-monitoring equipment works) would not belong in that paragraph; their presence would distract reader and writer alike from the intended focus and effect. Good prewriting and outlining will have separated all these issues, of course, but it is surprising how often an impulsive writer will mix things together again while composing the draft.

As readers, we expect authors to stick to one subject at a time, to show why they are discussing that subject, and to avoid confusing changes of approach. As writers, we owe our own audiences the same orderliness and clarity.

Unity of Topic

Everyone would probably agree that a good paragraph deals with only one subject. In practice, however, it is hard to achieve *unity of topic* unless the paragraph's subject is kept quite specific. Unity begins with the selection of a topic that can in fact be discussed adequately in a single paragraph of not more than, say, ten sentences. Obviously, ten miscellaneous sentences on the general subject of "Native Land Claims" would not constitute a unified paragraph. That topic is too large and diverse; to be properly explained, it would need to be broken down further into particular aspects (such as causes, kinds of problems, history, examples, possible solutions, and so forth) for treatment in many separate paragraphs.

The following muddled paragraph illustrates the same problem of disunity. While it does refer to a single situation, the writer seems indecisive about what to focus on. Several kinds of ideas are vaguely lumped together instead of being sorted out for clearer analysis in different paragraphs.

> The cave-in occurred at the Colanco mine near Loon Landing, Manitoba. Colanco is a wholly-owned subsidiary of the Raycorp Resources Corporation of Dallas, Texas. Three men drowned in flooded galleries and two others were found buried in collapsed chambers nearby. Some witnesses reported that mining and rockfalls had weakened the bedrock and floors at the 30-metre and 60-metre levels a week before the accident. The company employs an on-site engineer to supervise all technical aspects of production and to conduct regular inspections. These are not prosperous times for mining and smelting firms because the deflated value of basic metals hardly justifies the increasingly high costs of production. Miners are offered bonuses on the basis of how much material they mine during a shift. Jobs are hard to come by and unions are co-operating with management in order to keep people at work. Unstable layers of earth, clay, water, and gravel are liable to fall at any time. At the time of the Loon Landing tragedy, the mine administrator was absent, attending a conference in Montreal.

22.1
¶
Unity

The most confusing thing about the above passage is the writer's apparent inability to choose and stick to one topic. Superficially, of course, nearly everything in the paragraph concerns the Loon Landing cave-in, but different issues or sorts of information are introduced simultaneously. There is no unifying focus. Even if we overlook apparently irrelevant points such as the mine's ownership, we sense that the writer still has at least two differing subjects in mind: *facts* about the mine and the accident, and *implied causes* of the cave-in. These are both worth-while topics, but they don't belong in the same paragraph — unless it were completely rewritten as a direct cause-and-effect narrative or argument. In any case, the paragraph in its present form is inconsistent and inconclusive, and neither of its main concerns is ever adequately discussed.

Dividing indirectly related material into separate paragraphs is almost always a good idea. Besides encouraging you to think harder about your subject and about unified explanation, it promotes the fuller development and illustration of each new point. As shown above, the "miscellaneous" content of a disunified paragraph usually means that *nothing* receives a clear or complete treatment. Splitting a topic gives you more opportunity to be specific. For example, the well-built paragraphs below both deal with early Canadian commercial shipping, but the author has wisely divided that subject into two different aspects (inland and maritime) for more thorough analysis:

> From the first settlements, maritime Canada dominated the seaward approaches to continental Canada and the two were linked strategically. But they were never linked commercially and two separate mercantile systems developed. The commercial empire of the St. Lawrence was based on the exportation of staples from the interior; its transportation system was extended by canals and railways until it stretched across a continent. It served the needs of continental expansion but never developed a maritime extension. Not only was the strain on its resources for continental development demanding enough in itself, but there was never any economic need to develop a maritime extension — there was always sufficient cheap foreign shipping. For continental Canada, commercial maritime interests stopped at tidewater.
>
> In contrast, the commercial interests of maritime Canada began at tidewater. The commercial empire that developed was based on the fisheries, shipbuilding, and international seaborne trading. The period of greatest expansion of the Canadian fishing industry was from the 1830s to the 1880s after the European distant water fleets had largely withdrawn from the cod fishery. By 1878 the Canadian merchant marine numbered 7196 vessels and was the fourth largest in the world. The ships were mostly built and sailed for international trading and not as an economic extension of Canadian continental expansion. — Brian Cuthbertson, *Canadian Military Independence in the Age of the Superpowers*

Unlike the writer of the disunified Loon Landing passage, Cuthbertson has clearly identified and separated his two areas of interest, giving each of them a distinct and detailed treatment. Recognizing the historical differences between fresh-water and salt-water shipping, he has let that natural subdivision determine the organization of his information. A less orderly (or less precise) author might have discussed both topics in the same paragraph. Incidentally, notice that the opening of Cuthbertson's first paragraph actually tells the reader why and how the various aspects of a large and complicated subject have been sorted out. Clarity and unity of topic are maintained because the author has obviously divided and subdivided his material in advance, according to definite criteria: the *commercial* factors are distinguished from *strategic* ones, and then the commercial focus itself is further broken down into *continental* and *maritime* considerations. Altogether, the two paragraphs show how careful discrimination helps you unify and develop a paper's different points.

Disunified writing is especially frustrating for a reader because it neglects the basic function of all paragraphing: clarification of a subject by dealing *separately* with each of its important elements. Unity of topic is the primary principle of a good paragraph; otherwise, there would be virtually no reason for dividing a piece of writing into sections. Such division requires planning, of course, so unless you have done some analysis before writing—at the prewriting and outlining stages—you will probably have a lot of trouble organizing even the simplest subjects into paragraphs.

Following a topic outline.   Each paragraph in a paper covers just one aspect or key point of the main subject. If your prewriting and preliminary organizing have been fairly detailed, you can usually expect to have as many paragraphs as there are headings in the outline. The number of sections you need may also depend on the nature of the assignment and of the material; a long essay on an especially complex matter, for example, may require further subdivisions than your original plan would suggest. On the other hand, writing a short paper on a more familiar subject can present paragraphing problems of a different sort: you may have to reject a lot of interesting material in order to stay within the prescribed length and still compose detailed, unified paragraphs. In either case, thoughtful prewriting activity and a good topic outline will be your best guide to paragraph content and divisions.

Methods of prewriting that result, directly or indirectly, in a highly specific plan can greatly simplify the job of keeping different points in separate paragraphs. Imagine, for instance, that you are preparing a draft from the sentence outline found on page 277. As you can see, the subject of a Canadian Forces career has been organized sensibly into four general aspects (I.A., I.B., II.A., II.B), within which can be found a total of ten subtopics (all the items marked with Arabic numerals). Hence, your essay is probably going to require at least ten paragraphs of detailed explanation *in addition to* an introduction, a conclusion, and any "extra" paragraphs that may seem advisable. One of the subtopics (II.B.1) has been broken down into even finer points; these might or might not need separate treatment.

22.1

¶
Unity

Whether or not you actually compose all those paragraphs in that order, the outline should make it easy to build unified paragraphs. Indeed, the opening sentence for each draft paragraph is already written. Provided you don't put the wrong sort of evidence into a particular paragraph (mixing paid leave with retirement benefits, for example), disunity can be readily avoided.

Eliminating irrelevant material.   Paragraph unity is damaged by the insertion of incidental or irrelevant facts and ideas. Extraneous details are probably less confusing than general shifts of topic are, but both faults are indications of an uncertain or wavering focus. Always decide exactly what a particular paragraph is going to be about, and then ruthlessly exclude all material that isn't directly pertinent. The following passage includes unnecessary and distracting points:

> Among the oddities of the plant world, Venus's-flytrap is one of the most interesting. **Venus is the mythological goddess of love**. It is a carnivorous plant that catches and devours insects and occasionally even small birds. This is done by means of paired lobes that resemble the halves of an oyster or clam, **scientifically known as bivalves**. When the lobes are open, they expose a colorful interior that attracts insects in search of nectar. Once it is disturbed, the powerful lobes snap shut, and strong digestive juices go to work to break down and assimilate the body. **Some people have successfully grown these plants in their homes**.

The boldface statements in this example are not directly related to the subject of the paragraph, and in revision they should be omitted or transferred to another paragraph. The last sentence, for example, might be appropriate in a paragraph telling how to grow a Venus's-flytrap, but it is out of place in a description of the plant's physical qualities.

Unity of Purpose

Singleness of subject is not the only unifying force in a paragraph. Indeed, it is possible for a paragraph to stick carefully to one topic or focus and yet not *accomplish* anything in particular. As the headnote to this chapter states, a paragraph has a job to do — a point to make. A series of related statements about something would not constitute an effective paragraph unless all those details are working together to create one effect or illustrate some definite idea. Another way we can talk about paragraph unity, then, is to concentrate on how clearly and consistently the author's *purpose* is achieved.

For example, you may already have concluded that the real reason for the disunity of the Loon Landing passage (page 305) is that the author appears to have written aimlessly, or at least with confused purposes. We can't figure out what the point is. There is no controlling idea, no single impression, towards which the whole paragraph contributes. The disconnection and inconclusiveness of the various focuses (on background, on facts about the disaster, and on possible causes) may have resulted as much from lack of clear purpose as from lack of organizing. Indeed, if the writer had made up his or her mind about *why* the subject was worth writing about, the many different things covered in that paragraph could have been effectively integrated into a specific cause-and-effect analysis of the cave-in.

The important thing to remember is that you must decide what your purpose is, stick to that purpose, relate everything in the paragraph to that purpose, and make that purpose clear to your reader. No amount of factual knowledge and perceptive observation in a paragraph will make up for the frustration a reader rightly feels when confronted with information that apparently leads to no conclusion, that illustrates no particular idea, that seems unrelated to the main thesis, that requires the reader to *guess* what the point is. On the other hand, writing that communicates its purpose clearly and consistently makes even complicated material easy to grasp:

22.1
¶
Unity

> It is a mistake to confuse unemployment insurance with social welfare. Unemployment insurance is generally only available to those people who have worked in insurable employment, contributed premiums, and are out of work for reasons beyond their own control. A person collecting unemployment insurance must, unless incapacitated, be actively looking for work. At the end of a defined period of time, usually no longer than fifty-two weeks, unemployment insurance benefits are cut off. Anyone, rich or poor, is eligible for unemployment insurance benefits as long as he's a member of the plan.
>
> Social welfare, on the other hand, is only available to people with no other means of support. It is not insurance, but assistance, based on need and supported wholly by tax dollars under the various governments' health and welfare budgets. A person on social welfare can have no savings, have no income, and must, in effect, be virtually destitute. Welfare cases are carefully monitored and recipients receive regular visits from a social caseworker. Assistance lasts until welfare recipients are able to provide their own support. —William James Schneider and Lawrence Solomon, *A Practical Guide to Unemployment Insurance*

The obvious aim of that pair of paragraphs is to show, point by point, the often misunderstood differences between two forms of financial support. This purpose is announced at the beginning and maintained throughout. No other objective or kind of information is allowed to intrude, and the carefully matched structure of the two paragraphs confirms that the composition of the whole passage was governed by the intended effect (emphatic contrast). Both writing and reading are controlled and aided by this definiteness and unity of purpose.

However, suppose that the first sentence of the Schneider-Solomon excerpt were omitted, along with the phrase *on the other hand* at the beginning of the second paragraph. Those omissions would not alter at all the actual information presented, or its arrangement. But the point of the passage would suddenly be much less clear to a reader. Indeed, only after reading both paragraphs (perhaps twice) would the basic principle emerge, and even then the authors' reason for writing might not be plain. This experiment illustrates the importance of making your purpose explicit. The temptation to "let the facts speak for themselves" must be strongly resisted because facts *cannot* speak for themselves. A paragraph aims to show what the facts add up to, and you must make sure that your reader is kept aware of the particular idea or interpretation you expect the whole paragraph to communicate.

Topic Sentences

You can help your reader see a paragraph's topic and purpose by stating the main idea in what is called a *topic sentence*. This is a "covering" statement to which all the other sentences in the paragraph are related. If a paragraph can be likened to a "mini-essay," the topic sentence is its "mini-thesis" —the key point that you think your information illustrates.

The topic sentence typically comes at the start of the paragraph, as in the following judgment upon the Canadian Pacific Railway. The opening remark declares very clearly what the author's topic and point will be, and every other sentence in the paragraph provides examples or quotations to support the original assertion:

> **The CPR has always been all take and no give**. The tiresome litany of what it has given, to build a railway so as to bait the remote Pacific colony of British Columbia into confederation, is well-known. The pattern was set for what the *Grain Growers' Guide*, back in 1918, called "a government on wheels." Pierre Berton in *The Last Spike* detailed how the CPR purposely veered off government-surveyed routes and took more difficult mountain passes so as to control development. It slyly moved its lines three kilometres from the centre

of a young Calgary so as to create a new downtown. The Husky Tower and the core of Boomcity now sit on that land. The CPR was given 6,000 acres of what is now the most expensive land in Canada, in Vancouver, to do what it planned to do anyway: move the terminus 23 km closer to the sea. It still controls all the waterfront property in Vancouver and most of it in Toronto. Robert Chodos, in *The CPR: A Century of Corporate Welfare*, wrote, "There have been corporate welfare bums in this country almost as long as there have been corporations, and none has collected as much money over as long a period of time as Canadian Pacific."—Allan Fotheringham, in *Maclean's*

Placing the topic sentence at the beginning of the paragraph is a good habit to develop, since it can then guide both the writing and the reading of the passage. It is also the most direct way of expanding a sentence outline into full paragraphs; each introductory sentence will already have been drafted. Moreover, starting with a topic sentence is especially advisable if you are dealing with complicated or technical information that might otherwise become confusing.

Another method is to work *towards* the topic sentence, using it as a summation or conclusion for details in the paragraph. Although suspense is not ordinarily a desirable effect in non-literary writing, this arrangement can give a passage a climactic or cumulative movement, as in this example:

22.1
A Unity

The customs office, land office and, eventually, the post office were placed in the station area some two miles away, partly as a result of George Stephen's complaint to the Prime Minister that Dewdney had an interest in the Hudson's Bay section and was trying to place all the public buildings adjacent to it. As a kind of compromise between the two warring factions, the offices of the Indian Commissioner and North West Council were placed half-way between the station and the river. Later, when the registry office went up, it was on a block of its own. The queer community straggled for two and a half miles across the prairies, the various clusters of official buildings standing like islands in the prairie sea. **Regina was a city without a centre.**— Pierre Berton, *The Last Spike*

There is no rule requiring topic sentences to be either first or last. They may appear in the middle of a paragraph, and they may appear both first *and* last, as when a writer returns at the end to his or her main point. (See also 23.1, Inductive and Deductive Development.)

Topic sentences give you *control* over the information you are presenting. Without them, readers will have to reach their own conclusions about the meaning of the facts and ideas collected in your paragraphs. Never assume that the point of a paragraph is obvious, or that any intelligent reader ought to be able to figure out the intended meaning. Emphatic topic sentences ensure that *your* dominant idea will indeed govern both the writing and the reading of every passage, leaving nothing to chance.

Besides controlling the significance of particular paragraphs, topic sentences provide direction for the whole paper. They indicate how the paragraphs are related to each other and to the main thesis. An ideal topic sentence lends unity to its own section, reminds the reader that the subject of that paragraph is one aspect of a wider analysis, and includes some transitional reference to the previous paragraph. The following example is from a generally unfavorable book review:

> **Another organizational problem involves the use of statistics**. The editors are as much to blame as the authors for the awkward way statistics are incorporated into the narrative. I would defy any but the most dedicated friends of the authors to slog their way through the swamp of numbers that begins this book. It is one thing to provide a framework for understanding the period, but it is quite another to make a book unreadable. Throughout the book the narrative is all too frequently lost in a blizzard of figures. The authors seem to think that the way to introduce a subject is to quantify it. The book would be vastly improved if a lot of this number crunching was removed to an appendix. — Daniel Francis, in *Books in Canada*

In the above paragraph a very simple topic sentence manages to do three things. It identifies the dominant idea (*organizational problem*), the subject (*use of statistics*), and (by means of the transitional word *Another*) the paragraph's role in a series of related points. For further examples of the linking force of topic sentences, see 21.2, page 286, Controlling Direction, and 21.3, Relating Paragraphs in Sequence.

Like a thesis statement, a topic sentence should be specific and should not merely state an obvious fact. Vague topic sentences usually indicate that the writer's purpose is uncertain or that the paragraph itself is going to be too general. Moreover, a topic sentence stating a self-evident fact is of little value; it may mean that the writer doesn't see the information's significance, or that there actually is no significance.

> WEAK: Alcoholism is a serious social problem. [too general for one paragraph]
>
> BETTER: Family break-up is one of the serious social problems caused or aggravated by alcoholism.
>
> WEAK: Skiing is a very enjoyable winter sport. [too vague]

BETTER: Nothing can match the exhilaration of skiing perilously down icy slopes or bursting through fresh powder snow.

WEAK: The new Canadian Constitution was approved in 1982. [merely a fact]

BETTER: The new Canadian Constitution, approved in 1982, reflected compromises achieved only after years of fierce debate.

The important thing to remember is that a topic sentence *makes a point*. It states (or clearly implies) *exactly* what the paragraph is about and *why* the information is being presented. A wide variety of topic sentences is illustrated in the samples of effective paragraphing found throughout chapters 19, 21, 22, and 23. Leaf through these sections, noticing how the topic sentences do unify and control meaning. Even in descriptive and narrative writing a single sentence will often give the dominant impression that is borne out by the paragraph's remaining sentences.

Unity of Method

Another way to keep a paragraph unified is to emphasize one of the four kinds of writing—exposition, argument, description, or narration (see 19, What Writing Will Let You Do). If your paragraphing has singleness of topic and of purpose, you should have no trouble achieving *unity of method* by sticking mainly to one type of writing. Strict uniformity is not necessary, of course. Provided you don't lose track of your focus and aim, you are free to use two or more kinds of writing to develop the paragraph's main point. In principle, however, a paragraph's approach should be *basically* expository or narrative or descriptive or argumentative.

Suppose, for example, you were writing about the aftermath of a wild party at your apartment. A paragraph aiming to show the condition of the place the following morning would naturally call for mostly *descriptive* writing. Another paragraph, concerned with your embarrassing experiences at the police station after the raid, would be mostly *narrative*. To explain the pertinent provisions of the Riot Act and the Landlord-Tenant Act, a primarily *expository* paragraph would be required. If you included one or more paragraphs aiming to persuade your reader (or the judge) that you were blameless in the whole affair, you would use mainly *argumentative* writing in those sections. Avoid needless and distracting shifts of method within a paragraph. Begin a new paragraph if you see that a subtle change of focus is going to mean a significant change of mode.

The clue to which type of writing you should emphasize in a paragraph will usually be found in your topic sentence. Ask yourself what the topic sentence seems to promise. A story? An explanation? An argument? A description? If the point of the passage plainly requires two types of illustration (both an extended narrative and a related argument, for example), consider dividing the material into separate paragraphs. The main danger in mixing modes is that even an otherwise unified paragraph can become so inconsistent in *approach* that both writer and reader lose track of what the dominant effect is supposed to be. (See also 22.2, Paragraph Continuity, regarding the disruptive effect of switching methods in mid-paragraph.)

▶ **EXERCISES**

1. Which of the following are too general or pointless to be good topic sentences? Rewrite each unsatisfactory sentence to make it an *effective* opening (or closing) statement for a unified, purposeful paragraph.
   a. The quality of television programming is an interesting subject.
   b. Revelstoke is surrounded by mountains.
   c. Technology develops many new products every year, many of them useful.
   d. Never blame your mistakes on your secretary.
   e. Universities offer courses in economics and accounting.
   f. The Canadian envoys had various experiences on their way home.
   g. Usually, good reports are short reports.
   h. Perennials are plants that live longer than two years.

2. In the sample below, the first sentence is a topic sentence, and each following sentence in some way refers to it. Study the example, and then write similar paragraphs from the topic sentences provided.

   Example: **One popular linguistic myth is that people living in technologically unsophisticated cultures speak primitive languages**. / But the languages of native Canadian Indians such as the Cree, the Ojibway, or the Sarcee of Alberta are as complex in syntax and phonology as English or German. / The many languages of Africa, also, are just as rich and complicated as any language in the Indo-European family. / Even the Ainu — one of the most primitive people discovered thus far — prove to have a language that is capable of expressing the most subtle thoughts and needs of the speakers. / If there is such a thing as a "primitive" human language in existence anywhere on earth, the burden of proof now rests with those who glibly equate mechanization with linguistic superiority.

   a. Renovating old houses can be as expensive as building new ones.
   b. There has been a change in what most students want from a post-secondary education.

c. Men must combat sexism.
d. Wind power has one particular advantage over conventional kinds of energy.
e. The natural enmity between landlords and tenants seem to intensify when the renter is a student.

22.2 PARAGRAPH CONTINUITY

H Con **Rewrite the marked paragraph to make the relationships between ideas clear.**

A paragraph represents a chain of thought. Like the links in a chain, the sentences of a good paragraph are arranged in a particular order and are connected to each other. A paragraph that has *continuity* (or *coherence*) is a series of statements expressing ideas that are closely associated in your mind, and that you want the reader to see in that same relationship. The elements in most paragraphs should be related as closely as the elements in a sentence, where presumably the parts fit each other to make a whole. In the expository paragraph below, the relationships between successive statements are shown in brackets:

> The genetic structure of human cells is extremely difficult to study because of its incredible complexity [topic sentence identifying a specific problem]. A human cell contains an estimated 50,000 genes, compared to 5,000 in a fruit fly and fewer than ten in some viruses [factual details to illustrate opening statement]. The problem of studying human DNA is compounded by the fact that in higher organisms, such as man, not all genes are actively engaged in expressing themselves [a complication that further illustrates the opening statement]. To circumvent these difficulties, recombinant DNA can be used to divide the problem DNA into parts that are individually manageable [statement of the solution to the problem]. In order to study the DNA of higher organisms, scientists...cut it into pieces which are then inserted into micro-organisms, either bacteria or viruses [explanation of how the solution is implemented, with verbal echoes of all previous sentences]. —John Kingsbury in *Perspectives: Profiles of Research at Queen's University*; December 1981

22.2
H Con

Notice too that the key idea of the above paragraph is continually re-introduced, sentence after sentence, throughout the passage (*difficulty to study...incredible complexity...50,000 genes... problem of studying...problem DNA...In order to study*). Particular terms are also repeated or rephrased (for instance, *human...*

human...higher organisms, such as man...higher organisms). This whole pattern of careful repetition and transition keeps each new sentence on track, enabling the reader to follow even a complicated explanation easily. The connectedness or "flow" of a passage is not just a matter of style; it firmly establishes the relation of one idea to the next, making the whole paragraph a logical, step-by-step *process* of thought.

Methods of Showing Continuity

Readers should not have to "read between the lines" to supply missing connections. The most common ways of showing continuity between statements or within long sentences are called *transitional devices*. They include the following:

1. **repetition** of an important word from a previous sentence;
2. use of a **synonym**, a different word of much the same meaning as one already used;
3. use of a **pronoun** or demonstrative adjective referring to a word or idea in the preceding sentence;
4. use of a **connecting word**, an adverb or a conjunction that points out the relationship.

Examples of these signs of the relationship between statements are emphasized and identified in brackets in the following paragraph:

> The union of the two Canadas eventually failed to accommodate regional attachments and sectional frictions, **so** [conjunction signalling cause-and-effect relationship] a new system of government was proposed and **eventually** [repetition] instituted—a federal **union** [repetition] of the British North American colonies in 1867. A principal reason for the **failure** [repetition] of the **1841 union** [repetition] was that the Parliament was based on equal representation from **the two** [repetition] **sections** [synonym]. **Union** [repetition] by **this** [demonstrative adjective] **formula** [synonym] permitted the political recovery of French Canadians and, in Mason Wade's estimation, **it** [pronoun] **also** [adverb signalling expansion] provided for **French-Canadian** [repetition] cultural development. **However** [adverb signalling contrast], **in addition** [adverbial phrase signalling expansion], **sectional identities** [synonym] continued and **indeed** [adverb showing connection and emphasis] hardened.—David B. Knight, *Choosing Canada's Capital: Jealousy and Friction in the Nineteenth Century*

The thought of this paragraph is a unit, and each statement follows the other clearly. You cannot start reading it after the first sentence without realizing that something essential to the meaning has gone before.

We are inclined to overlook the absence of guides to the reader in our own writing, because the intended relationship of ideas is already clear to us, but we notice immediately when other writers forget to show the connection between ideas. Consider how the following unconnected paragraph is improved by showing the relationship between the statements:

> UNCONNECTED VERSION: Many people today believe that objectionable movies should be censored by provincial or local agencies. The recent emphasis in films on immorality and violence is outrageous. They are undermining morals and traditional values, according to many people. There may be some truth here. I agree with the diagnosis, but I cannot accept the cure. Censorship poses a greater threat to a democracy, in my opinion.

> RELATIONSHIPS SHOWN: Many people today believe that objectionable movies should be censored by provincial or local agencies. **These critics** have been outraged by the recent emphasis in films on immorality and violence. **Such films**, according to **them**, are undermining morals and traditional values. **This** may be true. **However**, although I agree with **their** diagnosis, I cannot accept **their** cure. It seems to me that censorship poses a greater threat to a democracy **than objectionable entertainment**.

Listed below are just a few examples of the many hard-working connective words and expressions that you should try to build into your paragraphs. Refer to this list when revising the final draft of a paper, to check that your sentences are effectively linked together in the relationships you want the reader to grasp. In addition to these particular devices, use repetition and synonyms to maintain continuity.

22.2

¶ Con

1. Personal pronouns: **he, she, they, it, his, her, their, its**.
2. Other pronouns: **both, either, several, some, many, most, all, another, latter, this, these, those, that, each other**.
3. Conjunctions: **but, yet, so, because, while, since, unless, if, whereas**.
4. Conjunctive adverbs: **however, moreover, nevertheless, therefore**.
5. Other adverbs: **also, next, then, consequently, otherwise, similarly, finally, meanwhile, indeed, subsequently, first, second, third** (and so on), **instead, earlier, further, besides, rather**.
6. Prepositional phrases: **for example, in fact, for that reason, in addition, in conclusion, in the same way, as a result, on the other hand, in other words**.

► **EXERCISE**

In the sample paragraph below, each sentence picks up a word, phrase, or idea from the preceding sentence. Using the topic sentences provided, write paragraphs following this model.

Example: Lots of Canadians talk about "getting in shape," but few do much about it. By "getting into shape" I don't mean taking a walk now and then or wearing a girdle. There is only one way to get in shape, and that is with regular exercise. And regular exercise means setting aside some time of the day, every day, for strenuous physical activities. Among the useful activities are jogging, push-ups, and sit-ups.

1. The road to riches is usually a muddy path, not a freeway.
2. The registration system at this institution is incredibly complicated.
3. Without the "missing link," evolution remains a theory.
4. The room in which my evening class meets is unsuited to any educational activity.

Continuity in Descriptive Paragraphs

The details in a descriptive paragraph should give the reader a clear, unified impression. Descriptive writing is more than simple enumeration. You need to choose the most effective details and arrange them so that the more important ones stand out. The following paragraph illustrates a lack of selection and focus. Some of the sentences focus on size, direction, and appearance. Others focus on busy activity. Too much attention is given to minor details, and as a result no single impression emerges:

> We entered the Roundup Room through a curtained entrance just past the checkroom. The Roundup room was a long ell-shaped affair with the end of the ell angling off to the left. It was about sixty metres long and probably fifteen metres wide. Along the wall on the left ran a long bar made of dark wood. Behind the bar five bartenders were busily filling orders and giving them to a dozen or so waitresses ranging in age from about twenty to forty-five. Above the bar mirror on the wall were paintings of western scenes and cartoons, like those I described on the outside of the building. Down the aisle in front of us there seemed to be a beehive of activity, with couples coming off and going on to the small dance floor. I say "small" because it couldn't have been more than eight square metres. On our right were small tables, all filled with customers, and on the right wall, farther down, were a number of small booths. We threaded our way through the smoky haze to an empty table.

If the writer intended to emphasize the overcrowding and confusion in this room, she should have concentrated on those features and omitted or briefly summarized such unnecessary details as the shape and dimensions of the room, the paintings above the mirror, the age of the waitresses, and so on.

When you are writing a descriptive paragraph, try to include only the material, facts, or images that will contribute to a single central impression. In the paragraph below, notice that everything is excluded except what contributes to the scene of grim austerity:

> The little crowd of mourners—all men and boys, no women—threaded their way across the market-place between the piles of pomegranates and the taxis and the camels, wailing a short chant over and over again. What really appeals to the flies is that the corpses here are never put into a coffin, they are merely wrapped in a piece of rag and carried on a rough wooden bier on the shoulders of four friends. When the friends get to the burying-ground they hack an oblong hole a foot or two deep, dump the body in it and fling over it a little of the dried-up, lumpy earth, which is like broken brick. No gravestone, no name, no identifying mark of any kind. The burying-ground is merely a huge waste of hummocky earth, like a derelict building-lot. After a month or two no one can be certain where his own relatives are buried. —George Orwell, "Marrackech"

Continuity in Narrative Paragraphs

When you are relating an experience, describing an incident, or summarizing the plot of a story or play, keep the action moving in one direction and avoid unnecessary interruptions. The boldface sentences in the following paragraph destroy the continuity of the narrative because they stop the action:

22.2

Ħ Con

> It was the seventh of August 1976. My friend and I were hitch-hiking from a small town in the northern part of the province. Unlike most adventurers, I did not notice the sky nor did I feel the impending danger. **I guess I don't make a very good hero. Now I must get back to my story.** After waiting by the side of the road for some time, we were picked up by two men in an old station wagon.

Later events in this narrative should show whether or not the writer is "a very good hero." This unnecessary remark not only slows down the action, but also suggests the outcome of the incident before it is unfolded.

The connection between statements in a narrative paragraph is usually simple, since it is controlled by time. Events follow each other as they happened in time or as they are imagined to have happened. The verbs usually carry this movement, and the continuity is made stronger by the repetition of the same grammatical subject from one sentence to another. Time may be emphasized and made more obvious by adverbs—*then, next, before, soon, later, presently* — or by adverbial phrases or clauses: *When he got to the corner . . . , After the last dance. . . .* The boldface verb forms and adverbs of time in the following passage show how large a part words of action and time play in giving continuity to a narrative paragraph:

> **Slowly** the clear place on the grass **enlarged**: oval, **then** round, **then** oval again. The sun **was rising** above the frost mists **now**, so keen and hard a glitter on the snow that instead of warmth its rays **seemed shedding** cold. One of the two-year-old colts that **had cantered** away **when** John **turned** the horses **out** for water **stood** covered with rime . . . , head down and body **hunched**, each breath a little plume of steam against the frosty air. She **shivered** but **did not turn**. In the clear, bitter light the long white miles of prairie landscape seemed a region alien to life. — Sinclair Ross, "The Painted Door"

To maintain continuity in narrative paragraphs, keep the tense of verbs consistent. If you start with one tense — the past or the present — don't shift without reason to another. (See also 19.4, Narration.)

▶ **EXERCISE**

Both of the following paragraphs lack continuity. Rewrite them, making whatever rearrangements, additions, or omissions are needed to make the continuity clear.

1. My grandparents still follow many of their national customs. They have lived in Canada for more than forty years. The traditional ceremony of the eggs begins on the night before Easter, when my grandmother prepares a dozen elaborately decorated eggs. Despite her age, she still has a very firm hand. The eggs are passed from hand to hand around the table, where the whole family has gathered. My grandfather chants a prayer meanwhile. The eggs are taken outside and buried in the garden, and everyone goes to bed for the night. Then everyone takes the candle he has left lighted in his window and returns to the garden. As dawn is breaking, the eggs are dug up and placed in a basket decorated with flowers. There is a sumptuous breakfast to celebrate the successful recovery, and humanity's redemption by Christ has been acted out.

2. When I got about thirty feet out into the lake, I saw that the water was rougher than I had thought. Several large breakers hit me full in the face, and I took in too much water for comfort. There are techniques good swimmers use to avoid getting swamped by breakers, but I had never learned them because I didn't think it was important at the time. I decided to head back toward the rocks, but I couldn't see the flat shelf where I had entered. In desperation, I headed toward a jagged group of rocks nearby. Just as I got close to it and was groping for a foothold, a large breaker threw me against a sharp edge and knocked me breathless. Being thrown against rocks in rough waters is a danger many inexperienced swimmers overlook.

22.3 PARAGRAPH CONTENT AND LENGTH

 # dev **The marked paragraph is not adequately developed. Add enough explanation or illustration to make the central idea clear and complete.**

In a well-developed paragraph the central meaning is clear and complete. Some ideas can be fully expressed in a few simple statements; others may require from a hundred to two hundred words or more of explanation or illustration in order to be complete.

Underdeveloped Paragraphs

The effect of underdeveloped paragraphs is illustrated by the following student narrative of a trip:

> Two years ago I took my first trip up the British Columbia coast. On this cruise there were only forty-five passengers. I learned from the steward that the usual number of weekly passengers ranged from seventy-five to two hundred.
>
> The fruit basket in each cabin was filled daily with apples, oranges, and other kinds of fruit. Since meals were included in the price of the ticket, we could choose anything we wanted from the menu without worrying about the price.
>
> We arrived at our first port, Ocean Falls, on a rainy day. We were told that the ship would be there for about four hours unloading cargo and that we could go ashore if we so desired. After taking a good look at the town, I decided that I would very much prefer to be on board ship.

22.3

 # dev

These paragraphs don't work well because they raise questions that the writer fails to answer: Why were there so few passengers on this trip? (This should be explained in the first paragraph or else not mentioned.) What is the point of the second paragraph, which jumps so abruptly from the introductory statements? the abundance of food? how cheap it was? how much the writer enjoyed it? Some statement is needed at the beginning of this paragraph to link it with the preceding one and to express the main idea ("Because there were so few passengers, we were offered more food than we could eat. . . ."). The third paragraph leaves the reader wondering what Ocean Falls looked like, what unpleasant things the writer saw that made him prefer to stay on the ship. Three or four explanatory sentences would have cleared up this point and would have made the paragraph more interesting.

The following paragraph is similarly underdeveloped. It is too brief to convey adequately the writer's ideas:

> People have been faced lately with many different ideas and systems of government. Each has tried to win the majority to its side, frequently by force or by unscrupulous propaganda. Each person thinks of himself or herself as being representative of the majority.

This paragraph could be improved by listing some specific examples after the second sentence (communism in Angola? monarchy in Spain?) and by using a separate paragraph to explain the third sentence.

A good way to avoid underdeveloped paragraphs is to explore all your ideas fully in the first writing, putting down everything that occurs to you. If the paragraph turns out to be too long or contains irrelevancies, it is easy enough to trim it in revision. To do the reverse — to fill out an underdeveloped paragraph with details and explanations — takes much more time. (See 21, Writing the First Draft.)

Typical Content of Paragraphs

No rule exists that says a paragraph *must* do this, or that, or the other. Paragraphs may have one sentence or many. One paragraph may state a point and amplify it with explanation and illustration. Another paragraph may be nothing but illustration of a point made in a preceding paragraph. A whole series of paragraphs may contain only episodes and illustrations to explain an earlier point.

Still, it is probably reasonable to say that *most* fully developed paragraphs are composed of three kinds of statements:

1. **General statements** in a paragraph may range from expressed attitudes and opinions (This is the better plan; You are wrong) to large generalizations (Everyone needs some form of artistic expression; Prison conditions are in desperate need of reform). General statements may also appear as *restatements*, where a general statement is put into different words for clarification, *summary statements*, where ideas already introduced are brought together, and *conclusions*, where material previously presented leads to a new judgment.

   The most important general statement in a paragraph is the topic sentence. It must "cover" everything else in the passage, providing unity of topic and purpose, so it is likely to be the broadest.

2. **Specific statements** are generally subtopics of a general statement. In a paragraph opening with the general statement "Going to Prince George by car is the better plan," the specific statement that followed might be something like "It has three particular advantages." Specific statements also provide any necessary *links* between general statements and particular examples. Definitions, elaborations, transitional remarks, comparisons, and other supplementary comments are often essential to the clarity or completeness of the paragraph.

3. **Details** are particular observations and facts (He is eleven years old; This violet is a Blue Akey; In two years the city's population increased by 11 460) and summaries of facts (All day the planes had been running late). Details *illustrate* the general statements, either as concrete examples or as careful supportive reasoning. Without ample detail a paragraph will be vague and unconvincing, and probably boring. The most effective writing is in fact made up largely of details, with some generalizations to hold them together and show their meaning, and with occasional specific statements to guide the reader's attention. The following paragraph contains all three of these elements:

> The needs for exotic adventure and self-discovery may well amount to the same thing, since adventure is commonly a way of testing oneself. In a sense every exploration of the world is an exploration of oneself. But I wonder if the designers of the survey realized that many people think exotic means erotic. Away from the constraints of their own circle, many outwardly demure persons are eager to indulge in erotic adventure. I think of the staid social worker in Italy, flushed with excitement as she sped away from her hotel on the pillion of a Vespa scooter behind the handsome bellboy. Or the grave church sidesman rioting through the red-light district of Hamburg like a small boy in a jam cupboard. — Kildare Dobbs, in *Leisure Ways*

22.3

¶ dev

The sentences in the above paragraph are successively more specific. The opening statement establishes a broad connection between exotic adventure and self-discovery, while the second sentence refers expressly to the self-exploration that comes with world travel. These first two sentences can be considered *general statements*. However, the third and fourth sentences illustrate the author's point by focussing narrowly on the association of travel and eroticism; these are *specific statements*. The final two sentences vividly present particular examples of sexual indulgence among vacationers; these are *details*. Paragraphs can, of course, have other patterns. But, whatever the structure or purpose of a passage is, its full development usually depends on adequate use of both details and more general statements.

A good balance of ideas and details is especially important if you are writing about an unfamiliar or difficult subject or if you are examining a familiar subject in an unusual way. In such cases you want to make the point, clarify it further, and provide specific examples. And to do so, you will need to use *expository* paragraphs that combine details with general statements and serve *to explain*. The following expository passage is a fairly technical explanation of the effects of relative humidity on personal comfort:

> The human body is constantly giving off moisture which evaporates into the air at a rate governed by the dryness of the air. The drier the air, the more rapid the evaporation. All evaporation requires heat, and this heat can only be taken from the film of moisture in contact with the surface of the body. It is easy, therefore, to understand that one will feel colder in dry air where evaporation is rapid than in conditions of higher relative humidity when evaporation is retarded.
>
> Recent studies show that at temperatures between 23 and 25°C. comfort actually is not directly connected with the relative humidity over a range of 30 to 80% RH, when light clothing is worn and no physical activity is taking place. Naturally, the amount of clothing, exertion, drafts and other factors will act to change the reaction. Another accepted measure of a desirable condition for optimum comfort is the skin temperature of the person. Ordinarily no discomfort is felt when this is in the 33-34°C. range. — Taylor Instrument Ltd., "Questions and Answers about Humidity"

The first paragraph gives general principles that explain why our sense of heat and cold is affected by the humidity of the air. The second paragraph shows in more specific detail the conditions and factors that govern personal comfort. To the best of the writer's knowledge, all this material is *factual*. Although comfort is not the same for all people, reference is made to "Recent studies" and "Another accepted measure" to assure readers that the information has general scientific validity.

In formal *argument* it is likewise essential to provide enough information of either kind (or of both kinds) to convince a reader to accept the disputable statement made in the topic sentence. In the complex paragraph below, an eminent philosopher combines reasoning and specific details to attack the unclear language used in some discussions of university education:

> Perhaps the felt necessity to be on terms of great friendship and deep understanding with the political authorities is bound to generate humbug. The real business of the university and the conditions under which it is best pursued are not easy to explain to a public that stands

outside the university world. Things may be thought to happen for the best when those who hold political power are themselves reflective about their own educational experiences and are prepared, if they are convinced they ought to, to stand by the interests of the universities without falling into the debased rhetoric that goes with much public talk about education. This rhetoric takes the form not so much of nonsense as of what I can only call *para-sense*. It sounds like sense: words, phrases, clauses, are gummed together to form what are grammatically speaking sentences. But since such pieces of discourse are filled with words and expressions that in their typical uses have neither sense nor reference — there is talk of 'open-ended situations,' 'meaningful relations,' 'catalysts' (where no catalysts, no matter how metaphorical, can be), problems which have 'parameters,' and the rest of the jargon that makes so much talk about education so painful, so idiotic — it is all as parasensical as the first verse of Lewis Carroll's *Jabberwocky*, as parasensical but not as amusing. Parasensical discourse is not likely to provoke public criticism, for the public, and here the universities may be blamed, has been persuaded that matters of deep import have to be talked about in this mystifying way. — J.M. Cameron, *On the Idea of a University*

The above paragraph is essentially a cause-and-effect argument. According to the author, many university people use "humbug" (empty or misleading language) in order to screen themselves from public and political criticism. He illustrates this idea by explaining the universities' difficult position, by describing the sort of evasive jargon that has become popular, by making an unfavorable comparison with *Jabberwocky*, and by quoting particular examples of hollow terms. There is also a suggestion (in the third sentence) about the attitude that politicians *should* have towards university matters.

22.3

¶ dev

Developing paragraphs by full use of details removes a frequent worry of beginning writers — "getting the required length." The bulk of the space in most papers should be taken up with specific statements and details, with occasional general statements to interpret or summarize their meaning.

▶ **EXERCISE**

Select one paragraph from each of three articles in a magazine, or from different magazines. Copy the paragraphs, numbering each sentence as you do so. Then determine what each sentence in each paragraph does and how it is related to the rest of the paragraph. Write down your observations in a phrase or two, numbering them to correspond to the sentences.

Appropriate Paragraph Length

Remember that a fully developed paragraph should cover a clear-cut division of the topic. A paragraph indentation is a mark of separation, indicating to the reader that one stage in the development of the topic has been completed and that another is about to begin.

The real test of paragraph length is not the number of words or lines but rather the answer to these questions: Why was indentation necessary? Does the paragraph express one aspect of the thesis in a unified, coherent, and thorough way? Should any one of the paragraphs be written as two, for clarity and emphasis? Are two so closely related that they should be combined? Appropriate paragraph length follows almost automatically from effective paragraph development.

In practice, however, you should probably expect that your essay's paragraphs will include between five and eight sentences. The requirements of different subjects and different types of projects can vary a lot, but a *typical* paragraph in most student writing should make that number of points. Anything shorter would probably be too vague; anything longer would probably begin to lose unity and continuity. Most of the model paragraphs reprinted in this *Handbook* (notably throughout chapters 19, 22, and 23) are of about that length. To get a further idea of how your paragraphs compare in length with those of experienced writers, examine some recent publications. But don't forget that the scope of any paragraph really depends on the writer's particular purposes and, to some extent, on the requirements or conventions of different situations.

Extended narration, for example, tends to employ longer paragraphs than other writing does. In a chronological account of events, especially in fiction or history, paragraphing may be determined more by the reader's need for regular relief than by definite stages in the story. Good writers of narrative do manage to end each section at a significant or logical point, but the breaks tend to be less frequent and less crucial than in expository or argumentative writing. For this reason, do not imitate in your non-narrative work the lengthy paragraphing found in, say, most novels. Even if you are writing narrative, try to divide very long passages into natural parts, as in the following passage:

> About three years ago when I started my final year in high school, a neighbor who was the captain of the local Naval Reserve unit paid me a visit. He started talking about the wonderful possibilities the

Reserve had to offer—training in radios, electronics, and other technical subjects. Evidently he must have been a good recruiting officer, for after he had talked for an hour, I fell for his argument and joined, thinking I might learn something. I did. [**Next sentence starts a new stage of the topic.**] After a few drill parades, I was able to draw some conclusions about this outfit and my place in it. All the fancy talk I had heard was just propaganda, for as soon as I got my uniform, they hustled me down to the naval dockyard. From then on, for a year, I spent most of my weekly drill parades scrubbing the harbor craft while the Petty Officers stood around talking about sports and women. Occasionally they would look busy when they saw an officer coming, but most of the time they loafed while I worked.

Since the discussion of recruiting clearly stops with "I did," the next sentence should begin a new paragraph.

Perhaps a more common fault of inexperienced writers is breaking up related statements into too many paragraphs. This practice distracts the reader and gives the writing a choppy effect:

The day of the game finally arrives and the first thing you do is look out the window to check on the weather.

As the paper predicted, it is a beautiful sunny morning with very little wind—real football weather. You try to pass the morning by reading about the game, while you are counting the hours and the minutes until the game starts.

Finally you start for the game, only to find the nearest parking lot over a mile from the stadium. You begin the long walk across the campus, joining the thousands of people all as eager as you are, all hurrying in the same direction.

As you pass the impressive Gothic buildings, memories of your undergraduate days come back to you, and you wish for a moment at least that you were back in school again.

22.3

¶ dev

The first two paragraphs concern the morning of the game and should be written as one; the last two paragraphs also deal with one topic—the trip to the stadium—and should similarly be combined.

Avoid imitating the very brief, often single-sentence, paragraphs that appear in most newspapers. These are abbreviated for fast reading and to permit last-minute editorial changes, and are not typical of general writing. Indeed, the fragments of factual information in newspapers, some magazines, and other publications (such as brochures and technical manuals) are not really paragraphs at all. They should not be confused with the carefully developed units or processes of thought described in this *Handbook*. Ordinarily, if there are more than two or three indentations on a single page of your paper, you have probably left ideas inadequately developed, or separated things that belong together.

This does not mean that a short paragraph is automatically a poor one: even a one-sentence paragraph can be used now and then to good effect. The contrast between it and your longer passages can emphasize a dramatic or ironic comment, for example, or indicate a major transition of thought. But such techniques lose their impact if overused. It is almost always better to develop every point fully, resorting to the occasional short paragraph when you have a good reason.

▶ **EXERCISE**

Take a good sampling of the length of paragraphs in your textbooks and in two or three magazines that you read. Take special note of paragraphs that are unusually long or short; how do you account for the atypical length?

23

Patterns of Paragraph Development

When a writer has decided what he wants to say, has chosen the mode of writing which he wishes to employ, and has considered some of the appeals to and expectations of his ideal audience, he might then make some important decisions about the specific methods he plans to use. — Don Gutteridge, *Language and Expression: A Modern Approach*

Much of the labor of writing consists of managing general statements and details, arranging them in sequences that move toward a point, or support a point, or move toward a transition, or achieve some other effect. A paragraph is the unit of discourse in which all that organizing is finally reflected. The qualities of all good paragraphs — unity, continuity, and thoroughness — are considered in chapter 22, Basic Paragraphing. But beyond those common features there are many different methods of effectively arranging and developing ideas.

It would be impossible to describe and give names to all the possible patterns of development that can be used in paragraphing. Every paragraph is unique, and many well composed passages of published writing can't easily be classified. Accordingly, this chapter should be regarded as one very selective and general way of looking at paragraph variety. For instance, our categorizing some patterns by *mode* (expository, argumentative, narrative, and descriptive) is a convenient, but rather artificial, distinction. Any kind of writing can usually employ any method of development, and paragraphs very often combine two or more modes. Furthermore, the patterns aren't mutually exclusive; a passage will often combine or adapt two or more of the approaches suggested here. Remember, then, that these "types" are really nothing more than characteristic ways of thinking that we go through as we mull things over and work them out.

Nevertheless, having some system of classification enables inexperienced writers to recognize differences in paragraph style and to see the importance of *choosing* a form that will best present their ideas. Many standard kinds of development are good and can be used deliberately to control emphasis and achieve variety. Sometimes, of course, any pattern will do. But in many other situations the success of a paragraph will depend greatly on a

23

¶ dev

careful integration of form and content. This chapter outlines some of those opportunities. Examples from a wide range of published sources are used extensively here to illustrate the different types of paragraphs commonly used by practising writers.

23.1 DEDUCTIVE AND INDUCTIVE DEVELOPMENT

The two basic patterns for developing the main idea in a paragraph are *deductive development*, supporting a main point made at the beginning of the paragraph, and *inductive development*, moving toward a main point at the end. Deductive and inductive development are often referred to as the methods of *support* and *climax*.

A deductive or support paragraph often has an emphatic opening, with the topic sentence at or near the beginning, followed by specific supporting details. It is the more common type. On the other hand, in an inductive paragraph, the early sentences provide the data on which the conclusion — usually in the last sentence — is based. (See also 22.1, Topic Sentences.)

Some people say that a deductive pattern is more forceful because its firm opening tends to establish and control the meaning of what follows. First impressions are lasting. But this doesn't mean that an inductive paragraph is a weak one; its climactic final comment gives the main point a different kind of prominence. Final impressions are also lasting. Ideally, a paper will contain some paragraphs of each type — if only for the sake of variety.

23.2 EXPOSITORY DEVELOPMENT

Probably, most of the paragraphs you write are explanatory. Organizing and presenting information are the commonest writing tasks at university or on the job. The purpose of exposition is to select and arrange *facts* and *verified ideas* to show their meaning or relationship. It differs from argument, for example, in this emphasis upon essentially unquestionable subject matter and conclusions; that is, its job is to *inform* reliably, not to persuade. (See 19.2, Exposition.)

Explaining can, however, take a great many forms. A paragraph itemizing in detail the latest technical changes in ski equipment is obviously not going to resemble one that tells skiers how to get from Vancouver to Grouse Mountain. A passage comparing the reproductive techniques of earthworms and elephants will be different from one that explains the difficulty of finding good sex education texts for Canadian schools. Indeed, adopting an unsuitable approach or paragraph structure can frustrate your efforts to develop a point clearly. Facts can be surprisingly hard to work with; their inexpressiveness means that a writer must search for the method of presentation that will best bring out their significance.

A few basic patterns of expository paragraphing are outlined in this section. You should also look in good books and magazines to see how many other ways there are of arranging information and ideas.

Deductive and Inductive Exposition

Although a passage of explanation can be developed either deductively (main point first) or inductively (main point last), the usual expository pattern is a *deductive* arrangement. It tends to be the simplest and clearest way of getting the message across and supporting it with factual material. In the following typical paragraph, for instance, the opening sentence establishes the author's basic idea and indicates why the subsequent details are going to be worth reading:

23.2

¶ dev

> **In Canada, we do have examples of communities that offer chances for individuals to develop as persons and as members of communities.** The Hutterite colonies in Alberta are held together by strong, religious and communal ties; the Hutterites balance change against stability. An ambitious young person first becomes thoroughly immersed in knowledge of his religion which stresses community. Then he his allowed to innovate — according to his religion, in areas where his knowledge and skills increase the community's well-being. The biggest opponents of the Hutterites have been farmers who see in this way of life a form of communism that is profoundly threatening. The simple fact is that the Hutterites are more efficient producers than these individualistic farmers. They look after the land better, and rely less upon government assistance. The Hutterites use sophisticated agricultural technology, but they also produce a lot of their own food and household goods. The fact that they are not avid consumers is also held against them. — Jim Lotz, *Understanding Canada*

Notice that the various facts and comments in the above paragraph lead *from* the controlling topic sentence. The Hutterites' situation is explained in order to illustrate the concept of *community* that is defined at the beginning. We are first told what to expect, and then that expectation is satisfied by specific information. Without its opening sentence, however, we wouldn't know what point the passage was attempting to develop. The deductive (or "support") method depends on its strong interpretive beginning to show *why* the data are being presented.

Expository paragraphs organized *inductively* are less common, but they too can be effective. The important thing to remember when composing an inductive passage is that every detail must really lead toward the final comment, as in the following example:

> In the past, Canadian consumers have had no information available on the absolute or relative efficiency of refrigerators offered for sale. Advertisements and brochures have offered no data that would assist a consumer in comparing the efficiency of alternative models. Even if a manufacturer had advertised the energy efficiency of a single model, the consumer would have no way of verifying that claim, and would have to rely on government or consumer policing of laws governing truth in advertising. The technical features that affect efficiency, such as the type of insulation, the design of the motor and compressor, and the efficiency of the condenser, are not subject to inspection and evaluation by the consumer. The energy use depends in part on the frequency of door openings and the load in the refrigerator. Once a refrigerator is installed, there is no way to determine its energy consumption. There is no separate electrical meter for that appliance, and a refrigerator uses a sufficiently small portion of total household electricity that one could not possibly determine whether a new model used more or less than an old model simply by comparing electrical bills. **Thus, the energy consumption of refrigerators is a characteristic that cannot be determined by inspection beforehand, and cannot be verified in any way after purchase.** — D.N. Dewees, "Energy Policy and Consumer Energy Consumption"

As explained earlier in 23.1, Deductive and Inductive Development, this particular pattern is most useful when you want details to accumulate gradually or to move toward a climactic conclusion, or when you wish to break away from an unvaried succession of deductive paragraphs. The sample passage above, for instance, *could* have been developed deductively. As it is, however, the information is effectively gathered and explained and directed toward the final summary statement.

Exposition by Examples

Sometimes a paragraph can effectively illustrate its topic sentence simply by providing specific examples. A single extended instance may occasionally be adequate, but the usual practice is to give several in order to develop the main impression more fully. This is especially advisable when a paragraph's purpose is to confirm the number or variety of items or ideas that the subject includes. Consider the following passage:

> **The arrival of a small family added to the hard work that a pioneer woman had to do.** Wash water was caught in a wooden rain barrel if it rained, or else it was carried from a nearby slough. The washing machine was a round wooden tub with a handle that was used to turn the machine back and forth until the clothes would be clean. It had a wringer, and a metal washboard and rinse tubs added to the equipment. There was the making of lye soap for laundry. When the creamy mixture was ready to pour, a box would be lined with a flour bag and the liquid soap poured in to set. This also helped to bleach the print from the flour bag, although Robin Hood must have been the best dye that could be had because he sometimes outlasted the article made from the empty bag and all of the lye soap bleachings. In the winter time the clothes had to be hung in the house to dry whether they were first frozen outside or not. The old sad irons were brought out and heated on top of the kitchen stove to do the ironing. In summer time it was a very hot job, and if it could be done at the same time as the bread was baked it saved an extra fire. — Marjorie M. Strum, "A Pioneer Lady"

The above paragraph is a good illustration of exposition by examples. Particular instances are accumulated to corroborate and expand the general statement made at the beginning. Gathering specific, concrete examples is also a helpful way of avoiding the vagueness that can creep into explanatory writing. Successful writers agree that, for the most part, a generalization should never be used when a particular example is available.

23.2

¶ dev

Exposition by Elaboration

Many complex or abstract ideas can't be developed by concrete examples alone. In such situations, the paragraph will probably consist instead of clarifying or elaborating sentences. These explanatory statements should show some careful order (of increasing specificity, for instance, or of step-by-step logic) so the reader can easily follow your analysis. The following paragraph uses elaboration to explain novelist Malcolm Lowry's use of film-like techniques:

> Certainly Lowry frequently used his knowledge of what might be called the film-experience to formulate the experiences of his charac-

ters in *Under the Volcano*, where each seems almost to be entranced by an omnipresent, frequently oppressive world of visual images. At times Lowry tried to use these very visual stimuli to re-create for the reader the actual, physical sense of certain of his characters' sensual experiences and, hence, of the emotions that these experiences evoked. . . . Physical, spatial, and, in part, temporal relationships between reader and image, and character and image, became parallel. As is so commonly the case with film, when character and viewer can literally be made to see the same image (though, to be sure, from different perspectives, in different contexts), the reader and the character could be said to share an experience. The central role of actual, visual stimuli in Lowry's technique might rightly remind one, then, of the function of the motion picture camera. Lowry was attempting to simulate the experience of film, where the viewer's response is rooted in the actual stimulation of the sense of vision. Similarly, Lowry's persistent attempts at the precise physical rendering of the appearance of visual objects which could not be reproduced typographically, indicate his desire to attain, here too, as great a sense of visual immediacy as written description would allow. — Paul Tiessen, "Malcolm Lowry: Statements on Literature and Film"

The passage above aims to show why Lowry sought to simulate in language the visual impact of film. Concrete examples are given elsewhere, but here the author's main point would not be aided by an emphasis on specific details. To explain *why* something happens requires instead a succession of logically related general statements. The paragraph about Lowry develops its idea primarily by means of sentences that analyse, compare, expand, and repeat.

In many situations, of course, you will be able to combine general statements with specific details. (See 22.3, page 322, Typical Content of Paragraphs.) Use whatever method is most appropriate for your paragraph's topic and purpose. Highly factual material, for example, should be developed mainly by concrete details; theoretical subjects will almost certainly require more elaboration.

Cause-and-Effect Exposition

Academic and professional writing frequently consists of (or includes) paragraphs explaining causal relationships. The reasons for many things are accepted as matters of fact. It is possible to explain confidently, for instance, how molecules of oxygen and hydrogen combine to form water, or why a person's tongue sticks to cold metal in the winter. Less definite, but not really disputable, are the reasons for such things as successful advertising techniques or the increasing cost of travel. Even a paragraph outlining the *possible* causes of some phenomenon (perhaps a controversial political decision) will still be expository as long as none of them is declared correct or perferable. Cause-and-effect writing ceases to be expository whenever the writer asserts the validity of a questionable cause (or effect). (See 23.3, Argumentative Development.)

The keys to developing a passage of cause-and-effect explanation are clarity and thoroughness. The reader must be shown exactly what the causal relationship is and what its implications are. One suitable pattern of this type opens with a firm cause-and-effect topic sentence, which is then expanded upon and illustrated:

> **The chief military weakness of the Iroquois was . . . the result of . . . their individualism and their total lack of discipline** [statement of two related causes]. These made it difficult for them to take concerted action or make a sustained effort [effects number 1 and 2]. They were like a ship without a rudder, manned by a quarrelsome crew, able to maintain a steady course only as long as the wind remained constant and some common danger forced the crew to cooperate [effect number 3]. — W. J. Eccles, *Frontenac: the Courtier Governor*

Another common method of cause-and-effect explanation is to begin by identifying the result instead of the cause. The result might be a problem, or an achievement, or simply a change. This information will create interest in the subsequent analysis of the reasons for that effect — as in the following paragraph:

23.2

 # dev

> The most striking thing about Canadian children's books is their paucity. Since 1952 only some thirty or forty have been published each year, and in the years before there were far fewer. This is an infinitesimal number in comparison with the children's books of other English-speaking countries. Some 6,000 are published each year — 3,000 in Great Britain and 3,000 in the United States. Canadian writers for children share all the problems that beset their colleagues in other fields of Canadian writing. **They still have a fairly small market in Canada for their output and therefore small financial incentive for work.** Often in choosing topics or a locale that would specially interest Canadians, our writers limit their sales potential outside Canada. A book on Captain Joseph Bernier, who claimed the Arctic for Canada, would not be read by many people in the United States, just as a recent children's book on the American President, James Polk, would not find its way into many Canadian libraries. But the potential readership for these books in their respective countries would vary considerably. Consider the difference in the two populations: 20 million and 196 million. While both countries yield to regionalism in book purchasing, a book with a Florida setting would

certainly have more readers in the United States than a book with a British Columbia or a Saskatchewan setting would have in Canada. — Sheila Egoff, *The Republic of Childhood*

A third method would be to identify and important fact or event at the beginning of the paragraph, and then illustrate its influence by itemizing the results or effects. Whatever arrangement you choose, be sure that the causal relationships are explained clearly and logically. Distinguish, for example, between direct and indirect causes (or effects), and beware of the fallacy known as *post hoc, ergo propter hoc* (see page 259).

Exposition by Comparison

Some ideas or situations are best explained by being compared with things that are like or unlike them. The exact character of your topic may be more fully illuminated in this way than if you look at it in isolation. The comparison could emphasize *differences* (as in the relative caloric expenditure of running and walking) or *similarities* (as in the parliamentary systems of Canada and Britain). The excerpt below illustrates development by contrast. The first few sentences explain a "traditional" male attitude toward a house; the second part of the paragraph ironically shows how the same situation differs for a "traditional" female:

> A house is all right for a man to work in. He brings his work into the house, a place is cleared for it; the house rearranges itself as best it can around him. Everybody recognizes that his work exists. He is not expected to answer the telephone, to find things that are lost, to see why the children are crying, or feed the cat. He can shut his door. Imagine (I said) a mother shutting her door, and the children knowing she is behind it; why, the very thought of it is outrageous to them. A woman who sits staring into space, into a country that is not her husband's or her children's is likewise known to be an offense against nature. **So a house is not the same for a woman**. She is not someone who walks into the house to make use of it, and will walk out again. She is the house; there is no separation possible. — Alice Munro, "The Office"

For further examples of contrast in exposition, see the paragraphs by Lotz (page 331) and Egoff (page 335). Developing a contrast through *paired* paragraphs is illustrated in the passages by Cuthbertson (page 306) and Schneider and Solomon (page 309).

Information can also be developed through describing similarities, as in the following passage about Dene and Inuit people. Notice that the comparison in this case is divided into two paragraphs: the first explains the main idea and one of the three points of similarity; the second covers the other, less detailed, points.

> There are, of course, distinct differences in lifestyles and other cultural patterns between the one tribe and another. **However, for the purpose of this discussion I should like to consider them as one — the "native" people of this part of the north. There are three basic reasons for this.** The first is that they have many things in common, notably their traditionally nomadic lifestyle. Also, each group seems to have been homogenous, doing little or no mixing with other people, even other people with similar origins. For instance, although the Indian tribes are collectively classed as Athapascan, they apparently did not integrate tribally. The Inuit, although they are now of Alaskan descent, were originally Mackenzie Eskimos in the main, and they too remained quite separate and distinct from the Copper Eskimos to the east and Alaskan Eskimos to the west.
>
> The second reason for considering them as one is based on the fact that theirs was a primitive culture, anthropologically speaking. They have been hunting and gathering societies using "primitive" weapons and tools and some of the earliest methods known to man. The third reason is that contact with the white man was experienced in very similar ways — through the trader and missionary, and all that they brought them, from sugar to disease to Christianity. — Alfred Aquilina, *The MacKenzie: Yesterday and Beyond.*

23.2

¶ dev

Additional examples of comparative development include the passages by Harrison (page 264), Erb (page 289), and Tiessen (page 334). These writers all illuminate their subjects by showing similarities between one thing and another.

Bear in mind that comparison must illustrate some idea. There is no point in listing differences or similarities unless these show us something or lead to some conclusion. A common weakness in comparative writing is the failure to indicate why the subjects are being looked at together or what we learn from that approach.

Exposition by Classifying or Defining

Especially when dealing with complicated or technical information, it is sometimes necessary to explain what class the subject belongs to, or what its own constituent parts are. You may also need to define unfamiliar terms or concepts. A whole paragraph can be developed by either of these means — classification and definition.

Classification is effective when your topic is characteristic of a certain type of subject that can be examined generally, or when it has different aspects of its own that might become confused. Sorting out these qualities or parts can help both you and your reader to understand its nature. In the following paragraph, classification is used to emphasize the authors' point about a "duality" in computer applications:

> For most purposes, it is useful to distinguish two aspects of any computer application. There are **data**, which are the substance that the computer processes and the **process** that the computer carries out using the data. The process is usually called a "*program*". It is useful to focus on this duality for a moment. We have had data (commonly called information) as part of our culture for millions of years; we are comfortable with data being "out there" for processing by human brains. Prior to 1950, and for practical purposes prior to 1978, when the first personal computers appeared—we had no significant device for processing information outside of a human skull. We now have the ability to externalize information processes as well as data. We are only just beginning to learn how to express such processes effectively, but the fact that we are doing it at all marks a significant shift in our intellectual capabilities. Perhaps it also marks a new era in what it means to be a human being, since much of being human derives from our information processing capabilities. — Robert S. McLean and Ruth W. McLean, "Microcomputers in Higher Education"

A paragraph of *definition*, on the other hand, explains an unfamiliar term or concept at some length. The meaning is usually developed with illustrations, background information, and other clarifying comments (such as distinctions or connotations). This fullness and variety of treatment makes the method different from, say, a mere dictionary definition. In essence, the paragraph of definition will be a brief expository essay — a clear and interesting illumination of some phrase or word that must be explained to help the reader understand your paper's main point more easily. The following passage about castles, for instance, clarifies terms that have changed meaning or that might otherwise be confused:

> Although in English studies of military architecture the word 'keep' is now generally used and understood, in the Middle Ages it was unknown. To contemporaries the shell keep was generally simply the 'motte' (Latin *mota*) and the tower keep the 'tower' (Latin *turris*) or, later, the 'donjon'. The custom of calling the tower keep simply '*the* tower' has survived of course with our 'Tower of London', where in fact the keep, the White Tower, has given its name to the whole castle. The words 'motte' and 'donjon' have both suffered much change of meaning. The first, in the form of our 'moat', has been shifted from the castle mound to the ditch or fosse which surrounds both the mound and the whole castle. 'Donjon' or 'dungeon', because the tower keep, as difficult to leave as to enter, was sometimes used as a prison, came to be used first, presumably, for the basement of the keep, and

subsequently for any subterranean, dark and dismal prison or cell, whether beneath a keep or any other building. — R. Allen Brown, *English Castles*

The definition pattern can also be used to show that you are employing a word in some special way; unusual meanings could include personal, obsolete, connotative, or humorous usages. See, for example, Bertrand Russell's paragraph defining *oligarchy* on page 437.

Passages of classification and definition are alike in being "supporting" paragraphs that really aren't part of an essay's main movement of thought. In fact, even important and well-integrated explanations of this sort actually interrupt the development of the overall thesis. For this reason, avoid needless or half-hearted sections of definition or classification. Obvious distinctions and expositions of familiar terms are considered insulting (as well as superfluous) by most readers. Moreover, defining and classifying don't always require paragraph-length treatment; the information can often be given in parantheses or, if necessary, in a footnote or endnote. Like all special forms, the full passage of classification or definition is most effective when used sparingly.

Explaining a Process

23.2

 # dev

When you are writing about how something should be done, or how something works or typically happens, you are explaining a *process*. The subject might be how to use a slide rule, or how a certain type of computer functions, or how a book is published and marketed. Because a process usually involves a time sequence, exposition of this sort can be very close to narration — especially when the past tense is employed. But the special character of a process analysis is its emphasis on a series of typical or habitual acts or steps.

The range of possibilities is indicated by the two sample passages below. The first tells us how to wash a car; the second explains the more complex and technical subject of how engines function:

> Wash your car at regular intervals, and to the extent that weather conditions permit and appropriate facilities are available, at least once a week under adverse conditions. When washing your car, begin by softening up the dirt on the underside of the body with a jet of water. Then rinse the entire body until the dirt has loosened up. After this, wash off the dirt with a sponge using plenty of water. A mild soap or detergent can be used, either one specialized for vehicles or a

general purpose dish-washing fluid mixed with fresh, clean luke-warm (not hot) water. After soaping, your car should be well rinsed down with clean water. —Consumer and Corporate Affairs Canada, *Anti-corrosion Code and Owner's Care Guide*. Reproduced by permission of the Minister of Supply and Services Canada.

· The conventional gasoline engine functions by drawing a vaporized mixture of gasoline and air into itself, compressing the mixture, igniting it and using the resulting explosion to push a piston down a cylinder. In the cycle of the diesel, only air is drawn in; the air is then very highly compressed so that it heats up naturally. In the next stage, a very accurately timed and measured quantity of fuel is injected into the cylinder, and because of the heat of the air, the mixture explodes spontaneously, which is why the diesel is sometimes referred to as a compression-ignition engine. —Tony Hogg, "That Old-time Ignition"

The important thing in explaining procedures or functions is clarity. Even the most apparently simple operations can be hard to present concisely and fully. Ambiguous references, unfamiliar terms, or omitted steps will be fatal to a reader's understanding, as will disorderly sequencing. The transitional expressions used in narration (*then*, *next*, *as a result*, *before*, and so forth) will help you to develop a coherent paragraph of process.

▶ **EXERCISE**

Compose effectively developed *expository* paragraphs according to the instructions outlined below. Feel free to modify the suggested topic sentences or subjects.

a. A *deductive* paragraph beginning with the topic sentence "The government issues driver's licenses only to people who can demonstrate in several ways their competence to operate a car."

b. An *inductive* paragraph ending with the topic sentence "Altogether, the facilities at _____ are everything an enthusiast could wish for."

c. A paragraph developed by *examples*, beginning with the topic sentence "Today's students are becoming more inventive in their excuses for late assignments."

d. A paragraph developed by *elaboration* on either the popularity of racquet sports *or* the purpose of family allowance cheques.

e. A *cause-and-effect* paragraph explaining one of the following:
   (i) indirect results of high energy costs
   (ii) why clothing styles change so often
   (iii) drinking and driving

f. A paragraph of *comparison* (or *contrast*) on one of the following:
   (i) hockey and lacrosse
   (ii) high school and university (*or* college *or* a job)
   (iii) the costs of driving a car and of public transit

g. A paragraph of *classification* beginning with the topic sentence "A professor has two main academic responsibilities: research and teaching."

h. A paragraph of *definition* on one of the following terms: *electronic*; *remedial course*; *seasonally adjusted rate of unemployment*; or *statistical validity*. In each case your explanation would be assisted by distinctions and examples.

i. A paragraph explaining a *process*, on one of the following:

    (i) how a garment (*or* a record album *or* a photographic print) is made

    (ii) how to find a summer job

    (iii) what to do when the smoke detector begins buzzing at 3:00 a.m.

23.3 ARGUMENTATIVE DEVELOPMENT

We write *argumentatively* when we want to convince readers to accept our interpretation of a disputable subject. You must remember that no matter how strongly you hold to an opinion, other viewpoints are also possible and supportable. To be persuasive, then, a paragraph must *defend* its main point so that an impartial reader will accept it as probably true. In some situations, this means showing why your conclusion is preferable to another. (See also 19.3, Argumentation.)

There are two key principles in developing a good paragraph of persuasive writing. First, the topic sentence must make a clear and debatable assertion—a definite statement with which it would be possible for people to disagree. (Factual topic sentences–indisputable ideas that need only to be illustrated–are inappropriate in argumentation.) Secondly, the remaining sentences in the paragraph must demonstrate logically the reasonableness of that proposition. In other words, your proof or support must satisfy the standard criteria of evidence and sound thinking. The success of an argumentative paragraph depends not on the strength of your own belief, but, rather, on the clarity and thoroughness with which you show why your readers should also accept it.

23.3
arg dev

A few of the patterns of expository paragraph development (see 23.2) are also used effectively in argument. Other forms, some borrowed directly from the practices of public debate, are more specifically suited to persuasive writing.

Deductive and Inductive Argument

The commonest method of argumentative paragraph development is the basic *deductive* arrangement. By emphatically stating the main proposition at the outset, you keep it uppermost in the reader's mind and retain control over the interpretation of the evidence that follows. The excerpt below illustrates this pattern of assertion-and-defence. Notice too that the paragraph isn't expository: it opens with a debatable statement and supports it with other learned (though not indisputable) opinions and logical inferences. The author continually indicates that the subject is problematic and open to question, and that his own approach requires justification:

> **And yet, while reading Biblical myth poetically is a more liberal exercise than reading it as factual history, trying to reduce the Bible entirely to the hypothetical basis of poetry clearly will not do.** There is no difficulty with Homer or the Gilgamesh epic, because they are poetic throughout, but large areas of the Bible are clearly not poetic. To put it another way, the Bible taken as a poem is so spectacularly bad a poem that to accept it all as poetry would raise more questions than it solves. Besides, we should have no criteria for distinguishing, say, Jesus from the prodigal son of his own parable, both being equally characters in fictions, and nobody would take such an approach to the Bible very seriously, whatever his degree of commitment to it. There are and remain two aspects of myth: one is its story-structure, which attaches it to literature, the other is its social function as concerned knowledge, what it is important for a society to know. We now have to consider this second aspect of myth, remembering that just as the poetic aspect had already developed toward literature by Biblical times, so the functional aspect had developed toward historical and political thought. — Northrop Frye, *The Great Code*

In the deductive paragraph above, the opening statement firmly governs a reader's interpretation of the reasons and suggestions provided afterward. We know what the writer is trying to prove, and we find every sentence adding support for that idea.

In an *inductively* organized passage, however, data accumulate gradually to lead the reader with a kind of inevitability *toward* one conclusion. The main point isn't explicitly declared until the end. This technique is less frequently found in argumentative writing than the deductive approach is, but it can be effective when you particularly want the weight or direction of the evidence to emerge naturally, as in the paragraph below:

> Certainly Canadian authors spend a disproportionate amount of time making sure that their heroes die or fail. Much Canadian writing suggests that failure is required because it is felt—consciously or unconsciously—to be the only 'right' ending, the only thing that will support the characters' (or their authors') view of the universe. When such endings are well-handled and consistent with the whole book, one can't quarrel with them on aesthetic grounds. But when Canadian writers are writing clumsy or manipulated endings, they are much

less likely to manipulate in a positive than they are in a negative direction: that is, the author is less likely to produce a sudden inheritance from a rich old uncle or the surprising news that his hero is really the son of a Count than he is to conjure up an unexpected natural disaster or an out-of-control car, tree or minor character so that the protagonist may achieve a satisfactory *failure*. **Why should this be so? Could it be that Canadians have a will to lose which is as strong and pervasive as the Americans' will to win?** — Margaret Atwood, *Survival*

The climactic movement of the paragraph above enables us to feel we have shared in the process of reaching the final conclusion. Such effects also add greatly to the stylistic variety of your paragraphing. Readers become weary when one pattern is used constantly — even (or especially) if it's a forceful one like the deductive method of assertion and support. An occasional paragraph arranged inductively will help to keep interest alive.

Development by Examples or Reasons

The main point of a typical argumentative paragraph can be supported either by specific facts or by logical reasoning, or by both. Depending on the topic and purpose of a passage, the writer will decide which of these methods is most appropriate and most convincing. No matter which technique is adopted, however, the author's interpretation of the evidence must satisfy the standard criteria for valid conclusions (see 19.3, Argumentation).

23.3

arg dev

Argument by factual examples.   One way of developing an argumentative point is to provide specific *examples* that corroborate the main point. If the details offered as evidence are accurate and representative, a writer may not need to add much additional comment. The kind of information that can be used in this approach includes statistics, historical facts, results of research, experts' testimony, and other verifiable data that readers will accept without much question. Such material – sometimes called "hard evidence" – can usually be *interpreted* in different ways, however, and this is where the argumentative element comes in. Your topic sentence must specifically indicate the conclusion to which you think the examples lead. In the following two-paragraph passage, for instance, the writer cites research findings in support of forceful topic sentences:

> **The differential rates of surgery between the sexes reflect a similar disrespect for women.** Women tend to receive more surgery than men, particularly in certain categories. Take gallstones. Dr.

Eugene Vayda, associate dean of community health at the University of Toronto's Faculty of Medicine, points out that Canadian women receive four times more gallbladder surgery than men, although an English study found the prevalence of gallstones to be about the same in both sexes.

Operations performed exclusively on women, such as hysterectomies, suggest another wrinkle to the sexual politics of sickness. Hysterectomy is now one of the most frequently performed operations in North America, a statistic that lends alarming credence to Barker-Benfield's belief that hysterectomy and mastectomy have replaced female castration as outlets for male aggression. A Saskatchewan study actually discovered that 25 to 30 percent of the hysterectomies done in that province were unnecessary. When the hospital boards were informed of their too liberal use of the scalpel, the rates dropped considerably. — Judith Finlayson, "The Sexual Politics of Sickness"

Unless there is some reason to challenge the author's facts, the only potentially disputable points in the excerpt above are her interpretations of the information. Readers who agree that such evidence about medical practices does suggest sexual politics or disrespect for women will be convinced. Readers who don't find those particular conclusions valid will not be convinced, and should be prepared to explain why. Of course, you would have to read the whole article before firmly making up your mind.

The advantage of an argumentative paragraph developed entirely (or primarily) by specific details and examples is its concreteness. When your idea *can* be illustrated and defended with factual data, you would be unwise to neglect so persuasive a form of evidence.

Argument by reasoning.   Certain important kinds of ideas can't easily be supported by concrete examples. Moral and philosophical principles, for instance, as well as many less abstract topics, need to be developed by *reasoning*. Reasons are logically related ideas (known as *inferences*) that demonstrate the probable truth of an assertion. Reasoning is usually more complex than illustration by example, mainly because its evidence isn't strictly factual. Instead, logical inferences emphasize the rationality or good sense of a conclusion. The reasonableness of any proposition or proof is judged by its adherence to established principles of sound thinking (see 19.3, Testing the Argument). In the following passage, the writer defends a controversial viewpoint by urging us to accept the logical consequences of a basic principle:

In negating all rights to the fetus we are saying something negative about what he or she is. And because the fetus is of the same species as the mother, we are inevitably faced by the fundamental question of principle. What is it about the mother (or any human being) that makes it appropriate that she should have rights while the fetus does not? The stark comparison between members of the same species unveils inescapably the terrible question. What is it about our species that makes it appropriate that we have rights at all? If the fetuses are accidental blobs of matter, aren't we also? It is this that is frightening about those who argue that the fetus in the womb has no rights. **In that affirmation is implied a view of human beings that destroys any reason why any of us should have rights.** —George Grant, "The Case against Abortion"

The above paragraph is typical of arguments on important subjects that lack "hard evidence." Such topics must be investigated and discussed by reasoning. Readers will be convinced (or not) by the logical consistency of the inferences. As always, a reader who does not accept the conclusions of an argument should be willing to explain what is faulty about them.

Combining examples and reasoning.   In most argumentative writing you will be able to use both factual details and reasons to support your thesis. Even within a single paragraph it's often possible–depending on the nature of the topic–to effectively combine examples with extended inferences. The excerpt below **23.3** illustrates this method. The authors begin by drawing out the logical implications of their research into writing instruction; then they mention a specific case that dramatizes those rather theoretical ideas:

Arg dev

> **The problem with the "current-traditional" rhetorical framework within which these teachers seem to be operating is not just that much is omitted concerning the process of writing but that, as a result of these omissions, the nature of the whole is distorted.** When teachers ignore the cognitive aspects of the process and focus only on the rhetorical features of the completed product, they ignore the interrelationship between the intellectual and rhetorical dimensions. . . . Further, when they focus only on the rhetorical dimensions of the writing, they may actually impede the intellectual growth. In the end, no doubt, these intellectual skills will develop anyway. But the short-run effects of such evaluation are probably to encourage students to operate on the safe levels they have already mastered in writing their essays, not to venture further. In Emig's study, Lynn, the precocious twelfth grader, when given a choice of topics, chose to shy away from the personally difficult, to stay with the easy task. . . . The kind of evaluation which rewards performance according to rhetori-

cal criteria and does not recognize intellectual leaps forward encourages students to take the same cautious stance in the intellectual sphere as Lynn did in the psychological. — Aviva Freedman and Ian Pringle, "Writing in the College Years: Some Indices of Growth"

Some combination of examples and reasoning is characteristic of many argumentative paragraphs. The two kinds of evidence complement each other: the details provide concreteness while the inferences extend the ideas beyond the realm of mere facts. It is a good idea, then, to include both general ideas and specific instances whenever you are composing a paragraph of argument. Your pattern of development can be either from the general to the particular (as in the Freedman-Pringle passage above) or from the particular to the general.

Concession Pattern

Because there are two (or more) sides to every worth-while argument, you will often find yourself wondering how to react to evidence that doesn't support your position. Indeed, points favoring the opposite side may be undeniable. It's unwise to simply ignore such potentially troublesome material; pretending it doesn't exist might suggest to the reader that your case is superficial or dishonest. Instead, you should willingly *concede* it, acknowledging that you recognize its relevance. Then you can go on to explain why those points are outweighed by the strength or number of other facts and reasons that do support your position.

A paragraph of argument by *concession* has a definite pattern. It begins with a sentence or clause mentioning the other side's good point, but attention is then shifted immediately to the development of your own position on that topic. Openings like the following are typical:

> **Although nuclear power is risky and expensive,** it is the only practical alternative to conventional energy sources. Danger and cost have to be weighed against the advantages of. . . .

> **Dogs and cats are obviously the most popular pets in North America.** But for exotic interest, no pet is superior to a tarantula. Uniqueness is important in a pet. . . .

In the two examples above, the worth of the other side's point is frankly admitted before the argument for a different position begins. The concession pattern, with full development of the writer's own viewpoint, is used similarly in the following paragraph about radar speed traps:

> **While radar is a useful control measure to stop speeding on residential streets, in school zones and in high accident areas**, there's no doubt it's also being used as a cash register by the police. This is made all the more peculiar by the fact municipalities don't get all the fines from speeding but only a percentage back from the province. Still, it's daily occurrence to see registers — we mean radars — being operated from illegally-parked cruisers in areas or at times where a speeder threatens no one. While there must always be upper limits to speed in urban areas, such radar traps are operated by more zeal than common sense. — *Canadian Motorist*

The paragraph by Northrop Frye on page 342 is a further example of development by concession. Like the author of the radar passage above, Frye has built a "while" clause into his own topic sentence.

The occasion for a concession paragraph arises when you sincerely believe that the overall strength of your case outweighs one or two undeniably strong aspects of an opposing view. This pattern thus permits you to demonstrate your fairness, your familiarity with both sides of the issue, and your ability to evaluate the relative significance of different facts and ideas.

Refutation Pattern

A *refutation* or *rebuttal* is a direct attack on the argument of the opposing side. Unlike a concession approach, it challenges the accuracy, logic, or importance of ideas that have been (or could be) advanced by the other side. Characteristically, a paragraph of refutation begins with a succinct and fair statement of the position the writer intends to deny; the rest of the passage is then devoted to a detailed criticism of that viewpoint. The pattern might open in the following way:

23.3
arg dev

> **Opponents of sex education in schools also claim that learning too soon about sexuality leads children into premature experimentation.** But premature experimentation is going to occur anyway, and it is more dangerous when kids are given no information or warnings. Moreover,. . . .

Sarcasm, oversimplification, and exaggeration should be avoided in your summary of the idea you are challenging; use wording that would satisfy its supporters. And be sure that your objections are clearly and logically developed.

For an example of development by refutation or rebuttal, see Gideon Rosenbluth's paragraph on page 253, which includes a note of concession: "It is true that. . . however,. . . ." Tactful acknowledgements of that sort can actually strengthen a paragraph of refutation by showing that even the apparent strengths of the other side's case are not damaging to your position.

The advantage of a good refutation is that it shows your familiarity with both sides of the issue and your ability to analyse logically the weakness of an opposing position. Used honestly (and in combination with positive arguments for your own viewpoint), this technique can greatly enhance the convincingness of your essay. But beware of basing a whole paper on negative or destructive points. It is one thing to anticipate the objections that might be made to your thesis, but quite another thing to concentrate entirely on finding fault with the other side's ideas. It's a fallacy to assume that disproving someone else's position is in itself an adequate proof of your own.

Argument by Comparison and Analogy

Comparison.   One good way of persuasively developing an idea is to compare or contrast it with another idea. Provided the two situations are truly comparable and the connection is logical, this technique can greatly illuminate and support a difficult point. In the following passage, for example, comparison is used to put the author's idea into a broader context:

> Some of this might be bearable if Canadian academics were paid the high salary that current myth assigns to them. But this is not so. If one looks at lifetime earnings, academic salaries are similar to many other callings in the community such as school teachers and carpenters. This is not to devalue the work of these professions, merely to point out that the notion of the highly paid professor is simply false. Furthermore, it is getting harder and harder to recruit new blood into the community, partly because there are so few jobs and, where there are jobs, the starting salaries are so low that it is difficult to recruit the best. It is, in fact, in many cases more attractive to work for the Post Office, than to become an assistant professor. — Donald C. Savage, in C.A.U.T. Bulletin

Although this kind of argument doesn't prove that academic salaries *should* be higher than (or equal to) those in certain other occupations, the comparisons do clarify the issue by dispelling myths about income levels.

Analogies.   Unlike comparison, argument by *analogy* is often a questionable technique. The trouble is that analogies are based on partial or incidental similarities between things that are otherwise unlike. For example, there is no real resemblance between rotting fruit and a corrupt government, nor any logical relation between the law of gravity and the principles of economic theory. Nor are "dirty" hands like "dirty" movies. All such analogies are, by themselves, merely figurative: they may be witty or picturesque, with strong emotional appeal, but they are inappropriate as a basis for argument. The differences between the things compared are much more important than any coincidental similarities.

An analogy can be effective, however, if it has logical similarities and if it is not treated as evidence. Even a partial resemblance between basically dissimilar situations may clarify or dramatize some idea that the writer wants to establish. In the example below, a vivid analogy is drawn between military sacrifice and economic sacrifice:

> Reliance on tight money and high interest rates are all too reminiscent of the propaganda tactics of the First World War. There, after the horrors of the Battle of the Somme, the generals decided that, rather than admit the errors of their ways, they would claim they were winning and that persistence was needed. The result was years more of outrageous bloodletting. Similarly, one would think that the central bankers in Western Europe, again with the exception of Italy, would realize that their monetary policies will not work, that tight money leads to a sharp drop in output and employment, years before there is a major and lasting effect on prices and wages. Tight money must be pursued into the "bloodletting" of a major depression in order to break the inflationary psychology. One would hope that there would be a recognition that this policy must be abandoned. — Bruce Whitestone, in the *Kitchener-Waterloo Record*

23.3
arg dev

Notice that the author isn't asking us to believe that war is a lot like economics. That would be a false analogy in this context. Instead, he urges us to recognize the principle of mass involuntary sacrifice that links the otherwise dissimilar situations. Not all readers will share his alarm, of course, but the analogy provides an interesting and original perspective on the issue.

▶ **EXERCISES**

Compose effectively developed *argumentative* paragraphs according to the instructions outlined below. Feel free to modify the suggested topics in order to keep your paragraphing specific and unified:

a. A *deductive* paragraph arguing that the women's movement is (or is not) a threat to men.

b. An *inductive* paragraph arguing that parents and civic groups have too much (or too little) influence on the public-school curriculum.

c. A paragraph using mainly *specific examples* to praise or criticize some aspect of a television program.

   d. A paragraph using mainly *reasons* to show why the salaries of elected officials should (or should not) be reduced.

   e. A *concession* paragraph beginning "Although it is often a bad idea for a student to have a part-time job. . . . "

   f. A *refutation* or *rebuttal* paragraph arguing against the view that professional athletes are overpaid.

   g. A *comparison* (or *contrast*) paragraph on one of the following:

      (i) A plagiarized essay is like a bad cheque

     (ii) Killing an animal is (or is not) the same as killing a human

    (iii) Government employees should (or should not) have greater job security than workers in private businesses.

23.4 NARRATIVE AND DESCRIPTIVE DEVELOPMENT

Certain kinds of ideas are best supported or illustrated by narrative or descriptive details. While these two modes can sometimes be used for their own sakes (especially in personal writing), their usual function in general and academic situations is to complement the development of mainly expository or argumentative projects. For example, if the topic sentence of a paragraph declares that something important *happened*, the natural method for that passage will probably be narrative—the particular incidents of the story. Similarly, if a topic sentence refers primarily to the *appearance* of something or somebody, the paragraph should probably consist largely of specific description—visual details that create an image in the reader's mind. In either case, the purpose of the paragraph is to confirm and particularize whatever dominant impression is intended by the author.

Bear in mind this principle that a successful narrative or descriptive paragraph does communicate some particular idea or effect. Like a good expository or argumentative passage, it is composed with a specific purpose and contributes an important point to the essay. Your reason for writing is to indicate the *significance* of the events and details you have selected. Although the topic sentence of a descriptive or narrative paragraph isn't always explicit (the main point can often be *implied* clearly enough), be sure that a unified and worth-while impression emerges.

Different types of narrative and descriptive development are outlined below. (See also these other pertinent sections of the *Handbook*: 19.4, Narration; 19.5, Description; 22.2 Paragraph Continuity.)

Narrative Patterns

Narration is story-telling—relating a series of events (real or imaginary) that establishes a unified impression or point. Narrative writing differs from factual (expository) discourse in this emphasis upon *action*. Depending on the writer's subject and aim, the sequence of occurrences in a narrative passage may be more or less particular or dramatic, but the effect is always one of *development through time*. Narration usually recounts events chronologically and employs the past tense.

In non-fictional writing, narration is commonly used to illustrate an expository or argumentative thesis. Professional historians, for example, are *interpreters* of the past; the events they narrate are chosen and offered as evidence in support of scholarly explanations of our history. Indeed, everyone who writes narrative needs to do so with some particular idea in mind that is confirmed or clarified by the story. No matter which pattern of development you select, don't forget to show (directly or indirectly) the paragraph's point.

Deductive and inductive narration.   While the order of events in all narrative writing is temporal, a story can be developed either deductively or inductively. That is, the author's own interpretation of or comment on the action may come either at the beginning of the passage or at the end. A paragraph of *deductive* narration opens with a statement of the author's idea, and then illustrates that point by relating a pertinent sequence of incidents. This pattern emphasizes the writer's position – the meaning he or she sees in the story – and employs the particular events mainly as supporting evidence. In the example below, the main point is announced at the outset and governs our reading of the subsequent details:

> **But this time he knew how to proceed. The full collaboration of the Inuit was already the key to his method.** It was to be a film not only about the Inuit but also a film by them. In line with this method, they soon became involved in every phase of the production, from "acting" in front of the cameras, to planning scenes and assisting in processing the exposed film, and repairing the equipment. As his principal character, Flaherty chose Nanook, a celebrated hunter in the district. Nanook became totally engrossed in making the film and was a constant source of ideas. One of his first suggestions was to film a walrus hunt, done as in the old days before the white men came with their rifles. It as an extraordinary event and the sequence became one of the most famous in *Nanook of the North*. —Peter Morris, *Embattled Shadows: A History of Canadian Cinema 1895-1939*

23.4

¶ dev

Like all deductively organized narratives, the above story develops from and serves to illustrate the author's opening assertion. Stress is being placed on the meaning of the events – the idea they are intended to confirm – rather than on the dramatic qualities of the action itself.

On the other hand, *inductive* narration reveals its dominant idea gradually, accumulating incidents that lead to some conclusion or comment at the *end* of the passage. In such cases, emphasis falls more noticeably on the "story quality" of the events, the author's ultimate point being less obtrusive than in a deductive paragraph. The passage below is typical of inductive technique. Notice how the author makes no judgment about the action until the final two sentences:

> On the two thousand mile voyage from Pennsylvania to Prudhoe Bay, the Manhattan got stuck in the ice a dozen times, freed by the relatively tiny (nine thousand tons) Canadian Coastguard icebreaker John A. MacDonald. With the engines rocking his big ship back and forth to free it from the ice that gripped it like a vice, Manhattan's Captain Roger Steward drawled, "You just gotta keep 'a-swinging'." In McClure Strait, north of Banks Island, the Manhattan was not doing much swinging. Caught in a pan of polar ice ten feet thick, with ridges twice as thick — sparkling crystal blue ice, centuries old and as strong as concrete — the Manhattan was stuck for thirty-four hours. From where I watched it, as a journalist back and forth between the two vessels on this journey, it seemed to me that the Manhattan would be there yet if it were not for the help of the Johnny Mac. **Still, the Manhattan did demonstrate that, if properly designed, an ice-breaker tanker could operate through these Arctic waters.** — Earle Gray, *Super Pipe*

Thinking about the purpose of your project will sometimes help you decide which of these two methods will be most suitable. If you are mainly interested in showing what the events prove or suggest, you may want to use deductive patterns most of the time. If, however, the action itself is of primary importance or interest, inductive organization may be the best way to give it the desired prominence. Emphasis can also be controlled by employing more or less explicit topic sentences: a strong statement focusses attention on your interpretation whereas a more casual (or merely implied) comment keeps the story in the spotlight. In addition, it is a good idea to change patterns now and then for the sake of variety; long narrative papers in which all the paragraphs have the same form can become very tedious for a reader.

Levels of generality in narration.   Another approach to writing narrative paragraphs is to concentrate on the *type* of action or incidents being presented. There are many kinds of stories, ranging from the extremely general (the history of the world) to the highly particular (your activities during the past two minutes), and effective development depends in part on where your material fits into this spectrum of generality. The following three excerpts from Helen Moore Strickland's *Silver Under the Sea* illustrate how the subject (and, of course, the purpose) of a narrative passage can affect the writer's treatment of the events. Each of these paragraphs presents a story to illustrate a point, but they deal with different kinds of events, cover different spans of time, and achieve different effects. The first is relatively general, summarizing the career of a nineteenth-century Canadian mining entrepeneur:

> **William Bell Frue was a man of distinguished talents, of great benevolence of character who, like a magician wrought a wonderful change in the Canadian wilderness of Silver Islet and the surrounding country.** He helped to transform the once lonely, desolate shore into a thriving and industrious settlement with churches, a schoolhouse, post office, store, custom house and substantial dwellings for over 500 men. It was the best harbour refuge on the northern shore of the lake, with a lighthouse on Silver Islet and range lights on the mainland. There were extensive wharfs for shipping ore and supplies, with basins protected by breakwaters, and with three steam tugs and a sectional dock for repairing vessels. Silver Islet itself had been enlarged to over two acres, well protected against storm and water, and covered with buildings for mining, assorting and packing the ore. All this was what William Frue walked away from, boarded a steamer at the landing and sailed away over the lake that he had bested through sheer guts and determination.

23.4

¶ dev

The passage above is fairly typical of good historical summary. Several events that each took a long time to happen are mentioned to confirm the opening statements that a "wonderful change" occurred. Considered as *narrative*, this information is very general; no attempt is made to illustrate in exciting detail the "magic" or "guts" of Frue's exploits. Uniformly long sentences unfold with calm detachment, relating *what* was done rather than *how*. Indeed, while the paragraph's controlling method is narrative, the general and factual nature of the story bring it very close to expository writing. Only the climactic final sentence presents a specific action (Frue's *walking*, *boarding* a ship, and *sailing away*), and even there the vividness and immediacy of the event are deliberately slight. In a paragraph intended to review a whole career, the author has wisely avoided graphic accounts of particular incidents.

A much different kind of story, from another part of the same book, is given below. In this passage the writer *does* dramatize specific and vigorous action. The excerpt is taken from her account of a mine disaster (sentences from the adjacent paragraphs provide a context):

> . . . . While the tumult raged, Dugan and Swanson kept up steam and the pumps running to hold the flooding in check. Suddenly, Frue heard a loud explosion.
>
> Dugan! Swanson! They were down there, trapped in the rapidly flooding boiler house. If he could . . . **but there was no time for anything.** Suddenly, where the boiler house had been there rose a geyser of water, timber and metal. Blow up! The boiler must have burst, its plates buckled by the ice-cold water smashing against the hot metal. Debris showered around Frue. A falling plank slashed him and sent him reeling. For a moment he fought for balance then fell into the swirling torrent. The water slammed him against a beam protruding from the shaft house and he grabbed it.
>
> As he clung there waiting for the flood to recede, he realized the lake had beaten him again. . . .

Notice the contrast between this narrative and the previous one, especially the differences in specificity and effect. Consider pattern, pace, elapsed time, tone, sentence lengths, and extent of authorial comment. The dominant impression in this second sample is one of violent physical activity and emotional turmoil. Emphasis is placed on the exactness and rapidity of events and on exclamations of horror and surprise — all occurring during the moments between the explosion and Frue's sad reflection. Everything is immediate and dynamic; nothing is generalized or distanced by overt interpretation. A very similar technique is used in Thomas Raddall's exciting paragraph about the Halifax explosion (see page 261).

Of course, not all narrative writing is either historical summary or fast-paced drama. In fact, most of the narration you are likely to use will probably fall somewhere between these extremes. In relatively short papers a blend of specific happenings and general comment is usually best; it helps you keep both your focus and your purpose clear. Moreover, the function of the narrative mode in academic and work-related projects is almost always to support a particular idea or assertion that you want the reader to accept. Hence a paragraph requires convincing details *and* controlling statements. The following paragraph, also from *Silver Under the Sea*, is typical of such writing:

> In the search house, every man was required, upon coming out of the

mine, to pull off his boots and clothes to be searched for silver. **This procedure did little to stop hijacking of silver.** In the winter, the men upon leaving the shaft and before reaching the search house would toss choice pieces of ore out on the ice and retrieve it after they had been thoroughly searched. In the summer they would fasten the ore to the underside of a log or plank, send it adrift towards Burnt Island and collect it later. They took their booty home, put it in whiskey kegs, and when these were full, buried them in their back-yards and cellars. Seventeen kegs were buried as far as is known. Many if not all of these kegs are probably still resting where they were buried for the miners did not have much opportunity to smuggle 17 kegs of silver off the island.

The level of generality in this paragraph could be called "medium" because although the actions are described precisely there is no moment-by-moment detail. A more general approach would not permit the exact accounts of highjacking techniques, and a more dramatically specific approach would distract the reader's attention from the main point. Many ideas, like the one stated in Strickland's topic sentence here, refer to past experience in a way that requires narrative illustration of this sort. She makes her point by recounting interesting and characteristic happenings that demonstrate the futility of search procedures.

Descriptive Patterns

23.4

Description aims to communicate the *sensory* qualities (usually the appearance) of its subject. Like the other types of writing, description consists of facts, ideas, and sensations that work together to establish some particular impression. In other words, a good descriptive passage is not merely ornamental: only in bad writing (including bad poetry) are visual images and other sensory details used just to create a "fancy" effect. Nor are occasions for descriptive writing limited to literary projects. Like narration, it is very commonly employed in non-fictional, even highly technical, situations.

The materials of descriptive writing are precise perceptual details — distinctive colors, shapes, sounds, atmosphere, and other sensory data about the subject. It differs from simply expository writing in this emphasis on vividly recreating what the eye sees, the ear hears, and so forth. The arrangement of these details will depend on the effect a writer is trying to create.

Deductive and inductive description.   Like narrative patterns, methods of descriptive development can be either deductive or inductive. In either case, however, your topic sentence should make clear the meaning or purpose of the various details in the paragraph. In the following *deductive* passage about an Inuit village, for example, the specific opening statement is necessary to show the intended significance of the whole:

> **Used to the ramshackle houses of the northern Indians, dotted about at random around a settlement, I found the tidy lay-out of the houses here a revelation.** They were mostly of the standard prefabricated Government type, the 'crackerbox' one room, and its larger cousins with two or three bedrooms. They had large windows and slightly sloping roofs, usually festooned with caribou antlers, sealskin frames or furs; all were oil-heated, water came from big, plastic tanks filled from the water tank, and sanitation was the standard model for a land where no subsoil drainage is possible — an outsize green garbage bag lining a pail and crowned with a plastic seat. Colours of houses varied according to individual whim. The white people, the Kabloonahs, had a somewhat more elaborate version, plus a bathroom, the exception being the nursing station, which consisted of two trailers. — Sheila Burnford, *One Woman's Arctic*

Without a firm topic sentence, the unifying principle of the descriptive details in that paragraph wouldn't have been clear. We wouldn't have realized that the passage aims to illustrate a "revelation" about the tidiness of Inuit living arrangements. Although the passage might still have presented an interesting picture, its apparent lack of relation to any general idea or purpose would have made it seem inconclusive.

A description organized *inductively*, on the other hand, keeps back its unifying comment until the end. Particular details gather gradually, creating an overall impression that is then summed up or assessed in a concluding remark. The following excerpt is an example of inductive development.

> It was a little south-facing dell, surrounded by dense thickets of brambles and dogwood; a kind of minute green amphitheater. A stunted thorn grew towards the back of its arena, if one can use that term of a space not fifteen feet across, and someone — plainly not Sarah — had once heaved a great flat-topped block of flint against the the tree's stem, making a rustic throne that commanded a magnificent view of the treetops below and the sea beyond them. Charles, panting slightly in his flannel suit and more than slightly perspiring, looked round him. The banks of the dell were carpeted with primroses and violets, and the white stars of wild strawberry. **Poised in the sky, cradled to the afternoon sun, it was charming, in all ways protected.** — John Fowles, *The French Lieutenant's Woman*

Inductive paragraphing lends variety to your paper, and it can sometimes be used to achieve an order of ascending interest within a passage. Most people consider it more dramatic than deductive writing; like spatial order (see below), it imitates the way in which we do look at things before forming judgments.

Spatial order.   Typical of much descriptive writing is the arrangement of objects in some logical spatial sequence, such as far to near, high to low, large to small, and so forth. This method gives a paragraph internal coherence and direction. It also appeals realistically to the reader's "mind's eye" by positioning the visual details in the order in which they might be noticed by an actual observer. Consider the systematic sequence (far to near) in which the elements of the following description of a valley are presented:

> The valley became narrower and its sides steeper. Road, river and canal made their way as best they could, with only a twenty-yard strip of wasteland — a tangle of rank weeds, elderberry bushes and rubble, bleached debris of floods — separating river and canal. Along the far side of the river squeezed the road, rumbling from Monday to Saturday with swaying lorry-loads of cotton and wool and cloth. The valley wall on that side, draped with a network of stone-walled fields and precariously-clinging farms and woods, came down sheer out of the sky into the backyards of a crouched stone row of weavers' cottages whose front doorsteps were almost part of the road. The river ran noisily over pebbles. On the strip of land between river and canal stood Top Wharf Pub — its buildings tucked in under the bank of the canal so that the towpath ran level with the back bedroom windows. On this side the valley wall, with overshadowing woods, dived straight into the black, motionless canal as if it must be a mile deep. The water was quite shallow, however, with its collapsed banks and accumulation of mud, so shallow that in some places the rushes grew right across. For years it had brought nothing to Top Wharf Pub but a black greasy damp and rats. — Ted Hughes, "Sunday"

23.4

¶ dev

Hughes has arranged his material very carefully, adopting the point of view of a person situated on the near side of the valley. He begins with a general prospect of the scene, and then focusses in turn on the far side of the valley, on the somewhat nearer river in the middle of the valley, on the even closer area between the river and the canal, on the canal in the immediate foreground, and finally on the muddy water itself (which seems to be at his feet). A grimly ironic concluding sentence suggests the author's purpose in developing the scene.

All descriptive paragraphs should exhibit some such concern for logical order. Examine the other sample passages printed in this section of the chapter, noticing the ways in which spatial arrangement and coherence are maintained.

Concrete detail in description.   Because the aim of all descriptive writing is to evoke precisely its subject's sensory properties, a special degree of exactness and definiteness is needed. The various excerpts in this part of the chapter illustrate that dependence on concrete details. Without it, a passage is merely expository, stating facts rather than creating visual impressions. For example, general terms like *beautiful*, *ugly*, *big*, *colorful*, *funny-looking*, *impressive*, or *old-fashioned* are too vague and abstract to render specific images. So, when you are developing a descriptive paragraph, concentrate on naming particular objects and qualities. The difference between vague and precise description is illustrated in the two paragraphs below. The first is a weakened and generalized "translation" of the second:

(a) Lizzie was unusual in appearance. Her shape was unique. She was heavy, short and was always wearing aprons and dull clothes. She moved rapidly and grumbled a lot. She had a foreign accent and spoke severely except when reading to us on religious subjects. Our mother was her favorite.

(b) No shapes remain on earth like the shape of Lizzie. As nature forgot the combination that produced the pterodactyl, so it forgot the formula for Lizzie. Fat is not the word. It was all in the way it was gathered up in sundry places. Five feet short, a presence stiffened by uncompromising stays, she appeared many-aproned. Black buttoned boots, black cotton stockings and long buff-coloured flannel underwear were the staple items of her wardrobe. Her boots squeaked. She never walked but moved at a bustling dog trot, muttering the while a kindly sort of scolding. Cockney born, her aitches remained flighty all the days of her life. Her voice never descended to the sentimental except when she read to us from her book of Bible stories; then, as she sat on a little rocker, steel-rimmed spectacles tipped low on the bridge of her nose, her eyes would water and her voice fill with a special religious prayer. Our mother was her spotless darling and we counted as nothing compared to 'Miss Mary'. — Anne Wilkinson, *Lions in the Way*

The contrast here between bland, abstract generalizations in the first passage and exact, lively impressions and images in the second is obvious. The first passage is so inexpressive that we would probably consider it essentially explanatory rather than truly descriptive.

Description is hence the mode of writing in which "originality" is most important. This doesn't mean that you must strive for strange or fanciful effects or that you require some sort of poetic inspiration. It does mean that you must look hard and honestly at your subject to identify its individual characteristics, and that you must choose language that will communicate those unique qualities with precision. See, for example, Naipaul's highly particularized paragraph about India (page 266).

Description by comparison.   Among the many ways of creating sharp visual images for your reader is the use of particular comparisons. Sometimes the peculiar quality or behavior of something, or the impression you want it to suggest, is otherwise hard to put into words. The following passage about an old horse, for instance, consists almost entirely of humorous comparisons, mostly similes:

> As grim as Don Quixote's Rosinante would look next to elegant Pegasus, that's how Malkeh would have looked next to Rosinante; she was U-shaped in side view, as if permanently crippled by the world's fattest knight lugging the world's heaviest armour. She sagged like a collapsed sofa with stuffing hanging low. She was bare as buffed mohair, her shoulders tanned from the rub of reins, her color an unbelievable combination of rust, maroon, purple, bronze, found elsewhere only in ancient sun-drenched velvets. Her tail was a Gibson Girl's worn discarded feather boa, its fly-discouraging movements ritualistic, perfunctory, more to let flies know that Malkeh wasn't dead than that she was alive. Her legs, like a badly carpentered table, were of assorted lengths, which made Malkeh move by shuffling off like a pair of aged soft-shoe dancers in a final farewell. Her hooves were fringed with fuzzy hairs like a frayed fiddle bow abandoned to rain and sun, her horseshoes dime thin, rusty as the metal hinges on her wagon's tailgate. To encourage Malkeh to see, Bibul covered her almost-blind eyes with a pair of snappy black racing-horse blinkers trimmed with shiny silver rivets, a touch to her decor like a monocle in the eye of a Bowery bum. — Jack Ludwig, "Requiem for Bibul"

23.4

 # dev

Naturally the tone and frequency of these particular comparisons would not be appropriate in all kinds of writing, but the passage does show how effectively a vivid visual effect can be established by citing similarities.

There are many methods of comparative description. See, for instance, the paragraph about Brock and Tecumseh on page 361, and the opening of Sheila Burnford's passage about native settlements on page 356.

Technical description.   It is important to realize that descriptive writing is by no means limited to the creation of so-called "liter-

ary" effects. A common and very practical use for clear description
is in technical writing — especially scientific, industrial, and consumer reporting. Such projects often require the accurate rendering
of an object's shape or color or other aspects of its appearance. The
following paragraph is just one example of this sort of writing; here
cartographers are describing the design of early Canadian maps:

> **On examining any of the early sheets of this series one is struck by
> the spartan appearance of the cartography.** The type used for the
> map title and number is a form black-letter type commonly used on
> posters. The remaining marginal information is in Roman but in point
> sizes that are far larger than necessary. The place names on the face of
> the map are somewhat less oppressive but still of a point size larger
> than that used on modern maps. The line work is coarse, with the lines
> of the land survey system dominating the whole presentation. In the
> original concept this series of maps was designed to give a simple
> presentation of the survey system and those topographic features that
> were necessary for the location of property boundaries, the whole to
> be shown in black and white at a convenient scale for use on the
> counters of the land registry offices. The poster-like appearance was
> probably intentional as no doubt the use of these sheets on the walls of
> railway stations, police posts and registry offices was commonplace.
> — N.L. Nicholson and L.M. Sebert, *The Maps of Canada*

Notice in particular the emphatic topic sentence that opens the
above excerpt. In technical description it is especially important
that the significance of the details be stated explicitly.

▶ **EXERCISES**

1. Compose effective *narrative* paragraphs according to the following
   instructions. Modify the subjects if you wish.
   a. A deductive paragraph about something that has occurred *over a fairly
      long period of time* in politics, sports, business, education, or another field
      of general interest.
   b. Compost a paragraph of *inductive* narration about some highly *specific*
      experience of your own — a humorous, exciting, or annoying event,
      perhaps, or a personal discovery, or even something you witnessed.
2. Compose worth-while *descriptive* paragraphs according to the instructions
   below. Remember the importance of spatial order and concrete detail. Modify
   the suggested topics if you wish.
   a. A *deductive or inductive* paragraph describing a park, a building or house,
      or someone's room or office.
   b. A paragraph of *comparison* (or *contrast*) about the clothing, hair style, or
      physique of one or more people you can see around you at this moment.
   c. A paragraph of *technical* description about a certain type of chair, design
      of car, or style of painting.

23.5 COMBINING PATTERNS OF DEVELOPMENT

It is certainly not necessary that every paragraph exhibit just one method of development. Choosing one pattern and sticking to it is an excellent way of practising stylistic control or achieving variety, but in many actual writing situations you will find two (or more) of these techniques converging in a single paragraph. Any passage, like a full paper, should employ whatever design best suits the subject and will be clearest to the reader.

In the following sample paragraphs, different methods or internal arrangements are effectively blended to enhance the total effect of the passage. Notice in each case how the approaches are combined without disunifying the author's main point:

Narration and description. The meeting of Brock and Tecumseh, as it comes to us through the pen and paintbrush of those who watched, is one of the most dramatic moments in Canadian history. Each had heard of the other. The general stood, tall and broad-shouldered in his scarlet tunic and white pants, his eyes blue and steady in a strong but amiable face framed by fair hair; the Shawanese chief was smaller, but supple and perfectly built. His copper face was oval, his hair shining black over dark piercing eyes that took the measure of Brock. Born within a year of one another, and with backgrounds worlds apart, fate was joining their destinies and they both seemed to know it. They would die within a year of each other, too. From this moment of their meeting a unique rapport was evident between them. Tecumseh smiled and said to one of his Indians in his own tongue, "This is a man!" On a later occasion his perceptive admiration of Brock's character was expressed in terse, simple words, "Other chiefs say, 'Go'—General Brock says, 'Come.' "—Enid L. Mallory, *The Green Tiger*

23.5

¶ dev

Narration, exposition, and argumentation. We are locked in the room for three hours; the guard stands over us, his rifle's shadow, like a cold draft from an unheated cellar, lies flat across the wall. We are each other's hostage, despite the guard and the row of buttons on the wall behind me, despite the rotunda just outside the door where another guard keeps us covered. This is a new society; the ultimate in authority, but recognizable in convention and etiquette, nuance and taboo, madness, and waste. It is a society based totally in the present —the future has been legislated out and the past is irrelevant. "We're the most dangerous men in Canada—DO WE LOOK IT?" "That button's in case we rush you—DO YOU THINK WE WILL?" No— you don't look like criminals, only like prisoners. Lining them up, who could pick the rapist from the hit-man? Or the journalist? No— they don't act like killers, they're courteous and respectful. Sometimes lucid, sometimes mad with theory and self-instruction. Yet they *could* rush me. They can kill. They don't feel guilt. In some profound way, they cannot be reached. It is a society based on a single premise satisfactory to all: that from nine months before they were born until three days after they die, they will have passed an abbreviated life without ever having been wanted by a single soul. They never had a childhood, nor did they ever grow up. —Clark Blaise, "Among the Dead"

Exposition and narration. The ideal rising temperature for bread dough is between 80 and 90 degrees Fahrenheit; if it is much cooler the rising is sluggish, if very much hotter the yeast might burn itself out. If the thermostat in your home is set at 80 you can put your bowl of dough anywhere. If your temperature is normal, a warm spot or high shelf in your kitchen might do, or you could turn on the heat in your oven at its lowest setting for 5 minutes, then turn it *off* and put the dough in. A friend of mine puts her bowl of coffee-cake dough on a board on top of a radiator. I put mine on a sunny window ledge. In winter I put it on shelf above an electric heating unit. While visiting at a summer cottage I found a perfect rising-place on a cool day was the seat of my car parked in the sun. And one shivery morning in September I mixed my bread dough at dawn and went back to my warm welcome bed. Like the slap of a frosty wet fish the thought struck me that dough won't rise well in the cold. I got up, brought the covered bowl to my bed and tucked it under the electric blanket. Of course I slept again. Of course the dough rose. Very quickly. —Edna Staebler, *Food that Really Schmecks*

As you can see, combining styles of development or types of writing is occasionally effective. But in your own work beware of throwing things together that may actually damage the unity or continuity or thoroughness of a passage. In general, it is probably best to plan on using only one pattern or type in most paragraphs. Remember, however, to employ combined development when the subject seems especially conducive to it.

EXERCISES

1. Look in books, journals, or good magazines for a few examples of combined development in paragraphing. Identify the different methods used in each case, and decide whether you think the blending of approaches strengthens or weakens the passage.
2. For practice, compose a paragraph that imitates one of the three sample passages reprinted in this part of the chapter (23.5). Use roughly the same patterns of development, but write about some other subject familiar to you.

24

Sentence Length and Economy

It is as important for the purpose of thought to keep language efficient as it is in surgery to keep tetanus bacilli out of one's bandages. — Ezra Pound, *Literary Essays*

One important sign of a mature style is *variety* in the length and pattern of sentences. Ideas can be expressed and combined in many different ways, even if you use virtually the same words in each case. Sentences can be long and leisurely, gradually unfolding a complicated idea or a series of intricately related facts. They can also be brief and emphatic. Regardless of length, moreover, their structure may be either elaborate or simple. Taking advantage of this diversity of forms can be a good thing for its own sake: it sustains your reader's interest by varying an otherwise monotonous and tiresome style, and through habit it makes you a more consciously versatile writer. But, more importantly, these options enable you to control the effectiveness of your presentation by adapting the form of each sentence to its particular purpose or intended effect.

The stylistic qualities of sentences are matters of choice and judgment rather than of rule. If there are rules, they are simply that you *must* choose, that the first version you try will not necessarily be the best, that you must at least consider other possibilities. Of course, it is conceivable that a whole paragraph or even a whole paper could consist entirely of short, simple, mechanically correct sentences, but if you wish to say something that cannot be said in that way you will need more suitable forms. Remember that re-reading your first-draft sentences critically and revising them can be extremely important in developing a strong, effective style.

24.1

This chapter is about the stylistic features of sentence *length*, including economy of wording. Chapter 25 considers the variety of forms, or *patterns*, that your sentences may take to communicate meaning.

24.1 SENTENCE LENGTH AS A MATTER OF STYLE

There is no special virtue in either long sentences or short ones. Written sentences should vary in length according to your purpose, the way in which you typically express your ideas, and the type of material you are presenting. In current writing, longer sentences (more than twenty words) generally dominate in fairly formal discussions of complex ideas; shorter sentences occur frequently in rapid narrative, simple exposition, and other general writing. The sentences in newspaper reports, for example, tend to be short because their subject matter is *factual*; notice, however, that good editorials and columns of analysis or opinion employ longer sentences because of the more complex nature of responsible *interpretation*. Beware of arguments (or advertisements) that can be expressed entirely in short, simple sentences; that sort of "reasoning" is usually assertive rather than logical. Since assignments at colleges and universities are ordinarily expected to be thorough, analytical, and well-reasoned, such projects should contain a high proportion of longer sentences. Some kinds of academic or business *reports* in which explanation or instructions (rather than analysis) is expected should ideally use brief, emphatic sentences more often.

Nevertheless, your sentences ought to be of whatever length *you* decide is best for the subject and occasion. Most important is the total effect of any passage in which the sentences are characteristically long or short. In the following paragraph by a well-known writer, the sentences are noticeably shorter than average for professional writers. The average length is just over fifteen words, and six of the thirteen sentences have fewer than fifteen words. Yet the form seems appropriate enough for its time and place.

> July 3, 1943
> We received a letter from the Writers' War Board the other day asking for a statement on "The Meaning of Democracy." It presumably is our duty to comply with such a request, and it is certainly our pleasure.
>
> Surely the Board knows what democracy is. It is the line that forms to the right. It is the don't in don't shove. It is the hole in the stuffed shirt through which the sawdust slowly trickles; it is the dent in the high hat. Democracy is the recurrent suspicion that more than half of the people are right more than half of the time. It is the feeling of privacy in the voting booths, the feeling of communion in the libraries, the feeling of vitality everywhere. Democracy is a letter to the editor. Democracy is the score of the beginning of the ninth. It is an idea that hasn't been disproved yet, a song the words of which haven't gone bad. It's the mustard on the hot dog and the cream in the rationed coffee. Democracy is a request from a War Board, in the middle of a morning in the middle of a war, wanting to know what democracy is. —E. B. White, "Democracy." From *The Wild Flag* (Houghton-Mifflin); © 1943 E. B. White. Originally in *The New Yorker*. Reprinted by permission.

The frequency of shorter sentences in the above passage makes its ideas forceful and memorable. Brevity and conciseness are also especially well suited to White's chosen pattern of *definition* ("Democracy is . . ."). But in another essay, the same writer decides that his intended effect or tone requires somewhat longer sentences (average length, twenty-two words) with a more leisurely tempo:

> I would rather train a striped zebra to balance an Indian club than induce a dachshund to heed my slightest command. For a number of years I have been agreeably encumbered by a very large and dissolute dachshund named Fred. Of all the dogs whom I have served I've never known one who understood so much of what I say or held it in such deep contempt. When I address Fred I never have to raise either my voice or my hopes. He even disobeys me when I instruct him in something that he wants to do. And when I answer his peremptory scratch at the door and hold the door open for him to walk through, he stops in the middle and lights a cigarette, just to hold me up. — E. B. White, "Dog Training." *One Man's Meat*

These two examples illustrate consistency and appropriateness in sentence length, and a writer's adaptability to different situations. But each of White's paragraphs (most obviously the one about democracy) aims at an *unusual* effect which would rarely be called for in most writing. Indeed, to use many successive sentences of similar length, without having a good reason for doing so, is probably unwise. Such writing can quickly become monotonous and unemphatic. Normally, abundant *variety* in sentence length is desirable in any passage.

So, during the revision stage of preparing your essay or project, be sure to check both the *average length* and the *variety in length* of the sentences in your draft. Be willing to rewrite sentences if necessary. The appropriate average length is determined mainly by your subject and method. For example, a factual report on fire-drill procedures will probably tend to use short sentences more often than will an argumentative essay on the politics of university financing. A high frequency of extraordinarily long sentences (forty words or more) or extraordinarily brief ones (ten words or fewer) is almost never advisable; a steady dose of either will weary most readers' patience. But neither should you strive for uniform sentence length, which is equally tedious. Remember that a sensible average length still leaves plenty of opportunity for the wide *variety* in length that really makes for a readable and effective style. Look at the following paragraph by Canadian historian:

> "There they are," exclaimed Montcalm, "where they have no right

to be!" His defensive position had been pierced, and he must now come directly to grips with the enemy. He had a choice between taking the offensive and attacking Wolfe before he could entrench and consolidate, or waiting behind the walls of Quebec until he could unite his forces with those of Bougainville and Vaudreuil and strike with his full strength. He may have feared that the latter course would mean a siege, which Quebec, with its weak defenses on the landward side and its supplies almost exhausted, had little hope of standing for long. His temperament, strained by months on the defensive, impelled him to immediate action. He decided to attack. —Edgar McInnis, *Canada: A Political and Social History*

Notice how natural emphasis and control is achieved by letting various aspects of the subject and its treatment determine variations in sentence length. The average length (about twenty words) is suited to this kind of introductory historical writing—a combination of narrative and explanation—but the passage's success results from a striking *diversity* in the length of statements. The long expository third sentence of forty-two words dwells in thorough, leisurely, and suspenseful detail on the nature of General Montcalm's dilemma. The climactic final sentence of just four words shows how dramatic brevity can be in narrative.

Length alone is seldom as important as variety and appropriateness. Your ability to use the form, long or short, that best suits your purpose and material will give emphasis and liveliness to your writing.

Choppy (Too Short) Sentences

Some sentences say too little because a simple idea has been broken up unnecessarily into two or more separate statements, as in this example:

I took my first course in mathematics. It was at Riverdale High School. This course was first-year or elementary algebra.

Most readers would resent being asked to invest their time in these individual sentences, which might better be combined:

I took my first course in mathematics, elementary algebra, at Riverdale High School.

A succession of very short sentences tends to give a piece of writing a halting, jerky effect. Such sentences also impede the flow of thought, for they fail to show how ideas are related:

We arrived at the recruit camp that afternoon. We were divided up. We were sent to barracks. They were reserved for recruits. The barracks were old. The floors were scrubbed almost white. Vague scars of cigarette burns marked them. I wondered how many wars had brought recruits here.

The choppy movement of this passage gives an incoherent effect the writer did not intend. The passage could be made smoother and less plodding by combining related statements:

> When we arrived at the recruit camp that afternoon, we were divided up and sent to the old barracks reserved for recruits. The floors were scrubbed almost white, but the vague scars of cigarette burns marking them made me wonder how many wars had brought recruits here.

Short sentences are useful in various writing situations—in dialogue, for emphasis, for creating a feeling of rapid action or of tension—but you must exercise judgment if you are to use them successfully. In the following passage, for example, the writer's intention was probably to convey a feeling of excitement, but the breathless style defeats this purpose because it goes on too long and has no variety in sentence pattern:

> It was my senior year in high school. Our basketball team had won the trophy the year before. This year the team was considered even stronger. Nearly every member of the pep club was seated. It was the final game. We had come all the way through the tournament without a defeat. This game would determine which team would be the champion. I looked toward the end of the gym. The referees were talking. They, too, were excited. Would that starting gun never go off! My hands were clammy. My cheeks burned.

24.1

SL

Examine closely any passage in your own writing that contains a noticeable number of consecutive sentences under eighteen words. Try reading the passage aloud to see whether it conveys the effect you intended or whether the writing is simply hasty.

Stringy Sentences

Avoid stringing together (with *and*, *but*, *so*, *and then*) statements that should be written as separate sentences or as subordinate elements. Sentences carelessly tacked together in this manner are not only monotonous to read but lose all their emphasis because every idea seems to be of equal importance:

> About fifty feet away I saw a buck deer running for safety **and so I** knelt on my right knee **and then I** brought the rifle to my right shoulder. He was still running, **so I** fired one shot at him, **but I** missed, **but** he stopped and looked at me, **and then I** had a much better target to shoot at.

Reading such sentences aloud should reveal their weaknesses and help you to revise them for better organization:

> About fifty feet away I saw a buck deer running for safety. Kneeling on my right knee and bringing the rifle to my shoulder, I fired once, but missed. He stopped to look at me, providing a much better target.

Stringy sentences often result from linking too many main clauses together (*Most people know that our agricultural system is the world's best* **and** *they have grown to expect great things from this system,* **and** *they should,* **and** *our farmers and politicians accordingly have a reputation to uphold*). The cure lies in cutting down the number of co-ordinating conjunctions (*and, but, so*) and in subordinating ideas of lesser importance.

▶ **EXERCISE**

Improve the style of the following paragraphs by rewriting them in sentences of *varying* lengths. Add or delete or change words if necessary.

1. Vegetables need lots of soil to grow in. They won't develop fully without it. Window boxes are too small and shallow. There isn't enough room for roots to spread. The soil dries out too fast. A tomato plant would require at least a bushel basket of soil. Cherry tomatoes will grow in ten-inch pots. Chives or radishes can grow in six-inch containers. Onions and parsley need at least ten-inch pots. Window boxes or patio planters can be used to start vegetables. Later transplanting in a garden plot is advisable. Full sunlight and plenty of rain are essential. Soil nutrients will also be more abundantly available.

2. Although a reliable sign of ripeness in watermelons is the change from white to a yellowish color on the underside of the melon, you can plug it (cut a test hole) if you're not sure whether it's ready to pick, but be sure to replace the plug in an unripe fruit and take care not to bruise the skin of the melon when handling it in the field or carrying it from the field. There is also a right way and a wrong way to transport a watermelon because dropping it, rolling it, shaking it, or piling others on top of it can cause serious internal damage (and consequent loss of taste and texture) that an unblemished exterior would not lead anyone, even the grower, to suspect. Serving and storing melon pieces is also an art that involves deciding between wedges and slices, between cutting vertically or horizontally, and, so far as storage is concerned, whether to refrigerate the uneaten pieces (which may reduce taste) or keep them in plastic wrap at room temperature (which may dry them out or induce pulping and rotting), choices that all aficionados know are crucial to the joys of melon-eating. Even the watermelon rinds afford opportunities for devoted horticulturalists who, having planted, nurtured, harvested, and enjoyed this delicious food, can now add the table scraps to a compost heap in the yard which in time provides rich fertilizer for a future generation of watermelon plants and thus perpetuates the pleasures, and the subtle arts, of true melon culture.

24.2 SENTENCE LENGTH AND MEANING

SL **Rewrite the passage marked to eliminate choppy or stringy sentences and to show the relationship of ideas.**

Sentences of unvarying length, most commonly short ones, are typical of inexperienced writers. There are times when you may be tempted to keep all your sentences deliberately brief. After all, it may seem safer: punctuation errors and other troubles are less likely to show up in short sentences. You may also remember that it is usually easier to read and grasp the meaning of short sentences; news reports, textbooks, and children's books use them a lot. Moreover, the language of the world around you — especially of the popular media — may sometimes seem to show that short statements are the characteristic form of human expression. The opening lines of magazine articles are often filled with short sentences. Radio disc jockeys usually speak in a staccato rhythm of short sentences. Television commercials and printed ads depend almost exclusively on short, presumably forceful, statements. An inclination to imitate this style — to try to write everything as simply as possible — is perhaps understandable. But consider how little real information, how little sustained thought, how little depth of explanation is conveyed in that manner. Are safety and simplicity all that count? Is the "simple" style of commercials a good model for responsible argument? There are some things that just cannot be said briefly, and there are many times when the brisk, assertive style of everyday *spoken* English cannot properly convey the fuller or more subtle ideas that comprise most *written* language.

24.2

SL

Don't be too cautious about grammatical complexity, and don't be too easily convinced that short sentences are clearer than longer ones. Brevity is not always efficient, and expansiveness in a sentence will often let you be more thorough, more honest. The novelist John Erskine once said that "When you write, you make a point, not by subtracting as though you sharpened a pencil, but by adding." The vagueness of most brief statements (which partly explains their attraction for advertisers) seriously hampers your efforts to communicate distinct ideas fully and precisely. As you add to sentences, more often than not they become more specific. Start with a basic sentence, for example:

Hockey is exciting.

The statement is extremely general. Its range of possible meanings is uncontrolled. Does it refer to *playing* hockey? to *watching* hockey? to a career in hockey? And what is meant by "exciting?" Different people are excited by different things. What, exactly, might the writer be trying to communicate? And what might be the personal feeling concealed behind so vague and conventional a statement? Notice what happens when we begin to add to the sentence:

1. Watching hockey is exciting.
2. Watching hockey is exciting because of the action and the fans.
3. Watching hockey is exciting because of the action on the ice and the exuberance of the fans.
4. Watching hockey is exciting because of the fast, rugged action on the ice and the infectious exuberance of the fans.

With each addition the meaning has become more clearly defined. Here an interesting paradox occurs: *by adding you take away.* The specific details actually *subtract* unintended meanings, narrowing the idea much more distinctly by eliminating other possible interpretations. The reader no longer has to guess at what the writer means. Even more importantly, perhaps, the statement has grown to be truly expressive of the writer's real feelings and values; a blunt, uninformative generality has become a particular and personal thought.

As a general rule, then, you will find it easier to be thorough and precise if you avoid the habit of consistently short sentences. Use brevity for variety or special emphasis, not just to be safe or evasive. The fullness of a mature presentation comes by *expanding* and *combining* ideas that inexperienced writers would tend to leave undeveloped.

▶ EXERCISE

Five short statements are listed below. For practice in adding texture to sentences, rewrite each one of them in at least three different ways, adding constructions as suggested in the following example:

Example: The police arrived at midnight.

Revision 1: The police, heavily armed and expecting the worst, arrived at midnight.

Revision 2: Although we had called them repeatedly since ten o'clock, the police arrived at midnight.

Revision 3: The police arrived at midnight, screeching to a halt in their patrol car.

Revision 4: When the police arrived at midnight, it was already too late.

Revision 5: The police, who had apparently been summoned by a bystander, arrived at midnight.

1. The shortstop hit a double.
2. Mrs Merriwether took the job.

3. Professor Gunning is an unfair marker.
4. This book is interesting.
5. The class inspired her.

24.3 AVOIDING WORDINESS

Wdy   **Make the marked sentence or passage less wordy and more direct.**

Although fullness and clarity are desirable in most sentences, remember that *wordiness* is not. Wordiness means *unnecessary* expansiveness and clutter—length that serves no worth-while purpose. No one likes to listen to a speaker who talks too much and says too little, and no reader likes to cut a path through a tangle of useless words or constructions to get at a relatively simple idea. Phrases, clauses, or other constructions that use many words to say what can be said more directly are called *circumlocutions*.

Practising economy does not always require stripping your sentences down to the bare minimum, as you might in composing a telegram or writing a classified ad. The previous section of this chapter explains why the shortest words and simplest constructions are not always the most economical, for they may fail to convey your exact or complete meaning. Economy of expression requires rather that you state your ideas in the most accurate and direct way possible.

24.3
Wdy

Often you can make a statement or idea more efficient by reducing an unnecessary sentence to a phrase or single word:

The snow lay like a blanket. It covered the countryside. [two sentences]

The snow, **which lay like a blanket**, covered the countryside. [One sentence contains the other, which has been reduced to a clause.]

The snow covered the countryside **like a blanket**. [One sentence contains the other, which has been reduced to a phrase.]

The snow **blanketed** the countryside. [One sentence contains the other, which has been reduced to a single word.]

One way to tighten sentence form is to eliminate unnecessary and ineffective verbs and their modifiers:

WORDY: He crawled slowly over the river bank, looking for the flint chips which would mean that he had found a campsite.

REDUCED: He crawled slowly over the river bank, looking for flint chips marking a possible campsite.

The two verbs that can most frequently be eliminated without any loss of meaning are *be* in its various forms and *have:*

> WORDY: **He is a native of the prairies** and knows the value of water conservation.
>
> MORE ECONOMICAL: **A native of the prairies**, he knows the value of water conservation.
>
> WORDY: A few of the fellows **who were less serious** would go into a bar **where they would have** a steak dinner and a few glasses of beer.
>
> MORE ECONOMICAL: A few of the **less serious** fellows would go into a bar **for** a steak dinner and a few glasses of beer.
>
> WORDY: **There is** only one excuse **that is acceptable**, and **that is** "I have a class this hour."
>
> MORE ECONOMICAL: **Only one excuse is acceptable**: "I have a class this hour."

If a number of your sentence begin with *There*, try to revise some of them so as to express the idea in a more direct way:

> WORDY: **There are two plays in our anthology**, and I like them both.
>
> MORE DIRECT: I like both plays in our anthology.
>
> WORDY: **There is a suggestion box** in almost all big business houses where employees may put ideas.
>
> MORE DIRECT: Most big business houses provide suggestion boxes for their employees.

While a writer's style and the general movement of the entire composition determine to a large degree whether shorter or longer constructions are more appropriate, the careless habit of consistently using two or more statements where one would be just as effective should be avoided in all styles of writing.

► **EXERCISE**

Rewrite the following paragraph, tightening it whenever possible by substituting words and phrases for clauses; eliminate all unnecessary words:

There were so many things to do and the summer was so short. We could go and chase rats in the barn, which was a dangerous and slightly sickening enterprise; we could teach a kitten how to play circus. We could climb to the roof of the corridor where we could watch the ducks file out to the pond, and crack dry mirthless jokes to one and another. We could help with the cider press, where all the apples with a rotten spot, those that had been claimed and contended for by the yellow jackets, disappeared into the hopper and gushed out the sides in a seethe of liquid that was brown and bubbly. There were so many things to do and the summer was so short.

24.4 REMOVING DEADWOOD

Dead   **Revise the marked sentence or passage to eliminate deadwood.**

Deadwood is a term for a particular kind of wordiness: lazy or pretentious words and phrases that clutter up a statement without adding anything to its meaning.

> Anyone acquainted with **the subject of** violin construction knows **it is a fact that** the longer the wood is seasoned, the better **the result will be as far as** the tone of the instrument **is concerned**.

Empty expressions like those in boldface above are excess baggage and do nothing to further communication. They often find their way into first drafts because they come to hand so readily, but you should take care to prune them out in revision. Eliminating deadwood will make a statement neater and more direct without changing its meaning in the least, as these examples illustrate (deadwood in brackets):

> Every thinking person these days seems to agree [with the conception] that the world has gone mad.
>
> Because [of the fact that] she had been ill, she missed the first two weeks of classes.
>
> After a delay of forty-five minutes, the audience [got to the point that it] became restless and noisy.

24.4

Dead

Some people imagine that a wordy style of speaking or writing will make their ideas seem more impressive or authoritative. Many politicians and other public officials, for example, cultivate a verbose manner in the hope of making themselves and their pronouncements appear important or sophisticated. But pretentious, superfluous phrasing actually annoys most listeners and readers. It is considered either thoughtless or phoney and contributes nothing favorable to one's "image." Let's face it: there is no good reason, for instance, to say "at this point in time" instead of simply saying "now."

Wordy formulas that people use habitually in casual conversation are more noticeable and irritating in written English than in speech. Roundabout expressions should be replaced in revision by terms that say the same thing more directly:

get in touch with	*means*	**call** or **see**
due to the fact that	*means*	**because** or **since**
in this day and age	*means*	**now** or **today**
at the same time	*means*	**while**

Certain words, generally in stereotyped phrasal combinations, account for much of the deadwood found in student writing. This list, while not exhaustive, illustrates phrases built upon the most common of these words:

Word	As Deadwood	Deadwood Eliminated
case	**In many cases** students profit from the research paper.	Many students profit from the research paper.
character	Her gossip was **of a sordid and ugly character.**	Her gossip was sordid and ugly.
exist	The soil conditions **that existed** in Manitoba became serious.	The soil conditions in Manitoba became serious.
fact	In spite of **the fact that** he is lazy, I like him.	In spite of his laziness, I like him.
factor	Speed is also **an important factor.**	Speed is also important.
field	Anyone interested in **the field of** Canadian history should take his course.	Anyone interested in Canadian history should take his course.
instance	**In many instances,** students write their papers just before the deadline.	Often students write their papers just before the deadline.
line	He always thought he would be successful **along agricultural lines.**	He always thought he would be successful in agriculture.
manner	He glanced at her **in a suspicious manner.**	He glanced at her suspiciously.
nature	She seldom talks on any subject **of a controversial nature.**	She seldom talks on any controversial subject.
seems	**It seems that** we have not lost a daughter, but gained another icebox-raider.	We have not lost a daughter, but gained another icebox-raider.
tendency	When I am supposed to be working, **I have a tendency to** clean my pipes and dawdle.	When I am supposed to be working, I clean my pipes and dawdle.
type	His father had an executive **type of** position.	His father had an executive position.

These words have definite meanings in some expressions (a *case* of measles, a minor *character* in the play, a *field* of clover, and so forth), but as used here, they are superfluous.

▶ **EXERCISE**

Read the following sentences carefully, looking for roundabout expressions and deadwood. Then rewrite them into direct and economical statements.

1. In university one must put away the childish thoughts of her girlhood and begin thinking of the future that lies ahead with adult ideas and responsibilities.
2. Throughout my previous school days, I have been the type of person who hasn't had to study a great deal to get grades above those obtained by the average student.
3. One of my bigger excuses was the fact that I claimed there were too many social activities currently in progress.
4. The method used to detect the approach of other ships is radar.
5. One lady aroused my indignation when she claimed that her son, who was six feet in height, was under twelve years of age.
6. Habits can be classified into two distinct types: one is the useful, progressive, uplifting kind while the other is of the nature that deteriorates character and often damages the physical body.
7. My scholastic averages give, in my opinion, a rather distorted picture of what my true knowledge actually is.
8. I have chosen this road of higher education to reach my goal, which is that of teaching children.
9. To reach this goal I must be well educated and have a thorough understanding of my subject.
10. The income from the tourist business is an important source of revenue for people who own businesses in Prince Edward Island.

24.5

Rep

24.5 AVOIDING REDUNDANCY AND CARELESS REPETITION

 Rep **Eliminate the ineffective repetition of words, meaning, or sound.**

Wordiness can also result from a careless habit of *redundant* and *repetitive* expression. Redundancy (useless repetition of meaning) always lengthens a sentence unprofitably, while the recurrence of particular words or sounds in a passage is stylistically clumsy.

Redundancy

Redundancy (or *tautology*) in writing is the pointless use of a word or phrase that merely repeats a meaning that is already clear. For example, the words and phrases printed in brackets in the following list of common expressions should be omitted. They are a kind of deadwood (24.4). They can easily be eliminated because they just repeat something that is already obvious.

yellow [in color]	rectangular [in shape]
a [true] fact	the [resultant] effect
a widow [woman]	sixteen [in number]
the modern world [of today]	massive [in size]
all [of the] new fashions	co-operate [together]
inside [of]	[illogical] fallacies
her age is nine years [old]	circulating [around]
refer [back]	continue [on]
my [fellow] classmates	repeat [again]
[past] history	[a pair of] twins

The abbreviation *etc. (et cetera)* means "and so forth." To write "*and* etc." is equivalent to saying "and and so forth." Avoid this non-standard expression; and avoid *etc.* in formal writing.

A more extended kind of redundancy is the "circular" statement —an assertion in which synonyms or other *equivalent* terms are weakly used to explain or illustrate one another. Consider the following sentence:

> Our optimistic chairman was always looking on the bright side of things.

This is an inefficient and virtually meaningless remark. Since *optimism* means the same thing as *always looking on the bright side of things*, one or the other of these expressions is superfluous. The statement should be revised to read either "Our chairman was optimistic" or "Our chairman was always looking on the bright side of things." The following examples illustrate similar tautologies:

> The **hazy** figures in the painting's background are **vague** and **indistinct**.
>
> This is a **popular** belief that **many people have faith in**.
>
> The public library **regulates** borrowing **by means of rules**.
>
> Layton is my **favorite** poet because I **like his poetry best**.

Another sort of redundancy is that of a "paragraph" in which a single idea is merely *rephrased* instead of being explained or illustrated. The following section of a student essay shows how tautological expression can mislead a writer into believing that the idea is being developed:

> Mass transit systems are the solution to today's urban transportation problems. They can move great numbers of people throughout the busy city. Our metropolitan centres need the facilities to transport efficiently a large population. Without large-scale public transit service, there will be no end to the present difficulties of city travellers. Urban transportation is a problem to which we can respond adequately only by acquiring methods and equipment capable of handling the requirements of contemporary urban life and work. We need mass transit, and we need it now.

Notice that the above passage is really just saying the same thing over and over again. In effect, the writer has simply re-asserted the topic sentence five times in different words. Because no actual argument or details are ever provided, the paragraph is ultimately unconvincing as well as redundant. Beware, then, of the many kinds of careless repetition that can make your *meaning* wordy or incomplete.

Useless Repetition

There is also a kind of thoughtless repetition that isn't related directly to either wordiness or meaning. It is the awkward recurrence of certain words or sounds. Such unintentional and unnecessary repetition is conspicuous in the following passage:

24.5

Rep

> When I was in high school, I would some**times** take a book home and maybe read it two or three hours at a **time. Most of the time** I would read **most** of my homework just in **time** to have it ready before class began. It was very easy **most of the time** to read the assignment and have it prepared when my **time** came to be called upon for recitation.

Repetition of this kind is weak and clumsy, for it unintentionally focusses attention on words rather than on ideas. It also suggests that the writer may be careless and unconcerned with what he or she is saying.

Repetition of words.   Repeat words in a passage only when you have good reason for doing so. Key words (such as the subject) may sometimes be repeated for clarity or emphasis, but less important terms should not be used more often than necessary.

> POINTLESS REPETITION: The **problem** of feeding its ever-increasing population is one of India's most acute **problems**.

REVISED: Feeding its ever-increasing population is one of India's most acute problems.

POINTLESS REPETITION: Many people think **that** if a **product** is endorsed by a prominent person **that** it is a good **product** to buy.

REVISED: Many people think that a product endorsed by a prominent person is a good one to buy.

Especially to be avoided is repetition of the same word when it has two different meanings:

If I **run**, I'll get a **run** in my stockings.
If I run, I'll **tear** my stockings.

Astrology is so popular in Hollywood that many movie **stars** won't sign a contract unless the **stars** are favorable.
Astrology is so popular in Hollywood that many of the movie stars won't sign a contract unless their **horoscopes** are favorable.

Repetition of sounds.   A sound should not be made conspicuous by careless repetition. The cumulative effect of certain suffixes like *-ly*, *-ment*, and *-tion* may be evidence of weak style:

The concept of such sanctua**ry** immuni**ty** unquestionab**ly** predomi-nant**ly** influenced the ene**my** to enter into the conflict.

Written permis**sion** of the administra**tion** is required for reregis-tra**tion** of those students who are on proba**tion**.

Alliteration—the repetition of the same sound at the beginning of words in a series—is out of place when it attracts attention to the words at the expense of the ideas:

I am looking for a shop that still has **p**leated **p**ants for **p**oor and **p**aunchy **p**rofessors.

He then made himself comfortable in a **r**ather **r**ickety **r**attan **r**ocker.

Even though your papers are not usually written to be read aloud, you should try to avoid unintentional sound patterns that may be momentarily irritating or distracting to a reader who has a well-tuned ear:

The enemy was re**port**ed to have seized this im**port**ant **port**, and reinforcements were hurrying up in su**pport**.

Effective Repetition

Sometimes repetition is essential for meaning or for sentence structure:

For three thousand years, poets have been enchanted and moved and perplexed by the power of their own **imagination**. In a short and summary essay I can hope at most to lift one small corner of that mystery; and yet it is a critical corner. I shall ask, What goes on in the mind when we **imagine**? You will hear from me that one answer to this question is fairly specific: which is to say, that we can describe the working of the **imagination**. And when we describe it as I shall do, it becomes plain that **imagination** is a specifically *human* gift. To **imagine** is the characteristic act, not of the poet's mind, or the painter's, or the scientist's, but of the mind of man. —Jacob Bronowski. "The Reach of Imagination," *American Scholar*

Intentional repetition may also be effective for emphasis:

There is no way of becoming **inaccurate** by industry, and if you deliberately try to be **inaccurate** you fail. **Inaccuracy** is perhaps the most **spontaneous** and the **freest** of **gifts** offered by the Spirit to the wit of man. It is even more **spontaneous** and more **free** than the **gift** of writing good **verse**, or that rarer **gift** which I have also written of here — the **gift** of writing abominably **bad verse**; exceptionally **bad verse**; criminally **bad verse**; execrable **verse**. —Hilaire Belloc, *On*

Some kinds of words must of course be used over and over again: articles (*a*, *an*, *the*), conjunctions (*and*, *but*, *or*), prepositions (*of*, *in*, *at*), and pronouns (*it*, *that*, *my*, *which*). Because their purpose is grammatical, the constant repetition of these words goes unnoticed.

24.5

Rep

▶ **EXERCISE**

Revise the following sentences to eliminate clumsy or pointless repetition of words, meaning, or sounds. If the repetition in any statement seems intentional and effective, explain what purpose it serves:

1. I admire those people whose objectives show that they have aims and goals in life.
2. The advantage of getting a broader perspective through travel is only one of the advantages of spending a summer travelling through Canada.
3. Many people live so compulsively by the clock that they have a fixed time for eating, a fixed time for bathing, and a fixed time for everything but enjoying life.
4. An application of lotion to the area of inflammation should relieve the pain.
5. Concrete and steel have both been used successfully in skyscraper construction, but buildings of concrete must have much thicker walls at the lower levels than those of steel. On the other hand, concrete has a far greater decorative potential than steel.

25

Sentence Variety, Control, and Emphasis

Look at it this way. If a person can write only simple sentences . . . he has very few choices with which to create his effects. He is trapped in a syntax which allows a very narrow range of effect. If he learns to write compound sentences well, he will expand his range of choices. If he adds complex and complex-compound sentences to his repertoire, his choices will be amazingly greater. . . . But — and this must be emphasized — he must know the language so well that he is making choices and deliberately creating certain desired effects. — W.D. Valgardson, in *The English Quarterly*

You can write just by putting down the words, phrases, and sentences that come to mind readily, but most of us can't write *well* that way. Good writers don't always accept the first words that occur to them, or the first sentences that take shape on their papers. The construction of sentences can be arranged and rearranged, and you can gain some control over the sentences you write and emphasize your meaning to make your points more effective and to assist your reader's understanding.

A good way to achieve greater versatility, control, and emphasis in sentence patterning is to become familiar with a few of the basic kinds of variation. This chapter explains and illustrates different ways of expressing and combining ideas within statements. The aim is to indicate how you might fairly easily increase the variety and complexity of your sentences without loss of clarity. At first it will probably seem "mechanical" to be reshaping perfectly correct statements according to the suggestions and models given here. But after a while it will become natural to use and adapt a wider range of forms than is found in your style now.

Matters of sentence length and efficiency are considered in chapter 24. Basic grammar and other conventions of sentence formation are covered in chapters 1 through 5.

25.1 SENTENCE VARIETY

Var Vary the sentence patterns in the marked passage to avoid monotony or to make your meaning clearer or more emphatic.

Often when we are reading good writing, we don't notice the sentences and we are unaware of their patterns. But if the patterns become monotonous, either in length or in arrangement, then we are likely to notice and react unfavorably, even irritably. An easy variety and flexibility customarily pleases us more and lets us move without vexation from sentence to sentence, as in this passage:

> After Cromwell had thoroughly subjected Ireland, there was mass confiscation of land on a scale which put Elizabethan measures in the shade. Henry Jones, Bishop of Clogher, was partly responsible. By exaggerating the massacres of 1641, he confirmed Cromwell in his view that he had fought a religious war and had to punish the Catholic murderers. He held all Catholics responsible for the excesses of some; when he had subdued the country 30,000 Irish soldiers were sent to the Continent, and thousands of Irish were deported as slaves to the Barbadoes. (The population in 1652 was about half a million.) Phelim O'Neill and fifty other leaders were executed for their part in the rising. Nine counties were confiscated to meet arrears of army pay. 'To Hell or Connaught' is said to have been Cromwell's maxim; it was certainly his policy. To Clare and Connaught the Irish gentry were sent; the labouring class were left to work for their new masters. The Down Survey, by Sir William Petty (nowadays an invaluable document of historical reference), was compiled to facilitate the Cromwellian plantation. — Terence de Vere White, *Ireland*

Although full of little-known information and names, this paragraph is readable and understandable at least partly because the movement is easy and natural, yet powerful, with variety in sentence structure. Of the ten sentences, only two (the sixth and seventh) are alike in form, and the paralleling of those two is itself an intended effect. The variations include differences of clause structure and arrangement, of beginning, of subject-verb-object order, of emphasis by position, of balanced elements, and so forth. There are also long, short, and medium-length statements, and both active and passive constructions.

25.1

Var

Getting accustomed to using a diversity of sentence patterns can help you refine and enliven what you want to say. But there is a corresponding danger that revisions made merely for the sake of change will cloud a meaning that was previously clear. Only through experimenting with various versions of many statements will you develop an instinctive awareness of what would be appropriate and effective in a particular situation. This section of the chapter aims to give you some opportunities to consider and practise sentence flexibility.

Loose and Periodic Sentences

Sentence patterns may also be varied by using both loose and periodic sentences.

Loose sentences.   In a loose sentence the main statement comes first, followed by subordinate elements that explain or amplify or alter its meaning. This pattern is the one most commonly used both in speech and in writing, for writers characteristically make points by adding information. Notice especially the second, third, and fifth sentences in this passage:

> Montreal this winter is the colour of a gray and white cat. It is furry like a cat, too, thick with snow-dusted trees and vegetation along the undulating flank and haunches of Mount Royal. Its factories hum and its traffic often snarls and the crowds along the sidewalk are thicker than fleas trying to escape extinction. Everyone is in a hurry, but less from exuberance than because it is a long-standing tradition in Montreal to be late for everything except hockey games. We blame our tardiness on overcrowded trams, on motorists who persist in their Gallic right to be individuals, on the fact that nearly everyone is working too hard. Certainly there has never been so much lettuce to be picked or more Montrealers busy gathering it. — Hugh MacLennan. "Letter from Montreal"

One particular kind of loose construction, called *prolepsis* in early rhetoric texts, can be useful. *Prolepsis* is the expression of a general statement, which is then followed by amplifying details:

> Once on the mound, he was a most unlikely looking pitcher, slouching, tangle-footed, absent, with the aspect of a lost goose.

> Modern homes have lost a tempo they once had — urban activities speed them up, television governs some hours, and separation from relatives and neighbors leaves them alone.

Such a construction can set the subject for a paragraph or short essay, determine its content, and act as an outline. The second sentence above, for example, could be amplified in an essay that had three key parts, each fully illustrating one of the three factors listed.

Loose, or *accumulating*, sentences are an interesting reflection of the writer. As you add to a sentence, amplifying and specifying your meaning, you show yourself in the *process of thinking*.

Periodic sentences.   A periodic sentence, however, is more often than not the statement of *completed thought*. Much less common both in speech and in writing, a periodic sentence is one in which the main statement is not completed until the end or near the end of the sentence:

> In these regions, as well as on the Melville Peninsula, polar bear traps erected by the Greenlanders have also been found. — T.J. Oleson, *The Norsemen in America*

> Without such parliamentary battles on little theatres, of which this was one of the first, Canadian democracy, as we know it, would never have emerged, — W.S. MacNutt, *The Making of the Maritime Provinces, 1713-1784*

Although periodic sentences occurred frequently in writing before this century, they are now much less common than loose sentences. They require planning beforehand and are more typical of a formal than of a general style. The very fact that periodic sentences are not widely used, however, gives the pattern all the more value as a means of achieving emphasis.

When you are framing a periodic sentence, make certain that the suspension is not awkward or unnatural, as it is in this example:

> The reader will probably agree after reading this essay **that the novelist's portrayal** of the woman who, after being married for a number of years and raising a family, gradually loses interest in most of her former outside activities, **is realistic**.

See also 25.4, Sentence Emphasis, for further illustration of how the climactic effect of periodic sentences can accentuate your key idea.

▶ EXERCISES

1. Make loose sentences by adding to the five simple sentences or independent clauses below. Try to add at least three additional units to each, as in the example.

   Example: It was a depressing day.
   Loose sentence: It was a depressing day, with black clouds obscuring the sun, a cold wind whipping through the trees, and even the birds hiding from the weather.

   a. This house is your dream house.
   b. The eastern third of China is the core of the nation.
   c. Railways played an important part in building Canada.
   d. The student council listened attentively.
   e. "Liberation" can mean a lot of different things.

2. Make periodic sentences by completing the sentences started below, as in the example.

   Example: After he found the candlestick on the rug, . . .
   Periodic sentence: After he found the candlestick on the rug, and after he learned that the fingerprints were those of the dead woman, and after he found the scratches on the lock, the inspector became convinced that this was a case of murder.

   a. When the sun went down . . .
   b. After finals were over for the seniors . . .
   c. Although regular class-attendance is important . . .
   d. While others might need lots of money . . .
   e. If you have followed the map carefully up to this point . . .

25.1
Var

Varying Types of Sentences

If you discover in scrutinizing your first draft that you have written an essay in which most of the sentences have the same kind of clause structure, you should consider combining, dividing, or reshaping your sentences. Quite aside from the question of variety, different kinds of sentences—simple, compound, complex, and compound-complex—are usually necessary for meaning and emphasis in university-level writing.

These types of sentences are defined in 1.4, Sentences Classified by Clause Structure. They are named according to the presence and combination of main (independent) and subordinate (dependent) clauses. Here is a review of the essential characteristics of each:

Simple Sentence (one main clause and no subordinate clauses):
Gertrude flew to Calgary yesterday.

Compound Sentence (two or more main clauses and no subordinate clauses):
Gertrude intended to return from Calgary first thing this morning, but her plans changed.

Complex Sentence (one main clause and one or more subordinate clauses):
Gertrude's plans to return from Calgary first thing this morning changed when she was invited to spend the weekend in Banff.

Compound-Complex Sentence (two or more main clauses and one or more subordinate clauses):
Gertrude, who flew to Calgary yesterday, intended to return first thing this morning, but her plans changed when she was invited to spend the weekend in Banff.

Increasing sentence complexity doesn't necessarily mean additional sentence length; many very long sentences may actually be simple in their structure. Compound-complex sentences do tend to be lengthy because of the number of clauses (at least three); they are more typical of formal writing on sophisticated topics than of general writing. Note too that the variable *arrangement* of the clauses in the four types of sentences is a further opportunity to diversify your patterning. See below, for example, regarding Sentence Beginnings and Interrupters.

Apart from style, the advantage of variable clause structure is that ideas can be related to each other in different ways. Depending on your intended meaning or emphasis (or on the demands of the topic), a draft sentence can be rearranged or combined with others until it conveys exactly the information you want to deliver. The sample sentences above represent four subtly different ways of looking at Gertrude's experience in Calgary. They vary in focus and in fullness. Of course, only the writer would know which version best communicates the *intended* effect, but we can see the importance of choosing and controlling the form of our statements. (See also 25.2, Subordination to Control and Clarify Meaning.)

The formal paragraph below from the field of political science, illustrates variety and appropriateness in the use of sentence types. All four classes of sentence are present. Three statements are simple in structure, two are complex, one is compound, and two are compound-complex. The relatively high proportion of complicated forms reflects the precise distinctions and qualifications required to explain an intricate subject like parliamentary procedures:

> A distinction must now be drawn between "private members' business" and "Government business". Any private member, on giving forty-eight hours' notice, may introduce any public bill or resolution which does not entail the imposition of a tax or an expenditure of public money. Financial matters of this kind are solely within the prerogative of the Government: such "money bills" must be recommended to the House by the Governor General (who acts constitutionally on the advice of the Government). Private members may nevertheless introduce resolutions related to finance by moving that the Government "consider the advisability of" adopting a course of action involving taxes or expenditures: the reason is that such motions, if passed, would not impose any financial obligation on the Government. Private members' public bills and resolutions have a very slight chance of being passed or even of coming to a vote. A limited time is allotted for their consideration and they must be dealt with in strict accordance with the order of precedence assigned to them by the Standing Orders. Obviously, they must command the support, or at least the acquiescence, of the supporters of the Government in order to stand even a slight chance of adoption. An hour is allotted on Mondays, Tuesdays and Thursdays for the consideration of private members' business, until forty such hours have been consumed, following which one hour only on each Thursday for the remainder of the session is so allotted. — E. Russell Hopkins, *Confederation at the Crossroads: The Canadian Constitution*

25.1
Var

The use of different sentence types in the above passage lends clarity and variety to a potentially confusing and dull exposition. Most significantly, perhaps, it adapts the form of each statement to the complexity of the idea it must express, defining relationships much more specifically than simple structures alone would permit. Some important things can be communicated only by the more elaborate techniques of language. At the same time, of course, other important things can and should be expressed simply. Needless complexity is as undesirable as none at all.

Questions.   Sometimes a question or directive makes an interesting variation from the usual declarative sentence:

> Is "painfully clear" an evasion of the too political "perfectly clear?" Certainly it is an example of the meaningless adverbial sludge which clogs inflated editorial writing. — Maurice S. Elliot, "Respecting Our Organs"

> You know, because you felt the pain in your own flesh, that evening when the police shot your son. Is it necessary to feel pain in our own flesh before we really know? More and more, I think that it probably is. — Margaret Laurence, "Open Letter to the Mother of Joe Bass"

Questions and commands can be effective if they serve a legitimate purpose, but like other sentence patterns they should not be used solely for the sake of variety. Unless the answer is self-evident ("Who would trade freedom for tyranny?"), don't raise a question without answering it. Never conclude a paper with a pointless, blunt question such as "What do *you* think?"

▶ **EXERCISES**

1. Compose sentences according to the following instructions:
   a. a *simple* sentence on some aspect of winter weather
   b. a *compound* sentence on some aspect of auto repairs
   c. a *complex* sentence on some aspect of cafeteria food
   d. a *compound-complex* sentence on some aspect of postal service.
2. Rewrite in a different structure each of the sentences you composed in Exercise 1 above. Delete or add to the wording or ideas wherever necessary. Identify the form you are using in each case, and notice the difference in meaning or emphasis that results from the change in structure and detail.
3. Try to combine the following ideas into *one* sentence in four different ways. Create a simple sentence, a compound sentence, a complex sentence, and a compound-complex sentence. Adapt the wording wherever necessary, but be sure that each of your sentences includes all the information.
   The oil discovery occurred at Leduc.
   It was the start of the Alberta energy boom
   Prosperity was brought to the province.
   It was a sudden change.
   Such changes naturally bring social problems too.
   Which of your four sentences conveys the message most clearly and effectively?

Varying Sentence Beginnings

When several consecutive sentences begin the same way — with a
noun subject, for example — the passage is likely to be monotonous
and to lack impact:

> **Meteorology** has made many advances in recent years. **Weather
> observation balloons** have been developed to gather data from the
> upper stratosphere. **Time-lapse photography** has improved the
> study of cloud formations and patterns. **Barometric instruments** of
> greater sensitivity are widely used. **Radar** is useful in detecting the
> approach of storms and precipitation.

The beginnings of sentences and main clauses can be varied and
made more interesting by occasionally starting with a modifier — a
word, phrase, or subordinate clause — as in the following paragraph about the battle at Batoche in 1885. Notice too that the third
"sentence" is an effective fragment in which the adverb *Fast*
assumes an uncustomary and dramatic opening position:

> **To an extent** Gabriel would always think like a hunter: **at any
> moment** Poundmaker's horsemen might appear on the west bank of
> the river and double his troops; or Wandering Spirit more than triple
> them. **But** he did not wait for that; he knew the Canadian guns now,
> and his resolute men had all been tried by fire: **he told** Riel they must
> strike. **Fast**, while Middleton sat immobile. **If they stampeded** all
> those horses chewing expensive hay, as they easily might, and killed a
> dozen soldiers while raiding their supplies for more rifles and the
> ammunition they had to have for a stand-up fight, Middleton would
> have to retreat and wait even longer for supplies and more troops.
> **Day after day** that big camp simply sat there on the river-bank,
> practising a few horse manoeuvres, shooting at targets, and chewing
> up supplies. **They** had not so much as dared cross Fish Creek Coulee
> to look into Isaac Tourond's hen-house! — Rudy Wiebe, *The
> Scorched-Wood People*

25.1

Var

To begin sentence after sentence with a modifier (or to overuse any
one kind of opening construction) would be no less monotonous, of
course, than to start every statement with the subject. But when
changing the beginnings of some of your sentences does seem
appropriate for variety or emphasis, you can choose from among
the different sorts of modifying elements outlined below. (See also
11.2, Commas After Long Introductory Elements.)

Introductory clauses.   A subordinate clause that might ordinarily follow the main subject can sometimes be used instead to open
the sentence. In some cases this repositioning actually improves the

natural logic of the statement or alters the emphasis. In other
situations the change may be made solely for the sake of variety
within a passage. Here are a few simple examples:

> **Because the car had a flat tire**, we arrived at the meeting an hour
> late.
>
> **After you have loosened the wheel nuts**, jack up the car.
>
> **Although I've watered it every day**, the lawn looks brown and dry.
>
> **That Ed needs help** nobody can deny.
>
> **When they reached the top of the hill** they could see for miles in
> every direction.

Naturally this pattern can also be used in longer and more complicated sentences. It is even possible to open with a series of
dependent clauses, as in the fourth sentence of Rudy Wiebe's
paragraph. That sentence presents four subordinate clauses before
the main clause: (1) *If they stampeded all those horses chewing
expensive hay*, (2) *as they easily might*, (3) *while raiding their
supplies for more rifles and the ammunition*, (4) *they had to have
for a stand-up fight*. The whole construction is conditional,
explaining the circumstances under which the action of the main
clause (Middleton's retreat) might happen.

Introductory phrases.   A phrase of one kind or another can be an
easy and effective opening construction. Phrases usually occur
after the subject and verb (I took three courses *during the summer*)
but may come first if there is no awkwardness (*During the summer*,
I took three courses). In some cases, like the first example given
below, the opening position is actually the clearest:

> **Under the circumstances**, discretion seemed to be the better part of
> valor.
>
> **For no apparent reason**, the plane began to shudder and lose
> altitude.
>
> **Without his magic sword**, our hero was no match for the dragon.
>
> **On the top shelf** was a dusty old pair of binoculars.
>
> **After Christmas** we will study research methods and bibliographical
> work.

The introductory forms illustrated above are all *prepositional*
phrases. But any of the three kinds of *verbal* phrases can also be
used at the beginning of a sentence for the sake of clarity or variety:

> **Wallowing from side to side in the heavy seas** [*participle phrase*],
> our little boat threatened to capsize at any moment.

Getting up at 3:00 a.m. to feed the new baby [*gerund phrase*] is one of the dubious pleasures of parenthood.

To avoid recognition [*infinitive phrase*], she wore sunglasses and a broad-brimmed hat.

For more information on the forms and functions of verbal phrases, see 1.3, Phrases and Clauses, and 4.1, Using Verbal Phrases. And remember not to "dangle" this kind of introductory modifier; the phrase must refer to the *subject* of the main clause, not to some other person or word. A careless sentence like "Cartwheeling across the floor, the announcer described the gymnast's technique" is illogical and unintentionally funny. (See also 4.4, Dangling Modifiers.)

Other introductory modifiers. Adjectives, adverbs, verbals, absolute constructions, and other forms can also be effective sentence openers. Briefer than introductory clauses or phrases, they are particularly good for achieving strong emphasis as well as stylistic variety. A few examples of such beginnings are given below:

All day long we languished in one long line-up after another.

Occasionally a bottle of this wine will taste corky.

Outside, it was beginning to snow heavily.

Tamed, a skunk is an affectionate and interesting pet.

Trembling, I slowly opened the garage door and peered in.

Lean and fit, the mountaineers were well prepared for their ordeal.

Incredibly, the child survived her fall from a sixth-floor balcony.

All things considered, we were lucky to lose by only thirty points.

25.1

Var

▶ **EXERCISE**

Compose effective sentences according to the following instructions. Try to avoid imitating too closely the examples in the text: use different topics and connective words as much as possible.

1. Three sentences that begin with *subordinate clauses*. See the examples on page 388.
2. Three sentences that begin with *prepositional or verbal phrases*. See the examples on page 388.
3. Two sentences that begin with any other kind of modifier. See the examples under Other Introductory Modifiers, but don't use those particular expressions in either of your sentences.

Varying S — V — O Order

A less common means of varying sentence patterns is changing the usual order of subject-verb-object or subject-verb-complement in declarative statements. This is called *inversion:*

> Supplementing the guitars and drums are a solo cello, a ragtime piano, an Indian sitar, sound effects of barnyard animals, and a complete symphony orchestra. — Peter Schrag, "Facing the Music"

Except in questions and requests, however, inversion should ordinarily be used only when the words put first really deserve special emphasis by withholding the subject. Inversion used solely for variety may have painful results, as in this reversal:

> A garden city, with one of the most delightful climates in the world, is Victoria.

Such awkwardness is too high a price to pay for stylistic variety. Inversions should be used sparingly, and only when they remain clear and fairly natural-sounding.

The effective examples below illustrate various forms of partially and completely inverted sequence. The fourth sentence contains two such inversions, parallelled for dramatic effect:

> Equally important are the geographical factors determining Canada's economic growth.

> From her English teacher's lips emerged a dangling participle!

> Insensitive and boorish is any woman who appears unexpectedly at her old flame's wedding.

> Her breach of good sense and good manners we might overlook, but her throwing sand instead of confetti nobody can forgive.

(See 1.1, Main Sentence Elements, for a review of the conventional relationships between subjects, verbs, objects, and complements.)

▶ **EXERCISE**

Rearrange the subject-verb-object or subject-verb-complement order of the following five sentences. See the examples above.

1. The startled child dashed back to the sidewalk.
2. The possible job opportunities in technical writing are even more interesting.
3. I do not appreciate that kind of criticism.
4. The boundless Barren Ground lay to the north, the grim forests to the south.
5. The idea of male and female principles (*animus* and *anima*) comes from Carl Jung.

Interrupters

Variety in sentence patterning can also be achieved by inserting long or short modifying constructions into the middle of some sentences. These elements dramatically interrupt the basic statement to add information or comment. They increase the detail and complexity of a sentence, and they also alter its pace and rhythm. Notice the effect on meaning and sound that different forms of interruption contribute to the excerpt below. In this passage the inserted elements (in bold face type) happen to be a verbal phrase, a subordinate clause, an appositive, and a prepositional phrase:

> The scores of thousands of rocky islands, **falling into the long curved rough lines of old mountain ridges**, are the roots that alone survived the grinding and pounding of primordial storms. In wartime, **as one looked at or lay on its smooth glacier-carved contours**, one could not fail to think piteously of the frailty of the world's cities being levelled to dust and of the ephemeral existence of man. Some parts of the Bay have limestone shores or sandy beaches; here we live on granite — **feldspar, quartz and mica, with seams of black basalt** — rock that once miraculously bore great forests. In the nineteenth century, **by ignorant and ruthless timbering**, the mainland was nearly denuded of its huge virgin pines and hardwoods; second-growth trees only were left. — Kathleen Coburn, *In Pursuit of Coleridge*

25.1

Var

Interrupters may be placed almost anywhere, depending on what word or idea they modify. But they always require strong punctuation — paired marks (commas, dashes, or parentheses) that signal the break in the statement. The element being added is usually grammatically "extra," so it needs to be set off in some definite way. Various types of interrupters and methods of punctuations are illustrated in the following sentences:

> Ancient rock deposits, **some of them dating back to the Upper Cretaceous period**, have yielded the fossilized remains of several dinosaur species.

> The difference in calories between lean and regular ground beef is small — **about 45 calories per patty** — but the lean beef costs a lot more.

> Several wind-driven turbines placed together in one windy location (**an arrangement known as a "wind farm"**) can generate electricity as cheaply as a conventional power plant.

> Union organizers, **when soliciting support for their association**, must not approach employees during actual working hours.

> Cases involving personal financial contracts (**"bounced" cheques,**

for example, or defaults in loan repayment, or arrears in rent) can
sometimes be settled in Small Claims Court.

My house plants, **however**, did not respond to classical music or,
alas, to jazz.

A polyethylene vapor barrier—**enveloping the heated side of the
insulation, preventing diffusion of moisture, and plugging air
leaks**—can be applied over large areas.

Formaldehyde, **which is thought to cause dizziness, headaches,
rashes, and respiratory problems**, is found in many common
house-building materials, including hardboard panelling.

An interrupter should be located immediately before or after the
sentence part it modifies. Changing its position can alter the
meaning or clarity of your statement. (See also 4.3, Misrelated
Modifiers, and 9.1, Position of Adjectives.)

▶ **EXERCISE**

Compose effective sentences according to the following instructions. Try to avoid
imitating too closely the examples in the text.

1. A sentence with an interrupter between *commas*.
2. A sentence with an interrupter between *dashes*.
3. A sentence with an interrupter in *parentheses*.
4. A sentence with an interrupting *clause*.
5. A sentence with an interrupting *series of appositives*, as in the third sentence
    in the Coburn excerpt on page 391.

25.2 SUBORDINATION TO CONTROL AND
CLARIFY MEANING

 Show the intended relationship between ideas by using
appropriate subordination, or correct the faulty
subordination.

By bringing related ideas together, you give continuity to your
writing and signal the direction of your thinking to your reader. But
even when ideas are so closely related that they belong in the same
sentence, they do not necessarily deserve equal weight. You must
decide, in every case, how contributing ideas can best be arranged
around a major idea, or how minor points can best accumulate to
help make a major point. This means that every sentence should be
composed.

An indiscriminate clustering of ideas in a sentence or paragraph is a disservice to the writer, to the subject, and to the reader. Ideas are *not* all the same: some are antecedents to others, some are conditions of others, some are less important than others. If you fail to show the relationship of one idea to another — whether in a single sentence or in a series of sentences — you may be informing your readers, in effect, that all your ideas are equally important or that you are too lazy to bother making your meaning clear:

> FAILURE TO SUBORDINATE: I worked hard and I turned out a first-rate manuscript, and I missed my deadline and my publisher was angry.

> IDEAS EFFECTIVELY RELATED: Although I worked hard and turned out a first-rate manuscript, my publisher was angry because I missed my deadline.

In the first version, four sentences are presented, and all are treated equally. In the revised version, the writer shows how the four are related. One of the statements was chosen as dominant ("my publisher was angry"). One was reduced and rewritten as a cause ("because I missed my deadline"), and the other two are presented as contrary conditions.

Subordination serves writers in several ways. You can put minor ideas into grammatically dependent constructions in order to stress your major point in an independent construction. And at the same time, if you are judicious, you can precisely relate the major and minor ideas. This principle is well illustrated in the passage by Kathleen Coburn on page 391. Its first and third sentences conclude with similar subordinate clauses that add significant detail and also link the sentences to the overall idea of geological age:

25.2

Sub

> ...roots **that alone survived the grinding and pounding of primordial storms**.

> ...rock **that once miraculously bore great forests**.

The second sentence of the Coburn excerpt contains an interrupting subordinate clause that provides a personal and dramatic context for the reflection expressed in the main clause:

> In wartime, **as one looked at or lay on its smooth glacier-carved contours**, one could not fail to think. . . .

The same careful disposition of major and minor points is demonstrated in other passages reprinted in this chapter of the *Handbook*. Examine, for instance, the first few sentences in the paragraph about Ireland on page 381. Notice how information is arranged there in such a way that supplementary ideas serve the main points. The opening sentence of that passage, for example, begins and ends with subordinate clauses expanding the basic statement that mass confiscation occurred. And look again at the fourth sentence of Rudy Wiebe's paragraph on page 387, statement in which *four* effectively related subordinate clauses modify the main clause.

Thoughtful subordination also allows you to move easily from sentence to sentence, using dependent constructions as transitions. Notice, for example, the subordinate clause introducing the last sentence of this passage:

> When you write, you make a point, not by subtracting as though you sharpened a pencil, but by adding. When you put one word after another, your statement should be more precise the more you add. **If the result is otherwise**, you have added the wrong thing, or you have added more than was needed. — John Erskine. "A Note on the Writer's Craft"

Because grammatical constructions are important controllers and signals of meanings, you should make certain in checking your first draft that you have not put major ideas into minor constructions, or minor ideas into major constructions — a fault known as inverted or "upside-down" subordination. (See also 3, Subordinate Clauses and Connectives, especially 3.5, Faulty Subordination.)

Reducing Subordinate Clauses to Shorter Elements

For the sake of conciseness, subordinate clauses should be reduced to briefer supporting constructions whenever possible. A phrase, an appositive, or even an adjective can often do the job of a subordinate clause more emphatically and in fewer words. Especially if your style tends to be complex and wordy, it is wise to practise transforming long modifying elements into short ones. The revisions below illustrate this principle:

Subordinate Clause: I am married to the woman **who is playing the tuba**.

Participle Phrase: I am married to the woman **playing the tuba**.

Two Subordinate Clauses: **Because they were exhausted**, the rowers collapsed over their oars **when they reached the finish line**.

Adjective and Prepositional Phrase: The **exhausted** rowers collapsed over their oars **at the finish line**.

Of course, short constructions can often be reduced even further: *travels in the north* are *northern travels*, and *the frustrations of a teacher* are *a teacher's frustrations*. Even when the difference in economy or emphasis is slight, revisions like these can add structural diversity to your sentence patterning. (See 25.1, Sentence Variety.)

▶ **EXERCISE**

Combine each of the following sets of statements into a single sentence by using subordinate clauses or, when appropriate, shorter elements. Reword as much as seems necessary.

Example: Canadian tourists travel in Europe.
            They wear maple-leaf pins.
            They don't want to be mistaken for Americans.
Possible Combination: Canadian tourists who don't want to be mistaken for
                        Americans wear maple-leaf pins when they travel in
                        Europe.
Another Possibility: Canadian tourists wear maple-leaf pins while travelling in
                        Europe because they don't want to be mistaken for
                        Americans.
Yet Another: To avoid being mistaken for Americans, Canadian tourists travelling
                in Europe wear maple-leaf pins.

1. The fans were chasing the rock star.
    The concert was over.
    He was tired.
    He was leaving the dressing room.
2. I saw a hippo sleeping blissfully in the mud.
    The hippo was smelly and fat.
    It reminded me of my roommate.
3. Edgar Christian kept a diary.
    He recorded in it his grim Arctic ordeal.
    He starved to death in the Barren Ground.
    The diary was found near his body.
4. Historians reconstruct the past.
    Psychology is the science of behavior.
    Sociology is the study of groups in action.
    Political Science examines government.
    Literature embraces them all.
5. Old Fort Garry has been restored.
    It is now in nearly its original condition.
    In its heyday the fur trade was booming.
    Those were exciting and dangerous times.

25.3 ◀
Paral
(//)

25.3 PARALLELISM

Paral
(//) **Make the sentence elements marked parallel in form.**

Ideas of equal value in a statement can be made parallel; that is, they can be expressed in the same grammatical form. Putting co-ordinate ideas in parallel constructions shows the reader that you regard two or more things as related and equal in importance; the *appearance* of parallel passages is a signal that they are closely related. Parallelism also helps the reader see in which direction the statement is going and makes for smoother writing, since it helps prevent unnecessary shifts in person and number and in the tense and mood of verbs.

Elements in Series

Words, phrases, and clauses in series are best stated in parallel form. The boldface words in the following sentence are parallel because each is the object of the preposition *with:*

> His mind was filled with artistic **projects, schemes** for outwitting his creditors, and vague **ideas** about social reform.

Structures are also effectively matched in the following examples. In the first sentence, compound predicates are parallel; in the second, verbal phrases are parallel:

> His dramatic attempt to take over the conduct of his own case **alienated** him from his counsel, almost **broke up** the trial, and probably **helped** to cost him his life. — Joseph Kinsey Howard, *Strange Empire*

> In the older part of the country there was political uproar, the English party **crying out** for a reform of the laws and the establishment of an assembly, the French party stoutly **defending** the existing system, and both parties, for opposite reasons, **fighting** the western demand for a partition of the province. — A.L. Burt, *Guy Carleton, Lord Dorchester, 1724-1808*

When co-ordinate ideas are not stated in parallel form, the statement is likely to seem awkward and unpolished:

> NOT PARALLEL: We were told **to write** in ink, **that we should** use but one side of the paper, and **we should** endorse our papers in the proper manner. [an infinitive phrase and two clauses]

> PARALLEL: We were told **to write** in ink, **to use** but one side of the paper, and **to endorse** our papers in the proper manner. [three parallel infinitive phrases]

A preposition or a conjunction should be repeated between the items of a series when necessary for clarity:

> PREPOSITION NOT REPEATED: These problems are currently of great concern **to** the school system, teachers, and many parents.

> CLEARER: These problems are currently of great concern **to** the school system, **to** teachers, and **to** many parents.

> CONJUNCTION NOT REPEATED: The opposing citizens argued **that** the

increased tax rates were exorbitant and the **school board** should find some other way to raise the money.

CLEARER: The opposing citizens argued **that** the increased tax rates were exorbitant and **that** the **school board** should find some other way to raise money.

Elements Being Compared or Contrasted

Elements that are compared or contrasted through the use of pairs of conjunctions such as *either...or*, *neither...nor*, *not only... but* (or *but also*) are usually clearer and more emphatic when they are stated in parallel constructions. Since readers expect similar constructions to follow pairs of conjunctions, they may be momentarily confused or sidetracked if the pattern is shifted:

SHIFTED: You may go to the ski jump either by special train or a chartered bus may be taken.

PARALLEL: You may go to the ski jump either by special train or by chartered bus.

SHIFTED: He admired the premier not for his integrity, but because of his political cunning.

PARALLEL: He admired the premier not for his integrity, but for his political cunning.

Making related ideas parallel is one of the jobs of revision. Similar forms for similar ideas help hold a sentence together.

25.3
Paral
(//)

Balanced and Antithetical Sentences

When parallel constructions, especially clauses, are noticeably equal in length and similar in movement, the sentence is called *balanced*. Balance is useful for emphatic statements, for comparing and for contrasting ideas:

He was no more willing to change these views than he was to stop drinking whisky. And he was known as a man with a powerful thirst. —Ramsay Cook, *Saturday Night*

The best model of the grand style simple is Homer; perhaps the best model of the grand style severe is Milton. —Matthew Arnold, *On Translating Homer*

When contrasting clauses occur in parallel constructions in a single sentence, the sentence is called *antithetical*. Such a construction fittingly emphasizes a striking or important contrast:

You may eat without danger our canned food, fresh and hot, from your own campfire; but you will drink in peril the dirty water, polluted and foul, from the nearby stream.

Antithetical sentences are occasionally effective to mark turning points in an essay—the first half of the sentence pulling together what precedes, the contrasting second half foreshadowing what follows.

▶ **EXERCISE**

Rewrite the following sentences, eliminating unnecessary words and making related elements parallel in form.

1. I wrote because it amused me, and I enjoyed correcting the work, too.
2. The town turned out to be hard to reach, a bore, and very chilly in the evening.
3. The squirrel in our front yard is a playful sort, and who mocks us from his tree.
4. He slogged his way through his homework, and finished off his notes, then turning on the TV.
5. The house was charming and a real buy, but it was not near enough public transportation nor quite large enough for our family.
6. People who have not been to the Yukon ask questions about the prices, how cold it gets in winter, and what is worth seeing.
7. I am tall and bald and have an ungainly gait.
8. This report is exceptionally complete and a fine example of concise writing.

25.4 SENTENCE EMPHASIS

Emph Rewrite the marked passage so that the position and expression of the ideas will show their relative importance.

In composing your sentences, you should help your reader to see your ideas in the same relative *importance* as you do—to distinguish among the most important, the less important, and the incidental. The arrangement of individual sentences can weaken or strengthen this effect. The sentences in the following paragraph, for example, are unemphatic because they are haphazardly constructed. They are wordy, the beginnings are weak, and the endings are unemphatic:

There are some interesting points about contemporary Canadian life in "The Mobile Society" by Herbert MacAdoo. Some of the things he notes are the paradoxes in it. The way a person often reduces his independence by relying more on mechanical devices is one example the author gives. A man may actually become the machine's slave instead of its master, as he thinks he is.

To make the statements more forceful and concise, the writer might have revised the sentence structure in this way:

> In his essay "The Mobile Society," Herbert MacAdoo points out some of the paradoxes in contemporary Canadian life. He notes, for example, that increasing reliance on mechanical devices often reduces a person's independence. Thinking he is the machine's master, he may actually become its slave.

Emphasis by Position in the Sentence

Important ideas can be stressed by putting them in emphatic positions in the sentence. In longer statements, the most emphatic position is usually at the end, the next most emphatic position at the beginning:

> It is obviously demanding the impossible in any existing society to ask that all individuals in it should be **so linked and united**. But freedom of expression, and other freedoms as well, can have only a precarious existence where the bulk of the people are not **so linked and united**. Thus freedom of expression has been best safeguarded in countries like Britain with a **profound sense of national unity**. — J.A. Corry, "Free Trade in Ideas"

25.4
Emph

Sentences — particularly those that introduce or sum up the main points of a topic — should end strongly. Statements that are qualified by a phrase or a word at the end usually undermine the force of your main idea:

UNEMPHATIC: The work at the mill was hard and often dangerous, but the mill hands didn't complain, or at least very seldom.

IMPROVED: The work at the mill was hard and dangerous, but the mill hands seldom complained.

UNEMPHATIC: These songs are dull and unoriginal, with few exceptions.

IMPROVED: With few exceptions, these songs are dull and unoriginal.

A periodic sentence, because it is not completed until the end, is frequently more emphatic than a loose sentence:

LOOSE: Sociology 101 should interest every thoughtful student with its discussion of the theoretical as well as the practical aspects of human behavior.

PERIODIC: Sociology 101, with its discussion of the theoretical as well as the practical aspects of human behavior, should interest every thoughtful student.

(See also 25.1, page 381, Loose and Periodic Sentences.)

A particular kind of periodic sentence, the *climax* sentence, directs the reader through phrases and clauses arranged in ascending order to the most important element at the end:

> We shall fight on the beaches, we shall fight on the landing-grounds, we shall fight in the fields and in the streets, we shall fight in the hills; we shall never surrender. — Winston Churchill, Speech following Dunkirk, 1940

Sentences that begin with *There is* or *There are* tend to be unemphatic as well as wordy; frequent use of these constructions will make your writing seem flat and uninteresting.

> FLAT: There were several people who objected to the commission's plan.

> IMPROVED: Several people objected to the commission's plan.

Emphasis by Separation

Ideas can be emphasized by setting them off from other parts of the sentence with strong internal punctuation. The idea being set off in this way can appear in the middle of the sentence, punctuated with commas or dashes (see 25.1, Interrupters). But putting it at the end — signalled by a separating colon, semicolon, or dash — is usually a better way to give it prominence (see above, Emphasis by Position in the Sentence). Here are two examples:

> Pierre Elliott Trudeau would like to be remembered for one thing above all: **repatriating the Canadian constitution**.

> The rock group produced a fourth album, aimed at a slightly more sophisticated audience; **it was their first commercial success**.

When the ideas warrant it, the most emphatic separation is into individual sentences. The effect is best achieved in fairly short sentences, as in the following illustration:

> Quiet scholarly professors are rarely the most popular teachers. Sometimes their students don't appreciate them until years afterward.

The occasional use of even briefer sentences is another way of giving extra impact to things you want to stress. Their abruptness makes for a dramatic contrast with material in the passage's longer statements:

Four years later, a bribery scandal ended the cabinet minister's political career and plunged his personal and professional life into ruin. **He died a broken man**.

A miner trapped underground should try to avoid panic and unnecessary activity while awaiting rescue, especially if the air supply seems to have been cut off. **Tension and exertion rapidly expend oxygen**.

For further discussion of the effects of varying sentence length, see chapter 24, Sentence Length and Economy.

Emphasis by Repeating Key Words

Statements can be made emphatic by judiciously repeating important words or phrases:

His highest hope is to **think** first what is about to be **thought**, to **say** what is about to be **said**, and to **feel** what is about to be **felt**. — Bertrand Russell, *Unpopular Essays*

In your reading, you will sometimes see a word or phrase repeated deliberately to create a special effect at the beginning of consecutive clauses or sentences:

Vimy was more than a battle. It has become for Canada a **symbol**. It is a **symbol**, as were many other and even bloodier battles, of the courage and the self-sacrifice of Canadian men. It is also a **symbol** of the coming of age of Canada as a nation, a nation which was brought to birth in the emotion of that time with a unity sealed by blood. — Lester B. Pearson, "Vimy — Fifty Years After"

25.4
Emph

This kind of rhetorical repetition is often found in political speeches, and can easily be overused or become tedious. In the hands of a skilled writer, these techniques can be highly effective, but they should be used very sparingly, and only when a serious subject can be honestly and appropriately conveyed in the deliberate manner they suggest.

Effective (and intentional) repetition should be distinguished from careless repetition, as discussed in 24.5.

Emphasis by Mechanical Devices

The least effective way to emphasize ideas is by underlining or capitalizing words, by setting them off in quotation marks, or by using emphatic punctuation marks (!!!). Certain kinds of advertising rely heavily on such devices:

"Oh, of course," you may reply, "it's just a matter of calories." But

IS it? Suppose you had to choose between a large glass of orange juice and half a sirloin steak? You would probably reach for the orange juice. Actually, *the steak would give you 15 times as many ENERGY-stimulating calories. Yet the total number* of calories in each is roughly the same! So, you see it ISN'T "just a matter of calories." It's the KIND of calories that makes the big difference.

In university and college writing, mechanical devices for emphasis should ordinarily be avoided; the wording of the statement or its position in the sentence should give it the emphasis it deserves.

▶ **EXERCISE**

Rewrite the following sentences so that the important points are correctly emphasized. In each case, consider ways of subordinating, repositioning, or rewording some of the information.

1. Television programs today are very adolescent in content, at least most of them.
2. There were two magnificent volcano peaks which towered over the valley.
3. Theoretically, the plan seemed flawless; its results, however, were disastrous.
4. Students on the campus were completely unaware that under the abandoned stands of Stagg Field scientists have produced, through concentrated day-and-night effort under rigid security precautions, the first controlled atomic chain reaction.
5. There is something the average voter doesn't realize — that his ONE vote really *can make a difference;* in fact, it can change the outcome of the WHOLE ELECTION!
6. Thumbing frantically through his calendar and clutching his registration cards in his sweaty hands while he stands in line is the typical freshman.
7. Sculpture is an excellent hobby, although it can be expensive and not everyone has the skill to pursue it.
8. Outside his office there were several customers waiting and they insisted there were other matters they had to attend to.
9. The recent civil defence drill — like all the preceding ones — showed that public apathy toward survival methods is immense.
10. Many juvenile delinquents (you'd be surprised *how* many) have parents who refuse to try to *understand* them.

26

Using a Dictionary

There was a time when the meaning of language presented no problem, when it was a simple matter, upon being challenged as to meaning, to call to witness the dictionary. But in our age of universal skepticism, we have come to know that dictionaries are not depositories of eternal meanings of language. Dictionaries are made by ordinary human beings, who have collected data from — of all people — you and me, the general users of the language. — James E. Miller, Jr., *Word, Self, Reality: The Rhetoric of Imagination*

While it certainly is more reliable than any one person, a dictionary is not a supreme authority to be quoted in settling all arguments about the meaning, pronunciation, and spelling of words. Although modern dictionaries aim to record the ways in which terms are actually used, none can possibly be a complete record. The pioneer lexicographer Samuel Johnson concluded long ago that it was foolish for a man to attempt to "embalm his language." But the notion still persists that a dictionary is — or should be — a code of law for language use.

For this reason, there has been considerable debate, and some heated argument, about whether a dictionary should *prescribe* or *describe* language use. Some people want a dictionary to tell us which pronunciation is right, which meaning is proper, which use of a word is correct.

Other people, including the editors of many dictionaries, declare that dictionaries are not intended to dictate use of language. Almost any rule that a dictionary could offer to govern pronunciation or definition would have originated in observation of how people at some time in the past actually pronounced and defined words. Thus, if a dictionary set out to be a system of law, the editors would be converting the *habits* of some past time into *rules* for the present.

The editors of most recently published dictionaries want to *register* how the language is used. To that end, they may offer a variety of acceptable pronunciations for many words, with no effort to dictate what is "best." Some editors, too, have begun to omit usage labels — which indicate that some words are *informal* (or *colloquial*) or *slang* — on the ground that the correctness or appropriateness of a word can seldom be determined out of context.

Contexts (the situations in which words are used) change, and language changes. It's understandable that we might sometimes wish for an authority to stop changes that are not good, such as those in which a unique or precise meaning of a word is lost. But changes often *are* good: for example, our language has for centuries been enriched and enlarged by the addition of words from other languages.

Since language changes—sometimes for the worse, probably more often for the better—a dictionary cannot control, but simply record the way it is actually used. The standards for determining what good language is rest in other hands (see Introduction).

26.1 SELECTING A DICTIONARY

A good dictionary, though not a final authority, is a basic reference tool for every student. Dictionaries answer questions about the meanings, spellings, origins, and pronunciations of words. They also give information about the grammatical forms of words (plurals, past tenses) and about idiomatic constructions (what preposition, for example, is commonly used with a particular noun or verb). Many also give usage notes explaining divided or non-standard usage (as the "double negative") and information about synonyms, doublets, and so on. One of the most valuable habits a writer can acquire is checking a dictionary for the meaning and spelling of words.

Dictionaries differ in size and purpose, but certain criteria apply in evaluating any dictionary for general use. First of all, it should be up-to-date. New words and expressions are continually coming into the language (*acrylic, ambience, détente, Francophone, Anglophone, mainstreeting, psychedelic*) and old words are always being used in new senses (a *crash* program, an advertising *flyer*, a publicity *handout*). Even spelling and pronunciation can change with time (*judgment, judgement; ab′ dəmən, abdō′ mən*). In addition, most dictionaries are somewhat encyclopedic, including information about prominent people and places. There are always new names to be added (*Nkomo, Namibia*) and new facts to be recorded.

In an effort to keep their entries up-to-date, most dictionaries make limited changes every few years. Check the copyright dates before you buy a dictionary to find out when it was last revised. You might also want to look up some words that have recently come into use to see if they are included.

In evaluating a dictionary, you should also consider the quality of its editing. A good dictionary of current English is not simply an updating of earlier editions; it reflects the research and judgment of a large staff of experts who record and analyse hundreds of thousands of examples of words in actual use. It is the responsibility of the lexicographer to make certain that the language has been sampled adequately and that all the most common uses of even uncommon words have been found. Then all new evidence must be carefully evaluated, some being discarded and some carefully edited. The result should be a concise yet reliable description of the words current in the language. Whatever "authority" a dictionary has, then, depends on the scholarship, discrimination, and judgment of its editors.

Dictionaries for General Use

The most complete descriptions of contemporary English are to be found in the various "unabridged" dictionaries. Though not practical for desk use, these large dictionaries are invaluable for reference, and at least one of them is available in every library of consequence. All English unabridged dictionaries are American, the best-known being *Webster's Third New International Dictionary* (the most complete record now available); *The Random House Dictionary of the English Language; Webster's New Twentieth Century Dictionary;* and the *New Standard Dictionary of the English Language*.

For everyday use, however, "college-size" dictionaries are more practical for college and university students. Among the best American dictionaries of this category are *Webster's New World Dictionary, Second College Edition*; the *Random House Dictionary,* College Edition; *Webster's New Collegiate Dictionary;* and the *American Heritage Dictionary*. Worthy of special attention is *Funk & Wagnalls Standard College Dictionary*, which gives more attention to Canadian words than the others; the Canadian Edition includes a great deal of lexical and other information pertaining to Canada, though it is still substantially American in content. Of comparable quality is the British *Collins Dictionary of the English Language*, which includes and identifies words that are characteristic of different parts of the English-speaking world, including Canada. Also to be considered are two other British dictionaries: the *Concise Oxford Dictionary* and the *Longman Modern English Dictionary*; both give considerable attention to Americanisms, very little, as yet, to Canadianisms.

Canada does not yet have an unabridged dictionary of its own. Nevertheless, there is an up-to-date and reputable general work in the adult "desk-dictionary" category: The *Gage Canadian Dictionary (GCD)*—the senior book in the graded Dictionary of

26.1◀

Dict

Canadian English series, which includes *The Junior Dictionary* and *The Intermediate Dictionary*. Although it is slightly less inclusive than most of the dictionaries mentioned above, the *GCD* is highly suited to Canadians, for it is intended to record usage in Canada, an objective not sought by American and British dictionaries.

Special Dictionaries

The general dictionaries — abridged and unabridged — are supplemented by a number of specialized dictionaries that may be consulted for information not to be found in general works.

Historical dictionaries.   Good general dictionaries are based in part upon scholarly dictionaries of international repute. *The Oxford English Dictionary*, twelve volumes and a *Supplement*, 1888 – 1933 — currently being supplemented by four additional volumes (1972–) — is a historical dictionary of the words and idiomatic phrases of the English language. It traces the various forms and meanings of each word, giving the date of its first appearance in recorded English and illustrative quotations from writers to show the word's typical use at various times in its history (a dozen or more columns are sometimes devoted to a single word). In many kinds of study, it is a basic tool for research. *The Shorter Oxford English Dictionary* (two volumes) is an abridgment of the larger work and somewhat easier to use.

The Dictionary of American English (four volumes), made on the same plan as the *Oxford*, gives the history of words as they have been used by American writers from 1620 to 1900. *A Dictionary of Americanisms* (two volumes) gives the history of words that originated in the United States and brings the record of American English down to 1944.

A Dictionary of Canadianisms on Historical Principles (1967) provides "a historical record of words and expressions characteristic of the various spheres of Canadian life during the almost four centuries that English has been used in Canada." Also available is an abridgment entitled *A Concise Dictionary of Canadianisms* (1972).

Dictionaries in special subjects.   Dictionaries of slang, usage, and other specialized language uses are available, and most special fields have dictionaries of their specialized vocabularies. For these and other sources of information, familiarize yourself with the reference shelves in the library.

26.2 LEARNING TO USE YOUR DICTIONARY

Dictionaries differ not only in the information they include but in the way they present it, and the best dictionary in the world will be of little value to you unless you know how to read and interpret the information it provides. Before using a new dictionary, read the front matter carefully. It will explain the organization of entries, the method of indicating pronunciation, the use of restrictive labels, and the meaning of abbreviations and symbols used in the definitions and etymologies. Then look carefully at a page of entries to see how words and phrases are handled. Test your understanding of the pronunciation guide by using it to pronounce some familiar words. Look through the table of contents to see what sections of information your dictionary provides in addition to the main alphabetical list of words. You may find a short grammar of English, a short history of the English language, a discussion of punctuation, a table of signs and symbols, a list of colleges and universities, or a guide to the preparation of manuscript copy.

A little time spent in learning to use your dictionary can make it immensely useful to you. The following sections describe the kinds of information found in most dictionaries; the sample entries on page 408 show how one dictionary presents this information, but most dictionaries are very similar.

▶ **EXERCISE**

To help you familiarize yourself with your dictionary, write out the following information about it, for discussion in class or to be handed in.

1. The title, the name of the publisher, and the most recent copyright date. This date may be found on the back of the title page.
2. A list of the sections following the introduction and preceding the dictionary entries (such as "How to Use the Dictionary," "A Guide to Pronunciation," "Usage Levels").
3. A list of the material in the appendix (if any), such as "Signs and Symbols," "Biographical Names," "Colleges and Universities."
4. Do the words appear in one alphabetical list or in separate lists (for biographical names, geographical names, abbreviations, and so on)?
5. Are derived forms (*cynical* and *cynicism* from *cynic*, for example) listed separately as main entries in the alphabetical list, or are they listed under the base form?
6. Do the etymologies come at the beginning or at the end of an entry?
7. The order of the definitions of the words. Does the older meaning or the current meaning come first in words such as *cute, ghastly, shrewd, liquidate, souse* (noun), *recession, sheriff, reeve, umpire*?

26.2◀

Dict

Sample Dictionary Entries

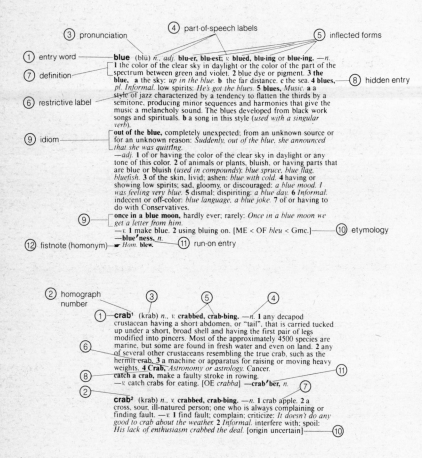

③ pronunciation

④ part-of-speech labels

⑤ inflected forms

① entry word

⑦ definition

⑥ restrictive label

⑨ idiom

⑧ hidden entry

blue (blü) *n., adj.* **blu·er, blu·est;** *v.* **blued, blu·ing** or **blue·ing.** —*n.*
1 the color of the clear sky in daylight or the color of the part of the spectrum between green and violet. 2 blue dye or pigment. 3 **the blue, a** the sky: *up in the blue.* **b** the far distance. **c** the sea. 4 **blues,** *pl. Informal.* low spirits: *He's got the blues.* 5 **blues,** *Music.* **a** a style of jazz characterized by a tendency to flatten the thirds by a semitone, producing minor sequences and harmonies that give the music a melancholy sound. The blues developed from black work songs and spirituals. **b** a song in this style (*used with a singular verb*).
out of the blue, completely unexpected; from an unknown source or for an unknown reason: *Suddenly, out of the blue, she announced that she was quitting.*
—*adj.* 1 of or having the color of the clear sky in daylight or any tone of this color. 2 of animals or plants, bluish, or having parts that are blue or bluish (*used in compounds*): *blue spruce, blue flag, bluefish.* 3 of the skin; livid; ashen: *blue with cold.* 4 having or showing low spirits; sad, gloomy, or discouraged: *a blue mood. I was feeling very blue.* 5 dismal; dispiriting: *a blue day.* 6 *Informal.* indecent or off-color: *blue language, a blue joke.* 7 of or having to do with Conservatives.
once in a blue moon, hardly ever; rarely: *Once in a blue moon we get a letter from him.*
—*v.* 1 make blue. 2 using bluing on. [ME < OF *bleu* < Gmc.]
—**blue′ness,** *n.*
☛ *Hom.* **blew.**

⑨ idiom

⑩ etymology

⑫ fistnote (homonym)

⑪ run-on entry

② homograph number

③

⑤

④

① **crab**¹ (krab) *n., v.* **crabbed, crab·bing.** —*n.* 1 any decapod crustacean having a short abdomen, or "tail", that is carried tucked up under a short, broad shell and having the first pair of legs modified into pincers. Most of the approximately 4500 species are marine, but some are found in fresh water and even on land. 2 any of several other crustaceans resembling the true crab, such as the hermit crab. 3 a machine or apparatus for raising or moving heavy weights. 4 **Crab,** *Astronomy or astrology.* Cancer.
catch a crab, make a faulty stroke in rowing.
—*v.* catch crabs for eating. [OE *crabba*] —**crab′ber,** *n.*

⑥

⑧

② **crab**² (krab) *n., v.* **crabbed, crab·bing.** —*n.* 1 crab apple. 2 a cross, sour, ill-natured person; one who is always complaining or finding fault. —*v.* 1 find fault; complain; criticize: *It doesn't do any good to crab about the weather.* 2 *Informal.* interfere with; spoil: *His lack of enthusiasm crabbed the deal.* [origin uncertain]

⑪

⑦

⑩

Spelling and Word Division

Develop the habit of using your dictionary to check the spelling in your papers. If you are unable to find a word because you are uncertain of one of the beginning letters, try to think of other possible spellings for the same sound. (Is it *gibe* or *jibe*?) Remember that dictionaries give the spelling not only of the base form of a word but also of distinctive forms—the principal parts of verbs, the plurals of nouns, the comparative and superlative forms of adjectives and adverbs—that are in any way irregular.

Your dictionary may give two spellings for a word when usage is divided (*hemoglobin—haemoglobin; adviser—advisor*). Use the spelling that the editors have indicated is the more common one. (The method of listing variants and of indicating their relative currency will be explained in the front matter of the dictionary.) American and British dictionaries are not always helpful for Canadians. (See the comments in 17.5, Variant Spellings.)

Dictionaries divide words into units (usually corresponding to spoken syllables) by means of small dots or spaces: *de•mar•ca•tion, de light ful*. This device will enable you to see each part of the word clearly and to notice if you have omitted or transposed any letters. In writing, divide a word at the end of a line only where your dictionary shows a division and never divide words pronounced as one syllable (as *clipped*). The word *reorganization*, for example, has five possible places for division: *re•or•ga•ni•za•tion*. Not all dictionaries divide every word in exactly the same way, but by following the practice of any good dictionary, you will avoid such careless blunders as dividing *bedraggled* into *bed-* and *raggled*. See also 17, Spelling, and 29.3, Manuscript Form.

▶ **EXERCISE**

26.2
Dict

What information do you find in your dictionary on the spelling of these pairs of words? Are the spellings interchangeable? If so, which form would you use and why?

aesthetic — esthetic	gaol — jail
carat — karat	ketchup — catchup
catalog — catalogue	licorice — liquorice
draft — draught	sac — sack
favor — favour	traveling — travelling

Pronunciation

Because English spelling is not consistently phonetic (there are over 250 ways to spell the forty-odd sounds in English), dictionaries use a system of special symbols to show how words are pronounced. The word *bamboozle*, for example, might be respelled this way after the entry word: *bam bü′ zƏl*. The pronunciation key at the bottom or top of the page will illustrate, with familiar words, the sounds represented by the symbols, (*a*), (*ü*), and (*Ə*). Since the consonants (*b*), (*m*), (*z*), and (*l*) have no special marks over them, you may assume that they are pronounced in the usual way. The accented syllable in (*bam bü′ zƏl*) is indicated by a heavy stress mark. Phonetic spellings also indicate secondary stress, when appropriate, usually by a lighter mark (′). Since the system for showing pronunciation varies somewhat from dictionary to dictionary, you should study carefully the explanatory notes in the front of your own book before attempting to use its pronunciation key.

Dictionaries often list two or more pronunciations for a word when usage is divided. Although the first pronunciation is usually the more common one, it is not necessarily "preferred," and you should use whichever pronunciation is customary in your own community.

▶ **EXERCISES**

To familiarize yourself with the pronunciation key in your dictionary, write out the following exercises:

1. What pronunciations does your dictionary list for each of these words? Is the first pronunciation given the one you hear most frequently? If not, tell how it differs, including the stress (accent):

address	creek	gratitude	pianist
adult	culinary	herb	poesy
Celtic	drama	implacable	research
coupon	gibberish	leisure	Oedipus

2. How is each of these words pronounced when used as a noun? As a verb?

confine	escort	impact	misuse
conflict	exploit	import	refuse
consort	ferment		

Meaning

Dictionaries are perhaps most important for what they tell us about the meanings of words. To a reader, a dictionary is useful for finding the meanings not only of unfamiliar words but also of familiar words used in new senses. To a writer, dictionary definitions are most useful for checking the meanings of words about which he or she is uncertain.

Dictionaries begin each definition, or group of definitions, with an abbreviation showing whether the word is being defined as a noun (*n.*), adjective (*adj.*), verb (*vb.*), or other part of speech. Sometimes, verbs are distinguished as being transitive (*v.t.*) or intransitive (*v.i.*). This information is important, for words usually have different meanings in different grammatical contexts. Sometimes the meanings are closely related (for example, the meanings of *advance* as a verb, a noun, or an adjective) but sometimes they are completely different (the meanings of *fly*, *plant*, and *court* as verbs or as nouns).

In looking for the meaning of a word in context, therefore, you must ordinarily isolate the right group of definitions before you can find the particular meaning you are looking for. Then you should look over all the definitions included in that group. Some dictionaries give the oldest meaning first and others the most common current one. Often, however, you will be looking for a more specialized meaning that comes later in the entry. At the end of the entry, or at the end of a group of definitions for one part of speech, you may also find one or more idioms listed.

In using dictionary definitions, you should keep two general principles in mind:

1. A dictionary does not *require* or *forbid* a particular meaning or use of a word; it merely *records* the most common ways in which a word has actually been used. Therefore, you must exercise judgment in deciding whether a particular word will be appropriate in a particular context.

2. A dictionary definition is for the most part a record of the *denotation*, or specific meaning, of a word; at best, it can only suggest the *connotation*, or suggestive qualities, which varies with context and with use. (See 27.1.) In general, it is better not to use a word until you have heard it or read it in context and know at least some of its connotations.

26.2

Dict

► **EXERCISES**

1. Answer the following questions by referring to the definitions given in your dictionary:
    a. In what kind of writing would it be appropriate to use the word *gimmick*?
    b. In what profession would the word *dolmen* most likely be used?
    c. Where would you be most likely to hear the word *legato*?
    d. When a woman *rests on her laurels*, what is she doing?

e. Which of the following expressions would be underlined in a paper to indicate they belong to a foreign language?

quid pro quo   de facto   sarong   apartheid   toccata   vice versa

2. Consult your dictionary and choose the best definition for the italicized word in each of these sentences:
   a. At ten he became a printer's *devil*.
   b. His *fellowship* expired at the end of the year.
   c. Luther objected to the sale of *indulgences*.
   d. The entrance fee was *fixed* at twenty dollars.
   e. She has extremely *catholic* reading tastes.
   f. They soon discovered that the resort was a *white elephant*.

Areas of Usage and Special Labels

Some words (or particular meanings for some words) are labelled in a dictionary as *dialectal*, *obsolete*, *archaic*, *foreign*, *informal* (or *colloquial*), *slang*, *Cdn.*, *Brit.*, *U.S.*, or are identified with some particular activity, field or region — *medicine*, *law*, *astronomy*, *music*, *hockey*, *Newfoundland*, *Maritimes*. Words that are not labelled in a dictionary are considered part of the general vocabulary.

Usage labels can serve as rough guides, but you should bring your own observation to bear on individual words. Certainly you would ordinarily avoid words marked *obsolete* or *archaic*, but many words that carry no label (*albeit*, *perforce*) would be equally out of place in most college writing. On the other hand, many words marked *Dial.* or *Informal* (such as *highbrow*) might fit perfectly well into both informal and general English. The label *colloquial*, used for *informal* in some dictionaries, means simply that a particular usage is more characteristic of conversation than it is of writing. The labels *Cdn.* or *U.S.* mean that the usage is associated with those countries rather than with other parts of the English-speaking world.

Most dictionaries of the English language include frequently used words and expressions from foreign languages. Some dictionaries indicate that such terms are generally considered foreign by indicating the language, as *German*, *Latin* or (lt.), (Gk.). Others use an identifying mark, such as a dagger or an asterisk, before all foreign-word entries. Such labels are useful because they help distinguish between words that are now considered part of the English vocabulary (*chalet*, *aria*, *junta*) and those that are still considered distinctly foreign (*dolce far niente*, *Weltanschauung*, *ibidem*) and must be underlined in a paper. (See 14.3, page 182, Italics for Foreign Words.)

► **EXERCISE**

Answer the following questions by consulting the *grammatical information* given
in the dictionary entry for each word:
1.   What is the past participle of *shear*?
2.   What is the past tense of *bear* in the sense of *carry*?
3.   What does *feign* mean when it is used intransitively?
4.   What does *gull* mean when followed by a direct object?
5.   What is the plural of *ghetto*?
6.   What is the plural of *stratum*?

Synonyms and Antonyms

Most dictionaries list words of similar meaning (*synonyms*) and
explain how these various related words differ slightly in meaning,
especially in connotation. Sometimes the entry for a word will also
list an *antonym*, a word of opposite meaning, as *cowardly* would
be an antonym for *courageous*.

There are several specialized books containing lists of related
words: *Webster's Dictionary of Synonyms*, Fernald's *Standard
Handbook of Synonyms, Antonyms, and Prepositions*, Soule's *A
Dictionary of English Synonyms*, *Webster's Collegiate Thesaurus*,
and Roget's *Thesaurus*. The *Thesaurus* is probably the most
widely used book of synonyms, but since it does not give definitions, its chief use is to remind writers of words they recognize but
do not use regularly. If you find words that appear to be appropriate
but you are not completely sure, check their definitions in a
dictionary.

Etymology

A dictionary not only tells how a word is used and pronounced but
also gives its origin, or *etymology*. Sometimes the etymology is
merely a notation of the language from which the word was
borrowed (as *decor* is from French and *Gestalt* is from German) or
a statement of how it was coined. But often the etymology is fairly
complicated; the development of the word *advance*, for example,
can be traced back through Middle English to Old French and
finally to Latin. The explanatory notes at the front of your dictionary include a discussion of etymology and a key to the abbreviations and symbols used in tracing a word's origin.

Knowing how a word originated will often help you understand
and remember it. Knowing that *philanthropy*, for example, comes
from the Greek words *philein* (to love) and *anthropos* (man) may

26.2

Dict

help fix its meaning in your mind. Beyond this, it may help you figure out other unfamiliar words by analogy (*philology, anthropocentric*).

Etymologies often illustrate how word meanings have changed from their original to their present use and are interesting as records of human thought and experience.

▶ **EXERCISES**

1. Consult the *etymologies* in your dictionary to answer the following questions:
    a. What is the origin of these words?

sandwich	assassin	lecture
robot	okra	semester
farm	radish	geology

    b. Which of the following words have retained most or all of their original meanings? Which have retained some? Which none?

bigot	fiasco	pilot
curfew	neat	silly
feeble	pedigree	tragedy

2. The following questions can be answered by finding the needed information in the dictionary. In some cases, this information will be found under the appropriate entry word; in others, special sections at the back or front of the dictionary must be consulted.
    a. Write sentences using the words shown below. Be sure your sentences distinguish among the similar words put together as sets:
        deviate — digress — diverge — swerve
        slim — thin — slender — skinny
        fictitious — legendary — mythical
        giggle — titter — snicker — chuckle
        latent — potential — dormant
    b. Give antonyms for the following words: *authentic, chaste, devout, futile, verbose*.
    c. Who was John Huss? When did he live?
    d. What was Camelot?
    e. Where are lemmings found?
    f. When was Napoleon Bonaparte born?
    g. What is a pronghorn?
    h. What does IPA stand for?
    i. What does the symbol B/L mean in business and commerce?
    j. Of what country is the cordoba the monetary unit?

27

The Meaning of Words

Respect for the word — to employ it with scrupulous care and incorruptible heartful love of truth — is essential if there is to be any growth in society or in the human race. — Dag Hammarskjöld, *Markings*

A word is dead
When it is said,
Some say.
I say it just
Begins to live
That day. — Emily Dickinson

We usually take for granted that we know the meanings of the words we use. Except when there is a question of accuracy (*infer* or *imply?*) or of appropriateness (*boss* or *supervisor?*), we rarely think about *selecting* our words. But if you are to use the words that will best convey your intended meaning, you need to do more than simply accept and use the first words that come to mind. You need to take an active interest in words as words. What gives a particular word its special meanings in different situations? In what different ways can a word be used? How will others take the words you use? Words have many possible meanings. If you are to choose those that best serve your purpose, you need to know first what the choices are.

27.1 KINDS OF MEANING: DENOTATION AND CONNOTATION

27.1

Mng

Words do not actually have "meaning" until they are used in speaking or writing. Then their meaning derives partly from the *context*, or the words around them, and partly from the *situation* in which they are used, which involves the attitudes and purposes of either a speaker and listener or a writer and reader.

Nor is the "meaning" of a word limited to the definite senses that a dictionary attempts to describe. Besides those explicit meanings, there are often implicit meanings or associated values (subtle powers of suggestion) that have become connected with its use. Impressions of this sort can be included or excluded by a writer's word choices. That is, words may be selected for either their narrowness or their breadth of possible meaning. Unless you choose your words carefully and show your readers the limits of meaning that you have in mind, they are at liberty to take your words in any way they wish.

Denotation: The Core of a Word's Meaning

When we first think about the meaning of words, we usually think of their *denotation*, what they have come to represent as a result of the ways they have been used. This is the meaning that dictionaries usually record and try to define for us.

Of course, a particular word can have two or more denotative meanings. In such cases the context shows us which one is intended. For instance, a word like *deck, run, fly,* or *match* can be used in several quite different senses, but usually in a particular sentence it can have only one meaning:

> Tomorrow we'll take a **run** up to the lake.
> You will have to **run** to catch the train.
> Frowning, she noticed the **run** in her stocking.
> McKay scored the third **run** after two were out in the seventh.
> He did a **run** of scales and decided that was enough practice.
> When the store opened on the morning of the sale, there was a **run** on leather goods.

The situation in which a word is used also helps clarify its meaning. The word *bill* in "The bill is too large" would mean one thing if the speaker were trying to identify a bird and another if he were discussing family finances.

There are, moreover, different kinds of denotation. Some words are more definite than others because the things they refer to are more specific or exact. The nouns *carnivore* and *cougar* are both denotative, yet the latter is obviously more specific than the former. Similarly, *angry* or *disappointed* would be more precise than *upset*. Depending on their definiteness, words may be classified into three groups:

1. Concrete words, words that name specific people, places, or objects, are the most exact in meaning: *Wilfrid Laurier, Lake Louise, my bicycle, the library, reindeer, a Boy Scout knife.*

2. Relative words, words that describe qualities, are less definite than concrete words and frequently depend for their meanings on the situation or on the writer's past experience with a term: *hot, pretty, honest, angry, silly, impossible.* In Toronto, a *tall* building might refer to any structure over twenty storeys, but in a city with no skyscrapers, *tall* might refer to any building higher than five storeys.

3. Abstract words,   words that refer to general concepts—acts, situations, relationships, conditions—are the least definite: *reasoning, citizenship, education, intelligence, society, objectives, art*. Since these words have a range of references (think of all the activities that may be included in *education*, for example), rather than a specific referent, they are more difficult to use precisely than concrete words. (See also 27.4, Concrete and Asbtract Words.)

Words in all three of these classes are denotative; they simply name, without qualification or implied judgment, things or ideas that can be defined. Though there is no such thing as an *entirely* "flat" or "neutral" word, denotative language comes closest to (or aims at) that condition of limited, factual, impersonal meaning. The ordinary or literal significance of a denotative word, the sense that every user shares, does not suggest any particular value judgment or attitude.

Denotative language is most appropriate and effective when you do wish to *narrow* your meaning to achieve as much exactness and detachment as possible. In such situations, words with multiple or subjective implications might tend to confuse or broaden the scope of a topic you are trying to clarify and limit. In practical and formal projects like reports, it is especially important to stick to words that have distinct, neutral meanings. For example, if you are preparing a political science essay on student protest rallies, you should confine yourself to denotative terms (*demonstration, protesters, ignore, government officials, reason*); and avoid words that are charged with emotion or personal judgment (*disturbance, radicals, scorn, bureaucrats, excuse*). Of course, an informal paper on the same topic might be an appropriate occasion for more subjectively colored language (see below regarding *connotation*).

27.1

Mng

Connotation: The Power to Suggest Meaning

In addition to their denotative meanings, many words are highly *suggestive* of other senses or values. Such words are sometimes described as "loaded" because they are strongly associated with emotional or qualitative impressions. These implicit extra associations—the suggestiveness and expanded "flavor" a word has acquired through use—are known as *connotative* meanings.

The word *twilight*, for example, has been used so often in association with melancholy or romance that we sometimes don't think of it simply as a time of day. And someone has suggested that the word *nightingale* could lose all its suggestion of beauty and be merely the name of a bird only to a tone-deaf ornithologist. Likewise, connotative terms such as *bureaucrat, radical, hierarchy*, and even *political* are so "loaded" with negative implications that most people use them mainly to signal disapproval.

Very often the chief difference between words of closely related denotation is in their connotation. Both *inexpensive* and *cheap* refer to low price, but *cheap* may also connote poor quality; *average* and *mediocre* both refer to the middle of a range, but *mediocre* suggests dispraise; *belief, faith, creed, dogma* all refer to ideas held, but they differ widely in suggesting how they are held. It is easy to see why some linguists say that there are no true synonyms.

Dictionaries try to suggest the shades of meaning that words may have, but the best way to discover the connotations of a word is to observe how it is actually used in current writing and speech. The connotative value of a word often changes over time. *Sly*, for example, once meant *skilful*, but as generally used now, it would fit into the same context as *devious* or *tricky*; it may even suggest *criminal* or, sometimes, *lecherous*. Words like *genteel* and *bucolic* have lost their favorable connotation as the values they represent have lost much of their appeal. Certain words, usually those whose referents arouse widely ranging responses, are extremely variable in connotation: *pop art, punk, intellectual, nuclear, socialism, jazz*. When you use such words, be cautious, making sure that your attitude is clear to your reader and that you are being fair to your subject. Words with highly emotive connotations, such as those associated with prickly controversies, may create special problems.

In such situations, the view of the whittler who sat in the town square may be instructive. This man, widely known for his uncannily realistic carvings of birds, when asked how he managed to achieve such realism in his carvings, said, "Well, I just whittle off all the wood that don't look like a bird." When you use words that have high emotive power, you may have to whittle away all the meanings that you do not want to express. This may mean taking the time to define, to set limits to what you are trying to say, to establish clearly how you want to use the words.

Take advantage of the richly connotative qualities of language whenever you do want to *extend* your meaning to include impressionistic or emotional qualities or ironic implications. In other words, control of connotation lets you indicate your *attitude* towards the things you are explaining, or lend *flavor* to objects or actions that would otherwise seem flat and ordinary. A descriptive or narrative passage will be livelier and more effective if your words are personal and suggestive than if they are detached and limited. "Golden" hair or "frenzied" preparations are more vivid than "yellow" (or "blonde") hair or "rapid" preparations. Students late for class "scramble" into the elevator; they don't just "move quickly." Moreover, your choice of words can, by itself, signal favorable or unfavorable judgments regarding your subject. Notice the range of possible attitudes in the following examples:

Favorable Connotation	Denotation (Neutral)	Unfavorable Connotation
normal	average	mediocre
traditional	old	antiquated
famous	well known	notorious
stability	permanence	stagnation
public servant	government employee	bureaucrat
patriot	nationalist	chauvinist
agreement	arrangement	deal

In writing situations that do not require the neutrality and detachment of denotation, you are free to let your language disclose personal attitudes. The important thing in this regard is *control*—knowing when and how to include (or exclude) kinds of meaning.

Argumentative writing can also be much more interesting and persuasive when vigorous connotative language is used; remember, however, that exclusively emotional appeals are considered to be dishonest in formal argument. Employed appropriately and responsibly, connotation greatly enriches and humanizes your meaning. Used irresponsibly (or when the definiteness of denotation is expected), it can create in the reader's mind a very unfavorable impression of your judgment and reliability. See 27.2, Fair Words and Slanted Words.

27.1
Mng

▶ **EXERCISES**

1. The meaning of a word often depends on the context in which it is used. Write two sentences using each of the following words to show how the meaning of the words can change as they move from one context to another: *realize, studio, elevation, pitching, cup, book, stack, feedback*.

2. The connotative value of words is very important in determining their use: for example, you might say "I am *plump*; you are *heavy*; he is *fat*"; three different pictures emerge. Arrange the following groups of words into columns, according to their connotation: favorable, neutral, or unfavorable.

a. student, scholar, bookworm
b. stubborn, firm, pigheaded
c. counterfeit, replica, copy
d. racy, obscene, blue
e. unusual, bizarre, unique
f. tolerant, flexible, wishy-washy
g. caustic, penetrating, sharp
h. reserved, aristocratic, snobbish
i. buffoon, wit, comic
j. officer, policeman, fuzz
k. svelte, skinny, thin
l. literary artist, hack, writer

27.2 FAIR WORDS AND SLANTED WORDS

Your readers don't always see things as you see them, or know them as you know them, just as you don't see and know things as they do. If you want your readers to see and know things as you do, at least for a moment, you have to show them where you are, how you have positioned yourself. Words chosen carefully for their connotative value can help you show your readers what your attitude is toward your subject. A fair and balanced presentation of your position is entirely appropriate. Sometimes, however, writers attempt to manipulate the emotions of their readers by using words chosen to influence the readers' responses in one way or another. This practice—intentional or otherwise—is called *slanted writing*.

Words Used Fairly for Effect

It is not possible to speak or write in completely neutral, objective language about anything that has fully engaged our interest. To write well about a subject, we must care about it enough to take a position or make a judgment concerning it.

In factual as well as in imaginative writing, interest, liveliness, and effectiveness depend greatly on the successful use of connotation. Our awareness of all the values that words have enables us to represent our subject precisely, to address our audience with a varied and appealing style, and to show where we stand in relation to our material. Fairly used, words with apt connotative value give *shape* and *texture* — as opposed to *slant* — to what we say.

Observe the power of suggestion in this passage about the erosion of English studies:

> In schools and universities, sensitivity sessions, the linking of hands . . . , mutual strokings, deep breathing . . . , and the communion of pot, have all been experimented with and in their turn abandoned in the search for some more immediate, less difficult, and more deeply unifying medium than mere human speech. — Geoffrey Durrant, "The New Barbarians"

Deeply concerned, the author uses connotation, irony, and shock to win support for his view that recent trends in educational practice must be re-assessed. The term *sensitivity sessions* suggests that such meetings are actually indulged in by the insensitive; the sexual images — expressed in ironically formal terms — suggest titillating but aimless and unproductive activities; and *communion of pot* suggests minds high on something other than the desire for learning. The slanting here is powerful and clearly intentional. Thus the point is fairly and effectively made that the merits of *human speech* as a *unifying medium* have been neglected and that it is high time due emphasis were given to teaching the art of using *mere* language effectively.

Slanted Words

The story is told of a harvester of enormous appetite who shortened the legs of the dining table on the side where he sat so that the food would slide toward him for instant availability. By exploiting the suggestive power of words, writers can similarly tilt arguments and meanings in their favor.

Sometimes slanting occurs only because writers, in their enthusiasm, allow words that are too intense to intrude in statements presented as fact. To say "All television programs are designed for the twelve-year-old mind" is to allow a personal distaste for television programming to displace good sense. Too often *all* or *most* are used when *many* would be accurate, or an exaggeration ("grotesque") is used when a less extreme word ("unattractive") is called for, or *only* or *nothing but* is used to the exclusion of other possibilities.

27.2
Slant

Much unfair slanting occurs in statements of opinion where a writer, knowingly or not, assumes that he or she is the only reliable authority. There is no slanting in a simple statement of one's likes or dislikes ("I can't stand people who dress sloppily.") But the same opinion stated as a general fact in slanted wording ("Slobs on the street in old overalls or sweat pants are disgusting signs of cultural decay.") implies that the writer expects the reader to share that opinion without thinking about it.

Just as writers who trust themselves as the only reliable authority are apt to slant their writing, so are writers who, in their enthusiasm for their own position, fail to consider more than one possibility. The following passage is from an essay in which the author argues that destroying the wilderness and its resources is a perfectly natural and appropriate human activity.

> The trumpeting voice of the wilderness lover is heard at great distances these days. He is apt to be a perfectly decent person, if hysterical. And the causes which excite him so are generally worthy. Who can really find a harsh word for him as he strives to save Lake Erie from the sewers . . . , save the redwoods from the . . . highway engineers, save the giant rhinoceros from the Somali tribesmen who kill those noble beasts to powder their horns into what they fondly imagine is a wonder-working aphrodisiac?
>
> Worthy causes, indeed, but why do those who espouse them have to be so shrill and intolerant and sanctimonious? What right do they have to insinuate that anyone who does not share their passion for the whooping crane is a Philistine and a slob? From the gibberish they talk, you would think the only way to save the bald eagle is to dethrone human reason. — Robert Wernick, "Let's Spoil the Wilderness"

Unexamined assumptions (wilderness lovers are hysterical) and unsubstantiated assertions (they speak gibberish) are the source of much slanting. For this reason, many of the most serious instances of slanting come in writing on social or political problems, especially when the words reflect prejudice. This type of slanted writing can be objected to on at least four grounds:
1.   it doesn't accurately represent the situation being discussed;
2.   it suggests that the writer is at best quite careless of what he or she says and at worst willing to distort the facts for his or her own purposes;
3.   it stands in the way of an intelligent and constructive approach to problems that affect the public interest;
4.   it is likely to antagonize the reader (unless similarly prejudiced) and so prevent clear communication.

Slanted writing, which is often clever and sometimes funny, does not always stress loaded words. The gentle ridicule that emerges from the following passage is largely implied by the asides and the tone:

> . . . the Trudeau aides, seeking as always to humanize his image before a working-class audience, suggested that he toss in a topical reference to Hank Aaron. Who *is* Hank Aaron? Well, ahem. It was explained that he is a baseball player who at the moment is set to surpass Babe Ruth's home-run record. *Who* is Babe Ruth? Well, er,

ahem, it was explained with some rolling of eyes, who Babe Ruth was. So came the speech and there was the prime minister, exhorting the voters not to give up on the Liberals because even Hank Aaron is allowed three strikes and . . . Hank Aaron was soon to break the home-run record of "Baby" Ruth. — Allan Fotheringham, in *Maclean's*

► EXERCISE

Practise shifting connotations by rewriting the first three paragraphs in two newspaper editorials so as to illustrate slanted writing. Bring to class some slanted passages from newspapers or magazines.

27.3 CHOOSING THE RIGHT WORD

W W   Replace the marked wrong word with one that accurately conveys your intended meaning.

In most factual prose, words should be used in their established forms and senses; if they are not, the reader may be misled or confused. A sentence such as "The scene *provoked* his imagination" (in which *provoked*, commonly meaning "angered," is inaccurately used instead of *stimulated*) interferes with communication. In revising your papers, check any words that you are unsure of, especially those that are not part of your regular vocabulary. Be particularly alert to words that are easily confused.

Distinguishing Words of Similar Spelling

27.3

In English there are many pairs of words that closely resemble each other in sound or spelling but have quite different meanings: *moral* and *morale*, *personal* and *personnel*, *historic* and *historical*. When writing hastily, you may accidentally substitute one word for another, but you can easily eliminate such errors by proofreading your work and by referring to a dictionary when necessary. When words of identical pronunciation, called *homonyms*, are confused in writing, the mistake may be called a spelling error (*bear* for *bare; there* for *their*). But your instructor is likely to label it WW (wrong word) if he or she suspects that you may not know the difference in meaning (*principal* for *principle; affect* for *effect*).

The following words are very often interchanged in writing. If you are not sure of the distinction between them, use your dictionary, or the glossary of usage on page 543.

accept — except	detract — distract
adapt — adopt	formally — formerly
affect — effect	human — humane
allusion — illusion	mantle — mantel
censor — censure	persecute — prosecute
cite — site	precede — proceed
complement — compliment	principal — principle
conscientious — conscious	respectful — respective
credible — creditable — credulous	stationary — stationery

▶ **EXERCISE**

Write sentences using the words listed above. Be sure that your sentences show clearly the differences in meaning.

Distinguishing Words of Similar Meaning

Word errors most frequently occur because the writer has failed to distinguish between words of similar meaning. A synonym is a word having *approximately* the same meaning as another:

angry — annoyed — indignant
frank — candid — blunt
multitude — throng — crowd — mob
strange — peculiar — quaint — bizarre

A few words have identical meanings and are therefore interchangeable (*flammable — inflammable; ravel — unravel; toward — towards*). But most synonyms, while they refer to the same idea or object, differ somewhat in denotation or connotation and thus cannot be substituted for each other without affecting the sense or tone of the statement. One term may be more formal than another (*coiffure — hair-do*); more specific (*tango — dance*); more precise (*charitable — kind*); or more personal (*dad — father*).

Usually it is not the more subtle distinctions between closely related words that cause trouble (*necessary — indispensable; intrinsic — inherent*), but the failure to distinguish between common words in different contexts:

The mysteries of the unknown arouse curiosity that must be **fulfilled**. [for *satisfied*]

We may expect food consumption to increase everywhere because of the **growth in people**. [for *increase in population*]

The only way to avoid such errors is to take notice how words of similar meanings are used in various contexts. Connotation as well as denotation should be considered. Notice, for example, how unexpected the last word in the statement is:

> In the 1890's, Dawson City was a gathering place for prostitutes, cardsharps, confidence men, thugs, and other **scamps**.

Scamps might be quite appropriate in referring to mischievous children, but the term is conspicuously out of place in this company. Moreover, certain synonyms are too heavy or too flippant for the context:

> The water was rougher past the next bend, and we had **difficulty circumventing** the rapids. [too formal: had *trouble getting around* would be more appropriate]
>
> I enjoyed studying Plato, because among other things **I got clued in on** what is meant by a Platonic friendship. [too informal: *learned* would be better]

But remember the principle of appropriateness. There are special situations in which such incongruities might be useful. T.C. Haliburton (Sam Slick) and Mark Twain, for example, could, by mixing different kinds of language, get comic effect from incongruity.

Writers sometimes use strings of fanciful synonyms to avoid repeating the same expression for an idea or object (*cats, felines, furry beasts, tabbies, nine-lived creatures*). Such "elegant variations" are pretentious and are usually more confusing than simple repetition. Readers expect key words to be repeated when they cannot be replaced by pronouns (*cats . . . they*). Factual synonyms (*these animals*) are also unobtrusive and will seldom strike the reader as repetitious.

27.3

Distinguishing Words of Opposite Meaning

Some words (such as *connotation* and *denotation*) that have contrasting or wholly opposite meanings are frequently confused, probably because the writer associates them mentally but has reversed their meanings. Among the most common antonyms or near antonyms are the following. Make sure that you know their meanings.

concave — convex	inductive — deductive
condemn — condone	infer — imply

explicit — implicit	prescribe — proscribe
famous — notorious	subjective — objective
former — latter	temerity — timidity

Confusing such pairs may result in your saying the very opposite of what you intend. Half-knowing a word is often more dangerous than not knowing at all.

▶ **EXERCISE**

Write sentences using the words listed above. Make sure that your sentences show clearly the difference in meaning.

Learning New Words

Although many word errors are caused by confusion or careless-ness, it's easy to use the wrong word (or settle for the almost-right word) simply because you do not know another one. Many papers are likely to deal with complex ideas and precise distinctions that may demand a larger vocabulary than the student has needed in the past.

It has been estimated that children enter first grade knowing about 25 000 words and add 5 000 every year, so that they leave high school with a vocabulary of perhaps as many as 90 000 words. The average vocabulary of college and university graduates is about twice this size. These estimates are for *recognition* (or *passive*) vocabulary, words understood in reading and listening. One's *active* vocabulary, the words actually used in writing or speaking, is considerably smaller.

Most people use only about a third as many words as they recognize. Thus, an obvious way for you to enlarge your working vocabulary is through conscious exercise. In making an effort to say precisely what you mean you should search not only among the words in your active vocabulary, but also among those you have learned to recognize. Frequently we find new words in reading (*cybernetics, rhetoric, apartheid*) and learn their meanings from the context or from a dictionary. Using these words in writing or speaking helps to make them more readily available for future use.

It is sometimes possible to guess the meaning of a word by knowing its parts. Many scientific words, for example, are formed with suffixes and roots from Greek or Latin:

mono- (one)	-graph (writing, written)	poly- (many)
bi- (two)	bio- (life)	macro- (large)
tele- (at a distance)	photo- (light)	micro- (small)

Since the combined meanings of the parts may only approximate the meaning of the whole, however, it is usually safer to use a dictionary and learn the entire word.

Ordinarily, we learn and remember words not for their own sake but for the meanings they represent. We have a good stock of words in the fields that interest us because facts and ideas are retained chiefly in verbal form. Thus, anything that extends the range of your ideas or experiences will help to enlarge your vocabulary. The typical college or university course adds to a student's vocabulary several hundred new words and new meanings for familiar words.

When you meet a new word that is likely to be useful, learn it accurately at the start — its spelling and pronunciation as well as its usual meaning. Students quite often have trouble in their courses because they only half know the specialized words essential to a subject. Using these words in conversation, when they are appropriate, or in reviewing course work with another student will fix them in your mind so that you can use them easily and accurately in examinations, papers, and class discussions.

▶ **EXERCISES**

1. The first word that comes to mind is not necessarily the best one, even if it means *approximately* what you intend. Read each of the following sentences carefully and choose the word in parentheses that most *exactly* expresses the intended meaning.
    a. The latest statistics (dispute, refute, rebuke) his claim that the economy is expanding.
    b. In time Einstein (convinced, persuaded, showed) most physicists that his theory was correct.
    c. Most cities have laws that (stop, deter, prohibit) littering.
    d. We stopped in our stroll on lower Mill Street to (give, donate, contribute) some money to a blind man.
    e. The remarks at the end of his speech (implied, inferred, insinuated) that he had some financial support for his plan.

    27.3

2. Examine the diction in the following sentences to determine whether some words are misused. If so, rewrite the faulty sentences, supplying more exact or more appropriate words. Be prepared to explain why you made each change.
    a. Within the next few days the assassin gained considerable renown.
    b. I do not like to be around him, for his perpetual pessimism aggravates me.
    c. A student who is writing a research paper should compulsively read through the leading works devoted to his subject.
    d. If we adopt the plan, how will the changes in procedure effect the goals?
    e. I found this poem extremely obtuse, and even after struggling over it for hours with a dictionary and an encyclopedia, I could not decipher many of its illusions.

27.4 CONCRETE AND ABSTRACT WORDS

Words can be classified according to the nature of their referents as *abstract* or *concrete* (pages 416-17). Abstract (general) words refer to ideas, qualities, acts, or relationships. Concrete (specific) words refer to definite persons, places, objects, and acts. This list demonstrates the differences between the two kinds of words:

Abstract (general)	Concrete (specific)
institution	King's College
work	running a bulldozer
men's organization	Lion's Club
a politician	the mayor of Vancouver
food	cheesecake
an educator	my history teacher
creed	Westminster Confession

Often a word cannot be classed as abstract or concrete until it is read in context:

ABSTRACT: Honest labor never killed anyone. [a generalization about all labor]

CONCRETE: In the GM contract dispute, labor seeks a ten percent wage increase. [in the context, a specific reference to the United Automobile Workers]

Effective Uses of Concrete and Abstract Words

Concrete words are essential in discussing situations, incidents, and processes that are based upon personal experience or direct observation: impressions of particular people or places or objects, discussions of plans for the future, explanations of the writer's specific attitudes or interests. Abstract words, on the other hand, are usually necessary in discussing general ideas ("The Intangible Values of Education"), for summarizing facts or stating opinions, or for analysing theoretical problems ("Is Specialization in Education Undesirable?").

Abstract words are more characteristic of formal than of general or informal English and are best used by writers with a good deal of experience in handling ideas. In this passage, for example, the writer uses very few concrete words, yet the meaning is clear to anyone who is interested in jazz:

Some of the most brilliant of jazzmen made no records; their names appeared in print only in announcements of some local dance or remote "battles of music" against equally uncelebrated bands. Being devoted to an art which traditionally thrives on improvisation, these unrecorded artists very often have their most original ideas enter the public domain almost as rapidly as they are conceived to be quickly absorbed into the thought and technique of their fellows. Thus the riffs which swung the dancers and the band on some transcendent evening, and which inspired others to competitive flights of invention, became all too swiftly a part of the general style, leaving the originator as anonymous as the creators of the architecture called Gothic. — Ralph Ellison, "The Charlie Christian Story"

But broad ideas can also be discussed in concrete terms. For example, the passage below is from an essay on Christian social values, an abstract idea:

Next winter at a theatre meeting that I had instituted on Sunday evenings, we had one evening devoted to public health. The City Health Officer gave a lecture on how disease could be prevented. This was illustrated by means of moving pictures which showed how the fly developed, how it flew from the decaying refuse to the sugar bowl or from a spitoon to the baby's feeding bottle. It was a horrible exhibition — one saw snakes all night after it; but it was tremendously effective. Even the poor foreigners who could not understand English could understand the pictures. But my church friends were shocked. Here was I, a minister of the Gospel, who had degenerated until I was running a moving picture show in a theatre on Sunday evenings! — J.S. Woodsworth, "Thy Kingdom Come"

Another way to think about the value of concreteness is to remember that poets and novelists rarely rely on abstract generalities to convey impressions. Their business is to *show*, not just to tell. For example, when Shakespeare in Sonnet 73 wrote about the sad longing associated with the loss of what we love, he didn't use abstract words, but instead presented images of autumn, twilight, **27.4** and a dying fire, concrete images that directly suggest ending, loss, *Abst* and longing. When Keats told of his excitement when he discovered Homer's works, he didn't write about *excitement, stimulation, amazement, discovery,* or other abstractions; instead, he pictured specific situations where such excitement would occur:

Then felt I like some watcher of the skies
    When a new planet swims into his ken;
Or like stout Cortez when with eagle eyes
    He star'd at the Pacific — and all his men
Look'd at each other with a wild surmise —
    Silent, upon a peak in Darien.
                    — "On First Looking into Chapman's Homer"

For a fuller discussion of *figurative language* as a means of preserving immediacy even in general writing, see 28.4, Figures of Speech.

Generalization is appropriate—even necessary—when a writer must summarize a large body of facts. This is frequently done in short papers on general subjects, where the writer's primary concern is to survey briefly the available facts and explain their significance. The important thing in such cases is to choose general words that *accurately* summarize the specific details examined, without distortion or unnecessary vagueness. A student writing a paper on conservation for example, might run across this passage:

> In the seven years from 1883 to 1890 the New South Wales Government was forced to spend not less than £1,543,000 in its attempt to control the scourge, and today rabbit control both in Australia and in New Zealand is a financial load upon every community. Many methods of eradicating this pest have been attempted. In Western Australia more than 2000 miles of fencing was erected at a cost of almost £500,000, but after it was all up it was found that some rabbits were already on the other side of the fence! Unfortunately, incidental to the compulsory use of poison for rabbits, there has been a very great destruction of wildlife as well as livestock, and phosphorus poisoning, employed for rabbit control, has been one of the principal causes of death among the marsupials and native birds.—Fairfield Osborn, *Our Plundered Planet*

In writing the paper, the student might effectively generalize from these facts as follows:

> Attempts to limit the rabbit population in Australia and New Zealand have been costly and destructive of other animal life.

It is perfectly proper to use abstract words when the material calls for them, if they can be used accurately and clearly. But writing on almost any subject gains force through the use of specific words. It is usually more convincing to generalize at the beginning or end of a paper, on the basis of a number of specific facts, than it is to pile up generalities throughout.

Excessive Use of Abstract Words

Abst   Replace the marked abstract expression with one that is more specific.

The most common fault in the wording of many student papers is a fondness for abstract terms where concrete words would be more meaningful and certainly more interesting. Even if an assigned topic is so worded that it seems difficult to discuss in specific terms ("The Importance of Education," "What Democracy Means"), a paper can be reasonably factual, concrete, and convincing if it is written in words that represent the writer's own experiences and beliefs.

Some students make the mistake of believing that the more general the expression, the more convincing and impressive it is. Others mistake the use of abstract words for intellectual discipline. The use of a general or indefinite expression where a concrete one would fit is annoying to readers:

> I began to participate in all of the different aspects of college pleasure.

We don't know if the writer began to drink, to study, to play bridge, to attend concerts, to sleep late, or to do all or none of these.

The excessive use of abstract words can become an unfortunate habit in writing. Some students apparently never take *physics, history, economics,* or *French*; instead, they encounter *various interesting courses of study*; instead of attending, say, Simon Fraser University, they attend *an institution of higher learning*; they do not play *golf, bridge, tennis,* or *baseball*, but *participate in various recreational activities*. Few traits of style are less convincing than the unnecessary use of vague, abstract terms for ideas that could better be expressed concretely.

► **EXERCISES**

1. The sentences below are general statements, and they may be somewhat vague. Rewrite each of them so that they use more concrete words and name more specific things. Don't worry about the length of your sentences — think instead about making them as specific as you can.

   a. City noises are sometimes raucous and distracting.
   b. Individuals who live in an urban metropolis can engage in more leisure activities.
   c. Fuel conservation will require some changes in our way of living.
   d. More people now are interested in keeping fit.

2. Sometimes you may need to generalize without citing specific information. Keep track of the information in each of the items listed below and then write out your generalization from each:

   a. one week's daily weather reports in a local newspaper
   b. one episode of a soap opera
   c. any two hours of listening to the same disc jockey on a radio station you are familiar with
   d. the letters to the editor in any three days' issues of a local newspaper.

27.4

Abst

28

The Effect of Words

Words are sounds, and written words are the musical score of meaningful sounds. . . . Those same symbols are given to us . . . to influence people. All we need do is choose them wisely and use them imaginatively. The person to whom you are writing will respond to some words while remaining indifferent to others. How can you expect to energize a reader into doing what you want him to do if you write stale and flat words in uninspired sentences? Mark Twain is quoted as saying: "The difference between right words and the almost right word is the difference between lightening and the lightening bug." — The Royal Bank of Canada Monthly Letter.

If words are to convey to a reader the impression you desire, they must be used *appropriately* as well as accurately. Besides being alert to actual connotative and denotative meanings (see 27.1), a writer needs to bear in mind the essay's *context*—its subject, purpose, and audience. The kind or "level" of language that will be most suitable in any particular situation depends on the nature of your assignment. An informal paper on your tastes in popular music would obviously call for a different vocabulary than a formal report on economic forces governing the entertainment business.

Because you can't judge the effect of words out of context, you must use good sense in choosing words that are consistent with both your meaning and the kind of writing you are doing. A dictionary is a useful guide to meaning, but it is of little help when it comes to deciding what words will do the job best.

There are three things you can do to help make your word choice more effective. First, you can choose more thoughtfully from the range of your own present vocabulary the words that best suit your purpose. Often we already know words that would be more precise and appropriate than the first ones we think of. Second, you can sharpen your judgment by paying closer attention to the language around you—the language of your classmates, your instructors, your parents, the people you hear speak on television and radio— and noticing the differences in usage that you hear and read. Third, you can read widely to familiarize yourself with the range and variety of writing. All written English is a bank you might draw on.

28.1 FORMAL WORDS

We may call vocabulary *formal* when it is noticeably more special- ized than typical spoken English. It deliberately employs a much wider range of word choices than we hear in casual conversation about topics of general interest. The need for this variety and increased precision arises when a writer is dealing with an especially complex subject or addressing an audience that expects a high degree of exactness in phrasing. In such situations, formality is appropriate and necessary. The limited range of ordinary spoken English would be inadequate for the refined discriminations that specialized analysis must make.

However, formality in language is too often overused by people who are trying to make their very ordinary and questionable ideas *sound* extraordinary and authoritative. This section considers the uses and abuses of formal words.

Appropriate Use of Formal Words

Formal words are not necessarily longer or more abstract or more elegant than the vocabulary of general English. Formality is really a matter of *subtlety*, of finding words that express finer distinctions or more complex ideas than can be discussed adequately in casual speech. The theoretical and technical details of any science, art, or business are very hard to explain precisely unless we do take full advantage of the meanings available to us in specialized English words. Some things cannot be said easily, or at all, otherwise. If the nature of your subject requires a formal vocabulary, as the following passages do, use it:

> The solid character of [David] Helwig's work, in terms of his **syntax**, his particular observation, his **persistent** moral awareness, has always been one of its main attractions. . . . If we note in addition Helwig's emphasis on reason, on **moderation**, on the plain moral **dimension** of human experience, we may conclude that [he] is closer to the spirit of Jonson's **classicism** than to that of many recent poetic movements. — D.G. Jones, in *Queen's Quarterly*

> Through the centuries (if not **millennia**) during which, in their retelling, fairy tales became ever more refined, they came to convey at the same time **overt** and **covert** meanings — came to speak simultaneously to all levels of the human personality, communicating in a manner which reaches the uneducated mind of the child as well as that of the **sophisticated** adult. Applying the **psychoanalytic model** of the human personality, fairy tales carry important messages to the conscious, the **preconscious**, and the unconscious mind, on whatever level each is **functioning** at the time. — Bruno Bettelheim, *The Uses of Enchantment*

28.1
Wds

The audience for such writing obviously consists of well-informed readers who understand specialized terms like *classicism* and *preconscious* and who are comfortable with other relatively uncommon expressions such as *covert*, *moral dimension*, and *psychoanalytic model*. Formal words are appropriate to people who use them easily and naturally and to situations that definitely require extraordinary precision.

But in using formal language when it isn't needed (or for a general audience), you run the risk of sounding pretentious or remote. Formality is not always appropriate. In particular, avoid the temptation to translate ordinary matters into "big words."

"Big Words" — Stilted Language

Big 24. Replace the stilted word or words with words from the general vocabulary.

"Big words," as the term is used here, are any and all expressions that are too heavy or too formal for the situation. Such words sound artificial and stilted, whether they are short or long, common or uncommon. A typical fault of inexperienced writers is the use of big words in a misguided effort to sound learned:

> It is difficult to filter out one specific cause for a social problem. Most often there are many minute factors interrelated and closely corre-lated. Our conception of a social problem today possesses more magnitude than that of two or three decades ago. We now consider the world as a unit rather than an aggregation of component entities.

Ideas are easier to understand and are more convincing if the wording is natural. It should be exact, not inflated beyond the requirements of the subject or the expectations of the reader. The language of the sentences just cited, for example, might be simpli-fied as follows:

> A social problem can seldom be traced to a single, specific cause. Today we are much more aware of the complexity of social problems than we were twenty or thirty years ago, for we have come to see that all societies are interrelated.

Writers are most likely to use stilted language when they are not certain what attitude they should take toward their material or toward their readers. They may use inflated diction because they honestly (though wrongly) believe that certain papers should be as formal and impersonal as possible. Other writers who strain to create an impression of formality and complexity imagine that big words are authoritative and "intellectual" or that exaggerated diction is humorous ("a fair damsel garbed in the mode of the moment" instead of "a fashionably dressed young woman"). Always write as plainly as accuracy will allow. Good readers are annoyed and suspicious when they see ordinary ideas "dressed up" in unnatural words or in big, blocky, pretentious language. The verbs *endeavor* and *utilize*, for example, are not preferable to *try* and *use* in any kind of writing.

Jargon

One extreme use of inappropriate big words is known as *jargon* or, sometimes, *gobbledygook*. It is language so inflated in sound and obscure in meaning that it seems to have lost all real contact with the matter being discussed. If you find yourself reading about things like *functional instrumentality of networked decision-making processes* (how to make choices carefully) or *methodologically beneficiary-oriented educational module delivery system* (teaching), you're reading jargon. Writing full of such language is often found in print today, especially in specialized journals, advertisements, government publications, and administrative manuals, but this does not make it good English.

In some cases, jargon is inappropriate simply because it is out of place. That is, it may impose on general writing certain terms and expressions borrowed without good reason from the technical vocabulary of highly specialized fields. Because we tend to be in awe of science itself, we are too easily impressed by big words that lend ordinary ideas the ring or flavor of scientific authority and respectability. The professional languages or codes employed in computer technology, psychology, sociology, and economics are also frequently imitated by people who wish to surround themselves and their opinions with the atmosphere of currently fashionable knowledge. In the following example (from a brief student paper on prison reform in Canada), the writer aims unnecessarily and unsuccessfully at the *sound* of theoretical psychology or sociology:

28.1

Big H

> Data on motivational factors in the area of recidivism should have had predictive value concerning concepts of normative behavior.

The terms are misused, and the meaning is very unclear. This writer probably wanted to say something like "Our knowledge of typical ex-convicts' problems should have forewarned us that many would eventually be back in prison." In any case, specialized language should be avoided (particularly by non-specialists) in general discussions. See also the following section, Technical and Foreign Terms.

A less innocent kind of gobbledygook is the selection, creation, or adaptation of big words in order to conceal or confuse meaning. A smokescreen of high-sounding but empty generalities is often the last resort of writers who want to disguise ignoble intentions or who really have nothing to say. Consider the following passage of evasive bureaucratic jargon:

> The committee corroborates the desirability in principle of contemplating a sensitized system of far-reaching reviews to identify, examine, evaluate, reconcile, and mediate the functions and roles that constitute the institution's perceived notion of its structural integrity, but recommends at the same time that the data base be strengthened and refined as a rich context for innovative decision-making at a somewhat projected point in time when renewed consideration would more productively be implemented.

This wordy bombast seems to mean "We can't [or *won't*] do anything until we get more information." But the writer evidently preferred not to be so clearly understood. The wording seems calculated mainly to confuse or to intimidate or to stall for time, but not to communicate. Unfortunately, the habit of deceptive or bullying gobbledygook is becoming more and more noticeable in the language adopted by influential public figures, institutions, and media. It is a tendency in current English usage that should be resisted by all writers, both in their own work and in their attitude towards what they read and hear daily.

The remedy for too many big words is simple: Read aloud what you have written, preferably some time after you have written it; if you find the language markedly different from what you would use in conversation, look at the words carefully to see whether you can find simpler and clearer synonyms.

Technical and Foreign Terms

In writing intended for a general audience, unfamiliar terms not made clear by the context should be defined or explained. Technical terms or unfamiliar expressions that often need explaining include

1. scientific terms (*isotope*, *lobotomy*, *gneiss*) and other expressions restricted to a specialized activity (*a cappella*, *heroic hexameter*, *escrow*, *chiaroscuro*, *farinaceous*, *binary*);
2. words used in special senses rather than in the usual way (the *spine* of a book, to *justify* a line of type, the *recorder* as a wind instrument, a *frog* as a fastener for a jacket);
3. words and phrases not customarily used by most people (*lex talionis*, *leitmotif*, *eisteddfod*, *de trop*).

You should not use an inexact or wordy expression in place of a necessary technical term. If, for instance, the subject of a paper is "Mountain Climbing," it is better to define and use a word like *piton* than to say "those little metal gadgets that ropes are tied to." Do not use unfamiliar words just to show off, but use and explain those that are essential to your subject.

Often a simple definition or explanation can be worked into the sentence where the foreign or technical term is introduced, as in the following examples:

> The ability of the heart to function depends primarily on the state of the heart muscle, or myocardium, as it is technically known.

> In the study of rhetoric we are first to consider *inventio*, or what we now refer to as the problems of pre-writing.

> In cold weather the Inuit wear mukluks (fur boots) and parkas (short fur coats with fur hoods).

Occasionally you may decide to define the term or expression in a footnote instead. The following example is a footnote from an accounting textbook:

> [3]When a corporation issues shares the result is an increase in both assets and shareholders' equity, and the issuance may be termed **primary distribution**. Except for the case of the so-called private company, shares are fully transferable. Thus, a shareholder is free to sell his shares, or a portion thereof, to any willing buyer. This type of transaction, termed **secondary distribution**, has no effect on the accounts of a corporation. The stock exchanges provide the markets in which most secondary distribution takes place.—Joan E. D. Conrod and John R. E. Parker, *Decision Problems in Intermediate Accounting*

Don't make a habit, however, of including a lot of explanatory **28.1** footnotes. Language that requires continual definition is probably inappropriate for your purpose and audience.

Big 21

As a rule, do not simply quote a dictionary definition, which may be too narrow, but compose one that fits the style and scale of your own paper. Compare a dictionary definition of *oligarchy* with this explanation of the term:

> I mean by "oligarchy" any system in which ultimate power is confined to a section of the community: the rich to the exclusion of the poor, Protestants to the exclusion of Catholics, aristocrats to the exclusion of plebeians, white men to the exclusion of colored men, males to the exclusion of females, or members of one political party to the exclusion of the rest. A system may be more or less oligarchic according to the percentage of the population that is excluded;

absolute monarchy is the extreme of oligarchy. — Bertrand Russell, *The Impact of Science on Society*

The crucial thing in defining a term is to give an adequate description of the way *you* are using it, with details and concrete illustrations to clarify the meaning.

▶ EXERCISE

Rewrite the following passages in clear and effective English. Be honest: don't copy down anything you can't understand. If you are unable to translate one (or more) of these passages, write instead about *why* you think it was composed so strangely.

1. *From a student composition:* Our high school was eminently well equipped for various recreational pursuits. For those of sportive inclinations, there was the capacious gymnasium, which resounded to multitudinous roars whenever our champions engaged a challenging contingent.

2. *From a term paper in an introductory literature course:* The dominant characters in this novelistic artifact experience severely fractionalized interpersonal interaction because of their low conceptualization of societal norms governing gender-specific roles. The thematic implication of their tragic terminus is that activity patterns of self-actualization are counterproductive by comparison with adaptive strategies for developing the potentiality of the status quo.

3. *From a professional journal for teachers:* This film demonstrates the progress of an idealized date, from the ideational impetus to the request, acceptance, the dating experience itself, and the final leave-taking, in the process raising some significant questions regarding dating and suggesting partial answers as discussional guides.

4. *From a letter to the editor:* Is the love of monetary remuneration such that it acerbates all else into obliviousness? Can we not conjure into our configurations and substratums of consciousness some other destination than the all-mighty dollar?

5. *From a landscape architect's report for a client:* Prioritized implementation of the enclosed analysis process would facilitate optimization of space articulation aesthetics, screening and climate control, activity nodes, directional orientation (including access/egress), an overall arboriculturalist concept, pedestrian walk-way hierarchy (and reduced conflicts with vehicular circulation pattern), and a scale-functionalized site theme.

28.2 INFORMAL WORDS

Informal words include those marked *informal*, or *colloquial*, in dictionaries and most of those marked *slang*. They are part of general English but may not be appropriate to all kinds of writing.

Appropriate Use of Informal Words

Informal words are often appropriate in discussions of informal or humorous situations, and activities such as sports. They are also sometimes fitting in discussions of more important topics, where the language is typically general English. You will find such words used in many reputable publications. Note the boldface words and phrases in the passage below:

> On the other hand, **shrinks** don't like small cities—the isolation sometimes **gets to them**. [One] is moving now to Toronto, where he plans to make $250,000 a year **shrinking Bay Street tycoons**.— "Inside Track," *Saturday Night*

There is usually no need to apologize for informal words by putting them in quotation marks. A word that needs apology shouldn't be used. Employ quotation marks only if you want to draw attention to some extraordinary use of a word or phrase (see 14.1, page 177, Popular and slang expressions).

Inappropriate Use of Informal Words

Inf   Change the informal expression to one that is more general.

It is disconcerting to a reader to encounter an informal expression in relatively formal writing. The unexpected colloquialism tends to diminish a serious statement, making the subject seem trivial and the writer's attitude casual:

> The displaced persons in Europe experienced many **tough breaks** after the end of the war. [more appropriate: *hardships*]

> The natives believe that they can expiate certain offenses against tribal customs by **throwing a feast**. [better: *giving a feast*]

28.2

Inf

In formal writing, informal words not only indicate a shift in variety of usage but may also suggest that you've grown careless toward your subject:

> When Desdemona failed to produce the handkerchief, Othello began to suspect that she **wasn't on the level**. Of course, he was just being **sucked in** by Iago's deceitful **caper**.

Be particularly careful about certain expressions so widely used that you may not realize (until the slip is called to your attention) that they are considered informal rather than general usage:

Plays of this sort are seldom seen **in our neck of the woods**.

Malcolm Lowry had **a funny habit** of writing long, rather compli-cated sentences.

▶ EXERCISE

Listen to the conversations of people around you and take note of occasions when you and they fall back on inappropriate or inaccurate informal words in place of more precise words. Record such instances on paper for discussion in class.

28.3 LIVE WORDS AND DEATH MASKS

Good writing, whether factual or fictional, captures a reader's interest and holds attention; other writing, concerned with similar facts or ideas, may strike a reader as lifeless and boring. In either instance the wording may be correct enough, but in the more enjoyable and memorable reading, the words are fresh and direct:

Multi-coloured kites bounced in the skies over the Heath. Lovers strolled on the tow paths and locked together on the grass. Old people sat on benches sucking in the sun. — Mordecai Richler, "Playing Ball on Hampstead Heath"

Supper was a young squirrel who had nevertheless achieved an elder's stringiness, roasted in foil on the embers, and a potato baked in the same way. — John Graves, *Goodbye to a River*

The search for fresh and direct expression does not require that you should strain obviously for effect, by searching for unusual expres-sions or words, any more than it requires that you should use eccentric punctuation or unconventional sentence structure. It does mean that you should take sufficient time and thought to put aside *death masks* in favor of live words.

A *death mask* is a casting made of someone's face just after death —and that seems to have little to do with words. Yet two ideas are brought together in the term to describe the effect of some words: they are dead, for they lack vitality and freshness; they hide or mask meaning. We have used the expression *death masks* as a general name for several kinds of words and expressions, including worn-out terms, euphemisms, incongruous figures of speech, or currently overworked expressions. Several varieties of death masks are discussed in the following sections.

Vogue Words

We naturally use words that are in current use. All of us from time to time resort too easily to "vogue words," words that our society has currently adopted as signals of value. *Meaningful* is such a word; *dialogue* is another, and *phenomenon* is a third. These words and others like them come into popular use in a number of ways, and then suddenly they are everywhere. The problem is that when we start using words and phrases such as "the bottom line," or "relevant," or "scenario," then the vogue words begin to take the place of thinking, and we use them automatically.

Other vogue words can be listed: *game plan, flat out, lib* (short form of *liberation*), words with *-put (input, output, throughput), counterproductive, societal, mass media, methodology, matrix, fantastic, gut feeling, pick up on, get it together*, and certain words ending in *-wise (profitwise, timewise)*. A useful activity would be for you to list the vogue words you hear or read.

Trite Expressions

Trite Replace the trite expression with one that is fresher or more direct.

Trite expressions, or clichés, are overfamiliar phrases that almost everyone is tired of hearing and reading. Given the first words, we can usually finish the expression without thinking:

This is going to hurt me more _____.
He is down but not _____.
Gone but _____.
It isn't the heat but _____.

28.3

Trite

Such language is a death mask because all originality and life have long since been sapped out of it by overuse. Similarly, the following overworked constructions (and others like them) should be avoided by writers who wish to be taken seriously:

Cliché	Comment
according to Webster	Did Webster write the dictionary you are using?
history tells us	A dubious personification, one that often leads to empty generalizations.
the finer things in life	Name two or three. No matter what they are—a good pipe, a Beethoven quartet, a cheesecake—they'll be

	more convincing to the reader than this nebulous phrase.
last but not least	Is the last item or fact *never* of least importance?
in today's society	Does this really mean anything more than *today* (or *now*)?

The problem with trite expressions is that you can use them without thinking. They are there in the air, and you can fill a gap on your page by plucking one; using them easily becomes habitual. But when you use trite expressions, they replace your own words and thoughts, and so they mask your own meaning.

Figurative language (28.4) adds interest to writing when it is fresh and appropriate, but stale comparisons and personifications only serve to bore the reader. It will not make anything seem cooler or neater if you describe it as *cool as a cucumber* or *neat as a pin*. Here is a short list of trite figures of speech; you can probably think of many similar expressions:

quick as a wink	at the drop of a hat
lost in thought	a watery grave
sly as a fox	run like a deer
rotten to the core	like a shot from a cannon
white as snow	brave as a lion
in a nutshell	Mother Nature
darkness overtakes us	spreading like wildfire
commune with nature	bull in a china shop
the rat race	the crack of dawn

Similarly, many famous quotations have now lost their vividness through overuse:

- a sadder but wiser man	all the world's a stage
stone walls do not a prison make	water, water, everywhere

There are many fresh, vivid, less-quoted lines, if you wish to enliven your writing with quotations.

When you find yourself using overworked expressions, look at them closely to see if they actually mean anything to you; usually you will decide that they really mean very little, and you will make your point another way.

Euphemisms

A euphemism is an evasive expression used in place of a more common term which the user fears might be considered impolite or offensive. Euphemisms are often used in conversation out of consideration for the listener's feelings: a teacher might tell parents that their child is *slow* or *exceptional* rather than *dull* or *stupid*; a salesperson is more likely to tell a customer that she has a *problem figure* than that she is *overweight* or *fat*. But although euphemisms are often necessary in social situations, they ordinarily sound affected when used in writing:

Euphemistic expression	Direct expression
a reconditioned automobile	a used car
underprivileged, disadvantaged	poor
senior citizens	old people
unmentionables	underwear
expecting	pregnant
pass away	die
lay to rest	bury
our statement apparently has escaped your attention	you haven't paid your bill
preferred customers	customers who pay their bills regularly

▶ **EXERCISE**

The sentences below contain clichés and trite expressions. Rewrite them in more direct language or, if you can, in fresh figurative language.

1. If he wins the election—and he may—we are all up the creek without a paddle.
2. Silence reigned supreme among us as the principal gave us a piece of his mind.
3. When he got to the campus post office and found his failure notice, it was a bitter pill to swallow.
4. Armed to the teeth with notes and coffee, he started to work on his research paper.
5. The chairman nipped the squabble in the bud and got the discussion down to brass tacks.
6. Each and every man should take out life insurance so that his loved ones will be well provided for when he goes to his eternal reward.
7. I told him straight from the shoulder that his work was no longer acceptable.
8. If it didn't mean showing my hand too soon, I would tell the newspapers that I intend to throw my hat in the ring.
9. Teachers are called upon to render services beyond the call of duty time and time again. Their unselfish devotion to the youth of Canada goes a long way toward making this a better world to live in.
10. The investigators didn't leave a stone unturned in their relentless search for the fugitive from justice.

28.3

Trite

28.4 FIGURES OF SPEECH

Figures of speech express ideas in a concrete (rather than abstract) manner. Instead of changing a vivid idea or experience into a pale generality, figurative language *preserves* or *embodies* its flavor in specific, immediate impressions. See 27.4, Concrete and Abstract Words. Consider, for example, the following metaphor:

> . . . meaning is an arrow that reaches its mark when least encumbered with feathers. — Herbert Read, *English Prose Style*

A theoretical principle could perhaps be extracted from that statement, but only with a great loss of freshness, directness, and power:

> The fewer words a person uses, the more quickly his or her meaning will be understood.

The second version means more or less the same thing as the first, but the idea has been deadened. Figures of speech maintain the natural images, comparisons, personifications, and associations that arise in our minds. They keep even the most formal writing personal and alive. Whenever possible, stick with these direct perceptions and images instead of "translating" them into abstract, unoriginal terms that may also be less clear:

> FIGURATIVE: Plotted on a graph, normal statistical distribution **looks like a bell**.

> NON-FIGURATIVE: Plotted on a graph, normal statistical distribution will represent itself as a symmetrical curve sloping up to and down from a central high point.

The figurative version above, which employs the method of comparison known as a *simile*, is briefer, clearer, more natural, and more memorable than the second statement. Many complex ideas are best visualized and explained in figurative terms.

Sometimes, the meaning or purpose of a passage is contained entirely (or almost entirely) in its figures of speech. Imagine, for instance, how different the following paragraph would be if stripped of all figurative expressions:

> Among the grim conifers, forever fighting to survive and forever doomed, the smooth limbs of maples search for the light, spreading jagged leaves to the sun, like supplicating hands, and in the bottom lands beside the streams the alders leap up overnight, with white-mottled bark, hand-painted. High in the coastal mountains the gray boles of yellow cedar are as antiseptic in their emanation as the smell of a hospital. Down in Saanich, which the evergreen forest has not yet

discovered, there are old oaks, with crooked arms, running across the
hillsides like frightened gnomes. — Bruce Hutchinson, "The Trees"

The use of figurative language is not limited to purely descriptive
passages or to "literary" subjects. You will find figures of speech
used freely and effectively in such diverse material as financial
articles, literary criticism, advertising copy, sports writing, and
political discussions. The chart on page 446 defines some of the
more common types of figurative expressions.

Effective Figures of Speech

Fig **Change the figure of speech to an expression that is more
appropriate to your subject and your style; avoid
inconsistent figures.**

Although figures of speech, if they are fresh and perceptive,
clearly have an appeal, they are *not* mere ornaments. Indeed, when
they seem to be ornaments, we can usually conclude that they are
used unnaturally and ostentatiously. If they are vivid and natural,
they make writing attractive, but they can accomplish much more
than this.

Each kind of figurative language has its special uses. Metaphor
and simile, for example, can enlarge our perception and understanding of a subject, and can say much in little space. If a writer
says, "The old cowpuncher's parenthetical legs were covered by
worn, brown chaps," we gain from the metaphor a pretty clear
picture of the cowboy's shape; some notion of his age and the
amount of time he has spent on a horse; and some insight into his
character and the writer's attitude toward him (the choice of
metaphor suggesting a familiar, even comic treatment). We can
learn something about a subject in one area by the light cast on it
from language of another area, much as we do in reading parables
and allegories, which, in a sense, can be considered extended
metaphors.

28.4
Fig

For these reasons, figurative expressions should be in keeping
with your subject and your style, and they should be accurate
enough to contribute to the meaning. Expressions that are too
strong or that strive too hard to be picturesque only confuse or
irritate the reader:

As fall comes in with its gentle coolness, Mother Nature **launches
her chemical warfare**, changing the leaves into their many pretty
colors.

My grandfather's barn was **like a medieval fortress shrouded in legend**.

Types of Figurative Language

HYPERBOLE: Deliberate exaggeration for interest and emphasis.

It was a day **to end all days**.
He's the **greatest** second baseman **in the world**.

IRONY: Use of a word or phrase to signify the reverse of its literal meaning.

For Brutus is an **honourable man**...Shakespeare, *Julius Caesar*
That's just **great**. [expression often signifying disgust]

LITOTES: An assertion made by the negation of its opposite.

Hemingway was **not a bad writer**.
Rome was **no mean city**.

METAPHOR: Implied comparison between two unlike things, often used to show some unexpected likeness between the two.

....Out, out, **brief candle**!
Life's but a walking shadow, a poor player
That struts and frets his hour upon the stage
And then is heard no more.... Shakespeare, *Macbeth*

METONYMY: Substitution of an associated word for what is actually meant.

Suited to the **plough**, he sought to live by the **pen**.

ONOMATOPOEIA: Use of words to create a sound appropriate to the sense.

It was a hot day in late July when I sat with Uncle Miles at Belting beside the **strippling ream**. The deliberate Spoonerism was Uncle Miles's, and it did seem to express something about the stream that rippled beside us as we sat on the spongy grass.
—Julian Symons, *The Belting Inheritance*

OXYMORON: Coupling contradictory terms.

At eleven, she **enjoyed the fright** of reading *Dracula*.
Life is a **bittersweet** experience.

PERIPHRASIS: Substitution of a descriptive phrase for a name, sometimes of a name for a descriptive phrase.

Be true to the **red, white, and blue**.
Hockey gave us the **Big Train** and the **Rocket**.

PERSONIFICATION: Attribution of human qualities to non-human or abstract things.

They turned and waved, and then the jungle **swallowed** them.

SIMILE: Stated comparison between two unlike things (see *Metaphor*).

> My mistress' bosom **is as white as the snow, and as cold**. — Joseph Addison, *The Spectator*

SYNECDOCHE: Naming a part when the whole is meant, or naming a whole when a part is meant.

> The poor man had twelve **mouths** to feed.
> **Calgary** plays Ottawa for the Grey Cup.

Straining for unusual expressions seldom results in effective writing. The figures to use are those that actually come to mind when you are trying to give an exact account of the subject. They should be fresh, if possible, but, even more important, they should fit their context and be natural.

Consistent Figures of Speech

A figure of speech should not begin with one kind of image and switch to another wholly unrelated one. These *mixed metaphors*, as they are usually called, often present a ludicrous, confused image instead of the fresh insight the writer intends:

> The nineteenth century **became a door** opened by some of the braver authors, through which many of the earlier ideas of writing for children, which had been **crushed or discarded, again sprang to blossom**, and spread into the many branches of children's literature that we have today.

If you can look at your own writing with some degree of objectivity, you can usually determine whether a figure is consistent or not. Sometimes an expression that seemed very vivid at the moment of writing proves, upon rereading, to be confusing or even ridiculous.

28.4
Fig

▶ EXERCISE

The critic I.A. Richards has speculated that we use figurative language more than we are aware. He maintains that we can barely get through three sentences without it. Try checking out this claim in any magazine you have handy. Go through an article or two, copying the figurative language that you find. Try classifying it according to the types of figures listed in the chart on pp. 446-47.
Example: There were nine *hands* on the ranch (synecdoche) who tended the cattle and also the fields of wheat that *rippled like waves* (simile) in the wind.

29

Revising and Submitting the Project

Do not be afraid to seize whatever you have written and cut it to ribbons; it can always be restored to its original condition in the morning, if that course seems best. Remember, it is no sign of weakness or defeat that your manuscript ends up in need of major surgery. This is a common occurrence in all writing, and among the best writers. — E. B. White, *The Elements of Style*

Revising your draft and preparing a final copy for submission are the last two steps in producing a paper. Inexperienced writers often neglect these important stages of the project, not realizing that *revising* means a lot more than just typing up or legibly recopying rough work. A draft is merely a draft: it is written to be rewritten, and you shouldn't become so committed to it that you don't notice opportunities for improvement. Nor is revising the same as simply altering your manuscript to conform to the conventional format of academic assignments. Correct footnote technique, for instance, is a waste of time if the essay itself gets no careful reconsideration. You needn't concern yourself about such details until you have thoroughly re-assessed and refined the organization and expression of your ideas.

When you have finished a nearly-final draft of a paper, put it aside for a while before revising it. Most people find it difficult to look at their own writing carefully while the ideas they have tried to express are still running about in their minds. For this reason, the first draft should be written as early as possible, so that you can wait a day or two (or at least several hours) before examining it. If the assignment gives you time to write a draft and put it aside for a *week or two*, you may be astonished to discover how perceptive a critic you are when you return to it for revision.

The purpose of revision is to *re-see* or to *re-scrutinize* what you have written so that you may add to it, subtract from it, rearrange it, improve the organization, alter the tone, shift the intention, as well as check the general form, spelling, grammar, and conventions of your writing. You will probably save time and improve the quality of your writing by going over your draft slowly and systematically. A hit-or-miss approach to revision is likely to be a waste of time, since you may catch only glaring faults or problems that just happen to attract your notice. The chart on pages 451-52 may help you keep some major points in mind as you revise.

29.1 RE-SEEING THE SUBJECT

No one else knows the thoughts you are trying to convey when you write. An experienced teacher can sometimes read your first efforts, ask some leading questions, and thus help you to understand what you want to say, but no one knows exactly all that is milling around in your mind. You have to be the first judge of what you are writing. Your first draft may be all right, even good, if you care about the subject, if you have a lot at stake in the writing, and if you have thought a long time about how to work your way through the writing. Most of the time, however, many of us find that even a good first draft isn't enough, isn't quite exact. Most of us have to keep working on what we write.

No one can predict exactly what you may have to do in order to revise your paper most usefully. Sometimes your work may need to be expanded to hold more—more details, more examples, more long sentences to slow the pace, more short sentences to speed the pace. Sometimes your work may need to be compressed where you have taken too long to say something, or where something needs to move more quickly. Sometimes you may need to change the tone— from angry to thoughtful, from heavy and ponderous to quiet and meditative, from aggressive to ironic. Sometimes you may need to rearrange the structure, moving a paragraph from here to there, shifting two sentences so that they end a paragraph. And sometimes you may need to spend considerable time tidying up, checking for punctuation, spelling, construction, trying to guarantee the intelligibility of what you have written.

Consider the example below. It is the second paragraph of a student's first draft about a boat trip to Alaska. A longer passage from the same first draft appears on page 321 in the chapter on paragraphs, where you'll find some comments and recommendations. In the first draft the introductory paragraph is brief; it tells only when the student took the trip and how many other passengers went along. The second paragraph is:

29.1
Rev. Draft

> The fruit basket in each cabin was filled daily with apples, oranges, and other kinds of fruit. Since meals were included in the price of the ticket, we could choose anything we wanted from the menu without worrying about the price.

This scarcely seems satisfactory. The author gives us two sentences which are not related to each other in any special way. Though each mentions food, the two together have no particular effect—the paragraph merely reports some items of information in a perfunctory way.

In the process of revision the author made what turned out to be some false starts. First, he decided to re-write the essay concentrating on what he saw. With that in mind, he reduced the significance of his first sentences. Here, he treats food as just one of many distractions and he reduces the two sentences to subordinate parts of a sentence that focusses on something else.

> Although there were distractions everywhere — games, entertainment, baskets of fresh fruit provided in my room every day, and meals at which I could choose anything I wanted from the menu — I was still impatient to reach our first port, Sitka, and to see Alaska.

But that didn't work. As the student acknowledged in a consultation with his writing instructor, although he enjoyed seeing parts of Alaska, that hadn't left the greatest impression on him. His greatest pleasure, it turned out, was in the voyage itself and the accommodations offered on the ship. Next he made another false start:

> The service on board ship was prompt and efficient. Every day a steward delivered a basket of fresh fruit to my room — apples, oranges, and other kinds of fruit. The meals were particularly fine. The waiters were careful and quick. The food was beautifully displayed, and it was delicious.

Although that wasn't it, either, it turned out that with this revision the student was closer to what fascinated him most about the trip. The student said that this was the only vacation his family had ever taken. His father and mother had begun planning the trip before they were married, and it had been a goal ever since. Gradually he began to remember more and more details and more and more of his feelings about the trip. Eventually, he realized that what had delighted him most about the trip was that for a few days he could enjoy luxury. Once the student came to that understanding of the experience, his tone changed. He re-wrote the essay, focussing on the things that had seemed particularly luxurious to him, and in re-writing this paragraph he focussed on food:

> By the second day I felt like a bad Roman emperor, reveling in daily banquets. They fed us food as if they had never heard of fat and we had never heard of cholesterol and heart attacks. Every day a steward delivered a basket of fresh fruit to our room. There were apples and oranges and sometimes peaches and tangerines and a slice of fresh pineapple. Once in a while a lush purple plum or two were hidden among the other fruit. The meals were beyond believing. For the first few minutes of the first meal I felt guilty, but then I realized I was in paradise. The cost of the meals was included in the price of the ticket; I could choose anything I wanted from the menu without worrying about the price. There were huge roasts of beef or thick slabs of ham,

shrimp, fried fish, baked fish, grilled fish. There were fruit salads, green salads, shrimp salads, and trays of sliced carrots, cauliflower, and piled olives and pickles. There were more vegetables than I could recognize. And then there was the dessert table — rich cakes, fat pies, ice cream, puddings, and a whole section of the table reserved for different varieties of chocolate dessert. It was probably my only chance to feel rich and decadent, and I loved every minute of it. I scarcely knew it when we reached Sitka, our first landing, and after that I ate my way from port to port.

Sometimes it takes a while to get your memory and your mind working. As you can see, the author of this passage didn't just change a few words or add a few commas in revising, but actually continued thinking and talking about what he wanted to say and how he wanted to sound. Revising needn't be just a matter of making the paper look neat, though that counts, too.

A Checklist for Revising

Checking the Content

1. Does your paper need more or better examples and illustrations?
2. Is information in your paper clear enough so that a reader unfamiliar with the subject can understand it?
3. Are there general statements that don't have accompanying details or illustrations?
4. Can you show that every statement is directly related to the topic?
5. Have you expressed your own convictions? Are the ideas your own, or are you merely repeating ones you have often heard?

Checking the Organization

1. Is it clear from near the beginning what the paper is about?
2. Does each paragraph clearly add something to the paper?
3. Do important ideas and statements stand out from less important ideas and statements?
4. Can you justify the order of the important statements?
5. Are all sentences and paragraphs tied together in a coherent way?
6. Is the ending clear?

29.1
Rev.
Draft

Checking the Wording

1. Are there words whose meanings you are not sure of?
2. Have you used any unfamiliar terms that need explanation?
3. Is there any unnecessary or awkward repetition?
4. Are any of your sentences too involved? Do you stumble over some passages as you read your work aloud?
5. Does the language sound like something *you* could reasonably be expected to say?
6. Have you used trite language (vogue words, phrases, or sentences) that you have often heard or read?

Checking for Accuracy

1. Have you checked your work specifically for any errors that you have made in earlier writing?
2. Have you checked a dictionary for doubtful spellings?
3. Can you account for your punctuation?
4. If a sentence seems doubtful or confusing, have you tried to analyse it grammatically for structure and punctuation?

Checking Again

1. Have you read the draft systematically?
2. Have you read the paper aloud at an easy, normal tempo?

29.2 REVISING A DRAFT

Another way of *re-seeing* a nearly-final draft of your paper is to anticipate the criticisms of an attentive reader, particularly those of a writing instructor. Going carefully through the checklist on pages 451-52 is one method of getting outside yourself and looking at the paper as a reader would. A further way is to compare your work with the advice and examples given in various chapters of this *Handbook*. You could look again, for example, at the sections on thesis clarity (18.3), or paragraph unity (22.1), or sentence variety (25). Indeed, it may be that those suggestions and warnings will be most useful to you only *after* you have had to struggle with the demands of composing and editing an actual project. In any case, only systematic revising is likely to be effective. Look for specific things, one at a time, instead of aimlessly reading and re-reading what you have written.

Some drafts, of course, may contain only minor errors, requiring the change of a few words or punctuation marks. Often, though, a satisfactory revision means sentences or even whole paragraphs must be rewritten or rearranged. For passages that require extensive changes, experiment with different versions. Then read the revisions through several times to determine which is the best one.

More particularly, it is important to learn from past mistakes. In composition, your *last* paper is a valuable resource because the instructor's markings and comments may let you see what kinds of errors, omissions, ambiguities, and other weaknesses may be habitual in your writing. This is the purpose of those corrections. They are meant to help students strengthen their writing by paying special attention to the advice of a qualified reader. Many instructors require their students to revise all corrected papers and resubmit them. But even if the instructor does not ask for revisions, it is worth your time to make a careful analysis of all correction marks and to revise or rewrite the paper accordingly. A cursory glance down the margins is not enough — if errors and weaknesses are not studied and corrected they will no doubt recur in other papers.

Two versions of a student essay are reproduced opposite each other on pages 454-55 and 456-57. The first version, which has been conscientiously edited, includes the corrective markings. In the second, much improved, version, those errors and ambiguities are eliminated. Study the marks on the original version and determine their meaning. Then examine the changes (underlined) in the rewritten paper. If you don't understand why certain of the revisions are necessary, consult the correction symbol key at the front of this *Handbook* and then reread the relevant section in the text. Do the same thing when your own assignments are marked and returned. Anything you still don't understand should be discussed with your instructor.

In the first version there are two broad categories of weakness. Poor word use has been marked in five instances: the inaccurate *consists of;* the poor connective *and;* the vague and inappropriate *a good mood;* the inflated *fatigued and stupefied by a plethora of chaotic data;* and the colloquial *call him a square*. In addition, the passages marked for sentence economy (Wdy) and awkwardness (Awk) are marred by poor word choice as well as faulty sentence construction. The writer shows little skill at selecting accurate, appropriate, and forceful language to express his or her ideas. To avoid word errors the author will have to become more alert to other writers' use of words, consult the dictionary frequently, and study his or her own first drafts critically to eliminate wordiness and pretentiousness.

Several passages have also been marked for sentence and para-

29.2

*Rev-
Draft*

ms

ⓤⓞod Study Habitsⓢ

It is important for every college student to develop good study
habits. A lucky few have already developed them in high school, but
for the majority of students the greater demands of college work   *Dic*
agr requires some adjustment. Good study habits consist primarily of two   *H H*
things: a mature mental attitude and appropriate physical techniques.

Going to college is a demanding full-time job, and students   *Dic*
should be prepared to spend about forty-five or more hours a week on
it. Like any other job, it requires effort and concentration. Some
students are indifferent toward required courses, which they feel are
// uninteresting or cannot see how they are related to their chosen
course of study. Students should remember that if colleges require
certain courses, usually of a general nature, this means that they   *Ref*
present basic knowledge that every educated person is expected to
wdy acquire while in college. If you are indifferent to such courses, you   *Shift*
are condemning yourself to a lopsided intellectual development, which
you will probably regret later on in life.

DM Whether attending class or studying at home, full concentration
is essential. Students sometimes complain that they do poorly in
courses even though they spend many hours studying everyday.   *✳*
"Studying" means inattentively running their eyes over a page between
frequent distractions from the radio, conversing with their roommates,   *¶*
// and daydreams. Five hours of this kind of studying is worth less than   *con*
an hour of uninterrupted concentration on the material. A student who
goes to a lecture without having done the assigned reading and without
No₃ having reviewed his notes from the last lectureⓞis not really in a
H H good mood to acquire new information and relate it to what he already
knows.

An erratic and undisciplined approach to study is usually
Sp disasterous. Many students ignore course assignments until just
before an examination. Then they frantically do all the required
reading in one or two nights, try to decipher sloppy, disorganized
notes, and stay up all night over black coffee cramming hundreds of

Good Study Habits

It is important for every college student to develop good study habits. A lucky few have already developed them in high school, but for <u>most</u> students the greater demands of college work <u>require</u> some adjustment. Good study habits <u>are</u> <u>based</u> <u>on</u> two things: a mature mental attitude and appropriate physical techniques.

Going to college is a demanding full-time job, <u>so</u> students should be prepared to spend about forty-five or more hours a week at it. Like any other job, it requires effort and concentration. Some students are indifferent toward required courses <u>because</u> <u>they</u> <u>consider</u> <u>them</u> <u>uninteresting</u> <u>or</u> <u>unrelated</u> <u>to</u> <u>their</u> <u>chosen</u> <u>field</u>. <u>They</u> should remember that <u>such</u> <u>courses</u> <u>are</u> <u>required</u> <u>because</u> <u>they</u> <u>provide</u> <u>general</u> <u>knowledge</u> <u>expected</u> <u>of</u> <u>every</u> <u>college</u> <u>graduate</u>. <u>Students</u> <u>who</u> <u>neglect</u> <u>these</u> <u>courses</u> <u>are</u> <u>limiting</u> <u>their</u> <u>intellectual</u> <u>growth</u> <u>and</u> <u>usually</u> <u>regret</u> <u>it</u> <u>later</u>.

<u>Full</u> <u>concentration</u> <u>is</u> <u>essential</u> <u>both</u> <u>in</u> <u>the</u> <u>classroom</u> <u>and</u> <u>in</u> <u>the</u> <u>study</u> <u>room</u>. Students sometimes complain that they do poorly in courses even though they spend many hours studying <u>every</u> <u>day</u>. <u>But</u> <u>to</u> <u>many</u> <u>of</u> <u>them</u> "studying" means inattentively running their eyes over a page between frequent distractions from the radio, <u>conversations</u> with their roommates, or daydreams. Five hours of this kind of studying is worth less than an hour of uninterrupted concentration. <u>The</u> <u>same</u> <u>principle</u> <u>applies</u> <u>to</u> <u>class</u> <u>attendance</u>. A student who goes to a lecture without having done the assigned reading and without having reviewed his or her notes from the last lecture <u>is</u> <u>not</u> <u>concentrating</u> <u>on</u> <u>acquiring</u> new information and <u>relating</u> it to what he or she already knows.

An erratic and undisciplined approach to study is usually <u>disastrous</u>. Students with poor study habits ignore course assignments until just before an examination. Then <u>they</u> frantically do all the required reading <u>in</u> <u>a</u> <u>day</u> <u>or</u> <u>two</u>, try to decipher <u>their</u> sloppy, disorganized notes, and stay up all night over black coffee cramming hundreds of facts into <u>their</u> heads. The result usually is that they come to the examination <u>not</u> <u>only</u> exhausted <u>but</u> <u>also</u> con-

29.2
Rev.
Draft

awk

facts into their heads. The result is usually that_he comes to the *Shift*
examination fatigued and stupefied by a plethora of chaotic data. All *Big N*
of this could have been avoided if the student had kept up with his
assignments and had gotten into the habit of taking neat, orderly
notes which were reviewed by him regularly. Studying for an examin- *Pass*
ation should involve only glancing over his notes and readings and
planning how to organize related facts to answer the questions most
likely to be asked.

Inf

Log

A student should not be afraid that his room mates and friends
will call him a square if he sets aside regular times for daily study
and refuses to be interrupted. On the contrary, most good students
are respected by their fellow students and popular because they devote
more time to social activities than students with poor study habits.

CORRECTION SYMBOLS

MS   Do not enclose titles of papers in quotes. Set them off from
the body of the paper by extra space.

Agr   Avoid blind agreement. Despite intervening words, subject and verb must agree: *demands* (S) *require* (V).

WW   Choose words for their exact meaning.

Dic   (1) *Most* is better. (2) Use a more exact connective (than
and) to show the relationship of ideas.

‖   Constructions joined by co-ordinating conjunctions
should be equivalent in rank and meaning.

Wdy   Express ideas as directly and economically as possible.

Ref   Pronouns should refer clearly to a definite antecedent. The
pronoun *they* might seem to refer to *colleges* or *students*
as well as to *courses*.

Shift   Avoid shifts in person (*they* to *you* in the second paragraph, *they* to *he* in the fourth).

fused by a mass of unrelated facts. They could have avoided all this by keeping up with their assignments, making orderly notes, and reviewing their notes regularly. Studying for an examination then would involve no more than glancing over the material and mentally organizing it in terms of the questions most likely to be asked.

Students should not be afraid that their roommates and friends will make fun of them if they set aside regular times for daily study and refuse to be interrupted. On the contrary, good students are usually respected for their scholastic achievements and, because they use their time more efficiently, are usually freer to participate in social activities than are students with poor study habits.

DM	The sentence should include the word to which the modifier refers.
¶ con	Make sure the relationships among ideas in a paragraph are clear to the reader.
No ,	Do not separate subject and verb by a comma: *A student* (S) *is* (V).
AWK	Smooth out awkward passages when revising a first draft.
Big W	Stilted, unnecessarily heavy language is out of place in all kinds of writing.
Pass	Avoid the awkward use of passive voice, especially an unnecessary shift from passive to active.
Inf	Writers should be consistent in their level of usage. The informal *call him a square* is out of place in this relatively formal paper.
Log	Make sure the logic of a statement is clear to the reader. Devoting a large amount of time to social activities does not necessarily make a student popular; neither do good study habits. The writer's intended meaning is made clear in the revision.

29.2
*Rev.
Draft*

graph weaknesses. The second paragraph concludes with two long, clumsy sentences (Wdy). The third paragraph lacks continuity (con), because the student has omitted certain words and expressions necessary to indicate connections and transitions between ideas. The fourth paragraph contains two jumbled, awkward sentences (Awk). In the correct version, the student has made each of these passages more clear and direct, and has gained valuable practice in expressing the ideas economically. To avoid weak sentences in future papers, he or she should read the sentences and paragraphs aloud to see whether they are difficult to follow, repetitious, or ambiguous. And to assure continuing improvement, the student should become more alert to sentence patterns used by other writers, particularly in published material.

Besides these stylistic and mechanical faults, the first version of the sample essay is frequently vague and unrealistic in its ideas. Even the corrected paper is pretty conventional and not very interesting. Improvements in insight and originality would probably require a more thorough rethinking of the topic than is ordinarily possible at so late a stage of revision. (See 29.1, Re-Seeing the Subject, and 18, Discovering What You Have to Say.) Nevertheless, systematic revisions in matters of detail are beneficial. One change may suggest another, and refinements that appear to be stylistic may actually strengthen your explanation itself. Most importantly, writers who form a habit of careful revising (and of following up on instructors' advice) will soon find an improvement even in their early drafts.

▶ **EXERCISES**

1. Mark up the following student essay as if you were the instructor, write a helpful comment at the end, and assign the paper a grade. Compare your suggestions and evaluations with others in the class.

"The Farmers and Food Prices"

When people complain about high food prices, the blame always ends up in the farmer's lap. "Those farmers are making a fortune and we're almost starving!" I hear people say. Well, I can tell you that the farmers do not make a fortune, and that compared to any other workers, farmers are overworked, underpaid, and have jobs with the most risk and least security.

Labor unions have decreed that laborers can work no more than forty hours a week without being paid overtime, which is time-and-a-half. And if you ask a laborer to work on Sundays or holidays, they get double-time. But the farmers have to work every day, often from sunup to sundown (which in the summer is over fourteen hours). Cows must be milked everyday, Sundays and holidays included. And when the crops are ripe, the farmer's must work to harvest them seven days a week until all are in. There is no forty-hour week, no overtime, no double-time, for farmers.

Laborers have unions which negotiate wage contracts for them. Members of the most powerful unions get longevety and cost-of-living raises yearly. But farmers get paid what the food processors feel like paying them. They cannot strike for higher wages. The only thing they can do is withhold their crops from the market until prices rise to where they think they should be. But if they do that, people think their just being greedy, when really their only doing what laborers are doing, trying to get a living wage.

If you asked a laborer to work at a job where all the products he works on, through no fault of his own, can disintegrate over night and where he will get no pay if this happens, he will just laugh at you. But farmers do just that. They must work to get out a product which may or may not materialize, depending on purely outside influences, particularly inclement weather. If there is a too-wet spring, they cannot plant in time. If there is a too-wet fall, the harvest is delayed or sometimes even ruined. If there are shortages of gasoline or fertilizer, farm work will be held up. The farmers are at the mercy of the elements and the various chemical shortages that can happen at any time.

So, its not the farmers who make a killing while your food bill goes up. Any money they make can never fully pay them for the risk they take and the hard work they do day in the day out, year after year.

2. Rewrite one of your own recent papers, paying particular attention to the comments of your instructor.

29.3 MANUSCRIPT FORM

ms   **Be sure the manuscript is in the appropriate form**

Make a neat and accurate copy of your revised paper to submit to your instructor. Follow the directions he or she gives you for the form: the size and the kind of paper; margins and spacing; numbering of pages; endorsement. Typical manuscript form is described in the following pages.

29.3
ms

Typed Papers

If you have a typewriter and know how to use it, it is a good practice to type all papers written outside class. Typed manuscript is easier to read than most handwriting.

In typing your final draft, use unlined white 21.5 cm x 28 cm paper, but not onionskin, for it lets the type show through.

Type everything *double spaced* except long quotations and footnotes. These should ordinarily be set off appropriately and single spaced.

Follow standard conventions in typing. For the figure 1, use lower case l (not capital I). For a dash, use two hyphens with no space between the words and the dash:

```
The book--a first edition--was missing.
```

Check your work carefully for typographical errors. Uncorrected typing mistakes are usually considered to be errors.

Handwritten Papers

If you cannot type, you may write the paper by hand—if the instructor concurs. Legibly written and neatly prepared, such papers are usually quite acceptable.

Use lined white paper 21.5 cm x 28 cm, with lines at least 13 mm apart. Remember to double-space (write on every second line). Do not use pages torn from spiral-bound notebooks, because their rough edges stick together. Use black or dark-blue ink.

Handwritten papers should be easy to read. If a word looks misspelled or is difficult to decipher, it may be marked as an error. Handwriting that is too small puts an unnecessary strain on the eyes of the reader; handwriting that is excessively large is no less difficult to read. Try to strike a happy medium in size. If you have developed what you consider to be an individual style of penmanship, make certain that it will be as legible to others as it is to you.

Margins and Spacing

Leave ample margins on both sides of the page. About 3.8 cm on the left and 2.5 cm on the right are customary margins in handwritten and typed papers. Leave at least 3.8 cm at the top and 2.5 cm at the bottom of every page.

Indent paragraphs uniformly. Five spaces from the left-hand margin is an acceptable indentation for typed papers, and about 2.5 cm for those written in longhand. Don't indent any line that is not the beginning of a paragraph, even though it is the first line on a page. The last line on a page should not be left partly blank unless it is the end of a sentence or paragraph.

Don't crowd your writing at the bottom of a page. Start a new page, even if it will contain only a line or two.

Division of Words

Div   **Divide the marked word according to the syllabication given in a reliable dictionary.**

If you leave plenty of room at the right-hand side of your page, you will not have to divide many words at the ends of the lines. It is a good idea to divide words only if writing them out or putting them on the next line would make the lines conspicuously uneven.

Words of one syllable must not be divided at all: *through, played, bright*. And avoid breaking a word if a single letter will be left at the beginning or end of a line. There is no point in dividing a word like *a-lone;* the single letter at the end of the line is less attractive than leaving space and carrying the whole word over to the next line.

Words spelled with a hyphen (*mother-in-law, self-confidence*) should be divided only at the hyphen.

Form of the Title

The title appears on the first page of your paper. On unlined paper, place it in the centre about 5 cm from the top of the page; on lined paper, write the title on the top line. Leave a blank line between the title and first line of the text.

Capitalize the first and last words in your title and all others except short words like *and, the, a, an,* and prepositions less than six letters long:

Breaking and Training a Horse   How Not to Become Overweight
The Art of Making Friends   Strength Through Community

No period should be put after a title. However, if the title is expressed as a question or as an exclamation, it should be followed by the proper punctuation:

Why not the NDP?   Man Overboard!

29.3

ms

Titles are not enclosed in quotation marks. Even when familiar quotations are used as titles, no marks are needed:

Blood, Sweat, and Tears   From Sea to Shining Sea

Numbering Pages

The first page of a manuscript is not numbered. Begin with the second page, using Arabic numerals (2, 3, 4...) for paging. Numbers are customarily put at the top of the page in the centre— or in the right-hand corner. Make certain that the pages of your paper are in the right order before you turn the paper in.

Long tables, diagrams, charts, and other material supplementary to the text itself are usually put on separate pages, placed near the part that refers to them, and numbered consecutively with the other pages.

It is not necessary to write "more" or "continued" at the bottom of each page or to put "Finis" or "The End" at the conclusion.

Covering Page

Cover your essay with a page that is blank except for the title, your name, course number (including section, if applicable), instructor's name, and any other factual information requested by the instructor. Find out if there is a preferred format or order for this information. Usually, it should be centred attractively on the sheet.

Ask your instructor how the papers should be submitted, whether folded, flat, or otherwise. Sheets should be held together by a paper clip or a staple only. Don't use folders or binders unless instructed to the contrary.

Proofreading

When you finish your final draft, put it aside for a while and then proofread it carefully before handing it in. No matter how perfect the finished product may appear, it will pay to give it one final check. Errors somehow creep into even the most careful writing. To find them, you will have to get away from the paper for a time so that you can look at it with a fresh eye.

Look for slips of the pen or typing errors, for the omission of words and marks of punctuation. And look particularly for mistakes of the kind marked on your previous papers.

Making Corrections in the Final Copy

Changes and corrections should be kept to a minimum, particularly on important papers. When you have to make major changes in the final copy (rewording sentences, revising paragraphs), do the page over. For minor changes (spelling, punctuation, adding or striking out a word), make the corrections neatly and according to standard practices.

To add a word, use a caret (∧) and write the missing word directly above it:

```
                       be
Manuscript should easy to read.
                  ∧
```

To strike out a word, draw a straight line through it (do *not* use parentheses or brackets):

```
Final copy should be as as accurate as possible.
```

To indicate the beginning of a new paragraph where you have failed to indent, write the symbol ¶ immediately before the first word of the new paragraph.

```
So ended my first day away from home. ¶ The second day....
```

To correct a misspelled word, draw a line through it and write the correct form directly above. This makes a neater and more legible correction than an erasure:

```
                             quantity
Quality is more important than quanity.
```

To indicate in typed copy that two letters should be reversed in order (transposed) use a curved line:

```
be⌓tween              recie⌓ve              Smith⌓s novel
```

Submitting Manuscript for Publication

If you are going to submit a manuscript for publication, you should type it (or have it typed) and follow the suggestions already given. Many publications have their own preferences about the form in which manuscripts should be submitted, and many will send guide sheets or samples of various kinds to writers who want to submit work.

Be sure that your name is on the manuscript. One way to identify your work is to put your complete name and address in the upper left-hand corner of the first page. It's also a good idea to put at least your last name on each page. A simple way to do this is to put it adjacent to the page number (for example: Jones, 2).

Enclose a stamped, self-addressed envelope with any manuscript you submit. Most publications will not take responsibility for returning manuscripts unless you do.

If you are serious about submitting a manuscript for publication, it's a good idea to study a reference such as *The Canadian Writer's Market*. Now in its fourth edition, the current volume includes detailed and comprehensive general advice for writers and information about various categories of magazine and book publication in Canada.

PART THREE

Practical Writing Situations

30

The Research Paper

. . . not to know what has been transacted in former times is to continue always a child. If no use is made of the labours of past ages, the world must remain always in the infancy of knowledge. — Samuel Johnson

One of the decisions you need to make in thinking out any paper is whether or not you know enough already to handle the subject. If you don't know enough, if the subject requires information you cannot supply, then any assignment may become a research assignment.

Often the planning and writing of a research paper (also called a library or reference paper) is a separate and special part of many courses. The preparation of a research paper has much in common with other writing assignments, but in addition it provides:

1. An opportunity to learn something new about a subject and to gain specialized, thorough knowledge of it.
2. Practice in exploring the possibilities of a subject and limiting it so that it can be treated adequately in a paper longer than those you will customarily write; research papers may often range from 1500 to 4000 words.
3. An introduction to the resources of the library and training in the most efficient ways of locating information.
4. Practice in using source material intelligently—choosing between what is useful and what is not, evaluating the ideas of others, organizing and interpreting the information.
5. Acquaintance with documentation and manuscript form typically expected in academic work and in reports and papers prepared for publication.

Because the reference paper is longer and more complex than most other compositions you may be asked to write, we discuss its main aspects here in successive steps:

1. choosing a topic (30.1)
2. locating appropriate source materials (30.2)
3. preparing the working bibliography (30.3)
4. evaluating your material (30.4)
5. taking notes (30.5)
6. planning the paper (30.6)
7. writing the first draft (30.7)
8. documenting the paper (30.8)
9. assembling the completed paper (30.9)

The actual task of preparing a reference paper, however, can seldom be divided into such neat categories. The steps overlap and certain operations must be repeated as work progresses. For example, as you get into your reading, you may decide that your chosen topic needs to be modified; and as you write your paper, you may discover gaps in your information that must be filled in by further research. The best advice, perhaps, is to start on the assignment early and to take particular care in choosing and defining your topic, so that both your research and your writing will have a clear focus.

30.1 CHOOSING A TOPIC

One important prerequisite for writing a good reference paper is that you have a genuine interest in the subject that you are going to investigate. In some courses, the subject field may be limited by the general assignment (perhaps to various aspects of the United Nations, or to the history of a specific geographic area, or to an author or work of literature you have studied); but more often the choice of a subject will be left up to you.

In either instance, you should be reasonably certain that the specific topic you select will be one that you will like to read about, to think about, and then to write about. Since a reference paper may take as much as five or six weeks to prepare, it can easily become a chore—and be largely a waste of time—unless you feel that what you are doing is of some interest and importance. The suggestions in 18.1, Finding Something You Want to Say, are as relevant to the reference paper as they are to other kinds of writing.

Choosing a Subject Area

Before making a definite decision on your topic, consider your various interests in and out of school. These general subjects may suggest particular topics that you might want to investigate:

30.1
Topic

1. A subject related to one of the courses that you are now taking or that you intend to take. For example, if you are going to major in business administration and you intend to take Canadian economic history next year, you might investigate the beginning of child-labor laws or early life insurance companies in Canada.

2. A subject related to your reading interests (biography, history,

science fiction, detective stories) or one related to your favorite hobby or sport (music, dress design, mountain climbing,
baseball).

3. A subject about which you now have an opinion but little
    actual information. Does capital punishment help prevent
    crime? Are children with high IQ's generally successful in later
    life? Do rapid readers retain more than slow readers?

4. A subject that has aroused your curiosity but that you have
    never had time or opportunity to investigate. Of what value are
    computers in education today? Do sunspots actually affect the
    weather? How has the popularity of television affected book
    sales?

It is easier to find a purpose and keep it before you if you select a
topic that ties in with one of your current interests.

Limiting the Topic

As soon as you know what general subject area you would like to
concentrate on, find a specific topic within that area that can be
treated adequately and profitably in a paper of the assigned length.
Keep these considerations in mind when you are narrowing your
topic:

1. **Length of the reference paper.**   An undergraduate refer-
    ence paper is not expected to be the last word on a topic;
    neither is it intended to be a disconnected listing of common-
    place facts or a superficial summary of a complex topic. Limit
    your topic enough so that your treatment of it can be reasona-
    bly thorough. The danger of selecting a topic that is too narrow
    is far less than the danger of choosing one that is too broad and
    lacks focus. (See 18.1, page 230, Limiting Your Subject.)

2. **Availability of source material.**   Before you begin to read
    and take notes, find out whether or not the more important
    books and periodicals that you will need are available in the
    library. Since half a dozen or more sources are usually required
    for a reference paper, you should be certain that enough
    material is available before you begin your research.

3. **Complexity of the source material.**   For some subjects
    (chemical structures of synthetic rubber, for example), the
    available material may be too technical for a general reader to
    understand — and perhaps too complicated for you to interpret

without a good deal of study. You will probably be better off, even in a technical area, with a topic of current general interest.

Here are some steps to take to help you determine your approach to your topic:

1. **Do some preliminary reading.** Spend a few hours reading background material in one or more general or special encyclopedias, in some magazine articles, and perhaps in newspaper articles, if your subject is of current interest and likely to be covered by the daily press.

2. **Check reference sources.** Look through the library card catalogue and the guides to periodical literature to see how the general subject you have chosen may be broken down into smaller units. A broad subject like *aviation* might first be limited to *commercial aviation*, then to the *functions of the Canadian Transport Commission (CTC)*, and then still further to *recent safety measures enforced by the CTC*.

3. **Define your idea as precisely as possible.** Even though you probably still will not be able to make a final statement of the central or controlling idea of your paper, your preliminary reading should have given you a reasonably accurate idea of the focus of your paper. This will help give direction to your research, so that you won't later have to discard much material as useless.

30.2 LOCATING APPROPRIATE SOURCE MATERIALS

One purpose of the research paper is to acquaint you with the resources of your library so that you can locate the information you need quickly and efficiently. On most subjects, the material in the library is so extensive and so varied in form (books, periodicals, **30.2** encyclopedias, newspapers, pamphlets, microfilm) that to keep from being hopelessly lost you need to know something about the *Lib* essential works on your subject, the methods used to index and catalogue material, and the quickest way to obtain this information.

This section deals with library facilities and the various aids that will help you find the material for a reference paper. Librarians are always willing to help students with their research problems, but every student should also have some knowledge of the standard sources of reference in a library.

The Library Card Catalogue

The card catalogue is an alphabetical card index of the items in the library. The cards, filed in drawers or trays, are located in the main reading room or some other central spot. Most card catalogues, in addition to listing all books in the library, give the titles of periodicals (and indicate what copies the library has), encyclopedias, government publications, and other works.

Almost all books are listed alphabetically in three places in the card catalogue of most libraries: by author, by subject, and by title. The cards issued by the Library of Congress, like those reproduced on page 471 for *Policeman* by Claude L. Vincent, are almost universally used for cataloguing.

You can save yourself many hours of thumbing through books that are not relevant to your subject by learning to interpret and evaluate the information given in the card catalogue. The subject card includes the following information (keyed to the circled numbers on the card):

1. **Subject**   The subject heading on the catalogue card tells in general what the book is about. In this instance, the general subject is police psychology. Also listed on the card (in item 7) are the other subject headings under which the book is catalogued.

2. **Call number.**   The call number in the upper left-hand corner tells where the book is located in the library. In some libraries, borrowers obtain books by filling out a slip with the call number, author, title, and the borrower's name and address. If you have access to the stacks, the call number will enable you to locate the book you are looking for.

3. **Author's name.**   If you are already familiar with the subject you are investigating, the author's name may tell you whether the book is likely to be authoritative.

4. **Title and facts of publication.**   The date of publication is sometimes an important clue to the usefulness of a book. For example, if you are looking for information on the ratio of male to female police officers in Canada in the 1980s, this book will not be helpful.

Subject card

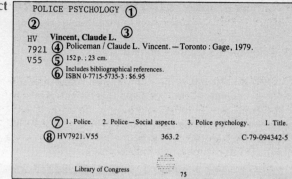

```
POLICE PSYCHOLOGY ①
②
HV      Vincent, Claude L.  ③
7921    ④ Policeman / Claude L. Vincent. — Toronto : Gage, 1979.
V55     ⑤ 152 p. ; 23 cm.
        ⑥ Includes bibliographical references.
           ISBN 0-7715-5735-3 : $6.95


        ⑦ 1. Police.   2. Police—Social aspects.   3. Police psychology.   I. Title.
        ⑧ HV7921.V55               363.2                    C-79-094342-5

                Library of Congress            75
```

Author card

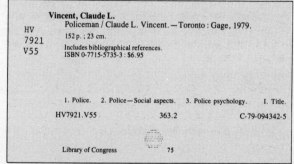

```
        Vincent, Claude L.
HV        Policeman / Claude L. Vincent. — Toronto : Gage, 1979.
7921      152 p. ; 23 cm.
V55       Includes bibliographical references.
          ISBN 0-7715-5735-3 : $6.95


          1. Police.   2. Police—Social aspects.   3. Police psychology.   I. Title.
          HV7921.V55               363.2                    C-79-094342-5

                Library of Congress            75
```

Title card

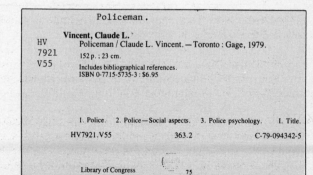

```
        Policeman.
HV      Vincent, Claude L.
7921      Policeman / Claude L. Vincent. — Toronto : Gage, 1979.
V55       152 p. ; 23 cm.
          Includes bibliographical references.
          ISBN 0-7715-5735-3 : $6.95


          1. Police.   2. Police—Social aspects.   3. Police psychology.   I. Title.
          HV7921.V55               363.2                    C-79-094342-5

                Library of Congress            75
```

30.2

Lib

5. **Number of pages, illustrations, height.** The number of pages in the book suggests how extensive its coverage is. This book is of medium length — 152 pages of text. The indication of height — 23 cm — is for librarians.

6. **Special information.** The catalogue card indicates that the book contains a bibliography that might prove helpful in directing you to other sources. None of the books listed, however, would be later than 1979, the year in which this particular book was published.

7. **Other subject headings.** The list of other subject headings under which the book is catalogued may provide ideas of other subject areas to look under for more material; it may also provide a further clue to the contents of the book.

8. **Facts for librarians.** The information at the bottom of the catalogue card — such as the Library of Congress classification (HV7921.V55) — is generally for the use of librarians.

See 30.3, Preparing the Working Bibliography, to see what information from the library catalogue card should be included on your own bibliography card.

The Library Microfiche Catalogue

In addition to the card catalogue, many libraries, especially those in large universities, have introduced a microfiche catalogue system. Situated in the same part of the library as the card catalogue, the microfiche copies are conveniently located next to the microfiche reader. The same information previously recorded on the cards (alphabetically, by author, by subject, and by title) is now stored on microfiche, making it possible to retain as many as 5400 individual entries on a single piece of microfilm (called a microfiche, or simply fiche) measuring 10 cm x 15 cm.

Each microfiche is divided into 270 sections which are identified vertically from A to O and horizontally from 1 to 18 (for example, A-1, A-2, . . . A-18, B-1, B-2, . . . B-18 to O-1, O-2, . . . O-18). An index listing the contents, alphabetically, of each section is recorded in the lower right-hand corner of the microfiche.

When the microfiche is inserted into the microfiche reader, an enlargement of the information is displayed on the screen. By following the schematic printed on each reader, it is easy to locate the section you require. If you have any difficulty locating the information or using the equipment, ask the librarian for assistance.

Trade Bibliographies

The bibliographies published for booksellers and librarians should be consulted to locate a library book not listed in the catalogue or to learn if a book is still in print. The most important include

> *Books in Print.* A listing by author and by title of books included in *Publishers' Trade List Annual*, which lists — by publisher — all books currently in print.
>
> *Canadian Books in Print.* A list by author and by title of books bearing the imprint of Canadian publishers or Canadian subsidiaries of international publishing firms and currently in print.
>
> *Cumulative Book Index.* The complete publication data on all books published in English, each listed by author and by title.
>
> *Guide to Basic Reference Materials for Canadian Libraries* (1974).
>
> *Paperbound Books in Print.* An especially useful source since some important books are available *only* in paperback.
>
> *Subject Guide to Books in Print.* An invaluable index to *Books in Print*.

Periodical Indexes

A great deal of essential material, particularly on current topics, is available only in periodicals, which may range from popular magazines and newspapers to technical journals and learned publications. This material is catalogued in various guides and indexes, some of them published monthly, others annually. Knowing how to use periodical indexes will not only simplify the task of research but will also enable you to make your reference paper more authoritative and up to date. Most libraries also have lists which tell where the periodicals they hold are indexed.

30.2

Lib

Readers' Guide. The most generally useful of all periodical guides is the *Readers' Guide to Periodical Literature*, which indexes the articles in a great many magazines of general interest. It is published monthly in paperbound volumes which are later assembled into large cumulative volumes covering a year or more.

The entries in the *Readers' Guide* are listed alphabetically both

by subject and by author. The abbreviations used in the listings—
for the titles of periodicals, the month of publication, and various
facts about the article itself—are explained on the first page of each
volume. A reproduction and explanation of a few consecutive main
entries from a monthly issue are shown below.

Other periodical indexes.   In locating sources for a reference
paper you may find it useful to refer to one of the specialized
periodical indexes listed below. Most of them appear annually; the
year after the title shows when publication began. The indexes are
listed alphabetically.

> *Applied Science and Technology Index* (1913—). Subject index to
> periodicals on science, technology, and related subjects.
>
> *Art Index* (1929—). Author and subject index for fine-arts periodi-
> cals and museum bulletins.
>
> *Bibliographic Index: A Cumulative Bibliography of Bibliographies*
> (1938—).
>
> *A Bibliography of Canadian Bibliographies* (2nd ed., 1972).
>
> *Biography Index: A Cumulative Index to Biographical material in
> Books and Magazines* (1946—).
>
> *Book Review Digest* (1905—). Author, subject, and title index to
> published book reviews; gives extracts and exact references to
> sources.
>
> *Business Periodicals Index* (1958—). Subject index to periodicals
> on all phases of business, including particular industries and trades.

Sample entries from the *Readers' Guide*

Recruiting of employees
   Help (still) wanted [industries now hiring] Money 11:114 F '82
Rectifiers. *See* Electric current rectifiers
Recycled buildings. *See* Buildings, Remodeled
Recycling (Waste, etc.)
      See also
   Refuse as fuel
   Scrap metal
   Water reuse
   Buying buildings bit by bit: architectural antiques. il Fam
      Handyman 32:26-7+ Ja '82
   Ensuring a sustainable society. D. Hayes. il USA Today
      110:45-7 Mr '82
   John Olberding's for-free (nearly) house [from landfill discards]
      R. Kidd. il Mother Earth News 73:118-19 Ja/F '82
   Recycling is a way of renewing the value of old things. J. R.
      Provey. il Fam Handyman 32:4 Ja '82
   Salvage and savoir-faire [New York brownstone of K. Mann]
      J. Kron. il NY Times Mag p46-7+ F 14 '82

Economic aspects

Local self-reliance. Mother Earth News 73:142 Ja./F '82
Red blood cells. *See* Erythrocytes
Red Brigades (Terrorists) *See* Terrorists, Italian
Red shift

A boundary for the quasars? [study by Maarten Schmidt and Richard F. Green] M. M. Waldrop. Science 215:388 Ja 22 '82
Deep redshift survey of galaxies suggests million-Mpc³ void [work of Robert Kirshner and others] B. M. Schwarzschild. il Phys Today 35:17-19 Ja '82
Red wines. *See* Wine
Redgrave, DeWitt

Preparing for your Paris adventure. World Tennis 29:14-15 Mr '82
Redistricting. *See* Apportionment (Election law)
Redman, Brian

Brian Redman and the Lola T600. L. Griffin. il pors Car Driv 27:94-101 Ja '82
Redman, Lloyd

Decimal multiplication for the ZX-80. il Pop Electron 20:63 F '82

From *Readers' Guide to Periodical Literature*, Vol. 82, No. 5 (May 1982).
New York: H.W. Wilson Co., 1982, p. 389.

Explanation

Most of the items in this selection are *subject entries*. For some, such as **Recruiting of Employees**, only one source is cited (**Money 11:114 F'82**). Under **Recycling** and **Red shift** more than one source is listed. Several subject entries simply make cross references to titles listed elsewhere under different headings. For example, for the entry **Red wines**, the reader is referred to the entry **Wine**.

Two of the items are *author entries*: **Redgrave, DeWitt** and **Redman, Lloyd**. These writers' articles are also listed elsewhere by subject (e.g. **Tennis**). Notice that **Redman, Brian** is not an author entry; racing car driver Brian Redman is the subject of an article by L. Griffin.

Standard abbreviations like *il* (*illustrated*) are explained in the *Guide*.

The Canadian Book Review Annual (1975 —).

The Canadian Essay and Literature Index (1973 —).

Canadian Government Publications (1953 —). A monthly catalogue.

Canadian Periodical Index (1938 —) A continuing serial which includes the index to *The Financial Post*; a valuable source for Canadian subject matter.

Catholic Periodical Index: A Guide to Catholic Magazines (1930 —).

A Checklist of Canadian Literature and Background Materials, 1628-1960.

30.2

Lib

The Education Index (1929-1964). Author and subject index for educational periodicals, books, and pamphlets.

Essay and General Literature Index. Author, subject, and title index to essays, articles, and miscellaneous works published in collections since 1900.

Humanities Index (1974—). Author and subject index to periodicals from various countries; devoted to articles in the humanities; valuable supplement to the *Readers' Guide*.

Poole's Index to Periodical Literature (1802-1881). Subject index to American and English periodicals, many of which are no longer published but still important; precedes coverage of *Readers' Guide*.

Social Sciences and Humanities Index (1907-1974). Author and subject index to periodicals from various countries; devoted chiefly to the humanities and social sciences; formerly titled *International Index to Periodicals*; now superseded by two separate indexes.

Social Sciences Index (1974—). Author and subject index to periodicals focussing on the social sciences; supplements *Readers' Guide*.

Ulrich's International Periodical Directory. Classifies international periodicals by subject area and indicates which periodical index covers them.

Vertical File Index: A Subject and Title Index to Selected Pamphlet Material.

Encyclopedias

The following general encyclopedias are authoritative and include many bibliographies and cross references; all are regularly revised and several are supplemented annually with yearbooks:

Catholic Encyclopedia	*Encyclopedia Americana*
Chambers' Encyclopaedia	*Encyclopedia Canadiana*
Encyclopaedia Britannica	*Encyclopedia of the Social Sciences*

Many subject areas, from art to science, are covered by more specialized reference works that go into greater detail than general encyclopedias, for example, Norah Story's *The Oxford Companion to Canadian History and Literature* (1967), a supplement to which appeared in 1973, edited by William Toye. You should be able to find most of these by browsing in the reference room of your library. The librarian will also be able to tell you what reference works exist for your area of interest.

Yearbooks and Annuals

The following annuals provide up-to-date facts and figures on a wide variety of subjects, particularly those of current interest.

> *Canada Year Book.* Annually updated facts, figures, and other valuable information about Canada.
>
> *Canadian Almanac and Directory* (1847 —).
>
> *Canadian Annual Review of Politics and Public Affairs* (1960 —).
>
> *Information Please Almanac, Atlas and Yearbook* (1947 —).
>
> *The World Almanac and Book of Facts* (1868 —). This is one general reference that any student can afford to own.
>
> *Yearbook of the United Nations.* Activities of the United Nations.

Guides to Reference Materials

Many other specialized reference works can be found by consulting the following guides:

> Barton, Mary N., comp. *Reference Books: A Brief Guide for Students and Other Users of the Library.*
>
> *The Reader's Adviser: A Layman's Guide to Literature.*
>
> Shores, Louis. *Basic Reference Sources: An Introduction to Materials and Methods.*
>
> Walford, Arthur, J., ed. *Guide to Reference Material.*
>
> Winchell, Constance M. *Guide to Reference Books,* updated 9th ed. by Eugene P. Sheehy (– 1980).

30.3 PREPARING THE WORKING BIBLIOGRAPHY

A working bibliography is a list—on note cards—of the books, magazine articles, and other works that you intend to consult when gathering material for your reference paper. The number of references you should collect will depend on the nature of the assignment, but it is always best to begin with more than you will probably need. If your working bibliography includes only a bare minimum of sources, you will probably have to take time later to find more: a book you want from the library may already be out on loan; one article on your list may prove to be too technical; another may merely repeat material you have already collected.

30.2

Lib

Sample bibliography cards

For a book by one author

> JS
> 1708
> H53
>
> Higgins, Donald. *Urban Canada: Its Government and Politics.* Toronto: Gage, 1977.
>
> ①

For a book, edited

> HV
> 6804
> C75
>
> McGrath, W.J., ed. *Crime and Its Treatment in Canada.* Toronto: Gage, 1980.
>
> ②

For a signed article in an encyclopedia

> Reference
> Room
> Shelf 12
>
> M[yers], R[aymond] R. "Paints, Varnishes, and Allied Products." *Encyclopaedia Britannica Macropaedia* 13, 1974
>
> ③

For a journal article

> Periodical
> desk
>
> Pearsall, Robert Brainard. "The Presiding Tropes of Emily Brontë." *College English,* 27 (January 1966), 266–273.
>
> ④

For a magazine article

> Periodical
> desk
>
> Francis, Diane. "Our New Export: Revitalized Cities." *Canadian Business,* August 1980, pp. 43-44, 47-49.
>
> ⑤

For an unsigned newspaper article

> Periodical
> desk
>
> "Unlucky Shiker." *The Globe and Mail,* September 27, 1978, p. 6, col. 1-2.
>
> ⑥

Whether your initial bibliography contains many sources or relatively few, you will probably want to add others as you get into your research and find new avenues you want to explore.

Each entry in your working bibliography should be written on a separate card, either a 12.7 cm × 7.6 cm or 10 cm × 15 cm. With only one reference on each, cards can be rearranged quickly for alphabetizing; new ones can be inserted in the proper places and useless ones discarded. You may want to use 12.7 × 7.6 cards for the working bibliography and 10 × 15 cards for taking notes, since the larger cards will obviously hold more data and will also be readily distinguishable from your bibliography cards.

Bibliography cards for different types of references are illustrated on page 478. Each card should include all the facts you will need to identify the reference and obtain it from the library. It should also have all the information you will need in preparing the final bibliography. The punctuation suggested here is a standard form for bibliographies (see page 493 for a detailed discussion of proper form):

1. **Author's name**   (with the last name first), followed by a period. If the book is edited, use the editor's name, followed by a comma, followed by ed. If the article or pamphlet is unsigned, write the title first on the card.

2. **Title of the book,**   underlined and followed by a period. The title of an article should be in quotation marks with a period inside the closing quotation mark.

3. **Facts of publication:**
   a. **For a book:**   the city of publication, followed by a colon; the name of the publisher, followed by a comma; and the date, followed by a period. Former practice often left out the publisher's name, and usage is still divided. However, unless you are told otherwise, it is always best to include it.

   b. **For a magazine article:**   the name of the magazine, underlined and followed by a comma; the date of the issue, followed by a comma; and the pages covered by the article, preceded by pp. and followed by a period.

   c. **For a journal article:**   the name of the journal, underlined and followed by a comma; the volume number in Arabic numbers; the date, in parentheses, followed by a comma; the page numbers, without p. or pp., followed by a period.

30.3

Biblio

    d. For a newspaper article: the title of the item (other than mere headlines) in quotation marks with a period inside the closing quotation mark; the name of the newspaper, underlined and followed by a comma; the date, followed by a comma; the section number, followed by a comma; the page number, preceded by p. and followed by a period. The column number may be added after the page number, separated from it by a comma, preceded by col., and followed by a period.

4.   **Library call number,**   or the location of a reference work in the library. This information, placed in the upper left-hand corner, should be written just as it appears in the card catalogue, so that you can easily relocate the reference if the need arises. (See also 30.9, page 499, The Final Bibliography.)

5.   **Index number,**   a number or code that you assign to the work, should be placed in the upper right-hand corner of the card. This same number should be used on any note cards you make that refer to this source.

The difference between a magazine and a journal will usually be apparent from content and format. Magazines generally have a wide public appeal and are published weekly or monthly, with dates corresponding to the issue. Each issue begins with page 1. Journals are of more limited appeal (e.g., *The Canadian Journal of Economics*) and are published less frequently than magazines (many are published quarterly); the date does not always correspond to the actual date of issue ("Autumn" could be issued between September and November). Therefore the volume and issue number are more important, especially since pagination is usually continuous throughout an entire volume (e.g., Volume 1, number 2, might begin on page 233).

30.4 EVALUATING YOUR MATERIAL

Since writing a reference paper is in part an exercise in critical judgment, it is important that you learn to evaluate the sources you use. Try to find and use the most informative books and the most authoritative material available.

Facts to Consider in Evaluating

Writers engaged in writing their first reference papers on unfamiliar subjects are not expected to know offhand that a work by author A is wholly worthless or that author B is considered the foremost authority on the subject. They can, however, arrive at a fairly accurate estimate of their sources by considering these facts:

1. **Date of publication.**   If your subject is one for which recent facts are important, see that the sources are up to date. The most recent edition of a book or an encyclopedia will generally be more useful and authoritative than an earlier one.

2. **Completeness.**   With magazine articles, it is better to read the original article as it was printed in full instead of a condensation or reprint of it. Similarly, books are usually more comprehensive than articles, though you should determine that the book's author is reputable. Check the bibliographies in the books you look at for sources often referred to. Encyclopedias should usually be used only as a place to start your search for information, and never relied on heavily.

3. **Facts and opinions.**   Distinguish carefully between an author's facts and opinions. Label the opinions "So-and-so thinks that. . . ." In general, pay more attention to *facts* (unless your paper is about various opinions), since you will need facts to support your own opinions.

4. **Objectivity of the source.**   A book or an article based in large part upon an author's opinions or biases — particularly when the subject is controversial — should not be used as your sole authority on the matter. Read material on the other side of the question before reaching a conclusion.

When you are in doubt about the reliability of a source, a librarian or your instructor may be able to give you advice. Reviews in the more specialized journals evaluate books in their own fields. *Book Review Digest* may also prove helpful. Taking the time to read reviews of books may help you judge their reliability. And, of course, after you have worked a while on your subject, you will be in a better position to evaluate the material yourself.

30.4
Eval

30.5 TAKING NOTES

Accurate and full notes are essential for writing a good reference paper. You can save time when taking notes if you approach the problem efficiently. Don't try to take down everything you read; instead, spend a little time looking over the book, the article, or the pamphlet to see if it contains the information you want. If you have given enough thought to formulating and narrowing your topic, you will have a pretty clear idea of what you are looking for.

Despite the increasing popularity of photocopying in research, note-making is still the best way to keep track of potentially useful information. It is much cheaper, of course, and it also encourages you to be selective and to record your reactions to what you read. Photocopying can certainly save time (and errors) when extended passages or charts need to be transcribed exactly, but it probably isn't more efficient in the long run than conventional research methods. Nor are machines always available.

When examining a book, look first at the index and the table of contents to see in what sections your subject is treated. See also if there are any tables, graphs, bibliographies, or further references that might be useful. Skim each chapter or article to find out what it covers. Then go over it again carefully, taking down the notes you will need.

Notes should be taken either on sheets of loose-leaf paper or on index cards. This technique enables you to rearrange the material later according to the plan of your paper. It is usually a waste of effort to try to take notes in numbered outline form since you probably won't know the final plan of your paper until you have finished your research. What is important is to have each sheet or note card accurate, clearly written, and clearly labelled. Each card or page should contain these essential parts, as illustrated by the sample cards shown on page 483:

1. The **heading** at the top of the sheet or card, showing what material it contains.
2. The **index number** to identify the source and **page number**, accurately noted.
3. The **content**, facts or opinions (summarized in your own words or directly quoted) accurately recorded.

Notes that cannot be readily interpreted a week or a month after they have been written are obviously of little use; so too are incomplete or carelessly written notes. You can avoid a good deal of tedious, unnecessary work, including rereading and rechecking, by following these simple rules:

Sample note cards

Direct quote

> Influences on Britain's development ①
> Fielding
> Hist. of Eng., 72
>
> "In these arts, as in all else, England
> was showing her dual nature: a child of
> the Roman Empire and an island of the
> North. The German Rhineland provided
> models for many of our churches: Scandi-
> navian and Irish influences sent the
> carving and the stone crosses of the
> north country."

Summarized material

> Incidence of neurosis ②
> among the poor
> Harrington
> Other Amer., 119
>
> Though there is a myth that the
> richer you are the more neurotic
> you are likely to be, the truth is
> just the opposite: poor people
> suffer from mental illness more often
> than people in any other social class.

Statistical data

> Enrolment in institutions   Stat. Abstract ③
> of higher education (1000's)   (1976) 112

	1940	1950	1960	1970	1975
Total	1708	1851	2008	2525	2747
Public	603	641	701	1060	1214
Private	1105	1210	1307	1465	1533

1. Use only *one side* of each page or card. Your material will then be easier to classify and arrange, and you won't run the risk of overlooking a statement on the back of a card or sheet.
2. Include only *one major point* or a few closely related facts from the same source on a single page or card. If the information is too extensive to write on one side, use two or three cards or sheets and number them in sequence.
3. Get all the information accurately the first time you consult a source so that you won't have to make extra trips to the library.
4. Put all *direct quotations* in quotation marks, including all

30.5
Notes

statements, single sentences, and phrases that you copy word for word from any source. If you omit a word or words in a direct quotation use ellipsis periods (...) to indicate the omission (see 14.2). If you are paraphrasing the source, state the idea in your own language. (See 30.8, page 491, Plagiarism.)

5. Write your notes in ink (pencilled notes may become blurred with frequent handling) so that you won't have to recopy them. When you use abbreviations, be sure that you will know later on what they mean.

It isn't necessary to write out all your notes in complete sentences; practical shortcuts such as the omission of *a*, *the*, *was*, and other such words are good for summarizing material. If the method you use for taking notes in lectures or on your own textbooks has proved successful, use it also for your reference paper.

Accurate notes are one of the chief tools of scholarship. Early and careful practice in taking them is excellent training that may be useful in later work.

30.6 PLANNING THE PAPER

The central or controlling purpose of a reference paper should be clearly in mind long before you have finished investigating all your resources. You should know, for instance, whether you are trying to reach a conclusion about two opposing viewpoints or whether you are trying to explain an event or situation. When you have gathered a sufficient amount of material to put your topic in focus, it is time to formulate a thesis sentence (see 18.3) that will state your controlling purpose, and to outline the order in which you will develop your material.

Examining and Arranging Your Notes

First read through all your notes to refresh your memory and determine the general order in which you will arrange your material. Then arrange the notes in piles, grouping together all the notes on a particular aspect of your subject. The headings at the top of each card or sheet will be useful in helping you sort and arrange your material. At this stage, you should note any gaps in your material that will have to be filled in with further reading before you start your first draft.

If any of the notes you have taken no longer seem relevant to your purpose in writing, put them aside in a tentative discard pile or folder. Almost anyone engaged in research finds that a good deal of carefully recorded material has to be discarded. Don't succumb to the temptation to include material that has no bearing on your thesis simply because it is interesting or because you worked hard to find it.

Making a Preliminary Outline

When you have arranged your notes to your satisfaction, state the central idea or conclusion of your paper in a thesis sentence (not in two or more sentences nor in the form of a question). Then make a rough outline showing the order in which you intend to present your material. Each point in the outline should contribute in some way to the development of your central idea or thesis. Often your instructor will want to see your working outline before you go much further with the work. To crystallize your plan and to make it possible for your instructor to examine it and make suggestions, you should follow standard outline form. At this stage, a topic outline is generally sufficient; if necessary, you can later expand the entries into complete sentences. (See 20, Organizing Your Material, for a discussion of outlining and outline form.)

Neither your preliminary outline nor your thesis sentence needs to be considered as final. It is better, in fact, to make a reasonably flexible outline so that you can make whatever changes seem desirable as you write and revise your first draft.

30.7 WRITING THE FIRST DRAFT

A reference paper should represent your writing at its best—in terms of organization, sentence structure, wording, and emphasis. The most convincing proof that you have actually learned something new from your research is the way you have evaluated, organized, and expressed your material. Instructions concerning the proper form for footnotes or endnotes (30.8) and for the bibliography (30.9, page 499) should be followed to the letter. The paper should be as neat as you can possibly make it, with each part in its proper order and all errors in spelling and punctuation carefully corrected.

30.7

Draft

Make certain that you are thoroughly familiar with your material before you begin to write. You should have the information on your note cards so well in mind that you can write rapidly and with confidence once you start. For this reason, it is a good idea to review your notes once more just before you begin writing.

Most reference papers are written in a rather formal, impersonal style. Usually there's no need to refer to yourself at all, but if you do, the reference should be brief. (It's also better to say "I" rather than use "the writer" or other third person references.) Remember, however, that impersonal writing does not have to be flat or lifeless. The information itself will provide the interest if you express it clearly and directly.

The first draft of your research paper should be written in the same way you would write the first draft of any other important assignment (as discussed in 21, Writing the First Draft), but with ample room left for documentation. You can leave spaces between the lines or at the bottom of the page to note the necessary footnotes for that page. Some writers insert the documentation in the text of the first draft to help determine final placement and estimate space requirements:

```
    The theory reserved the most desirable characteristics for northern

people.  Those of the south were pictured as jealous, superstitious,

cowardly, lascivious, cruel, and inhuman. [Philip Butcher. "Othello's

Racial Identity," Shakespeare Quarterly, 3 (July 1952), 246.] Because

of this belief, Shakespeare's choice of Othello as the victim of Iago's

plot is especially convincing to the audience.
```

Or the footnotes may be put all together on a separate page or handled in any other way that will be convenient when you make the final copy.

If a passage seems to need more facts or further documentation, don't interrupt your writing to do the necessary additional research. Put a question mark or some other notation in the margin, continue with your writing, and look up the material after you have finished the first draft.

30.8 DOCUMENTING THE PAPER

Any paper based partly on the writing of others should specifically acknowledge each and every source from which an idea or statement is taken. In a reference paper, formal acknowledgments are made in notes—either *footnotes* at the bottom of the page or *endnotes* collected at the end of the paper. These notes, showing exactly where the information was obtained, are numbered to correspond with numbers entered after the pertinent passage in the essay.

There is no consensus about whether footnotes or endnotes are preferable in student writing. There has been a trend toward endnotes, but each method has its advantages. The use of endnotes is most convenient for writers and typists, and is now a common practice in academic publishing. Footnotes are naturally easier for readers, and are certainly recommended if publication in the form of microfilm or microfiche is contemplated. Either format is "correct" and will usually be acceptable in student papers, though it would be wise to find out if your instructor has a strong preference.

Where Footnotes or Endnotes Are Needed

When drawing on the work of another writer or researcher, you owe him or her the courtesy of giving credit where credit is due. You also owe your *readers* the courtesy of providing the sources of your information so that they can judge them for themselves and find additional information, if desired. Failure to document borrowed information is at best carelessness; at worst, it is plagiarism, which means offering material written by someone else as if it were your own work (see page 491). Footnotes or endnotes are essential in two situations:

1. **After direct quotations.** Each statement taken word for word from a printed source should be placed within quotation marks, have a reference number at the end, and have its source fully identified in a note. The only exceptions to this rule are well-known expressions, such as familiar Biblical quotations ("Blessed are the poor"), famous lines from literature ("Something is rotten in the state of Denmark"), and proverbs ("A bird in the hand is worth two in the bush").

2. **After all important statements of fact or opinion taken**

30.8

Doc

from written sources and expressed in your own words. Facts include figures, dates, scientific data, and descriptions of events and situations about which you have no first-hand knowledge, such as what happened at a session of the United Nations, how coffee is cultivated in Brazil, or the role of Madagascar in World War II. Opinions and interpretations that are not actually your own would include ideas such as one writer's reasons for the growing popularity of soccer in Canada, or an opinion on seal hunting from a newspaper editorial.

Documentation is *not* needed for statements that would pass without question. These include obvious facts ("Certain chemicals cannot be used in the preservation of foods in Canada"), matters of common knowledge ("The British North America Act was passed in 1867"), general statements ("The medical and biological sciences have made great progress in the last twenty years"), and expressions of the writer's own opinion.

As for the practice of using footnotes or endnotes to add comments or additional information, this should be avoided in research papers if at all possible. If a statement is worth making, it usually belongs in the text.

If you have a full page in your draft without any references, you should probably check it again to see if any documentation is needed. On the other hand, a lot of references on a single page may indicate that some of the material could better be combined or rephrased to simplify documentation.

The following sections discuss some things to consider in integrating footnoted material into the text of your paper.

Using Direct Quotations

When incorporating reference material into your research paper, you will often have to decide whether to quote directly or to restate the material in your own words. In general, direct quotations are preferable only in these situations:

1. **Important statements of information, opinion, or policy.** Whenever the *exact* wording of a statement is crucial in its interpretation, it should be quoted in full:

   Faced by much opposition, Mackenzie King, in 1942, described his government's policy on conscription as: "Not necessarily conscription but conscription if necessary."[2]

2. **Interpretations of literary works.** When a statement or opinion in your paper is based on a passage in a poem, essay, short story, novel, or play, quote from the passage so that the reader can see the basis for your interpretation:

There are differences that defy all understanding. For example, Indians do not lie. As Big Bear explains, "no Person will deny what he has done." Then, he concludes, "White law is the way it is because Whiteskins are liars."[14] Otherwise, why the proceedings of a court. Crime itself depends on the point of view. Stealing horses, for example, is one way the young men traditionally prove themselves. Yet Big Bear realizes the white authorities do not abide by their custom. Therefore, they do not steal from whites: "Once, when I took a horse away from one of my young men he was so enraged he beat me with a stick. I let him, and he stood ashamed."[15] — John Moss, *Sex and Violence in the Canadian Novel: The Ancestral Present*

When you are writing a paper that requires frequent references to a literary work, however, you need to footnote or endnote the edition of the text you are using only *once*, the first time you use a quotation. Thereafter, you may identify quotations by giving (immediately after the quotation, in parentheses) the page numbers for fiction, the line numbers for poetry, the act and scene for drama (followed by the line numbers if in verse):

Man, who once stood at the centre of the universe, confident that he was the end of Creation and could claim kinship with the angels, is now shrouded in a "mist" that isolates him from God and shuts off all his questioning about the problems of ultimate order. As Webster says of the Cardinal in *The Duchess of Malfi*, Man,

which stood'st like a huge pyramid
Begun upon a large and ample base,
Shalt end in a little point, a kind of nothing. (V.v.96-98)

3. **Distinctive phrasing.** If your source states some idea or opinion in a particularly forceful or original way that would be weakened by paraphrasing, quote the exact words:

Russell does not believe that our age lacks great ideas because religion has declined: "We are suffering not from the decay of theological beliefs but from the loss of solitude."[13]

30.8

Doc

A quotation should be smoothly integrated into the text of your paper. Even though its source is given in a footnote or an endnote, it should be preceded by some brief introductory remark such as "one leading educator recently said that . . ."; "as Desmond Morton points out . . ."; "an editorial in *The Canadian Forum* argued that. . . ." The best way to learn about integrating quotations is to observe how professional writers handle them:

> Another English critic described Canada as "a sort of half-way house in letters between U.K. and U.S.A.," and therefore found no surprise in Leacock's having discovered "the hilarious mean between American and English humour":
>
> > His fantastical ideas are often in the nature of American hyperbole — but they are developed in English fashion as a rule, in a quiet and close-knit narrative which has none of the exuberance of the typical American humorist.[8]
>
> The notable exception is J.B. Priestly, who finds specific and positive qualities in Leacock's "outlook, manner, and style," which, he says, not only "belong to the man but . . . to the nation". . . .[9] — R.E. Watters, "Stephen Leacock's Canadian Humor"

See 14.1, page 173, Quotation Marks Around Quoted Material, for a discussion of ways to set up long and short quotations from both prose and poetry.

Paraphrasing

Although a reference paper relies heavily on the writings of others, it should not consist simply of a long string of word-for-word quotations from sources. As always, it should reflect your own thinking and your own style. Except in the situations described in the preceding section, information from secondary sources should be *paraphrased* — restated or summarized in your own words. Otherwise the paper will have a jumbled, patchwork effect that may distract or confuse the reader. Compare the two following passages for effectiveness:

> TOO MANY DIRECT QUOTATIONS: Authorities disagree about the dating of these pyramids. Professor Sheldon Muncie says, "The preponderance of evidence collected by investigators in recent years points to a date no earlier than 1300 A.D. for the construction of the lowest level."[1] Professor William Price basically agrees with him: "Bricks of this type were not used in the surrounding areas until the late fourteenth century."[2] But Robert McCall found that "The radiocarbon readings are completely out of line with the standard textbook dates; the original substructure is at least 700 years older than Muncie's earliest estimate."[3]
>
> BETTER(PARAPHRASED): Authorities disagree about the dating of the pyramids. Professors Sheldon Muncie and William Price con-

cluded, on the basis of the type of brick used and other evidence, that the pyramids were begun no earlier than the fourteenth century.[1] But Robert McCall's radiocarbon readings indicate a date earlier than 600 A.D.[2]

The best way to paraphrase a passage is to absorb the content and then to write it down from memory in your own words. When you have finished, you should check it for accuracy and any unconscious borrowing of phrases and sentences. Remember that even though the words are your own, the information or ideas are not; you will still have to use a footnote or endnote to identify the source.

Plagiarism

Although the research paper you eventually produce will be your own original analysis of the topic, the supporting data (statistics, technical details, theories, expert opinions, or whatever) are still the property of the authors in whose books or articles you found the information. The sources of all borrowed material must be identified. The acknowledgments lend authority to your paper and protect you from accusations of *plagiarism* — a form of academic stealing or cheating.

Almost everyone realizes that copying someone else's work word for word without crediting the author is considered plagiarism. But many people are uncertain (or careless) about less obvious forms of borrowing. For example, they may assume that this practice is frowned on only when long passages are involved — whole pages or paragraphs. Consequently, they feel free to copy phrases and sentences without using quotation marks and notes. Or they may suppose it is all right to adopt ideas or interpretations from published sources so long as word-for-word copying is avoided. These and other unfortunate misconceptions cause a lot of grief for those college and university students who subsequently find themselves charged with plagiarism.

Actually, any uncredited use of another's information, ideas, or wording is plagiarism. Under the mistaken notion that they are paraphrasing, students often reproduce sources almost exactly, changing only a word here and there. An honest paraphrase, however, is one in which the *ideas* of the source are stated in the writer's *own words*. The following examples show the difference between genuine paraphrase and plagiarism of source material:

30.8

Doc

ORIGINAL SOURCE: (from J.A. Corry, "Free Trade in Ideas," *Our Sense of Identity*, Malcolm Ross, ed., p. 277): "It will be urged here that most of the arguments of [John Stuart] Mill's *Essay on Liberty* still apply. . . . Freedom of expression is a necessity of life for the free flexible society which admits that it is not sure of final answers and wants to feel its way by experiment, by trial and error. It is meaningless to talk about proceeding experimentally unless we have the fullest possible observation and report on the result of the experiments. Every individual is now deeply affected by the social and political experiments we undertake daily. Our society is so complex and it is so difficult to know exactly what the results of these experiments really are that we need the widest possible ventilation of grievances."

STUDENT VERSION (PLAGIARISM): Nineteenth-century arguments for liberty still apply. For the free society that confesses to not knowing all the answers must grope its way by trial and error. Therefore, full observation and report on the result of such experiments must be available. This is so because every individual is daily influenced by social and political experiments. Thus, in our complex society the widest possible airing of grievances is a must.

By omitting any reference to Corry and Mill, the writer implies that the ideas are his or her own. In organization the paragraph follows the source very closely—a similar order of ideas and the same number and structure of sentences. Many of the words and phrases are taken directly without the use of quotation marks to indicate this fact. In other cases, word order has been simply rearranged and synonyms substituted (*confesses* for *admits*, *grope* for *feel*, *influenced* for *affected*, *airing* for *ventilation*). These problems are avoided, however, in the different version below:

ACCEPTABLE STUDENT VERSION: J.E. Corry, citing Mill's *Essay on Liberty*, stresses the continuing need for freedom of speech in a society which admits to not knowing all the answers and which must therefore proceed experimentally. He concludes that because these experiments—both political and social—affect everyone in our complex society, great latitude must be allowed for dissent.[1]

Notice that the writer admits, both in the text and in a footnote, that the ideas used are Corry's. They are stated in the student's own words and do not slavishly follow the source. Quotation marks are unnecessary, since none of the actual phrases are Corry's.

Numbering and Spacing of Notes

In the text of the paper, the note number is placed *at the end of the quotation or statement* for which the source is being given; it is never placed before the borrowed material. The number is raised slightly above the line and is placed outside the end punctuation of the statement to which it refers: "...nearly 400 000 in 1978."[13]

Footnotes and endnotes are generally numbered consecutively throughout the paper in Arabic numerals beginning with 1. If the last note on the first page is numbered 3, the first note on the second page will be numbered 4, and so on. It is impossible to say how many notes should appear in a paper of a given length because frequency varies with the type of subject and the kind of sources used; however, the typical student reference paper contains from two to four notes on a page. Studying some footnoted or endnoted articles and books will help you see how the system works.

In typed manuscript, notes are single spaced (but separated from each other by an extra line of space) and the first line of each is indented as for a paragraph. Set *footnotes* apart from the text with a short line extending about 2.5 cm from the left margin.

Footnote and Endnote Form

Generally, each note should contain at least four essential facts (the information a reader would need to locate the source): the name of the author(s), the title of the work, the facts of publication (publisher, place, and date), and the specific page or pages for the information used.

Practices in footnote and endnote *form* vary, chiefly in punctuation and kinds of abbreviations. This section follows the form recommended by the second edition of the *Style Sheet* of the Modern Language Association (MLA), the form most often used in academic writing in the humanities. Alternative systems are frequently used in scientific papers (see 30.8, page 498, Alternative Forms). Follow carefully any changes your instructor may want made in the form described here.

Footnotes or Endnotes for Books

30.8

First reference. Study the sample notes below, noting the order of the information and the punctuation used between each element. The first time you refer to a book in a note, include as much of the information as is relevant. For example, if the author's full name has been given in the text, it need not be repeated in the endnote or footnote. This is sometimes called a *split note*.

A book with one author:

[1]Pierre Elliott Trudeau, Federalism and the French Canadians (Toronto: Macmillan, 1968), p. 10.

Two or three authors:

[2]Alan Bowd, Daniel McDougall, and Carolyn Yewchuk, Ed. Psych. A Canadian Perspective (Toronto: Gage, 1982), p. 283.

More than three authors:

[3]Patricia A. Fitzgerald, and others, Business: Its Nature and Environment (Toronto: Gage, 1979), p. 568.

[The Latin abbreviation *et al.* may be used instead of *and others*.]

An edited book:

[4]Journals and Papers of Gerard Manley Hopkins, ed. Humphry House, completed by Graham Storey (London: Oxford University Press, 1966), p. 192.

[If the editor's name is most relevant to the citation, put that name at the beginning of the note: Humphry House, ed., *Journals and Papers of Gerard Manley Hopkins*.]

An article in an edited book of selections written by various authors:

[5]George Whalley, "Where Are English Studies Going?" In the Name of Language, ed. Joseph Gold (Toronto: Macmillan, 1975), pp. 131-60.

A translated book:

[6]M. H. Scargill, "Le développement de la langue anglaise au Canada," Histoire littéraire du Canada, ed. Carl F. Klinck et al., trans. Maurice Lebel (Québec: Université Laval, 1970), pp. 308-17.

A book for which no author is given:

[7]A Manual of Style, 12th ed. (Chicago: University of Chicago Press, 1969), p. 27.

A revised edition:

[8]Michael D. Moore, Walter S. Avis, and Jim W. Corder, Handbook of Current English, 2nd Canadian ed. (Toronto: Gage, 1983), pp. 345-49.

A multivolume work, all volumes published in the same year:

[9]John E. Robbins, ed., Encyclopedia Canadiana, rev. ed. (Ottawa: Canadiana Co., 1972), VI, 316-18.

[If the note includes a volume number, the abbreviation *p.* or *pp.* is omitted.]

A multivolume work, the volumes published in different years:

[10]Harold Child, "Jane Austen," in The Cambridge History of
English Literature, ed. A. W. Ward and A. T. Waller, XII (London:
Cambridge University Press, 1914), 231-33.

[The volume number in this instance precedes the facts of publication:]

A book that is part of a series:

[11]Garth Stevenson, Unfulfilled Union, 2nd ed., Canadian
Controversies Series, ed. Robert J. Jackson (Toronto: Gage, 1982),
p. ix.

Subsequent references.   For subsequent references to the same work that do not immediately follow the original reference, a short form should be used: the author's last name only, if not more than one work by the same author is being cited, and the page number:

[12]Trudeau, p. 150

If two sources by the same author have been previously cited, the short form must also include the title, to make clear which work the note re-refers to. A shortened form of the title may be used:

[13]Trudeau, Federalism, p. 150

If the book has no author, the title should be used:

[14]A Manual of Style, p. 92.

See page 497 for the use of *ibid.* in footnotes and endnotes.

Footnotes or Endnotes for Magazine, Journal, and Newspaper Articles

Footnotes and endnotes referring to magazine and newspaper articles are handled in much the same way; the volume number is used in noting an article from a scholarly journal and may also be included for a magazine if thought necessary.

Signed article in a magazine:

[15]Gary Geddes, "The Writer That CanLit Forgot," Saturday Night,
November 1977, p. 84.

30.8
Doc

Unsigned article in a magazine:

[16]"Canada's Heritage Sites," The Financial Post, November 1977,
p. 36.

Article in a scholarly journal:

[17]Arthur R. M. Lower, "History as Pageant," Dalhousie Review, 54
(Spring 1974), 5.

[The abbreviation *p.* or *pp.* is omitted if the volume number is given.]

Signed article in a newspaper:

> [18]Patrick Watson, "The Odds on Canadian Pay-TV," The Globe and Mail (Toronto), 1982 05 13, p. 7.

[Locate newspaper articles by section or column, if possible.] Unsigned articles and subsequent references to the same article are handled in the same way as unsigned articles in magazines. Subsequent references to articles in periodicals may be shortened in the same way as those for books (see page 495).

Footnotes or Endnotes for Other Sources

These sample entries will help you arrive at a form for various source materials you may use.

Encyclopedia articles:

> [19]Dorothy MacPherson, "Indians of Canada," Encyclopedia Canadiana, rev. ed. (Ottawa: Canadiana Co., 1975), V, 249.

[If the article is unsigned, begin with the title. Notice that the volume number is given in Roman numerals, and that the abbreviation *p.* or *pp.* is omitted.]

Biblical citations:

> [20]Matthew 6:26-30.

[Often this identification is given in parentheses immediately following the quotation, rather than in an endnote or a footnote. Very familiar quotations, such as "Thou shalt not steal," are not noted.]

Material at second hand:

> [21]Robert M. Stamp, "Canadian Education and the National Identity," Journal of Educational Thought, December 1972, p. 17, in Canadian Schools and Canadian Identity, ed. Alf Chaiton and Neil McDonald (Toronto: Gage, 1977), p. 29.

[Both the original source and the source from which the material was taken are given.]

Bulletins and pamphlets:

> [22]The Labour Force, December, 1976, Statistics Canada, Labour Force Survey Division, Cat. No. 71-001 (Ottawa: Statistics Canada, 1977), p. 24

Unpublished dissertations and theses:

[23]H. J. Matte, "The Dialect of Lunenburg County, Nova Scotia,"
Diss. Dalhousie University, 1980, p. 48.

[Titles of unpublished works are usually enclosed in quotation
marks.]

Use of *ibid*. in footnotes or endnotes.   The abbreviation *ibid*.
(for the Latin *ibidem*, "in the same place") means that the reference is to the same book or article as the preceding note. It can be
used only to refer to the work listed in the note *immediately*
preceding and *only* if the two notes appear on the same page:

[24]Frank H. Epp, Mennonites in Canada, 1920-1940 (Toronto:
Macmillan, 1982), p. 114.

[25]Ibid., pp. 135-36.

Because it stands first in an endnote or a footnote, ibid. is capitalized; because it is an abbreviation, it is followed by a period. Ibid.
is not usually italicized, but usage varies; follow the recommendation of your instructor.

The use of ibid., and of Latin abbreviations in general, is
decreasing in academic writing. Usually it is just as simple to use a
shortened reference to author and title (as described in 30.8., page
495, Subsequent references) as it is to use ibid.

Other abbreviations in footnotes or endnotes.   Standard
abbreviations such as those for provinces and territories (*White-
horse*, *YT*; *Oshawa*, *ON*; *Brandon*, *MB*) are commonly used in
notes. The following abbreviations may also be used to save space.
(Follow the recommendation of your instructor about whether to
underline for italics those from Latin.):

anon.	anonymous
ca. or c. (*circa*)	about a given date (*ca*. 1490)
ch., chs.	chapter, chapters
col., cols.	column, columns
ed.	edited by or edition (2nd ed.)
et al. (*et alii*)	and others (used with four or more authors); you may also simply write "and others"
e.g. (*exempli gratia*)	for example (preceded and followed by a comma; note the periods)
ibid. (*ibidem*)	in the same place (explained above)
i.e. (*id est*)	that is (preceded and followed by a comma)
l., ll.	line, lines (in typewritten copy it is better to write these out, to avoid confusion with figures 1 and 11)

30.8
Doc

MS., MSS.	manuscript, manuscripts
n.d.	no date of publication given
n.p.	no place of publication given
p., pp.	page, pages (the word *page* is never written out in footnotes)
rev.	revised edition or revised by
sic	thus (placed in brackets after an error in quoted material to show that you are aware of the error; seldom used by contemporary writers)
trans. or tr.	translated by
vol., vols.	volume, volumes

Alternative Forms for Footnotes

Research papers in the sciences and social sciences often use systems of reference to sources quite different from the system just described, which is one generally used in the humanities. The references have the same purpose — to give the author, title, and facts of publication of articles and books used, to acknowledge the source of materials, and to make it possible for a reader to go directly to a source for further information. However, the details of form vary considerably among the different scientific and technical fields and often among the books and journals within a field. If you are writing a paper for a course in the sciences, you will need to follow your instructor's specification of which system to use or study the form of a particular journal or style manual and follow its practice. Whatever system you follow, do not shift from one system to another in your paper: consistency in form is essential in the use of footnotes or endnotes.

Any description of notes makes their use seem much harder than it really is. If you have maintained good records of your reading, it is relatively simple to keep track of the sources in the first draft and to place them in the final paper in the proper form.

30.9 ASSEMBLING THE COMPLETED PAPER

In preparing the final copy of your research paper, refer to the suggestions given in 29.3, Manuscript Form. You will also find it useful to study the sample student paper on pages 502–10. Proofread your final copy carefully before turning it in. A well-researched paper can be seriously marred by careless errors and inconsistencies.

The Final Bibliography

The finished research paper concludes with a bibliography of the sources used in the paper. If the list includes only those books, articles, and other sources that have been documented in the notes, the bibliography is titled "List of Works Cited." If the list also includes references that you have explored in depth but have not cited directly, the bibliography should be labelled "List of Works Consulted." Your instructor will tell you which form you should use.

Your bibliography cards (see 30.3) should contain all the information you need to compile the final bibliography. The form for a bibliography differs somewhat from footnote or endnote form:

Footnote or endnote entry:

```
¹John Porter, The Measure of Canadian Society:  Education,
Equality, and Opportunity (Toronto:  Gage, 1979), p. 253.
```

Bibliography entry:

```
Porter, John.  The Measure of Canadian Society:  Education,
    Equality, and Opportunity.  Toronto:  Gage, 1979.
```

Follow these general guidelines and the examples that follow for an acceptable bibliography form:

1. List all entries in alphabetical order, by the author's *last name*, or, if the author's name is unknown, by the first significant word of the title (disregard *A* or *The*). When two or more works by the same author are listed, use a line of twelve dashes, followed by a period, in place of the author's name for all but the first work.
2. Do not give the page numbers for books, but do list the inclusive pages for articles in periodicals and newspapers.
3. Do not separate the list according to kinds of publications. Since the bibliography for most student papers is short, all sources should appear in the same list.
4. Do not number the entries.

Punctuation varies in different bibliographic styles, mainly in the use of commas, colons, and parentheses. The form shown in the examples illustrates one widely used style, but be sure to note carefully any different practices your instructor may want you to follow.

30.9

Biblio

Bibliography Form for Books

One author:

```
Munro, Alice.  The Moons of Jupiter.  Toronto:  Macmillan, 1982.
```

Two or three authors or editors:

Daymond, Douglas, and Leslie Monkman, eds. Literature in Canada.
    Toronto: Gage, 1978.

[Notice that only the first author's name is listed last name first —
for purposes of alphabetizing.]

More than three authors:

Blair, Walter, and others. The Literature of the United States.
    3rd ed. 3 vols. Glenview, Ill.: Scott, Foresman, 1969.

Two books by the same author:

Davies, Robertson. Fifth Business. Toronto: Macmillan, 1970.

_____. The Manticore. Toronto: Penguin, 1976.

[Notice that these books are arranged alphabetically by title.
Remember to disregard *A* and *The* when alphabetizing.]

An edited book, especially one of another writer's work:

Shakespeare, William. The Complete Works of Shakespeare. Rev. ed.
    Hardin Craig and David Bevington, eds. Glenview, Ill.: Scott,
    Foresman, 1973.

An edited collection; date of publication unknown:

Reed, William L. and Eric Smith, eds. Treasury of Vocal Music. 6 vols.
    Boston: Branden Press, n.d.

A translation:

Maillet, Antonine. La Sagouine. Trans. Luis de Céspedes. Toronto:
    Simon and Pierre, 1979.

An encyclopedia article:

McG[uire], W[illiam] J. "Persuasion." Encyclopaedia Britannica.
    Macropedia 14, 1974.

A Canadian government document:

Indian Claims Commission. 1977. Commissioner on Indian Claims:
    A Report, Statement and Submissions. Ottawa: Department of
    Supply and Services.

Reprint:

Dexter, Walter. The London of Dickens. 1923; rpt. Philadelphia:
    Richard West, 1973.

Bibliography Form for Periodicals

Signed article in a magazine:

Wanzel, Grant. "Architecture as Cultural Action." Canadian Forum,
    September 1978, pp. 20-23.

Unsigned article in a magazine:

"Canada's Last Growth Industry." Saturday Night, December 1977, p. 3.

Article in a scholarly journal:

Hill, Archibald A. "The Green Knight's Castle and the Translators."
    The Canadian Journal of Linguistics, 17 (1972), 140-58.

Newspaper article:

Strauss, Marina. "Prisons Replace Guards with Electronic Alarms."
    The Globe and Mail (Toronto), 1982 09 14, p. 4.

Unpublished dissertation:

Eaton, J. D. "The Rhetoric of the New 'Arcadia.'" Diss. University
    of British Columbia, 1979.

Final Order of Contents

The final version of the research paper should contain all the parts
in the order assigned. Typically, the completed paper has the
following units. Make sure that you include any other material
(such as your first outline or first draft) that your instructor asks for.

1. **Title page.**   The title of the paper should be centred; your
    name, the date, the course number, and any other information
    your instructor requests should be put in the lower right-hand
    corner — unless you are told otherwise.

2. **Outline.**   Some instructors will expect you to turn in your
    final outline (topic or sentence outline) and the thesis sentence.
    The revised outline should correspond to the organization of
    the final paper.

3. **Text of the paper.**   The final copy of the paper must be
    complete with footnotes or endnotes, charts, and diagrams
    wherever needed. The numbering of the text normally begins
    on the second page, with Arabic numerals centred at the top or
    at the top right-hand corner.

4. **Bibliography.**   The bibliography follows the text but begins
    on a new page, each page being numbered as a part of the text.

This extended explanation may suggest to you that writing a
research paper is an impossible task to accomplish in a mere five or
six weeks of work. It isn't. Done carefully, with due attention to
each of the stages outlined in this section, it may be accomplished
with no more effort than you would use for your other course work.
And if your research paper represents your best effort, you will find
the assignment a satisfying one and good training for later work.

    The following pages present a brief sample student paper,
complete with outline, text, and bibliography. It may be helpful for
you to study its style and content as well as the way quotations and
endnotes are handled.

30.9

Biblio

HAZARDS OF CAFFEINE:

THE EXPERIMENTAL BACKGROUND

Tom Woodhead
English 105 (Section K)
Professor L. Mann
1982 12 17

HAZARDS OF CAFFEINE: THE EXPERIMENTAL BACKGROUND

Thesis statement: Caffeine is a part of our everyday life and yet, because
it is a drug, we should be aware of the forms and amounts in which we consume
it, of its mental and physical effects, and of the problems that may arise
from its use.

A. Introduction

  1. Widespread use of caffeine

  2. Term psychotropism

  3. Thesis (warning about dangers)

B. Technical Background

  1. Pharmacological definition

  2. Known connection with medical problems

  3. Dietary and other sources of caffeine

C. Discoveries about Caffeine's Ill Effects

  1. Examples of scientific findings (e.g. birth defects)

  2. Problems of validating such conclusions

  3. Example of children and caffeine

D. Supposed Beneficial Effects of Caffeine

  1. Alertness

  2. Cure for intoxication

  3. Need for Further Research

E. Conclusion

  1. Probability of serious hazards

  2. What precautions should be taken now, while research continues.

HAZARDS OF CAFFEINE: THE EXPERIMENTAL BACKGROUND

The most commonly used drug in Canada is probably caffeine--a psychotropic (mood-altering) chemical compound found in a variety of drinks and
foods. Anyone who does not consume caffeine daily in some form is part of
a tiny minority. According to R. M. Gilbert of the Canadian Medical Association, "more than 90% of adults drink a caffeine-containing beverage each day."[1]
The Canadian Pharmaceutical Journal reports that "caffeine has become one of
the world's most widely-used psychotropic drugs and part of our daily diet."[2]
Caffeine is a part of our everyday life and yet, because it is a drug, we
should be aware of the forms and amounts in which we consume it, of its mental
and physical effects, and of the problems that may arise from its abuse.

Caffeine is pharmacologically defined as a xanthine alkaloid related to
two other widely-used drugs called theophylline and theobromine. All of these
drugs stimulate the central nervous system, the heart, and the kidneys.[3]
Although heavy drinkers are known to develop a certain amount of tolerance for
caffeine, excessive use can lead to a disorder known as caffeinism, the symptoms of which are similar to those of an anxiety attack. The symptoms are
"nervousness, irritability, agitation, headache, tachypnea (rapid respiration),
tremulousness, reflex hyperexcitability and occasional muscle twitching."[4]

----

[1]R. M. Gilbert, et al., "Caffeine Content of Beverages as Consumed."
Canadian Medical Association Journal, 114 (1976), 205.

[2]Candace J. Gallant, et al., "Caffeine: A Hazardous Drug?" Canadian
Pharmaceutical Journal, (1981), p. 212.

[3]Gallant, p. 213.

[4]Gallant, p. 213.

2

Because caffeine is an addictive drug, the user may experience uncomfortable withdrawal symptoms (dysphoria) upon reducing or eliminating his or her caffeine intake. The symptoms of caffeine withdrawal closely resemble those of caffeinism.[5] Caffeine is also known to constrict blood vessels in the brain (cranial vasoconstriction), raise blood pressure, heart rate, fatty acid and cholesterol levels.[6]

The pharmaceutical and medical technicalities of the preceding paragraph are not likely to mean much to most people. For the average Canadian, a more obvious source of concern will be the physical and mental disorders that can result from overuse of caffeine. Overuse is nevertheless hard to define. One of the problems in caffeine research arises from the various ways and dosage in which the drug is consumed. It is found in coffee, tea, cola, and other drinks, in cocoa and chocolate products, and in many prescription and non-prescription drugs such as stay-awake pills and medications for headaches, colds, and allergies. The following table illustrates the difficulty in assigning standard caffeine levels to different beverages and foods:

Variation of Caffeine Content of Common Sources

Item Consumed	Caffeine per serving (mg)*
Coffee	
Percolator	39-168
Filter	56-176
Instant	29-117
Tea	8-91
Cola Drinks	1-65
Cocoa	5-40
Chocolate bar	25

*Serving volume ranged from 140-250 ml for coffees, teas, and cocoa; 140-335 ml for colas. Chocolate bars were approximately 35g.[7]

[5]Gallant, p. 213.

[6]Gallant, p. 213

[7]Gallant, p. 212

3

This variation makes it impossible to arrive at an average caffeine consumption in milligrams. We can best conceive of the average caffeine intake by considering instead the number of caffeine-containing beverages consumed. Statistics show that the average person in Ontario, fifteen years of age or over, consumes 2.6 cups of coffee and 1.9 cups of tea daily. The same survey showed that 25 percent of Ontario's adults drink five or more cups of coffee or tea each day.[8]

Some of the effects of caffeine abuse are extremely serious. Besides its evident relatively mild results (such as sleeplessness), the drug has been linked to major problems including cancer. For example, according to the Canadian Pharmaceutical Journal,

> Caffeine has been linked with cardiovascular disease, benign breast lumps, cancer of the lower urinary tract and pancreas, gastric ulceration, cardiovascular disease, teratogenicity, as well as with the more familiar problems of irritability and diuresis.[9]

The same source connects caffeine with pregnancy complications such as spontaneous abortion, stillbirth, and prematurity.[10] It is also possible that cyanosis and birth defects are related to a mother's excessive use of caffeine. Scientists who injected large quantities of coffee into the stomachs of laboratory animals have concluded that the caffeine crosses the placenta into the fetus and causes body deformities.[11]

---

[8] Gallant, p. 212.

[9] Gallant, p. 212.

[10] Gallant, p. 214.

[11] Marc Leepson, "Caffeine Controversy." Editorial Research Reports, 214 (1980), 740.

4

   Many problems naturally arise concerning the validity of applying such
experimental evidence to what happens in humans. The laboratory animals
were fed large doses of caffeine all at once, but people generally drink
coffee relatively slowly, and several times throughout the day, not all at
once. Also, the large doses injected into the animals are, for their body
weight, well above the amounts humans consume. It is also not known if the
test animals can metabolize caffeine in their bodies the same way that
humans do.[12] As a result, health experts claim that experimental evidence
cannot definitely prove caffeine has caused or can cause birth defects in
humans; it can only support the theory.

   Caffeine's effect on children is not merely prenatal, however. The
caffeine content of colas and chocolate seems minimal, but it is important
to consider the child's body weight relative to that of an adult:

> A 27 kg child who in a day consumes five servings of
> Pepsi-Cola and three small chocolate bars (which con-
> tain approximately 25 mg of caffeine each) would be
> ingesting more than 7.7 mg of caffeine per kg of body
> weight, which is considerably more than the caffeine-
> dependent adult need drink.[13]

It is conceivable that a child could form a daily caffeine habit in this way.
Hyperactivity is considered one of the consequences. Parents' awareness of
the hazard is advisable, and young people today can be better educated about
caffeine use than was possible for previous generations of children.

   Of course, no drug becomes popular if it has only adverse consequences.
Even the most familiar and tolerable ill effects of caffeine would have greatly
discouraged or limited its use had there been no perceived benefits to the user.

---

[12]Facts about Caffeine, Addiction Research Foundation (1980).

[13]"Caffeine in Cola." Canadian Consumer, 10:1 (1980), 30.

5

Besides mere habit, then, the main reason for widespread heavy consumption of caffeine is the belief that it enhances mental alertness. It is widely considered to promote speed and clarity of thought, to assist intellectual effort, and to reduce drowsiness or fatigue.[14] However, modern psychiatry has cast doubts on the mental and psychological benefits of caffeine. In an article published in the Canadian Medical Association Journal, for example, K. Z. Bezchlibnyk and J. J. Jeffries express concern about both the mental and the physical effects of caffeine on psychiatric patients. They conclude that the results of using this drug are often not considered because caffeine is "the most popular psychotropic drug (not excluding alcohol) in North America."[15] They also believe that caffeine is a hazard in psychiatric treatment because it may lead to mistaken diagnoses or even aggravate an existing condition: "Caffeinism or caffeine withdrawal may be indistinguishable from anxiety neurosus, and each condition may potentiate the other."[16] These experts note too that heavy caffeine consumption has a high correlation with incidence of anxiety, psychosis, depression and schizophrenia.[17]

Likewise, it is generally believed that caffeine cures alcoholic intoxication. However, although it does reduce stomach tissues' absorption of ethanol, it cannot restore sobriety or co-ordination to someone who is already drunk.[18]

---

[14]Gallant, p. 213.

[15]K. Z. Bezchlibnyk and J. J. Jeffries, "Should Psychiatric Patients Drink Coffee?" Canadian Medical Association Journal, 124 (1981), 357.

[16]Bezchlibnyk, 357.

[17]Bezchlibnyk, 357.

[18]Gallant, p. 214.

6

Fluid intake of any kind may help the body recover gradually from excessive alcoholic ingestion, but coffee apparently has no special virtue in this regard. Such popular misconceptions illustrate how little we know about what caffeine does in our bodies.

Unfortunately, there has so far been insufficient research into the claims made for the benefits of caffeine use. Nor has it been possible to demonstrate whether taste, habit, real effects, imagined effects, or some other reason is actually the prime inducement to caffeine abuse. Further investigation of this "positive" side of the drug's use, together with continued research into the suspected medical and other consequences, may eventually resolve some of our uncertainties. Addiction Research Foundation publications such as Drug Use and Driving and Interaction of Alcohol and Other Drugs include bibliographical references to international research in the field.

Many scientific discoveries and theories now relate high caffeine consumption to various human disorders. While studies have not shown conclusively that caffeine is solely responsible for such symptoms, the drug would probably be available only by prescription if it were being introduced today. As research continues, public health authorities would be well advised to recommend caution in the use of caffeine. At the very least, the continuing accumulation of evidence about its dangers should be made better known. Moreover, caffeine-containing products should perhaps be labelled, like cigarettes, as potentially hazardous to health.

7

List of Works Consulted

Barnes, T. H., et al., eds. Drug Use and Driving: A bibliography of the scientific literature on the effects of drugs other than ethanol on driving or simulated driving of automobiles, piloting or simulated piloting of aircraft, and driving-related mental and motor performance. Toronto: Addiction Research Foundation, 1974.

Bezchlibnyk, J. Z., and J. J. Jeffries. "Should Psychiatric Patients Drink Coffee?" Canadian Medical Association Journal, 124 (1981), 357-58.

"Caffeine in Cola." Canadian Consumer, 10:1 (1980), 28-30.

Facts about Caffeine. Toronto: Addiction Research Foundation, 1980.

Gallant, Candace J., et al. "Caffeine: A Hazardous Drug?" Canadian Parmaceutical Journal, (1981), pp. 212-15.

Gilbert, R. M., et al. "Caffeine Content of Beverages as Consumed." Canadian Medical Association Journal, 114 (1976), 205-08.

Leepson, Marc. "Caffeine Controversy." Editorial Research Reports. Washington: Congressional Quarterly Inc., 214 (1980), 737-56.

Polacsek, E., et al., eds. Interaction of Alcohol and Other Drugs: An annotated bibliography of the interaction of ethanol and other chemical compounds normally absent in vivo. Toronto: Addiction Research Foundation, 1970.

31

Examinations, Letters, and Reports

Though often letters, speeches, and reports must be written in a hurry and,
because of the countless considerations that clear writing involves, are bound in
some way to fall short of the full intended meaning, conscientious people will
always regret this necessity and arrange their affairs as far as possible to avoid it.
— Robert Graves and Alan Hodge, *The Reader Over Your Shoulder*

Course assignments are not so different from final examinations or the practical, business, or technical writing that you may do outside of school. A letter of recommendation, for example, is both informative and persuasive, just as many school papers are. It offers information about a person's past (usually narrative) and about that person's present (often descriptive) in order to make an argument for his or her future. A letter in which you apply for a job is a kind of specialized personal essay, not entirely different from some personal writing that you will do in a composition class except that in the letter of application you may pay closer attention to your audience.

Practical and vocational forms of writing are different from in-course assignments, however, in at least one major respect. In a sense, such writing is not your own. Ordinarily, the occasion and the purpose are determined by some institutional need, not by your own choice. Even essay examinations in school may be expected to conform to a kind of established, non-personal form. They are, at any rate, not occasions for free-swinging experiments in writing. In most forms of practical and vocational writing, your writing is a medium serving a company, an institution, or something other than your own personal preferences. You can still be yourself, but you may also need to fulfill the expectations of others.

The following pages discuss some of what is expected in various forms of practical and vocational writing: examinations, business letters, and reports.

31.1

Exam

31.1 ESSAY EXAMINATION ANSWERS

Answering an examination question in essay form is similar to writing a short expository or argumentative paper. In studying for the course, you have become familiar with a fairly wide range of information; to answer a specific question, you must recall the relevant material, organize it, and present it in essay form.

Reading the Questions

Because most examinations have a time limit, students often begin writing feverishly after no more than a glance at the questions. The results of such frantic haste are usually disappointing. You can use the allotted time far more profitably if you take a few minutes at the start to read all the questions and directions. If a choice is offered, decide which questions you are best prepared to answer and cross out the others. If the questions have different values, plan the amount of time to spend on each: a question worth 10 percent, for example, should not take up 30 percent of your time. Try to save a few minutes at the end to check your answers.

Before beginning to write, be sure to read the question thoroughly. Many answers are unsatisfactory simply because students misinterpret or forget the question in their hurry to fill the paper with words. Examine each question carefully and decide what kind of answer it requires. Don't misread or overlook key words. Notice in the following questions how a change in one word would affect the whole question:

Explain the effects [causes] of the Quebec Act of 1774.
Describe the reproduction [digestion; development] of the frog.
Discuss the structure [sources; significance] of *Moby Dick*.

Since the verb often determines the nature of the answer, take particular care to interpret it properly. Here are some of the verbs instructors commonly use in essay questions:

analyse: give main divisions or elements, emphasizing essentials
classify: arrange into main classes or divisions
compare: point out likenesses
contrast: point out differences
criticize: give your opinion as to good and bad features
define: explain the meaning, distinguish from similar terms
describe: name the features in chronological or spatial order
discuss: examine in detail
evaluate: give your opinion of the value or validity
explain: make clear, give reasons for
illustrate: give one or more examples of
interpret: give the meaning or significance
justify: defend, show to be right
review: examine on a broad scale
summarize: briefly go over the essentials

Writing the Answers

Before beginning to write an answer to a question, remember that the instructor expects you to demonstrate *specific* knowledge on the subject. A succession of vague generalities will not be acceptable. Even if you are discussing a fairly broad general topic, support whatever generalizations you make with specific illustrations. Do not omit essential particulars because you assume the *instructor* is familiar with them already; the main purpose of the examination is to find out what knowledge *you* have acquired.

A scratch outline (see chapter 20) of the main points you plan to develop in your answer may be useful as a guide in writing. But whether you make an outline or not, make a concentrated effort to set your thoughts down in some logical order: all the sentences should relate to the question asked, and each should lead to the next in an orderly fashion. Many essay answers are unsuccessful because students, although well-informed, present information in a haphazard, unrelated fashion, giving the impression that they are thoroughly confused on the subject. It is often useful to repeat the key terms of the questions and the main points you'll be making about the terms in a thesis statement at the beginning of your answer. This can serve as an organizational guide for your writing.

Remember that the *length* of the answer is not the criterion of its worth: choosing the right facts and organizing them sensibly will impress the reader far more. Avoid throwing in unrelated material just to demonstrate your knowledge or to disguise your ignorance of more pertinent information. Since the time you have to write your answer is limited, you should confine yourself strictly to what you know about the specific questions asked. Your instructor is not likely to give you much credit for a short essay on the wrong subject, no matter how good it may be.

Examination answers should be written in acceptable general English. Although instructors do not expect an essay written in class to be as fully developed and polished in style as one written at home, they do expect it to be adequate in grammar, usage, and the mechanics of writing. Even if a paper is otherwise accurate, frequent misspellings do much to lower the reader's opinion of it. Take particular care to spell and use correctly any technical terms or names that have been used in the course: *myosis, mercantile, assize, neurosis, imagery, Lamarck, Malthus, Schopenhauer.* Instructors are understandably disturbed if they think you have paid scant attention to terms you have heard in class and read in the text numerous times. Careful proofreading of the answers will help you eliminate any careless errors you may have made and will also give you a chance to fill in gaps in information.

31.1

Exam

Examples of Essay Answers

Printed below are essay answers in biology, history, and literature. Read each question carefully, decide what sort of answer is required, and compare the two student answers. Then read the criticisms that follow. The sentences in the answers are numbered to facilitate discussion.

QUESTION: Define *dominant* as it is used in genetics.

ANSWER A: (1) In genetics, dominant is the opposite of recessive. (2) Different characteristics are inherited by the individual by means of genes acquired from the male and female parents. (3) These genes are arranged, or carried, on chromosomes, and are paired, one from each parent. (4) A good deal is still unknown about the behavior of genes, although the science of genetics is making rapid progress. (5) Gregor Mendel, a monk, made discoveries in heredity by doing experiments with sweet peas. (6) He found that certain traits are stronger (dominant) and others are weaker (recessive). (7) Therefore, if two genes carry the same characteristic, one will be dominant over the other. (8) Examples of this are dark eyes, normal color vision, etc.

ANSWER B: (1) The term *dominant* as used in genetics refers to that situation in which one gene in a pair takes precedence over another in determining a given characteristic in the individual. (2) For example, if a child inherits a gene for blue eyes from one parent and for brown eyes from the other, he will have brown eyes. (3) This is because the brown-eyed gene is *dominant*; the blue is *recessive*. (4) He still carries both genes and may transmit either to his offspring, but one has masked the effect of the other in his physical appearance. (5) Clear dominance does not occur in all pairings, however. (6) Sometimes *mixed dominance* occurs, as in the case of sweet peas, where a cross between a red and a white parent produces pink offspring. (7) Some cases of dominance are *sex-linked*; the gene for color blindness in humans, for instance, is dominant in the male and recessive in the female.

CRITICISM: Answer A contains irrelevant general information (sentences 2-5) and does not give a clear definition of *dominant*. You cannot explain the meaning of a word simply by naming its opposite (sentence 1). "Stronger" and "weaker" (sentence 6) are poor synonyms because they have such a variety of meanings. The answer also misleads by oversimplification: sentence 7 implies that complete dominance occurs in *all* pairings of genes. It is also not clear to what species of life the two examples in the last sentence (dark eyes and normal color vision) refer.

Answer B is satisfactory. The term is clearly defined in the first sentence. Sentences 2-4 give an example of its use, distinguish it from its opposite, and add an important qualification. Sentences 5-

7 note two important variants in the meaning of the term. There is no irrelevant material.

QUESTION: Compare and contrast English and Spanish colonial methods in the New World.

ANSWER A: (1) The Plymouth colony suffered many hardships in the early years of its existence. (2) This was also true of the Roanoke colony, but it eventually failed and did not survive. (3) The climate was more promising there, but it seemed as if the kind of people it included, like gentlemen unused to work, adventurers, and renegades, did not have the patience and religious fervor of the New England settlers. (4) The same was true of the Spanish colonies in Florida and elsewhere — the climate was good, but the men were selfish and had no direction. (5) The Spanish were more cruel toward the Indians than the English, and there was nothing constructive in their aims.

ANSWER B: (1) The Spanish generally thought of the New World as a reservoir of riches to be taped. (2) The great Spanish conquerors, like Cortez and Pizarro, were explorer-adventurers whose main aim was to subjugate the native population and wrench from them whatever riches and power they possessed. (3) The Spanish method was usually to impose a military dictatorship upon a restive populace; the domination depended on military force. (4) The English, on the other hand, thought of the New World colonies as a *permanent* extension of English civilization. (5) Their methods were not to immediately extract native riches, but to plant the seeds of English life in the new continent. (6) Unlike the Spaniards, the English generally emigrated in family units, placated rather than subdued the native inhabitants, invested labor and capital in the New World soil, and awaited long-term fruits. (7) Settlement was their aim rather than exploitation.

CRITICISM: More than half of answer A (sentences 1-3) contrasts *two English colonies* rather than *English and Spanish colonial methods*. Mention of climate in sentences 3 and 4 is also irrelevant to a question dealing with methods. "Selfish" and "had no direction" need further explanation, as do "cruel toward the Indians" and "nothing constructive."

Answer B is much more satisfactory than A. The basic differences in aim and the consequent differences in method are fairly well stated. The first section of the answer (sentences 1-3) describes Spanish methods; the second (sentences 4-7) presents the significant differences in English aim and method.

31.1

Exam

QUESTION: Explain the significance of E. J. Pratt's *Brébeuf and His Brethren* in the development of Canadian poetry.

ANSWER A: (1) *Brébeuf and His Brethren* by E. J. Pratt was published in 1940 in the midst of WW II. (2) It is a long poem about the Jesuits. (3) It won the Governor-General's Award for poetry and

has been widely praised. (4) Among Pratt's contemporaries were F. R. Scott, A. J. M. Smith, and Dorothy Livesay. (5) It is an important poem because it is concerned with
1) Canadian history
2) myth-making
3) realism
4) narrative
(6) Other writers in this tradition are Oliver Goldsmith, Dorothy Livesay, Isabella Valancy Crawford, Archibald Lampman, and Don Gutteridge. (7) *Brébeuf and His Brethren* combines in a single narrative all the themes of the earlier narratives. (8) Therefore, it is truly significant.

ANSWER B: (1) E. J. Pratt's *Brébeuf and His Brethren*, the winner of the Governor-General's award for poetry in 1940, is an important landmark in Canadian poetry. (2) A narrative poem describing the martyrdom of the Jesuit missionaries of seventeenth-century Canada, Pratt's poem represents the high point of a tradition of Canadian narrative poetry begun in the late eighteenth century. (3) Nineteenth-century narratives such as Oliver Goldsmith's *The Rising Village* (1825) and Isabella Valancy Crawford's *Malcolm's Katie* (1884) introduce contrasted states of order versus chaos, nature versus civilization, and isolation versus community; a similar treatment may be observed in *Brébeuf and His Brethren*. Abandoning the vague imagery and sentimental diction of many of his predecessors, Pratt introduces a mosaic structure and a new level of documentary detail which focus attention on the most dramatic incidents involving the Jesuits in Canada. In his concern with re-examining and re-evaluating the past, Pratt becomes a contemporary myth-maker. Consequently, *Brébeuf and His Brethren* is the most important model for narrative poems by such later Canadian writers as Dorothy Livesay, Don Gutteridge, and John Newlove.

CRITICISM: In Answer A, sentences 1 and 4 do not specifically relate to the question. The heart of the answer seems to be sentence 5, but the unexplained list of headings conveys nothing. If these points are important, each should be developed in a separate sentence or two. Sentences 6 and 7 also seem to be relevant but are vague. *What* were the poems and *when* were they published? *What* themes from earlier narratives does Pratt use?

In Answer B, the points merely listed in A are developed and made specific. The relation of the poem to both earlier and later poetic traditions is explained. All sentences are relevant and are well related to each other.

31.2 BUSINESS LETTERS

Although letter-writing is not always taught in composition

courses, it is one of the most important forms of written expression. In many situations, letters are the only means you have to make yourself heard. They deserve your best effort.

What you say in a letter and the way you say it will depend on your purpose, the person you are writing to, and, above all, upon the way you customarily express yourself. Courtesy and reasonableness, even in a letter of complaint, are always best in business correspondence. Beyond that, you should be familiar with the standard conventions of correspondence, so that the form and appearance of your letters will make the intended impression. The form established for business letters is standard for most kinds of formal correspondence.

Neatness, clarity, and directness are the chief virtues of a business letter. It should include all relevant information (such as dates, prices, description of merchandise) and should be as brief as possible and still be clear. The tone should be courteous, even if you are complaining about an error or poor service.

The sample letter of application on page 525 illustrates the form and tone of a typical business letter. Notice the position and punctuation of the heading, inside address, greeting (salutation), and close.

General Appearance

Select stationery of appropriate size and good quality, with envelopes to match. Good stationery costs little more than an inferior grade, and it will make a much better impression on the person who receives your letter. For business letters the standard sheet is 21.5 cm × 28 cm, the same size as regular typing paper.

Typed letters are expected in business correspondence, and they are increasingly popular for personal correspondence. In typing your letter, leave generous margins and centre the body of the letter so that the page will look well balanced. Space paragraphs distinctly, using either block or indented form. Block paragraphs are set flush with the left margin of the letter; they are separated by a line of space, as shown in the sample on page 521. For indented paragraphs, begin five spaces from the left-hand margin. Be consistent in form. If a letter runs to more than one page, use a separate sheet of paper for each page and number the pages at the top.

The heading.   A heading should be typed in the upper right-hand corner, giving the writer's complete address and date. The standard form is the block pattern, with end punctuation omitted. The name

31.2

Let

of the city, the province, and the date are typed as illustrated below:

```
902 21 St. S.W.
Calgary, AB    [or Alta.]
T2M 0L5

1983 01 05   [or January 5, 1983]
```

If you use a letterhead which includes the address, type the date below it, flush with the right-hand margin or centred, depending on the design of the letterhead.

Inside address and greeting.   The inside address of a business letter gives the full name and address of the person or firm to whom it is directed. It appears flush with the left-hand margin, at least one line below the last line of the heading. No punctuation is used at the ends of the lines. If you wish to mention the person's title or position in the firm, put the designation immediately below the name in the inside address:

```
Ms. Linda Peterson
Personnel Director
Allen, Swift and Company
4863 Portage Avenue
Winnipeg, MB   [or Man.]
R3L 1B1
```

The greeting, or *salutation*, appears below the inside address, separated from it by a line of space. In business letters, it is followed by a colon. If the letter is addressed to a particular individual in a firm, you may use either the name or an impersonal greeting:

```
Dr. Mr. Keiser: [or Dear Sir:]     Dear Miss Jenkins: [or Dear Madam:]
```

Until recently it was customary to use the masculine form of address (*Gentlemen: Dear Sir:*) if the letter was addressed to the firm as a whole or to an individual whose name was unknown. Since the recipient is just as likely to be a woman as a man, however, alternative salutations are becoming more widely used. One acceptable salutation is simply the name of the company or, if appropriate, the title of the individual or department:

```
Dear Sir or Madam:    Dear Editor:    Dear Matthews Camera Company:
```

Close and signature.   A conventional expression called the *complimentary close* is used at the end of the letter. Only the first word of the close is capitalized and a comma customarily follows. The general tone of the letter will suggest how formal the close should be:

Formal	Less formal
Yours truly,	Sincerely yours,
Yours very truly,	Sincerely,
Respectfully yours,	Yours sincerely,

The close can be either flush with the left-hand margin or in the middle of the page.

The signature is always written in longhand below the close. For clarity, however, you should type your name below your signature. A woman may indicate her marital status in parentheses if she wishes, but this practice is dying out among businesswomen.

Addressing the envelope.   Both the address of the person to whom you are writing and your own address should be clear and complete on the front of the envelope. A block style — with the left-hand margin even — is the standard form for both addresses.

No punctuation is used at the end of the lines in this form. A comma is used between the names of a city and the province, which are put on the same line; the postal code is placed directly below; a space separates the second letter from the second number.

```
Grande Prairie, AB
T8V 3X7
```

When you abbreviate street designations, use the standard forms (*St.* for *Street, Ave.* for *Avenue, Blvd.* for *Boulevard*). For names of provinces, use those abbreviations given in your dictionary (*Alta., Ont.*) or the new two-letter abbreviations being introduced by Canada Post (AB, ON).

Use an envelope that matches your stationery and fold the letter to fit. With long business envelopes, a standard sheet (21.5 cm × 28 cm) is folded horizontally into three sections. With short business envelopes, it is folded once across the middle and then twice in the other direction.

Some Criteria for Business Letters

Private (or *personal*) letters are likely to be extended, long-distance forms of private conversation, though some may in the course of time come to have public uses and be publicly displayed. On the other hand, *business* letters are a part of public discourse; they are typically not written forms of private or intimate conversation. They are written, usually, where there is work to be done, where public decisions are to be made and registered, where records must be kept. But that doesn't mean that official letters must, as a consequence, be impersonal, cold, or non-human.

Many public letters — letters of recommendation, job applications, information letters, and others — are stylized, ritualized performances. Their authors sometimes fall into the habit of using a

31.2

Let

stiff, impersonal style that is remote and official-sounding, or they lapse into the jargon of a particular trade or profession, or they fall into the strange world where bureaucratic dialects are accepted as good English, where simple things become complex and complex things become impossible.

It's not uncommon, for example, to find business, professional, technical, and semi-technical letters depending excessively on current fad words—*parameter*, for example, and *viable* and *dialogue*. It's easy enough to fall into the habit of overusing some words and phrases, such as these:

> *After a dialogue with* (for *after talking with*)
> *Implementing a decision* (for *deciding*)
> *Making a survey in depth* (for *studying*)
> *Causative factor* (for *cause*)
> *Optimum* (for *most* or *best*)

The list might go on and on. There are at least three reasons why we all sometimes use such stylized, pompous, trite, or unnecessary words and phrases. In the first place, we see so much of such language—in income tax instructions, political prose, legal documents, sales agreements, and elsewhere—that it's natural for us to conclude that there is an "official" kind of language—a special dialect that should be imitated. See 28.1, page 434, "Big Words" —Stilted Language. What's actually needed, however, is clear and direct language.

In the second place, many people who write business, professional, and technical letters have to write *many* such letters. If a person has to write, let's say, thirty or forty letters in a single day, it's certainly understandable if he or she relies on certain phrasings and words, repeating them again and again. It's understandable, but it's not desirable: when a writer depends upon certain habits of phrasing, then those habits of language become binding, and limit what a writer can say.

Third, we often depend upon standardized forms when we write public letters. If you have to write twelve letters in one afternoon requesting payment for a bill, it's likely that you will use the same or nearly the same form in each letter. Many companies, in fact, have some standardized forms that can be used in writing the various company letters that go out from the company. If we often depend upon standardized forms, then we may often depend also upon standardized, "official-sounding" language.

Natural Style.   A business letter does not have to be written in an "official" language. Even when you are writing as a representative of a company, for example, you can still sound like yourself. That doesn't mean that you should write public letters that are cute or highly personal or full of folksy, backslapping chatter.

The letter below was written in response to a customer's letter of complaint about gas mileage in a new car recently purchased from an automobile manufacturer's sales dealer. The customer's letter was mailed directly to the manufacturer's public representative in Oshawa. The representative sent the letter back to a local company agent who replied to the customer's original letter (the names have been changed to protect the innocent and the guilty):

1982 04 15

Mr. Patrick G. Wayne
7313 Arena Drive
Saskatoon, Saskatchewan
S7N 0W2

Dear Mr. Wayne:

This will acknowledge receipt of your letter of 25 March to Oshawa which has been referred to this office for handling.

We have been unable to contact you by phone during normal working hours; however, we have reviewed your gas consumption problem with the service manager at Westside Reo Motor Company, Mr. Ted Warsaw. We suggest you call him for an appointment that can be arranged when our service department manager will be at the dealership in order that he may implement procedures for checking out your vehicle.

We do thank you for writing.

Very truly yours,

B. M. Bell

B. M. Bell
Customer Relations Manager

31.2

Let

Now this is not a "bad" letter. It is typical of much business correspondence, and its meaning is plain enough. But since all letters are written by human beings to be read by other human beings, they might as well *sound* human. The opening sentence of the above letter, for example, might just as easily read as follows:

```
I have the letter you sent to our Oshawa office.
```

or

```
Our Oshawa office has sent me your letter.
```

In the original opening sentence the customer has been turned over to "this office" for "handling," which sounds altogether impersonal. Nowhere does the original letter acknowledge that the customer is a thinking person who *might* be right in his complaints about the car. A new second sentence or an addition to the first might be helpful:

```
I have the letter you sent to our Oshawa office, and I am

sorry to learn of the problems you have had with your new Reo.
```

or

```
Our Oshawa office has sent me your letter.  I hope we can

work out the problems you have had with your new Reo.
```

In the second paragraph, the original letter gets a bit better. There is, however, no good reason for the writer to use *we; I* would do as well. *Vehicle* in the last sentence is too vague. *Car* is more specific. The customer, seeing the word *car*, might believe that the letter writer actually knew which kind of vehicle was under discussion.

A human being ought to show up even in the most public letters. Impersonal language is not more accurate or official than natural, human language.

Providing a Context.   Readers should know the context in which a letter is written. They should know why a letter is written, its origins, or what the letter is responding to. They need to be able to see your connections and follow the sequence of your thoughts. If they can't, then your letter is likely to seem either abrupt and rude or tyrannical, expecting readers to agree with your assertions simply because they are yours.

Consider a typical good example. This letter is from a university student to an attorney; the writer is asking the reader to participate in a survey:

51 Farnham Road
Winnipeg, MB
R2J 2R1
1982 10 21

Mr. J. R. Abernathy
Abernathy & Swartz
28 Woodrow Place
Winnipeg, MB
R3G 1J3

Dear Mr. Abernathy:

You and several other prominent local lawyers were recently
quoted in the Free Press in a discussion of current problems
in education, especially problems in language use. The discussion and your comments so interested me that I decided to
write my term paper in Political Science 1953 on "The Legal
Profession's View of Today's Pre-law Education."

I hope you will be willing to complete the enclosed questionnaire. All you will need to do is to check yes or no in response to each of the questions. Your answers will be kept
confidential. If you wish, I will send you a summary of the
results based on my survey of fifty lawyers in this area.

Your answers, of course, will be useful to me in writing my
paper. More than that, I believe they will be useful in discussions of changes in education. I hope you will check the
answers and return the questionnaire in the enclosed self-
addressed envelope.

Sincerely yours,

Stacy Johnston

The letter provides the information necessary for the reader to
understand the context. The first sentence tells how the writer, a
stranger, came to be writing, and the second sentence establishes
the occasion. The second paragraph makes a specific request and
states the terms the writer offers. The last paragraph tells the
potential uses of the information that the writer is seeking.
Throughout the letter the writer has explained his mission clearly,
making it possible for the recipient to respond easily and conveniently. The sample letter of *complaint* printed on page 527 has
these same qualities of clarity, simplicity, and courtesy.

31.2

Let

Whether you are writing to an institution or to a person, to a
stranger or to an acquaintance, be sure that you tell readers enough
for them to follow the sequence of your thoughts. The sample
letters that follow show you what other people characteristically do

when they write certain kinds of public letters; both the content and the tone may help you in your own letter writing.

Letters of Application

Most prospective employers now prefer to receive a short letter of application accompanied by a résumé. Although the letter should be fairly brief, it is often helpful to make references to why you want to work for a particular company or what you feel you can offer the company. The letter should follow standard business-letter format (see page 525).

A résumé is a one-page summary of pertinent information about yourself, including personal data, educational background, and employment record. The form shown on page 526 would usually be considered acceptable, although it is not always necessary to define your objectives. It is a good idea to indicate the nature of the work you did at your places of employment, along with any specific accomplishments. You should also list any awards or honors and publications, if appropriate. If you wish to name references or people who would be willing to recommend you, a list can be inserted at the end of the résumé.

Always ask the permission of people you list as references. Give their complete addresses and correct titles (Professor, Dr., Mrs.). *Mr., Mrs., Ms.*, and *Dr.* are the only titles that are abbreviated. All others are written in full.

If you are asked to include documents (such as photographs, transcripts of academic records, or photostats), use a crush-proof envelope. If you want the enclosures returned to you, include a self-addressed, stamped envelope.

Letters to Editors and Public Figures

People in a democratic society often wish to express their opinions to newspapers, magazines, or influential public figures. Such communications should be written in standard business-letter form and should be brief and pointed. Even if you are expressing disagreement with some opinion or policy, try to be reasonable and courteous. Your letter is much more likely to have the desired effect if it relies on facts and logic than it if presents an impassioned subjective reaction. Formal greetings and closings are usual in these letters.

Consult the appropriate section of a dictionary or an etiquette book for the proper forms of address for cabinet ministers, members of Parliament, and other governmental officials.

856 East Hillside Drive   **Heading**
Burnaby, BC
V5B 1K4
1982 06 15

Dr. Robert Gruen   **Inside address**
Director of Research
Bloch-Peterson Foundation
780 West Augusta Boulevard
Vancouver, BC
V0N 1B3

Dear Dr. Gruen: **Salutation**

   I would like to apply for the position of bacteriologist
advertised by the Foundation in the current Journal of Pathology.

   I am currently employed in epidemological research with the
Vancouver Board of Health. My work involves assisting Dr.
Lucille Lesiak, mainly in her study of communicable diseases
among school-age children. I am responsible for the experimental and analytical laboratory aspects of that project, and
for supervising a small staff of technicians and clerical as-
sistants. This valuable experience has confirmed my desire to
pursue a career in applied research in microbiology.

   While completing my M.Sc. studies in bacteriology at UBC,
I also took courses in computing and in technical writing to
keep abreast of current scientific techniques and trends. I
have some practical and theoretical background in statistical   **Body**
analysis as well, and biological lab experience obtained at
McGill and the University of Guelph.

   The enclosed résumé outlines details of my academic and
professional background. Please let me know if you require
any additional information, or if you would like the names of
people who could comment on the quality of my work.

   Because of my training and on-the-job experience, I feel
confident that I could contribute to the Foundation's research
program. I would like very much to speak personally with you
about the advertised position. I am available for an interview
at your convenience.

                        Sincerely yours,   **Close**

                        Joanne Trestrail

                        Joanne Trestrail

JOANNE MARY TRESTRAIL

Address	856 East Hillside Drive Burnaby, BC V5B 1K4 (213) 267-1927
Personal	Birthdate: April 30, 1957 (Lennoxville, Québec) Marital Status: Single Health: Excellent Objective: Applied research, especially in some area of disease control and prevention
Experience	June 1980-present Vancouver Board of Health Assisting Dr. Lucille Lesiak in epidemological studies, concentrating on communicable diseases among Vancouver elementary-school children. Analytical laboratory work and supervisory responsibilities. Summer 1979 McGill University, Montréal, Québec Helped Dr. Joseph Roth prepare the statistical tables for his recently published <u>Tropical Diseases</u> Summer 1978 Laboratory Assistant, Department of Bacteriology University of Guelph, Guelph, Ontario References available on request
Education	1979-80 University of British Columbia, Vancouver Master of Science in Bacteriology 1975-79 University of Guelph, Guelph, Ontario Bachelor of Science in Biology Summer 1978 McGill University Seminar in microbiology and statistical techniques
Organizations and Activities	League of Women Voters Apollo Music Club Capilano Tennis Club Local Canvassing Co-ordinator, Canadian Mental Health Association

Director of Customer Complaints
Bolton's Stores Inc.
197 Townley Blvd.
Fredericton, NB
E3A 4N4

Dear Sir or Madam:

Thank you for delivering the FX-31 pocket calculator
that I ordered through your 24-hour phone service.
I was pleased to find that you carried the specific
model that I needed.

However, I'm sorry to say that the calculator has
not produced the results that were advertised. Instead of showing eight digits, this machine has five.
The independent memory bank also does not record more
than one entry.

I am sure that this particular instrument is not
typical of your products and that you will see that
the enclosed FX-31 is properly repaired or replaced.

As a regular customer of Bolton's, I am generally
pleased with your merchandise and hope to continue
shopping at your store.

Sincerely,

John Neal

31.2

Let

31.3 REPORTS

A *report* presents the results of an investigation. Almost any subject can be the basis for a report, and there are many types of reports, but the term is usually applied to the detailed presentation and analysis of *technical information* for an immediate *practical administrative purpose*. A report might be submitted to an office manager, for example, on anything from the costs of photocopying to the advantages of changing the staff pension plan. A town council could require a report on anything from police uniforms to snow-removal methods. Reports in academic settings present the results of scientific laboratory experiments, of scholarly research programs, and of individual projects in fields such as geography or business administration. Common to all such report-writing situations are thorough research (collection of technical data), clear summary, and objective analysis. In other words, a typical report organizes and simplifies some specialized body of facts to enable the reader (or client) to make some decision or take some action.

Some Criteria for Reports

Three particular qualities of reports are worth special notice. You may remember discussions in various places throughout this book of basic differences among kinds of writing. Some kinds of writing are personal or expressive; they give authors the opportunity to make themselves known. Some kinds are active or persuasive. Some kinds are referential; they explain or account for things without necessarily attempting to persuade readers.

In a report, the author may be deeply involved with the subject, and he or she is surely responsible for the report. But although an author may appear in a report as a spokesperson or as an investigator (even using the first-person), the author is not part of the subject. A report is not meant to be an occasion for self-expression. Neither is it usually meant to be persuasive, though some reports end with recommendations. More often than not, a report simply examines or discusses a subject; decisions or actions are made by the readers.

For example, in a business, one department—say market research—may report to another—product development—on the habits and preferences of a certain segment of the market, without recommending how a certain kind of product be developed. A research report that you are likely to write in college may suggest various courses of action to resolve an issue and what you think the results might be, but you wouldn't necessarily have to recommend which course should be followed. The sample report on pages 531-42, prepared by a student as a technical writing project, happens to be in the form of a proposal. That is, the information has been collected and presented in order to support the author's recommendation to the town council. But in all other respects — layout, style, factual detail, and so forth — it is similar to reports in which the writers' own ideas are kept in the background.

Finally, because reports are *referential* and intended to convey *information*, they are almost always based on some research. Characteristically, they describe an investigation, and don't depend on meditation or personal opinion. A report may have to be documented — that is, you may need to show the sources of your data by means of notes or references. Methods of research and documentation are explained in chapter 30.

Methods of Writing Reports

Remember that you needn't reinvent the wheel every time you write something new; that is, remember that other writers have probably used forms and organization similar to those you will need. You should make use of these methods whenever you can.

If you must write reports for your work, you might examine earlier reports in your company's files. If your university course work requires you to write reports, your instructors may suggest particular plans or formats for the work, or show you examples of other reports. In either instance — at work or at school — remember that almost any library, regardless of size, will have books on business and professional writing that will usually include guides to report writing. Other people have written reports; you don't have to start from scratch.

The occasions on which reports must be written are so diverse and the kinds of reports that may be called for are so numerous that no single guide can show you how to write every kind of report. However, there is a basic organizational pattern common to many reports:

Introduction:
> a statement of the problem and its importance
> the occasion or need for exploring the problem
> anticipated or proposed method for exploring the problem

Middle:
> an account of the procedure followed in exploring the problem
> an account of the information resulting from the investigation — tests, samplings, interviews, questionnaires, statistical investigations, library research of any kind

End:
> a presentation of the final findings, last suggestions, or proposals; a display of results, conclusions, and sometimes recommendations

31.3

Rpt

Not all reports, of course, will have all these parts, and not all reports will follow this order. Many reports do follow a pattern much like this, but some have special requirements:

1. **A memorandum,** for example, may present only the *end* of a chain of thought or an investigation.

2. **A progress report** may present the *middle* steps suggested above. A progress report is an account of what has been done so far in a given investigation or procedure.

3. **A briefing report** is meant, usually, to anticipate what is going to happen, to anticipate what should be known or done first, last, and in between, to anticipate problems. A *briefing* is intended to prepare someone or some group for what is to come.

4. **A proposal** is similar to a briefing report, except that the writer's purpose is to describe and recommend some idea or plan. The sample report on pages 531-42 is of this type.

5. **A critique or evaluation** looks at an enterprise or a piece of work after it is over. One way to write a *critique* is to look back at the beginning to see if the work was begun at the best place and at the middle to see if everything was done that should be done, in order to look at the conclusion to see if it can be validated.

Whatever form you follow, remember that within your writing you can call upon most of the methods used in other kinds of writing. Reports depend upon description, narration, exposition, and argumentation, and each of the other chapters of this book is relevant to report writing. You may want to review especially chapter 21 and the account there of various methods for developing and exploring material — definition, illustration, comparison, contrast, classification, cause-and-effect analysis, and the others.

Finally, as you prepare your own reports or as you study the reports of others, keep these questions in mind:

1. Is the language clear and direct, free of jargon?
2. How does the author show up in the work?
3. How is a context established for the work?
4. In what sense is the work referential? Does the subject dominate the work, or do other factors interfere?
5. Is the subject clearly examined? Are questions left unasked and unanswered?
6. What kind of investigation supports the work?
7. How is the work organized?
8. What methods of development are used?

In addition to these special requirements for reports, of course, you should bear in mind the criteria for *all* good writing. See the checklist on pages 451-52.

A New Look for the Ice Palace

A report to the Embro Town Council,
prepared by Susan L. Pye

1982 12 03

English 228 (Technical Writing)

Fall Term 1982

Instructor: L. M. Hancock

INTRODUCTION

At present, Matheson Park in Embro has no permanent concession stand.
But it does have an unused old arena, the Ice Palace, which many
people regard as an eyesore that should be torn down. This report
will explain the feasibility of converting the Ice Palace into a
much-needed concession stand and open-air pavilion.

The proposed alteration has three main features or stages.
The first is the removal of the existing metal-sheeting walls to
create an open-air pavilion. The second is the replacement of the
broken cement floor. The third phase is the construction of a large
enclosed commercial booth at one end.

This report will cover five aspects of the proposed conversion:
(1) the present condition of the building; (2) the renovations
necessary for its new role; (3) the benefits of conversion; (4) costs
and funding; and (5) community support for and involvement in the
project.

1. THE BUILDING AT PRESENT

Function: Although used formerly as an ice rink and as the home of
exhibits for the Embro Fair and the Caledonian Games, the Ice Palace
has now become a storehouse for the bleachers and garbage containers
used during the Highland Games each July. This equipment occupies
only about 700 m^2 of the total floor area (2000 m^2).

Actually the building gets more use from local vandals who
enjoy spraying paint, lighting fires, breaking lights, shooting holes
through it, and generally contributing to its ruination. A potentially

2

useful public facility is in idleness and decline.

Description: The Ice Palace is the largest of five buildings in
Matheson Park, as well as the most unsightly. It is situated in
the south-west corner of the park, facing directly onto Argyle
Street. There is plenty of adjacent parking space. The building
is constructed mainly of lumber, cement, and sheet metal, with an
outside measurement of 24 m x 84 m. The walls, set on a 22 cm
foundation, are 3.5 m high; the roof peaks another 3 m to a total
height of 6.5 m. The floor is a cement pad of about 2000 m^2.

2. RENOVATIONS NEEDED

Exterior: Much of the metal sheeting on the roof and sides is
rusting, loose, and unsightly. Since the side sheeting is to be
removed, the best of it could be used to replace any poor pieces
discovered during the renailing of the roof. (The balance could
be sold to defray other costs.) The roof should be resilvered
(as is done with barns) to fill the smaller holes, retard rusting,
and improve the building's appearance.

Interior: Preparation of the building's interior for the construction
of the new booth will take several days. This involves replacing
the floor and dismantling the existing facilities.

(a) Floor. The cement floor, originally the base for an ice surface,
is the worst feature of the building. It is cracked and heaved in
many places. There are two possible solutions. The first is to fill
the cracks and cap the floor with a thin layer of new cement to provide
a smooth surface; the second and recommended solution is to remove the

3

existing pad and pour a new floor.

The 22 cm cement lip or foundation surrounding the existing
pad should also be removed. Cement casings should be poured around
the bases of all upright beams to give the building's frame greater
stability.

(b) Existing Facilities. The booth, office, and upstairs observation
room at the west end are all in very poor condition and must be removed to make way for the proposed new concession booth. This involves dismantling an upper compartment, a set of stairs, a great
deal of wooden framing and wire, and a wooden platform. The fuse box
and hydro outlets located in this area should be checked and, if
necessary, re-wired.

(c) Construction of Booth. Construction, which will require about 500
hours of labor, can begin as soon as the preparatory work (including
floor replacement) is finished. First, the booth's cement-block
walls should be erected, to a height of 3.5 m all around, leaving
door and window spaces. Then the two open ends should be closed in
up to the roof with studs and plywood. Serving and storage facilities inside the booth (counters, cupboards, and the like) could be
added by the organization that assumes responsibility for running
the pavilion.

Design assistance and labor (including electrical work)
have been promised by local service clubs. Henry Dastuch, a site
foreman for Pritchard Construction Company, has volunteered to
supervise the project provided it is done evenings and weekends.

4

3. BENEFITS OF CONVERSION

<u>General Summer Use</u>: The concession booth could be operated profitably
on a daily basis during the summer, serving refreshments to the many
people who come to enjoy the park's other facilities. Weekend service
would be especially welcome and successful. At present the nearest
store is five blocks away -- an inconvenience for everyone and a danger
for children. Altogether the booth's presence would almost certainly
encourage greater general use of the park itself.

While daily winter operation would not be profitable, the
large number of people who use the skating rink and cross-country
trails on weekends would justify weekend service. For special events
such as Mardi Gras Night at the rink, or group outings like skating
parties and cross-country field days the booth could be opened or
rented.

<u>Baseball Season</u>: A very obvious need for refreshment service arises
during ball season. Ours is the only park in the league without a
permanent and regularly operating booth. Players and fans alike would
appreciate a drink or snack on warm days; first-aid supplies and ice
could also be available as they are at other league parks. The Ice
Palace is less than 75 m from the ball diamond.

Improvement of the park would also make it possible to hold
baseball tournaments, which are popular and successful elsewhere.
Tournaments require a headquarters area (the pavilion would be ideal)
and ample refreshment facilities. Moreover, sponsors such as Labatt's
and Molson's will provide publicity, a beer tent, and some prize money

5

to tournaments for senior (over age 19) teams. The calibre of ball and the beer tent draw large crowds to these events, and a great deal of money can be raised for the local team and for the park.

Highland Games: Each July the Caledonian Society's Highland Games attract a huge crowd to see the bands, the dancers, and the athletic competitions. The proposed pavilion would add a large sheltered area and the traditional Scottish food could be served in the booth rather than in a rented tent.

Because the park was donated to Embro by the Matheson clan, the Caledonian Society should be permitted free use of the new facilities. Members of the society's executive have nevertheless suggested that a percentage of profits might be contributed to the renovation fund as a gesture of encouragment.

Concerts, Dances, and Club Events: The new building could be used for open-air band concerts and dances like those successfully operated each summer elsewhere. The cement pad is as large as the dance floor in the community centre, and the booth could be a liquor outlet for licensed events.

Events like bingo and other worth-while fund-raising socials could also be held in the pavilion during summer. The Lions Club has expressed interest in this possibility.

Family and Group Picnics: Currently, Embro has only one public picnic area: the Mud Creek campground outside of town. Unlike Matheson Park, it lacks recreational equipment, and is really unsuitable for anything but camping. Its only attraction is a regularly operating snack stand.

6

A new facility in Matheson Park would more fully and conveniently serve the needs of local picnickers. The pavilion could also be reserved on weekdays for annual company picnics.

Field Days and Boy Scout Jamboree: Many schools, athletic organizations, and other associations hold competitions or field days that would be enhanced by the presence of a pavilion and booth. The Boy Scout Jamboree held here each fall is just one example of such gatherings. The winter campers who use Matheson Park every year are another group that would welcome the availability of a large covered shelter.

4. COSTS AND FUNDING

Cost of Materials: To estimate the direct costs of the conversion, prices for the necessary lumber, blocks, and cement were obtained from local suppliers. Since the proposed renovation is a community project, only dealers in the Embro-Woodstock area were considered.

Table 1

1400 Cement Blocks (8" standard #1)			
Supplier	Boehmers	CBM	Wallace
Cost per Block	85¢	75¢	75¢
Discount	10%	none	none
Delivery Charge	$10	$15	none
Total	$1081	$1065	$1050

7

Table 2

40 Bags of Cement					
Supplier	Allen	Boehmers	CBM	Saveway	Wallace
Price per Bag	$5.30	$3.80	$3.98	$4.75	$5.00
Discount Rate (40-bag lift)	$4.75	$3.50	none	none	none
Delivery Charge	$14.00	$10.00	$15.00	$12.00	none
Total	$204.00	$150.00	$174.20	$202.00	$200.00

Table 3

Lumber: Studs, 2 x 4s, and Plywood Sheets				
Supplier	Allen	Beohmers	Saveway	Wallace
40 10' studs (2 x 4) studs total:	$2.50 each $100.00	$2.00 each $80.00	$2.10 each $84.00	$2.27 each $90.80
120' 2 x 4 lumber 2 x 4 total:	25¢/ foot $30.00	20¢/ foot $24.00	21¢/ foot $25.20	19¢/ foot $22.80
14 pieces 3/8" select plywood total:	$14.10 each $197.40	$15.78 each $220.92	$14.95 each $209.30	$15.00 each $211.54
Discount	none	10%	none	none
Delivery Charge	$14.00	$10.00	$12.00	none
Totals	$341.40	$302.43	$330.50	$325.14

8

Taking the lowest figure from each of these tables, the estimated total
cost of supplies is as follows:

      Blocks (Wallace) $1050.00 + $73.50 sales tax = $1123.50

      Cement (Boehmers) $ 150.00 + $10.50 salex tax =   160.50

      Lumber (Boehmers) $ 302.43 + $21.14 sales tax =   323.57

      Nails, hinges, etc. 50.00

      Door (in frame) 100.00

      Miscellaneous 100.00

      TOTAL $1857.57

Additional Costs: The additional costs to make the booth fully op-
erational would be the responsibility of the organization(s) holding
the concession rights. These expenses would include equipment (such
as sinks, a refrigerator, grills and fryers, and a freezer), shelving
and storage space, and updated electrical service. These furnishings
should quickly pay for themselves if the booth is operated regularly.

Funding: Several organizations, businesses, and private individuals
have already offered financial support for construction if the project
is approved. These pledges now total approximately $800. Additional
funds may be available from such sources. However, since service
clubs are already donating labor and other assistance, and since
they will probably be bearing much of the equipment costs, most of the
$1000 still needed must be found elsewhere.

It is suggested that town council grant partial funding by
adding some of the Ice Palace conversion costs to next year's parks
budget.

9

Secondly, community fund-raising events such as paper drives and raffles could be specially organized to help finance the project. In conjunction with a general public appeal for donations, this approach could soon yield whatever amount is not included in the town council grant.

Final financial arrangements must be discussed if and when town council gives approval in principle to the conversion project.

5. PUBLIC INVOLVEMENT AND SUPPORT

Several local organizations have already offered to help with either the renovation or the operation of the facility. Other groups may also be willing to participate once the project is approved.

Optimist Club: The Optimists, the major service club in the Embro and West Zorra area, lend a hand in many worth-while community activities. This group supports the Ice Palace plan, and will provide the labor required to reconstruct the building. At a recent town council meeting, the club president confirmed the Optimists' commitment and added that some direct financial assistance might also be extended.

Opti-Mrs. Club: The members of the Opti-Mrs. Club are the wives of the Optimists. This group also helps with community projects and fund-raising drives. The Opti-Mrs. agree that the booth is needed in Matheson Park, and they would consider donating funds for equipment. The club is also interested in operating the booth occasionally during special events.

Lions Club: The Lions Club is mainly interested in obtaining the

10

concession rights and regularly operating the booth as a money-raising
venture during peak season. Their profits would go to charitable and
other worthy causes. In return for a firm agreement concerning the
concession, the Lions would either make a direct donation to the renovation fund or turn over a percentage of profits until expenses have
been recovered.

Embro Minor Ball: The Minor Ball Association will be one of the
principal beneficiaries of the conversion. The executive endorses
the project, but is not in a position to make a donation. The
association and the parents of the players would, however, be prepared to staff the booth during games and tournaments and turn over
the profits to the Ice Palace renovation fund.

Caledonian Society: The Highland Games' organizers have agreed to
give up their storage space and to encourage the conversion project.
Direct financial assistance would be limited to a percentage of
profits from operation during the Games.

Public Attitude: A questionnaire survey was conducted in Embro to
determine public attitude toward the Ice Palace. Results show that
the existing structure is considered a disgrace that should either
be torn down or converted to some good use. Setting up tennis courts
on the pad was one good suggestion. The proposal that a concession
booth and open-air pavilion be built received general approval.
Most respondents said that such a facility would encourage them to
use the park more often. Many also agreed to help with the work if
approached, or to make a small donation if a fund-raising campaign
is announced.

11

The survey results indicate that the public is concerned about the condition and uselessness of the Ice Palace and that many people are thinking about the building's future.

CONCLUSIONS AND RECOMMENDATIONS

There is a definite need for a permanent concession booth in Matheson Park, and it would be useful if associated with an open-air pavilion. Since something must soon be done about the old Ice Palace, conversion to the proposed facility is the ideal solution. The costs of this project would be much lower than those of demolition and reconstruction.

An important consideration is the advantages for the community. Organizations and the public favor it, and the renovation would be carried out and largely financed by the people of Embro. The community wants and needs the proposed facility.

Town council is accordingly urged to discuss this report and to consider acting upon the following recommendations:

1. that the Ice Palace conversion project described in the report be approved;

2. that funds be voted to make up the difference between the cost of construction and the amount of pledged community financing;

3. that a member of council (or some other appropriate person) be appointed to organize and supervise the project in co-operation with interested local groups;

4. that concession rights, for regular and special-event operation, be assigned;

5. that a budget be prepared and a fund-raising campaign be organized to defray equipment costs and any unexpected construction costs.

Prompt action would permit an almost immediate start on renovations. Any further information that might help the council in its deliberations will be provided upon request.

Glossary of Usage

This glossary lists the words and constructions that most often cause confusion in writing; it is not, however, a replacement for a good dictionary. Many of these items are discussed in more detail in the relevant chapter of the *Handbook*, for example, *lay, lie* in chapter 8, Verbs, and *who, whom* in chapter 7, Pronouns. Use the index to locate usage entries that appear in other sections of the *Handbook*.

a, an.   The choice of *a* or *an* depends on the initial sound of the following word rather than the initial letter. Use *a* before words beginning with a consonant sound, *an* before words beginning with a vowel sound: **a** boat, **a** used boat, **a** European country, **an** alligator, **an** F, **an** hour.

accept, except.   *Accept* means "receive" or "approve of"; *except* means "exclude" or "with the exclusion of":

> Everyone has **accepted** the invitation **except** Sam.

advice, advise.   *Advice* is a noun meaning "counsel" or "recommendation"; *advise* is a verb meaning "give advice" or "make a recommendation":

> I **advise** you to follow your instructor's **advice**.

affect, effect.   *Affect* is a verb meaning "influence" or "assume the appearance of"; *effect* is a noun meaning "result":

> The weather **affected** our tempers.
> The frightened child **affected** a defiant look.
> The **effects** of radiation are not yet completely known.

Affect is also a noun, a technical term used in psychology meaning "emotion," and *effect* is a formal verb meaning "to bring about."

aggravate, irritate.   In formal English, *aggravate* means "make worse" and *irritate* means "annoy": *aggravate* the condition; an *irritating* habit. In general and informal usage, *aggravate* and *irritate* both mean "to annoy": his voice *aggravated* me; the mosquitoes were *irritating*. But since the use of *aggravate* to mean "annoy" might irritate some readers, it is better to maintain the formal distinction.

ain't.   A non-standard contraction meaning "aren't" or "isn't." *Ain't* is not considered appropriate in writing (or in speech) in Canada.

all ready, already. *All ready* is an adjective phrase meaning that everything or everyone is prepared; *already* is an adverb meaning "previously":

> Finally the car was loaded and we were **all ready** to leave.
> The train had **already** left when we got to the station.

all right. The only acceptable spelling. Avoid *alright* or *alrite*.

all together, altogether. *All together* is an adjective phrase meaning "in a group"; *altogether* is an adverb meaning "wholly":

> The sale items were **all together** on one table.
> That's **altogether** another matter.

allude, refer. To *allude* is to make indirect mention of something; to *refer* is to state directly:

> I knew that her remark about trees **alluded** to the unfortunate incident at the picnic.
> He **referred** to the second chapter in order to make his point.

allusion, illusion. An *allusion* is a brief, indirect reference to a person, event, literary work, or the like. An *illusion* is a misleading appearance:

> She made an **allusion** to Yeats' "Second Coming."
> The little boy's smile created an **illusion** of innocence.

almost, most. *Almost* is an adverb meaning "very nearly"; *most* is an adjective meaning "the greater part of":

> He **almost** wrecked the car.
> **Most** drivers try to be careful.

Although in speech *most* is sometimes used to mean *almost*, the two words are not interchangeable.

a lot. Always two words. Do not use *alot*.

a.m., p.m. (or A.M., P.M.) The abbreviations should always be used with numbers to refer to a specific time:

> The train leaves at 5:56 **p.m.**

Do not use the word "o'clock" with *a.m.* or *p.m.* [not *eight o'clock p.m.*]; do not use *a.m.* or *p.m.* without a specific time [not *We're going to a party this p.m.*].

among, between.   *Among* usually refers to more than two; *between* refers to two only. However, *between* is sometimes used in informal English for more than two. *Between* is always used when the reference is to individual items, even though an "item" might consist of more than one unit.

> We had to choose **between coffee and cake** [as one item] **and punch and cookies**.

Do not use *or* between the items: *between him and her* [not *between him or her*].

amount, number.   In general and formal usage, *amount* is used to refer to something as a mass: a large *amount* of black dirt; a certain *amount* of money. *Number* is used to refer to individual items which are countable: a large *number* of plants, a *number* of people.

and etc.   The use of *and* with *etc.* is redundant because *etc.* (*et cetera*) means "and so forth."

and which, but which.   The use of *and* or *but* with a relative pronoun (*who, which, that*) in an adjective clause is superfluous and defeats the subordination; only the pronoun should be used:

> The sea anemone is a fascinating creature **which** [not *and which*] looks more like a plant than an animal.

anymore.   Except in negative constructions (*He doesn't go to school anymore*), this adverb is not in general use in the sense "these days." *The team is losing a lot of games anymore* is an inappropriate usage.

anyone, any one.   These words are not interchangeable. *Any one* refers to one of a certain number of items or people; *anyone* is a singular, indefinite pronoun and refers only to a person:

> You may choose **any one** of those books to read.
> **Anyone** who pays the entrance fee may enter the race.

Everyone, every one, and *someone, some one* are similar.

as. When used as a conjunction to introduce adverb clauses, *as* is often less exact than other adverbs such as *while, when,* or *because*:

> While [not *as*] we were eating, we talked about the election.
> We stopped to rest under a tree because [not *as*] the sun was so hot.

awhile, a while. *Awhile* is an adverb meaning "for a certain period of time." *A while* is a noun:

> Can you stay **awhile?** [adverb modifying *stay*]
> Can you stay for **a while?** [noun, object of the preposition *for*]

bad, badly. *Bad* is the adjective, *badly* the adverb. Although *bad* is the preferred form following a linking verb (I feel *bad*; the situation looks *bad*), *badly* is sometimes used, especially after *feel* (she feels *badly* about hurting you). Many people object to such uses of *badly*, however, and it's just as well to avoid them in writing. Similarly, avoid using *bad* when *badly* is called for: The day started off *badly* [not *bad*] and got worse.

because. See *reason is because*.

behind. Most Canadians use *behind* rather than *in back of*: The bike is *behind* the garage

being. The present participle of the verb *be* is overused by many writers. It is superfluous in sentences like the following:

> **Frustrated** [not *Being frustrated*] by my roommate's untidiness, I'm moving out as soon as I can find another place.
> Witnesses described the suspect **as** [not *as being*] tall, thin, and fair-haired.

being that. To introduce a dependent clause of reason or cause, *being that* is an unacceptable substitute for *because, since,* or *for*:

> **Because** [not *being that*] I was so tired, I decided not to go to the party.

but that, but what. Even though *but that* and *but what* are used informally in dependent clauses, *that* is preferable in most writing:

> I don't doubt **that** [not *but that*] he'll be there.

but which. See *and which*.

can be, able to be.   *Able to be* is an awkward expression when used with a passive infinitive: Canoes are *able to be* carried easily by two people. *Can be* is preferable: Canoes *can be* carried easily by two people.

can, may.   In written edited English, *can* is used to express ability, *may* to express permission:

> **Can** you dance? **May** I have this dance?

Can is frequently used informally in the sense of permission (*Can* I go too?), but it is best to avoid this use in writing.

can't hardly.   Such common expressions as *can't hardly* and *couldn't scarcely* are double negatives, because *hardly* and *scarcely* mean "almost not." Use *can hardly* instead: I *can hardly* hear you.

can't help but.   This an established idiom, but many writers avoid it, using instead *cannot but* (formal) or *can't help*:

> **I cannot but** feel sorry for him.
> **I can't help** feeling sorry for him.

capital, capitol.   The *capitol* is the building which houses the state or national legislative bodies in the United States. For all other meanings, use *capital*.

case.   Often deadwood that should be removed.

> AS DEADWOOD: **It was often the case that** we stayed in town for dinner.
> BETTER: We often stayed in town for dinner.

censor, censure.   *Censor* means "repress" or "remove objectionable parts of"; *censure* means "condemn" or "disapprove," often in an official sense:

> Some restricted movies have been **censored**.
> The MP who used foul language in the Commons was **censured** by the Speaker.

centre around.   Although this is a commonly used expression, it is considered illogical by many. Use *centre on* instead.

cite, site. *Cite* is a verb, most often used in the sense of "quote" or "refer to"; *site* is a noun meaning "location," or a verb meaning "place in a certain location":

> Dictionaries often **cite** the way a word has been used by different writers.
> We've found the perfect **site** for a picnic.

complement, compliment. *Complement* is a noun or verb referring to completion or fitting together; *compliment* is a noun or verb suggesting praise:

> She saw a hat that would be the perfect **complement** for her suit.
> Nancy **complimented** Theodore for having the sense to come out of the rain.

conscientious, conscious. *Conscientious* is an adjective meaning "scrupulous" or "upright"; *conscious* is an adjective meaning "awake" or "aware":

> Pamela was **conscientious** about every responsibility she took on.
> Stephen was **conscious** of the noise in the background.

considerable, considerably. *Considerable* is the adjective, *considerably* the adverb. Using *considerable* as an adverb is nonstandard:

> It was a **considerable** amount of money.
> The weather was **considerably** [not *considerable*] colder last year than this.

contact. Although in wide use, *contact* in the sense of "get in touch with" (I'll *contact* you soon) is disapproved by some; in formal edited English a more precise word is preferable: *see*, *call*, or *write*.

continual, continuous. Although the distinction has largely disappeared, *continual* refers to an action that occurs repeatedly over a period of time, *continuous* to an action that is uninterrupted flow:

> The **continual** ringing of the phone began to annoy Joe.
> Many old people live with a **continuous** fear of being robbed.

could of, would of.   These are mistaken expressions derived from the spoken contractions *could've* and *would've*. Use *could have* and *would have* in writing.

credible, creditable, credulous.   *Credible means "capable of being believed"* (a lie can be credible); *creditable* means "worthy of being believed" (a lie should not be creditable); but *credulous* means "willing to believe on the slimmest evidence."

data.   Although *data* is widely used in informal usage for both the singular and plural, *datum* is used as the singular in formal writing. Other commonly used plurals derived from Latin and Greek include the following:

PLURAL FORM	SINGULAR FORM
media	medium
criteria	criterion
curricula	curriculum
strata	stratum

See also the glossary entry for *phenomena*. Be careful to maintain subject-verb agreement when using such words in formal writing:

Statistical data **are** included in the report.
What criteria **determine** success in job applications?
The electronic media **are** subject to government licensing.

detract, distract.   *Detract* means "take away from"; *distract* means "to turn aside" or "divert the attention."

The amount of litter on the ground **detracted** from the pleasantness of the park.
The wailing sirens **distracted** us from our conversation.

different from.   This is the general idiom, but *different than* may be used to avoid an awkward sentence:

Life in a small town is **different from** life in a large city.
Living on a farm involves a **different** life-style **than** living in a city does.
OR: Living on a farm involves a life-style **different from** that in a city.

disinterested, uninterested.   Even though both words are commonly used to mean *uninterested*, a distinction should be maintained. Use *disinterested* to mean "impartial": *Disinterested* judges are better than *uninterested* ones.

done, don't. All varieties of standard English call for *did* in the past tense in all persons: I, you, he, she, it *did* [not *done*]. The past participle in all persons is *have* or *had done*. *Don't* is the contraction for *do not*; *doesn't* is the contraction for *does not*: I, you *don't*; he, she, it *doesn't* [not *he don't*].

due to. Although widely used to mean "because of" (Due to the rain, he stayed home.) many insist on using this phrase only with forms of *to be*: His absence was *due to* the rain, where *due* is an adjective modifying *absence*. Nevertheless, *due to*, like *owing to*, is now widely used by many established writers.

due to the fact that. In most situations, this phrase is deadwood: His failure was **due to the fact that** he didn't study. Better: He failed because he didn't study.

either...or. Singular subjects joined by *either...or* or *neither...nor* are generally considered singular, and take a singular verb:

Either the bicycle or the moped **is** the transportation of the future.

If both subjects are plural, the verb is plural:

Either bicycles or mopeds **are** the transportation of the future.

eminent, imminent. *Eminent* is an adjective meaning "noteworthy" or "famous": an *eminent* ambassador. *Imminent* is an adjective meaning "about to happen": The storm is *imminent*.

enthuse. This verb is a back formation from *be enthusiastic about* or *show enthusiasm*. While *enthuse* is fairly common in speech, it is generally better to use another form in writing.

etc. The abbreviation for *et cetera*, "and so forth." Do not use *and etc.* and avoid *etc.* in essays.

every one, everyone. See *any one, anyone*.

exist. Often deadwood: The traffic jams that *exist* at rush hour cause a lot of hot tempers to flare. Better: Rush-hour traffic jams cause a lot of hot tempers to flare.

expect. Colloquial in the sense of "suppose," "presume," or "think": I *expect* it's about time for dinner. Use a more precise word in most writing.

farther, further. In formal English *farther* is used to refer to measurable physical distance: How much *farther* do we have to walk? *Further* refers to abstract degree: We will study these suggestions *further*. The distinction is not always adhered to in informal writing. If in doubt, it is better to maintain the distinction.

fewer, less.   *Fewer* is used to refer to countable items, *less* to something considered as a mass:

> **Fewer** people are here today than yesterday.
> If there are **fewer** people, it means **less** work for the clean-up crew.
> This cash register is for customers with six items or **fewer**.

flaunt, flout.   Although frequently confused, these words are not synonyms: *flaunt* is to make a show of, or display something ostentatiously: *flout* is to disregard, or treat with scorn:

> Everyone was tired of the way he **flaunted** his wealth.
> Some people always **flout** the traffic laws.

former, latter.   Used to refer to the first or last of two items only. If there are more than two items, use *first, last*.

get, got, gotten.   In North America, both *got* and *gotten* are acceptable forms of the past participle of *get*:

> He could have **gotten** [or **got**] more for his money.

Many idioms with *get* are standard in all levels of writing: *get up, get away from, get ahead*. But some expressions are considered informal and should be avoided in student writing: *get on one's nerves, get away with murder, gets me* (for "annoy"), *get* in the sense of "hit" or "struck."

good, well.   *Good* is an adjective: a *good* time; this cake tastes good. *Well* is either an adjective, in the sense of one's health, or, more usually, an adverb: The team plays *well* together. Since *good* is an adjective, it shouldn't be used in place of the adverb *well*: The car is running *well* [not *good*] since it was tuned up.

half.   Both *a half* and *half a* are standard; the choice usually depends on sound and idiom: He ate *half a* pie; He ate *a half* serving. *A half a* is redundant.
   The number of the verb is determined by the noun accompanying *half*: Half the children **are**. . . . Half the pie **is**. . . .

hang.   People are *hanged*, pictures and other objects are *hung*. This distinction is not always made for people, but it is for objects.

hardly.   Since *hardly* is a negative that means "almost not," don't use another negative with it. See *can't hardly*.

he/she, his/her.   These and other "slash forms" such as *and/or* are a kind of shorthand that should be avoided in formal writing. Use neutral plural forms (they, their) whenever possible; otherwise, write *he or she* and *his or her*. Don't make masculine forms (*he, his, him*) stand for both sexes.

hisself.   Non-standard for *himself*.

imply, infer.   *Imply* means "suggest"; *infer* means "assume" or "draw a conclusion" from a suggestion or implication:

> Even though she didn't say anything, her expression **implied** that she thought her friend was acting foolishly.
> We **inferred** from the manager's remarks that we would not be getting a raise this year.

Because *infer* is sometimes used to mean *imply*, your context should also make your meaning clear. In any case, maintain the distinction between the two words.

in, into.   *In* generally refers to a location within, *into* to the action of going toward the location:

> She decided to sit **in** the chair that she had bumped **into** in the dark.

in back of.   See *behind*.

incredible, incredulous.   *Incredible* means "very hard to believe"; *incredulous* means "not believing, skeptical":

> The Olympic gold-medal winner showed **incredible** precision and control on the balance beam.
> John was **incredulous** at the story the old soldier was telling.

irregardless.   Non-standard for *regardless*. Since both *ir-* and *-less* are negative affixes, *ir-* is redundant.

is when, is where.   Often incorrectly used to introduce an adverb clause as a definition:

> INCORRECT: Theatre-in-the-round **is when** the audience surrounds the stage.
> BETTER: A theatre-in-the-round is one in which the audience surrounds the stage.

its, it's. These two words are often carelessly confused. *Its* is the possessive form of the pronoun *it*: everything in *its* place. *It's* is the contraction for *it is* or *it has*: *it's* raining; *it's* begun.

kind, sort. *Kind* and *sort* are singular when used with *this* or *that* and should be used with a singular noun and verb: *this kind* of book is my favourite, *that sort* of person annoys me. If the idea is plural, use *these* and *those: these kinds* of books are..., *those sorts* of people....

kind of a, sort of a. Although frequently occurring in speech, *kind of a* is considered informal in writing: We'll never see that *kind of a* day again. The *a* is unnecessary. Use *that kind of day*.

last, latest. *Last* refers to the final item in a series of something that is completed: the *last* chapter, *last* inning. *Latest* refers to the most recent in an ongoing series: the *latest* book I read (I'll read others), the team's *latest* defeat (we hope it's the last).

later, latter. *Later*, a comparative adjective, refers to time: the *later* the hour, the longer the shadows. *Latter*, an adjective or a noun, refers to the second of two items named. See also *former, latter*.

lay, lie. *Lay* is a verb meaning "to put or place"; it takes an object: *lay* the books on the desk. *Lie* is a verb meaning "to recline"; it does not take an object: **lie** down for a nap. The principal parts of *lay* are *lay, laid, laid*: He *laid* the books on the desk. The principal parts of *lie* are *lie, lay, lain*: She *lay* down for a nap.

learn, teach. The student *learns*, the instructor *teaches* the student. The use of *learn* for *teach* is considered non-standard [not *I'll learn you some manners*].

leave, let. *Leave* means "depart or abandon"; *let* means "permit": *Let* us *leave* this place. Using *leave* for *let* is considered non-standard.

let's us. Since *let's* is a contraction for "let us," *let's us* includes a redundancy and is, therefore, a misusage.

lie, lay. See *lay, lie*.

like, as. To introduce a prepositional phrase of comparison, use *like*:

> He looks **like** [not *as*] his father.
> Some people **like** the Joneses try to keep up with their neighbors.

To introduce a clause of comparison (with a subject and verb), use *as, as if,* or *as though*:

> It looks **as if** [not *like*] his father is not coming.
> She wanted to be a lawyer **as** her mother had been.

The use of *like* as a conjunction has become more widespread recently, but it is ordinarily better to use the preferred forms *as, as if,* and *as though*.

likely, liable, apt. Both *likely* and *liable* suggest that something will occur, but in formal usage *liable* is restricted to an unpleasant or disastrous occurrence:

> The tornado is **liable** to damage a large part of town.
> BUT: The tornado is **likely** to veer away from town.

The use of *apt* to suggest an occurrence is colloquial: She's *apt* to appear soon. In formal usage, *likely* is preferred in this instance; *apt* is used only in the sense of aptitude: She is very *apt* at needlepoint.

line. Often overused, *line* in the following sense can be considered deadwood: He was in the legal *line* of work. Better: He was in law.

loose, lose. The spelling of these words is sometimes confused. *Loose* is an adjective meaning "not tight" (*loose* sleeves), or a verb meaning "release" (*loosen* the rope). *Lose* is a verb meaning "misplace" (don't *lose* it).

may, can. See *can, may.*

may be, maybe. *May be* is a verb phrase suggesting possibility; *maybe* is an adverb meaning "perhaps":

> He **may be** the next mayor.
> **Maybe** it will rain this afternoon.

moral, morale. The adjective *moral* means "ethical" (a *moral* code of conduct); the noun *moral* refers to the ethical significance or practical lesson (the *moral* of a story). The noun *morale* means "state of mind": If all the workers do their share, the *morale* of the group will be good

myself.   A reflexive or intensive pronoun, used to refer back to *I* in the same sentence:

> I hurt **myself. I, myself,** am the only one to blame.

It is not more elegant to substitute *myself* for *I*, as in this sentence: My friend and *myself* were invited. Avoid this usage.

nohow, nowheres.   *Nohow* is non-standard for "not at all"; *nowheres* is non-standard for "nowhere."

not...no.   Constructions such as "I don't have no money," or "The tickets will not cost you nothing" are called double negatives, because the second negative needlessly repeats the meaning of the first one. They are common in some dialects, but are not appropriate to written or spoken standard English.

number, amount.   See *amount, number*.

of, have.   Do not use *of* for *have* in expressions such as *could have* and *would have*. See *could of*.

of which, whose.   *Whose*, the possessive form of the pronoun *who*, is generally used to refer to persons; *of which* is the possessive form most often used for inanimate objects:

> One of the most interesting colonial Canadians was Joseph Howe, **whose** ideas still sound very modern.
> It was a huge house, the rooms **of which** were dank and mildewed.

Often, however, *of which* is awkward: *whose* is generally used in such cases: "...the room *whose* walls were painted orange."

off of.   A colloquial expression that means no more than *off*: He jumped *off* [not *off of*] the cliff.

party.   Colloquial in the sense of "person"; Are you the *party* who wanted to see me? Use *person* in your written work.

piece, peace.   Do not confuse the spelling of these homonyms: *piece* means "portion"; *peace* means "absence of hostility."

phenomena.   The plural of *phenomenon*, a fact or event. If you use *phenomena*, be sure to use a plural verb. See *data*. The adjective *phenomenal* is greatly overused; try *remarkable* or *extraordinary* or *amazing* instead, depending on the intended meaning.

plenty.   As an adverb, *plenty* is colloquial: This coffee is *plenty* hot. Use *very, quite*, or a more precise word in your writing. In the sense of "more than sufficient," the general phrase is *plenty of*: We have *plenty of* time.

plus.   *Plus* is a preposition meaning "with the addition of"; its use as a conjunction (John *plus* Mary went to the dance) is best avoided; use *and*. A phrase using *plus* should not affect the number of the verb; *together with* is preferable to *plus*:

> The old apartment complex, **plus** the new townhouse section, contains a total of 225 units.

Plus is also used as a noun. (The new lights are a *plus* for the city), but many consider this usage journalese or jargon.

practicable, practical.   The two words are not interchangeable. *Practicable* means "feasible or usable, but not necessarily proved successful." *Practical*, on the other hand, implies success in its application to living. An electric car may be part of a *practicable* solution to urban pollution problems; putting on the spare tire is the *practical* method of dealing with a flat tire.

precede, proceed.   *Precede* means "to go before"; *proceed* means "to continue," "to move along":

> The mayor's car **preceded** the lieutenant-governor's in the parade.
> Let's **proceed** with the meeting.

principal, principle.   *Principal*, both as an adjective and a noun, means "chief" or "foremost": the *principal* of a school, the *principal* reason for success. *Principle* is a noun meaning "rule of conduct or action"; the *principle* governing the operation of a windmill, *principles* for living.

raise, rise.   *Raise* is a transitive verb, taking an object, meaning to cause (something) to move up; *rise* is an intransitive verb meaning to go up:

> Every morning when I get up **I raise** the window shade.
> Yeast causes bread dough to **rise**.

As a noun, *raise* meaning "an increase in pay" is typically Canadian; *rise* is British.

real, really.   *Real* is an adjective, *really* an adverb, although in speech *real* is often used as an adverb: We had a *real* good time. In writing, distinguish between the two:

> Their disagreement was **real**.
> You did a **really** fine job.

reason is because.   This phrase contains a redundancy since *because* means "the reason that." The preferred phrase is "the reason is that":

> The **reason** we are late **is that** [not *because*] an accident tied up traffic for hours.

A closely related redundancy is *the reason why*; the word *why* is unnecessary: "Another *reason* [not *reason why*] we are late is..."

reckon.   Informal or colloquial for "think": Who do you *reckon* will win the Grey Cup? In writing, use "think" or "feel."

regarding.   In various modifying phrases employing the verb *regard*, *regard* can usually be replaced effectively by *about* or *concerning*. But if you insist on the *regard* constructions, try to use only recognized forms:

POOR	BETTER	PREFERABLE
in regards to	regarding	concerning
in regard to	with regard to	about
with regards to	as regards	on [*weak*]

respectful, respective.   *Respectful* is an adjective meaning "considerate of" or "honoring"; *respective* is an adjective meaning "particular" or "in a certain order":

> He is very **respectful** of his instructors.
> Each application was placed in its **respective** file.

semi-.   The prefix *semi-*, derived from Latin, means *half* or *partly* in words like semi-transparent or semi-conductor. Except in technical terms like these, it is better to use more common English forms: *half*-sérious, *partially* finished, *somewhat* tough. Never use *semi-* as an independent adverb ("The dog's bad habits were *semi* a result of its master's laziness"). Other prefixes of this sort that can give trouble include *pseudo-* (counterfeited), *quasi-* (seemingly), and *anti-* (opposed to).

set, sit.   The verb *set*, meaning "put (something) down," is transitive, taking an object: *Set* the plants on the balcony. The verb *sit* (as in a chair) is intransitive, not taking an object: *Sit* down.

shall, will.   In current Canadian usage, *will* is generally used with all persons in the verb for the future tense. In formal usage, however, *shall* is used in the first person for the simple future (I *shall ask*), *will* in the second and third persons (she *will ask*). For the emphatic future, the use is reversed: *will* is used in the first person (I *will win*), *shall* in the second and third (they *shall leave*). *Shall* is not a more elegant term than *will*.

sic.   *Sic*, a Latin word meaning "thus" or "so," is used only in quoted material, within brackets, to indicate an error in the source. It is used less often today than formerly.

sit, set.   See *set, sit*.

some.   *Some* used as an adverb (I was *some* tired) is regional; edited English would use *somewhat* or a more precise descriptive word. *Some* used as an adjective (That was *some* concert) is informal; it is best avoided in writing.

someone, some one.   See *anyone, any one*.

sort.   See *kind*.

somewheres.   Non-standard for *somewhere*.

stationary, stationery.   *Stationary* is an adjective meaning "fixed in position," "immobile." *Stationery* is a noun referring to writing matrials. One way to remember the difference is to recall that both *stationery* and *letter* contain *er*.

supposed to, used to.   Because in speech the *-d* ending of *supposed* is assimilated to the *t-* of *to*, the *-d* is sometimes left off when phrases such as *supposed to* and *used to* are written. Remember that they are regular verbs in the past tense, and thus require the final *-ed*.

sure, surely.   In conversation, the adjective *sure* is often used in place of the adverb *surely*: We *sure* enjoyed the new exhibit at the museum. Avoid this "bob-tailed" adverb in writing, *surely* being the adverb:

> We **surely** enjoyed the new exhibit at the museum.
> *Better*: We **certainly** enjoyed the new exhibit at the museum.

suspect, suspicion.   *Suspect* is a verb meaning "distrust" or "imagine": The police *suspected* foul play. *Suspicion* is a noun; used for *suspect*, it is inappropriate in writing.

their, there.   Confusion of these two words is usually a careless error in spelling: *their* is the possessive form of *they: their* house, *their* problem. *There* is most often used as an adverb or an anticipating subject: she is over *there*. *There* are five horses in the corral.

themselves, theirselves.   *Themselves* is a plural reflexive or intensive pronoun: they hurt *themselves*. *Theirselves* is not a standard English form.

that kind.   See *kind, sort*.

till, until.   Interchangeable as prepositions or conjunctions: Wait *till* [or *until*] I get there. Notice that *till* is not a shortened form of *until*, and should not be spelled with an apostrophe. The form *'til* is occasionally seen, especially in "poetic" writing, but is an unnecessary contraction and does not appear in most dictionaries. The spelling *untill* is obsolete.

to, too.   Confusion of these two words is usually a careless error in spelling. The preposition *to* is far more common than the adverb *too*, which means "also," "besides," or "very."

too, very.   Don't confuse the adverbs *too* (meaning *excessively*) and *very* (meaning *greatly*). The problem usually arises only in negative constructions, as in illogical statements like *his play wasn't too impressive* or *she wasn't feeling too well*. In such cases, use *very* — or nothing at all.

try and, try to.   Both are accepted idioms: *try and* is the more common in colloquial English: *Try and* get your work done on time. *Try to* is the preferred form in formal English: *Try to* get your work done on time.

type of.   The shortening of this phrase to *type* (as in *this type car*) should be avoided. The preferred form is *this type of car*.

unique. Although a common enough practice, avoid using *more unique* and *the most unique* in writing. Many people find these usages distasteful because *unique* applies to things in a class by themselves: a *unique* design.

used to. See *supposed to*.

wait on. A localism in the sense "Wait for." In writing, this phrase should be used only in the sense "serving a customer."

want, want to, want that. In the sense "ought" or "should," *want* is informal: You *should* [rather than *want to*] review your notes before the test. In statements of desire or intention, *want to* is the standard idiom: *I want you to get* [not *for you to get* or *that you get*] all you can from this year's work. In such constructions, *want that* and *want for* are non-standard.

was, were. *Was* is the past tense of *be* (*is*) in the first and third person singular: I, he, she, it *was*. *Were* is the past tense for second person singular (you *were*) and first, second, and third person plural: we, you, they *were*. "We was" or "you was" are non-standard.

we, I. *We* (the "editorial we") should not be used when I is meant: I [not *we*] base my [not *our*] conclusions on information I received from several hotel managers.

who, whom. Although the distinction between *who* and *whom* is disappearing in many contexts, follow this general guideline: use *who* when it is the subject of a verb, even in subordinate clauses; use *whom* in all object positions (object of the preposition, direct object):

> **Who** is going to the play?
> **Whom** are you taking to the play? (You are taking whom?)
> He is a man **who** never compromises his principles.
> He is a man of **whom** it has been said, "He never compromises his principles."

whose. See *of which, whose*.

-wise. This suffix is well established in many words (*likewise, otherwise*); but it is bad form to use this suffix indiscriminately by making your own combinations, as *business-wise, politics-wise*.

would of. An error for *would have*. See *could of, would of*.

Index entries in *italics* are words that commonly cause difficulty in meaning or in grammatical construction.

Deduction, as pattern of paragraph
development, 330-32
Deductive argument, 341-43
Deductive description, 356-57
Deductive exposition, 331-32
Deductive narration, 351-52, 356
Definition, 437, 438
as pattern of development, 337-39
and subject of paper, 233, 292
Definitions, in dictionaries, 338, 410-
11
Degrees, of adjectives and adverbs,
134-36
Degrees (academic), abbreviations of,
198-99
Deity, capitalization of, 190
Demonstrative adjectives, 128
Demonstrative pronouns, 92 (table)
Denotation, 411, 415-19, 424
Dependent clauses. *See* Subordinate
clauses.
Dependent construction, 393
Description, 266-69, 313, 355-62, 419
by comparison, 359-60
modifiers in, 125
spatial order in, 285, 357-58
technical writing in, 359-60
verbless sentences in, 39-40
Descriptive details, 40
desert, dessert, 213
Details
as beginning of paper, 293
in description, 323, 325, 355, 356,
358-59
for interest and support, 323
in narration, 264-65
parentheses enclosing, 169
selecting and arranging, 267-69
detract, distract, 424, 549
Development of ideas in writing, 284-
88, 361-62
answers to essay questions, 511-16
argumentation, 252-60
exposition, 248-51, 324
organizing a paper, 270-81
paragraph development, 329-62
paragraph sequences, 289-91.
See also Outlining, in prewriting.
Diagrams, placement of, 462
Dialect, xvii, 7-8, 11, 15 (table)
as dictionary label, 412
Dialect modifications, 10
Dialogue
punctuation of, 168, 173
short sentences for, 39-40, 366-67
Diction, 415-47
abstract and concrete words, 417,
428-31
clichés, 441-42
connotation, 415-16, 417-19
context, 415-19

deadwood, 373-75
denotation, 415-17
economy of expression, 371-72
euphemisms, 442-43
figures of speech, 444-47
foreign words, 436-38
formal words, 432-38
informal words, 438-40
meaning of words, 410-11, 415-31
repetition, careless, 375, 377-79
slang, 2, 10, 296, 412
slanted words, 421-23
stilted language, 434-35
technical words, 436-38
trite expressions, 441-42
wordiness, 371-72
Dictionaries, xvii, xix, 2, 403-14
Canadian, xvii, 219, 405-06
college, 405-06
definitions in, 403, 411
etymology in, 413-14
foreign words in, 412
for general use, 405-06
grammatical information in, 410-11
historical, 406
idioms in, 411
imported, xix
labels in, 412
meaning of words in, 410-11
pronunciation in, xix, 403, 409-10
selection of, 404-06
special, 406
special labels in, 412
special subjects in, 406
spelling in, xix-xx, 209, 403, 409-
10
synonyms and antonyms in, 413
unabridged, 405
using, 403-14
word division in, 409
different from, 549
Direct address, 152
Direct discourse, 173
indentation of, 173
punctuation of, 173
Direct object, 26, 29. *See also*
Objects.
Direct questions, 141-42
Direct quotations, 483 (table), 488-90
footnotes for, 487
punctuation of, 157-58, 172-79,
189
note cards for, 483 (table)
disinterested, uninterested, 549
Dissertations
bibliography form for, 501
footnote form for, 497
distract, detract, 424, 549
Division of words, 409, 461
do, idioms with, 112
do, did, done, 112